GREEN GUIDE TO ANTIQUING IN NEW ENGLAND

SEVENTH EDITION

Praise for previous editions …

"… a wonderful compilation. … I am really impressed with this superb guide to New England antique shops."

Wendell Garrett, Senior Vice President, Sotheby's

"… the best of the guidebooks …"

The *Maine Antique Digest*

" … the ultimate source for those with a passion for vintage."

amazon.com

"Everything you need to know for a New England treasure hunt."

The Boston *Globe*

"When antiques are the mission."

The New York *Times*

"… indispensable to antiques collectors in the Northeast."

Early American Homes

Praise for the Green Guide to Antiquing in the Midwest

"Looking for antiques in the Midwest? Look no further than the Green Guide."

The *Maine Antique Digest*

"A MUST for anyone traveling to or interested in buying or selling in this Midwest Market."

New Hampshire Antiques Monthly

"Finally, the Midwest has an antiques directory that affirms the word 'antique'!"

Antique Review

Green Guide to Antiquing in New England

SEVENTH EDITION

EDITED BY LISA FREEMAN & JOHN FISKE

The Globe Pequot Press

GUILFORD, CONNECTICUT

Produced by AntiqueSource, Inc., P.O. Box 270, Belmont, VT 05730 USA; (802) 259-3614. Visit us on the World Wide Web at www.antiquesource.com.

ISBN: 0-7627-0511-6
ISSN: 1051-6719

Manufactured in the United States of America
Seventh Edition/First Printing

Contents

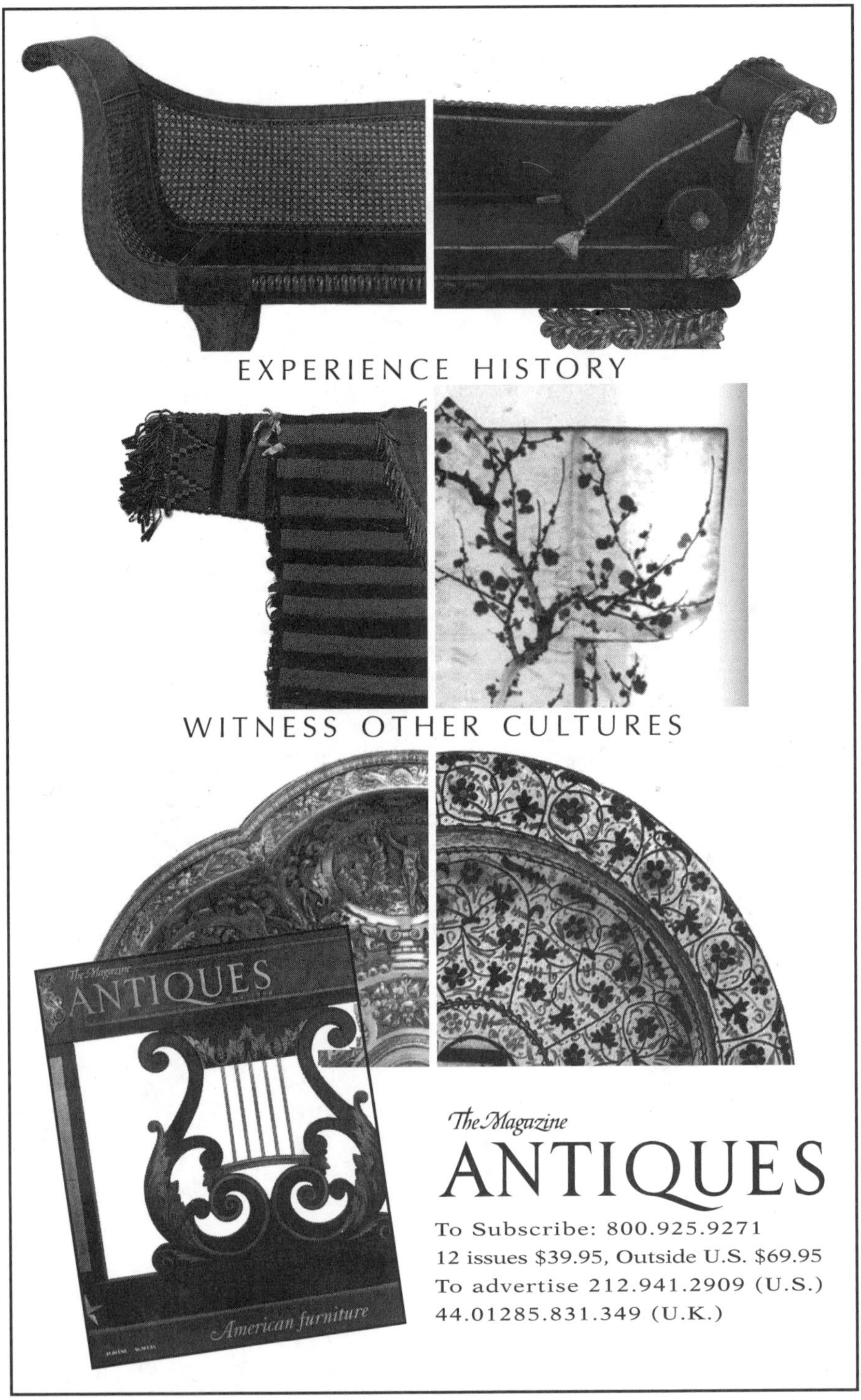
EXPERIENCE HISTORY
WITNESS OTHER CULTURES
The Magazine
ANTIQUES
American furniture
The Magazine
ANTIQUES
To Subscribe: 800.925.9271
12 issues $39.95, Outside U.S. $69.95
To advertise 212.941.2909 (U.S.)
44.01285.831.349 (U.K.)

Maps

From the Editors

Once again, we are delighted to present a new edition of the AntiqueSource *Green Guide to Antiquing in the New England*. This seventh edition contains over 3,000 listings for antiques dealers and services throughout the New England states of Connecticut, Maine, Massachusetts, New Hampshire, Rhode Island, and Vermont. This edition also includes expanded coverage of Upstate New York and Long Island.

Since publishing our last edition of the New England Guide (November 1997), we have brought out a new *Green Guide to Antiquing in the Midwest* (October 1998) and have watched the activity on our web site (www.antique-source.com) grow to nearly 4,000 visitors a day. Despite our own (largely positive) experiences with the Internet and the notable growth in on-line auction sites, sales of the print editions of our Guides continue to rise, suggesting that many people still prefer to search for antiques in person.

In previous editions of the Guides, we noted an increase in the number of group shops and the concomitant decrease in the number in single-owner shops. Both trends appear to have slowed if not stopped altogether, although many individual dealers now prefer to run their businesses primarily on an appointment-only business. We have listed many more of these businesses in this edition, frequently without their street addresses (at the dealer's request), but we encourage you to call and make an appointment. Dealers are always more than happy to open their shops to receive an interested visitor.

As always, we have many people to thank for their help with this edition. Raye Lin Collins and Amy Bannon assisted with (among other things) the time-consuming task of verifying the over 3,000 entries that comprise this edition. Mike Ahearn and the staff at Imagesetters of Rutland, Vermont, again did an excellent job with ad creation, typesetting, and design. Joy Hall of The Globe Pequot Press kept the final stages of production moving ahead without a hitch. And Terry Brown Pittaro kept the book orders flowing at a time when our minds were elsewhere. We could not have done this without them.

The dealer listings contained in the Green Guides are available free of charge on the World Wide Web at www.antiquesource.com thanks to Michael Jensen. For advertising rates or information about inclusion in future editions, or to order a copy of either the New England or Midwest Green Guides, please contact us at AntiqueSource Inc., P.O. Box 270, Belmont, Vermont, 05730; (888) 875-5999 (toll free); or at info@antiquesource.com.

Please remember to tell the dealers you visit that you "found them in the Green Guide." Happy antiquing!

Lisa Freeman & John Fiske
Editors
June 1999

How to Use this Guide

The *Green Guide* is a comprehensive guide to antiquing in New England. It has been compiled with collectors, dealers, and passionate antiquers in mind and is designed to enable you to easily identify antiques shops, publications, services, and antiques-related institutions that meet your individual needs. The Guide is divided into three basic parts.

Following a general introduction to Antiquing in New England, Part I consists of nine individual state-by-state sections listing dealers in Connecticut, Maine, Massachusetts (with a separate section devoted to Cape Cod, Martha's Vineyard, and Nantucket), New Hampshire, New York (with separate sections devoted to Long Island the New York City metropolitan region and Upstate New York), Rhode Island, and Vermont. Each of these sections begins with a map of the state to assist you in your travel planning. Each state section is organized alphabetically by town name and within each town, alphabetically by business name.

Each individual dealer entry begins with the business name, address, and phone number, as well as fax and toll-free numbers, email address, and web site if available. (If no street address is listed, the dealer has requested that we not publish his or her address but is willing to be contacted in advance for an appointment.) This basic information is follow by a brief description of the inventory. Following this is additional information concerning the price range of the dealer's inventory (**Pr**), the year in which the business was established (**Est**), the days and hours of business (**Hrs**), the size of the retail space (**Sz**), associations to which the dealer belongs (**Assn**), charge cards accepted (**CC**), directions to the shop (**Dir**), and the shop owner's name (**Own**). Group shops are noted by the designation "G" followed by the number of dealers in brackets immediately after the business name. A full listing of association acronyms appears on p. xv.

Finally, each entry includes both QuickCodes and Service QuickCodes to indicate categories of antiques or services that the business sells or provides (**QC**). The letter "**S**" in front of a QuickCode indicates that this is a Service QuickCode (for example, **S2** is Appraisal, whereas **2** is Antiquities). A list of the Quick Codes and Service Quick Codes appears on p. xiii and on one of the bookmarks that come with the Guide.

Part II of the Guide begins with a section listing Service Providers. Included here are appraisers, auctioneers, suppliers of period building materials, and clock repair specialists, as well specialists in the repair, restoration, and conservation of furniture, porcelain, glass, art, and metalware. We have also included a brief listing of businesses specializing in the reproduction and replication of antiques and parts for antiques. Part II also provides background information on several related aspects of antiques collecting, including periodicals that cover the New England and national antiques trade. A listing of historic homes and museums in New England follows, as well as a listing of the major antiques show promoters in the region.

Part III of the Guide includes three indexes. Index I is arranged alphabetically by business name (*Alphabetical Index to Dealers*). The Quick Codes and Service Quick Codes provide the bases for Indexes II and II (*Quick Code Index to Specialties* and *Quick Code Index to Services*). Dealers and service providers are listed under their appropriate QuickCodes by state. To use this index, first determine the QuickCode for the type of antique or service in which you are interested (say Furniture, Period American, which is 52) by looking at the list of QuickCodes on p. xiii or on the QuickCode bookmark. Turn to that heading in the *Quick Code Index to Specialties* and note that dealers who carry Period American Furniture are listed alphabetically by state and town under this heading. Conversely, if you note that a dealer lists QuickCodes 9, 33, and 60 in her entry, you can quickly determine that she carries Art (Marine/Nautical), Coins/Medals, and Garden Antiques by looking up the QuickCodes on p. xiii or on the handy bookmark. The Service QuickCodes work in a similar manner.

When using the Guide, please note the following usages:

By appt only	By appointment only (always call ahead)
By chance/appt	By chance or appointment (call recommended)
Daily	Seven days a week
Shop Sizes	S = Under 500 sq ft
	M = 501-2,000 sq ft
	L = 2,001-10,000 sq ft
	H = 10,000+ sq ft

Quick Codes

1 Americana
2 Antiquities
3 Architectural Antiques
4 Arms/Military
5 Art Deco/Art Noveau
6 Arts & Crafts
7 Art (General)
8 Art (Landscapes/Townscapes)
9 Art (Marine/Nautical)
10 Art (Miniatures)
11 Art (Objets d'Art)
12 Art (Portraits/Figures)
13 Art (Religious)
14 Art (Sporting)
15 Art (Still Life)
100 Art Glass
101 Art Pottery
16 Baseball Cards
17 Baskets
18 Books/Manuscripts
19 Books on Antiques
20 Brass/Copper
21 Buttons/Badges
22 Ceramics (American, General)
23 Ceramics (English/Continental, General)
24 Ceramics (Oriental, General)
25 Ceramics (Chinese Export)
26 Ceramics (Creamware/Pearlware)
27 Ceramics (Delft/Faience)
28 Ceramics (Imari)
29 Ceramics (Redware/Yellowware)
30 Ceramics (Staffordshire)
31 Ceramics (Stoneware)
32 Collectibles
33 Coins/Medals
34 Country Antiques
35 Clocks/Watches
36 Decorative Accessories
37 Decoys
38 Dolls
107 English Antiques
39 Ephemera
40 Fireplace Accessories
41 Folk Art (General)
42 Folk Art (Native American)
43 Folk Art (Theorems/Frakturs)
44 Folk Art (Trade Signs)
45 Folk Art (Weathervanes)
46 Folk Art (Wood Carvings)
47 French Antiques
48 Furniture (General)
49 Furniture (Arts & Crafts/Mission)
102 Furniture (Country)
50 Furniture (Oak)
51 Furniture (Paint)
52 Furniture (Period American)
53 Furniture (Period Continental)
54 Furniture (Period English)
55 Furniture (Pine)
56 Furniture (Reproduction)
57 Furniture (Shaker)
58 Furniture (Victorian)
59 Furniture (Other 20th Century)
60 Garden Antiques
61 Glass/Bottles (General)
103 Glass (Pattern)
104 Glass (Blown)
62 Iron
63 Jewelry (Costume)
64 Jewelry (Estate)
65 Lighting
66 Maps/Globes
67 Memorabilia
68 Mirrors
69 Musical Instruments
70 Nautical/Marine Antiques
71 Oriental Antiques/Export Trade
72 Pewter
73 Photography
106 Primitives
74 Prints
75 Rugs (Hooked/Braided)
76 Rugs (Oriental)
77 Scientific/Medical Instruments
78 Silver
79 Sporting Antiques
80 Textiles (General)
81 Textiles (Lace/Linen)
82 Textiles (Needlework/Samplers)
83 Textiles (Vintage Clothing)
84 Textiles (Quilts)
85 Tin/Toleware
86 Tools
87 Toys
88 Treen
105 20th C Decorative Arts
89 Victoriana
90 Vintage Cars/Carriages
91 Wicker

Service Quick Codes

S1 Appraisal
S2 Auction
S3 Bookbinding/Restoration
S4 Building Materials
S5 Cabinetmakers
S6 Chair Caning
S7 Clock Repair
S8 Consignment
S9 Consultation/Research
S10 Display Stands/Glass
S11 Doll Hospital
S12 Estate Purchases
S13 Framing
S14 Insurance
S15 Interior Design
S16 Repair/Restoration/ Conservation
S17 Reproduction/Replication
S18 Services to Period Homes
S19 Shipping/Packing/Storage
S20 Upholstery

Association Acronyms

AAA	Appraisers Association of American
AAAA	American Antiques Appraisers Association
AADA	Associated Antique Dealers of America Inc
AADLA	Art & Antique Dealers League of America Inc
ABAA	Antiquarian Booksellers Association of America
AC	Antiques Council
ACDA	Antique & Collectible Dealers' Association
ADA	Antiques Dealers' Association of America
AIC	American Institute for Conservation of Historic & Artistic Works
ANS	American Numismatic Society
AR	The Appraisers' Registry
ARLIS/NA	Art Libraries Society of North America
ASA	American Society of Appraisers
ASJH	Association of Jewelry Historians
AWI	American Watchmakers Institute
BCADA	Berkshire County Antiques Dealers Association
BHI	British Horological Institute
CADA	Connecticut Association of Dealers in Antiques Inc
CAGA	Certified Appraisers' Guild of America
CAI	Certified Auctioneers Institute
CCADA	Cape Cod Antique Dealers Association Inc
EAPGS	Early American Pattern Glass Society
ESA	Ephemera Society of America
GIA	Gemological Institute of American
GSAAA	Granite State Antique Dealers & Appraisers Association (NH)
HAAD	Hockomock Association of Antiques Dealers Inc (MA)
HADA	Hudson Antique Dealers Association (NY)
IIC	International Institute for Conservation of Historic & Artistic Works
ILAB	International League of Antiquarian Booksellers
ISA	International Society of Appraisers
ISFAA	International Society of Fine Arts Appraisers
MAA	Maine Auctioneers Association
MABA	Maine Antiquarian Booksellers Association
MADA	Maine Antiques Dealers Association Inc
MARIAB	Massachusetts & Rhode Island Antiquarian Booksellers
MBADA	Madison-Bouckville Antiques Dealers' Association (NY)
MSAA	Massachusetts State Auctioneers Association
NAA	National Auctioneers Association
NAADAA	National Antique & Art Dealers Association of America Inc
NADA	National Association of Dealers in Antiques Inc
NAWCC	National Association of Watch & Clock Collectors
NEAA	New England Appraisers Association
NEBA	New England Booksellers Association
NECA	New England Conservation Association
NHAA	New Hampshire Auctioneers' Association
NHABA	New Hampshire Antiquarian Booksellers Association
NHADA	New Hampshire Antiques Dealers Association Inc
NTHP	National Trust for Historic Preservation
ORRA	Oriental Rug Retailers of America
PSMA	Professional Show Managers Association
PVADA	Pioneer Valley Antiques Dealers Association
SSADA	South Shore Antiques Dealers' Association (MA)
SADA	Suburban Antique Dealers Association (MA)
SNEADA	Southeastern New England Antique Dealers Association Inc (MA)
SPNEA	Society for the Preservation of New England Antiquities
UCADA	Ulster County Antique Dealers Association (NY)
VAA	Vermont Auctioneers Association
VABA	Vermont Antiquarian Booksellers Association
VADA	Vermont Antiques Dealers' Association Inc
WADA	Woodbury Antiques Dealers Association (CT)

A view of one of the rooms in our gallery showing part of our large collection of American Federal furniture and American paintings.

ARTEMIS GALLERY

Stop by on your way to or from New England. We are just off Route I-84 at the NY-CT border.

Carol & Jesse Goldberg
North Salem, New York 10560

In Westchester County, one hour north of New York City.

914-669-5971
Anytime by appointment.

DAVID C. MOREY

AMERICAN ANTIQUES

103 MAIN STREET
P.O. BOX 368
THOMASTON, MAINE 04861
(207) 354-6033

Whether you are a discriminating, advanced collector or are simply decorating your home with period antiques, I have a large shop and inventory of the finest Eighteenth Century American country furniture with emphasis on original or early surface and condition, as well as Eighteenth and early Nineteenth Century American decorative and folk arts. New England redware and English ceramics related to the American experience are always available. I guarantee each item purchased as to authenticity, period, and condition, as I have represented it, on a money back basis.

Hours: Nov. 1 to May 31 Wed., Fri. & Sat. 10:00 - 5:00
June 1 to Oct. 31 Mon. through Sat. 10:00 - 5:00

Antiquing in New England

The reason so many people go antiquing in New England is, obviously, the antiques. There are more antiques here than in most other parts of the country, they come in a wider variety of forms and prices, and they have a distinctive, appealing character. But antiques do not appear out of nowhere. They are part of an architecture of symmetry and clapboarding, part of a townscape that groups houses, church, and meeting house around a village green, part of a landscape that sends roads winding around hillsides and rivers tumbling down rocky valleys; they are, in other words, part of New England.

New England is serious about antiques. The six New England states of Maine, New Hampshire, Vermont, Connecticut, Massachusetts, and Rhode Island are home to literally thousands of dealers. There are frequent auctions and shows, numerous monthly (and one weekly) periodicals covering the New England antiques scene, and thousands upon thousands of people who talk about antiques, read about them, study them, buy, sell and trade them, restore and repair them, gossip about the personalities involved, and exchange stories about the one that got away, or, better yet, the one that didn't. You simply cannot come to a better place in the United States to find, learn about, and enjoy antiques.

If it is furniture you are after, New England has it. You will be able to search out high-end pieces made in Boston or Newport at the height of colonial prosperity and confidence. On the other hand, if like most of us your bank balance is lower than your taste, you will be able to find wonderful pieces made by local cabinetmakers who maintained the fine proportions of metropolitan pieces but who simplified them and made them, in the best sense of the word, more homey. They domesticated the imposing chests, tables, and chairs of the cities, which is not to say that they made pieces that were merely functional (though of course, like any true New Englander, each piece had to serve its purpose), but for New England craftsmen, look was as important as the function. A piece of furniture had to please the eyes of its owners as they went about their daily lives. And it had to please the family, rather than impress the visitor, for it was more important to make the house a pleasure to live in — that is, comfortable — than it was to announce the high status of its owners.

This high country, or domesticated formal, furniture, made by a cabinetmaker who may well at some stage have worked in a city, had a more country cousin: furniture made by local craftsmen, who besides repairing wagons would have built houses and barns in the summer, made furniture in the winter, and constructed coffins all the year round. The most "country" of all was what we call "primitive" and was made by the householder for his own use. New England is full of this very characterful and regionally distinctive country furniture, whose prices can range from bargain basement up to levels approaching those for high-end formal furniture, especially if the piece has that rare and highly desired "original surface."

But whatever its style or price, you will find that New England furniture has a certain Yankee look to it. There's an economy of line and decoration that makes form serve function. Yankee cabinetmakers achieved their effects through harmony of proportion and the beauty of local woods rather than by means of rich carving, elaborate paint, or applied decoration. The block front, a New England invention, is so beautiful because it gives to what would otherwise be the flat surface of a desk or chest a subtle movement of concave and convex curves flowing into straight planes; the spectator sees the wood from every possible angle at the same time, and thus receives all the colors and textures that well-worked mahogany or cherry can offer. When carving was added to the blocking, as it often was in Newport, it was restricted to crisp, clean shells.

This is not to say that New England furniture is merely plain and simple. Makers in Boston and along the North Shore used wonderfully contrasting inlays and veneers to highlight the beauty of local and imported woods, and in New Hampshire, intricate silhouettes were given to aprons, cabriole legs and cornices.

In New England, independence started long before the Boston Tea Party. It showed itself not just in Yankee self-sufficiency (that was a necessity as well as a desire), but also in design and taste. Although styles of furniture and architecture were strongly influenced by those of old England, the early settlers quickly developed new designs to express their distance from the mother country. In the Connecticut River Valley, Hadley chests were painted and carved with flowing foliage that no European could match, and other New Englanders produced such new forms as the butterfly table that were never seen east of the Atlantic.

Although these early examples of Yankee inventiveness are highly sought after and thus highly priced, the tradition that produced them informs much more readily available furniture. A country Chippendale chest of drawers has a quiet confidence about it as if it knows it has descended from William and Mary forebears, who, in their turn, could trace their lineage back to the Pilgrim century

People with the taste for such elegant forms in furniture and architecture were not ones to fill their houses with junk. Although porcelain was generally imported from Europe during the Colonial period, New Englanders were highly selective in their choices; the quality of the European porcelain that can be found in New England antiques shops today reflects this good taste. Later and more primitive forms of American tableware such as redware and wooden treen bowls and implements are also widespread.

As with porcelain, most pewter, brass, and silver were imported during the Colonial period, but some New England craftsmen began making their own. These native pieces are rare and expensive. After independence, however, pewter and silversmithing blossomed, and locally made pewter and silver stocked the homes of the early nineteenth century and the antique shops of today. The more humble ironware, however, was almost all made locally from the Pilgrim century onwards. Cooking utensils and tools, fat lamps and candleholders, hearth equipment and hinges, clasps and bolts were all made by the local blacksmith for local use. Highly collectible, early ironware is still a reasonably affordable yet authentic decorative accessory.

Women of the Colonial period were as productive in the home as the men were in the workshop. They wove and made lace, they made quilts and sewed samplers, they painted theorems and stenciled patterns on walls and floors. Their work, intricate and highly individualized, can also be hunted out and collected but beware the burgeoning market for later reproductions.

And finally, if furniture or smalls are not your interest, New England is also home to dozens of superb antiquarian bookshops, numerous print and map dealers, and a wide range of art galleries featuring everything from early American folk art to fine marine art, landscapes of the Hudson River Valley school, and formal portraits.

Where to Buy Antiques

There are many different ways to buy antiques in New England. The simplest may be through the group shop or antique mall. Here the wares of a dozen to as many as several hundred dealers are brought together under one roof. Picking through the tens of thousands of items requires a sharp eye and patience, but the chances of finding your particular treasure are high. A rule of thumb: the larger the mall, the greater the variety, the younger the stock, and the lower the prices. Smaller group shops are more selective in their dealer mix and tend to carry earlier, higher quality antiques. Each state has a handful where the quality is as high as that of the single owner, specialist shop.

The single-owner shop may occasionally offer the variety if not the quantity of a mall, but in general it will reflect the taste or special interest of the owner. This will range from a more general line to carefully selected, specialist items for the serious collector. In the single owner shop you can talk to the owner, you can pick his or her brains and learn all that you can about the piece you are considering. Most dealers will guarantee what they sell, will describe it and its origin on the sales receipt, and will buy it back if it turns out to be other than represented. In most malls and group shops, however, sales are final.

Specialty dealers often do not keep regular shop hours but welcome visitors by chance or appointment. By chance is as chancy as it sounds, particularly in the off season, and you are well advised to accept the dealer's invitation to call ahead for an appointment. Don't feel that you are under any obligation to buy because the dealer has stayed in or opened up especially for you. Dealers expect collectors, especially serious ones, to search thoroughly before buying, and they know that they may not have the item you are looking for. You will put more miles on your car searching out single owner shops than you will if you go to a mall, but those miles will be over some of the most beautiful roads in the country, you will meet some fascinating and knowledgeable dealers, and you will have a real experience of New England.

Another quintessential experience for the New England antiquer is that offered by the antiques show. A show gathers together dealers of comparable quality offering their best stock at their best prices (it is a myth that dealers raise prices for shows). Shows provide plenty of opportunity for comparison shopping, plenty of antiques to browse among, and plenty of dealers to talk to. Outdoor, tented shows are often on the grounds of beautiful old mansions where you can combine antiquing with admiring the gardens and the view; they may also be held in an open field tucked under a mountain, on a village green, or on the state fairgrounds. They may be commercially run, or held to benefit the local historical society, the library or the botanical gardens, the hospital or the women's club. Most provide decent, and sometimes excellent, home-cooked food. An antiques show makes a wonderful day out for the antiquer.

The antiquer has plenty of shows to choose from during the season. But noone should miss the nationally famous Antiques Week in New Hampshire (the second week in August) with its three major shows, numerous "tailgate" shows, and important auction, all held in Manchester (New Hampshire). A new development is what is now being called "Antiques Week in Vermont." On the last weekend in September and the first in October, there are eight shows in southern Vermont, all within easy driving distance of one another. Headed by the Vermont Antiques Dealers' Association Show in Manchester (Vermont) and beautified by the fall color, these shows provide the antiquer with a wonderful opportunity to sample the full range of New England antiques. Equally famous but for different reasons are the huge shows at Brimfield (Massachusetts) and Farmington (Connecticut), where the antiquer will be able to find anything from Colonial furniture to granny's china. A list of the primary New England show promoters appears beginning on p. 477. Call or write for their annual schedules.

Auctions are an equally important part of the New England antiques scene. Many people consider their summer incomplete if they have not attended at least one on-site auction, held in a marquee or on the open lawn where a local estate is being sold.

Auctions take various forms, from those where major firms sell high-end antiques that they have spent up to a year assembling, to weekly local auctions where householders and dealers consign more everyday items. The items in the specialist sales have been carefully selected by the auctioneer, but in estate or regular sales, anything may turn up in any condition. And prices can be as unpredictable as the merchandise. Sometimes collectors will bid against each other and send prices far above those that the antiquer would pay in a dealer's shop. At other times the only bidders are dealers, and the price is wholesale. And at yet others, the bidders seem to sit on their hands, and the price is a giveaway. Auctions are great fun so long as you have learned about what you are buying before you bid. Your enjoyment of outdoor auctions will be greatly enhanced if you remember to bring an extra folding chair or two, a decent sun hat, some sunscreen, and some insect repellent.

Final Thoughts

All experienced antiquers know the value of the old adage ''buy the best you can afford. Be prepared to stretch your definition of affordable if you come across the piece that really speaks to you. Writing a slightly larger check than you'd planned may make you catch your breath as you sign it, but in six months' time, you'll be glad that you did. It is always preferable to have fewer but better antiques, not least because when you wish to "trade up" (and all collectors eventually do), the higher quality piece will have held or increased its value and will be the easier to resell.

In an age in which mass production and global distribution threaten to erase the unique and even to wipe out history and geography, uniqueness is the primary appeal of the antique. The Benetton sweater you can buy in Rome, New York, or Singapore has no history; it was produced, and can be used, anywhere. It has no anchor in time or place. Use it, discard it, and buy another. It doesn't matter.

Antiques, however, do matter. Each is unique. Each has written into it the place where it was made and used. The wear on its surface is the history of the hands that have used it, each dent or scratch is a sign of an accident that happened to it, and it alone. Antiques are not just objects, they are objects plus history, plus location, plus imagination.

Antiques thus do much, much more than merely furnish or decorate a home. They link that home to the past and the future, for owning an antique is not like owning a pair of shoes. Antiques are not to be used and discarded, but to be used, cared for and passed on to the next generation. To possess an antique is to hold something in trust for the future from the past. The antique collector is a trustee rather than an owner.

Antiquing is participating in history, and New England is the best place in the country to do it. Enjoy your antiquing, enjoy your antiques, and come back again to New England.

John Fiske and Lisa Freeman
Belmont, Vermont
June 1999

Part I

Dealer Listings By State

Connecticut

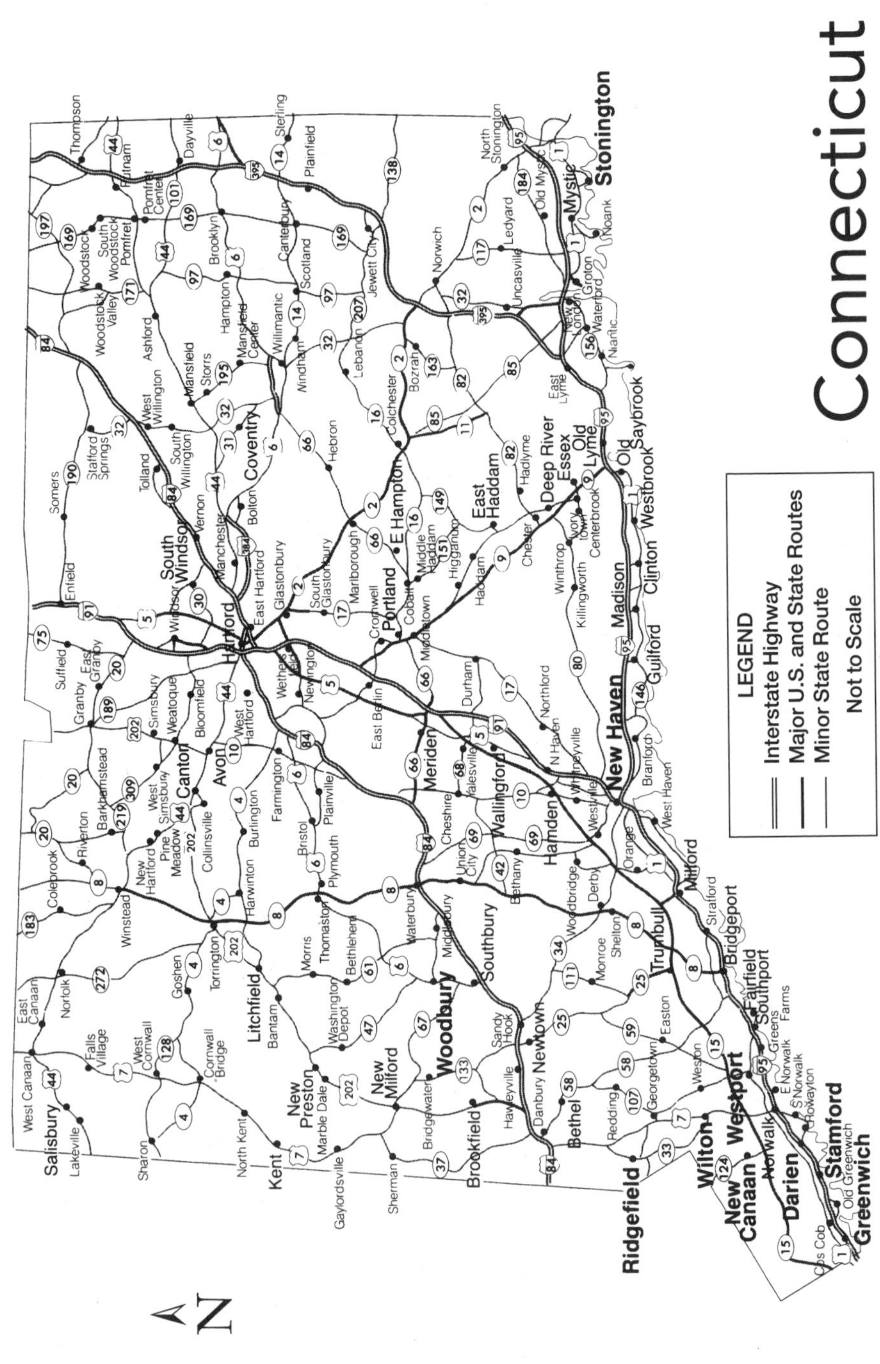
Connecticut
LEGEND
Interstate Highway
Major U.S. and State Routes
Minor State Route
Not to Scale
N
Hartford
New Haven
Bridgeport
Stamford
Greenwich
Norwalk
Westport
Darien
New Canaan
Wilton
Ridgefield
Danbury
Bethel
Brookfield
Newtown
Woodbury
New Milford
New Preston
Kent
Salisbury
Litchfield
Torrington
Canton
Avon
Meriden
Wallingford
Hamden
Milford
Trumbull
Southbury
Middletown
Portland
E Hampton
East Haddam
Deep River
Essex
Old Lyme
Old Saybrook
Westbrook
Clinton
Madison
Guilford
Stonington
Mystic
South Windsor
Coventry
Glastonbury
Enfield
Windsor

Ashford

Merrythought

271 Ashford Ctr Rd (Rte 44) • 06278
(860)429-8827 • (860)429-8977 (fax)
gdunphy@juno.com

18th & 19th C country antiques, furniture & accessories: ship models, fireplace cooking equipment, weather vanes; handcrafted reproduction weathervanes & copper lighting fixtures by order. **Pr:** $25-5,000 **Est:** 1987 **Hrs:** Sat-Sun 10-5 or by chance/appt. **Sz:** M **CC:** V/MC **Dir:** Rte 44 approx 1 mi E of Rte 89, next to Scout Camp entrance, look for Sign of the Swan. **Own:** Jeri Dunphy. **QC: 34 70 45 S18**

Avon

Antiques at Old Avon Village

1 E Main St • 06001
(860)676-2180
dw coll41@aol.com

Specializing in art glass: Venetian, Fenton, Contemporary, Cambridge, Duncan, Fostoria, Heisey, Tiffany, cut glass, carnival glass, Victorian glass, glass animals & glass figurals. **Est:** 1979 **Hrs:** Tue-Sat 10-5. **Sz:** M **CC:** AX/V/MC **Assn:** NCC HCA MCA FAGCA Tiffany Collectors **Own:** David Walker. **QC: 100 61**

Moosavi Persian Rugs

45 E Main St (Rte 44) • 06001
(860)676-0082 • (860)676-0089 (fax)

Large selection of antique & semi-antique fine, tribal & oversized Persian rugs, needlepoint & Aubusson weave. **Est:** 1979 **Hrs:** Mon-Sat 9:30-5:30, Thu til 7:30, Sun 1-4. **CC:** V/MC/DIS **Dir:** In Old Avon Village. **Own:** Ali Moosavi. **QC: 76**

Ruth Troiani

1 Mulberry Ln • 06001
(860)673-6191 • (860)673-5843 (fax)

Fine 17th to early 19th C accessories of all kinds, portraits of animals & children, 18th C glass, metal & a huge selection of fine samplers & memorials. **Est:** 1963 **Hrs:** By appt only. **Assn:** NHADA **Dir:** I-84 Farmington Exit. Call for directions. **QC: 12 36 82**

Edith Whitman Interiors

Old Avon Village, Bldg 21 • 06001
(860)677-5000 • (860)677-6909 (fax)

A variety of antiques, accessories, furniture, rugs & art work in a broad price range. **Pr:** $25-25,000 **Est:** 1968 **Hrs:** Mon-Sat 10-5. **Sz:** M **CC:** AX/V/MC **Dir:** Rte 44: 1/4 mi on L behind the big rocking chair. **Own:** Edith Whitman. **QC: 36 48 74 S15**

Bantam

Bantam Fine Arts

352 Bantam Lake Rd • 06750
(860)567-3337

19th & 20th C American & European paintings, period frames & sculpture. **Est:** 1980 **Hrs:** Jul-Aug Thu-Sun 11-5; Sep-Jun Sat-Sun 11-5; call ahead advised. **Own:** Thomas Pikul. **QC: 8 9 15**

Bradford House Antiques

895 Bantam Rd (Rte 202) • 06750
(860)567-0951 • (860)567-4896 (fax)
bradford@wtco.net

Fine Americana, jewelry & sterling. **Hrs:** Daily 11-6. **CC:** AX/V/MC **Own:** Jeff & Sandra Russak. **QC: 78**

The Old Carriage Shop Antiques Center [G20]

920 Bantam Rd (Rte 202) • 06750
(860)567-3234 • (860)496-9996 (fax)
dgrieco@snet.net

Antique furnishings including beds, chests of drawers, chairs, tables, desks, mirrors & decorative accessories. Collections of pottery, books, glassware, 1940-50s kitchenware, Jadite, lamps, rugs, linens, vintage clothing, sterling & jewelry. **Pr:** $5+ **Est:** 1990 **Hrs:** Wed-Sun 11-5. **Sz:** L **CC:** AX/V/MC **Dir:** 3-1/2 mi W of Litchfield Green. **Own:** John & Deborah Grieco. **QC: 48 32 36 S8 S19**

Weston Thorn Antiques

Rte 202 • 06750
(860)567-4661 • (860)567-4661 (fax)
LCA@litchfieldauctions.com

An attractive collection of antique English, Continental & American furniture & old reproductions, paintings, silver, porcelain & rugs, housed in a 2-story building & barn in scenic Litchfield County. **Pr:** $1-10,000 **Est:** 1982 **Hrs:** Fri-Sun 11-5, Sat 11-5:30, or by chance/appt. **Sz:** L **Assn:** AAA **Dir:** 4 mi SW of Litchfield. **QC: 48 7 78**

TNT Antiques & Collectibles

898 Bantam Rd (Rte 202) • 06750
(860)567-8823
tntique@snet.net

Huge selection of collectibles, antiques & junque; emphasis on trains, toys, vehicles, miniatures, kitchenware, tools & nostalgia. **Pr:** $2-500 **Hrs:** Thu-Sun 1-5 or by chance/appt. **Dir:** 3 mi W of the Litchfield Green. Old house with lots of junk on the porch. **Own:** Tom Pirone. **QC: 32 87**

Barkhamsted

Williams Fine Art & Antiques

78 N Canton Rd (Rte 179) • 06059
(860)379-8880

American & Continental furniture, specializing in fine art, sterling & plated silver as well as older books & fine smalls. **Hrs:** Sum Sat-Sun 10-5 or by chance/appt. **CC:** V/MC.

Bethany

Whitlock Farm Booksellers

20 Sperry Rd • 06524
(203)393-1240

Rare & unusual books in all fields: Americana, Connecticut, farming, gardening & horticulture, natural history, prints & maps. **Hrs:** Tue-Sun 9-5. **CC:** V/MC **Assn:** CAB **Own:** Gilbert & Everett Whitlock. **QC: 18 66 74**

Bethel

Nick of Time Antiques

219 Greenwood Ave • 06801
(203)730-9348

Furniture, pinball machines, jewelry & coins. **Hrs:** Thu-Mon 12-5. **Own:** Paris Caporale. **QC: 63 33**

Winston House Antiques & Fine Furnishings Ltd

219 Greenwood Ave • 06801
(203)730-9348 • 914-669-8004 (fax)

19th & 20th C collectibles. **Est:** 1999 **Hrs:** Thu-Mon 12-5. **Own:** Michael Winston. **QC: 32**

Bolton

Grand View Antiques

22 Hebron Rd • 06043
(860)643-9641

Antique furnishings & accessories of the 18th, 19th & early 20th C. **Hrs:** By appt only. **CC:** V/MC **Dir:** I-84E to Rte 384: Exit 5, turn R, 2 mi to Bolton Ctr, bear R at fork. **QC: 36 48**

Hailston House Inc

59 West St (Rte 85) • 06043
(860)646-2877

Two authentic New England barns brimming with traditional furniture, decorative accessories & eclectic lighting, situated in a charming country setting accented with garden ornaments. **Est:** 1976 **Hrs:** Sat & Sun 10:30-6 or call for appt. **Dir:** Rte 84 to Rte 384 Bolton Exit: Rte 85 S 1-1/2 mi. **QC: 34 48 60**

Branford

The Clocktower Antiques [G]

824 E Main St (Rte 1) • 06405
(203)488-1919

Featuring furniture, early iron, glass, china, books, ephemera, clocks, architectural items, carriages & sleighs. **Hrs:** Tue-Sun 10-5. **Dir:** I-95 Exit 56: N to Rte 1, go R on Rte 1, on the L.

Stony Creek Antiques

172 Thimble Island Rd • 06405
(203)488-4802 • (203)432-8471 (fax)
david.parsell@yale.edu

Jewelry, sterling silver, paintings, prints & mirrors. Also fine china, glass & pottery. 18th & 19th C furniture as well as decorative arts & accessories. **Pr:** $5-2,000 **Est:** 1992 **Hrs:** May-Dec daily 10:30-5:30; Jan-Apr Thu-Mon 10:30-5:30. **CC:** V/MC **Assn:** CADA **Dir:** I-95 Exit 56 toward Stony Creek, straight at 4-way stop, 1/4 mi on L next to Stony Creek Market. **Own:** Linda & David Parsell. **QC: 64 78 7**

Antiques of Wilderwood [G30]

764 E Main St • 06405
(203)483-5406 • (203)483-5336 (fax)
wilderwood@msn.com

Est: 1998 **Hrs:** Tue-Sun 10-5:30. **CC:** V/MC **Dir:** I-95 betw Exits 56 & 57. **Own:** Cheryl Conroy.

Yesterday's Threads

206 Meadow St • 06405
(203)481-6452

Vintage clothing (1800s thru 1960s) for men, women & children. Evening & day wear, accessories including hats, gloves, costume jewelry of all eras. Large selection of men's tuxedos, neckwear, cufflinks, tie bars & studs. **Pr:** $1-1,000 **Est:** 1977 **Hrs:** By appt only. **Sz:** M **Dir:** I-195 Exit 54 (Cedar St) to ctr of town. L onto Main St, R at end of town green onto Montowese St, 4th R on Meadow. Shop on R in white bldg w/purple trim. **Own:** Judith Young. **QC: 83 63**

Bridgewater

The Doll Room

9 Stuart Rd W • 06752
(860)354-8442 • (860)355-0546 (fax)
dollrm@aol.com

In an 1800s farmhouse, a doll shop with an abundant display of French & German antique & collectible dolls. Doll accessories including clothing, books, stands, furniture & doll house items. **Pr:** $25-2,000 **Est:** 1976 **Hrs:** By chance/appt. **Sz:** S **Dir:** Hutchinson Pkwy to 684N to Exit 9W onto Rte 84 to Exit 9. L to 1st light, R onto Rte 133 over bridge 2 mi to shop on L. **Own:** Walter & Diane Domroe. **QC: 38 S1 S11**

Bristol

Dick's Antiques

670 Lake Ave • 06010
(860)584-2566 • (860)314-0296 (fax)
rjblaschke@snet.net

Oak, walnut & Victorian furniture & accessories. Curved china cabinet glass. **Est:** 1960 **Hrs:** Jan 1-Jun 31 & Sep 1-Dec 31 Mon & Wed-Fri 10-5, Sat 12-5; Jul 1-Aug 31 Mon 9-5. **Sz:** L **CC:** V/MC **Dir:** I-84 Exit 31. **Own:** Richard Blaschke. **QC: 50 58 S10 S16 S17**

Wheels & Wings

78 Maple St • 06010
(860)589-1793
weselltoys@aol.com

Old toys: Ertl, First Gear, Matchbox, Racing Champions, Hess, Wilco, Servco, all airplanes, Texaco series always in stock, filling station memorabilia. **Hrs:** Mon-Fri 12-6, Sat 10-3. **CC:** AX/V/MC **Dir:** Near Clock Museum. **QC: 87**

Brookfield

McCaffrey & Booth Antiques & Restoration

436 Federal Rd • 06804
(203)775-1629

Antique & reproduction formal furniture. **Hrs:** By appt only. **CC:** V/MC **Dir:** I-84 to Rte 7, L onto Federal, on Rte 202. **QC: 48 56 S16**

Old Favorites

9 Arrowhead Rd • 06804
(203)775-3744 • (203)740-2743 (fax)

General line of fine antiques & collectibles. Specializing in Fiestaware. **Est:** 1969 **Hrs:** By appt only. **Assn:** NEAA **Own:** Rita Barg.

Brooklyn

Heirloom Antiques

8 Wolf Den Rd • 06234
(860)774-7017
marciabow@webtv.net

Period furniture & accessories, some formal, some country. Large inventory of lamps & lampshades. Lamp repair. **Pr:** $2-5,000 **Hrs:** Thu-Tue 12-5. **Sz:** M **CC:** V/MC **Assn:** NEAA **Own:** Marcia Laporte. **QC: 65 48 36 S1 S8**

Burlington

Hadsell's Antiques

191 George Washington Tpke • 06013
(860)673-2344

Two floors of Depression glass, quality glass & related items of the era. **Pr:** $25-500 **Est:** 1982 **Hrs:** Anytime by chance/appt. **Sz:** M **Dir:** From Unionville Ctr, S on Rte 177, R at 2nd light after bridge (Burlington Rd), at next SS, R on Geo Washington Tnpk, 1 mi. **Own:** Luther Hadsell. **QC: 32 61**

Canterbury

Cackleberry Farm Antiques

16 Lisbon Rd • 06331
(860)546-6335

A small shop featuring country collectibles. **Pr:** $1-3,000 **Hrs:** By chance/appt. **Sz:** M **Dir:** Rte 395 Exit 89: Rte 14W to Canterbury, 1st L past firehouse, 600 yds from corn on L. **Own:** Robert Forrest. **QC: 32 34**

Stone of Scone Books & Firearms

19 Water St • 06331
(860)546-9917
boomer@cyberzone.net

Located in the rural setting of Connecticut's quiet corner, featuring a large selection of rare & out-of-print books. New England history a specialty. Antique firearms & rare caliber reloading tools, antique & Indian jewelry & general line of smalls. **Pr:** $10-3,000 **Est:** 1976 **Hrs:** Sat 11-5, Sun 12-5, call for wkdy hrs. **Sz:** L **CC:** V/MC **Dir:** I-395N Exit 83A: L on Rte 169 8 mi, L at Rte 14 3 mi. L onto Water St, 500 ft on R. **Own:** Tom & Jan Stratton. **QC: 4 18 86**

Canton

Balcony Antiques [G17]

81 Albany Tpke (Rte 44) • 06019
(860)693-6440

Oldest group shop in CT: furniture, decorative accessories including a large selection of paintings, porcelain, china & silver. **Est:** 1972 **Hrs:** Mon-Sat 10-5, Sun 12-5. **Sz:** H **CC:** V/MC.

Antiques at Canton Village [G35]

220 Albany Tpke (Rte 44) • 06019
(860)693-2715 • (860)693-9636 (fax)

Authentic American & European period furniture, clocks, fine paintings, Oriental rugs, porcelains, silver, early lighting, Americana & art glass of the highest quality, many in period room settings. **Pr:** $50-5,000 **Est:** 1988 **Hrs:** Mon-Sat 10-5, Sun 12-5. **Sz:** L **CC:** AX/V/MC **Dir:** From Hartford, I-84W Farmington Exit: follow signs to Farmington Ctr. R on Rte 10 to Avon, L on Rte 44 to Canton (beyond Green). **Own:** Edwin Humphrey. **QC: 48 7 35**

The House of Clocks

148 Albany Tpke (Rte 44) • 06019
(860)693-2066

Antique clocks & watches bought, sold & restored. Specializing in restoration of wooden cased Federal, Empire & Victorian American clocks. Complete restoration of brass & wooden movements & refinishing. Free estimates. **Pr:** $50-7,500 **Est:** 1976 **Hrs:** Tue, Thu & Sat 10-1, Wed & Fri 10-4, Sun 2-5 or by appt. **Assn:** NAWCC **Dir:** I-84 to Farmington Exit Rte 4: W to Unionville N on Rte 177 to Rte 44, W 1/8 mi On L next to Margaritaville Restaurant. **Own:** Robert Galbraith Jr. **QC: 35 S7 S16**

Richard H Jenkins

(203)693-8968

Victorian jewelry, Oriental antiques, Arts & Crafts, Art Nouveau, Art Deco, snuff, vinaigrette, nutmeg, pommander, counter, vesta & pill boxes. **Est:** 1977 **Hrs:** By appt only. **Dir:** 17 mi W of Hartford off Rte 44. **QC: 78 71 64**

Decorating Glass

Prunt: A roundish blob of glass added as decoration to a piece of glassware.

Threading: Decorating glass by applying a thread of glass to a formed piece.

Lily pad: A coating of glass laid over a formed piece and tooled to a lily pad design. Originally Dutch, but taken up by New Jersey glassmakers.

Looping and swirls: Patterns made by incorporating threads of colored glass into a piece, particularly characteristic of Nailsea.

Engraving: Cutting a design into the surface of glass by a diamond point or a fine engraving wheel.

Etching: Using acid to "frost" a design on glass which results in whitish, opaque lines and areas.

Cutting: Cutting deeply into heavy, clear glass, usually in diamond patterns, to produce a faceted, sparkling design.

Enameling: Painting a design on glass that was then reheated to fix the enamel.

Gilding: Applying gold leaf to glass (see "Decorating with Gold").

Cranberry Glass: Glass of a deep red color produced by adding gold to the glass while hot.

Prunts, threads, lily pads, loops, and swirls were all applied while the glass was still hot: engraving, etching, and cutting were performed after it had cooled. Colored glass became popular only after the Civil War. The peak period for cut glass was about from about 1880 to 1915.

Centerbrook

Brush Factory Antiques [G]

33 Deep River Rd (Rte 154) • 06409
(860)767-0845

Offering a wide assortment of collectibles & quality antiques at affordable prices. **Est:** 1988 **Hrs:** Daily 11-5. **CC:** V/MC **Dir:** I-91 to Rte 9S Exit 4: R off ramp 1/2 mi on L. From I-95 Rte 9N, Exit 4: 3/4 mi on L. **Own:** Miriam Henderson.

Centerbridge Books

33 Deep River Rd (Rte 154) • 06409
(860)767-8943
LgraceL@aol.com

A fine selection of used & collectible books. **Hrs:** Wed-Sun 11-5. **CC:** AX/V/MC **Dir:** N of Essex. **QC: 18**

Essex Emporium Curious Goods

19 Deep River Rd (Rte 154) • 06409
(860)767-1869 • (860)767-3984 (fax)

Large shop of antique toys, furniture, folk art, garden & decorative accessories. **Hrs:** Fri-Sat 10-5 or by chance/appt. **Sz:** L **CC:** V/MC **Dir:** I-95 Exit 3: Rte 9N, turn L & follow Rte 154 N. **Own:** D I Feldman. **QC: 87 60 36 S11 S12 S19**

Chaplin

MacKay & Field

329 Chewink Rd • 06256
(860)455-1055

American country furniture in original paint &/or surface; appropriate decorative accessories including lighting, samples, portraits & a large selection of used & out-of-print reference books on antiques, all in the 1787 Jonathan Ashley house. **Pr:** $25-10,000 **Hrs:** Anytime by chance/appt. **Dir:** From int of Rte 6 & Rte 198, 1 mi W to yellow flashing light, then turn onto Lynch Rd. On Lynch, 1.5 mi to end, corn Lynch & Chewink. **Own:** Susan MacKay & Peter Field. **QC: 1 19 51**

Cheshire

The Magnolia Shoppe

908 S Meriden Rd • 06410
(203)272-3303

Antique furniture, decorative accessories, vintage linens & estate jewelry in excellent condition. **Pr:** $10-2,500 **Est:** 1984 **Hrs:** Tue-Sat 11-5, Sun 12-5. **Sz:** M **CC:** V/MC **Assn:** CADA **Dir:** Rte 10 in Cheshire to Academy Rd to int of Rtes 68 & 70, L on Rte 70 for 2 mi. Shop on R in Curtiss Homestead Village. **Own:** Louise Barto. **QC: 36 81 64**

Chester

One of A Kind Antiques

21 Main St • 06412
(860)526-9736 • (860)526-9759 (fax)
tom@oneofakindantiques.com
www.oneofakindantiques.com

Fine collection of American & European furniture, paintings, prints, estate jewelry, silver, Arts & Crafts, Modernism, Orientalia, lighting from the 17th-20th C. Original condition is a priority. **Est:** 1975 **Hrs:** Wed-Sat 10-5, Sun 12-4, Mon 10-5. **Sz:** M **CC:** AX/V/MC/DIS **Assn:** NEAA **Dir:** Rte 95N or S to Rte 9N Exit 6. R 1 m. Rte 84 to Rte 9S Exit 6, L 1 m. **Own:** Thomas & Cheri-Ann Perry. **QC: 64 52 53 S1 S8 S14**

William L Schaeffer Photographs

41 Main St • 06412
(860)526-3870

Specializing in vintage 19th & 20th C photographs by American, English, French & Italian photographers. **Hrs:** By chance/appt, best to call ahead. **Dir:** I-95 Exit 69: N of Rte 9 to Exit 6. **QC: 73**

Spiritus Mundi Antiques

122 Middlesex Tpke • 06412
(860)526-3406
marta.daniels@snet.net

18th & 19th C country antiques, stoneware, prints & stringed musical instruments. **Hrs:** Daily 10-5 or by chance/appt. **Dir:** Rte 9 Exit 6: Rte 148 E to Rte 154 S, 3 blks up hill on L. **QC: 102 74 69**

Willow Tree

4 Water St • 06412
(860)526-4297

Vintage clothing & accessories, linens, lace, hats, walking sticks, decorative accessories & collectibles. **Hrs:** Wed-Fri 11-5, Sat-Sun 12-5. **QC: 83 81 36**

Clinton

Barker & Chambers Antiques on Main Street

100 E Main St (Rte 1) • 06413
(860)664-9163
ambarker@snet.net
www.clintonct.com/barker

19th C decorative arts & furniture. **Hrs:** Thu-Mon 11-5. **Dir:** Rte 1 in the historic district of Clinton. **QC: 36 48**

Clinton Antique Center [G75]

78 E Main St (Rte 1) • 06413
(860)669-3839

Antiques & collectibles including furniture, china, glass, jewelry, military, toys, clocks, books & pottery. **Est:** 1992 **Hrs:** Daily 10-5; Oct-Apr Thu-Tue 10-5. **Sz:** L **CC:** V/MC/DIS **Dir:** I-95 Exit 63: Rte 1 E. **Own:** Jerri Case. **QC: 32 48 61**

Miriam Green

88 E Main St (Rte 1) • 06413
(860)664-4200

Books & period accessories. **Hrs:** Daily or by chance/appt. **Dir:** I-95 Exit 64: R onto Rte 1 to E Main St.

John Street Antiques

23A W Main St (Rte 1) • 06413
(860)669-2439

Jewelry, collectibles, dolls, toys, oak, country, walnut & mahogany furniture, advertising & architectural items. **Est:** 1989 **Hrs:** Thu-Sun 11-4. **Dir:** I-95 Exit 63: to Rte 1, 1 blk W of Rtes 81 & 1 on N side of the road. **QC: 32 38 63**

The Loft & the House Next Door [G6]

57-59 W Main St (Rte 1) • 06413
(860)669-4583

A corn crib building displaying glass, pottery, jewelry, linens, stoneware, unique wood & metal pieces. The 1800s house next door offers antique furniture & decorative accessories in room settings. **Pr:** $25-500 **Est:** 1985 **Hrs:** Daily 12-5. **Sz:** M **Dir:** I-95 Exit 63: S on Rte 81 to Rte 1, turn R on Rte 1. Across from Friendly's restaurant. **Own:** David Cramer.

Miller's Antiques

327 E Main St (Rte 1) • 06413
(860)399-9254

Country furniture & antiques in the rough. **Hrs:** Fri-Mon 9-6, Tue-Thu by chance. **CC:** V/MC/DIS **Own:** Russ Miller. **QC: 102**

Square Rigger Antiques Center [G]

350 E Main St (Rte 1) • 06413
(860)664-9001

Furniture, primitives, jewelry, lighting, rugs, paintings, collectibles & bric-a-brac. **Hrs:** Tue-Sun 11-7. **CC:** V/MC **Dir:** Rte 1 on the Clinton Westbrook town line. **Own:** Robert Denaro.

Hale Van Carter Fine Art

5 Post Office Sq • 06413
(860)669-4313

Fine American paintings, watercolors & prints with an emphasis on Connecticut & New England artists. Art appraisal to the trade with a computer bank of over 16,000 American & Canadian artists with auction records. **Pr:** $300-20,000 **Hrs:** By appt only. **Assn:** NEAA **Dir:** I-95 Exit 63: S on Rte 81 for 1/2 mi, R on Boston Post Rd (Rte 1), 6th bldg on L. **QC: 7 S1 S9**

Waterside Antiques

109 E Main St (Rte 1) • 06413
(860)669-0809

Primitives, country antiques & small accessories. Unique shop for country decorating. **Hrs:** Mon & Wed-Sat 11-4, Sun by chance. **QC: 34 106**

Wooden Wheelbarrow

327 E Main St • 06413
(860)669-3533

Country furniture, primitives, kitchenware — specializing in Fiesta & Royal Doulton china, books, jewelry & small accessories. **Hrs:** Thu-Mon 10-5, Tue & Wed by chance. **QC: 102 106**

Cobalt

Arthur Collins Antiques

Cobalt Ctr • 06414
(860)342-1144

Americana, folk art & furniture. **Est:** 1963 **Hrs:** Daily 10-5. **Sz:** L **Dir:** Jct Rte 66 & Rte 15. **QC: 1 52 41 S12 S1**

Colchester

Nathan Liverant & Son

168 S Main St • 06415
(860)537-2409 • (860)537-0577 (fax)

Large & varied inventory of fine Americana including some of the finest examples of New England regional furniture, paintings & related accessories of the 17th, 18th & 19th C. **Est:** 1920 **Hrs:** Mon-Sat 10-5. **Assn:** ADA NAADAA NHADA **Dir:** Betw Hartford & New London on Rte 85. **Own:** Israel "Zeke" & Arthur Liverant. **QC: 1 52 7**

Philip Liverant

267 Lebanon Ave • 06415
(860)537-2449

A general line of furniture & related items, large variety of early glass & art glass, lamps. **Est:** 1946 **Hrs:** Sun & Mon 10-4. **Sz:** M **Assn:** AAA **Dir:** Rte 2 S from Hartford, Rte 16 E from Middletown. **Own:** Philip Liverant. **QC: 48 61 S1**

Collinsville

Collinsville Antiques Company [G35]

1 Main St (Rte 179) • 06022
(860)693-1011

On the scenic Farmington River antique oak, walnut, pine & mahogany furniture, lighting, clocks, rugs, art, silver, glass, jewelry & collectibles in the Historic Collins Axe Factory. **Hrs:** Wed-Mon 10-5. **Sz:** H **CC:** V/MC **Assn:** NEAA **Dir:** I-84 Exit 39: follow Rte 4 W to Rte 179 into Collinsville, 1st R over bridge. **Own:** Doug Szydlo. **QC: 32 36 50 S1 S12**

Village Green Antiques [G29]

41 Bridge St • 06022
(860)693-1972 **Est:** 1992 **Hrs:** Daily 10-5. **CC:** V/MC/DIS **Own:** Michael LaMott

Columbia

Freudenwald Antiques

26 Rte 87 • 06237
(860)228-1245

Americana, folk art, pottery (including Red Wing), art & collectibles. **Hrs:** Sat-Sun 10-5. **Dir:** 1 mi S from Rte 6, 3 mi N of Rte 66 approx 900 ft off Rte 87. **QC: 1 41 22**

Cornwall

Ballyhack Antiques
16 Furnace Brook Rd • 06753
(860)672-6751 • (860)672-0005 (fax)

American country furniture, much in original paint & surface, as well as folk art & decorative objects. **Hrs:** By appt only. **Own:** Mary Sams. **QC: 1 41 51**

The Brass Bugle
Rte 45 • 06754
(860)672-6535

In an 18th C barn: furniture, primitives, collectibles, fabrics, quilts, dolls, glass, china, lamps & tools. **Est:** 1962 **Hrs:** May-Nov daily 8-5. **CC:** V/MC **Dir:** 1/2 mi off Rte 7 on Rte 45. **Own:** Louise Graham. **QC: 34 61**

G K Holmes Antiques
131 Kent Rd • 06754
(860)672-6427

Specializing in 18th & 19th C American country & formal furniture, accessories, toys & dolls; also William & Mary, Queen Ann, tavern tables & Windsor chairs. **Pr:** $25-5,000 **Est:** 1959 **Hrs:** Daily 7-7. **Sz:** M **CC:** V/MC **Dir:** 45 mi N of Danbury; 45 mi E of Poughkeepsie, NY; 45 mi S of Pittsfield, MA; 45 mi W of Hartford, CT. **QC: 52 S16**

Frederick I Thaler
(860)672-0052

A selection of 19th & early 20th C American paintings, American painted furniture & related objects. **Hrs:** By appt only. **Assn:** NHADA. **QC: 7 51**

Coventry

Memory Lane Countryside Antique Center [G50]
2224 Boston Tpke (Rte 44) • 06238
(860)742-0346

Three bldgs of silver, china, glass, furniture, primitives, jewelry, quilts, flow blue, mulberry, tools & toys. **Pr:** $10-7,000 **Est:** 1985 **Hrs:** Wed-Sun 10-5. **Sz:** L **CC:** V/MC **Assn:** ACDA **Dir:** I-84 Exit 67: 2 mi S to corn of Rtes 31 & 44. **Own:** Gail & Gene Dickenson. **QC: 48 61 32 S12**

Special Joys Antique Doll & Toy Shop
41 N River Rd • 06238
(860)742-6359

Doll, toy & Steiff shop specializing in antique & collectible children's items with some general antiques. Also a doll museum & B&B. **Hrs:** Apr-Oct Wed-Sun 11-5, Nov-Mar Thu-Sun 11-4:30. **Dir:** Off Rte 31. **QC: 38 87**

Village Antiques [G27]
1340 Main St (Rte 31) • 06238
(860)742-5701

Shop located in a reproduction of an 1890s village: a potpourri of antiques & collectibles, on two floors of an old barn. **Pr:** $1-5,000 **Est:** 1973 **Hrs:** Thu-Sun 10-5. **Sz:** L **CC:** V/MC **Dir:** Corn of Rtes 31 & 275. **QC: 32**

Cromwell

Broyles Barn
521 Main St (Rte 99) • 06416
(860)635-5957

Victoriana, primitives, Art Deco antiques & collectibles. **Hrs:** Sat-Sun 10-5 or by appt. **QC: 89 106 5**

Custom House
6 Kirby Rd • 06416
(860)828-6885

A specialty shop for custom lamp shades: hand sewn, pierced, botanical, fabric & paper lamination, displayed on antique furniture with a selection of antique accessories, Chinese porcelains, early oil & kerosene lamps. **Pr:** $25-5,000 **Est:** 1968 **Hrs:** Sep 15-July 15 Tue-Fri 10-4, Sat 9:30-12. **Sz:** M **Dir:** I-91 Exit 21: 1st R, 2nd L. **Own:** Eunice Buxton. **QC: 41 65 S16 S17**

Elizabeth's Antiques & Collectibles

196 Shunpike Rd (Rte 3) • 06416
(860)635-8464

Antiques, collectibles, vintage furniture, china, glass, porcelain, pottery, oak & costume jewelry. **Hrs:** Wed-Sun 10-5. **CC:** V/MC/DIS **Dir:** Rte 9 Exit 19: Rte 3 N 1 mi. I-91 Exit 23: Rte 3 S 2 mi.

Steamboat Landing

38 River Rd • 06416
(860)613-0820
rstars@internet-95.com

Antiques & collectibles. **Hrs:** Sat-Sun 11-3 or by appt. **Dir:** Rte 9 N to Exit 18: 1stt R onto South St to end, R onto River Rd. Shop on L. Rte 9 S to Exit 19: L onto West St to end, L onto Main St (Rte 99) 2nd L.

Danbury

Antiquity

66 Sugar Hollow (Rte 7) • 06810
(203)748-6244

Furniture & art, Victorian to Deco, decorative accessories & countless smalls including Depression glass, Staffordshire, Nippon, Limoges, pottery, toys, porcelain pipes & steins & costume jewelry. **Hrs:** Wed-Sun 12-4. **Dir:** I-84 Exit 3 on Rte 7 S on the Danbury-Ridgefield line.

Time After Time

5 Padanaram Rd N (Ridge Plaza) • 06811
(203)743-2801
www.bca-pool.com/tat/

Billiards supplies & custom & antique tables from the mid-1800s, run by a billiards historian. **Est:** 1958 **Hrs:** Mon-Sat 10-5, Jul-Aug closed Mon. **Sz:** L **CC:** V/MC/DIS **Assn:** BCA **Dir:** Rte 84E to Exit 5, bear L at 5th light, 1st R beyond McDonalds; Rte 84W to Exit 6, R to light, L at light, 1st R beyond McDonalds. **Own:** Ed O'Connell. **QC: 79**

Danielson

Lou's Olde Tyme Sheet Music Shop

229 Cook Hill Rd • 06239
(203)779-2183

Specializing in every category of sheet music from the Civil War to the 1980s. **Hrs:** Thu-Sat 9-4. **Dir:** I-395 Exit 93: call for directions. **Own:** Al Sanderson. **QC: 69**

Darien

Antiques of Darien [G8]

1101 Boston Post Rd • 06820
(914)961-9010 • (924)961-9010 (fax)

Formal, country & Continental furniture, Oriental carpets, paintings, prints & cases of smalls. **Est:** 1977 **Hrs:** Mon-Sat 10-5, Oct-May Sun 1-4:30. **Sz:** L **CC:** V/MC **Dir:** 300' off I-95 Exit 11. **Own:** Sarah Heintz. **QC: 7 36 48**

Emy Jane Jones Antiques

770 Boston Post Rd • 06820
(203)655-7576 • (203)655-1298 (fax)

Seven rooms of furniture in oak, pine, walnut & mahogany, beautiful antique jewelry & accessories. **Est:** 1974 **Hrs:** Mon-Sat 10-5, Sun 1-5. **CC:** AX/V/MC **Assn:** NEAA **Dir:** In the heart of Darien. **QC: 50 55 64**

Catherine Sylvia Reiss

1072 Post Rd • 06820
(203)655-8070

Antique prints including botanicals, birds, prints for children, national historic town views. **Est:** 1977 **Hrs:** Mon-Sat 10-5. **CC:** V/MC **Dir:** I-95 Exit 12. **Own:** Sylvia & Ken Reiss. **QC: 74**

Mary Stasik Antiques / Andrew Stasik Fine Arts

395 West Ave • 06820
(203)327-7456

Antiques & fine art. **Hrs:** By appt only. **CC:** V/MC.

Village Clock Shop
1074 Post Rd • 06820
(203)655-2100

A full line of antique shelf, wall & tallcase clocks in all price ranges. **Pr:** $25-25,000 **Est:** 1991 **Hrs:** Tue-Sat 10-5, Sun by chance. **Sz:** M **CC:** V/MC **Assn:** NAWCC BHI AWI **Dir:** I-95 Exit 11: 1/10 mi E on Rte 1 (Post Rd) directly across from movie theatre. **Own:** Karyn Critelli. **QC: 35 S7**

Windsor Antiques Ltd
(914)723-3993

Specialists in samplers & related needlework. Large stock of 18th & 19th C English & American furniture, Chinese export porcelain, Staffordshire, folk art, sporting art, paintings & fireplace equipment. **Est:** 1975 **Hrs:** By appt only. **CC:** V/MC **Own:** David & Jackie Kemp. **QC: 82 52 25**

Deep River

Jas E Elliott Antiques
453 Winthrop Rd • 06417
(860)526-9455

Specializing in British pottery & porcelain of the 18th & 19th C, Federal, Empire & Regency furniture, fine quality decorative accessories. **Pr:** $50-10,000 **Est:** 1959 **Hrs:** By appt only. **Sz:** M **Assn:** AADLA CINOA NEAA **Dir:** I-95 Exit 64: Rte 80, jct of 145. **QC: 36 23 52 S1**

Riverwind Antiques [G20]
68 Main St (Rte 154) • 06417
(860)526-3047

Nine rooms featuring antique furniture, china, silver, fine jewelry, books & collectibles. Owner-operated group shop. **Pr:** $5-5,000 **Est:** 1985 **Hrs:** Wed-Sat 10:30-5, Sun 12-5 or by chance/appt. **Sz:** M **CC:** V/MC **Assn:** NEAA **Dir:** I-95 Exit 69: to Rte 9, Exit 5 E to Rte 154 (Main St) to corn Spring St. **Own:** Peggy Maraschiello. **QC: 32 55**

Don Slater & Sons Antiques
246 S Main St • 06417
(860)526-9757 • (860)526-9757 (fax)
irshpine@connix.com

An enormous selection of Irish country antiques, all hand-picked from throughout Ireland, containers arriving regularly. Custom-made items also available, as well as a large selection of antiques & reproduction items from Indonesia. **Est:** 1980 **Hrs:** May-Sep Wed-Sun 10-5; Oct-Apr Thu-Sun 10-5. **Sz:** L **CC:** AX/V/MC **Dir:** Exit 4 off Rte 9; L approx 1 mi to the int of Main St & Union St. **QC: 55 56 S17**

The Way We Wore
116 N Main St • 06417
(860)526-2944

Two floors with vintage clothing & vintage accessories, furniture, glass, jewelry & assorted collectibles. **Hrs:** Mon-Sat 11-5, Sun & hols 12-5 or by appt. **Sz:** L **Dir:** Rte 9 Exit 5: on Rte 154 (Main St) in large yellow Victorian bldg. **Own:** Norma Watrous-Smith. **QC: 32 63 83**

Durham

Staneika Antiques
(860)349-1527

18th & early 19th C American furniture with an emphasis on original surface & condition as well as examples of early lighting & other quality smalls. **Hrs:** By appt only. **Assn:** NHADA. **QC: 52 65**

East Berlin

Clint & Pat Bigelow American Antiques
174 Main St • 05143
(860)828-1868

Specializing in Shaker furniture & accessories as well as 18th & 19th C furniture & accessories in original as-found condition. **Hrs:** By appt only. **Assn:** VADA. **QC: 57 102**

East Haddam

Howard & Dickinson Antiques

48-50 Main St • 06423
(860)873-9990

English & American antiques, decorative accessories, paintings & miniatures. **Hrs:** Daily 10-6. **Sz:** L **CC:** V/MC **Dir:** I-95 Exit 7. **QC: 7 10 36**

Millers Antiques

Rte 82 • 06423
(860)873-8286

Stone age to Moderne. North & South American Indian artifacts. Vintage clothing, country furniture, hanging lamps & exotic jewelry. **Est:** 1939 **Hrs:** Sat-Sun 12-6 or by chance. **Sz:** M **Dir:** CT Rte 95 to Rte 9 N Exit 7: Follow signs to Gillette Castle on Rte 82. **Own:** Jim & Louise Miller. **QC: 65 42 83**

Antiques at Society Hall

23 Main St (Rte 149) • 06423
(860)873-8286

Stone age to modern, architectural, vintage clothing, country furniture & lighting. **Pr:** $5-5,000 **Est:** 1999 **Hrs:** Wknd afternoons or by chance/appt. **Dir:** I-95 to Rte 9 N Exit 17: cross river, go behond Opera House, L at fork, Society Hall on L. **Own:** Chris & Gerry Miller.

East Hampton

Antiques at 70 Main Street [G]

70 Main St • 06424
(860)267-9501

Antiques & collectibles. **Pr:** $25-3,000 **Hrs:** Wed-Sun 10-5, Fri til 8. **Sz:** M **CC:** V/MC **Dir:** Rte 66 E to E Hampton, turn R at 2nd light, 1/2 mi on R.

The Iron Horse Antiques & Nostalgia

64 Main St • 06424
(860)267-7623

Eclectic assortment of 19th & 20th C bottles, books, garden accessories, kitchen items, decorative accessories, lighting & prints, paintings, small period furniture, pottery, sports related antiques, early tools & vintage appliances. **Pr:** $25-500 **Est:** 1993

Furniture Tops

Cornice: A flat, overhanging top on a tall piece of furniture, usually molded.

Pediment: An architectural element in the form of the shallow triangular end of a roof which was frequently applied to the cornices of bookcases, secretaries, and cabinets in the 18th century. More common in English than American furniture.

Broken Pediment: A pediment where the apex of the triangle has been cut away to allow for a bust or finial to be set on a pedestal rising from the base of the triangle.

Bonnet top: A strongly curved pediment, shaped like a cupid's bow, and "broken" at the top to allow for a bust or finial, as in a broken pediment. Often the two broken ends are embellished with rosettes. In England, often called a "swan's neck" pediment because of its resemblance to two swans' necks. In English furniture the swan's neck pediment is frequently only a facade, whereas in America it often extends to the whole depth of the piece. Typically used on secretaries, highboys, chests on chests, and clocks.

Blind bonnet top: A bonnet top in which the space behind the central finial is closed by a vertical board.

Hrs: Wed-Sun 1-5:15. **Sz:** M **Dir:** Main St in E Hampton, CT, off Rte 66. 8 mi E of Middletown, CT. **Own:** Mary Ann D Manzara. **QC: 32 36 39 S1 S8 S12**

Mechantiques
26 Barton Hill • 06424
(860)267-8682 • (860)267-1120 (fax)
(800)671-6333

Specializing in antique mechanical music, disc & cylinder music boxes, band organs, organettes, some phonographs, coin pianos, mechanical birds. Always something interesting & always looking to buy better antique mechanical musical instruments. **Pr:** $5-20,000 **Hrs:** By appt only. **Sz:** M **Dir:** Call for directions. **Own:** Martin Roenigk. **QC: 69**

Old Bank Antiques [G30]
66 Main St • 06424
(860)267-0790

Over 300 pieces of furniture from 1840-1940 in an old bank complete with vault, accented with glassware, lighting, clocks, mirrors, china & jewelry. **Pr:** $5-8,000 **Est:** 1984 **Hrs:** Wed-Sun 10-5, Fri 10-8. **Sz:** L **CC:** AX/V/MC **Dir:** I-91 Exit 25: onto Rte 2 E, Exit 13, R onto Rte 66, L at 3rd light. **Own:** Ray & Judy Laubenstein. **QC: 48 65 68**

Past & Present
81 Main St • 06424
(860)267-0495

Antiques, jewelry, collectibles & quality used furniture. **Hrs:** Wed-Sun 11-5. **Dir:** 20 mi S of Hartford. I-91 S to Rte 66 E for 9 mi into E Hampton. R onto Main St. **Own:** Doreen Pierce.

East Woodstock

Rivers Antiques
(860)974-3578

Samplers, quilts, coverlets, textile-related items & country furniture of the 18th & 19th C. **Hrs:** By appt only. **Assn:** GSAAA **Own:** Joyce & Charles Rivers. **QC: 80 82 102**

Eastford

Still Waters Antiques
Jct Rtes 44 & 198 • 06242
(860)974-3500

Antiques, textiles, vintage clothing & hats galore. **Hrs:** Thu-Sun 10-5. **Dir:** Located on N side of jct of Rtes 44 & 198. **QC: 83**

Ellington

Paul & Karen Wendhiser
(860)872-9600

18th & early 19th C Americana including painted country furniture, accessories & hearth iron, English pearlware & creamware. **Assn:** ADA NHADA VADA GSAAA. **QC: 1 51 26**

Enfield

Old Hickory Antiques
144 Candlewood Dr • 06082
(860)749-2213

High style American country furniture & accessories. **Hrs:** By appt only. **Assn:** GSAAA **Own:** Tom & Ann Corcoran. **QC: 102 34**

Essex

Arne E Ahlberg Antiques
145 Westbrook Rd • 06426
(860)767-2799

Early American furniture. **Hrs:** Tue-Sat 11-5. **QC: 52**

Frances Bealey American Arts / Gunn Gallery Inc
3 S Main St • 06426
(860)767-0220

18th & 19th C decorative arts, American furniture & paintings. **Hrs:** Tue-Sat 11-4. **Dir:** Located in the Old Public Library building in Essex. **QC: 7 36 52**

Bonsal-Douglas Antiques

One Essex Square • 06426
(860)767-2282 • (860)345-3914 (fax)

European & American paintings, Delft, British & American furniture & rugs. **Est:** 1984 **Hrs:** Tue-Wed 10:30-1:30, Thu-Sat 11-5. **Sz:** M **Assn:** NEAA **Dir:** I-95 Exit 69 to Essex Village, 1st gallery on R (Main St). **Own:** Isabelle Douglas Seggerman. **QC: 7 27 54 S1 S12**

Hastings House

4, 6 & 8 N Main St • 06426
(860)767-8217 • (860)767-0748 (fax)

Oriental art, garden furniture & statuary; European furniture & accessories from the rare to the whimsical; pieces from the 17th to the early 20th C. **Est:** 1965 **Hrs:** Spr/Sum/Fall Mon-Sat 10:30-5:30, Sun 12-5:30. **Assn:** AADLA **Dir:** Rte 95 to Rte 9 N Exit 3: go R into village, shop on Main St. **Own:** P Hastings McNemer & M A Barnes. **QC: 60 71 53**

Latitudes

Novelty Ln • 06426
(860)767-3001

18th & 19th C antiquarian maps & marine charts of New England, Atlantic Coast, Florida Keys, Caribbean; Nantucket prints/views; CT decoys, nautical & fishing items. **Est:** 1977 **Hrs:** Mon-Fri 9-4. **Sz:** M **Dir:** Rte 9 Exit 3; I-95 Exit 65. **Own:** Tom Lazor. **QC: 9 66 70 S1 S9 S16**

A Matthews Anderson Antiques

Rte 154 • 06426
(860)767-1617

Country furniture, china, Oriental rugs & lamps, collectibles, dolls & toys. **Hrs:** Thu-Sun 11-4:30 or by appt. **Dir:** Corn Rte 154 & Captain's Walk. **QC: 102 76 65**

Phoenix Antiques

10 Main St • 06426
(860)767-5082 • (860)767-0071 (fax)

Furniture & accessories. **Est:** 1992 **Hrs:** Daily 10-5. **CC:** V/MC **Dir:** Rte 3 to Exit 3, follow signs for historic district. **Own:** Joseph O'Neal.

Valley Farm Antiques

134 Saybrook Rd (Rte 154) • 06426
(860)767-8555

A large & varied collection of period & country antique furniture, guns & clocks. Specializing in American Indian, African, oceanic artifacts, Taconic, Shaker & Indian baskets. The largest collection of toys in New England. **Pr:** $25-18,000 **Est:** 1963 **Hrs:** Apr-Dec Tue-Sat 10-4. **Sz:** L **CC:** V/MC **Assn:** NEAA **Dir:** I-95 to Rte 154 N, 1 mi N of Essex Saybrook Antique Village. **Own:** Ellsworth Stevison. **QC: 48 61 87**

The Yankee Trader

55 Main St • 06426
(860)767-7659
yankeeart@aol.com
www.publiconline.com/~yankeetrader

Antique & vintage prints & posters. **Hrs:** Mon-Sat 10-5, Sun 12-5. **Dir:** Diagonally across from the Griswold Inn. **QC: 74 S13 S17**

Fairfield

James Bok Antiques

1954 Post Rd (Rte 1) • 06430
(203)255-6500

Period furniture, early brass & accessories. **Hrs:** By chance/appt. **Assn:** NHADA **Own:** James Bok. **QC: 20 36 52**

Martin Chasin Fine Art

1125 Church Hill Rd • 06432
(203)374-5987 • (203)372-3419 (fax)
(888)446-9441

Specializing in works of art on paper & canvas. English sporting art from the 18th & 19th C, English & American 18th C & 19th C antiques, Tiffany & English silver. **Pr:** $3,000-50,000 **Hrs:** Sun-Fri 10-6. **Sz:** M **Assn:** AAA NEAA **Dir:** Merritt Pkwy to Exit 46; Stratford Rd toward Long Island Sound to Church Hill Rd. **Own:** Martin Chasin. **QC: 54 7 78**

Gallery Orient

1828 Post Rd • 06432
(203)255-6777

19th & 20th C Asian furniture, porcelain & decorations. **Hrs:** Tue-Sat 11-5. **Dir:** I-95 betw exits 19 & 21. **QC: 48 24**

Madeline L Groark

26 Old Oaks Rd • 06432
(203)334-8937

American furniture, brass & ceramics. **Hrs:** By appt only. **Assn:** AC **Own:** Madeline & Owen Groark. **QC: 52 20 25**

Winsor Antiques

43 Ruane St • 06430
(203)255-0056

Specializing in fine early English & French country furniture, Delft & early accessories. **Hrs:** By appt only. **Own:** Paul & Barbara Winsor. **QC: 54 47 27**

Farmington

ANTIQ'S LLC

Hyde Rd. • 06032
(860)676-2670 • (860)676-9393 (fax)
info@antiqs.com
www.antiqs.com

A privately owned shop in a large post-and-beam barn offering 18th & 19th C antiques, formal & country furniture & all the appropriate accessories of the periods with an emphasis on American lighting & historic pieces of Farmington & the Valley. **Pr:** $10.00-20,000 **Est:** 1987 **Hrs:** Wed-Sun 11-4, other times by appt. **Sz:** L **CC:** V/MC **Own:** Thomas P McCarthy. **QC: 52 58 65 S1 S12**

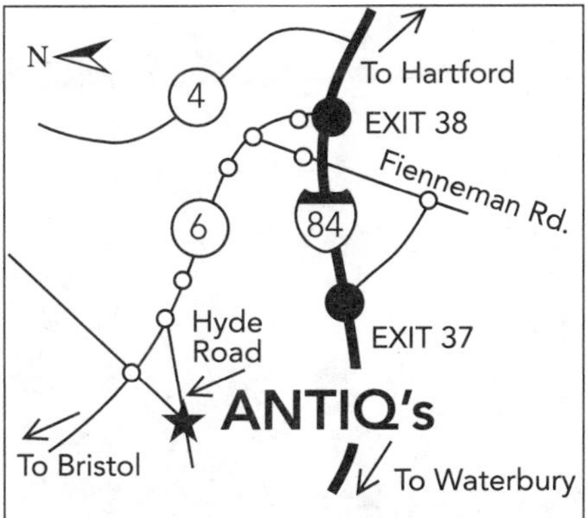

How to Find Antiq's

From Hartford, CT: Rte 84 West to Exit 38 (Rte 6, Bristol): Beginning at bottom of exit, go 5 traffic lights (don't count the blinking light). Left at the 5th light onto Hyde Rd. Shop is 3,000 feet on the right.
From Waterbury, CT: Rte 84 East to Exit 37, the Fienneman Rd exit. At end of exit, take a left, go to the second light, and take another left onto Rte 6. Continue on Rte 6 to 3rd traffic light (don't count the blinking light). Left at the 3rd light onto Hyde Rd. Shop is 3,000 feet on the right.

Farmington Lodge Antiques [G]

185 Main St (Rte 10) • 06032
(860)674-1035
(888)768-8310

In a 1763 Colonial mansion, an ever-changing selection of antiques & decorative accessories in room settings. **Hrs:** Tue-Sat 10-5, Sun 12-5. **Dir:** I-84 Exit 39: 1/4 mi to Rte 10 S, 1.2 mi on L. **Own:** Michael & Lisa Richard.

Gaylordsville

Bittersweet Shop [G14]

Jct Rtes 7 & 55 • 06755
(860)354-1727
mestab4730@aol.com

Formal & country furniture, quilts, paintings, baskets, porcelain & glass. **Pr:** $25-4,000 **Est:** 1978 **Hrs:** Mon-Tue, Thu-Sat 12-6, closed Wed. **Sz:** L **CC:** V/MC **Dir:** 40 min N of Danbury on Rte 7; 10 min S of Kent. **Own:** Mark Estabrooks. **QC: 84 32 48**

Deer Park Books

609 Kent Rd • 06755
(860)350-4140 • (860)350-4140 (fax)
deerparkbk@aol.com

Rare non-fiction, Americana, first editions, children's & illustrated, printing history, art, sports & military books, postcards, autographs, engravings & ephemera. **Est:** 1986 **Hrs:** Sun-Mon 12-5, Tue-Sat by appt. **Sz:** M **CC:** V/MC/DIS **Assn:** CABA ESA **Dir:** I-84 Exit 7: "Super" Rte 7 to end, R onto Rte 7 proceed 13 mi N, shop in on L. Sign over mailbox reads "Old Books Bought & Sold." **Own:** Barbara & Richard Depalma. **QC: 1 18 39 S1 S9 S12**

Michael Hall Antiques

711 Kent Rd (Rte 7) • 06755
(860)355-4750

American & European furniture, pottery, porcelain, glassware, textiles, linens, lighting fixtures, 19th C vintage photography, 18th & 19th C prints & Oriental works-of-art. **Hrs:** Sat-Sun 1-6 or by chance/appt; Sum Thu-Mon 12-5 call ahead advised. **Dir:** From Gaylordsville Iron Bridge, on Rte 7 less than 1/4 mi on Housatonic River side, traveling N. **QC: 65 71 80**

Glastonbury

Black Pearl Antiques & Fine Art

2217 Main St • 06003
(860)659-3601 • (860)659-2387 (fax)

Period furniture, fine arts, sculpture & Asian antiquities. **Hrs:** By appt only. **QC: 52 7 2**

Mary S Swift Antiques

1401 Main St • 06033
(860)633-2112
efhiker@aol.com

A small friendly shop in an 18th C house, with painted country furniture & interesting accessories including decoys, tools, wrought iron, quilts. **Pr:** $25-5,000 **Est:** 1972 **Hrs:** Daily by chance/appt. **Sz:** M **Dir:** Main St is Rte 17 in Glastonbury. **Own:** Mary Swift. **QC: 51 34 37 S1**

Tobacco Shed Antiques [G40]

119 Griswold St • 06033
(860)657-2885

In a renovated tobacco barn with two huge floors of furniture, glassware, china, paintings, quilts, silver, lamps, clocks & jewelry as well as an annex featuring estate furniture from local homes. Fresh items daily. **Est:** 1991 **Hrs:** Wed-Sun 10-5. **Sz:** L **CC:** V/MC **Dir:** I-95 to 91 N to Wethersfield Rte 3 (Putnam Bridge) to Glastonbury. 1st exit across bridge, L at light, straight 3/4 mi on L. **Own:** Gary Voerg. **QC: 48 36 32 S12 S1**

Granby

Salmon Brook Shops [G20]

563 Salmon Brook St • 06035
(860)653-6587

Antiques, collectibles, ephemera, art, books, frame shop & price & reference guides. **Pr:** $1-1,000 **Hrs:** Daily 10-5. **Sz:** L **CC:** V/MC **Dir:** I-91 Exit 40; I-90 Exit 3. On Rtes 10 & 202, 1/2 mi S of the MA line. **Own:** Betty Messenger. **QC: 19 32 39 S13 S12**

Greenwich

The Antiquarian at Greenwich

44 W Putnam Ave • 06830
(203)625-0060

18th C French, English & Italian decorative pieces & furniture. **Hrs:** Mon-Sat 10-5. **Sz:** M. **QC: 54 53**

Church Street Antiques Inc

77 Church St • 06830
(203)661-6309

A wide selection of small scale furniture, artwork, lamps, mirrors, smalls & unusual decorative accessories. **Pr:** $50-1,000 **Est:** 1992 **Hrs:** Mon-Thu & Sat 10:30-5, Fri 1:30-5. **Sz:** M **CC:** V/MC **Dir:** Off Putnam Ave, Rte 1, near Greenwich Hospital. **Own:** Ann Davidow. **QC: 36 48 7**

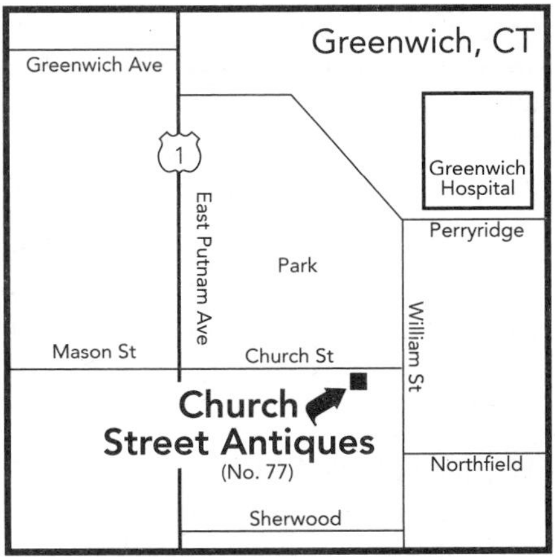

Eggplant & Johnson Inc

58A William St • 06830
(203)661-5335 • (203)869-6052 (fax)
jmcaselli@aol.com

Charming small shop featuring American, French, English, Neo-Classical & period pieces & decorative objects as well as architectural & garden pieces, paintings, objets d'art, sterling silver, crystal, prints & framed art. **Est:** 1993 **Hrs:** Tue-Fri 10-5, Mon & Sat by chance. **Sz:** S **CC:** V/MC **Dir:** I-95 Exit 3. **Own:** Jim Caselli. **QC: 53 36 54**

Estate Treasures of Greenwich

1162 E Putnam Ave • 06878
(203)637-4200 • (203)637-3493 (fax)

Estate jewelry, furniture, china, glass, sterling & collectibles. **Hrs:** Mon-Sat 10-5:30, Sun 12-5:30. **Dir:** I-95 Exit 5: L off ramp, shop is located on L. **Own:** Lillian London & Harriet Roughan. **QC: 64 32 48**

French Country Living

34 E Putnam Ave • 06830
(203)869-9777 • (203)869-9790 (fax)

Specializing in antique French country furniture & decorative accessories & custom-made furniture in the style. **Hrs:** Mon-Sat 9:30-5:30, Sun 12-5. **Sz:** M **CC:** V/MC **Own:** Jenny Caroli. **QC: 47**

Guild Antiques

384 Greenwich Ave • 06830
(203)869-0828

Two large rooms of quality English & American furniture, Chinese export porcelain & decorative accessories handsomely displayed. At competitive prices. **Est:** 1979 **Hrs:** Mon-Sat 10-5. **Sz:** L **CC:** V/MC **Dir:** I-95 Exit 3: 2 mi at the foot of Greenwich Ave. **Own:** Regina & George Rich. **QC: 41 52 54**

Hallowell & Co

340 W Putnam Ave (Rte 1) • 06830
(203)869-2190 • (203)869-2190 (fax)
hallowellco@mindspring.com
www.hallowellco.com

Fine vintage sporting & collector firearms. **Pr:** $500-50,000 **Est:** 1983 **Hrs:** Tue-Sat 10-6. **Sz:** M **CC:** V/MC **Own:** Morris Hallowell. **QC: 79 4 S1**

Henri-Burton French Antiques

382 Greenwich Ave • 06830
(203)661-8529 • (203)661-0938 (fax)

A handsome shop with quality 18th & 19th C French & Irish furniture & accessories from country to formal; armoires, commodes, long case clocks, farm tables & shop specialty of 19th C gold leaf mirrors. **Est:** 1987 **Hrs:** Mon-Sat 10-5. **Sz:** L **CC:** V/MC/DIS **Dir:** I-95 Exit 3: From NYC turn L, from New Haven turn R. Follow to Greenwich Ave, turn R, at the foot of Greenwich Ave. **Own:** Anne Satterthwaite. **QC: 47 34 68**

House of Weltz

522 E Putnam Ave • 06830
(203)661-8244 • (203)661-4551 (fax)
bobweltz@aol.com

English, French & American furniture, silver, paintings & prints. **Pr:** $25-25,000 **Est:** 1963 **Hrs:** Mon-Sat 10-5. **Assn:** AAA **Dir:** Exit 4 to Post Rd (Putnam), L at light, bldg on R. **Own:** Robert Weltz. **QC: 7 48 78 S1 S8 S9**

The Ivy Urn

115 Mason St • 06830
(203)661-5287

Featuring garden accessories: iron pieces, urns, plant stands & decorative items. **Est:** 1992 **Hrs:** Mon-Sat 10-5. **Sz:** M **CC:** AX/V/MC **Dir:** Betw Lewis & E Elm St, 1 blk E of Greenwich Ave. **Own:** Connie Lowenstein. **QC: 60 36**

Layton Antiques

115 Mason St • 06830
(203)661-0066 • (203)661-0911 (fax)

18th & 19th C European antiques & accessories. **Est:** 1998 **Hrs:** Tue-Sat 10-5. **Sz:** M **Dir:** I-95 Exit 3: R off ramp under RR bridge. Take immediate R onto RR Ave. Straight thru 2 lights Maison St on L. Shop is 1/4 mi on R. **Own:** Ingrid Layton.

Manderley Antiques

134 E Putnam Ave • 06830
(203)861-1900 • (203)861-1916 (fax)

18th & 19th C English furniture, paintings & accessories. Specializing in sporting motif. **Est:** 1986 **Hrs:** Mon-Sat 10-5. **Sz:** L **CC:** V/MC **Dir:** Off Milbank Ave. **Own:** Katherine Post. **QC: 54 7 79**

Off the Avenue

104 Bruce Park Ave • 06830
(203)622-7500 • (203)622-7226 (fax)

An eclectic selection of antique furniture & accessories, antique jewelry & handcrafted gifts. **Hrs:** Mon-Sat 10-5. **CC:** AX/V/MC **Own:** Paula Greenstein.

Provinces de France

22 W Putnam Ave • 06830
(203)629-9798

Three rooms of fine French 18th & 19th C antiques: a large collection of formal & country furniture & accessories, paintings, faience, armoires, desks & tables. **Est:** 1987 **Hrs:** Mon-Sat 10-5:30 & by appt. **Sz:** L **CC:** AX/V/MC **Dir:** I-95 Exit 3: 1/2 blk from Greenwich Ave, on Rte 1. **Own:** Jenny Berry. **QC: 47 53 34**

Donald Rich Antiques

23 W Putnam Ave • 06830
(203)661-6470

A large bright showroom of 18th & 19th C formal & country English & American furniture, paintings & decorative accessories. **Est:** 1990 **Hrs:** Tue-Sat 10-5 or by appt. **Sz:** L **CC:** AX/V/MC **Dir:** 1 blk W of the int of Greenwich & Putnam Aves. **Own:** Donald Rich. **QC: 36 52 54**

rue Faubourg St Honore

44 W Putnam Ave • 06830
(203)869-7139 • (203)869-2918 (fax)

In a small shop a large selection of handsome old fireplace tools, fenders, screens & mantels, cleaned & polished to perfection. Special tools for oversize fireplaces custom made. Chandeliers, wall sconces & umbrella stands are also available. **Est:** 1961 **Hrs:** Tue-Sat 10-5. **CC:** V/MC **Dir:** I-95 Exit 3: W of Greenwich Ave on Putnam. **Own:** James Ryan.

Sophia's Great Dames

One Liberty Way • 06830
(203)869-5990

Quality antique clothing, linens & textiles; furniture, glassware, costume jewelry, nostalgia & collectibles, as well as an extensive collection of costumes for rental. **Est:** 1981 **Hrs:** Mon-Sat 10-5:30. **Sz:** L **CC:** AX/V/MC **Dir:** I-95 Exit 3: 1/2 blk off Greenwich Ave betw Lewis & Elm Sts. **Own:** Sophia Scarpelli. **QC: 32 63 83**

Tudor House Antiques

30 E Putnam Ave • 06830
(203)869-4355 • (203)661-7186 (fax)

18th & 19th C English furniture, paintings & objets d'art. Custom-designed furniture created to blend with fine antique furniture. Drapery & restoration service. Painting murals. **Hrs:** Mon-Sat 10-5:30. **CC:** V/MC **Own:** Clive Blunt. **QC: 54 11 7 S15 S22**

Guilford

Arne E Ahlberg Antiques

1090 Boston Post Rd (Rte 1) • 06437
(203)453-9022

18th & early 19th C American country & formal furniture & decorative accessories. **Hrs:** By chance/appt. **Dir:** On the corn of Fair St. **QC: 36 52 102**

Country Home Antiques

260 River St • 06437
(203)458-2263 • (203)458-2263 (fax)

Country furnishings, antiques & collectibles. **Hrs:** Mon-Sat 10-5, Sun 11-5. **QC: 102 34**

Guilford Antique Center

1120 Boston Post Rd • 06437
(203)453-7077

Oriental rugs, sterling silver & collectibles. **Hrs:** Daily 11-6. **Dir:** I-95 N Exit 57: R off ramp, continue 1 mi. I-95 S Exit 57: L at light on Rte 1, L about 500 yds. Located in Napa Auto Parts Plaza. **QC: 76 78 32**

Gustave D Balacos

2614 Boston Post Rd • 06437
(203)453-9922

Furniture, glass, china & clocks. **Est:** 1969 **Hrs:** Fri-Sun 12-5 or by appt. **Dir:** I-95 Exit 57: W approx 2 mi on L.

A Summer Place

37 Boston St • 06437
(203)453-5153

American wicker & quilts. **Hrs:** By chance/appt. **Dir:** Near the Green. **QC: 91 84**

Yesterday's Treasures

2311 Boston Post Rd (Rte 1) • 06437
(203)453-1650

Furniture, glassware, trunks, country & Victorian, oak, mahogany & pine. **Hrs:** Tue-Sat 10-5:30. **CC:** AX/V/MC/DIS **Dir:** I-95 Exit 57.

Haddam

Hobart House Antiques
943 Saybrook Rd • 06438
(860)345-2015 • (860)345-2015 (fax)

English pre-1840 Georgian silver & American prints. **Hrs:** By appt only. **QC: 78 74**

Hadlyme

Black Whale Antiques
Rte 82 • 06439
(860)526-5073

An attractive selection of American & English furniture, appointments & Oriental accessories in eight rooms. **Est:** 1984 **Hrs:** Tue-Sat 10-5; Win Sat-Sun 10-5. **Sz:** M **CC:** V/MC **Dir:** At the jct of Rtes 82 & 148 at Rattleberry Farms in Hadlyme Four Corners. **Own:** Tom Rose. **QC: 48 60 65**

T F Vanderbeck Antiques
32 Town St (Rte 82) • 06439
(860)526-3770

Large selection of period Continental, English & New England furnishings. Mirrors, lighting, old garden iron, old prints, Continental & Oriental porcelain. **Pr:** $100-10,000 **Est:** 1972 **Hrs:** Sat-Sun 11-5 or by appt. **Sz:** L **Dir:** I-95 Exit 70: Rte 156 N to Rte 82 W. 1/4 mi N on Rte 82 from Hadlyme Four Corners. **Own:** Tom Vanderbeck. **QC: 53 54 52**

Hamden

Antiques on Whitney
1648 Whitney Ave • 60517
(203)287-9015

Fine furniture, linens, lamps & decorative accessories. **QC: 81 36 48**

Gallery 4
2985 Whitney Ave • 06518
(203)281-6043

Small shop jam-packed with antiques, silver, cut glass, Limoges, linens, books, trade cards, jewelry, china, pattern glass, quilts, fine art, large collection of Eskimo, American Indian & Oriental art. **Est:** 1976 **Hrs:** Mon-Sat 10:30-6; Dec Mon-Sat 10-8, Sun 12-5. **CC:** V/MC **Dir:** Merritt Pkwy Exit 61: 1.9 mi N on R; I-91 Exit 10: 200 yds N on R in Mt Carmel Ctr. **QC: 39 64 89 S10 S12 S13**

Hampton

Linda & Michael Whittemore
279 Main St • 06247
(860)455-9385

18th & early 19th C high-country American furniture & appropriate accessories with emphasis on original surface & condition. **Hrs:** By appt only. **Assn:** NHADA. **QC: 1 52**

Hartford

Bacon Antiques
95 Maple Ave • 06114
(860)524-0040

Furniture, decorative accessories, glass & china. **Est:** 1947 **Hrs:** Mon-Sat 9-5, Jul-Aug closed Sat. **Dir:** 100 yds from Main St in Hartford's South End. **QC: 48 61 60**

The Unique Antique
Hartford Civic Center • 06103
(860)522-9094

Specializing in antique & estate jewelry. **Est:** 1977 **Own:** Joanne Douglas. **QC: 64**

Hebron

David & Dale Bland Antiques

124 Slocum Rd • 06248
(860)228-3514 • (860)228-3514 (fax)

Early American furniture & accessories. **Pr:** $250-10,000 **Hrs:** By appt only. **Dir:** Call for directions. **QC: 52**

Higganum

Ron Chambers Antiques

7 High St • 06441
(860)345-3863

18th & early 19th C American furniture & accessories, American & English pewter. **Pr:** $100-10,000 **Hrs:** By appt only. **Sz:** S **Assn:** VADA **Dir:** Rte 91 S to Rte 9 S Exit 9: L off ramp onto Rte 81. Rte 81 dead ends at light turn R, 1st R onto High St shop is 1st house on R. **Own:** Ron Chambers. **QC: 52 72 102 S1**

Never Say Goodbye Inc

660 Killingworth Rd • 06441
(860)345-4329

Vintage clothing, jewelry, linens, glassware & furniture. **Hrs:** Wed-Fri 11-4, Sat-Sun 11-5:30. **Dir:** Rte 9 Exit 9: R on Killingworth Rd, 1 mi on L.

Jewett City

Griswold Antique Center [G5]

65 S Main St • 06351
(860)376-6953

Hrs: Thu-Sun 10-4. **CC:** V/MC.

> Use the Specialty QuickCode indexes at the back of the book to find dealers who specialize in your area of interest.

Kensington

Derik Pulito Antiques

381 Percival Ave • 06037
(860)828-0588

18th & 19th C high-style country American furniture in original condition & surface with related period accessories & art. **Hrs:** By appt only. **Assn:** NHADA. **QC: 1 52 41**

Kent

The Company Store Antiques

30 Kent Cornwall Rd • 06757
(860)927-3430 • (860)927-3430 (fax)

A restored company store offering furniture, folk art, American Indian artifacts, paintings, clocks, original grain-painted furniture, decoys, silver, tools, estate jewelry & accessories. **Pr:** $20-13,000 **Est:** 1989 **Hrs:** Daily 11-5. **Sz:** M **CC:** AX/V/MC **Dir:** Opposite Sloane-Stanley Museum. **Own:** Robert Bear. **QC: 106 102 101 S16**

Vivian G Forrer Antiques

92 N Main St (Rte 7) • 06757
(860)927-3612

Early American country & formal furniture, accessories, pattern glass, pewter, toys, banks, tools, folk art & Staffordshire china. **Est:** 1959 **Hrs:** Daily 9-5 by chance/appt. **Sz:** M **CC:** AX/V/MC **Dir:** 30 mi N of Danbury. **QC: 30 52 61**

Harry Holmes Antiques

Rte 7 & Carter Rd • 06754
(860)927-3420 • (860)927-3420 (fax)
sculptaire@snet.net

18th & 19th C furniture, clocks & accessories, large dining tables & many sets of chairs. **Pr:** $25-2,500 **Est:** 1968 **Hrs:** Thu-Tue 9-5. **CC:** AX/V/MC **Dir:** 5 mi N of Village of Kent, just below Kent Falls State Park. **Own:** Jeanette & Harry Holmes. **QC: 35 48 S6**

Kent Antiques Center [G8]

Kent Station Sq, Main St • 06757
(860)927-3313

Quality country antiques, accessories & collectibles from the 18th-20th C located in a restored 150 year-old farmhouse. Featuring English silver, early tools, paintings/prints, toys, quilts & early glass. **Hrs:** Fri-Wed 11-5; Jan-Mar Sat-Sun only 11-5. **Sz:** M **CC:** V/MC **Dir:** On Rte 7 behind the RR station, N of the monument. **Own:** Robert Howard. **QC: 78 86 34**

Main Street Antiques [G2]

8 N Main St • 06757
(860)927-4916

American, English & French country antiques, decorative accessories, textiles & apothecary tastefully displayed in a one-room gallery in the heart of Kent. **Est:** 1995 **Hrs:** Mon & Thu-Sat 11-5, Sun 12-5. **Sz:** S **CC:** V/MC **Dir:** Rte 7 N of traffic light. **Own:** Susanne Edgerly & Barbara McLean. **QC: 34 36 80**

Elizabeth S Mankin Antiques

123 Route 341 E • 06757
(860)927-3288
esmankin@snet.net

American furniture, English pottery & accessories. **Hrs:** Mon-Sat 10:30-5 by chance/appt. **QC: 23 48 36**

Pauline's Place

79 N Main St (Rte 7) • 06757
(860)927-4475

Exclusively antique & estate jewelry including Georgian, Victorian, Edwardian, Art Deco & Retro. **Est:** 1978 **Hrs:** Fri-Mon 12-5 & by appt. **CC:** V/MC **Dir:** Approx 1/4 mi N of Main St monument. **Own:** Pauline Simring. **QC: 64**

Killingly

The Prop Shop

172 Hall's Hill Rd • 06239
(860)774-5972

A c 1750 building with a frequently changing stock of unusual collectibles & antiques. **Hrs:** Mon-Wed & Fri 10-4, Sat-Sun by chance/appt. **QC: 32**

Killingworth

Acorn Antiques

628 Rte 148 • 06419
(860)663-2214
richard@acornbedandbreakfast.com
www.acornbedandbreakfast.com

Rustic old hickory & country furniture, art & accessories. **Pr:** $10-2,800 **Hrs:** Wed-Sun 9-5 or by appt. **Sz:** S **CC:** AX/V/MC/DIS **Dir:** 3 mi from Rte 79; 4 mi from Rte 81. **Own:** Carole & Richard Pleines. **QC: 7 34 55 S1 S12 S16**

The Bergerons Antiques

294 Rte 81 • 06419
(860)663-2122

Furniture including English oak pub tables, Continental armoires, American furniture & accessories. **Pr:** $25-5,000 **Est:** 1972 **Hrs:** By chance/appt. **Sz:** L **CC:** V/MC **Assn:** CADA **Dir:** I-95 Exit 63: 7.5 mi N on Rte 81. From Rte 9S Exit 9: 5.8 mi S. **Own:** Lloyd Bergeron. **QC: 52 53 50**

Country Squire Antique Shoppes

243 Rte 80 • 06417
(860)663-3228

Americana through Victoriana housed in an historic 18th C inn. **Hrs:** Wed-Mon 11-5. **CC:** AX/V/MC **Dir:** E of Rte 81 traffic circle. **QC: 1 10 89 S16**

Lewis W Scranton Antiques

224 Roast Meat Hill • 06419
(860)663-1060

Specializing in New England redware & slipware, early furniture, silhouettes & decorated tin. **Est:** 1968 **Hrs:** By appt only. **Assn:** ADA NHADA **Dir:** I-95 Exit 63: Rte 81N, 5 mi, R at circle onto Rte 80, approx 1 mi, R at 1st crossroads, 3rd house on R. **QC: 52 85 29**

Lakeville

Burton Brook Farm Antiquarians

299 Main St (Rte 44) • 06039
(860)435-9421

Fine Chinese & Japanese period art & porcelains; antique furniture & accessories in elegant room settings; antique & estate jewelry. **Est:** 1990 **Hrs:** Daily 10-5:30 by chance/appt. **Sz:** M **CC:** AX/V/MC **Assn:** BCADA **Dir:** On Rte 44 4 blks E of the PO; 2 hrs from NYC, 1 hr from Hartford. **Own:** Virginia Rosen. **QC: 64 36 24 S1**

Lisbon

Mr & Mrs Jerome Blum

45 Ross Hill Rd • 06351
(860)376-0300

Specialists in American country & formal furniture of the 18th C & appropriate period accessories; creamware, Weldon, saltglaze, Prattware, delft & mochaware, brass, early lighting & fireplace equipment. **Est:** 1950 **Hrs:** By appt only. **Dir:** I-395 Exit 84: Jewett City. Call for directions. **Own:** Selma Blum. **QC: 52 23 65**

Visit our web site at www.antiquesource.com for more information about antiquing in New England and the Midwest.

Litchfield

Black Swan Antiques

17 Litchfield Commons • 06777
(860)567-4429

17th to 19th C English & Continental country & formal furniture, framed engravings, paintings, prints & decorations. **Est:** 1985 **Hrs:** Thu-Mon 11-5, Sun 12-5. **Dir:** E on Rte 202 on R side of Litchfield Green. **Own:** Susan & Hubert van Asch van Wyck. **QC: 53 54 36**

Samuel Herrup Antiques

33 West St • 06759
(860)567-2644

Continental & American furniture of the 17th, 18th & 19th C, Continental & Oriental decorative arts, Chinese export porcelain, ceramics, paintings, brass, wrought iron & American redware. **Est:** 1972 **Hrs:** Wed-Mon 11-5. **Sz:** L **Assn:** ADA **Dir:** On the Green. **QC: 53 52 29**

Linsley Antiques

499 Bantam Rd • 06759
(860)567-4245 • (860)567-4245 (fax)
(800)572-2360
linsley.antiques@snet.net

Exceptional English country pine, period oak, formal yew wood, mahogany & walnut furniture & accessories displayed on three heated & air-conditioned floors. **Pr:** $100-20,000 **Est:** 1976 **Hrs:** Mon-Tue & Thu-Sat 11-5, Sun 12-5. **Sz:** L **CC:** AX/V/MC **Dir:** 2 mi from Litchfield Green on Rte 202 adjacent to the White Memorial. **Own:** Andrew Murray. **QC: 54 36**

Thomas McBride Antiques

62 West St • 06759
(860)567-5476

Furniture, decorations, silver & American & European paintings. **Est:** 1966 **Hrs:** May-Dec 15 Mon-Fri 9:30-5, Sat-Sun by appt only. **Dir:** Red barn next to Town Hall. **QC: 61 7 78**

Roberta's Antiques [G10]

Rte 202 • 06763
(860)567-4041

Est: 1995 **Hrs:** Thu-Mon 10-5, Tue-Wed by chance/appt. **CC:** V/MC **Own:** Roberta Cremese.

John Steele Book Shop

15 South St • 06759
(860)567-0748 • (860)567-3394 (fax)
jsteelebks@wtco.net
www.litchfieldcty.com

Antiquarian & second-hand books, including a strong collection of books on Connecticut & local history, postcards. **Pr:** $1-600 **Est:** 1985 **Hrs:** Tue-Sat 11-5, Sun 1-5 & by appt **CC:** V/MC **Assn:** CAB **Dir:** Next to the Litchfield Historical Society near the Green. **Own:** Bill Keifer. **QC: 18 19 39 S1 S12 S19**

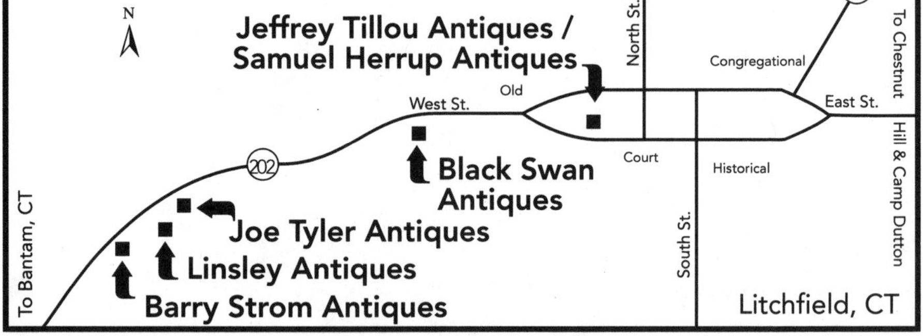

BLACK SWAN ANTIQUES

17 Litchfield Commons • Litchfield, CT
860•567•4429

Early English and Continental furniture and accessories, including framed engravings, paintings, prints, lighting.

Thursday–Saturday & Monday 11 a.m. to 5 p.m.
Sunday Noon to 5 p.m.

LINSLEY ANTIQUES

Litchfield, Connecticut 860 567 4245

Exceptional British Country and Formal Antique Furniture and Accessories

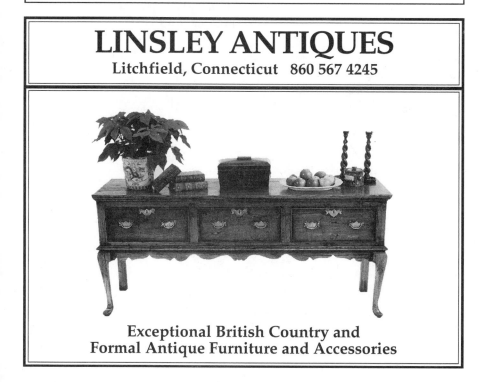

Oil on canvas,
Hudson River, ca 1860

Barry Strom Antiques LLC

503 Bantam Rd • 06759
(860)567-2747 • (860)567-9767
barry.strom@snet.net

17th to 19th C American & Continental furniture with an emphasis on Northern Europe & decorative accessories. **Est:** 1971 **Hrs:** Sun-Sat 11-5 or by appt. **Sz:** M **QC: 52 53**

Harry W Strouse

322 Maple St • 06759
(860)567-0656

Two rooms of 18th & 19th C antiques & decorations in a 1749 house. Specializing in silver, objets d'art, furniture, glass, china, rugs, tools, paintings, prints, fabric, pewter, crocks, andirons, books, brass, copper & wrought iron. **Pr:** $25-5,000 **Est:** 1971 **Hrs:** By chance/appt. **Sz:** M **Dir:** 1-1/2 mi N from Rte 202, just past Our Lady of Grace Church. **QC: 48 11 78**

Jeffrey Tillou Antiques

33 West St on the Green • 06759
(860)567-9693 • (860)567-2781 (fax)
jtillou@esslink.net
www.artnet.com/jtillou

Specializing in fine 18th & 19th C American & English furniture & related accessories, paintings & folk art. **Pr:** $500-50,000 **Hrs:** Mon & Wed-Sat 10:30-5, Sun 11-4:30. **Dir:** On the Green in Litchfield. **QC: 52 54 7**

Peter H Tillou Fine Arts

109 Prospect St • 06759
(860)567-5706

European & American paintings of 17th-19th C, 18th C American furniture, sculpture, American folk art, ethnic works of art & fine accessories. **Est:** 1955 **Hrs:** By appt only. **Own:** Peter & Trace Tillou. **QC: 41 7 11**

Tyler Antiques & Appraisals LLC

495B Bantam Rd (Rte 202) • 06759
(860)567-0755

17th-19th C Continental & English furniture, a variety of decorative accessories, Americana, paintings & ethnographic art. **Pr:** $300-15,000 **Est:** 1996 **Hrs:** Thu-Mon 11-5, Tue-Wed by chance. **Sz:** M **CC:** V/MC **Assn:** ASA **Dir:** 2 mi W of Litchfield on Rte 202. **Own:** Joseph W Tyler. **QC: 53 54 36 S1**

Madison

Kirtland H Crump

387 Boston Post Rd (Rte 1) • 06443
(203)245-7573
(800)246-3191 (CT only)

18th & 19th C tall-case clocks, pillar & scroll shelf clocks & mantle clocks & period time-pieces. **Est:** 1976 **Hrs:** By appt only. **Assn:** ADA BHI NAWCC **Dir:** I-95 Exit 61: approx 1 mi. **QC: 35 S16 S7**

P Hastings Falk Inc

859 Boston Post Rd • 06443
(203)245-3327 • (203)245-5116 (fax)
info@falkart.com
www.falkart.com

Major gallery specializing in late 19th to early 20th C American art including important emerging contemporary realists & impressionists. Also publisher of *Who Was Who in American Art* & other leading art reference books. **Pr:** $150-30,000 **Est:** 1976 **Hrs:** Mon-Fri 10-5, Sat 11-5, Sun 12-5. **Sz:** M **CC:** AX/V/MC **Assn:** ARLIS **Dir:** I-95 Exit 61: S to Boston Post Rd (Rte 1), turn L. Gallery is 1/2 mi on L, parking on site. **QC: 7 8 15 S1 S9 S12**

Lawton Fine Art & Antiques

837 Boston Post Rd (Rte 1) • 06443
(203)245-4949 • (203)245-7082 (fax)
lawton.antiques@snet.net
www.lawtonantiques.com

Specializing in 19th & 20th C fine art, furniture, glassware, china, porcelain, silver & decorative accessories. **Est:** 1997 **Hrs:** Sum Wed-Mon 11-5. Call for other times. **Sz:** M **CC:** AX/V/MC **Dir:** I-95 N or S to ctr of Madison (Rte 1/Boston Post Rd). Turn L. **Own:** Kristin Donlin, Marcia L Kalayjian & Marcia Wrubel. **QC: 7 61 48 S12 S9 S8**

Nosey Goose

33 Wall St • 06443
(203)245-3132

Specializing in country furniture & related accessories in early paint, garden items, baskets, textiles, pottery, folk art & primitives. **Pr:** $20-900 **Est:** 1980 **Hrs:** Mon-Sat 10-5:30, Sun 12:30-4:30. **CC:** AX/V/MC **Dir:** I-95 Exit 61S: Rte 1, L at light, 1st L off Rte 1. **Own:** Betty-Lou Morawski. **QC: 51 34 60**

Manchester

Books & Birds

519 E Middle Tpke • 06040
(860)649-3449

50,000 antiquarian books: general stock used & rare, including birds, nature, Connecticut, antiques, arts, collectibles, hunting & fishing, military & history, gardening, cooking & children's books. **Hrs:** Daily 10-5, Thu til 8. **CC:** V/MC **Dir:** 1 mi E of Main St on Rtes 6 & 44. **Own:** Gil Salk. **QC: 18**

Lighting and Dowsing Candles

Tinder: Dry flammable material such as scorched cotton designed to be ignited easily by a spark from a flint. Sometimes this happened. More often, particularly if the tinder was more than a day or two old, ignition was chancy, rarely instantaneous, and frequently frustrating.

Flint: A sliver of flint stone held in the striker.

Tinderbox: A box holding tinder, flint, and steel striker.

Tinderbottomed: A type of candleholder, usually tin, whose base is a tinderbox.

Candle snuffers: Implements used to trim the wick when a candle started smoking. They resemble scissors fitted with a small box to catch the trimmed wick. Introduced about 1725, they were made first of iron and later of silver or brass. They often stand on small trays, or, more rarely, fit vertically into elaborate holders. They range from simple, functional household tools to elaborate objects of ostentation. To snuff, we should note, originally meant to trim not to extinguish.

Candle dowser or candlecone: A conical device on a handle for extinguishing candles. Candlecones are often hung on hooks fitted to the handles of chambersticks.

Lest We Forget Antiques

503 E Middle Tpke • 06040
(860)649-8187
b7777lest@aol.com

Period furniture as well as Art Deco, paintings, glass, dolls, toys & prints. **Hrs:** Tue-Sat 10-5, call ahead if coming a long distance. **CC:** V/MC. **QC: 48**

Vintage Jewels & Collectibles

190 W Middle Tpke • 06040
(860)645-1525 • (860)533-9529 (fax)
vinjewels@aol.com
www.theplace2b.com/VintageJewels

Antique, vintage & collectible costume jewelry from 1850-1960s, vintage clothing, handbags, hat, linens, lace, china, pottery, paintings, print, glassware, toys, flatware, Christmas ornaments & furniture. **Pr:** $20-2,000 **Est:** 1994 **Hrs:** Wed-Sat 10-5, Thu til 6, extended hrs during holiday season. **Sz:** M **CC:** AX/V/MC/DIS **Dir:** I-84 E Exit 60: R off ramp to Shaw's Grocery, then L on Broad. R at next int onto Middle Tpke W. 3rd bldg on R. 10 min E of Hartford. **Own:** Deborah Robinson. **QC: 63 5 64 S8 S12 S19**

Mansfield

Button Box Antiques

301 Gurleyville Rd • 06268
(860)429-6623

Antiques, collectibles, wide range of glass, furniture, early prints, lithographs, etchings, advertising & early kitchen utensils. **Hrs:** Daily 1-4. **Dir:** 1 mi E off Rte 195. **QC: 61 74**

Two Sisters Antiques

937 Storrs Rd (Rte 195) • 06268
(860)429-5207

A charming house listed in the National Historic Register, filled with quality smalls, furniture & accessories. **Hrs:** Fri-Wed by appt only. **Dir:** 2 mi S of U Conn. **QC: 36**

Marble Dale

Earl J Slack Antiques

Rte 202 & Wheaton Rd • 06777
(860)868-7092

English & American furniture, paintings, fine English, European & Oriental porcelains thoughtfully displayed in a 19th C house. **Est:** 1968 **Hrs:** Sat-Sun 11-5. **CC:** V/MC **Dir:** Betw New Milford & Litchfield by a red brick church. **QC: 52 54 7**

Meriden

Dee's Antiques

600 W Main St • 06450
(203)235-8431

Victorian furniture & smalls. **Hrs:** By appt only. **Dir:** I-691 W Exit 4: L off exit, R at 2nd light. **QC: 58 89**

Second Generation Antiques [G]

819 Hanover Rd • 06451
(203)639-1002 • (203)235-1536 (fax)
secndgan@snet.net
www.geocities.com/eureka/park/1566

Silver, glass pictures, oak & mahogany furniture. **Hrs:** Sat-Sun 9-4. **Sz:** L **CC:** V/MC/DIS **Dir:** I-691 Lewis Ave Exit (Meridan Square Mall): R off exit at stop sign, R on Hanover, shop 3 mi on R. **Own:** Beth Pieines. **QC: 78 50**

Middle Haddam

Middle Haddam Antiques

Rte 151 • 06456
(860)267-9221

Country & Victorian smalls in a carriage house surrounded by extensive perennial gardens. **Pr:** $10-700 **Est:** 1983 **Hrs:** Daily 10-5. **Dir:** Rte 66 from Portland CT to jct with Rte 151. R onto Rte 151, 1 blk down on R. **Own:** Janet Freidenberg. **QC: 32 34**

Middlefield

Country Depot Antiques
24 West St • 06455
(860)349-0165

Antique furniture & decorative accessories. **Est:** 1991 **Hrs:** Wed & Sat 11-4, Sun by chance. **Dir:** Next to Lyman's Orchard. **QC: 36 48**

Middletown

Country Antiques of Middletown
808 Washington St • 06457
(860)344-8536

Specializing in oak furniture & antique office furniture. **Hrs:** Fri-Sun 11-5, Mon 12-4 & by appt. **Dir:** Rte 66 across from Caldor's Plaza. **QC: 50**

Margaret & Paul Weld
(860)635-3361

Early American country & painted furniture, folk art & unusual accessories, craftsmen tools & architectural elements in wood & iron for period restorations. **Hrs:** By appt only. **Assn:** ADA NHADA. **QC: 41 51 86 S18**

Milford

Antiques of Tomorrow
95 Gulf St • 06460
(203)878-4561

General line of antiques & collectibles specializing in Victorian & oak furniture. **Pr:** $25-1,000 **Est:** 1974 **Hrs:** Daily 9-2:30 or by chance. **Sz:** M **Dir:** 4 min from either Merritt or Wilbur Cross Pkwys. 2 1/2 min from I-95. **QC: 50 7 71**

Gallery on the Green
162 New Haven Ave • 06460
(203)874-6047

Antiques, Oriental rugs, painted furniture & art. **Hrs:** Tue-Fri 10:30-5, Sat 10-4, Sun by chance. **CC:** V/MC. **QC: 51 7 S16 S13**

Milford Green Antiques Gallery Ltd
969 Bridgeport Ave • 06460
(203)874-4303

Ephemera, antiques, collectibles, prints, posters, magazines, autographs, postcards, advertising signs, books on collecting, featuring Norman Rockwell & Maxfield Parrish. **Pr:** $25-5,000 **Est:** 1987 **Hrs:** Tue-Sat 12-5. **Sz:** M **Assn:** AAA CADA **Dir:** I-95 Exit 36 to Plains Rd to Post Rd (Rte 1). Go straight across to W Clark St. Follow Clark St to end, turn R at light onto Bridgeport Ave. 500 ft on L. **Own:** Dave & Trudy Williams. **QC: 32 39 74 S13 S16**

New Beginnings
107 River St • 06460
(203)876-8332
winbegin@aol.com

Victorian, golden oak, antiques, collectibles & European imports. **Hrs:** Mon-Tue Thu-Fri 10:30-5:30, Wed 10-5, Sat 9:30-6, Sun 11-4. **CC:** AX/V/MC/DIS **Own:** Michael Winer. **QC: 32 50 58 S16**

Treasures & Trifles
580 Naugatuck Ave • 06460
(203)878-7045

Furniture, glassware, jewelry, clocks & watches. **Hrs:** Daily 11-4. **Dir:** 1/2 blk off of Rte 1. **Own:** Billy Byrnes & Jim Stewart.

Twin Chimneys Antiques
250 Gulf St • 06460
(203)874-8691

Small antiques & quality collectibles displayed in keeping room of a c 1745 Gambrel Saltbox. Formerly 1800 House Antiques, Phillipston, MA. **Pr:** $10-1,500 **Est:** 1986 **Hrs:** Daily 10-5 by chance/appt. **Sz:** S **Dir:** I-95 Exit 39A (Milford): to Post Rd (Rte 1) to Cherry St. Exit L onto Gulf St. **Own:** June & Don Poland. **QC: 23 32 65**

Monroe

Barbara's Barn Antiques [G8]

418 Main St (Rte 25) • 06468
(203)268-9805

Victorian, country, deco, ephemera, costume jewelry, bakelite, Nuttings, prints, frames, small furniture, primitives, buttons, bottles, canning jars & collectibles. **Est:** 1980 **Hrs:** Tue-Thu 11:30-4, Fri-Sun 11:30-5. **Sz:** L **Dir:** E off Rte 84 on Rte 25; W off Merritt Pkwy (Rte 95) to Rte 25. In red house at Pepper St & Rte 25. **Own:** Barbara Gilmore. **QC: 29 102 63**

Mystic

Church Street Antiques

5 Church St • 06355
(860)572-0457
csantiq2@aol.com

Art pottery, glassware, jewelry, books, silver & collectibles. China, porcelain, flow blue, oil paintings, linens, lace, lamps & mirrors. **Hrs:** Mon-Thu, Sat-Sun 10-6. Fri by chance. **CC:** AX/V/MC. **QC: 101 63 22**

Mystic Antiques Co

40 Washington St • 06355
(860)536-4819 • (860)536-4829 (fax)
mysticantiques@uconect.net
www.mysticantiques.com

Country & primitive furniture, clocks, jewelry, glass, sleighs, buggies, folk art, paintings, nauticals, pottery, dolls, amusement park collectibles, quilts, Americana, toys, stuffed bears, tools, signs, lamps, coin operated games, military. **Est:** 1997 **Hrs:** Tue-Sun 10-5. **Sz:** H **CC:** AX/V/MC **Dir:** I-95 Exit 90: Rte 27 S, R onto Washington St. **Own:** Tom & Georgette Beebe. **QC: 32 48 35 S8 S12**

Second Impression Antiques

59 Williams Ave • 06355
(860)536-4041

Specializing in antique wicker furniture: Victorian, Bar Harbor, Art Deco, Lloyd

Necessaries

Close stool or necessary stool: A box-like stool containing a chamber pot originating around 1500 and made for the next 300 years. The close stool is thus, predictably when we think about it, one of the earliest forms of furniture. The term is also used to refer to an 18th century chair, often of the highest quality, used for the same purpose.

Night table: A small stand, originating in about 1750, with a cupboard to hold a chamber pot. The cupboard door may be hinged, or, on finer examples, tambour. Chippendale designed elaborate versions, often disguised as small chests of drawers — polite society obviously liked the furniture for its natural functions to be as discrete as its words for them.

Commode: This French word for "convenient" was originally applied to a small, highly decorated chest of drawers, but the Victorians used it to refer to a piece of furniture designed for the "conveniences," that is, a chamber pot, wash basin, and pitcher.

Commode chair, or, in the vernacular, **potty chair:** A chair with a hole in the seat to accommodate a chamber pot, usually with deep seat rails to hide it.

Sideboard: Perhaps a surprising inclusion in this group of terms, but in the 18th century, one of the cupboards at each end of a sideboard often contained a chamber pot, so that, when the women had withdrawn after dinner, the men need not allow the calls of nature to interrupt their man-talk and their drinking.

Plumbing: A 19th century invention which, thankfully, rendered all of the above obsolete.

Loom, American pine furniture & accessories. **Hrs:** May-Oct daily 11-5. **CC:** AX/V/MC **Own:** Dan & Rosemary Pokorski. **QC: 5 55 91**

Trade Winds Gallery

20 W Main St • 06355
(860)536-0119

Antique map & antique print specialist, also offering contemporary New England art & custom framing. **Pr:** $25-2,500 **Est:** 1974 **Hrs:** Jun-Sep Mon-Sun 10-8; Oct-Apr Mon-Sat 10-6, Sun 10-6. **Sz:** M **CC:** AX/V/MC/DIS **Dir:** Just W of the drawbridge in downtown Mystic. **Own:** Thomas Aalund. **QC: 66 74 S13**

Naugatuck

Architectural Antiques LLC

149 Maple St • 06770
(203)723-1823 • (203)723-8706 (fax)

Two large floors of architectural antiques, fine country furnishings, collectibles & curiosities located in the old Odd Fellows Centennial Lodge. **Est:** 1990 **Hrs:** Mon-Sat 10-5, Tue by chance. **Sz:** L **CC:** AX/V/MC **Dir:** Rte 8N Exit 26: from S Main St, turn R onto Maple St. Rte 8S Exit 27: L onto Maple St. **Own:** Charles & Therese Wasoka. **QC: 3 34 48**

Eugene Joseph Antiques & Collectibles

1307 New Haven Rd (Rte 63) • 06770
(203)729-6669
ejoseph@snet.net
www.pages.cthome.net/ejoseph/

General line of antiques & collectibles. Roseville, prints, paintings, lamps. **Pr:** $5.00-2,000 **Est:** 1995 **Hrs:** Wed-Sun 10-5. **Sz:** M **CC:** V/MC **Dir:** I-84 to Rte 8 S Exit 26: S toward New Haven.1/4 mi past Wal-Mart. **Own:** Skip & Sue Seely & Susan Monsam. **QC: 22 34 59 S1 S12**

New Britain

Vintage Antiques Shop

61 Arch St • 06051
(860)224-8567

Lighting, including chandeliers, dressers of oak, mahogany, china & glass. **Hrs:** Wed-Sat 10-4. **QC: 48 65 61**

New Canaan

Butler Fine Art

134 Elm St • 06840
(203)966-2274 • (203)966-4694 (fax)
butlerfineart@prodigy.net

Specializing in 19th & early 20th C American paintings. **Est:** 1989 **Hrs:** Tue-Sat 10-5. **CC:** AX/V **Dir:** Merritt Pkwy Exit 38: N on Rte 123 to Rte 106, turn L & go to 2nd light, directly on L. **Own:** Jane Butler. **QC: 7**

Elisabeth de Bussy

(203)966-5947 • (203)966-0496 (fax)

17th-19th C antiques, brass, delft, Oriental porcelain, pottery & Continental high-country furniture. **Est:** 1987 **Hrs:** By appt only. **Assn:** AC. **QC: 20 53 24**

English Heritage Antiques Inc

13 South Ave • 06840
(203)966-2979 • (203)966-5382 (fax)
english-heritage@worldnet.att.net
www.english-heritage.com

Large gallery specializing in fine 18th & 19th C English formal furniture set off by an extensive collection of English 19th C paintings, prints & porcelain. **Pr:** $100-75,000 **Est:** 1978 **Hrs:** Mon-Sat 10-5. **Sz:** L **CC:** AX/V/MC **Assn:** AADLA CINOA NEAA **Dir:** Merritt Pkwy Exit 37: N 2 mi, opposite Mobil, 1 hr from NYC. **Own:** Cecily Megrue. **QC: 7 54 23 S9**

Evans & Co Antiques

114 Main St (Rte 124) • 06840
(203)966-5657 • (203)966-2598 (fax)

Specializing in 18th & 19th C European & English furniture, decorative accessories, mirrors, ceramics & glass. **Pr:** $100-40,000 **Est:** 1991 **Hrs:** Mon-Sat 10-5. **Sz:** M **CC:** V/MC **Assn:** AC **Dir:** Merritt Pkwy Exit 37. Near int with Elm St. **Own:** Barbara Evans. **QC: 53 54 68 S15**

Dora Landey Antiques

120 Main St • 06840
(914)533-2643

An extensive collection of early blue & white Staffordshire china, colored transferware, colored ironstone including Mason's, Davenport, Hicks & Meigh. **Est:** 1990 **Hrs:** Mon-Sat 10-5. **Dir:** At Scotts Corners. **QC: 23 30**

Main Street Cellar Antiques [G8]

120 Main St • 06840
(203)966-8348

A spacious group shop emphasizing American country furnishings, quilts, decorative accessories, architectural elements, folk art & Americana. Garden furnishings seasonally. **Est:** 1983 **Hrs:** Mon-Sat 10-5. **Sz:** L **CC:** AX/V/MC **Dir:** I-95 Exit 15: Rte 7 to Rte 123N to Rte 106S, L on Main St; From Merritt Pkwy: Exit 38, Rtes 123N & 106S as above. **Own:** Richard Campbell. **QC: 34 36 3**

New Canaan Antiques [G7]

120 Main St • 06840
(203)972-1938

Fine quality period American, English & French furniture, 19th C paintings, 18th & 19th C porcelains, brass & silver beautifully displayed in 7 rooms in one of New Canaan's earliest buildings. **Est:** 1984 **Hrs:** Mon-Sat 10-5. **Sz:** L **Dir:** Merritt Pkwy Exit 37 or 38: to Ctr of New Canaan, corn of Main & Elm Sts. **Own:** Jane McClafferty. **QC: 52 7 53 S1**

Sallea Antiques Inc

66 Elm St • 06840
(203)972-1050 • (203)972-1567 (fax)
kaltman@ibm.net
www.artnet.com/sallea.html

Specializing in fine English & French boxes of all sizes, shapes & styles; also fine furniture, Chinese export porcelain, Japanese Imari, brass, fireplace equipment, paintings, lamps & more. **Hrs:** Mon-Sat 10-5, sometimes Sun. **CC:** V/MC **Dir:** On the corn of Elm St & South Ave. **Own:** Sally Kaltman. **QC: 36 28 24 S9**

New Fairfield

Apple Tree Hill Antiques

402 Rte 37 • 06812
(203)746-7250

A country barn full of furniture & accessories. **Pr:** $2-1,000 **Est:** 1989 **Hrs:** By chance/appt. **Sz:** L **Dir:** 4-1/2 mi from ctr of New Fairfield (N on Rte 37); 3 mi E of Rte 22 (NY) via Havilland Hollow Rd. **Own:** Terry Froehlich. **QC: 34 36 51 S15**

New Hartford

Gallery Forty Four

Rte 44 • 06057
(860)379-2083 • (860)379-3455 (fax)
mhaller@snet.net

Specializing in 19th & early 20th C American paintings. **Est:** 1966 **Hrs:** Tue-Sat 10-5. **CC:** V/MC **Dir:** 7 min from Rte 8 & Rte 44 in Winsted CT opposite the PO. **QC: 7**

New Haven

Edwin C Ahlberg

441 Middletown Ave • 06472
(203)624-9076

A large selection of late 18th & early 19th C American furniture & paintings. **Est:** 1928 **Hrs:** Mon-Fri 8-5, Sat 8-12 or by appt. **Dir:** I-91 Exit 8: On Rte 17. **QC: 52**

Antique Corner

859 Whalley Ave • 06515
(203)387-7200

Oil paintings, antique & estate jewelry, art glass, quilts, silver, crystal & china. New & vintage hats, clothing & accessories. **Est:** 1981 **Hrs:** Mon-Fri 10:30-5, Sat-Sun 12-4 or by chance/appt. **Sz:** M **CC:** AX/V/MC/DIS **Dir:** Merritt Pkwy Exit 59. **Own:** Rhona Harris. **QC: 78 64 83**

The Antiques Market

881 Whalley Ave • 06515
(203)389-5440

Two floors of period English & American antiques & specializing in antique Irish Belleek & 18th & 19th C Wedgwood. **Est:** 1968 **Hrs:** Mon-Sat 10:30-5, Sun 12-4. **Sz:** L **CC:** AX/V/MC **Assn:** CADA **Dir:** Merritt Pkwy Exit 59: turn R to Westville Village. **Own:** Nancy Levine Ochman. **QC: 54 7 23**

ARK Antiques

(203)498-8572 • (203)776-4397 (fax)
crshburn@ct1.nai.net

Fine American silver, jewelry & metalwork of the early 20th C, with special focus on the Arts & Crafts Movement. **Pr:** $50-35,000 **Est:** 1972 **Hrs:** By appt only. **Dir:** Call for directions. **Own:** Aram & Rosalie Berberian. **QC: 6 64 78**

W Chorney Antiques

827 Whalley Ave • 06515
(203)387-9707 • (203)387-9707 (fax)
w.chorney@juno.com

Specializing in antique office furnishings & arcade items including jukeboxes, pinball machines, clocks, soda fountain items, gumball machines, gramophones & victrolas, telephones, theater & film prop rentals, toys & antique firearms, 50s & 60s funky. **Pr:** $25-15,000 **Est:** 1955 **Hrs:** Sum Tue-Sat 11:30-5; Win Tue-Sun 11:30-5 other hours by appt. **Sz:** L **CC:** AX **Dir:** Merritt/Wilbur Cross Pkwy Exit 59: Go R on Whalley 1-1/3 mi, on L. **Own:** Wayne Chorney. **QC: 50 32 105**

Thomas Colville Inc

58 Trumbull St • 06510
(203)787-2816

Specializing in 19th C American & French Barbizon paintings, drawings & watercolors for the serious collector. **Est:** 1972 **Hrs:** By appt only. **Dir:** I-91 Exit 3. **QC: 7 S1**

Giampietro

(203)787-3851
www.giampietro.com

American folk art, sculpture, paintings & painted furniture. **Hrs:** By appt only. **Assn:** ADA VADA **Own:** Fred Giampietro. **QC: 41 51 7**

Sally Goodman Antiques

901 Whalley Ave • 06515
(203)387-5072

One of New Haven's largest dealers in antique & estate jewelry. Large selection of sterling silver. Dealer trade welcome. **Est:** 1976 **Hrs:** Oct-Dec daily 10-5; Jan-Sep Tue-Sat 10-5. **Sz:** M **CC:** AX/V/MC **Assn:** GIA **Dir:** Merritt Pkwy Exit 59: 1-1/2 mi down road on L. **Own:** Steven Goodman. **QC: 64 78**

Shannon Fine Arts Inc

PO Box 3570 • 06525
(203)393-2033

American paintings from 1840-1940 featuring Hudson River painters, American Impressionism & select European works. **Est:** 1976 **Hrs:** By appt only. **Dir:** Call for directions. **Own:** Gene & Mary Anne Shannon. **QC: 7**

R W Smith, Bookseller

130 Cold Spring St • 06511
(203)776-5564 • (203)776-5564 (fax)

25,000 books, exhibition catalogs & periodicals on art reference, especially American; photography, architecture & 20th C design & American decorative arts. **Pr:** $10-3,500 **Est:** 1975 **Hrs:** By chance/appt. **Assn:** ABAA ARLIS/NA CABA ILAB NEBA **Own:** Raymond Smith. **QC: 18 19**

New Milford

Bit of Country

24 Park Lane Rd (Rte 202) • 06776
(860)354-6142 • (860)355-4766 (fax)

Amish oak, Shaker cherry, rustic pine. **Est:** 1981 **Hrs:** Mon-Sat 10-5:30, Sun 11-4. **CC:** AX/V/MC/DIS **Dir:** I-84 Rte 7 exit. **QC: 34 57**

The Browser's Box

148 Candlewood Mt Rd • 06776
(860)354-4932

Orientals with emphasis on Japanese, glass, one-of-a-kind items & miniature lamps. **Hrs:** By appt only. **Own:** Doris & Ray Poirot. **QC: 61 65 71**

Cricket Hill

92 Park Lane Rd • 06776
(860)354-8872

Antiques, fine furniture & porcelain.

New Preston

Ray Boas, Bookseller

6 Church St • 06777
(860)868-9596
rayboas@snet.net
www.rayboasbookseller.com

Antiquarian & out-of-print books. Specializing in antique reference, business history, Americana. Over 12,000 carefully selected non-fiction titles in a unique & memorable bookshop overlooking the historic New Preston waterfall. **Pr:** $10+. **Est:** 1980 **Hrs:** Fri-Mon 10:30-5:30 or by chance/apt. **Sz:** M **CC:** AX/V/MC/DIS **Assn:** ABAA **Dir:** Off Rte 202, Rte 45 toward Lake Waramaug & New Preston village. At town, turn L onto Church St. Cross bridge & park. Shop on L on the waterfall. **Own:** Ray & Cathy Boas. **QC: 18 1**

Books About Antiques

168 New Milford Tpke (Rte 202) • 06777
(860)868-1611 • (860)868-1620 (fax)

Largest bookstore in New England selling new books on antiques, collectibles & decorative arts. **Pr:** $5-350 **Est:** 1988 **Hrs:** Mon-Sat 9:30-5, Thu til 6, Sun 12-5. **Sz:** M **CC:** AX/V/MC/DIS **Assn:** ABA **Dir:** At Stone Mill Commons. **Own:** Greg Johnson. **QC: 19**

City House, Country House

13 E Shore Rd • 06776
(860)868-3322

Eclectic mixture of Continental & American furniture & decorative accessories as well as garden furniture. **Pr:** $25-25,000 **Hrs:** Thu-Fri & Mon 11-5, Sat 10-5, Sun 12-5 **Dir:** I-84 to Rte 7 N to New Milford. Take Rte 202 in New Milford to New Preston, turn L onto Rte 45. **Own:** Addie Troup. **QC: 53 36 60**

Dawn Hill Antiques

15 E Shore Rd • 06777
(860)868-0066

A great selection of unique garden antiques including furniture, garden tools, plant stands, urns & edging tiles. Also Staffordshire china, Majolica & quilts. **Hrs:** Thu-Mon 11-5. **QC: 30 84 60**

Deja Vu

Main St • 06777
(860)868-1671

Custom antique lighting, jewelry, period furniture & decorative accessories. **Hrs:** Thu-Mon 12-5. **CC:** V/MC **Dir:** In the ctr of New Preston Village. **QC: 65 48 63 S12**

Garden House

18 E Shore Rd • 06777
(860)868-6790

Antique & garden furnishings. **Hrs:** Wed-Sun 11-5. **QC: 60**

Recherche Studio

Rte 202 • 06777
(860)868-0281

Antiques & traditional china, glassware & silver; fine 19th C formal & country furniture; also garden statuary & distinctive garden items. **Est:** 1987 **Hrs:** Fri-Sun 10:30-6 & by appt. **CC:** V/MC/DIS. **QC: 48 61 60**

Reid & Wright Books & Antiques [G40+]

287 New Milford Tpke • 06777
(860)868-7706 • (860)868-1242 (fax)
reidbook@ct1.nai.net
www.reidbook.com

Specialties include art, architecture, decorative arts, maps & prints, as well as antiques for the library. **Pr:** $5-1,000 **Est:** 1992 **Hrs:** Mon & Wed-Sat 10-5, Sun 12-5. **Dir:** On Rte 202: 6 mi E of New Milford & 15 mi W of Litchfield **Own:** Rodger Reid. **QC: 74 18 66 S1**

Trumpeter Inc

Five Main St • 06777
(860)868-9090 • (860)868-9929 (fax)

English antiques & decorative accessories with a decidedly masculine appeal, framed autographs & antique prints. **Est:** 1978 **Hrs:** Thu-Mon 12-5. **CC:** AX/V/MC **Dir:** Just past jct of Rtes 202 & 45. **Own:** Peter Constandy. **QC: 74 107 36 S13**

Village Barn & Gallery

13 E Shore Rd • 06777
(860)868-0501

Lighting, formal & country furniture, decorative accessories. Specializing in lighting repair & making. **Pr:** $10-8,000 **Est:** 1984 **Hrs:** Thu-Mon 12-5:30, Sat 10-5:30. **Sz:** M **CC:** AX/V/MC **Dir:** Off Rte 202 on Rte 45 in the ctr of the village. **Own:** Craig Nelson. **QC: 65 36 S1 S16 S8**

Newtown

McGeorgi's Antiques

129 S Main St (Rte 25) • 06470
(203)270-9101
www.connix.com/~mcgeorgi

Antiques, furniture, collectibles, lighting fixtures, architectural antiques & painted furniture. Costume jewelry, textiles, sterling silver. **Est:** 1990 **Hrs:** Tue-Thu & Sat 10-6, Fri til 5, Sun 12-5. **CC:** AX/V/MC/DIS. **QC: 65 48 S8**

Repairs and Restorations I

Restoration: The attempt to return a damaged antique to its original condition so skillfully that the restoration is invisible to all but the expert eye. The restorer often uses new materials but makes them look old.

Repair: Work done on a damaged object that enables it to continue to serve its original function. Often a repairer uses no new material, but glues or mends the original. A good repair is unobtrusive, but not invisible. The line between restoration and faking can sometimes be a fine one: good repairs are open and "honest."

Replacement: The replacement of working parts, such as handles, hinges, and latches, that become worn and broken with use. Also used to refer to the restoration of a whole component of a piece of furniture, such as the top of a candlestand or the base of a chest on frame.

Refinish: The replacement of an original surface that has become worn with a new one that makes the piece look like it did when it was new. A "finish" is a protective coat, such as varnish or French polish, that allows the natural wood to show through. Refinishing involves stripping the piece back to the bare wood and putting on a new finish. This is an irrecoverable process that destroys patina and reduces the value of an American piece by at least 50% and probably more (on an English piece it may have little or no effect on value).

The Pages of Yesteryear

9 Old Hawleyville Rd • 06470
(203)795-6282

Antiquarian books, maps & prints. **Assn:** GSAAA **Own:** John Renjilian. **QC: 18 66 74**

Norfolk

Joseph Stannard Antiques

Station Place • 06058
(860)542-5212

An extensive collection of 18th & 19th C furniture, lighting, decorative accessories, fine art & Oriental rugs. The collection is generously French, including selectively imported French granite garden elements & other antique garden furnishings. **Est:** 1992 **Hrs:** Wed-Sun 11-5 or by appt. **Sz:** L **CC:** V/MC **Assn:** BCADA **Dir:** Berkshire foothills, 15 min from Rte 7, off Rte 44 in town ctr, just N of Village Green. **QC: 47 53 60 S9 S15**

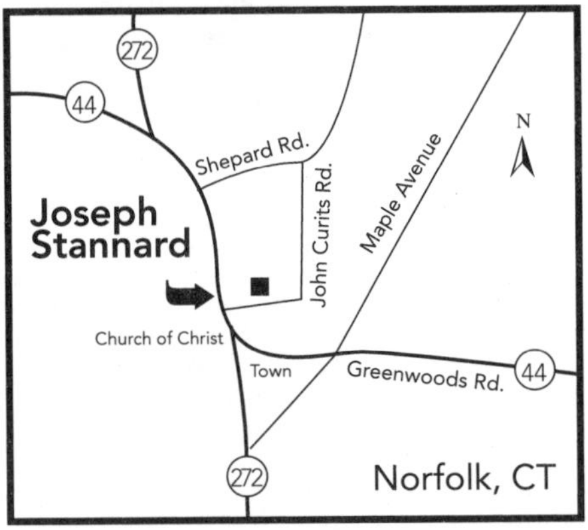

North Haven

Farm River Antiques

26 Broadway • 06473
(203)239-2434 • (203)239-6691 (fax)
antiques@farmriver.com
www.farmriver.com

Museum-quality American furniture of the Victorian period (1830-1890) in original & authentically preserved condition shown in a restored firehouse. **Pr:** $500-50,000 **Est:** 1972 **Hrs:** Sat 9-5:30, Tue-Fri by chance/appt, closed New Year's. **Sz:** H **Dir:** From New Haven: I-91N Exit 11: 1st 3 R turns to Broadway; from Hartford: I-91S Exit 12: L on Washington, R on Broadway. **Own:** George Morgio & Michael Yuhas. **QC: 50 52 58**

Norwalk

Doxtois Antiques

6 James St • 06850
(203)847-3315

Specializing in fine old tools, Heisey glass, pattern glass, English & export ceramics, 19th C brasses & animals, especially dog figurines. **Pr:** $25-500 **Est:** 1987 **Hrs:** By appt only. **CC:** V/MC **Assn:** CADA **Dir:** Just off Rte 7 at Cannon Crossing (Cannondale RR station). **Own:** Eva & Joe Hirsh. **QC: 23 61 86 S1 S12 S19**

Eagles Lair Antiques

565 Westport Ave (Post Rd Rte 1) • 06851
(203)846-1159 • (203)438-8024 (fax)

18th & 19th C American, English, Continental & Oriental furniture, pottery, porcelain, paintings, bronzes & smalls. **Pr:** $25-6,000 **Est:** 1968 **Hrs:** Tue-Sun 12-6. **Sz:** L **CC:** AX/V/MC **Dir:** Merritt Pkwy Exit 41: S 1 mi to Westport, Rte 1, L 1 mi. **Own:** Alexis Mihura. **QC: 1 23 107**

Koppels Antiques

4 First St • 06855
(203)866-3473

Direct importers of antique European country furniture including pine chests of drawers, armoires, tables, cupboards, bookcases, pine benches & original painted blanket boxes. **Hrs:** Mon-Sat 10:30-5. **CC:** AX/V/MC/DIS. **QC: 102**

Norwich

1840 House Antiques
47 8th St • 06360
(860)887-2808

Country furniture & accessories. **Est:** 1967 **Hrs:** By chance/appt. **Sz:** S **Own:** Olive Buddington. **QC: 34 102**

Norwich Antique Center [G15]
221 W Thames St • 06360
(860)887-1870

Pine, oak & walnut furniture, glassware, country accessories, coins, toys, dolls, pottery, tin, Art Deco & statuary. Estate jewelry. **Hrs:** Tue-Sat 11-5. **CC:** AX/V/MC **Dir:** Rte 32S, 1/4 mi from Norwich Inn along the Thames River.

Old Greenwich

New England Shop
250 Sound Beach Ave • 06870
(203)637-0326

China, glassware, rugs & furniture. **Hrs:** Daily 9-5. **Dir:** In the business district. **Own:** Barbara Reagan.

Old Lyme

Antiques Associates
11 Halls Rd • 06371
(860)434-5828

Fine formal furniture, paintings, rugs, estate jewelry, silver, architectural items & artist painted country pieces from 1800s thru 1950s. **Hrs:** Wed-Sat 11-4, Sun by chance. **QC: 64 3 7**

Jeffrey F Clark Fine Art
(860)767-1497
fineart@jclark.com
www.jfclark.com

19th & 20th C American paintings & prints. **Hrs:** By appt only. **QC: 7 74**

The Cooley Gallery Inc
25 Lyme St • 06371
(860)434-8807 • (860)434-7526 (fax)
jeffrey.cooley.01@snet.net

Specializing in fine American paintings from the 19th & 20th C including work by artists of the Hudson River School, American Expatriates, Tonalists & Impressionists. **Est:** 1984 **Hrs:** Mon-Sat 10-5 or by appt. **Assn:** ADA **Dir:** I-95 Exit 70. **QC: 7 S16**

Cove Landing
248 Hamburg Rd • 06439
(860)526-3464 • (860)434-3103 (fax)

18th & 19th C English & Irish furniture, Continental furniture including Biedermeier & unusual objects, beautifully displayed in an award-winning restored bldg. **Pr:** $500-25,000 **Est:** 1997 **Hrs:** Fri-Sat 12-6, Sun by appt. **Sz:** L **Dir:** I-95 Exit 70: 5 mi on Rte 156 W. **Own:** Angus Wilkie & L A Morgan. **QC: 53 54 36**

Mary Jean McLaughlin Antique Wicker
(860)434-1896

Large selection of fine antique wicker at reasonable New England prices; a good selection of quilts, hooked rugs & other textiles. **Pr:** $25-10,000 **Est:** 1982 **Hrs:** By appt only. **QC: 84 80 91 S15**

Morelock Antiques
12 Lyme St at the Village Shops • 06371
(860)434-6333
morelockantiques@earthlink

Specializing in French & Continental 18th & 19th C furniture, decorative objects, clocks, prints, drawings, lighting & paintings. **Pr:** $100-15,000 **Est:** 1988 **Hrs:** Thu-Sat 11-5, Sun 12-4. **Sz:** M **CC:** V/MC **Own:** Carlene Safdie. **QC: 11 47 53**

Oriental Rugs Ltd
54 Halls Rd • 06371
(860)434-1167 • (860)434-1168 (fax)
orientalrugs@snet.net
www.orientalrugsltd.com

A fine selection of antique carpets in excellent condition. **Est:** 1980 **Hrs:** Wed-Sat 10-5 or by appt. **CC:** V/MC **Assn:** ADA NHADA **Own:** Ralph & Karen DiSaia. **QC: 76 S16**

L Pedersen & Company
28 Lyme St • 06371
(860)434-0841 • (860)434-7476 (fax)
isgallery@aol.com

Antiques & decorative arts, 18th & 19th C Chinese furniture, porcelain & paintings. **QC: 71**

T F Vanderbeck Antiques
10 Lyme St • 06439
(860)434-2349

Period Continental, English & New England furnishings, regional paintings, old prints, European & Oriental porcelains, mirrors & lighting. **Pr:** $100-10,000 **Est:** 1972 **Hrs:** Thu-Fri 11-5 or by appt. **Sz:** M **Dir:** I-95 Exit 70 to Lyme St (historic district). **Own:** Tom Vanderbeck. **QC: 53 54 52**

Old Mystic

Holly Hock Farm Antiques
41 Main St • 06372
(860)536-4700 • (860)572-9911 (fax)
sales@hollyhockfarmantiques.com
www.hollyhockfarmantiques.com

18th & 19th C furniture as well as early 20th C custom made furniture. Specialize in dining room furniture by Margolis & Fineberg of Hartford as well as older Kittinger, Sacks & others. **Est:** 1978 **Hrs:** Daily 10-4. **Sz:** L **CC:** V/MC **Dir:** I-95 Exit 90: 1 mi N on Rte 27. **Own:** Cheri Page. **QC: 48 36 68 S16 S15 S12**

Old Saybrook

Antiques at Madison
869 Middlesex Tpke • 06475
(860)388-3626

American, English & French furniture & antique decorative objects. **Pr:** $100-3,000 **Est:** 1986 **Hrs:** Apr-Jan 15 Wed-Sat 11-5, Sun 1-5; Jan 16-Mar Sat 11-5, Sun 1-5. **Sz:** M **CC:** AX/V/MC **Own:** John Fernandez. **QC: 52 53 55**

Oil Lamps

Betty lamps, unlike the women who used them, were cheap, smelly, and comparatively inefficient. When whale or sperm oil became available in the middle of the 18th century, the oil lamp quickly evolved. It consisted of a domed foot supporting a covered font that held one or two wicks vertically. The earliest oil lamps were made of pewter or tin, and in the 19th century glass and brass became popular. The oil lamp underwent three major improvements: the wide flat wick adjusted by a spiked wheel appeared toward the end of the 18th century. In 1783 the Argand round burner and wick was invented. It gave the brightest and steadiest light yet seen but was itself improved even further by the invention of the glass chimney. "Invention" may not be quite the right word here, for the chimney appears to have resulted from a happy accident in which one of Argand's workmen broke the bottom of a glass font he was heating, and noticed how well the flame was drawn up through hollow cylinder. History does not tell us if he got promoted or fired.

Font: The part of a lamp that holds the oil or grease.

Wick: A piece of cotton, flax, rag, or rush used to soak the oil out of the font where it can be lit.

Antiques Depot of Saybrook [G95]

455 Boston Post Rd • 06475
(860)395-0595 • (860)395-0018 (fax)
gwoods@cannix.com
www.antiquesdepot.com

Largest selection of quality furniture on the shoreline, glassware, china, artwork, estate jewelry, toys, clocks, collectibles & architectural items. **Pr:** $20-10,000 **Est:** 1990 **Hrs:** Tue-Sun 10-5. **Sz:** H **CC:** AX/V/MC/DIS **Dir:** I-95N Exit 67: R on Rte 154, 1st R after light; I-95 S Exit 68: 1 mi to light, L onto Rte 154, 200 yards on R; Rte 9 S on Rte 154 1.7 mi — "at the train station." **Own:** Gary Woods. **QC: 61 36 48 S1 S19 S12**

Corner Cupboard Antiques

853 Middlesex Tpke (Rte 154) • 06457
(860)395-0796

Country antiques, china & glass, sewing items & linen. **Est:** 1957 **Hrs:** Wed-Sun 10-5. **QC: 34 103 81**

James Demorest Oriental Rugs

5 Great Hammock Rd • 06475
(860)388-9547

Specializing in the sale, purchase & appraisal of antique oriental rugs. **Hrs:** By appt only. **QC: 76**

Essex Saybrook Antiques Village [G120]

345 Middlesex Tpke • 06475
(860)388-0689 • (860)881-1179 (fax)
www.esavantiqs.com

Extensive offerings from jewelry to furniture & books. **Pr:** $1-1,000+ **Est:** 1978 **Hrs:** May 25-Jan 1 daily 11-5; Jan-May 24 closed Mon. **Sz:** L **CC:** AX/V/MC **Dir:** I-95 Exit 67 N: N on Rte 154 1/2 mi on L. Rte 9 S Exit 2, R on Rte 154 1 mi on R. **Own:** Judy Ganswindt. **QC: S9 S10 S19**

Hanlon's Antiques

816 Middlesex Tpke (Rte 154) • 06475
(860)388-6297

Antiques & collectibles including jewelry, glass, china, tools & toys. **Hrs:** Daily 10-5.

Stephen & Carol Huber

40 Ferry Rd • 06475
(860)388-6809

Leading dealers in American samplers, silk embroideries & schoolgirl art. Always the finest selection of needlework available. Always interested in purchasing collections or single pieces. **Pr:** $500-100,000 **Hrs:** By appt only. **Sz:** L **Assn:** ADA **Dir:** I-95 N Exit 67: R off ramp, L at light 1-1/2 mi to 40 Ferry Rd on R; I-95 S Exit 68: L 1/2 mi on R. **QC: 82 S1 S8 S16**

Little House of Glass

1560 Boston Post Rd (Rte 1) • 06475
(860)399-5127

Antiques & collectibles: furniture, china & glass. **Est:** 1956 **Hrs:** Thu-Tue 10-5 or by appt. **Dir:** I-95 Exit 66: approx 2 mi. **QC: 61 60**

Old Saybrook Antiques Center [G125]

756 Middlesex Tpke (Rte 154) • 06475
(860)388-1600
osac@connix.com
www.oldsaybrookantiques.com

18th & 19th C furniture, fine porcelain, glass, estate jewelry, silver, quality collectibles & a large selection of prints & paintings. **Pr:** $100-10,000 **Est:** 1995 **Hrs:** Mon-Sat 10-5, Sun 11-5. **Sz:** H **CC:** V/MC **Dir:** From Hartford: I-91 S Exit 2: L at end of ramp, 3/10 mi on R. from New Haven: I-95 Exit 67: bear L at end of exit, L onto Rte 154 1-1/2 mi on R. **Own:** Yolanda Moskal. **QC: 7 48 64 S1 S12**

Presence of the Past
488 Main St • 06475
(860)388-9021 • (860)388-2025 (fax)

Haviland & Noritake china. **Est:** 1977 **Hrs:** By appt only. **Dir:** Call for directions. **Own:** Jan Fenger. **QC: 23 24**

Sweet Pea Antiques
851 Middlesex Tpke (Rte 154) • 06475
(860)388-0289

Estate jewelry, sterling silver, china & glassware. **Est:** 1983 **Hrs:** Wed-Sat 11-5, Sun 12-5. **CC:** V/MC **Dir:** 5 min from I-95, to Rte 154N, on the L. **Own:** Jill Bellivean. **QC: 64 78**

Touch of Class Wicker
1800 Boston Post Rd • 06475
(860)399-6694

Specializing in antique & reproduction wicker. **Est:** 1977 **Hrs:** Mon-Sat 10-6, Sun 11-5 in season. **CC:** V/MC **Dir:** I-95 Exit 66: S on Rte 1. **QC: 91 S16**

Van's Elegant Antiques
998 Middlesex Tpke (Rte 154) • 06475
(860)388-1934

Antique dolls & related items, glassware, furniture, vintage clothing, linens & jewelry. **Hrs:** Daily 11-5 or by appt. **Sz:** M **CC:** V/MC **Own:** Barendina Blais. **QC: 38 61 83**

Orange

Tranquil Time Antiques
76 Shepherd Ln • 06477
(203)795-6282

British biscuit tins & decorative accessories. **Assn:** GSAAA **Own:** Rena Goldenberg. **QC: 85 36**

Plainfield

Plainfield Trading Post
260 Norwich Rd (Rte 12)
(860)564-4115

A diversified shop offering an extensive assortment of tools, farm equipment, glass. **Hrs:** Tue & Thu-Sat 10-12:30 & 1:15-4. **Dir:** I-395 betw Exits 88 & 89. **QC: 86 61**

Plantsville

Plantsville General Store Antiques [G27]
700 S Main St (Rte 10) • 06479
(860)621-5255

Depression & art glass; primitive, country & formal furniture; toys & dolls, ephemera, pottery, linens, silver & estate jewelry. **Pr:** $25-5,000 **Est:** 1974 **Hrs:** Oct-Dec Mon-Sat 10-5, Sun 12-5; Dec 25-Sep closed Mon & Tue. **Sz:** L **CC:** AX/V/MC/DIS **Dir:** I-84 Exit 30 (from Hartford): L at end of ramp; (from NY): R to SS. Follow blue hospital sign, R at 1st light, 4th bldg on R. **Own:** Elaine Maloney. **QC: 48 61 64**

Plantsville Station Antique Shoppes
75 W Main St • 06479
(860)628-8918

Fine china, early glass, furniture, dolls, lamps, primitives, pottery, collectibles, vintage clothing, coins & automobilia. **Hrs:** Wed-Sat 10-5, Sun 12-5. **CC:** V/MC **Dir:** I-84 Exit 30. **QC: 48 50 32 S1 S12 S9**

Village Antique Shoppe
61 W Main St • 06479
(860)628-2498

Dolls, toys & Victorian furniture. **Hrs:** Wed-Sat 10-4. **Assn:** ISA **Dir:** I-84 Exit 30. **Own:** Kathleen Connelly. **QC: 38 87 58 S1**

Pomfret

Pomfret Antique World [G90]
Rtes 101 & 44 • 06258
(860)928-5006

Furniture, pottery, porcelain & country paintings. **Est:** 1984 **Hrs:** Thu-Tue 10-5. **Sz:** H **CC:** V/MC **Dir:** I-395 Exit 93: To Pomfret, W from int of Rtes 169 & 101. **Own:** Robert Burrows. **QC: 7 101**

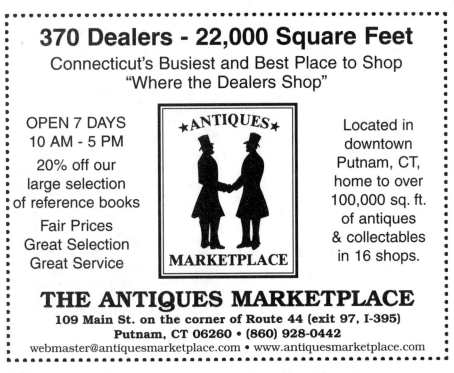

Washburn's This-n-That Shop

23 Wolf Den Rd • 06258
(860)928-3316

Unique & popular items including pictures, lamps & cabinets. **Est:** 1971 **Hrs:** Daily 10-5. **Dir:** S off Rte 44, opposite Pete's Stand, 3rd house on the L on Wolf Den Rd. **QC: 65 36**

Erik Wohl

(860)974-3483

18th & 19th C American furniture & accessories. Specializing in country painted furniture, art, iron, treenware, stoneware & folk art. Emphasis on original condition & surface. **Est:** 1989 **Hrs:** By appt only. **Sz:** M **Assn:** GSAAA NHADA **Dir:** I-395 Exit 93: Rte 101W to Rte 169 S approx 1 mi. **Own:** Erik Wohl. **QC: 7 34 41 S8 S12 S18**

Portland

Robert T Baranowsky Antiques

66 Marlborough St • 06480
(860)342-2425

A general line of quality antiques specializing in early 19th C to Art Moderne including furniture, fine art & jewelry. **Pr:** $50-5,000 **Est:** 1971 **Hrs:** Wed-Fri 10-4:30, Sat 12-4:30. **Sz:** L **Dir:** I-91 to Rte 9S to Middletown, R onto Rte 66 over the bridge into Portland. **QC: 48 64**

Putnam

Antiquary — Frank Racette

215 Park Rd • 06260
(860)928-4873

19th C antiques. **Dir:** I-395 Exit 95: L past JD Cooper's restaurant, shop on the R.

Antique Corner [G]
112 Main St • 06260
(860)963-2445
members.aol.com/antiquecor.htm

Wide variety of antiques & collectibles: china, glass, pottery, jewelry, toys & 50s modern. **Hrs:** Wed-Mon 11-5. **Own:** Steve & Donna Wisnewski. **QC: 32**

Antiques Marketplace [G370]
109 Main St (Rte 44) • 06260
(860)928-0442
webmaster@antiquesmarketplace.com
www.antiquesmarketplace.com

Over 50,000 items on three floors from general line to museum quality: furniture, paintings, glassware, china, art pottery, sterling, estate jewelry, kitchenware, sporting collectibles, advertising, toys, books, prints & Oriental. **Pr:** $1-10,000 **Est:** 1991 **Hrs:** Daily 10-5. **Sz:** H **CC:** V/MC **Dir:** I-395 Exit 97: 2 mi W on Rte 44. **Own:** Jerry Cohen. **QC: 34 48 S12**

Artisans' Alley [G]
39 Front St (Rte 44) • 06260
(860)928-4122
artisansalley@cyberzone.net

Furniture, reproductions, collectibles, jewelry, pottery, stained glass, baskets, lamps & Christmas items. Specializing in vintage quilts. **Pr:** $1-1,000 **Est:** 1998 **Hrs:** Tue-Sat 10-5, Sun 12-5. **Sz:** M **CC:** V/MC **Own:** Lynne Campagnano Bass. **QC: 36 84 102 S6 S15**

Mrs Bridge's Pantry
136 Main St • 06260
(860)963-7040

Antiques, collectibles, gifts, books. **Hrs:** Daily 10-5. **QC: 32 73**

Brighton Antiques
91 Main St • 06260
(860)928-1419

Quality 18th, 19th & 20th C furniture & accessories. **Hrs:** Wed-Sat 11-5, Sun 12-5. **QC: 52**

Century Antiques
127 Main St • 06260
(860)963-7982

Furniture, clocks, watches, glassware & pottery. **Hrs:** Daily. **QC: 48 35 61**

Cranberries Antiques & Collectibles [G20+]
5 Canal St • 06260
(860)928-5300

Antiques & collectibles from around the world. Specializing in fine English furnishings, silver, cocktail shakers & other distinctive smalls. **Est:** 1998 **Hrs:** Daily 10-6. **Sz:** L **CC:** V/MC **Dir:** Mass Pike Exit 10 to I-395 S to Exit 97 (Rte 44). Rte 44 W to Main St. Corner of Main & Canal St. **Own:** Shirley & Larry Fournier. **QC: 78 48 32 S8 S12**

Grams & Pennyweights [G50]
626 School St • 06260
(860)928-6624

Antiques, Victorian furniture, art glass, art pottery, lamps, silver, large collection of ivory, cut glass, paintings, coins, jewelry, Rolex watches & pocket watches. **Pr:** $50-30,000 **Est:** 1987 **Hrs:** Mon & Thu-Fri 11-4, Sat-Sun 10-5. **Sz:** H **CC:** V/MC **Dir:** I-395 Exit 97: W on Rte 44, commercial bldg on R. **Own:** Paul Kenyon. **QC: 58 22 78 S1 S12 S22**

Grandpa's Attic
10 Pomfret St • 06260
(860)928-5970

General line. **Hrs:** Daily.

Jeremiah's Antique Shop [G80]
26 Front St • 06260
(860)963-9485

Antiques & collectibles ranging from early country & centennial pieces to coins, fine estate jewelry & collectibles. **Est:** 1995 **Hrs:** Daily 9:30-5. **Sz:** L **Dir:** I-395 N Exit 95 or I-395S Exit 97: W on Rte 44 into town.

The Jewelry Court
91 Main St • 06260
(860)928-1419

Fine estate jewelry. **Hrs:** Wed-Sun 11-5. **Dir:** Located in Brighton Antiques. **Own:** Edmund DiMeglio. **QC: 64**

Little Museum Company
75-83 Main St • 06260
(860)928-2534

English & French antique furniture & accessories & oriental rugs. **Hrs:** Wed-Sun 10-5.

Palace Antiques
130-134 Main St • 06260
(860)963-1124

Extensive inventory of quality antiques & collectibles. **Hrs:** Wed-Sun 12-5, Mon-Tue by chance/appt. **Own:** Bob Rubenoff.

Pink House Antiques [G30]
80 Main St • 06260
(860)963-0422

Antiques & collectibles. **Hrs:** Daily 10-5. **Own:** Rebeka & Andrew Tanacea. **QC: 48 32**

Putnam Antique Exchange [G100]
75-88 Main St • 06260
(860)928-1905 • (860)928-6412 (fax)

Antiques & collectibles, specializing in architecturals & including art pottery, stained glass, lamps, art glass, furniture, paintings, Oriental antiques, antique & costume jewelry, antique guns. **Est:** 1989 **Hrs:** Wed-Sun 10-5. **Sz:** H **CC:** AX/V/MC **Dir:** On Rte 44. **Own:** Greg Renshaw. **QC: 70 32**

G A Renshaw Architecturals
83 Main St • 06260
(860)928-1905 • (860)928-1905 (fax)

Specializing in large architectural elements. **Hrs:** Wed-Sun 10-6. **QC: 3**

Riverside Antiques [G20+]
58 Pomfret St • 06260
(860)928-6020

Antiques, collectibles & clocks priced with the dealer in mind. **Est:** 1997 **Hrs:** Wed-Sun 10-5. **Dir:** I-395 Exit 95. R onto Kennedy Dr. At traffic light, L onto Pomfret St, 200 yds on L. **Own:** George & Cathy Dunham. **QC: 48 32 35 S7**

Strausberg Estate Jewelry
83 Main St • 06260
(860)928-6078

Estate jewelry. **Hrs:** Daily. **QC: 64**

Redding

Mellin's Antiques
(203)938-9538

Specializing in Canton Chinese export porcelain as well as high-quality 17th, 18th & 19th C brass & tea caddies. **Pr:** $25-10,000 **Est:** 1977 **Hrs:** By appt only **Sz:** M **Assn:** ADA **Dir:** Call for directions. **Own:** Gail Mellin. **QC: 20 25 S1**

Lincoln & Jean Sander
235 Redding Rd (Rte 107) • 06896
(203)938-9873

Varied selection of fine 18th & early 19th C American furniture, both country & formal & their appropriate period accessories. Most in old or original finish. **Est:** 1973 **Hrs:** By appt only. **Assn:** ADA **Dir:** 12 mi from Rte 84, 2 mi from Rte 7, 10 mi from Merritt Pkwy. **QC: 52**

Ridgefield

Antique Poster Gallery
17 Danbury Rd (Rte 35) • 06877
(203)438-1836
www.georgejgoodstadt.com

A gallery devoted to authentic lithography & vintage posters from 1840-1930 including Calder, Cassatt, Chagall, Delaunay, Dubuffet, Dufy, Kandinsky, Klee, Miro, Leger & Picasso. **Est:** 1969 **Hrs:** Tue-Sat 10-4, Jul-Aug Mon-Fri 10-4. **CC:** MC/V/AX **Dir:** Rte 35 Girolmetti Court. **Own:** George Goodstadt. **QC: 74**

Branchville Antiques & Collectibles

280 Ethan Allen Hwy (Rte 7) • 06877
(203)438-5375

Military, collectibles, art, glassware, china & toys. **Hrs:** Thu-Fri & Mon 12-4, Sat-Sun 1-5. **Own:** Eileen Corrado.

Branchville Junction Antiques & Collectibles

59 Ethan Allen Hwy • 06877
(203)544-8121

Hrs: Thu-Mon 11-5 (Sat til 5:30).

Country Gallery Antiques

346 Ethan Allen Hwy • 06877
(203)438-2535

In a charming 200-year-old barn: European antique pine furniture, custom crafted tables & decorative accessories. **Hrs:** Mon-Tue & Thu-Sat 10-5, Sun 12-5. **Sz:** M **CC:** MC/V **Dir:** Merritt Pkwy Exit 40: Rte 7 N to Ridgefield; on Rte 7 just past Rte 102 on R. Rte 84 (Danbury): Rte 7 S exit just past Rte 35. **Own:** Lisa Cassagrande. **QC: 34 55 41**

Deja Vu

23 Catoonah St • 06877
(203)431-8176

An eclectic gathering of fine & gently used furniture, oak/mahogany/pine, gilded mirrors, art pottery, silver & pewter, porcelain & china, estate jewelry, architectural elements, wicker, wrought iron, paintings, rugs, dolls & toys. **Hrs:** Tue-Sat 11-5, Sun 12-5. **CC:** AX/V. **QC: 48**

Repairs and Restorations II

Repaint: The application of a coat of paint over the original. Some repainted pieces can be stripped back to their original paint and will still be desirable, though they will have lost some patina and therefore some value. Pieces that have had heavy use, such as windsor chairs, have often been repainted more than once, and, if the final coat is not recent, and the older and/or original coat(s) can be detected where the paint has been worn or chipped, the chair will be valued for its "paint history," though it will still be less valuable than one in original paint.

Reconfiguration: Changing the structure or appearance of a piece to make it more useful or fashionable. A not-uncommon example of major reconfiguration is the conversion of large and almost useless 19th century wardrobes into breakfront bookcases or display cabinets. Some larger Hepplewhite and Sheraton sideboards have had their original depth of 28 or 30 inches reduced by six or eight inches to make them fit better into smaller rooms, and some highboys and chests on chests have had their height reduced by the removal of one drawer level for similar reasons. Less major examples of reconfiguration include glazing the blind doors of a secretary, scalloping the apron of a Queen Anne tavern table, or carving the knees or top of a Chippendale tilt top tea table — all of which were, in the 19th or early 20th centuries, common ways of enhancing unfashionably plain pieces.

Marriage: The creation of a piece of antique furniture by joining two parts that were originally from different pieces. Tables or candlestands sometimes have tops married to bases, but the most common marriages are found in large two-part case pieces such as highboys, secretaries, and chests on chests. A good marriage is when the two parts are of the same period and each was originally a part of the same form. A bad marriage is when the periods are not the same. The worst marriages of all are those that create a new form, as when as slant front desk is given a bookcase top that it was never designed to have, or when the bottom of a chest on chest is fitted with the top of a secretary to make a linen press.

Gerald Grunsell & Associates

450 Main St • 06877
(203)438-4332 • (203)431-9200 (fax)

Fine European 18th & 19th C clocks.. **Est:** 1953 **Hrs:** Wed-Sat 10:30-4. **Assn:** NAWCC **Dir:** 20 min N of I-95. **QC:** 35 S1 S16

Monkey Shines Antiques

199 Ethan Allen Hwy (Rte 7) • 06877
(203)438-0943

A menagerie of whimsical antiques & decorative accessories for the fun & unique home. Architectural, painted metal, French, Italian & Ganden, all things quirky yet sophisticated. **Pr:** $10-1,850 **Est:** 1995 **Hrs:** Thu-Sun 12-5, Mon-Wed by appt. **Sz:** M **Dir:** Rte 7 exit off either Rte 84 or I-95. Go S on Rte 7 off Rte 84 or N on Rte 7 off I-95. Located betw Rtes 102 & 35 on Rte 7. **Own:** Kendra Stetser. **QC:** 3 105 36 S15

The Red Petticoat

113 West Ln (Rte 35) • 06877
(203)431-9451

Ridgefield's oldest & largest antique shop. 18th & 19th C antique furniture & accessories, collectibles, folk art, lighting, early iron, pewter, brass, plus authentic reproductions by D R Dimes. **Pr:** $5-10,000 **Hrs:** Tue-Sat 10-5:30, Sun 12-5. **Sz:** L **CC:** V/MC **Dir:** 4/10 mi S of fountain. **Own:** Gloria Perschino. **QC:** 34 52 56

Ridgefield Antiques Center [G24+]

109 Danbury Rd • 06877
(203)438-2777

18th, 19th & 20th C furniture, paintings, porcelain, glass, textiles, country pieces & decorative accessories. **Est:** 1989 **Hrs:** Mon-Sat 11-5, Sun 12-5. **Sz:** M **CC:** V/MC **Dir:** In front, next to Southwest Cafe. **Own:** Marion North, Susan Fogerty & Mary McInerney.

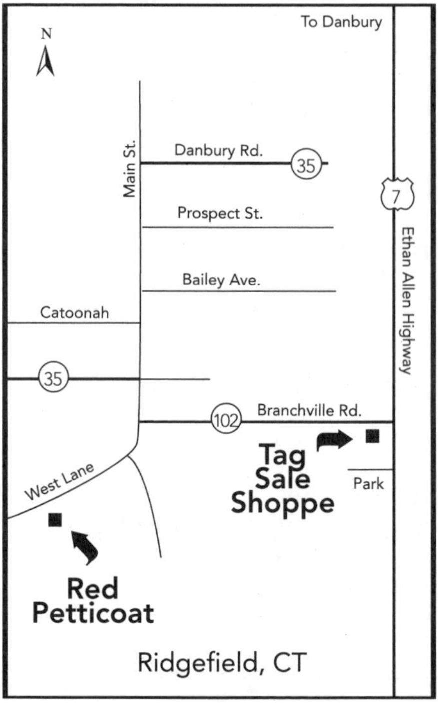

The Tag Sale Shoppe

47 Ethan Allan Hwy (Rte 7) • 06877
(203)544-8535 • (203)544-9973 (fax)

Six display rooms plus an annex of fine furniture, art, silver, jewelry, art pottery, Depression glass; period, country & vintage furnishings; large selection of smalls. **Pr:** $10-5,000 **Est:** 1987 **Hrs:** Daily 10:30-5:30. **Sz:** L **CC:** MC/V/DIS **Dir:** Merritt Pkwy to Rte 7: 10 mi N at Jct of Rtes 7 & 102 I-84 Exit 3: Rte 7 S 10 mi to Jct Rtes 7 & 102. **Own:** Miriam & Daniel Buckley. **QC:** 52 22 36 S8 S12

Riverside

Betty & Joel Schatzberg

(203)637-2943 • (203)637-3121 (fax)
bschatzber@aol.com

Folk art & Americana specializing in decorated American stoneware, American folk art, trade signs & painted smalls. **Hrs:** By appt only. **Assn:** NHADA VADA. **QC:** 1 41 31

Rocky Hill

Connecticut Antique Wicker

(860)721-7781 • (860)666-4684 (fax)

A large selection of antique wicker, rattan & bamboo from Victorian to Bar Harbor. **Est:** 1980 **Hrs:** By appt only. **Dir:** Call for directions. **QC: 91 S16 S15**

Stepney Antiques Gallery [G]

38 Town Line Rd • 06067
(860)257-0233 **Est:** 1999 **Hrs:** Tue-Sat 10:30-5:30, Sun 12-5. **Sz:** L **Dir:** I-91 Exit 24: N on Silas Deane Hwy, L on Town Line Rd. Gallery is located on the L in Great Meadows Plaza.

Roxbury

Thomas Chipman Antiques

Five Mine Hill Rd • 06783
(860)354-8911

17th, 18th & 19th C American antiques & accessories. Specialists in period building materials: wide board flooring, raised paneling, fireplace mantels, interior & exterior doors, beams, hardware & architectural ornamentation. **Pr:** $25-110,000 **Hrs:** Sat-Sun 9-5 or by appt. **Dir:** I-84 Exit 15: Rte 67 N to Roxbury Station. **QC: 3 S18 S15**

Charles Haver Antiques

Rtes 67 & 317 • 06783
(860)354-1031

In the historic Phineas Smith house, 18th & 19th C American furniture, hooked rugs, baskets, paintings & period accessories. **Hrs:** Thu-Sat 11-5, Sun 1-5. **Dir:** At the int of Rtes 44 & 41, Exit 15 off I-84. **QC: 1 51 52**

Salem

Down the Road Antiques

594 Norwich Rd (Rte 82) • 06420
(860)859-3561

Antiques, art deco, country & Victorian by beautiful Gardiner Lake in an old dance hall. **Pr:** $5-2,000 **Est:** 1989 **Hrs:** Thu-Sun 11-5. **Sz:** L **CC:** AX/V/MC/DIS **Dir:** I-395 Exit 80: On Rte 82 E of the int with Rte 354. 3 mi E of Rte 85, 6 mi W of Rte 395. **Own:** Peter & Audrey Wolcott. **QC: 34 48 65**

Salisbury

Barbara Ardizone Antiques

(860)435-3057

Specializing in painted American furniture, folk art & fine small accessories. Displaying during the summer at Marston House in Wiscasset, ME. **Hrs:** By appt only. **Assn:** ADA NHADA. **QC: 51 41 36**

Buckley & Buckley Antiques

84 Main St (Rte 44) • 06068
(860)435-9919

American William & Mary, country Queen Anne & other high forms of painted furniture (1680-1860). Paintings, early lighting, accessories. **Est:** 1976 **Hrs:** Wed-Mon by chance/appt. **Sz:** M **Assn:** BCADA **Dir:** 1/4 mi W of Town Hall. **Own:** Don & Gloria Buckley. **QC: 52 65 51**

Salisbury Antiques Center [G]

46 Library St • 06068
(860)435-0424

Formal English & American country furniture, paintings & smalls. **Est:** 1981 **Hrs:** Fri-Sun 11-5 or by appt. **CC:** V/MC **Dir:** Off Rte 44 in downtown Salisbury behind the Library. **Own:** Nick Collin.

Sandy Hook (Newtown)

The Mill Antiques [G50]

75 Glen Rd • 06482
(203)426-4469 • (203)426-8864 (fax)
QQJY47A@prodigy.com
www.themillantiques.com

18th, 19th & 20th C furniture & accessories displayed in room settings in an historic building. **Pr:** $25-10,000 **Est:** 1996 **Hrs:** Daily 10-5. **CC:** V/MC **Assn:** MADA **Dir:** I-84 Exit 10 into Sandy Hook: L onto Glen Rd Mill is 1 mi on L Use 2nd drive. **Own:** Jane Apuzzo. **QC: 36 41 48**

Seymour

Seymour Antiques Company [G80+]

26 Bank St • 06483
(203)881-2526
seymourantiques@mindspring.com

Featuring antique oak, walnut & mahogany furniture; lighting, clocks, glassware, jewelry, accessories, artwork & collectibles from the 18th, 19th & 20th C in an elegant turn-of-the-century storefront. **Est:** 1995 **Hrs:** Jan-Nov 15 Tue-Sun 10-5; Nov 16-Dec 24 Tue-Wed, Fri-Sun 10-5, Thu 10-8. **Sz:** H **CC:** V/MC/DIS **Dir:** Rte 8 Exit 22, at Rte 67 in the historic Humphreysville District. **Own:** Joseph Mignani. **QC: 52 74 32 S1**

Simsbury

Simsbury Antiques [G25]

744 Hopmeadow St • 06070
(860)651-4474

Furniture in all styles: desks, bureaus, armoires, tables, chairs as well as glass & china, lamps, mirrors, clocks, jewelry, books, oils, prints & etchings. **Hrs:** Mon-Sat 10-6, Thu til 8, Sun 10-5. **CC:** V/MC.

Somers

Antique & Folk Art Shoppe

62 South Rd (Rte 83) • 06071
(860)749-6197

Antique & country items, tables, early china, glassware, cupboards, chests, lamps, linens, stoneware, folk art, paintings & mirrors. **Est:** 1984 **Hrs:** Tue-Sat 10-4, Sun 12-4. **Sz:** M **Dir:** I-91 Rte 47 E Exit to Rte 190. **Own:** Carole Falkowski. **QC: 34 41 22**

Somerhouse Designs

62 South Rd • 06071
(860)763-4458 • (860)668-1283 (fax)

Bedroom sets, diningroom furniture, linens, Staffordshire, lamps, silver. **Hrs:** Tue-Sat 10-4, Sun 12-4. **Own:** Jean Matejek **QC: S15**

South Kent

The American Heritage Shop

248 Bulls Bridge Rd • 06785
(860)927-3749 • (860)350-3407 (fax)
gary.trabucco@snet.net
www.mypage.ihost.com/Heritage/

Early American reproductions & primitives. Accessory antiques such as tin, iron, wood items. **Est:** 1992 **Hrs:** Daily 11-5 **Sz:** L **Dir:** On Rte 7 15 mi N of New Milford at Bulls Bridge; 5 mi S of Kent. **Own:** Gary & Kathy Trabucco. **QC: 56 1 106 S17**

South Meriden

Fair Weather Antiques

763 Hanover Rd • 06451
(203)237-4636

Decorative antiques, furniture, postcards, ephemera & collectibles. **Hrs:** Mon & Thu-Sat 11-4. **QC: 39 48**

Use the Service QuickCode indexes at the back of the book to find restorers, appraisers, refinishers, and other specialty services.

South Norwalk

Old Well Antiques
135 Washington St • 06854
(203)838-1842

Fresh local 18th, 19th & 20th C objects. **Pr:** $1-5,000 **Est:** 1985 **Hrs:** Tue-Sat 11-5, Sun 12-5. **Dir:** I-95 Exit 15. **Own:** Patrick Padula. **QC: 34 51 32**

South Windham

Bartizek's Antiques
59 Bush Hill Rd • 06266
(860)423-8876

1700-1850 New England furniture & furnishings. **Dir:** Located S of downtown Willimantic, W off Rte 32 to S Windham Rd, W to Bush Hill Rd.

South Windsor

Country Barn Collectibles
1135 Sullivan Ave • 06074
(860)644-2826

Country furniture & accessories, painted & refinished fine oak & walnut, all displayed in a 19th C barn. **Pr:** $10-5,000 **Est:** 1982 **Hrs:** Thu-Tue 10-5. **Sz:** L **Dir:** I-84N S Windsor Exit: L on Buckland to Sullivan Ave. **Own:** Jo & Hugh Patelli. **QC: 34 50 41**

Horace Porter Antiques
16 Shares Ln • 06074
(860)644-0071

Early American furniture & accessories. **Hrs:** By appt only. **Dir:** I-84 Exit 63: R on Rte 30, then R on Shares Ln. Look for sign just before turn. **Own:** David & Dale Bland. **QC: 52**

Time Past
673 Main St • 06074
(860)289-2119

American, English & Continental clocks & fine American furniture. **Est:** 1981 **Hrs:** Mon-Fri 10-5; other times by appt only. **CC:** V/MC **Assn:** NAWCC **Dir:** Just across the Bissell Bridge off Rte 5; 6 mi N of downtown Hartford. **Own:** Ronald Johnson. **QC: 35 52 S1 S7**

Treasure Trunk Antiques
1212 Sullivan Ave • 06074
(860)644-1074

Barn & shop full of antiques & collectibles, fine line of advertising, prints, toys, furniture & more. **Pr:** $3-7,000 **Est:** 1973 **Hrs:** May-Sep daily 10-5; Oct-Jan daily 11-3; closed Jan-May **Sz:** M **Own:** John & Barbara Callahan. **QC: 87 48 32**

South Woodstock

Whispering Hill Farm
Rte 169 • 06267
(860)928-0162

Specializing in hooked rugs, Victorian clothing, dolls, antique sewing items & pine furniture. **Est:** 1989 **Hrs:** Thu-Mon 10-5, Tue & Wed by chance. **CC:** V/MC **Dir:** Located at Woodstock-Pomfret line on scenic Rte 169, red farm on hill. **QC: 55 38 75**

Southbury

Heritage Antiques Center [G100+]
Heritage Rd • 06488
(203)262-8900 • (203)264-3347 (fax)
www.heritageantiquescenter.com

A wide & diverse selection of original antiques, fine art & vintage collectibles displayed in a beautiful, modern, air-conditioned setting. On-site absentee auction monthly. **Est:** 1996 **Hrs:** Mon-Sat 10-6, Thu til 9, Sun 11-5. **Dir:** I-84 Exit 15: N on Rte 67, L onto Heritage Rd at light. Follow signs (1 mi from interstate). **Own:** Mark Marsh. **QC: 32 48 7**

Le Manoir Country French Antiques

(203)264-4650

Direct importer of authentic 18th & 19th C provincial French furniture in cherry, oak & walnut; decorative accessories, paintings, prints, lamps & old Quimper faience. **Pr:** $35-15,000 **Est:** 1979 **Hrs:** By appt only. **QC: 47 53 23**

Gayle O'Neill Fine Jewelry

Main St S • 06488
(203)264-0600 • (203)262-1244 (fax)

Antique, estate & contemporary jewelry from the Victorian, Edwardian, Art Nouveau & Deco periods. **Hrs:** Daily 10-6, call for extended hrs. **CC:** AX/V/MC **Dir:** I-84 Exit 14: R at light Union Square on the R at the next traffic light. On Southbury Green. **QC: 64 78 S16 S1**

Towne Apprentice of Woodbury

1208 Main St N • 06798
(203)263-2233
questman@wtco.net
www.townapprentice.com

Wide range of Americana since the age of exploration to 20th C folk art. Specializing in early lighting, fine scientific instruments, rare 17th & 18th C accessories to native arts of the American Indian. **Hrs:** By chance/appt. **CC:** V/MC **Assn:** GSAAA **Own:** Jonathan Thomas. **QC: 1 77 65**

Southport

Chelsea Antiques [G12]

293 Pequot Ave • 06490
(203)255-8935

Pine & 18th & 19th C furniture, decorative accessories, porcelain, estate & antique jewelry, silver plate & sterling. **Pr:** $10-2,000 **Hrs:** Tue-Sat 11-6. **CC:** AX/V/MC/DIS **Dir:** I-95 Exit 19 or 20. **Own:** Pat Everson. **QC: 64 78 48**

Pat Guthman Antiques

340 Pequot Rd • 06490
(203)259-7069
pguthman01@snet.net

18th & early 19th C furniture & accessories for the keeping room & cooking at the hearth including iron, ceramics, woodenware & furniture as well as 19th C prints & contemporary wood carvings. **Pr:** $100-10,000 **Hrs:** Thu-Sat 10-5 or by appt. **CC:** AX/V/MC **Dir:** From NYC I-95 Exit 19 (Southport): R onto Center St, L onto Pequot. **QC: 1 34 51**

Hansen & Company

244-246 Old Post Rd • 06490
(203)259-7337
(800)571-7337

Guns, swords, knives, war letters, souvenirs, photographs, documents, decoys, power cans, old ammunition, calendars, paintings & old gun company sporting art. **Hrs:** Tue-Fri 10-6, Thu til 7, Sat 9-4. **Assn:** AAA. **QC: 4 67 79**

Ten Eyck-Emerich Antiques

342 Pequot Ave • 06490
(203)259-2559

18th & 19th C English & American furniture, porcelain & decorations. **Hrs:** Tue-Sat 11-5. **Dir:** I-95N Exit 19: to Southport Center. **QC: 52 54 60**

Maria & Peter Warren Antiques Inc

340 Pequot Ave • 06897
(203)259-7069 • (203)762-0475 (fax)

18th & early 19th C American & English furniture & American paintings. Specializing in early creamware, pearlware & other fine English ceramics. **Hrs:** Thu-Sat

10-5 or by appt. **CC:** AX/V/MC **Assn:** AADLA AC. **QC: 52 54 23**

Stamford

The Antique & Artisan Center [G100+]

69 Jefferson St • 06902
(203)327-6022 • (203)327-4858 (fax)
www.antiqueandartisan.com

Period & decorative furnishings, exquisite porcelains, glass, silver, fine art & bronzes displayed tastefully in spacious room settings. One of New England's finest group shops, catering to the discriminating shopper. **Hrs:** Mon-Sat 10:30-5:30, Sun 12-5. **Sz:** H **CC:** V/MC **Assn:** CADA **Dir:** I-95 S Exit 7: L at bottom of ramp, L at 2nd light onto Jefferson; I-95 N Exit 8: R at 2nd light onto Canal, 1st L onto Jefferson. **Own:** Ron Scinto & Mark Candido.

The Arcade

614 Shippan Ave • 06902
(203)975-8400

Furniture, garden antiques, crystal, porcelain & decorative accessories. **Hrs:** Daily. **QC: 48 60 36**

Debbie's Stamford Antiques Center [G150]

735 Canal St • 06902 • (203)357-0537 (fax) (888)329-3546 **Est:** 1997 **Hrs:** Mon-Sun 10:30-5:30. **CC:** AX/V/MC **Dir:** I-95 N Exit 8: Atlantic St R onto Canal St; I-95 S Exit 7: L onto Canal St. **Own:** Debbie Schwartz.

Harbor View Center for Antiques [G75+]

101 Jefferson St • 06902
(203)325-8070 • (203)325-3938 (fax)

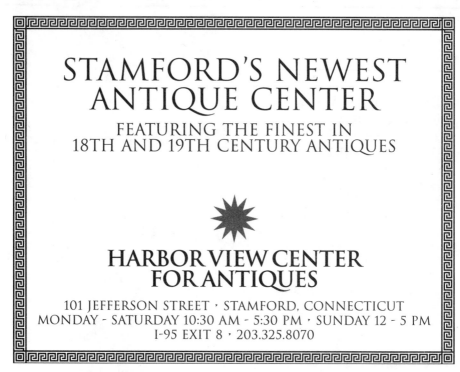

18th & 19th C furniture & decorative accessories. **Est:** 1999 **Hrs:** Mon-Sat 10:30-5:30, Sun 12-5. **Sz:** H **CC:** AX/V/MC/DIS **Dir:** I-95 Exit 8. **Own:** Gary Rubenstein, Michael Ortenau & Doreen Winston. **QC: 48 36**

Hiden Galleries [G60]

481 Canal St • 06902
(203)323-9090 • (203)977-0644 (fax)

Michael Kessler Antiques Ltd

77 Harvard Ave • 06902
(203)324-9100 • (203)324-9100 (fax)
(877)515-2772
michaelkesslerantiques@msn.com
www.michaelkesslerantiques.com

Offering a fine collection of English & Continental furniture, accessories, lighting fixtures & paintings of exquisite quality. **Est:** 1984 **Hrs:** Mon-Sat 10-5:15. **Sz:** L **CC:** AX/V/MC. **QC: 54 12 60 S16 S12 S5**

Steve Newman Fine Arts

112 Revonah Ave • 06905
(203)323-7799 • (203)327-9216 (fax)
barye1@aol.com
www.stevenewmanfinearts.com

19th & 20th C American & European sculpture, including figures, busts, reliefs & animal sculpture; garden fountains & figures. **Hrs:** By appt only. **QC: 11 S1 S16**

Peter Suchy Jewelers

1137 High Ridge Rd • 06905
(203)327-0024

Antique & estate jewelry. **QC: 63 64 S1**

United House Wrecking Inc
535 Hope St • 06906
(203)348-5371 • (203)961-9472 (fax)
www.united-antique.com

Connecticut's largest antique store & emporium. Unique, unusual & one-of-a-kind antiques, featuring architectural pieces, collectibles, doors, furniture & stained glass plus a large selection of outdoor furniture, concrete fountains & statuary. **Hrs:** Mon-Sat 9:30-5:30, Sun 12-5. **Sz:** H **CC:** AX/V/MC **Dir:** I-95 Exit 9S: R on to Courtland Ave (Rte 106), L on Glenbrook Rd, R on Hope St, 1/2 mi down on R side. **Own:** Ross Lodato. **QC: 3 36 60**

The Warehouse
425 Fairfield Ave • 06902
(203)975-7177

Treasure trove of American vintage furniture manufactured between 1880 & 1945. Largest selection of mahogany bedroom & diningroom sets, available as found or refinished to customer specifications; accent pieces, sofas, chairs, prints & mirrors. **Est:** 1990 **Hrs:** Mon & Thu-Sat 10-5, Sun 11-5. **Sz:** H **CC:** V/MC/DIS **Dir:** I-95 Exit 6: Call for directions. **Own:** Elyse & Bernie Kuhn. **QC: 48 50**

Sterling

Riversedge Collectibles & Antiques
13 Pond St
(860)564-7951

Lionels, antiques & collectibles. **Hrs:** Wed-Sun 10-5. **QC: 87**

Stonington

William A Cyr Jr Inc
145 Water St • 06378
(860)535-4700 • (860)535-4700 (fax)
www.williamacyrjr.com

Pilgrim C, William & Mary & Queen Anne period furniture, folk art & other American decorative arts related to the period. **Pr:** $2,000+ **Est:** 1996 **Hrs:** Thu-Sun 11-5. **Sz:** M. **QC: 52 41 1**

Grand & Water Antiques
135 Water St • 06378
(860)535-2624

Quality furniture & accessories, specializing in diningroom tables, chairs, chest of drawers, desks, silver & china. **Hrs:** Mon-Tue & Thu-Sat 10-5, Sun 12-4, Wed by chance. **CC:** V/MC/DIS **Dir:** In the village. **Own:** Deborah Norman. **QC: 48**

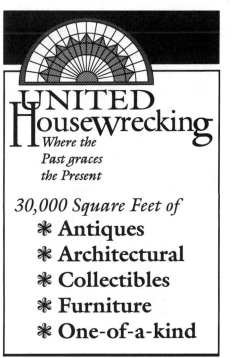

Orkney & Yost Antiques

148 Water St • 06378
(860)535-4402
orkyost@javanet.com
www.orkneyyostantiques.com

18th & 19th C American & Continental furniture, antique Oriental rugs, estate jewelry & silver, paintings & decorative accessories of all periods. **Pr:** $25-25,000 **Est:** 1972 **Hrs:** Mon-Sat 10-5. **Sz:** L **CC:** AX/V/MC **Dir:** I-95 Exit 91: Follow signs to Stonington Borough, 3 min off I-95, in the village. **Own:** Neil Orkney. **QC: 7 52 76**

Orkney & Yost Stonington Antique Center [G50]

71 Cutler St • 06378
(860)535-8373

Featuring 18th, 19th & 20th C furniture, accessories, Oriental rugs, architectural & art; a unique exchange for designers, decorators, dealers & bargain hunters. **Pr:** $50-5,000 **Hrs:** Tue-Sun 10-5. **Sz:** H **CC:** AX/V/MC **Dir:** I-95 Exit 91: Follow signs to Stonington Village (under the viaduct). **Own:** Neil Orkney. **QC: 34 36 48**

Peaceable Kingdom

122 Water St • 06378
(860)535-3434 • (860)535-3434 (fax)

Furniture, pottery, glassware, porcelain & silver. Specialize in the rare & unusual. **Est:** 1977 **Hrs:** Wed-Mon 10-5 or by appt. **Sz:** M **CC:** V/MC **Dir:** In the village. **Own:** Bertrand Bell. **QC: 61 78 S8**

Quester Gallery

77 Main St • 06378
(860)535-3860 • (860)535-3533 (fax)
questergal@snet.net
www.artnet.com/quester.html

Extensive collection of 19th & 20th C marine, sporting & impressionistic paintings, bronze sculptures & prints. Exceptional ship & yacht models, campaign furniture, sea chests & other maritime decorative arts. **Pr:** $500-500,000 **Est:** 1860 **Hrs:** Mon-Sat 10-5 & by appt. **Sz:** L **Assn:** ISA NEAA **Dir:** From N: I-95 Exit 91: L for 1/3 mi, L on N Main thru light, L at stop sign, R at next stop sign, over RR overpass, L on High St, 1 blk. **Own:** James Marenakos & Ann Bilby. **QC: 9 7 70 S1 S8 S16**

Quimper Faience

141 Water St • 06378
(860)535-1712 • (800)470-7339 (fax)
mail@quimperfaience.com
www.quimperfaience.com

The US retail store for Quimper. Some antique Quimper as well as pieces made currently in the original factory in Quimper, France. **Pr:** $25-500 **Est:** 1978 **Hrs:** Mon-Sat 10-5. **CC:** AX/V/MC **Dir:** In the village. **Own:** Elizabeth A Ladwig. **QC: 27**

Marguerite Riordan

8 Pearl St • 06378
(860)535-2511 • (860)535-0580 (fax)
41050@msn.com

Antique furnishings & works of art including needlework, New England furniture, primitive paintings & fine examples of the American decorative arts. **Est:** 1965 **Hrs:** By appt only. **Sz:** L **Assn:** NAADAA **Dir:** In the village. **QC: 1 52 82**

Water Street Antiques

114 Water St • 06378
(860)535-1124

English & Continental furniture, paintings & accessories. **Est:** 1987 **Hrs:** Daily 10-5 & by appt. **CC:** V/MC **Dir:** In the village. **Own:** Anne Murphy. **QC: 53 54 7**

Stony Creek

Taken for Granite Antiques

409 Leetes Island Rd • 06405
(203)488-0557 • (203)488-1650 (fax)

Decorator items for the home & garden keeping up with the trends of French country to "shabby chic." An array of art, pottery, lamps & mirrors. **Pr:** $5-1,000 **Est:** 1984 **Hrs:** Daily 10:30-5:30. **Sz:** M **CC:** V/MC **Dir:** I-95 Exit 56 (Stony Creek & Thimble Islands): 1.5 mi to Welcome to Stony Creek sign across from 3 way stop. Shop is located at the 3-way stop. **Own:** Michele Ward. **QC: 3 51 65 S12 S8 S15**

Stratford

America's Past

82 Boston Ave • 06497
(203)378-7037

Specializing in 19th & 20th C American paintings. **Hrs:** Wed-Fri 11-4. **Dir:** I-95 Exit 32: 4 min away. **Own:** Ivan Seresin. **QC: 7**

Natalie's Antiques
2403 Main St • 06497
(203)377-1483

Period to Victorian to Art Deco: furniture, glass, art, art glass, linen, vintage & estate jewelry & porcelain. Sterling silver, pottery, Chinese export porcelain. **Pr:** $25-50,000 **Hrs:** Mon & Wed-Sat 10-6, Sun 12-5. **Sz:** M **CC:** V/MC **Assn:** AAA **Dir:** From I-95 Exit 32 (from S): W Broad St straight to stop light, turn L on Main St. Go 3 blks to shop on L. **Own:** Nathalie Fisher. **QC: 25 101 48 S1 S12**

The Stratford Antique Center [G200]
400 Honeyspot Rd • 06497
(203)378-7754 • (203)380-2086 (fax)
www.stratfordantique.com

Antiques & collectibles. **Est:** 1992 **Hrs:** Daily 10-5. **Sz:** H **Dir:** I-95 Exit 31: Large blue bldg next to Hojo's. **Own:** Ken & Jan Wynn.

Suffield

Nikki & Tom Deupree
480 N Main St • 06078
(860)668-7262
deupree@concentric.net

American folk art & garden antiques. Small, top-quality inventory constantly changing, with emphasis on design & condition. **Pr:** $100-30,000 **Hrs:** By appt only. **Dir:** 5 mi N of Bradley International Airport. **QC: 41 60 51**

Tolland

The Homestead
46 Tolland Green • 06084
(860)872-0559

Antiques & collectibles, country crafts & furnishings, baskets, candles, cards, candy. **Pr:** .01-$1000. **Est:** 1981 **Hrs:** Jan-Sep Tue-Sat 10:30-5; Oct-Dec Tue-Sun 10:30-5. **Sz:** M **CC:** V/MC **Dir:** I-84 Exit 68 E: turn L 1/4 mi on R. I-84 Exit 68 W: turn R 1/4 m. **Own:** Judith & Harold Shaffer. **QC: 34 48 61**

Z's Antiques & Restorations
Rte 74 & Shenipsit Lake Rd • 06084
(860)872-7735

Specializing in American oak furniture. **Hrs:** Thu-Sat 11-5, Sun by chance. **Sz:** L **Dir:** Rte 84 Exit 67. **QC: 50**

Torrington

Northwood Antiques
47 Main St • 06790
(860)489-4544

Fine furniture, original art, decorative items & accessories. **Hrs:** Wed-Sat 12-6, Thu til 8, Sun 1-5. **Sz:** L.

Pure Silver & Gold
8 Water St • 06790
(860)489-0019

Specializing in antique & estate jewelry. **Hrs:** Tue-Sat 10-4:30. **Dir:** Rte 8 Torrington Exit: in ctr of downtown area. **Own:** Bret Van Scteras. **QC: 64 S1**

Remember When [G25]
111 Main St • 06790
(860)489-1566 • (860)489-1566 (fax)
remwhen@esslink.com

Specializing in the 1920s through the 1950s. Large inventory of lamps, chandeliers, wall sconces, floor lamps & table lamps. Service dept includes fabric & glass replacement lampshades. Vintage decor & ladies accessories. Always the unique in art deco. **Est:** 1989 **Hrs:** Mon-Tue, Sat 10:30-6, Thu-Fri 10:30-8, Sun 12-5. **Sz:** L **CC:** AX/V/MC/DIS **Assn:** NEAA **Dir:** Rte 8 N to Exit 44. Downtown Torrington next to Yankee Pedlar Inn. **Own:** Karen O'Donnell. **QC: 5 48 65 S16 S12 S1**

Wright's Barn [G40]
Wright Rd • 06790
(860)482-0095

Furniture, glass, china & jewelry on two floors of an old dairy barn. **Pr:** $0.50-1,000 **Est:** 1982 **Hrs:** Sat-Sun 10-4:30. **Sz:** H **Dir:** Rte 8 Exit 44: at 2nd light (approx 200 ft) turn L (W) onto Rte 4 about 3-1/2 mi on R. **Own:** Mildred & John Wright. **QC: 23 102 61**

Trumbull

Zimmers Heirloom Clocks
124 Strobel Rd • 06611
(203)261-2278

Wide variety of clocks including banjo, long case, mantel & others. **Hrs:** By chance/appt. **QC: 35 S7**

Unionville

Antiques on the Farmington [G30]
218 River Rd (Rte 4) • 06085
(860)673-9205
www.antiquesonfarmington.com

Fine 18th, 19th & 20th C antique & vintage furniture, clocks, glass, china, silver & accessories located in an historic 19th C grist mill on the banks of the Farmington River. **Est:** 1990 **Hrs:** Daily 10-5. **CC:** AX/V/MC **Dir:** I-84 W to Exit 39: Rte 4 W to River Rd. L at River Rd, L into parking lot. **QC: 48 64 79**

Wallingford

Antique Center of Wallingford [G3]
28 S Orchard St • 06492
(203)269-7130

A renovated barn filled with oak & other furniture, country items, pottery, pressed glass, tinware, postcards, books & collector's items. A browser's paradise. **Pr:** $1-5,000 **Est:** 1966 **Hrs:** Daily 1-5. **Sz:** M **Dir:** 1 blk E of Rte 5, across from the cemetery. **Own:** Lyn Livingstone. **QC: 34 36 50**

The Curiosity Shop
216 Center St • 06492
(203)294-1975

Antiques, collectibles & vintage items. **Hrs:** Wed-Sat 11-5, Sun 12-4. **Own:** Heidi Pariato.

Hunts Courtyard Antiques [G25]
38 N Main St • 06492
(203)294-1733

Furniture, quilts, art pottery, postcards, china, silver, Depression glass, estate jewelry & collectibles. **Hrs:** Thu-Mon 10-4. **Sz:** L **Dir:** I-91 Exit 14: N on Rte 150 (Center St) 2 mi to N Main St.

Images Heirloom Linens & Lace
32 N Colony (Rte 5) • 06492
(203)265-7065

American & European estate linens/lace & other early textiles: linen sheet sets, shams, banquet cloths, hard-to-find large tablecloths, rounds, squares, runners, doilies, pillowcases, quilts & coverlets. **Pr:** $2-1,200 **Est:** 1988 **Hrs:** Mon-Fri 10-4, Sat 11-4. **CC:** V/MC **Dir:** I-91 Exit 13: 4 mi; Merritt Pkwy Exit 64: 2 min. **Own:** Debra Bonito. **QC: 36 39 80**

Keepsakes Antiques Company
214 Center St • 06492
(203)265-4242

Fine 19th C thru the 1940s American & Victorian furniture & accessories as well as estate jewelry. **Pr:** $10-5,000 **Est:** 1993 **Hrs:** Thu-Sat & Mon 10:30-4:30, Sun 12-4. Closed Sun in Jul & Aug. **Sz:** S **CC:** V/MC **Dir:** I-91 Exit 14 or Rte 15 (Merritt/Wilbur Cross Pkwy) Exit 64. **Own:** Peter & Marianne Zablocki. **QC: 48 64 S8**

Madison Trust II [G]

118 Center St • 06492
(203)269-3030
www.connix.com/mt2

In the heart of Wallingford's antique district, featuring ten rooms of quality antiques, books, collectibles & fine furnishings. **Hrs:** Tue-Sat 10-4, Sun 12-4. **QC: S8**

Memories, Treasures Old & New

200 Center St • 06492
(203)269-2224

Antiques & collectibles. **Hrs:** Mon & Wed 10-4, Fri 10-6, Thu & Sat 12-4, Sun by chance/appt. **Dir:** I-91 Exit 14 or Wilbur Cross Pkwy Exit 64. Located in the middle of downtown Wallingford's antique district.

Rick's Antiques & Coins

428 North Colony St • 06492
(203)269-9888

Hrs: Mon-Sat 9-5.

Wallingford Center Street Antiques [G4]

171 Center St • 06492
(203)269-8439 • (203)269-8436 (fax)
sjabt@prodigy.net

Three rooms of Victorian, country & oak furniture, fine art, clocks, silver, Oriental rugs, lighting, fine glass & china, including flow blue, ironstone & antique accessories. **Pr:** $25-10,000 **Est:** 1991 **Hrs:** Sat-Sun 11-4 or by appt; Jul-Aug closed Sun. **Sz:** L **Assn:** CADA NAWCC **Dir:** I-91 Exit 13 or Merritt Pkwy Exit 64: Center St near the corn of So Orchard. **Own:** Steve & Joan Abt. **QC: 35 48 65**

Wallingford General Antiques

202 Center St • 06492
(203)265-5567

Hrs: Win Mon & Wed-Sat 10:30-4:30. **Dir:** I-91 Exit 14 or Wilbur Cross Pkwy Exit 64.

Watertown

A's Pool Tables

711 Main St • 06795
(860)274-7508

Specializing in antique pool tables with over two dozen on display including tables by Brunswick, JE Came, Wentco, Kling, Collender & Oliver Briggs; vintage jukeboxes & games. **Pr:** $3,000-20,000 **Est:** 1975 **Hrs:** Mon-Fri 10-5, Sat 9-4. **CC:** V/MC. **QC: 79**

DeBare Saunders & Ronald Mayne Antiques & Interior Design

(860)274-2293 • (860)945-3369 (fax)

In an historic Victorian mansion, masterworks of 19th C America (1840-1885); Egyptian Revival, Renaissance Revival, Gothic Revival, Aesthetic movement, American & Continental antiques. **Hrs:** By appt only. **Sz:** M **Dir:** I-84 Exit 17: N on Rte 63. 5 mi E of Woodbury on Rte 6; 9 mi S of Litchfield on Rte 63. **QC: 52 58 S18 S15**

West Cornwall

Barbara Farnsworth Bookseller

Rte 128 • 06769
(860)672-6571 • (860)672-3099 (fax)
bfbooks@snet.net

Marvelously organized antiquarian books on two floors in the old Masonic Hall building: extensive selections on horticulture, food & beverages, the arts, antiques, literature, printing & decorated trade bindings. **Pr:** $5-1,000 **Est:** 1978 **Hrs:** Sat usually 9-5 or by chance/appt **Sz:** 40,000 books **Assn:** ABAA CAB **Dir:** From I-84 E in Danbury turn N on Rte 7 35 mi to W Cornwall. Turn E on

Rte 128 past covered bridge, shop on R. **Own:** Barbara Farnsworth. **QC: 18**

Michael D Trapp
7 River Rd • 06796
(860)672-6098 • (860)672-3489 (fax)

Specialist in architectural fragments including columns, cornices, urns, textile fragments & other interesting objects. Period European furniture & accessories. **Hrs:** Fri-Sun 11-5, Mon-Thu by chance/appt. **Dir:** Second L through village. **QC: 3 54**

West Hartford

Metzgers
15 S Main St • 06107
(860)232-1843

Specializing in antique lighting. **Est:** 1925 **Hrs:** Tue-Sat 9-5:30. **CC:** V/MC **Dir:** I-84 Exit 41: R for 18 mi on L underneath the clock. **QC: 65 S16**

The Perfect Blend Antiques
1086 New Britain Ave • 06107
(860)570-0010

Fine period furniture, porcelains, glassware, jewelry, ephemera & collectibles. **Hrs:** Tue-Sat 10-6, Sun 10-4. **QC: 48 61 39**

West Haven

Joseph Louis Nacca
52 Fern St • 06516
(203)933-4668
j.l.nacca@snet.net

Formal 18th & 19th C furniture & smalls. **Pr:** $100-5,000 **Hrs:** Mon-Fri 8-4:30, Sat 9-12, appt suggested. **Dir:** I-95 Exit 43: make a R U-turn, go up Highland St, 2nd L is Fern, 2nd house on R. **QC: 52 36 S16**

West Simsbury

Mary & Ken Vincent Antiques
(860)658-0689

15th-19th C metalware including mortars, candlesticks, lighting, food molds, bed-warmers; objets de vertu including snuff mulls, quill cutters, vinaigrettes, nutmeg graters; porcelain including blue-and-white transferware. **Hrs:** By appt only. **Assn:** VADA. **QC: 62 22 85**

Taking Tea

Tea caddy: A fine box for storing tea, usually made of mahogany or rosewood, and later of papier mache. Most are fitted with two lidded compartments, one each for green and black tea, and some have a glass mixing bowl. Most caddies were made in the Sheraton through the Victorian periods.

Tea canister: A lidded jar-like container, usually of silver, pewter, or porcelain, for storing tea. The precursor of the tea caddy, and sometimes called caddies, canisters date from the early 1700s.

Tea poy: A tea caddy on an integral stand, usually tripod, and often of the highest quality. Most commonly made from 1800-1825.

Urn stand: A small stand for the urn that was used to fill the teapot with hot water. Most stands have four splayed legs and a gallery, and some have a pull-out slide on which to rest the teapot. Most were made in the Chippendale period.

Tea strainer: A small strainer that fit over the cup to catch tea leaves. Made from about 1750 onwards.

West Willington

Ronald & Penny Dionne

55 Fisher Hill Rd • 06279
(860)487-0741

Painted country furniture, folk art, weathervanes, redware & paintings. **Hrs:** By appt only. **Assn:** ADA NHADA **Dir:** I-84 Exit 69. Call for directions. **QC: 51 41 45**

Westbrook

Antique & Fine Furniture Restoration

433 Essex Rd • 06498
(860)399-2500 • (860)399-1840 (fax)
r.bambino@snet.net

Antique & fine furniture & complete restoration. **Est:** 1972 **Hrs:** Tue-Sat 10-3 or by appt. **Sz:** S **Dir:** I-95 N Exit 65: L off ramp onto Rte 153, approx 1/3 mi on L. I-95 S Exit 65: R off ramp onto Rte 153, approx 1/3 mi on L. **Own:** Robert Bambino. **QC: 52 54 56 S5 S16 S17**

Joseph Goclowski

374 Essex Rd • 06498
(860)399-5070

Decorative antiques. **Hrs:** Tue-Sat 10-4. **Dir:** I-95 Exit 65: 1/4 mi N to Rte 154.

Hanes & Ruskin

203 Essex Rd • 06498
(860)399-5229

Specializing in 18th & 19th C American country furniture & appropriate period accessories. **Est:** 1946 **Hrs:** By appt only. **Assn:** AC NHADA ISA MADA VADA **Own:** Joyce Ruskin Hanes & Lee Hanes. **QC: 52 26 7**

Lovejoy Antiques

150 Boston Post Rd (Rte 1) • 06498
(860)664-9015

Pottery, glass, trunks & furniture. **Hrs:** Daily 11-5. **Own:** Loren Lugg.

The Shops at Tidewater Creek

433 Boston Post Rd (Rte 1) • 06498
(860)399-8399

Antiques & collectibles from primitives to the 1950s. **Hrs:** Daily 10-5. **Dir:** I-95 betw Exit 64 & 65.

The Source

374 Essex Rd (Rte 153) • 07498
(860)399-6308

Antiques & interesting stuff. **Hrs:** Tue-Sat 10-4, Sun by chance. **Dir:** I-95 Exit 65.

Trolley Square Antiques

1921 Boston Post Rd (Rte 1) • 06498
(860)399-9249

A lovely shop full of antiques & collectibles, including jewelry, glass, china, tools, furniture, toys & miscellaneous items. **Pr:** $5-2,500 **Hrs:** Daily 10-5. **Sz:** M **CC:** V/MC **Dir:** I-95 Exit 66: to Boston Post Rd. R to Old Kelsey Pt Rd. From New Haven: I-95 Exit 65: to Boston Post Rd, turn L to Trolley Sq. **Own:** Ann & Dick Doran. **QC: 61 64**

Westbrook Antiques

1119 Boston Post Rd (Rte 1) • 06498
(860)399-9892

Toys. **Hrs:** Daily. **QC: 87**

Westport

Circa Antiques

11 Riverside Ave • 06880
(203)222-8642 • (203)222-3807 (fax)

European antiques, accessories & garden ornaments. **Hrs:** Tue-Sat 10-5, Sun 12-5 or by appt. **QC: 60**

Coleman-Kohn Decorative Antiques Group [20+]
263 Riverside Ave • 06880
(203)227-3401

Antiquarian & leatherbound books, furniture, art, sterling & plate, lighting, antique jewelry, dishes, stemware, mirrors, folk art, garden accessories, quilts, rustic, collectibles, architectural, rugs & dolls. **Hrs:** Mon-Sat 11-5. **QC: 18 48 S1 S8**

Charles Cooke Antiques & Art
125 Main St • 06880
(203)454-5242

Fine art, glass, 19th C furniture & painting restoration. **Hrs:** Mon-Sat 11-6, Sun 1-5. **QC: 7 48 61 S16**

The Family Album
283 Post Rd E • 06880
(203)227-4888

Antique jewelry, quilts, vintage prints & folk art. **Hrs:** Mon-Sat 10-6. **CC:** AX/V/MC **Dir:** Merritt Pkwy Exit 40 or 41: next to Westport County Playhouse. **Own:** Wendy Heyman. **QC: 41 64**

Jordan-Delhaise Gallery Ltd
238 Post Rd E • 06880-3614
(203)454-1830 • (203)221-7574 (fax)
mgdelhaise@aol.com

Eclectic 18th & 19th C European & American furniture & accessories &19th & early 20th C works of art. **Est:** 1982 **Hrs:** Tue-Sat 10:30-5. **Sz:** M **CC:** V/MC **Dir:** I-95 Exit 18: L on Rte 1. Merritt Pkwy Exit 41: Rte 33S, L on Rte 1. **Own:** George E Jordan & Michel G Delhaise. **QC: 53 7 52 S1 S9**

Leonce Antiques & Consignments
1435 Post Rd E • 06880
(203)254-8448 • (203)254-7944 (fax)

Antiques, decorations & sterling flatware. **QC: 36**

Lillian August
17 Main St • 06880
(203)838-8026

European pine furniture, antiques & Americana. **Hrs:** Mon-Sat 10-5, Sun 12-5. **QC: 55 1**

Parc Monceau Country French Antiques
1375 Post Rd E • 06880
(203)319-0001 • (203)255-5790 (fax)
parc.monceau@snet.net
www.parcmonceau.com

18th & 19th C country French furniture & accessories featuring buffets, armoires, chairs, clocks & tables. Custom tables — round, oval & rectangular. Outstanding collection of clocks in excellent working order. **Pr:** $50-15,000 **Est:** 1983 **Hrs:** Mon-Sat 10-5:30, Sun 12-5:30. **Sz:** L **CC:** V/MC **Dir:** I-95 Exit 18: R on Rte 1. Merritt Pkwy Exit 41 S: L on Rte 1. **Own:** Gene & Joanna Farber. **QC: 34 35 47**

Pepper Golden
14 Punch Bowl Dr • 06880
(203)227-2060

Fine American country furniture, folk sculpture, paintings & accessories of the 18th & 19th C. **Hrs:** By appt only. **Assn:** ADA NHADA. **QC: 51 41 7**

Prince of Wales
1032 Post Rd E • 06880
(203)454-2335 • (203)226-3039 (fax)

High-quality pine armoires, cupboards, desks & Welsh & Irish dressers & tables of all kinds & sizes. **Hrs:** Mon-Sat 10-5, Sun 1-5. **Dir:** I-95 Exit 18: to US 1, R 1/4 mi on R.

J B Richardson
6 Patrick Ln • 06880
(203)226-0358

American folk art, early painted & decorated furniture & Oriental rugs. **Est:** 1974 **Hrs:** By appt only. **Assn:** ADA **Dir:** Merritt Pkwy Exit 41. **QC: 41 51 76**

Silk Road Gallery
131 Post Rd E • 06880
(203)221-9099 • (203)221-9099 (fax)

The best of the Far East in a distinctive collection of furniture, paintings, carvings, ceramics, lacquer, baskets, architectural elements & other decorative accessories to complement Western homes. **Hrs:** Tue-Sat 10-6, Sun 12-5. **Sz:** M **CC:** AX/V/MC **Dir:** I-95 Exit 17: L at bottom of ramp, approx 1 mi to Post Rd, R 2 mi (two traffic lights), on L side of street. **Own:** Barbara Loeding. **QC: 36 48 71**

Sam Sloat Coins Inc
606 Post Rd E • 06881
(203)226-4279

Buy & sell coins, sports cards, sports memorabilia & precious metals. **Est:** 1961 **Hrs:** Mon-Fri 9-5, Sat 10-5. **CC:** AX/V/MC/DIS **Dir:** I-95 Exit 18 or Merritt Pkwy Exit 42. **Own:** Bruce Thompson. **QC: 33 79**

George Subkoff Antiques Inc
260 Post Rd E • 06880
(203)227-3515 • (203)227-1884 (fax)

American, English, European & Oriental furnishings, paintings & accessories. One of Connecticut's largest eclectic collections. **Hrs:** Tue-Sat 10-5:30, Sun 12-5; Jul-Aug closed Sun. **Sz:** L **CC:** AX/V/MC **Assn:** AADLA. **QC: 52 54 53**

Willington

1728 Hillview House Antiques
18 Sharps Mill Rd • 06279
(860)429-3634

18th C to turn-of-the-century furnishing, artwork & collectibles. **Hrs:** Daily 10-4 or by chance/appt. **Dir:** First L off Rte 32 S. **QC: 7 48 32**

River Road Antiques [G]
333 River Rd • 06279
(860)487-8611

Victorian & American furniture, vintage clothing, toys & porcelain. **Hrs:** Wed-Sat 10-5, Thu til 7, Sun 12-5. **Dir:** I-84 Exit 69: to Rte 74 E, at jct Rtes 74 & 32 across from Repko Design. **QC: 89 87**

Willington Antiques
7 Glass Factory Rd • 06279
(860)429-6562

Specializing in fine 17th, 18th & early 19th C American furniture & appropriate accessories, mostly high country, all items guaranteed. Rapidly changing inventory. Glass, folk art, needlework, porcelain, metalware, mirrors & treen. **Pr:** $1-6,000 **Hrs:** Tue-Sun 10-5. **Sz:** H **Dir:** I-84 Exit 69: Bear R off exit & follow Rte 74 through light up hill. R 1/4 mi on Glass Factory Rd. **Own:** Steve Kochenburger. **QC: 1 36 52**

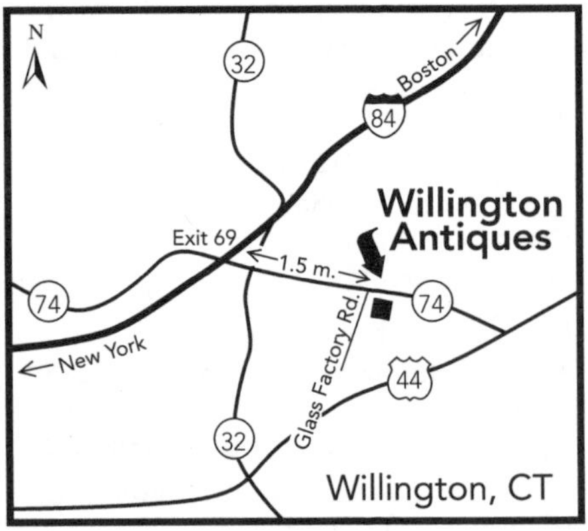

Wilton

Blue House Antiques
384 Ridgefield Rd • 06897
(203)761-9809

18th & 19th C American furniture & unusual English & American accessories. **Pr:** $8-

8,000 **Hrs:** By appt only. **Sz:** M **Dir:** On Rte 33. **Own:** Mike & Peg Jones. **QC: 52 36**

Peter Curran Antiques & Appraisals

444 Danbury (Rd Rte 7) • 06897
(203)762-5469
petercurran@sprintmail.com

Mostly American furniture, paintings & decorative arts from the 18th, 19th & early 20th C. **Pr:** $1000-1,000,000 **Hrs:** By appt only. **Assn:** AAA **Own:** Peter Curran. **QC: 52 7 36 S1**

Emerald Forest Antiques

951 Danbury Rd • 06897
(203)544-9441

Furniture including armoires, dining tables, chairs, country cupboards & trunks; chandeliers & smalls. **Hrs:** Thu-Sun, Tue 11-5:30. **CC:** V/MC **Own:** Kristin Keeler. **QC: 48**

Greenwillow Antiques

26 Cannon Rd (Cannondale) • 06897
(203)762-0244

An old-fashioned antique shop in a country setting with furniture, early glass, china, jewelry, art glass, American pottery & silver. **Est:** 1979 **Hrs:** Tue-Sun 11-5. **Dir:** From Merritt Pkwy: Rte 7N to Cannon Rd, 1 blk to Cannon Crossing. From I-84: Rte 7S to Cannon Rd. **Own:** Lynn Brinker. **QC: 48 61**

Simply Country

392 Danbury Rd • 06897
(203)762-5275

Antiques & collectibles. **Hrs:** Tue-Sat 10-5:30, Sun 12-5. **Dir:** Across from Wilton High School.

Vallin Galleries

516 Danbury Rd • 06897
(203)762-7441 • (203)761-9469 (fax)

A fine selection of period Chinese & Asian art & antiques, fine porcelains, pottery, paintings, textiles & Oriental garden ornaments from Neolithic through 19th C for the discerning collector. **Est:** 1940 **Hrs:** Wed-Sat 10-5, Sun 1-5, other times by appt. **CC:** V/MC **Assn:** AADLA ASA CINOA **Dir:** I-95 Exit 15 N; Merrit Pkwy Exit 39B. **Own:** Peter Rosenberg. **QC: 60 71 24**

Wilton Lamp Light & Shade

11 Danbury Rd • 06897
(203)762-3004

Antique chandeliers, lighting & decorative mirrors. Expert lamp repair & restoration. **Hrs:** Mon-Sat 10-6, Sun 12-5. **Dir:** Rte 7 across from Staples & TJ Maxx. **QC: 65 S16**

Windsor

Central Street Antiques

25 Central St • 06095
(860)688-3635
rookwood@tiac.net
www.antiquenetwork.com

Art glass, pottery, bronzes, sterling, dolls, furniture & toys. Also period American & country furniture. **Hrs:** Tue-Fri 10-6, Sat 10-5, Sun 11-5. **Sz:** L **Dir:** 5 min from Hartford. **QC: 52 65 101 S1**

Pottles & Pannikins

(860)683-0026

18th & 19th C lighting, iron for the hearth, country furniture & accessories. **Hrs:** By appt only. **Own:** Marvin & Barbara Eliot. **QC: 65 102 34**

Winsted

Laurel City Coins & Antiques

462 Main St • 06098
(860)379-0325 • (860)379-0325 (fax)

Estate jewelry, diamonds, sterling, antique toys, dolls, furniture, lamps, art glass & coins. **Est:** 1966 **Hrs:** Tue-Fri 10-4:30, Sat 10-4 or by chance/appt. **QC: 33 64 78 S1**

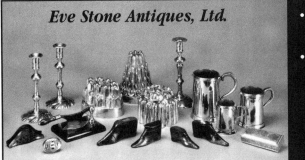

Woodbridge

Allan Katz Americana

175 Ansonia Rd • 06525
(203)393-9356 • (203)389-1906 (fax)
alkatz@concentric.net

American folk art. Specializing in wood carvings, painted furniture, weathervanes, tobacco figures, early American advertising signs & decorative arts. **Hrs:** By appt only. **Assn:** ADA VADA **Dir:** Merritt Pkwy Exit 57. 20 min from Woodbury Antique District. **Own:** Allan & Penny Katz. **QC: 41 44 51**

David M Lesser Fine Antiquarian Books

One Bradley Rd, Ste 302 • 06525
(203)389-8111 • (203)389-7004 (fax)
dmlesser@pcnet.com

Hrs: By appt only. **Assn:** CABA **Own:** David Lesser. **QC: 18**

Eve Stone Antiques Ltd

22 Selden St • 06525
(203)389-6665 • (203)389-6103 (fax)
(800)833-1665
estone@connix.com

The finest, most unusual inventory of English metalware, including copper cookware, brass lighting, fireplace equipment & decorative accessories as well as tobacco-related objects including snuff & tobacco boxes from the 17th-19th C. American furniture. **Est:** 1969 **Hrs:** Mon-Fri 10-4. **Sz:** M **CC:** AX **Own:** Eve Stone & Susan Stone. **QC: 20 88 1 S8**

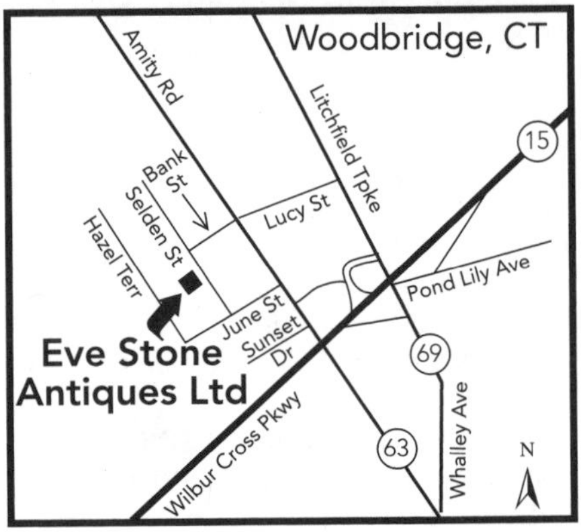

Woodbury

Antiques at the Parsonage

270 Main St S • 06798
(203)266-0555
parson@wtco.net

Wonderful selection of authentic 18th & early 19th C American antiques including furniture, paintings, clocks, nautical, folk art, export china & pewter. **Hrs:** Mon-Sat 10:30-5, Sun 12-5. **Sz:** M **CC:** AX/V/MC **Assn:** WADA NAWCC **Dir:** Rte 84 Exit 15: Rte 6 E to Woodbury. Shop at jct Rtes 6 & 317. **Own:** Gordon Titcomb & Patricia Roe. **QC: 1 52 36 S1**

Antiques on the Green

6 Green Cir (North Green) • 06798
(203)263-3045 • (203)263-3008 (fax)
nteak@aol.com

Quality formal, country & painted furniture, rugs, lighting, silver, botanical prints, decorative accessories & old tools displayed in an historic 1823 heated & air-conditioned barn. **Pr:** $25-10,000 **Hrs:** Daily by chance/appt. **CC:** AX/V/MC **Dir:** I-84 Exit 15: to Rte 6, 5.2 mi to North Green. **Own:** Carol Cogliati. **QC: 34 36 48 S16**

Authantiques

480 Main St • 06798
(203)266-9121 • (203)266-9121 (fax)

English & French 18th & 19th C furnishings, accessories, lighting. Specializing in Canadian & American country antiques with original surface, folk art & collectibles. Emphasis is on high design with authenticity. **Hrs:** Daily. **Sz:** M **Assn:** WADA. **QC: 53 54 102**

Autumn Pond Antiques

(203)263-4909 • (203)263-4712 (fax)
hcole.autumnpond@att.net
www.haroldcoleautumnpond.com

18th & early 19th C American furniture in original surface, 17th & 18th C Delft & English delftware, folk art & fine art. **Hrs:** By appt only. **Assn:** WADA MADA **Dir:** Call for directions. **Own:** Harold E Cole & Norma Chick. **QC: 52 27 41 S1**

Beaux Arts Gallery / Miller Frame Studio

16 Sherman Hill Rd • 06798
(203)263-3939 • (203)263-3939 (fax)
goldagate@aol.com

Featuring 17th-19th C etchings & engravings with occasional stock of 19th C & early 20th C paintings in our new gallery in the heart of Woodbury. Specializing in conservation framing, French matting, restoration of period frames & gold leafing. **Est:** 1983 **Hrs:** Mon-Fri 9:30-5:30, Sat 9:30-4:30, Sun 11-4:30. **Sz:** M **CC:** AX/V/MC **Assn:** PPFA SG FACTS **Dir:** I-84 Exit 15: Rte 6 N to Woodbury; at int Rtes 6 & 64, turn R, then 1st driveway on R. **Own:** Shelly & Peter Miller. **QC: 7 74 S13 S16**

British Country Antiques

50 Main St N (Rte 6) • 06798
(203)263-5100

Eleven spacious house & barn showrooms of beautifully finished 18th & 19th C English pine & French fruitwood country furniture, bamboo antiques, reproduction chairs & many unusual period accessories; direct importers. **Est:** 1977 **Hrs:** Wed-Sun 10-5. **Sz:** L **CC:** V/MC **Dir:** I-84 Exit 15: Rte 6 E for 5 mi, on R, 1 hr 45 min from NYC. **Own:** Ed & Connie Adolph. **QC: 47 34 55**

David Brooker Fine Art

113 Main St S • 06798
(203)263-0046

English & European 18th-early 20th C paintings. **Hrs:** Wed-Sat 11-5, Sun 12-5. **Assn:** WADA.

Taking Tea II

Tea infuser: A perforated container, shaped like a small egg on a handle, to hold the tea leaves within the pot. A 19th century development.

Slop bowl or waste bowl: A small bowl to receive the dregs from the bottom of the cup. Slop bowls were usually made in sets with teapots, creamers, and sugar bowls.

Cordial glass: A tiny, stemmed glass for drinking the sweet liqueurs that were often sipped as an accompaniment to tea in colonial times.

Cup plate: A small plate, 3" to 4" in diameter, made of porcelain or glass, on which to set the cup while the saucer was being used to cool the tea. This was a uniquely American custom, so cup plates are invariably of American origin. A cup plate was sometimes made in a matching set with a cup and saucer.

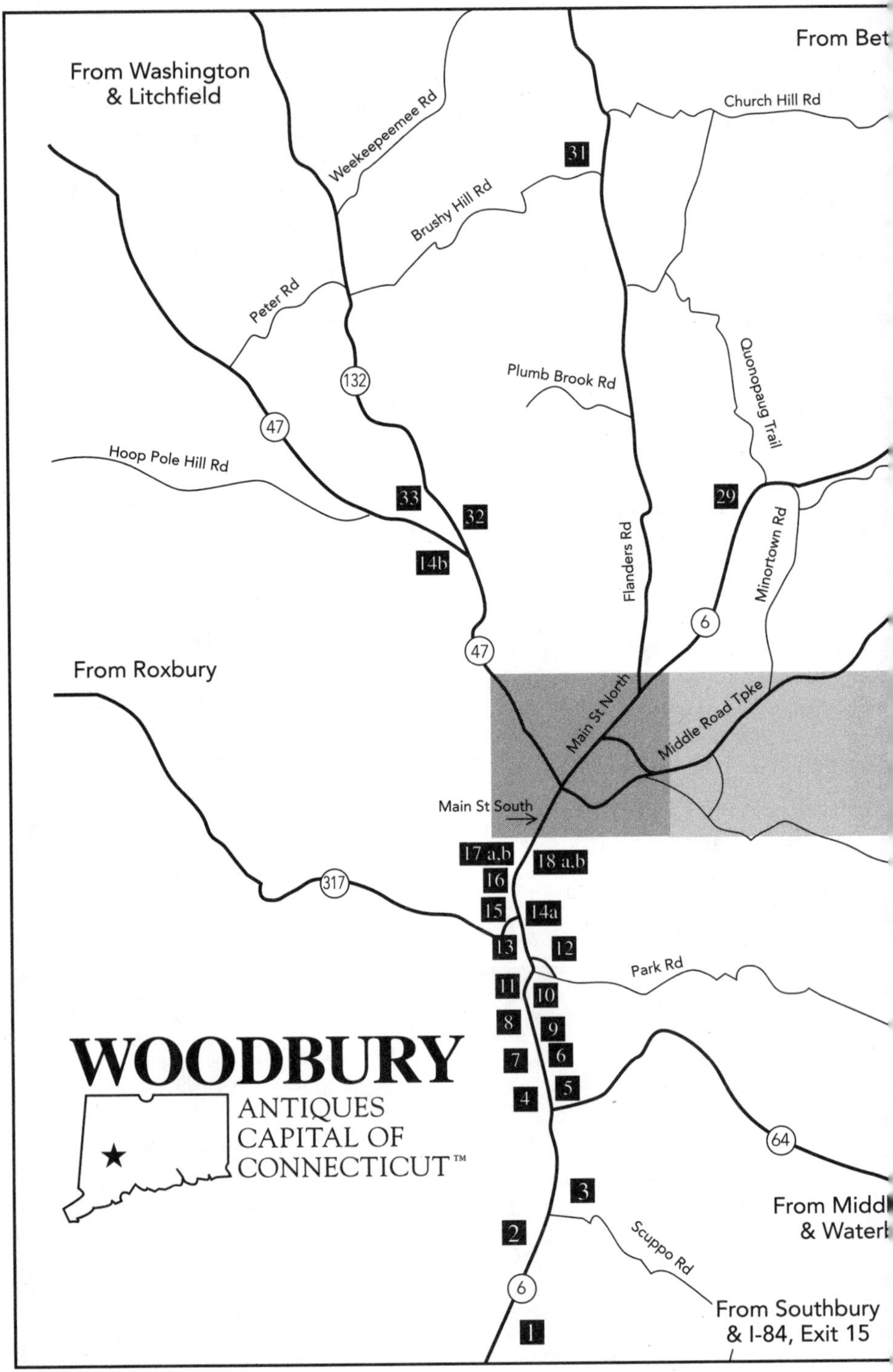
From Washington & Litchfield
From Bet
Church Hill Rd
Weekeepeemee Rd
31
Brushy Hill Rd
Peter Rd
132
Plumb Brook Rd
Quonopaug Trail
47
Hoop Pole Hill Rd
33
32
29
14b
Flanders Rd
Minortown Rd
6
47
From Roxbury
Main St North
Middle Road Tpke
Main St South
17 a,b
18 a,b
16
317
15
14a
13
12
Park Rd
11
10
8
9
7
6
5
4
64
WOODBURY
ANTIQUES CAPITAL OF CONNECTICUT™
3
From Midd & Water
2
Scuppo Rd
6
From Southbury & I-84, Exit 15
1

Woodbury Antiques Dealers Association Directory

1. Jennings & Rohn Antiques
2. Monique Shay Antiques
3. Thomas Schwenke Antiques
4. GLS Antiques
5. Country Loft Antiques
6. Eleish-Van Breems Antiques
7. Authantiques
8. Joel Einhorn Antiques
9. Tucker Frey Antiques
10. Heller-Washam Antiques
11. Martell & Suffin Antiques
12. Nancy Huebner Antiques & Interiors
13. Wayne Pratt Antiques

14a,b. Nancy Fierberg Antiques

15. Antiques At The Parsonage
16. William T. Drakeley-American Antiques

17a. Hitchcock House Antiques
17b. David A Schorsch, American Antiques
18a. David Brooker Fine Art
18b. Winsor Antiques

19. Old Tea Room Antiques, Lisa DeMuro
20. Woodbury Guild

21a. Grass Roots Antiques
21b. Reruns

22. Charles and Rebekah Clark
23. Daria of Woodbury-American Antiques
24. G. Sergeant Antiques
25. Douglas Samaha Oriental Rugs
26. Hamrah's Oriental Rug Co.
27. Three Generations
28. Nutmeg Auction Gallery
29. Eagle Antiques
30. Mill House Antiques
31. Robert S. Walin-American Antiques
32. David Dunton
33. West Country Antiques

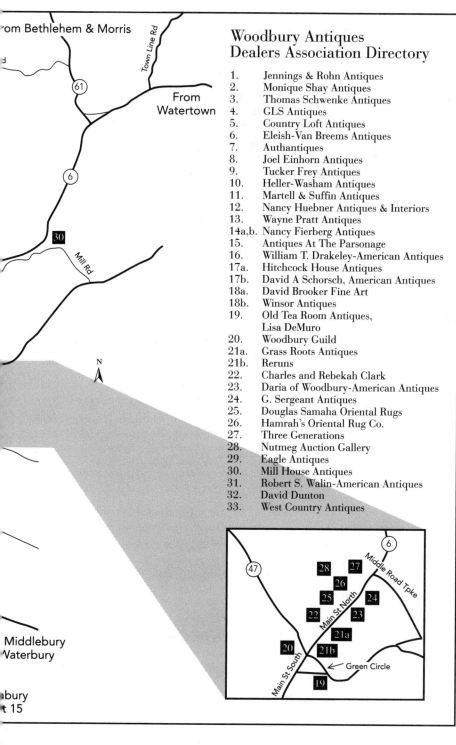

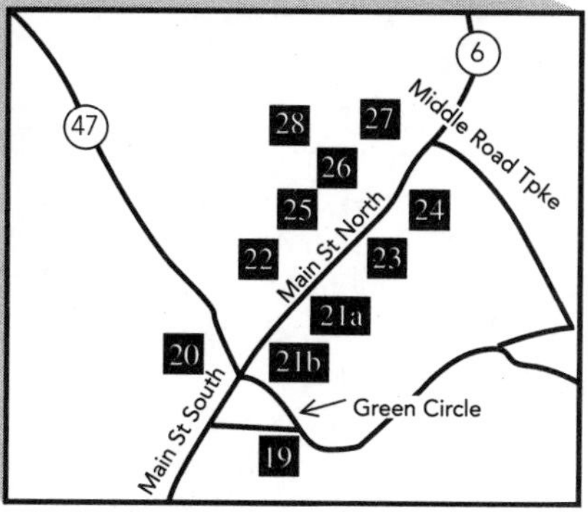

Charles & Rebekah Clark

35 Main St N • 06798
(203)263-7004
www.artnet.com/crclark.html

Classical American furniture & appropriate decorative accessories. **Hrs:** By chance/appt. **Assn:** WADA. **QC: 52**

Country Loft Antiques Inc

557 Main St S • 06798
(203)266-4500 • (203)266-4502 (fax)
french@wtco.net
www.countryloftantiques.com

Serenely situated on 19 acres of natural beauty located in historic Woodbury. Barns, loft & silo are filled with 18th & 19th C French furniture, faience, lighting & accessories. Wine objects from the cellars of France shouldn't be missed. **Pr:** $40-30,000 **Est:** 1980 **Hrs:** Mon & Wed-Sat 10-5, Sun 12-5, Dec-Apr closed Tue. **Sz:** L **CC:** AX/V/MC **Dir:** I-84E Exit 15: 4.3 mi N on Rte 6. **Own:** Carole Winer. **QC: 60 47 34 S15**

Daria of Woodbury

82 Main St N • 06798
(203)263-2431

18th & 19th C American country & formal furniture, folk art, paintings, glass, ceramics, brass & early decorative accessories. **Est:** 1968 **Hrs:** Daily 10-5. **Assn:** WADA **Own:** Daria, John & Wayne Mattox. **QC: 34 41 60 S1**

Des Jardins Oriental Rugs

289 Main St S • 06798
(203)263-0075

Specializing in prestigious antique & decorative Oriental rugs from around the world; also a highly selective inventory of new hand-woven rugs. **Hrs:** Wed-Sun 10-5 or by appt. **QC: 76**

William T Drakeley American Antiques

256 Main St S • 06798
(203)263-4336 • (203)263-4368 (fax)

In a pre-Revolutionary house, American 18th & early 19th C country & formal furniture. **Est:** 1992 **Hrs:** By chance/appt. **Assn:** WADA **Dir:** I-84 Exit 15: On Rte 6 near int of Rte 371. **Own:** Joyce & Bill Drakeley. **QC: 34 52 102**

David Dunton/Antiques

Rte 132 • 06798
(203)263-5355
www.artnet.com/ddunton.html

Formal antiques of the highest quality from the American Federal period with appropriate American, English & French accessories of the late 18th & early 19th C. **Est:** 1974 **Hrs:** Thu 1-5, Fri-Sat 11-5, Sun 1-5 & by chance/appt. **Sz:** L **Assn:** WADA **Dir:** I-84 Exit 15: Rte 6 to Rte 47, L on 47 to Rte 132, R onto Rte 132, 2nd house on L 10 min from I-84. **Own:** David Dunton. **QC: 36 52 7**

Eagle Antiques

615 Main St N • 06798
(203)266-4162 • (203)266-4162 (fax)

American, Continental & English furniture & decorative accessories from the 18th to early 20th C, rugs, carpets & tapestry. Frame restoration. **Est:** 1995 **Hrs:** Call ahead advised. **Sz:** M **Assn:** WADA NEAA **Dir:** I-84 Exit 15 (Southbury): L off ramp onto Rte 6, 4 mi on L. **Own:** Joseph Kiss. **QC: 52 53 54 S16 S13 S5**

Joel Einhorn Antiques

452 Main St S • 06798
(203)266-9090 • (203)266-9191 (fax)

Fine American formal & painted furniture, clocks, ship paintings & decorative accessories with special emphasis on fine American clocks, Federal & Classical furniture & portraits of American ships. **Pr:** $40-100,000 **Hrs:** Daily 11-5 (closed Tue sometimes); call ahead advised. **Sz:** M **Assn:** ADA WADA **Dir:** I-84 Exit 15: 7-1/2 mi N on Rte 6. **QC: 35 52 9**

Eleish-Van Breems Antiques

487 S Main St • 06798
(203)263-7030 • (203)263-7032 (fax)
evbantiq@wtco.net
www.evbantiques.com

Specializing in 18th & 19th C Scandinavian

& northern European antiques, garden elements & decorative accessories. **Hrs:** Mon & Wed-Sat 10-5; Sun 12-5. **Sz:** L **CC:** AX/V/MC/DIS **Assn:** WADA **Dir:** In the Thompson House. **Own:** Rhonda Eleish & Edie van Breems. **QC: 51 20 60 S15 S19**

Nancy Fierberg Antiques

289 Main St S • 06798
(203)263-4957

Americana including country & garden furniture, weathervanes, paintings & an emphasis on folk art. **Hrs:** Tue-Sat 11-5, Sun 1-5. **CC:** AX/V/MC **Assn:** WADA. **QC: 1 41 60**

Tucker Frey Antiques

451 Main St S • 06798
(203)263-5404

18th & early 19th C American furniture, paintings & decorative accessories; all items guaranteed. **Est:** 1992 **Hrs:** Tue-Sat 10-5. **Assn:** WADA. **QC: 52 7 41**

GLS Antiques

586 Main St S • 06798
(203)263-1923

18th & 19th C French, Continental & American furniture, decorative accessories, oil paintings & sterling. **Assn:** WADA. **QC: 53 52 36**

Gothic Victorian's Antiques [G14]

137 Main St S • 06798
(203)263-0398 • (203)263-5845 (fax)
gothicvic@aol.com

Eclectic country & Victorian furniture, accessories & collectibles. **Est:** 1991 **Hrs:** Mon-Fri 11-4, Sat-Sun 12-5. **Sz:** M **CC:** V/MC **Dir:** Next door to the blacksmith shop, directly across from St. Theresa's Church. **Own:** Dione Carbone-Hutton & Dorothy Carbone. **QC: 48 89 32 S8**

Grass Roots Antiques / Reruns

12 Main St N • 06798
(203)263-3983 • (203)266-4277 (fax)

19th C decorative accessories, furniture, mirrors, silver, china & unusual smalls. Distinctive estate & antique jewelry. **Est:** 1972 **Hrs:** Tue-Sat 11-5, Sun 1-5, call ahead in Sum. **CC:** V/MC **Assn:** WADA **Dir:** I-84 Exit 15: Just N of Rte 47 on Rte 6. **Own:** Ethel Greenblatt. **QC: 36 64 48**

Hamrah's Oriental Rugs

115 Main St N • 06798
(203)266-4343 • (203)266-4347 (fax)

Vast, peerless collection of Persian & European rugs & tapestries in pristine condition as well as washing & restoration services & complimentary appraisals. **Est:** 1895 **Hrs:** Wed-Mon 10-5. **CC:** AX/V/MC **Assn:** WADA **Dir:** N of the int of Rte 47. **Own:** Claire Falk. **QC: 76 S16 S1**

Heller-Washam Antiques

451 Main St S • 06798
(203)263-6099

18th & 19th C American furniture & accessories, paintings, textiles, folk art, garden furnishings & architectural elements. **Pr:** $500-50,000 **Est:** 1980 **Hrs:** By appt only. **Assn:** NHADA MADA AC WADA **Own:** Donald Heller & Kimberly Washam. **QC: 1 52 60 S1 S12**

Hitchcock House Antiques

244 Main St S • 06798
(203)263-3131 • (203)263-3622 (fax)

Featuring a large selection of American antiques & decorative arts from the 18th & 19th C. Specializing in American country style including painted furniture, quilts, hooked rugs, paintings, weathervanes, trade signs, pottery, mirrors, lamps & frames. **Est:** 1997 **Hrs:** Wed-Mon 11-6 or by appt. **Sz:** M **Assn:** WADA **Dir:** Located on the first floor of the historic Hitchcock House (c 1783). **Own:** Eileen Michaelis. **QC: 102 7 45**

Nancy Huebner American Antiques & Interiors

403 Main St S • 06798
(203)266-4021 • (203)263-3909 (fax)

Carefully selected 18th & early 19th C American furniture & accessories, all sold with a guarantee. Complete interior design services with a specialty in historically accurate American interiors. **Pr:** $500-10,000 **Hrs:** Thu-Sat 11-5, Sun 1-5. Call ahead advised. **Sz:** M **Assn:** WADA **Dir:** Across from the cannon & Civil War monument on Main St. **QC: 1 52 7 S15**

Jennings & Rohn Antiques

1153 Main St S • 06798
(203)263-3775

16th - 20th C fine & decorative European furniture, lighting, accessories, old master paintings & drawings. **Pr:** $10-5,000 **Est:** 1988 **Hrs:** Mon & Thu-Sat, Sun 12-5. **Sz:** M **Assn:** WADA. **QC: 36 53 7**

Frank Jensen Antiques

142 Middle Rd Tpke • 06798
(203)263-0908

17th, 18th & 19th C American furniture, accessories & country primitives. **Est:** 1953 **Hrs:** By chance/appt. **Dir:** I-84 Exit 15: R at 3rd light, off Rte 6, 1/2 mi on R. **QC: 34 52**

Madeline West Antiques

373 Main St S (at War Memorial) • 06798
(203)263-4604

Decorative accessories for the intermediate & advanced collector, Oriental paintings, prints, fine porcelain & Staffordshire plates. **Est:** 1960 **Hrs:** Daily 11-4. **Dir:** At the S end of town. **QC: 71 74**

Martell & Suffin Antiques

428 Main St S • 06798
(203)263-1913

18th & 19th C Continental & English furniture & decorative accessories, including candlesticks, mirrors, lamps, Chinese & oriental porcelains & art. **Pr:** $150-15,000 **Est:** 1976 **Hrs:** Wed-Sat 11-5, Sun 12-5, Mon by chance/appt. **Assn:** WADA **Dir:** I-84 E Exit 15: Rte 6 E to Woodbury; I-84 W Exit 17: Rte 64 W to Rte 6 E to Woodbury. **Own:** Wade R Martell & Michael S Suffin. **QC: 36 53 54 S1**

Mill House Antiques

1068 Main St N • 06798
(203)263-3446 • (203)266-4326 (fax)

Nestled in several cottage-like buildings, one of largest collections of English & French antique furniture, accessories, chandeliers & works of art thoughtfully displayed in 17 showrooms. Replenished by frequent buying trips to England & the Continent. **Est:**

> Use the Specialty QuickCode indexes at the back of the book to find dealers who specialize in your area of interest.

1964 **Hrs:** Wed-Mon 9-5. **Sz:** L **Assn:** WADA **Dir:** I-84 Exit 15: 9 mi N, just 4 mi N of Woodbury. **Own:** Leslie White. **QC: 47 54 65**

Gerald Murphy Antiques Ltd

60 Main St S • 06798
(203)266-4211 • (203)263-6002 (fax)
gmurphy2@earthlink.net
www.gmurphyantiques.com

Fine quality 17th-19th C English & American furniture, clocks, barometers, period accessories. All items sold with a guarantee. **Pr:** $200-25,000 **Est:** 1984 **Hrs:** Wed-Sun 11-5, call ahead advised. **Sz:** L **CC:** V/MC **Dir:** I-84 Exit 15: 5 mi E on Rte 6. **Own:** Patricia & Robert Sadlier. **QC: 36 52 54**

Old Tea Room Antiques

14 Green Cir • 06798
(203)263-7195 • (203)263-7196 (fax)

18th, 19th & early 20th C American antiques & antique reproduction four poster beds. **Hrs:** Sat 10-5 or by chance/appt. **Assn:** WADA **Dir:** Located behind the gazebo on the North green. **Own:** Lisa Demuro.

Art Pappas Antiques

161 Main St S • 06798
(203)266-0374 • (203)266-0374 (fax)
paptiques@aol.com

Early American antiques, architectural elements & building materials. **Est:** 1983 **Hrs:** Wed-Sat 11-5, Sun 1-5. **Sz:** L **CC:** AX/V/MC/DIS **Dir:** I-84 Exit 15: follow Rte 6 to ctr of Woodbury, approx 5 mi. **Own:** Art Pappas. **QC: 1 3 56 S12 S18**

Leatrice Platt

113 Main St S • 06798
(203)263-0046

American & European furniture of the 19th C, specializing in decorative objects, garden & architectural elements. **Hrs:** Wed-Sat 11-5, Sun 12-5. **Dir:** In the Main Street Antiques Center.

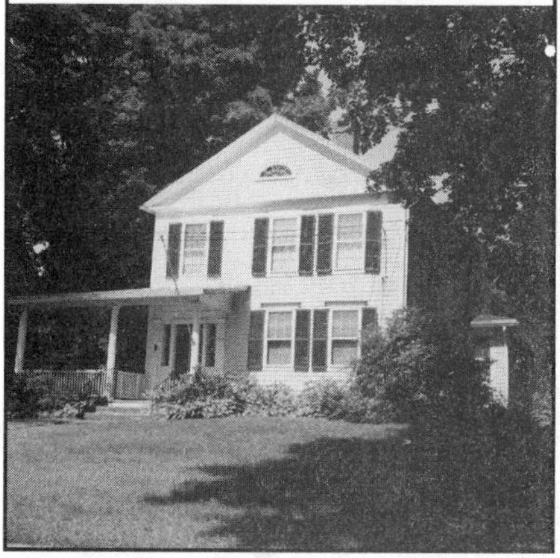

Wayne Pratt Inc

346 Main St S • 06798
(203)263-5676 • (203)266-4766 (fax)

Fine American 18th & 19th C furniture with an emphasis on original finish. Custom-made copies of rare antiques. Garden furniture/accessories a specialty. **Hrs:** Wed-Sat 10-5, Sun 12-5. **Assn:** WADA **Dir:** Exit 15 off I84, 90 min from Boston or New York. **QC: 52 60**

Rosebush Farm

Rte 317 • 06798
(203)266-9114

Direct importers of outstanding European antiques, accessories, garden antiques & architecturals. Designers paradise! **Hrs:** Mon-Sat 11-5, Sun 1-5. **Dir:** Corn Rtes 6 & 317. **QC: 3 60**

Douglas Samaha Oriental Rugs

97 Main St N • 06798
(203)263-4243

Wide variety of antique, decorative & collectible oriental rugs. Specializing in Heriz roomsize & Caucasian scatters. Expert restoration, washing & appraisal services available. **Hrs:** Thu-Fri 12-5 or by chance/appt. **Assn:** WADA. **QC: 76 S1 S16**

David A Schorsch American Antiques Inc

244 Main St S • 06798
(203)263-3131 • (203)263-2622 (fax)

Specializing in 18th & 19th C American antiques, painted furniture, folk art & Shaker. Large selection of period picture frames. **Est:** 1976 **Hrs:** Wed-Mon 11-6 or by appt. **Sz:** M **Assn:** WADA **Dir:** Located on the second floor of the historic Lamson-Hitchcock House (c 1783). **QC: 52 41 37**

Thomas Schwenke Inc

865 Main St S • 06798
(203)266-0303 • (203)266-0707 (fax)
fedfurn@schwenke.com
www.schwenke.com

America's foremost specialist in Federal furniture from 1780-1820 as well as Neoclassical furniture of English & Continental origin. Originator of American Federal Classics (TM), an exclusive line of American Federal replicas. **Hrs:** Wed-Sat 10-5, Sun 12-5 or by appt. **Assn:** ADA WADA. **QC: 52 S1 S17 S16**

G Sergeant Antiques

88 Main St N • 06798
(203)266-4177 • (203)266-4179 (fax)
www.gsergeant.com

Distinctive 17th, 18th & 19th C English, Continental & American furnishings from fine estates as well as designer fabrics & accessories. **Est:** 1989 **Hrs:** Mon & Wed-Sat 11-5, Sun 12-5. **Sz:** S **Assn:** AAA WADA CINOA **Own:** Gary Sergeant. **QC: 3 52 53 S12**

Monique Shay Antiques & Design

920 Main St S • 06798
(203)263-3186 • (203)263-3415 (fax)
euqinom@aol.com

Specializing in country Canadian farm house antiques with three large barns of 19th C furniture including painted armoires, cupboards, tables, chairs & accessories. **Pr:** $100-10,000 **Hrs:** Mon-Sat 10-5, Sun 12-5. **Sz:** H **Assn:** WADA **Dir:** I-84 Exit 15: Rte 6N, 3 mi on L. **QC: 34 51 36**

Taylor-Manning Antiques

107 Main St N • 06798
(203)263-3330

English & American antique furniture of the 18th & early 19th C, important period & signed silver pieces through the 20th C, mirrors, paintings & interesting decorative objects. **Hrs:** Wed-Sun 11-5; or by appt. **QC: 78 52 54**

Three Generations Inc / Stephen Liebson

121 Main St N • 06798
(203)263-6873 • (203)263-6867 (fax)
(888)543-2766
tiques@wtco.net

Suppliers of period & old reproduction American, English & Continental furniture, furnishings, paintings, rugs, objets d'art with an emphasis on quality estate furnishings. **Est:** 1940 **Hrs:** Wed-Sat 10:30-5:30, Sun 12-5. **Sz:** L **Assn:** WADA **Dir:** I-84 Exit 15 N to Woodbury. **QC: 11 53 54 S12 S2 S1**

Fat or Grease Lamps

Lamps probably predate candles. Most early civilizations had vessels that held oil or grease in which a wick was suspended.

Cruisie: The cruisie is the simplest form of lamp of all. It consists of a shallow tin or iron bowl with one, two, or four "spouts" in which the wick was laid.

Betty lamp: A betty lamp is technically a cruisie in which the spout for the wick, and sometimes the whole bowl, is covered over, but in practice the name is often used to refer to cruisies as well.

Phoebe lamp: A phoebe lamp is a betty with a bowl under the font and shaped like it to catch the drippings. It is sometimes called a double betty lamp.

Betties, phoebies and cruisies were hanging lamps usually on chains with spikes and/or hooks to hang from, but similar lamps were made on stands. Lamps were usually made of iron or tin, and sometimes of pewter. Standing lamps were also made of earthenware.

The word "betty" derives not from the name of some architypal housewife (as giving it a capital B would suggest), but from *betynge* — the early English word for the fat and oil left after cooking. Cruisie on the other hand refers to the vessel not its contents: a *cruse* or *crusekyn* was a 14th century vessel with a spout and handle. Where the name phoebe came from is a mystery. The moon was sometimes called Phoebe, and this is a possible origin of the name.

Names for antiques, like those for people, go in and out of fashion: "phoebe," for instance is rarely used today, whereas "cruisie's" popularity increased after 1950s. "Betty," whether used broadly to refer to all lamps of this type or specifically to ones without wick covers, is the name that never goes out of fashion, and if the technically incorrect capital B stimulates us to imagine the hard-working and highly skilled colonial women who used the lamps, then so much the better.

Robert S Walin American Antiques

547 Flanders Rd • 06798
(203)263-4416

18th & 19th C American high country, painted & formal furniture. Brass, fireplace equipment, folk art & other accessories **Est:** 1966 **Hrs:** Oct 10-May 30 Mon 9-5, Sat-Sun 9-4:30. **Sz:** M **Assn:** WADA **Dir:** I-84 to Rte 6, from Woodbury to int of Flanders Rd & Rte 6, N on Flanders Rd 3 mi to sign on L. **QC: 52 40 42 S16**

West Country Antiques

Rte 47 • 06798
(203)263-5741 • (203)266-0848 (fax)

Wide selection of 18th & 19th C French & English country furniture & decorative accessories. **Est:** 1982 **Hrs:** Mon-Sat 10-5, Sun 12-5, closed holidays. **Sz:** L **CC:** AX/V/MC **Assn:** WADA **Dir:** I-84 Exit 15: 1-1/2 mi N of Main St on Rte 47. **Own:** Judy & Ralph Mueller. **QC: 36 47 54**

Winsor Antiques

113 Main St S • 06798
(203)263-7017 • (203)255-0368 (fax)
pdwinsor@aol.com

Specializing in English & French country furniture & English Windsor chairs, furnishings from the 17th to 19th C, architectural elements & garden furniture. **Pr:** $25-20,000 **Est:** 1983 **Hrs:** Wed-Sun 11-5. **CC:** V/MC **Assn:** WADA **Dir:** Located in Main Street Antiques Center. **Own:** Paul & Barbara Winsor. **QC: 36 47 54**

Woodbury Blacksmith & Forge Co & New England Firebacks

125 Main St S • 06798
(203)263-5737 • (203)263-2388 (fax)

Early American wrought iron hardware, custom fireplace tools, accessories, brackets, hangers & hooks, latches, hinges, door knockers & foot scrapers, also reproduction of American 18th C firebacks. **Est:** 1976 **Hrs:** Mon-Fri 10-5, Sat 10:30-2. **Dir:** On Rte 6 off I-84. **Own:** Charles Euston. **QC: 40 62 S17 S16 S18**

Woodbury Guild

4 Main St S • 06798
(203)263-4828 • (203)354-8778 (fax)
wdbrygld@wtco.net

18th-early 19th C American & European antiques, sporting art & contemporary bronzes by international artists, custom-crafted furniture & accessories by local independent artisans & American folk art. **Pr:** $100-10,000 **Est:** 1996 **Hrs:** Wed-Mon 10-5. **Sz:** M **CC:** AX/V/MC **Assn:** WADA **Dir:** On the Main St of Woodbury at the int of Rte 47 and Main St. **Own:** Michael Bird. **QC: 1 14 52 S17 S8 S18**

Woodbury House

Main St N • 06798
(203)263-3407
burbery@ibm.net

Constantly changing inventory of merchandise fresh from local area homes, fine books in all categories, bindings, Americana & clocks. **Est:** 1968 **Hrs:** By appt only. **Assn:** CADA ISA NEAA NADA NAPPA **Own:** Bernie McManus. **QC: 1 35 S1**

Woodstock

Woodstock Hill Antiques

182 Child Hill Rd • 06281
(860)928-6148

Large collection of 18th & 19th C furniture, textiles & accessories displayed in a central chimney cape. **Est:** 1982 **Hrs:** Afternoons by chance/appt. **Dir:** Located 8/10 mi off scenic Rte 169, just N of the Woodstock common. **Own:** Cheryl Wakely. **QC: 48 80**

Maine

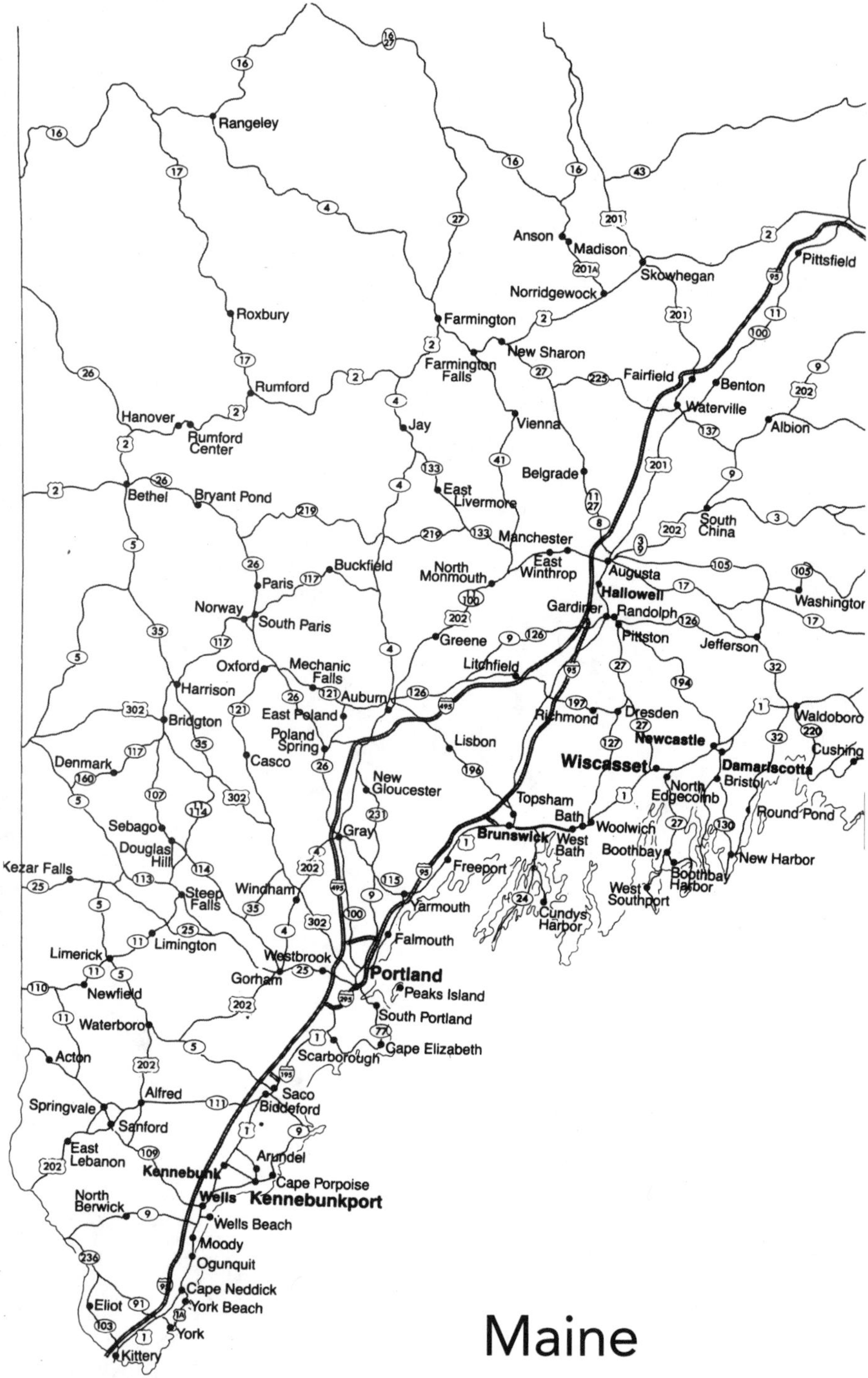
Rangeley
Anson
Madison
Skowhegan
Pittsfield
Norridgewock
Roxbury
Farmington
New Sharon
Farmington Falls
Fairfield
Benton
Rumford
Waterville
Hanover
Rumford Center
Jay
Vienna
Albion
Belgrade
East Livermore
Bethel
Bryant Pond
South China
Manchester
Buckfield
North Monmouth
East Winthrop
Augusta
Paris
Hallowell
Washington
Norway
South Paris
Gardiner
Randolph
Pittston
Jefferson
Greene
Oxford
Mechanic Falls
Litchfield
Harrison
Auburn
East Poland
Richmond
Dresden
Waldoboro
Bridgton
Poland Spring
Lisbon
Newcastle
Cushing
Denmark
Casco
Wiscasset
Damariscotta
New Gloucester
North Edgecomb
Bristol
Topsham
Bath
Round Pond
Sebago
Gray
Brunswick
West Bath
Woolwich
Douglas Hill
Boothbay
New Harbor
Kezar Falls
Freeport
Steep Falls
Windham
West Southport
Boothbay Harbor
Yarmouth
Cundys Harbor
Limington
Falmouth
Limerick
Westbrook
Portland
Gorham
Newfield
Peaks Island
South Portland
Waterboro
Cape Elizabeth
Scarborough
Acton
Saco
Alfred
Biddeford
Springvale
Sanford
East Lebanon
Arundel
Kennebunk
Cape Porpoise
Wells
Kennebunkport
North Berwick
Wells Beach
Moody
Ogunquit
Cape Neddick
Eliot
York Beach
York
Kittery

Maine

Garland
Orono
Bangor
Brewer
Holden
East Holden
Pittsfield
Hampden
Orrington
Troy
Winterport
Benton
Waterville
Bucksport
Albion
Stockton Springs
Ellsworth
Steuben
East Sullivan
Searsport
Trenton
Hulls Cove
Belfast
Castine
Blue Hill
Bar Harbor
Winter Harbor
South China
Liberty
Belmont
Somesville
Northport
Lincolnville Center
North Brooklin
West Brooklin
Lincolnville
Hope
Washington
Northeast Harbor
Dark Harbor
Deer Isle
Bernard
Southwest Harbor
Jefferson
Union
Camden
Rockport
Warren
Rockland
Waldoboro
Thomaston
Cushing
Damariscotta
Spruce Head
North Edgecomb
Bristol
Round Pond
Tenants Harbor
New Harbor
Boothbay Harbor
N
LEGEND
Interstate Highway
Major U.S. and State Routes
Minor State Route
Not to Scale

Albion

Cock Hill Farm

Bessey Ridge Rd • 04910
(207)437-2345
chfantiques@ctel.net
www.ctel.net/~thronsjo

Folk art, primitives, comic books, toys & memorabilia. **Hrs:** Jul-Sep by appt only. **Assn:** MADA **Own:** Barbara J Thornsjo. **QC: 39 41 87**

Alfred

DeWolfe & Wood — Antiquarians on the Green

Waterboro Rd • 04002
(207)490-5572
dwlfwdbk@biddeford.com

Large general selection with emphasis on Americana, Maine & Shakers. Also ephemera, postcards, photography, prints, manuscripts & autographs. **Est:** 1993 **Hrs:** May-Oct daily 9-4; Nov-Apr by chance/appt. **CC:** V/MC **Assn:** MABA **Dir:** On the Green. **Own:** Scott DeWolfe & Frank Wood. **QC: 18 39 74 S1 S13 S16**

Shiretown Antique Center [G50]

Rte 202 • 04002
(207)324-3755

Antiques & collectibles. **Hrs:** Jun-Sep daily 10-5; Oct-May Mon & Wed-Sat 10-5, Sun 1-5. **Dir:** 1 mi E of Village Sq. **Own:** Joan Sylvester.

Arrowsic

James E Arsenault Rare Books

(207)443-1510 • (207)443-1510 (fax)
jararbks@gwi.net

Fine & rare books with an emphasis on American art, architecture, landscape architecture, illustrated books, photographic literature, literary first editions, signed & inscribed books. Prints, paintings, photographs, maps, autographs, ephemera. **Hrs:** By appt only. **Dir:** Call for directions. **QC: 18 39 74**

Arundel

Antiques USA [G300]

Rte 1 • 04046
(207)985-7766 • (207)985-2315 (fax)
(800)USA-1114
ausa@mediaone.net
www.antiquesusamaine.com

Antiques USA - the antique superstore - Maine's largest. A vast & diverse selection of furniture, pottery, fine glassware, art, collectibles & other smalls. **Pr:** $5-3,000 **Est:** 1992 **Hrs:** Daily 10-5 exc Christmas, New Year's & Thanks. **Sz:** H **CC:** AX/V/MC/DIS **Dir:** From Boston: I-95 N Exit 3 (Kennebunk): L on Rte 35 1 mi to Rte 1, L on Rte 1 for 2.8 mi, on R. From Portland: I-95 S Exit 4 (Biddeford): R on Rte 1 S 3.5 mi on L. **Own:** Ron Koocher. **QC: 61 48**

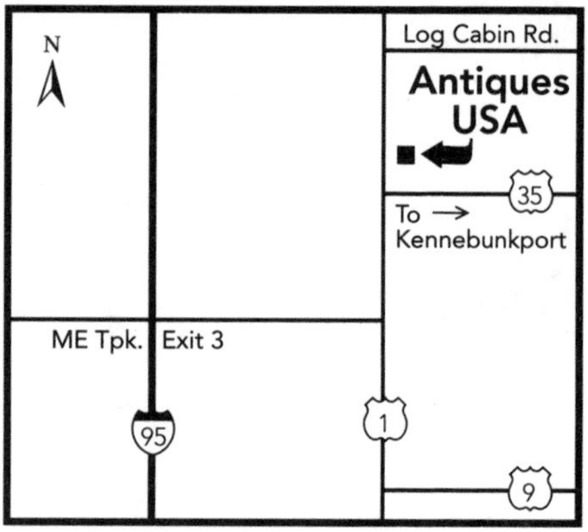

Arundel Antiques [G200+]

Rte 1 • 04046
(207)985-7965

A wide selection of antiques. **Hrs:** May-Oct 15 Mon-Fri 10-5, Sat-Sun 8-6; Oct 16-Apr daily 10-5. **Sz:** L **CC:** AX/V/MC **Dir:** Betw Biddeford & Kennebunk. **Own:** Joanne Desjardins.

Nothing New Antiques

2796 Portland Rd (Rte 1) • 04046
(207)286-1789

American Victorian furniture in oak, walnut & mahogany; rare & unusual accessories, stained glass windows, lamps, advertising, toys & architectural antiques. **Hrs:** Thu-Tue 11-5 **Own:** Richard & Linda Kontoff. **QC: 89 58**

Auburn

Morin's Antiques

195 Turner St • 04210
(207)782-7511

Specializing in refinished oak for home & office, always at least 300 pieces in stock. Also Amish reproductions & Winners Only reproductions. **Hrs:** Mon-Fri 6:30-3:30, Sat 10-2. **Own:** James Betsch. **QC: 50 56**

Orphan Annie's

96 Court St • 04210
(207)782-0638

Art glass by Tiffany, Durand, Steuben, Galle, Daum & Leverre Francais; decorative lighting from Art Nouveau & Art Deco periods; perfumes, jewelry, vintage clothing, pottery, silver, Oriental antiques, furniture & collectibles. **Pr:** $5-5,000 **Est:** 1977 **Hrs:** Mon-Sat 10-5; Sun 12-5; warehouse sale Mon 10-1. **Sz:** L **CC:** AX/V/MC **Dir:** I-95 Exit 12: 4 mi to Auburn, R at 3rd light, 4 blks, on R, across from County Court House. **Own:** Danny Poulin. **QC: 5 61 63**

Augusta

Meader's Stony Brook Antiques

Rte 3/202 • 04330
(207)623-0076

Shop located in rural setting with lush gardens. Barn contains country furniture, primitives & trunks, cupboards, tables, bureaus, benches, stands, wooden bowls, stoneware, coffee grinders, churns, molds, scales, lamps, baskets, glass, tools & kitchen. **Pr:** $5-1,000 **Est:** 1988 **Hrs:** Apr-Nov Mon-Sat 9-6, Sun 9-12:30 & 2-6. **Sz:** M **Dir:** From Augusta Rte 202E to Rte 3/202 6.4 mi from start of Rte 3 on L. **Own:** Harold & Charlotte Meader. **QC: 34 50 55**

Pine Tree Stables Antiques

1095 Riverside Dr • 04330
(207)622-4857

Art glass, baskets, primitives, watches, clocks, cut glass, flow blue, majolica, lamps, lanterns, prints, brides baskets, rose bowls, Roseville, Nippon, other fine glass & china. **Hrs:** May-Dec Tue-Sun 10-5 or by appt. **Assn:** MADA **Dir:** 6 mi off Rte 201. **Own:** Harold & Lois Bulger. **QC: 61 41**

Riverside Antiques

907 Riverside Drive • 04330
(207)621-0994

Dolls, doll carriages, cribs & chairs, linens, jewelry, glass, china & a general line. **Est:** 1984 **Hrs:** May-Sep Tue-Sun 9:30-5 or by chance/appt. **Dir:** Rte 201: Augusta to Waterville Rd. **Own:** Lou & Mary Bowen. **QC: 38 61 32**

Bailey Island

James & Nancy Glazer Antiques

Rte 24 • 04003
(207)833-6973

18th & 19th c Pennsylvania & New England paint decorated furniture & folk art. **Hrs:** Tue-Sat 10-4:30. **Assn:** MADA.

Bangor

Alcott Antiques [G]

30 Central St • 04401
(207)942-7706
pjalcott@aol.com

A selection of Maine country furniture, primitives, folk art, hooked & braided rugs. **Est:** 1977 **Hrs:** Tue-Sat 10-4:30. **Own:** Patricia Alcott. **QC: 34 39 74**

Thomas J Jewett Antiques

(207)548-2640

Specializing in folk art, Maine country furniture in original paint, architectural items, country smalls, Victorian jewelry, American & European art & early New England hooked rugs. **Hrs:** By appt only. **Assn:** MADA GSAAA **Dir:** Call for directions. **Own:** Thomas J Jewett. **QC: 41 3 102**

Bar Harbor

Albert Meadow Antiques

10 Albert Meadow • 04609
(207)288-9456

Locally acquired antiques & collectibles including Mexican, Bakelite, estate & costume jewelry, sterling silver, art pottery, childhood items & dolls. Specializing in Art Noveau, Arts & Crafts & Art Deco. **Pr:** $50-750 **Est:** 1987 **Hrs:** May 15-Oct 15 daily 10-5. **Sz:** S **CC:** AX/V/MC **Dir:** Downtown Bar Harbor, 100 ft from black clock on village green, on Albert Meadow. **Own:** Diana Doherty. **QC: 63 38 05**

Elizabeth Moore Antiques

(207)288-5873

English, Continental & American antiques & decorative accessories as well as garden ornaments. **Hrs:** Jul-Sep daily 10-5. **QC: 52 53 54**

Shaw Antiques at Chiltern Inn

3 Cromwell Harbor Rd • 04609
(207)288-0114 • (207)228-0124 (fax)
shawantiques@acadia.net

Very fine formal & country American & English furniture, 19th C paintings & decorative accessories for the serious collector. **Pr:** $100-10,000 **Est:** 1990 **Hrs:** May 1-Nov 1 Mon-Sun 10-6; Nov 2-Apr 30 by appt. **Sz:** M **CC:** V/MC **Dir:** Follow Rte 3 to stop sign on Main St in downtown Bar Harbor (a park is on your L). R at stop, go several blks R at Cromwell Harbor Rd. Chiltern Inn 1st bldg on R. **Own:** John Shaw & Pat Monhollon. **QC: 7 24 52 S1 S12 S15**

Bath

Brick Store Antiques

143 Front St • 04530
(207)443-2790

Country, Victorian & decorative pieces large & smalls in an old brick bldg. **Hrs:** Daily 10-5. **Own:** Barbara Boyland & Polly Thibodeau. **QC: 34 89 36**

Cobblestone & Co

176 Front St • 04530
(207)443-4064

18th, 19th & early 20th C country to formal furnishings, jewelry, art, rugs, textiles, glass, pottery, architectural accents, baskets, books & ephemera. **Hrs:** Daily 10-5. **Own:** Susan Belanger & Janice Bensing.

F Barrie Freeman — Rare Books [G5]

190 Front St • 04112
(207)443-8098 • (207)442-8452 (fax)
freemanfb@delphi.com

Books, ephemera, photographs, prints, manuscripts & maps. **Pr:** $2-5,000 **Est:** 1969

Hrs: Mon-Sat 10-5, Sun 11-3, exc hols. **Sz:** M **CC:** V/MC **Assn:** MABA **Dir:** Historic downtown Bath at the N end of the business ctr (Front St). **Own:** F Barrie Freeman. **QC: 18 36 66**

Front Street Books [G5]

190 Front St • 04530
(207)443-8098

Clocks, Staffordshire, flow blue, Mulberry, Limoges, silver, paintings, prints, dolls, Victoriana, primitives, 19th & 20th C furniture, rugs, quilts, jewelry, agateware, oak, 20th C kitchen items. Also general stock of used, old & rare books & ephemera. **Hrs:** Mon-Sat 10-5, Sun 11-3. **Own:** Barbara Weinz. **QC: 18 55 80**

Pollyanna's Antiques [G5]

182 Front St • 04530
(207)443-4909

General line including primitive, country & Victorian antiques as well as tools, Oriental antiques, jewelry, Civil War memorabilia, furniture, textiles & vintage clothing. **Hrs:** Daily 10-5 or by appt. **Dir:** From US 1 take downtown Bath exit and look for signs for Front St. **QC: 34 89 86**

Timeless Treasures

104 Front St • 04530
(207)442-0377

Antiques, pottery, jewelry, prints, art, pewter, sterling silver & custom cabinetry & furniture-making. **Hrs:** Tue-Sat 10-5. **CC:** AX/V/MC/DIS **Own:** Carol Grose. **QC: S5**

Trifles

70 Front St • 04579
(207)443-5856

Hrs: By chance/appt. **Dir:** Rte 1 E of the Kennebec River. **Own:** Matthew & Helen Robinson.

Belfast

Belfast Antiques & Books

40 Miller St • 04915
(207)338-5239

American & Continental furniture, quality & decorative accessories, garden & architectural fragments & books. **Hrs:** By chance/appt. **Dir:** Corn Miller & Congress. **Own:** Ann Ellen & Stuart Phelps. **QC: 3 52 53**

The Booklover's Attic

Rte 1 • 04915
(207)338-2450

Americana, aviation, military, hunting/fishing, music, children's books, American first editions, records (LPs): jazz, Broadway, sound tracks, opera, classical vocals & classical pop. **Hrs:** May-Oct Mon-Sat 10-5, Sun 11-4. **Assn:** MABA **Own:** Peter & Estelle Plumb. **QC: 18**

Frederica deBeurs — Books

92 Cedar St • 04915
(207)338-4122
debeursbooks@acadia.net

Antiquarian books: specializing in fine & decorative arts, Maine authors, mathematics, science & technology. **Pr:** $1-1,000 **Est:** 1981 **Hrs:** Mar-Dec Wed-Sun 10-5, call ahead on Sat. **Assn:** MABA **Dir:** Rte 1 exit for Rte 3: to downtown Belfast. Cedar is 5th st on R after Shop & Save sign. **Own:** Frederica deBeurs. **QC: 18 19 S1**

Kendrick's Antiques

213 Northport Ave (Rte1) • 04915
(207)338-1356 • (207)338-1356 (fax)
kendrick@mint.net

Specializing in furniture: country painted, formal period, Victorian & turn-of-the-century oak; mirrors, folk art & interesting accessories. **Est:** 1978 **Hrs:** Daily-call ahead advised. **CC:** V/MC **Assn:** MADA **Dir:** US Rte 1: 2.2 mi S of Rte 3 int. **Own:** Carol & Al Kendrick. **QC: 48 41 68**

Landmark Architectural Antiques

108 Main St • 04915
(207)338-9901

Broad offering of house & garden accessories: fireplace mantels, pedestal sinks, clawfoot bathtubs & iron fencing & fanciful array of outsized collectibles & artwork in an 1878 Victorian Gothic bank in historic seaside town. As seen in Travel & Leisure. **Pr:** $50-15,000 **Hrs:** May-Dec Mon-Sat 10-5:30, Sun by chance/appt. **Sz:** M **CC:** V/MC **Dir:** 20 min from Camden by Rte 1 N. **Own:** Mark Martelon. **QC: 3 60 S12**

Penobscot Bay Traders

127 Main St • 04915
(207)359-2031

A "discovery shop" full of fresh finds for the home & garden including American country furniture, folk art, architectural elements & accessories. **Hrs:** Mon-Fri 9-2, Sat 10-12, call ahead advised. **Assn:** MADA GSAAA **Dir:** At Post Office Sq. **Own:** Peg Grindell & Jude Nickerson. **QC: 102 41 3**

Belgrade

Borssen Antiques

Rte 135 • 04917
(207)495-2013

A large selection of country furniture, wholesale & retail, as well as pottery, baskets, books & paintings. **Est:** 1965 **Hrs:** Daily 9-5 **Dir:** Mins from I-95 Rte 27 to Rte 135; 1-1/2 mi S of Town Hall. **Own:** Arne Borssen. **QC: 102 39**

Benton

Beane's Antiques & Photography

92 River Rd • 04917
(207)453-6790
dbeane@mint.net
www.metiques.com/catalog/beane.html

Paintings, paper, toys, advertising, photography & primitives. **Hrs:** Daily, but please call ahead **Own:** Dave & Becky Beane. **QC: 39 S2**

C & G Antiques

469 River Rd • 04917
(207)453-2248

Refinished oak turn-of-the-century furniture, pottery, china, glass, kitchenware, tools, primitives, baskets, pine furniture, wicker & country smalls. **Hrs:** Mon-Sat 9-5, Sun 10-5. **Own:** Gerald & Cindy Gagnon.

Bernard

Antique Wicker E L Higgins

12 Main Rd • 04612
(207)244-3983 • (207)244-7088 (fax)
elhwickr@downeast.net
www.antiquewicker.com

Generally 300-500 pieces of wicker on hand from 1870-1940. Maine's largest quality antique wicker dealer. From Victorian sets to 40s stick wicker all in good to great condition. **Est:** 1972 **Hrs:** Apr-Oct daily 10-5, or by chance/appt. **Sz:** L **CC:** AX/V/MC **Dir:** Rte 1 0r 3 to Ellsworth, Rte 3 to Trenton, Rte 102 to Bernard, L to Bernard. Shop in yellow 2 story bldg. **Own:** Edward Higgins. **QC: 91 58 32 S6 S12 S16**

The Old Red Store

2 Steamboat Wharf Rd • 04612
(207)244-3349

China, glass, small furniture & collectibles. **Est:** 1974 **Hrs:** Jul-Sep 15 Mon-Sat 10-1 & 2-5, or by chance/appt. **Dir:** From Ellsworth off Rte 102. **Own:** Paul R Hinton. **QC: 61 60**

Berwick

Patricia Fulton Antiques

310 Blackberry Hill Rd • 03901
(207)384-2474

Featuring a diverse stock of 18 & 19th C furnishings from New England homes & catering to the special needs of dealers & collectors. Bed & breakfast accommodations & guided tours to New Hampshire & Maine. **Est:** 1962 **Hrs:** By appt only. **Assn:** MADA.

Bethel

Playhouse Antiques

46 Broad St • 04217
(207)824-3170

In a charming playhouse behind one of the town's prettiest houses, a good selection of vintage clothing, books, textiles, tools, quilts, china, glass, collectibles & furniture. **Hrs:** May-Oct 12-5; Nov-Apr by chance/appt. **Sz:** 1500 sq ft **Dir:** Across from the Bethel Inn. **Own:** Sally & Dick Taylor. **QC: 61 80 32**

Blue Hill

Blue Hill Antiques

8 Water St • 04614
(207)374-8825 • (207)326-9772 (fax)

Specializing in a wide range of American & French antiques including Federal furniture, Windsor chairs, painted pine, French country antiques, ceramics, early photography, nautical items, paintings, prints, drawings, as well as a selection of modernism. **Hrs:** Mon-Sat 10-5, Win by appt. **Sz:** L **CC:** V/MC **Dir:** In the village, just off Main St. **Own:** M Kernan & A Strong. **QC: 52 47**

Dwayne Dejoy

RR 1 Box 3388 • 04614
(207)374-3552
dejoy@panax.com

Pre- & postwar art, architectural, garden elements & a large smattering of the odd & obscure. **Est:** 1997 **Hrs:** By chance/appt. **Sz:** S **Dir:** 3 mi from Blue Hill village on the Surry Rd. **Own:** Dwayne Dejoy. **QC: 3 7 36 S1 S12 S18**

Emerson Antiques

Main St • 04614
(207)374-5140
bwemerson@acadia.net

Antiques & decorative accessories, mostly New England & pre-1845 including sophisticated country furniture, porcelains, fine prints, hooked & Oriental rugs, quilts & yacht models. **Est:** 1963 **Hrs:** May-Oct Mon-Fri 10-5, Sat 10-4, Sun by chance/appt. **Sz:** M **CC:** V/MC **Own:** Brad Emerson. **QC: 34 52 60**

Liros Gallery

Main St • 04614
(207)374-5370
(800)287-5370 (ME only)
liros@hypernet.com

19th & 20th C American & European paintings, watercolors, prints & maps. Russian icons a specialty. **Est:** 1966 **Hrs:** Sum Mon-Fri 9-5, Sat 10-5, Sun 12-5 (open year round). **CC:** AX/V/MC **Dir:** Int of Rte 15 & Rte 172. **Own:** Serge Liros. **QC: 7 74 66 S1 S13 S16**

Anne Wells Antiques

Ellsworth/Surry Rd (Rte 172) • 04614
(207)374-2093

American & European country furniture specializing in decorative objects, prints & painted furniture. **Est:** 1993 **Hrs:** Jun-Oct Mon-Sat 10-5 or by chance/appt **CC:** V/MC **Dir:** From Main St, 1/2 mi up hill on Rte 172 toward Ellsworth; shop on R in white cape house. **Own:** Anne Wells. **QC: 34 102 51**

Gail White Antiques

Rte 177 • 04614
(207)374-5759

18th & 19th C New England furniture, paint/early surfaces, lighting, textiles & related period accessories. **Est:** 1996 **Hrs:** May-Oct Tue-Sat 11-5, Sun by chance/appt. Off season call for appt. **Sz:** S **Assn:** MADA **Dir:** 3 mi N of Blue Hill Village. **QC: 34 51 102**

Boothbay

Sweet Woodruff Farm

Rte 27 • 04537
(207)633-6977

Wonderful country shop & herb farm in the barn of an early sheep farm. Painted country antiques are the specialty. **Est:** 1988 **Hrs:** May-Dec most days 10-5, call ahead advised. **CC:** V/MC **Assn:** MADA **Dir:** Rte 27 Boothbay (5 mi from Rte 1). **Own:** Mel & Evelyn Shahan. **QC: 34 51**

Albert Meadow Antiques

8 McKown St • 04538
(207)633-3021

A quality gallery devoted to the romance of the turn of the century. Antique diamond & estate jewelry, fine sterling silver, Tiffany, Galle, Rookwood, period bronzes, Maxfield Parrish prints, Art Nouveau & early Art Deco. **Pr:** $200-10,000 **Est:** 1985 **Hrs:** Jul-Sep 10 Mon-Sat 10-5, Sun 12-5. **Sz:** S **CC:** AX/V/MC **Dir:** Shop is located downtown across from the library. **Own:** David Doherty. **QC: 64 78 100**

Bay Street Antiques

2 Bay St • 04538
(207)633-3186

Art glass (Tiffany, Daum, Galle, Schneider), early 20th C American art pottery (Newcomb, Ohr, Rookwood, Grueby), paintings, American Indian rugs & pottery, pre-Columbian figures, Arts & Crafts, Art Deco, African wood & bronzes, folk art & ephemera. **Pr:** $5-20,000 **Est:** 1980 **Hrs:** Jun 20-Oct 1 daily 10-4. **Sz:** M **Assn:** AADA MADA **Dir:** Follow Atlantic Ave to Bay St, turn L (E side of Boothbay Harbor). **Own:** Tom Cavanaugh. **QC: 100 7 101**

Collector Shop

Lakeside Dr & Middle Rd • 04575
(207)633-2215

Furniture, glass, china, clocks, lamps, tin & postcards **Est:** 1982 **Hrs:** Most days 10-5. **Dir:** 5th business on L after Boothbay PO. **Own:** Ed Swett. **QC: 35 48 61**

Gleason Fine Art

15 Oak St • 04538
(207)633-6849

19th & 20th C American paintings, with emphasis on artists who have ties to the Boothbay Harbor region, including Monhegan Island. **Pr:** $5-10,000 **Est:** 1987 **Hrs:** Tue-Sat 10-5 or by appt. **CC:** AX/V/MC **Assn:** MADA **Dir:** Rte 27 to Boothbay Harbor, across from the Memorial Library. **Own:** Dennis & Martha Gleason. **QC: 7**

Marine Antiques
31G Townsend Ave • 04538
(207)633-0862

Selected marine antiques including ship paintings, scrimshaw, models, instruments & carvings, also campaign furniture. **Pr:** $500-50,000 **Hrs:** By chance/appt. **Sz:** L **Dir:** S of town on E side of the rd. **Own:** John Newton. **QC: 70 41 79**

The Palabra Shops
53 Commercial St • 04538
(207)633-4225
palabra@clinic.net
www.users.clinic.net/palabra

Art glass, Moses bottles, silver, glass, china, pottery, dolls (old & new), estate jewelry, marine items, tools, turquoise, scrimshaw, UK coronation & commemoratives, collectibles. **Est:** 1962 **Hrs:** Mar 15-Dec 15 daily 9-5, Sum 9-9. **CC:** AX/V/MC/DIS **Own:** Pal Vincent & Valerie Snow Vincent. **QC: 100**

Brewer

Center Mall Antiques [G56]
39 Center St • 04412
(207)989-9842
ctrmall@mint.net

Oak, pine, mahogany & country furniture; glass, china, pottery, linens, books, magazines, picture frames, toys, dolls, sporting memorabilia, advertising, military items, coins & jewelry. **Est:** 1990 **Hrs:** Daily 10-5. **Sz:** H **CC:** V/MC **Dir:** In the Thompson & Lyford Hardware Bldg on Penobscot Sq. **Own:** Thomas & Sharon Cole.

Bridgton

The Lamp & Shade Shop
95 Main St • 04009
(207)647-5576
lampshds@pivot.net

Specializing in restored early electric lighting & oil lamps & handcrafted shades. **Hrs:** Mem Day-Col Day daily 10-5; Win by chance/appt. **CC:** V/MC **Dir:** On Rte 302, 35 mi W of Portland in the Lakes Region. **Own:** Carol Honaberger. **QC: 65 S16**

Wales & Hamblen [G]
134 Main St • 04009
(207)647-3840
judie@antiquesmaine.com

Hrs: Sat 9-5, Sun 12-5. **CC:** AX/V/MC/DIS **Own:** Judie Lesh.

Bristol

Jean Gillespie
Rt 32 • 04539
(207)529-5555

Books, prints & ephemera. **Hrs:** Daily 12-5. **QC: 39 74**

The Maples
424 Bristol Rd • 04539
(207)563-2645 • (207)563-1452 (fax)

Country collectibles & primitive furniture (smalls) with a unique collection of Santa buoys & folk art. Also architectural corbels, window frames & mantel pieces. **Pr:** $25-1,000 **Est:** 1986 **Hrs:** Mid-May-Oct Tue-Sun 10-5 or by appt. **Sz:** L **Dir:** From Damariscotta just 2 mi S on Rte 130. **Own:** Pat Bell. **QC: 3 34 106**

The Backward Goose
Rte 130 • 04539
(207)677-2017

Glass, china, oak & pine furniture & primitives. **Hrs:** Daily 10-4. **Own:** Elizabeth Huff. **QC: 50 55**

Pioneer Antique Barn
Lower Round Pond Rd • 04539
(207)563-1008

Pottery, glass, open salts, china, Limoges, Haviland, Nippon, Wedgewood, slag glass, paintings, prints, jewelry (new, old & costume), sterling, country furniture, linens & decorative accessories. **Hrs:** Mid-May-Oct Mon-Sat 10-5, Sun by chance/appt. **Dir:** Next to the Bristol Mills PO on Rte 130. **Own:** Paula Foster.

Brooklin

Pineflower Gifts & Antiques

Naskeag Pt Rd • 04616
(207)359-4627

Furniture as found & refinished or painted with milk paint. Decorative lamps of many eras, tinware, bowls, yellowware; braided & woven rugs, quilts, kitchen items, jewelry, toys & games, all collected locally & displayed with local handicrafts. **Hrs:** May-mid Oct Sun-Fri 10-5. **Own:** Kathie Barbett.

Brunswick

Cabot Mill Antiques [G]

14 Maine St • 04011
(207)725-2855 • (207)725-9500 (fax)
cma@gwi.net

Fine antiques attractively displayed inside a restored 1820s mill on the scenic Androscoggin River in historic Brunswick. **Hrs:** Daily 10-5 **CC:** AX/V/MC/DIS **Dir:** Off I-95 & Rte 1.

Day's Antiques

153 Park Row • 04011
(207)725-6959

Country, Victorian, Deco & European furniture combined with wonderful carpets, exceptional glass, china, silver & accessories. **Hrs:** Mon-Sat 10-5; Jan-Mar closed Tue-Wed. **Dir:** Town Brunswick. **Own:** David Day. **QC:** **102 58 36**

Bryant Pond

Mollockett Books & Collectibles

Rte 26 • 04219
(207)665-2397

General stock with specialties in Maine writers, nature, history & travel, plus ephemera. **Pr:** $1-100 **Est:** 1968 **Hrs:** May 15-Oct 15 Thu-Mon 11-5; Oct 16-May 14 by chance/appt **Assn:** MABA **Dir:** Located on Rte 26 betw S Paris & Bethel. **Own:** Basil Seguin. **QC:** **18 S1**

Camden

ABCDef Books

23 Bay View St • 04843
(207)236-3903 • (207)230-0877 (fax)
(888)236-3903
abcbks@midcoast.com

Used, out-of-print, rare & unusual books. Specialties include Americana, nautical, literature cooking & gardening. **Hrs:** Apr-Jan Mon-Sat 10-4; Sun 12-5 **CC:** V/MC **Assn:** MABA **Own:** Barrie Pribyl. **QC:** **18**

American Country Collection

27 Mountain St (Rte 52) • 04843
(207)236-2326

Tools, folk art, woodenware, tinware, kitchenware, iron, textiles, glass & china. Specializing in country accessories. **Hrs:** By chance/appt. **Dir:** Across from the library. **Own:** James & Marjorie Tenety. **QC:** **34 41 80**

Downshire House Ltd

49 Bayview St • 04843
(207)236-9016 • (207)236-3445 (fax)

Fine quality antique longcase clocks, wall regulators, telescopes & selected pieces of fine furniture. **Pr:** $3,000-50,000 **Hrs:** May-Nov Mon-Sat 10:30-5. **CC:** V/MC **Assn:** MADA **Own:** Alan Spanswick. **QC:** **35 77 S1**

Rufus Foshee Antiques

Rte 1 • 04843
(207)236-2838

Specialist in American & English pottery & porcelain (1650-1880) for serious collectors. **Hrs:** Daily Apr-Oct by appt only. **CC:** V/MC **Assn:** MADA **Dir:** Rte 1 35 mi N of Camden betw Camden & Lincolnville Beach. **QC:** **22 23**

Dennis J Petrick Interiors

5 Elm St • 04843
(207)236-2135

Fine decorative antiques & accessories of Continental style with emphasis on porcelain from the 18th-20th C. Also interior design service & appraisal consultation by appointment. **Hrs:** Jan-May Mon-Sat 9-5; May-Dec daily 9-5. **Dir:** At Camden Home Fashions. **QC: 23 36 S1 S15**

The Richards Antiques

93 Elm St (Rte 1) • 04843
(207)236-2152

Furniture & accessories for the discriminating collector, lamps a specialty. Large inventory of Woodstock & other fine lamp shades. Lamp repair & electrifying. **Pr:** $1-5,000 **Est:** 1948 **Hrs:** Jun-Oct 10-5 or by appt. **Assn:** MADA **Dir:** Rte 1 on L entering Camden from S. **Own:** Chad Richards. **QC: 34 52 65**

Schueler Antiques

10 High St (Rte 1) • 04843
(207)236-2770

In a renovated carriage house, a range of 18th & 19th C American furniture, decorative accessories, complimentary art, decoys & paintings are attractively displayed. **Est:** 1947 **Hrs:** May 15-Oct 15 Tue-Sat 10-5, Sun 1-5, Mon by chance/appt only. **Sz:** M **Assn:** MADA **Dir:** Thru Camden heading N, R at top of town (where Rte 1 heads toward Belfast), 4th house on L. **Own:** Dick & Gay Schueler. **QC: 34 36 52**

Somerset Antiques

47 Bay St • 04843
(207)236-1013

Estate jewelry, antique garden accessories, fine decorative antiques & antique Oriental carpets. Appraisal consultations by appt. **Hrs:** May-Dec daily 9-5. **QC: 61 60 36 S1**

Starbird

17 Main St • 04843
(207)236-8292

Unusual portable country antiques & furniture. **Hrs:** Daily 10-5. **CC:** AX/V/MC/DIS **Dir:** Two doors from the library. **Own:** Alect Sutherland. **QC: 34**

Stone Soup Books

35 Main St • 04843
(207)763-3354

Out-of-print hardcover books & a general collection of select hardcover, reference books, vintage paperbacks & records. Specialties are nautical, Civil War & 20th C art. **Hrs:** May-Oct daily 10:30-5; Nov-Apr closed Sun. **Assn:** MABA **Own:** Agnes & Paul Joy. **QC: 18**

Suffolk Gallery

47 Bayview St • 04843
(207)236-8868

Fine English silver, blue & white transferware, porcelain, Staffordshire figures, furniture, paintings & decorative accessories. **Hrs:** May-Oct daily 10-5 or by appt. **Assn:** MADA **Own:** Marjorie Jones. **QC: 36 23 78**

Canaan

Architectural Antiques by Allan Soll

Rte 2 • 04924
(207)474-5396
solantiq@somtel.com
www.somtel.com/solantiq

Maine's largest selection of American antique leaded, beveled & stained glass windows; doors; lighting; Victorian & empire furniture. **Hrs:** By appt only. **Dir:** 9 mi E of Skowhegan in Canaan Village. **Own:** Allan Soll. **QC: 3 89 S18**

Drake / Haiss Antiques

Rte 2 • 04924
(207)474-5753
collweb@skow.net
www.skow.net/biz1/top.html

Buttons, toys, lanterns, pottery, tools, photographs & bottles. **Est:** 1995 **Hrs:** May-Oct daily 10-5, but please call ahead. **Dir:** Canaan village.

Cape Elizabeth

Two Lights Antiques aka Hanson's Carriage House

3 Two Lights Rd • 04107
(207)767-3608

Pieces of a primitive nature, constructed by hand for a specific purpose of homemaking in an earlier America, by homemakers, Native Americans & Shaker communes. Baskets, spinning & weaving equipment, kitchen, carriage, logging & marine tools. **Pr:** $3-1,250 **Est:** 1978 **Hrs:** Late Jun-Sep Mon-Sat 10-5. **Sz:** S **Dir:** From ME Tpke to Rte 1 following signs to Rte 77 (Coastal) near lighthouses. Located at int of Two Lights Rd & Wheeler Rd. **Own:** Jane (Jean M) Hanson. **QC: 34 57 80**

Cape Neddick

The Barn at Cape Neddick [G80]

Rte 1 • 03902
(207)363-7315

American country & period furniture, collectibles, Oriental & early pottery, folk art & decorative items attractively displayed in a pristine barn. **Est:** 1986 **Hrs:** Daily 10-5. **CC:** V/MC **Dir:** I-95 York Exit: Rte 1, 3 mi N. **Own:** Stephen Le Blanc.

Blanche's Antiques

Rte 1 • 03902
(207)646-5230

Victorian furniture & accessories & European religious art. **Hrs:** May-Oct. **QC: 58**

> Use the Specialty QuickCode indexes at the back of the book to find dealers who specialize in your area of interest.

Columbary Antiques [G]

Rte 1 • 03902
(207)363-5496

Furniture, framed prints, mirrors, collectibles, glass & china. **Hrs:** Daily 10-5; Nov-Feb closed Tue-Wed. **CC:** V/MC **Own:** Lynn Leisentritt.

Cranberry Hill Antiques & Lighting

1284 Rte 1 • 03902
(207)363-5178 • (207)351-2940 (fax)
www.cranberryhill.com

General line of antiques in as-found condition. Largest lamp shade/lamp parts selection N of Boston. Custom lighting services, reproduction & antique lighting with design capabilities. **Pr:** $1-3,000 **Est:** 1971 **Hrs:** Wed-Sat 10-5, Sat 12-5 & by chance. **Sz:** L **CC:** AX/V/MC/DIS **Dir:** I-95N York Exit: E to Rte 1N, L onto Rte 1N, 3-1/5 mi on L diagonally across from Cape Neddick Inn. **Own:** Anthony & Dorothy Anni. **QC: 25 65 36 S12 S16 S15**

The Gold Bug [G]

Rte 1 • 03902
(207)351-2707 • (207)363-3149 (fax)
antiques@thegoldbug.com
www.thegoldbug.com

18th & 19th C furniture, accessories, glass, pottery, fabrics & oddities. **Hrs:** Year round. **Own:** Cesar Chanlatte.

Caribou

The Barn Door

896 N Main St • 04736
(207)492-0432

Cupboards, primitives, clocks, oil lamps, quilts, tools, tin, woodenware, furniture, advertising items, brass bells & wooden sculptures. **Est:** 1968 **Hrs:** Apr-Dec Tue-Sat 9-5. **Dir:** Just N of the airport. **Own:** Valeska Lombard. **QC: 106 34**

Carroll

Duck Blind Antiques

Rte 6
(207)738-2065

General line of country, furniture, quilts, lamps & shades, glass, kitchen items & store items. **Est:** 1968 **Hrs:** Apr-Dec daily 8-6 **CC:** V/MC **Dir:** 25 mi E of Lincoln on Rte 6. **Own:** Jackie & Chuck Vandermeulen. **QC: 34**

Castine

Leila Day Antiques Gallery

Main St • 04421
(207)326-8786

Thoughtfully chosen period & decorative antique furniture, paintings, quilts, hooked rugs & folk art in the historic restored Federal Parson Mason House. **Est:** 1978 **Hrs:** May-Oct 10-5, Nov-Apr by appt only. **CC:** AX/V/MC **Dir:** 1 blk up Main St from town dock. **QC: 36 51**

Dolphin Books & Prints

Rte 166 • 04421
(207)326-0888 • (207)326-0888 (fax)
pete@media2.hypernet.com
www.dolphin-book.com

Books in all subjects with emphasis on nautical, art & architecture, American & English literature. Also original hand-colored prints, maps & framed art. **Pr:** $10-300 **Hrs:** May-Sep Mon-Sat 10-5 or by chance/appt **CC:** V/MC **Assn:** MABA **Dir:** Rte 1N through Bucksport toward Ellsworth/Bar Harbor. Take Rte 175 to Rte 166. White cape on R, with attached grey barn. Sign out front. **Own:** Leon H & Elizabeth S Ballou. **QC: 18 74 66 S13**

Barbara Falk — Bookseller

Rte 166A • 04421
(207)326-4036

Selected stock of 17th to 20th C books with emphasis on literature, women writers, poetry & better children's, with a growing stock of ephemeral material, particularly literature. **Hrs:** May-Oct by appt only. **Assn:** MABA **Own:** Barbara & Richard Falk. **QC: 18 39**

Cornish

Cornish Trading Company [G40]

Main St (Rte 25) • 04020
(207)625-8387
www.cornishtrading.com

18th & 19th C Americana, garden ornaments & architectural elements; decorator items; sporting, rustic & advertising. **Hrs:** Apr-Oct Wed-Mon 10-5; Nov-Dec Fri-Sun 10-5. **Assn:** MADA NHADA **Dir:** 30 mi W of Portland in the Masonic Hall next to the park in the ctr of town. **Own:** Francine O'Donnell.

Cumberland

Meadowood Farm Antiques

(207)829-5318

18th & 19th C furniture & accessories including early lighting, fireplace equipment & appropriate china. **Hrs:** By appt only. **Assn:** GSAAA **Own:** Barbara & Henry Milburn. **QC: 52 65 40**

Ben-Loch Books

19 Stony Ridge Rd • 04110
(207)781-2534

Civil War, Revolutionary War, War of 1812, World War II, American history & biography & Jack London. **Hrs:** By appt only. **Sz:** L **Assn:** MABA **Own:** Howard M Foley. **QC: 18 4**

Cushing

Neville Antiques & the Barometer Shop

576 Pleasant Point Rd • 04563
(207)354-8055

Barometers purchased, sold & repaired. Also fine English & Chinese porcelains & Staffordshire figures. **Pr:** $50-3,500 **Est:** 1951 **Hrs:** By chance/appt. **Sz:** S **CC:** V/MC **Assn:** MADA **Dir:** 9 mi S of Thomaston off Rte 1. **Own:** C Neville Lewis. **QC: 23 70 77 S12 S16 S19**

Damariscotta

Another Season

930 Biscay Rd • 04543
(207)563-1056

Country furniture & accessories. **Hrs:** Call ahead in win. **QC: 102 34**

Antiques at the Brannon — Bunker Inn

Rte 129 • 04543
(207)563-5941

Furniture, clocks, ephemera, military & political items. **Hrs:** Daily 10-6. **Dir:** 1.8 mi from the Rte 130 fork. **Own:** Joe & Jeanne Hovance. **QC: 4 39 48**

Antiques at the Mills

370 Bristol Rd • 04543
(207)563-6777

Country furniture. **Hrs:** By appt only. **QC: 101**

Arsenic & Old Lace Antiques

Main St • 04543
(207)563-1414

Large selection of restored vintage linens, tablecloths, napkins, dresser scarves, pillowcases, hand towels, christening gowns & aprons; also china, sterling & silverplate. Always buying linens & lace. **Hrs:** Mon-Sat 10-4; Win Tue-Sat 10-4. **Assn:** MADA **Own:** Shirley Frater. **QC: 80 81**

Cooper's Red Barn

Bus Rte 1 • 04543
(207)563-3714

Two-story barn filled with a large selection of modern & antique furniture, pine, oak, walnut, mahogany & maple; glass, china, metalware, old tools, linens, books & ironware. **Est:** 1945 **Hrs:** Daily 9-5 by chance/appt. **Sz:** L **Dir:** 3/4 mi heading E out of Damariscotta. **Own:** Calvin & Marjorie Dodge. **QC: 61 86 48**

The Ditty Box

Rte 1 • 04543
(207)882-6618

In an 1840 meeting house: a large collection of country & period American furniture, Staffordshire portrait figures, samplers & Currier & Ives lithographs. **Pr:** $10-3,000 **Est:** 1963 **Hrs:** Mid-Jun to mid-Oct. **Sz:** M **Assn:** MADA **Dir:** W side of Rte 1, on N Edgecomb/Newcastle line, 2 mi N of Wiscasset Bridge. 2 mi S of Foster's Auction Gallery. **Own:** Muriel E Lewis. **QC: 30 52 74**

Oriental Rugs

Main St • 04543
(207)563-6611

Antique Kilims, pillows & nomadic Orientals. **Hrs:** Mon-Sat 8-4. **QC: 76**

Patricia Anne Reed Antiques

148 Bristol Rd • 04543
(207)563-5633
patreed@lincoln.midcoast.com

18th & early 19th C country, formal & painted furniture & accessories, paintings & artwork of all periods, Chinese export, porcelain, Delft, Quimper, Indian, Arts & Crafts, pottery, rugs, architectural & garden, toys, dolls, decoys, silver, treen & tin. **Est:** 1969 **Hrs:** May 24-Oct 12 Mon-Sat 10-5:30, Sun by chance/appt. **Sz:** M **Assn:** MADA NHADA ISA **Dir:** I-95 N of Portland to Brunswick Exit: Rte 1 to Newcastle-Damariscotta ramp. Go thru town. R on

Rtes 129-130. Shop is located 1/2 mi on L. **Own:** Patricia Anne Reed. **QC: 7 51 41 S1 S9 S18**

Peter & Jean Richards Fine Antiques

152 Bristol Rd (Rtes 129/130) • 04543
(207)563-1964 • (207)563-1965 (fax)

Offering a large selection of 18th & 19th C American & English furniture (mostly formal but some country), silver, brass, prints & other period accessories. **Hrs:** May-Nov daily 10-6; Dec-Apr by chance/appt. **Sz:** L **CC:** AX/V/MC **Assn:** NHADA **Dir:** Rte 1, Bus Rte 1 into Damariscotta, S on Rtes 129/130, toward Pemaquid Point & Bristol, 7/10 mi to shop in red barn on L. **QC: 52 54 78 S12 S19**

River Gallery

Main St • 04543
(207)563-6330

19th & early 20th C fine paintings. **Hrs:** By appt only. **QC: 7**

Schooner Galleries

998 Biscay Rd • 04543
(207)563-5647

Specializing in antiques & country collectibles, paintings & prints. **Hrs:** Mon-Sat 10-5 by chance/appt. **QC: 34 74**

Stars

Elm St • 04543
(207)563-5488

Estate jewelry. **Hrs:** Mon-Sat 9:30-5:30 **CC:** AX/V/MC/DIS **Dir:** In the Day Block. **Own:** John & Freida Hanlon. **QC: 64 S1 S16**

This & That Shop

137 Walpole Meetinghouse Rd • 04543
(207)563-3739

Glass, china, kitchenware & collectibles. **Hrs:** Apr-Oct Wed-Mon 10-5; Win by appt. **Own:** Barbara Westheaver. **QC: 61**

Deer Isle

Belcher's Antiques

RR1 Box 359 • 04627
(207)348-9938
belchers@acadia.net
www.belchersantiques.com

Three large rooms & two floors in attached barn of a 19th C farmhouse featuring country antiques, folk art, nautical & advertising items. **Pr:** $50-2,500 **Est:** 1984 **Hrs:** Jun-Oct 11 daily 10-5, Oct-May by chance/appt. **Sz:** L **CC:** V/MC **Assn:** MADA **Dir:** Rte 15 S on Deer Isle; 2/10 mi from the Reach Rd monument. **Own:** Linda Friedman & Jean Hutchinson. **QC: 34 41 70**

Parish House Antiques

Rte 15 • 04681
(207)348-9964

Vintage linens; 20s, 30s & 40s kitchenware; clothing, jewelry & pottery. **Hrs:** Mid-Jun-Oct Mon-Fri 11-6, Sat-Sun 2-6. **Own:** Janice Glenn. **QC: 63 81**

Dexter

Adrienne's Attic

142 Shore Rd • 04930
(207)924-6923

Country, vintage clothing, toys, stoneware, milk bottles & agate collectibles. **Est:** 1984 **Hrs:** Daily by chance/appt; please call ahead. **Dir:** 8/10 mi off Rte 23. **Own:** Barry & Adrienne Strout. **QC: 32**

The Gray Barn Antiques

59 Maple St • 04930
(207)924-6419

Refinished oak & country furniture, collectibles, prints & paintings, tools, tins, advertising, glassware, agateware, jewelry, crocks, milk bottles, baskets, lamps, linens & antique frames. **Hrs:** Daily by chance/appt. **Own:** Phil & Carolyn Theriault. **QC: 50 32**

Dover-Foxcroft

Jenkin's Antiques
56 W Main St • 04426
(207)564-7781

A general line. **Est:** 1940 **Own:** Joyce & Ruel Cross.

Dresden Mills

Mathom Bookshop & Bindery
38 Blinn Hill Rd • 04342
(207)737-4512 • (207)737-4512 (fax)
(800)485-0253
mathom@gwi.net
www.bibliofind.com/mathom.html

First edition English & American literature, literary correspondence & signed books. 5,000 books. **Pr:** $10-2,500 **Est:** 1979 **Hrs:** Jul 1-Sep 30 Thu-Sat 10-5 or by appt; Oct 1-Jun 30 By appt only. **Sz:** M **CC:** V/MC **Assn:** MABA **Own:** Lewis Putnam Turco. **QC: 18 39 S1**

East Andover

Birches Antiques
Andover Rd • 04226
(207)392-2211

Refinished oak, walnut, mahogany, pine; glassware, kitchen collectibles & country Victoriana. **Hrs:** Wed-Sun 10-4 or by appt. **Dir:** Rte 5 from Rumford Point to Andover; R at four corners 15 mi on E Andover Rd. **Own:** Harold & June Hutchins.

East Holden

Country Store Antiques
Bar Harbor Rd (Rte 1A) • 04429
(207)843-7449 • (207)843-6689 (fax)

In an 100-year-old country store, two floors of American country & period formal furniture as well as wicker & appropriate accessories of all periods. **Est:** 1985 **Hrs:** Jun-Oct Tue-Sat 10-5 or by appt. **CC:** V/MC **Dir:** 10 min from Bangor, 20 min from Ellsworth Jct 1A & 46. **Own:** Francine & Benjie Grant. **QC: 41 102 7**

East Lebanon

Country Antiques
Milton Mills Rd • 04027
(207)457-1014

Country, furniture, textiles & folk art. **Est:** 1969 **Hrs:** By chance/appt. **Dir:** 2 mi off Rte 202, 8 mi from Rochester, NH. **Own:** Fran & Dick Thoresen.

East Orland

East Orland Antique Mall [G14]
Rte 1 • 04472
(207)469-1000 • (207)469-1000 (fax)
bcburkes@aol.com

Large selection of costume jewelry including Bakelite & old sterling, also kareted pieces; Wade figurines, including full sets of nursery rhyme characters; primitives; table & floor lamps; glass & china; Nippon, Noritake, Depression glass, furniture. **Pr:** $1-500 **Est:** 1989 **Hrs:** Apr-Dec daily 10-5; Jan-Mar Fri-Sun 10-5. **Sz:** L **CC:** V/MC/DIS **Dir:** Rte 1 N 8 mi from Bucksport on L; Rte 1 S 12 mi from Ellsworth on R. **Own:** Georgia Burke. **QC: 18 63 32**

East Poland

Barton's Antiques
707 Empire Rd • 04230
(207)998-2936

19th C Staffordshire (soft paste, transferware, ironstone, tealeaf, mulberry, flow blue) & some furniture & country items. **Hrs:** Daily by chance/appt. **Sz:** L **Dir:** Rte 122 E 12 mi, bear L 3 mi on Empire Rd. **Own:** Robert & Suzanne Barton. **QC: 30**

East Sullivan

Flanders Bay Antiques
Rte 1 • 04664
(207)422-6408

Country furniture: tables, cupboards, chair sets, beds, bureaus, Victorian & Empire furniture & numerous country accessories. **Hrs:** Daily 10-6. **Dir:** 12 mi downeast of Ellsworth. **QC: 34 102**

East Winthrop

Lakeside Antiques [G50]
Rte 202 • 04364
(207)377-2616

Two floors of pine, oak, walnut, Victorian furniture, cupboards, chests, tables, tools, toys & Victorian accessories. No children under 16 allowed. **Est:** 1986 **Hrs:** Daily 7-5. **Sz:** L **Dir:** 4 mi W of I-95 Exit 15 on Rte 202. **Own:** Juliette & Ormond Piper. **QC: 48**

Easton

Memory Lane Antiques & Collectibles
Station St • 04740
(207)488-3663

Specializing in quality oak, walnut & mahogany furniture, glass, clocks, linens, dolls, vintage clothing, jewelry & kitchen collectibles. **Est:** 1989 **Hrs:** By chance/appt. **Dir:** 7 mi from Presque Isle off Rte 10. **Own:** Rita Henderson & Frank Brown. **QC: 50**

Edgecomb

J Partridge Antiques Ltd
Rte 1 • 04556
(207)882-7745

A large barn full of fine period antiques including 18th C English & American furniture, paintings & prints. **Est:** 1949 **Hrs:** May 15-Oct 15 Mon-Sat 10-5; other times by appt. **Sz:** L **Dir:** 2 mi N of Wiscasset on R side of Rte 1 at Dodge Rd. **Own:** Tatiana Partridge. **QC: 9 52 54**

Eliot

Books & Autographs
287 Goodwin Rd • 03903
(207439-4739 • (207)438-9993 (fax)

Signed & limited editions of 20th C writers, autographs, letters, photographs, with emphasis on the performing arts including opera, movies & theater. **Hrs:** By appt only. **Assn:** MABA **Own:** Sherman R Emery & Harold P Merry. **QC: 18**

Ellsworth

Big Chicken Barn Books & Antiques [G55+]
Rte 1 • 04605
(207)667-7308 • (207)667-3925 (fax)
bcb@acadia.net
www.bigchickenbarn.com

Maine's largest antiquarian book dealer & antique shop filled with books & antiques including Maine, nautical, religion, Americana, mysteries, children's, cookbooks, nature & medical. **Hrs:** Spr & Fall daily 9-5, Sum 9-7, Win 10-4. **Sz:** L **Assn:** MABA **Dir:** Halfway betw Bucksport & Ellsworth **Own:** Annegret Cukierski. **QC: 48 18**

Cindy's Antiques
596 Bucksport Rd • 04605
(207)667-4476 • (207)664-0472 (fax)
mclough@acadia.net

General line including formal & period antiques; country, Victorian & primitive antiques; silver items, art pottery, paintings, prints, lamps, bronzes, porcelains & export china. Wholesale to the trade. **Hrs:** By chance/appt **Assn:** MADA **Dir:** 3 mi S of Ellsworth on Rte 1. **Own:** Lawrence Clough. **QC: 48 78 34**

Eastern Antiques
52 Dean St • 04605
(207)667-4033

Furniture: pine, oak, wicker, walnut, country; glass & china, silver, primitives, paintings, advertising items, dolls, Victorian to 1940s vintage clothing & textiles. **Est:** 1972 **Hrs:** Sum Mon-Sat 10-6 or by chance/appt. **Dir:** In town. **Own:** Al Sale Jr. **QC: 39 48 83**

His & Hers Antiques
512 Bucksport Rd (Rte 1) • 04605
(207)667-2115

Toys & pedal cars, Coke machines & advertising, automotive parts & literature, gas station memorabilia, kitchen collectibles, fruit jars & bottles. **Est:** 1979 **Hrs:** May-Sep daily; Win by chance/appt. **CC:** V/MC **Dir:** 28 mi S of Ellsworth Ctr on Rte 1. **Own:** Ed Weirick. **QC: 87 39 32**

Mill Mall Treasures [G55]
240 State St • 04605
(207)667-8055
www.metiques.com/catalog/mmt.html

Furniture, clothing, textiles, clocks, musical instruments, tools, quilts, art pottery, toys & fishing items **Hrs:** Daily 10-5. **CC:** V/MC/DIS. **QC: 48 32 61**

Sandy's Antiques
111 Oak St • 04605
(207)667-5078

Primitives, Victorian, glass & a good selection of freshly picked items. **Est:** 1973 **Hrs:** Sun-Fri 8-4. **Dir:** W of the int of Bucksport Rd & Rte 1A. **Own:** Sandy & Charlie Lounder. **QC: 61 106 89**

Fairfield

Connor-Bovie House Antiques
22 Summit St • 04937
(207)453-4919
pkelley@mint.net

Fine antique china. Specializing in English, Continental & Oriental porcelain & pottery; Staffordshire, blue & white transfer, flow blue, Leeds, pearlware, Derby, soft paste, Torquay, Dresden, Paris, Chinese & Japanese ceramics. **Est:** 1984 **Hrs:** By appt only. **Sz:** S **CC:** V/MC **Assn:** MADA **Own:** Monique Casavant Kelley & Patrick Kelley. **QC: 23 30 24**

Poulin Antiques
199 Skowhegan Rd (Rte 201) • 04975
(207)453-2114

Two barns full of antique oak, walnut & mahogany furniture, accessories & smalls. **Est:** 1967 **Hrs:** Mon-Sat 10-4, call ahead is advised. **CC:** V/MC/DIS **Dir:** I-95 Exit 36: 1 mi. **Own:** Steve & Jeannine Poulin. **QC: 48 50**

Falmouth

Hard Cider Farm Oriental Rugs
45 Middle Rd (Rte 9) • 04105
(207)775-1600 • (207)780-1713 (fax)

Fine Oriental rugs: antique to modern. 1200+ Persian & tribal rugs on two floors. **Est:** 1974 **Hrs:** Tue-Sat 10-5. **Sz:** M **CC:** V/MC/DIS **Dir:** I-295 Exit 10: Rte 9W, L onto Middle Rd, 1-4/5 mi. **Own:** Robert Tirrell. **QC: 76 S1 S9 S16**

Port 'N Starboard Gallery
53 Falmouth Rd • 04105
(207)781-4214

Marine antiques, paintings & folk art. **Pr:** $250-25,000 **Est:** 1984 **Hrs:** By appt only. **Assn:** MADA **Own:** Michael Leslie. **QC: 9 41 70 S1 S8 S9**

Farmingdale

Clark's Antiques
415 Main Ave (Rte 201) • 04344
(207)622-0592

Flow blue, Blue Onion, Blue Willow, blue-and-white transfer, Limoges & English porcelain, some pottery; silver, brass, stands, paintings & prints & decorative accessories. **Hrs:** By chance/appt. **Dir:** I-95 Exit 27, R to Rte 201. After Hasson St. **QC: 23 78 36**

Farmington

Antiques
71 N Main St (Rte 4) • 04938
(207)778-6358

Linens, prints, books, kitchenware, dishes, militaria, small furniture. **Hrs:** Mon, Wed, Fri, Sat 9-5. Nov-Apr closed. **Own:** Dorothy Drosdik. **QC: 80 32 74**

Lake Androscoggin Books & Prints
6 & 8 Greenwood Ave • 04938
(207)778-4437
gardner@inetme.com

Select variety of quality books from five centuries for collectors & serious readers, including antiquarian, art, first editions, illustrated, literature, private press, scholarly volumes & lithographs, prints & paintings by Maine artists. **Hrs:** By appt only. **Assn:** MABA **Own:** Bonnell TC Gardner. **QC: 18 74**

Maple Avenue Antiques
23 Maple Ave • 04938
(207)778-4850

Fine collection of early country furniture, paintings & great old things from area homes. **Hrs:** By chance/appt. **Assn:** MADA **Dir:** From Rte 2, turn onto Maple Ave betw Irving Filling Station & Pro Service Station. **Own:** Frank Dingley. **QC: 102 48 7**

The Old Barn Annex Antiques
30 Middle St #3 • 04938
(207)778-6908

19th & 20th C toys. **Assn:** MADA **Own:** Emery Goff & Bill Carhart. **QC: 87**

Powder House Hill
North St • 04938
(207)778-2946

Specializing in quality tools of yesteryear; over 500 functional & collectible trade tools on display. **Pr:** $5-850 **Est:** 1977 **Hrs:** By chance/appt. **Dir:** At Court House take Anson St for 3/4 mi, R on North St, 1st house. **Own:** Wendell Sweatt. **QC: 86**

Tom Veilleux Gallery
30 Broadway (2nd fl) • 04938
(207)778-0784

American 19th & 20th C paintings including contemporary artists. **Est:** 1972 **Hrs:** By appt only. **Dir:** Call for appt & directions. **QC: 7 74 S9**

Freedom

Roy & Kathy Bryant Antiques
Rte 137 • 04941
(207)382-6405

Music boxes; oak, Victorian & country furniture; cast & wrought iron architectural antiques, lighting, brass, iron beds. **Hrs:** Daily, but please call ahead. **Dir:** Just off Rte 137. **Own:** Roy & Kathy Bryant. **QC: 3 69 48**

Freeport

The Red Wheel Antiques
291 Rte 1 • 04032
(207)865-6492

Buttons, badges, military items, brass, primitives, copper, glass, lamps, china, reproduction shades & lamp parts. **Est:** 1960 **Hrs:** Daily 9-4. **Sz:** L **CC:** V/MC **Own:** Edward Collett. **QC: 4 21**

Elizabeth Simpson Antiques
1550 Rte 1 • 04032
(207)865-3836

Quality antiques including Staffordshire, Royal Doulton & Royal Copenhagen to German & French porcelain, Sandwich to cut glass, jewelry, sterling & smalls. No collectibles. **Est:** 1965 **Hrs:** By chance/appt. **Sz:** M **Dir:** 3 mi N of Freeport Village on Rte 1. **Own:** Elizabeth Simpson. **QC: 103 33 23**

Gardiner

McKay's Antiques
75 Brunswick Ave • 04345
(207)582-1228

Over 20,000 pieces of glass & china: cut, early pattern, Nippon, Noritake, ironstone, crystal, Blue Willow; kitchenware; crockery; lamps; mirrors; furniture; baskets; paintings; collectibles. **Hrs:** Sum Tue-Sun 10-5; Win by chance. **Own:** Clarence & Irene McKay. **QC: 61 22 23**

David L Spahr 19th & 20th Century Photographs
51 High Holborn St • 04345
(207)582-0402
dspahr3d@stereoviews.com
www.stereoviews.com

Stereoviews, daguerreotypes, ambrotypes, tintypes, cabinet cards, CDVs, most other types of photographs, ephemera, stereoscopes, some cameras. **Est:** 1990 **Hrs:** By appt only. **Assn:** NSA **Dir:** I-95 N Exit 27 (Rte 201): 4 mi to High Holborn St. **QC: 73 39 S1 S12**

Kenneth E Tuttle Antiques
Rtes 194 & 27 • 04345
(207)582-4496

Fine 18th & early 19th C American furniture, both country & formal. **Est:** 1967 **Hrs:** By chance/appt. **Assn:** MADA **Own:** Kenneth & Paulette Tuttle. **QC: 52**

Glenburn Ctr

Hometown Antiques
(207)942-8096
mgall10705@aol.com

Fine stoneware, antique marbles, country smalls, decorative boxes, jewelry, decoys & the odd lot. **Pr:** $20-15,000 **Est:** 1988 **Hrs:** By appt only. **Sz:** M **Assn:** MADA **Own:** Rachel & Michael Gallant. **QC: 1 34 67**

Gorham

Country Squire Antiques
105 Mighty St • 04038
(207)839-4855 • (207)839-7007 (fax)

Specializing in early hooked rugs, early American refinished country furniture, glassware, vintage jewelry & collectibles. **Est:** 1972 **Hrs:** Daily Apr-Dec. **Sz:** M **Assn:** MADA GSAAA **Dir:** ME Tpke Exit 8: Rte 25 to Gorham, 4 mi from ctr of Gorham, 1 mi off Rte 114N. **Own:** Edwin & Jane Carr. **QC: 75 102 63 S1 S19 S12**

Longview Antiques
20 Longview Dr • 04038
(207)839-3020

Primitives, quilts, paintings, hooked rugs & country furnishings in a three-room shop in a country setting. **Hrs:** By chance/appt. **Assn:** MADA **Dir:** From Gorham Ctr 2 mi N on Rte 114, Longview Dr on R, 3rd house on L. **Own:** Helen Woodbrey. **QC: 7 41 80**

Gouldsboro

William W Fontneau Antiques
Rte 1 • 04607
(207)963-7748

Pine cupboards & chests of drawers, military items & a large supply of laces & linens. **Est:** 1989 **Hrs:** Sum daily 9-6. **CC:** V/MC. **QC: 102 4 81**

Gray

The Barn on 26 Antique Center

361 Shaker Rd (Rte 26) • 04039
(207)657-3470

Oak, walnut, mahogany & Victorian furniture & collectibles. **Est:** 1977 **Hrs:** Wed-Fri 10-4, Sat-Sun 9-5. **Sz:** M **CC:** AX/V/MC/DIS **Dir:** I-95 exit 11: 3-1/2 mi N of village, Rte 26 toward Poland Springs & Shaker Village. **Own:** Alice E Welch.

Greene

Wilbur's Antiques

Rte 202 • 04236
(207)946-5711

A large barn full of furniture, country & Victorian, as well as Roseville, carnival glass, Depression glass, white ironstone & collectible furniture. Also linen, china, quilts & lamps. **Est:** 1961 **Hrs:** Daily 10-3. Call ahead if coming a distance. **Dir:** 7 mi N of Lewiston. **Own:** Rena Wilbur. **QC: 102 58 100**

Hallowell

Acme Antiques

165 Water St • 04347
(207)622-2322

20th C "wacky tack," 50s textiles & collectibles. **Hrs:** Daily May-Dec; Jan-Apr by chance/appt. **Dir:** I-95N Exit 30A. **Own:** Al & Kathy Waller. **QC: 38 83**

Brass and Friends Antiques

154 Water St • 04347
(207)626-3287

Restored antique lighting: chandeliers, sconces, floor & table lamps. In addition, fireplace accessories & antique mirrors. **Est:** 1987 **Hrs:** Mon-Sat 10-5, Sun 12-4. **CC:** V/MC **Dir:** Near the int of Union & Water St. **Own:** Robert Dale. **QC: 65 68 40**

Dealer's Choice Antique Mall [G55]

108 Water St • 04347
(207)622-5527
antiques@dlchoice.com

Two floors of antiques: china, glassware, furniture, postcards, lamps, toys, country primitives, dolls, oil on canvas, prints, Oriental antiques, jewelry, sterling, vintage clothing & photographica. **Est:** 1989 **Hrs:** Daily 10-5. **Sz:** L **CC:** V/MC/DIS **Dir:** I-95 Exit 27: Rte 201. **Own:** Dave Lovejoy & Jill Newton.

Johnson-Marsano Antiques

172 Water St • 04347
(207)623-6263

Victorian, Art Nouveau, Art Deco, Moderne & Bakelite jewelry; sewing implements; sterling silver; prints by Nutting, Sawyer & Davidson & unusual smalls. **Est:** 1984 **Hrs:** Open most days 10-5. **CC:** V/MC/DIS **Own:** Richard & Judith Johnson Marsano. **QC: 5 63**

Josiah Smith Antiques

181 Water St • 04347
(207)622-4188

Emphasizing early glass & ceramics (British transferware & American blown glass), Chinese export, Japanese pottery & baskets a specialty, art pottery, art from all periods, decorative furniture & accessories. **Pr:** $25-2,500 **Est:** 1980 **Hrs:** Mon-Sat 10-5, Sun by chance/appt. **Dir:** On Rte 201 (Water St). **Own:** Bruce Weber & Jeff Wainoris. **QC: 23 104 24**

James H LeFurgy Antiques & American Indian Art

168 Water St • 04347
(207)623-1771

American furniture & accessories pre-1850 in original condition, 19th & 20th C American paintings, Americana & Native American art, nautical antiques, toys & folk art. **Pr:** $10-10,000 **Est:** 1979 **Hrs:** Mon-Sat 10-5. **Sz:** M **CC:** V/MC/DIS **Dir:** I-95 Augusta Exit: Rte 202 toward Augusta. At rotary turn R on State St. S to Hallowell (State St becomes Water St). **QC: 7 42 70**

John Merrill Used & Rare Books

108 Water St • 04330
(207)623-2055

A general stock of 20,000 used & rare books in many subject areas; emphasis on literature & history. **Est:** 1988 **Hrs:** Tue-Sat 10-5, call ahead advised. **CC:** V/MC **Assn:** MABA **Dir:** Downtown Hallowell (Rte 201). **QC: 18**

Newsom & Berdan's Antiques

151 Water St • 04347
(207)622-0151

18th & 19th C painted & period furniture, folk art, baskets, paintings & country antiques. Emphasis on form, surface & Americana. **Est:** 1963 **Hrs:** By chance/appt. **Assn:** MADA NHADA **Own:** Betty M Berdan & Michael Newsom. **QC: 41 51 52**

Hanover

Lyons' Den Antiques

Rte 2 • 04237
(207)364-8634
lyonsden@megalink.net

Glass, china, primitives, early tools, clocks, furniture, prints, paintings & rugs. **Est:** 1964 **Hrs:** May 1-Nov 1 call for hrs; Nov 1-May 1 by appt only. **Sz:** L **CC:** V/MC **Dir:** 11 mi W of Rumford, 11 mi E of Bethel. **Own:** Elmer & Nancy Lyons. **QC: 48 103 86**

Harrison

Mr Oak

82 Main St • 04040
(207)583-4206

Turn-of-the-century oak furniture. **Est:** 1970 **Hrs:** Daily 8-5. **QC: 50**

Holden

McLeod Military Collectibles

703 Main Rd • 04429
(207)843-6205 • (207)843-6950 (fax)

Maine's only shop devoted to military antiques, all wars & all nations: Nazi, Japanese, GI, Viet Cong, Union or Confederate. **Pr:** $1-1,000 **Est:** 1964 **Hrs:** Mon-Fri 10-5, Sat 10-1. **CC:** AX/V/MC/DIS **Dir:** Rte 1A Holden on R side of Rd. 3 mi from I-395 Rte 1A interchange. **Own:** Ralph McLeod. **QC: 4**

Hollis

Sharon's Shed Antiques

(207)727-3714

Large barn with primitives, furniture, linens, clothing, tribal arts, pottery, books, tools, rugs, jewelry, glass, china, toys & baskets. **Est:** 197 **Hrs:** Daily from late Jun to Lab Day. **Dir:** 1-1/2 mi SW of Hollis Center. **Own:** Sharon & Danny Kleitman.

Houlton

Mountain & Meadow Books

59 Bangor St • 04730
(207)532-9285
youffer@ainop.com

Growing collection of used, out-of-print & scarce books. **Hrs:** Mon-Sat 10-4, call ahead advised **Sz:** 2,500 **Assn:** MABA **Own:** John Folsom. **QC: 18**

Hulls Cove

Hulls Cove Tool Barn

Breakneck Rd • 04644
(207)288-5126 • (207)288-2725 (fax)
sbrack@acadia.net
www.jonesport-wood.com

Large selection of old woodworking tools, also paintings, books & prints. **Hrs:** Jun-Oct 15 daily 9-5; Nov-May Thu-Sun 9-5 or by appt. **CC:** V/MC/DIS **Dir:** Rte 3 toward Bar Harbor, turn onto Breakneck Rd at the Hulls Cove General Store. **Own:** Skip Brack. **QC: 7 86 18 S12**

Jefferson

Bunker Hill Antiques

18 Vose Rd • 04348
(207)563-3167

Early painted country furniture & accessories, folk art, hooked rugs, paintings & Jasper pottery. **Hrs:** By chance/appt, call ahead advised. **Assn:** MADA GSAAA **Dir:** N of Newcastle. **Own:** Joanne & Erland Johnston. **QC: 34 41 51**

Garland's Antiques

484 Augusta Rd • 04348
(207)549-7589

Country furnishings, collectibles, glass, country accessories & primitives. **Est:** 1981 **Hrs:** Daily by chance/appt. **Dir:** 2-1/2 mi from Rte 17; 12 mi from Rte 1; at the former Weeks Tavern. **Own:** Bill & Ruth Garland.

Jonesport

Jonesport by the Sea

Main St • 04649
(207)497-2590

Nautical items: ship models, compasses, port & starboard lights, telescopes, microscopes & scientific instruments; also some furniture, bronzes, toys, pewter, glass & china. **Est:** 1991 **Hrs:** By chance/appt. **CC:** AX/V/MC **Own:** Richard Deegan. **QC: 70 77**

Jonesport Nautical Antiques

Cogswell & Main St • 04649
(207)497-5655 • (207)497-5954 (fax)
bsund@nauticalantiques.com
www.nauticalantiques.com

Marine art, nautical antiques, nautical collectibles, binnacles, telegraphs, compasses, life rings, sextants, telescopes, helmets & dive dresses. **Est:** 1992 **Hrs:** By chance/appt. **Sz:** M **CC:** V/MC **Dir:** Rte 187 in ctr of Jonesport. **Own:** Bernie & Bobbie Sund. **QC: 70 9 77 S19 S9 S17**

Moospecke Antiques

The Marina • 04611
(207)497-2457

Specializing in country furniture & accessories, paintings, prints & some glass. **Hrs:** Jun-Dec Tue-Fri 10-12 & 1-4; Sat by chance/appt. **CC:** V/MC **Own:** Jewell D Griggs Miller. **QC: 34 7**

Kennebunk

Americana Workshop

111 York St • 04043
(207)985-8356
cindy@americanaworkshop.com
www.americanaworkshop.com

Country antiques & accessories. **Est:** 1998 **Hrs:** Daily 10-5, closed Tue-Wed in Win. **CC:** AX/V/MC/DIS **Own:** Cynthia Hamilton. **QC: 102 36**

Antiques on Nine

75 Western Ave • 04043
(207)967-0626

American, Canadian, English & Continental furniture & accessories, country & formal, refinished & in as-found condition; books, paintings, architectural elements & garden antiques. **Pr:** $10-10,000 **Est:** 1989 **Hrs:** Daily 9-5:30, Sum 9-6. **Sz:** L **CC:** V/MC **Dir:** On the Kennebunk-Kennebunkport town line, Rte 9, 3-1/2 mi E of Rte 1, betw Wells & Kennebunk Exits 2 & 3 off I-95. **Own:** Beverly Bangs. **QC: 47 52 53**

Cattails Antiques
Rte 35 • 04043
(207)967-3824

Country furniture, accessories, folk art, paintings, nautical, wicker, Shaker items, hooked rugs, linens. B & B available in home. **Pr:** $5-2,500 **Est:** 1977 **Hrs:** Daily in Sum 10-4 or by chance/appt. **CC:** AX/V/MC **Assn:** MADA **Dir:** I-95 Exit 3: S on Rte 35, 4-5 mi, on L in lower village, upstairs at Gallery. **Own:** Roger & Kathy Ellenberger. **QC: 34 41 80**

Chocolate Tree Antiques
54 York St (Rte 1 S) • 04043
(207)985-7779

Country & formal American furniture, paintings, garden & architectural & decorative accessories, jewelry & silver. **Pr:** $25-5,000 **Est:** 1983 **Hrs:** Daily 9-5, call ahead advised. **Sz:** M **CC:** V/MC **Dir:** On the E side of Rte 1 across from Econo-Lodge. **Own:** Richard & Patricia Jennings. **QC: 1 36 60**

Heritage House Antiques
10 Christensen Ln • 04043
(207)967-2580

Specializing in clocks, porcelain, art glass, cut glass, silver & pottery. **Hrs:** Mon & Wed-Sat 10-4. **Assn:** MADA **Dir:** Off Rte 35 opp Ocean Nat Bank. **Own:** Fae Weiss. **QC: 35 61 100**

Rivergate Antiques Mall [G100]
Old Post Rd (Rte 1 N) • 04043
(207)985-6280

Featuring furniture, quality glassware, china, silver, country, linens, jewelry, pottery, books, dolls, miniatures & ephemera. **Est:** 1987 **Hrs:** Daily 10-5, Nov-Mar closed Tue. **CC:** V/MC **Dir:** 1/2 mi N of Kennebunk on Rte 1. **Own:** Monique Dumont.

Victorian Lighting Inc
29 York St (Rte 1 S) • 04043
(207)985-6868

Victorian & turn-of-the-century chandeliers, wall sconces, floor & table lamps in a 132-year-old carriage barn. Kerosene, gas & early electric lighting in original condition or completely restored. **Pr:** $5-30,000 **Hrs:** Mon-Sat 9:30-5, Sun by chance/appt. **Sz:** M **CC:** AX/V/MC/DIS **Dir:** I-95 Exit 3: to Kennebunk, Rte 1S, look for watertower which is at back of property. **Own:** Judy Oppert. **QC: 65 S16**

Antiques Kennebunkport [G12]
55 Western Ave (Rte 9) • 04046
(207)967-8033

An antiques center in beautifully designed space featuring period American, high country, painted & Victorian furniture, prints, porcelain & textiles. **Pr:** $25-8,000 **Est:** 1991 **Hrs:** May-Nov daily 10-5. **Sz:** L **CC:** AX/V/MC **Dir:** I-95 Exit 2 Wells: Rte 109 to Rte 1 N to Rte 9N, 4 mi N on Rte 9 From I-95 Exit 3: Rte 35 to Rte 9 S, 1/4 mi on R. **Own:** Helen Benner. **QC: 1 52 7**

Maritime Museum Shop
Ocean Ave • 04046
(207)967-4195

Nautical & general antiques, bronzes, paintings, campaign & camphorwood furniture, scrimshaw & navigational instruments. **Hrs:** May 15-Nov 15 Mon-Sat 10-5, Sun 11-5. **Dir:** At Booth Tarkington's former Boathouse. **QC: 70 9 77**

Old Fort Antiques
Old Fort Ave • 04046
(207)967-5353

Primitives, country furniture, tools, tin, advertising items, glass & china. **Pr:** $25-900

Hrs: Apr 15-Dec 15 daily 9-6; Win by chance/appt. **CC:** AX/V/MC/DIS **Assn:** MADA **Dir:** I-95 Exit 3: L on Rte 35, follow signs to Kennebunkport, over drawbridge, R to Ocean Ave, L at Colony Hotel, R, 1/4 mi. **Own:** David & Sheila Aldrich. **QC: 37 55 41**

Old River House Gallery

52 Ocean Ave • 04046
(207)967-3886

Paintings, small memorabilia, china, primitives, dolls, baskets, jewelry, linen, quilts, vintage clothing & textiles. **Est:** 1973 **Hrs:** Daily by chance/appt. **Own:** Penny Weidul.

John F Rinaldi Nautical Antiques

(207)967-3218

Specialist in marine antiques & paintings, scrimshaw, 19th & 20th C American paintings, campaign furniture & prisoner-of-war work. **Est:** 1972 **Hrs:** By appt only. **Sz:** M **Dir:** 1-1/2 hrs from Boston, 1/2 hr from Portland. **Own:** John Rinaldi. **QC: 70 9 77**

Windfall Antiques

Ocean Ave • 04046
(207)967-2089

American & English silver, Staffordshire, Oriental antiques, 19th C art, bronze & selected antiques. **Hrs:** Jun-Oct Thu-Mon 11-4:30; May wknds only. **Assn:** MADA NEAA **Dir:** Near Colony Hotel. **Own:** Ken & Anne Kornetsky. **QC: 71 30 78**

Winter Hill Farm

Wildes District Rd • 04046
(207)967-5879

Country furniture & antique pond sailers. Custom-built reproduction tables & other furniture available. Specializing in the restoration of fine antique furniture. **Pr:** $10-3,000 **Est:** 1985 **Hrs:** Daily 10-5, call ahead advised. **Sz:** M **Dir:** From Kennebunkport, Rte 9E to Main St, bear L at fork, 1/2 mi on Wildes District Rd, on L atop hill. **QC: 102 S17 S16**

Kittery

Essence of Time

15 Wallingford Sq • 03904
(207)438-9911

General line of antiques & collectibles, estate jewelry & art. **Hrs:** Tue-Sat 10-5, Sun 10-3. **Dir:** I-95 Exit 2 to Kittery. **Own:** Dena Flanagan.

Samplers II

By the early 19th century, as women became busier with household management, visiting, and shopping, the time-consuming intricate needle work of the earlier generation gave way to simpler, quicker styles. The quality of samplers declined, and by the middle of the century they were no longer part of a genteel girl's education.

An unmarried girl worked hard with her needle, not just to fill her dowry chest, but also to present herself as an attractive young woman, particularly when a young man had come to visit. As she sewed she sat prettily, her hands were occupied, showing her industry, her eyes looked down, showing her demureness, yet her ears and mind were open to the young man paying court. In genteel families, needlework was as close as a girl could come to flirting.

Needlework was a two-edged sword in a woman's life. On the one hand it was an art form in which she could express her imagination and creativity, on the other it confined her to a narrow female propriety, in which her hands were active, but her mind and voice were not.

Liberty

Liberty Tool Company
Main St • 04644
(207)589-4771 • (207)288-2725 (fax)
sbrack@acadia.net
www.jonesport-wood.com

A large selection of antique & second-hand tools, four floors of used tools, books, prints, paintings, furniture & collectibles. **Hrs:** Jun-Oct 15 daily 9-5; Nov-May Thu-Sun 9-5 or by appt. **Sz:** M **CC:** V/MC **Dir:** 17 mi W of Belfast, 1-1/2 mi off Rte 3. **Own:** Skip Brack. **QC: 86 18 7 S12**

Limerick

Tom Joseph & David Ramsay
(207)793-2539

Select furniture from painted country to 20th C decorative as well as garden & architectural elements, lighting, folk art, figural andirons & decorative accessories. **Hrs:** By appt only. **Assn:** NHADA. **QC: 51 3 60**

Lincolnville

Beach House Antiques & Books
Rte 1 • 04843
(207)789-5323

Antiques, books, art, estate jewelry, furniture & tools. A well-rounded collection of used, rare & out-of-print books for the reader & collector including Maine, nautical, literature, art, children's, sporting. **Est:** 1995 **Hrs:** Sum daily 10-6 or by chance/appt. **CC:** V/MC **Assn:** MABA **Own:** Paul Turnbull. **QC: 18**

Deer Meadows
Rte 1/RR 3 • 04849
(207)236-8020

Furniture, fine art, Oriental rugs, bronzes & rare jewelry. **Hrs:** Daily 9-5. **Dir:** Two shops on opp sides of Rte 1: one in red barn, the other in the red canopied bldg. **Own:** Irene Crossman. **QC: 32 48 64**

Fieldwood Antiques
F R 53 • 04849
(207)763-3926

Antique country furniture, decorations & accessories. **Hrs:** May-Oct Fri-Wed 10-5. **Dir:** Follow Rte 52: 5 mi from Camden. **Own:** Arlene Winters Lepow. **QC: 34 102**

Old Mill Shop
Rte 173 • 04849
(207)763-3504

Country collectibles, antiques & primitives. **Hrs:** By chance/appt. **Dir:** On Rte 173 N of Lincolnville, 1/4 mi from Gen Store. **Own:** Sharon Pendleton. **QC: 34 106**

Olde Home Farm Antiques
Rte 173 • 04849
(207)789-5178

Glass, china, pottery & collectibles. **Hrs:** Jun-Sep by chance/appt. **Dir:** 1 mi N of beach. **Own:** Shirley Bunker Butler. **QC: 61**

Goose River Exchange
Rte 1 • 04849
(207)789-5241 • (207)236-8670 (fax)
goosrivr@midcoast.com

Specializing in paper Americana & photography, advertising, books, magazines, ephemera, postcards, comics & posters. **Est:** 1977 **Hrs:** Sum daily 10-5. **Own:** Ken Shure. **QC: 39 73**

Mainely Antiques
Rte 1 • 04849
(207)236-6809

Large selection of refinished country pine furniture, advertising items, decoys & primitives. **Hrs:** Apr-Oct by chance/appt. **Assn:** MADA **Dir:** 10 houses S of Lincolnville beach blinker. **Own:** Bev & John Black. **QC: 55 39**

Painted Lady
Rte 1 • 04849
(207)789-5201 • (207)789-5201 (fax)

American & European country furniture, folk art, decorative accessories & painted pieces. **Hrs:** Daily 10-5 by chance/appt. **Own:** Sherry McGrath. **QC: 102 36 41**

Quarter Cape Antiques Gallery [G25]
Atlantic Hwy (Rte 1) • 04856
(207)236-4274
folklore@midcoast.com

A gallery shop set in Maine's only quarter cape coach house buying & selling fine ceramics, period furniture, folk art, paintings, paint decorated smalls, hooked rugs & accessories. **Pr:** $10-10,000 **Est:** 1999 **Hrs:** May 1-Dec 5 Tue-Sat 10-4, Sun 12-4; Dec 6-Apr 30 by appt. **CC:** V/MC **Assn:** MADA **Dir:** US Rte 1 N of Camden, ME. **Own:** Ray Cushing. **QC: 23 52 41**

Lisbon

Lisbon Schoolhouse Antiques
273 Lisbon Rd (Rte 196) • 04050
(207)353-6075

Victorian schoolhouse with a wide variety of furniture, decorative items, silver, pottery & rugs. **Hrs:** Apr-Dec Wed-Thu, Sat 10-4 or by appt. **Assn:** MADA **Own:** Burtt & Donna Warren. **QC: 48 36**

Locke Mills

Mt Mica Rarities
Rte 26 • 04255
(207)875-2030 • (207)875-3065 (fax)

Antiques & collectibles; glass, china, prints, paintings, coins. Oxford County new & used costume & estate jewelry as well as Maine gemstone jewelry. **Est:** 1992 **Hrs:** Daily 9-5. **CC:** AX/V/MC/DIS **Dir:** Bright purple bldg on Rte 26. **Own:** Ann & Phillip McCrillis. **QC: 63 64**

Manchester

Charles Robinson & Sons Rare Books
Pond Rd • 04351
(207)622-1885
rarebks@aol.com

Rare & fine books in many fields. Fine bindings, illustrated books, science, medicine & travel. Prints, lithographs & books containing original art. Verve, Derriere le Miroir & XXth Siecle. **Hrs:** By appt only. **Assn:** MABA. **QC: 18 74**

Montville

Stonewall Farm Antiques
Pierce Hill Rd • 04952
(207)342-5886

Specializing in Portland, Sandwich & other early American glass, china & other early American glass for the beginner & the advanced collector. **Pr:** $50-5,000 **Hrs:** By appt only. **Assn:** MADA NAGC **Dir:** Call for directions. **Own:** Virgil Fowles Jr. **QC: 61 103 104 S1**

Moody

The Gray's Antiques [G7]
32 Post Rd (Rte 1) • 04054
(207)646-8938

Victorian & country furniture, mirrors, lamps, china, dolls, doll houses & related accessories, brass, copper, iron & dog related items on 2 floors in the shop & in an attached barn. **Est:** 1987 **Hrs:** Daily 10-5; Nov-Apr closed Tue. **CC:** V/MC **Dir:** Just over the Ogunquit line. **Own:** Jean Gray.

Mt Desert

Weyhe Art Books

(207)288-4281
ok@acadia.net

A large collection of rare & out-of-print books on the fine & applied arts, architecture & decoration. Also decorative prints, botanicals, Daumier, maps & textile designs. **Hrs:** Tue-Sat afternoons by appt **Assn:** MABA **Own:** Donald & Deborah W Kiley. **QC: 18 74 66**

New Portland

Nora West Antiques

Rte 27 • 04954
(207)628-2200 • (207)628-4194 (fax)

Varied range of interesting objects & furniture in "as found" condition from local homes. Kitchenware, tools, china, pine & oak furniture, stoneware, prints, iron, camp items, postcards & graniteware. **Est:** 1983 **Hrs:** Anytime by chance/appt, please call ahead. **Sz:** M **Dir:** Rte 27 N from Farmington 20 mi at int of Rtes 27 & 146 on L. **Own:** Nora West. **QC: 32 34 S5**

Newcastle

Connell Fine Arts

Rte 215 • 04553
(207)563-6871

Late 19th & early 20th C paintings. **Hrs:** By chance/appt. **QC: 7 S1**

Different Drummer Antiques

Glidden St • 04553
(207)882-5520

A fine selection of country & formal furniture & accessories, toys & textiles. Specializing in early 18th & 19th C lighting. **Hrs:** By appt only. **Assn:** MADA NHADA GSAAA **Own:** Judy Waner. **QC: 34 65 80**

Mary Hodes Antiques

54 Mills Rd (Rte 215) • 04553
(207)563-5151

Furniture, pewter, tin, china, silver, tools & sewing items neatly displayed in a large red barn. **Est:** 1970 **Hrs:** May 1-Oct 15 Mon-Sat 11-4. **Dir:** 1 mi from Rte 1, 1/4 mi from Newcastle Sq. **Own:** Mary Hodes. **QC: 86 78 68**

Kaja Veilleux Antiques

Newcastle Sq (Bus Rte 1) • 04553
(207)563-1002 • (207)563-3445 (fax)
(800)924-1032

18th & 19th C American country & formal antiques; selection of American & European paintings; estate jewelry; sculpture; period furniture. **Hrs:** Sum Mon-Fri 9-5, Sat 10-4; Win Mon-Sat 9-5. **Sz:** L **Assn:** MADA NEAA **Dir:** Rte 1 Damariscotta exit: on Bus Rte 1, Newcastle Sq. **Own:** Kaja Veilleux. **QC: 52 64 7 S1 S9**

Nobleboro

Adelaide's Antiques [G3]

63 Rte 1 • 04555
(207)563-6693

A general line of antiques & collectibles. **Pr:** $2-1,500 **Est:** 1995 **Hrs:** May-Oct daily. **CC:** V/MC **Dir:** 2 mi N of Damariscotta on Rte 1 betw Ma's Antiques & the Nobleboro Dinner House in the Glendon Inn. **Own:** Delly Schweighauser. **QC: 48**

Norridgewock

Black Hill Antiques & Collectibles [G10]

Main St • 04938
(207)634-5151
dndg@wworx.net

Steins, toys, tools, books, sports memorabilia, magazines, clocks, glass, china & collectibles. **Hrs:** Daily 10-5 (Win closed Wed). **Sz:** M **CC:** V/MC **Own:** Dick & Dot Guilmet.

North Anson

Glad Rags

Main St • 04958
(207)635-2698
info@vintagegladrags.com
www.vintagegladrags.com

Specializing in vintage clothing & accessories from 1800-1950. **Hrs:** Fri-Sat 10-4:30 or by appt. **CC:** AX/V/MC/DIS **Own:** Sherry Walrath. **QC: 83**

North Berwick

Brick House Antiques

Rte 9 & Main St • 03906
(207)676-2885

Reverse painted lamps, Bohemian glass, Art Nouveau, fine porcelain, quality furniture, steins & objets d'art. **Est:** 1993 **Hrs:** Apr-Nov Wed-Mon 10-4; Dec-Mar Fri-Mon 10-4. **Dir:** 7 mi from Wells & Ogunquit. **Own:** Ingo Lange.

The Village Exchange

41 Main St • 03906
(207)676-5771 • (207)676-2124 (fax)
villex@psouth.net

Glass, porcelain, books, furniture, Hummels, linens, prints, tools & toys in the quaint village of North Berwick. **Est:** 1992 **Hrs:** Mon & Thu-Sat 10-4. **Own:** Chuck & Carol Gale.

North Edgecomb

Edgecomb Book Barn

534 Cross Point Rd • 04556
(207)882-7278

Out-of-print & scarce books in many categories. Rural location overlooking the sea in Boothbay Harbor region. **Est:** 1959 **Hrs:** Sum daily 11-6 or by appt. **Own:** Frank McQuaid. **QC: 18**

North Turner

Nancy T Prince

(207)224-7823
ntprince@aol.com
www.maineada.com

Specializing in Native American art & American folk art. **Hrs:** By appt only. **Assn:** MADA. **QC: 42 41 102**

Northeast Harbor

Pine Bough

Main St • 04662
(207)276-5079

Select, uncommon & interesting antiques from the 18th-20th C; treen, glass, ceramics, Eastern Woodlands Indian objects; American early lighting a specialty. Also, out-of-print books in a broad range of subjects. Shop newly expanded. **Pr:** $1-10,000 **Hrs:** Jun-Aug Mon-Sat 10-5, other times by chance/appt. **Sz:** M **CC:** AX/V/MC/DIS **Assn:** MABA **Dir:** Within 5 mi of Acadia Nat'l Park, at head of Sea St, on Main St in heart of village. **Own:** J & R Fuerst. **QC: 1 18 65**

Wikhegan Old Books

117 Main St • 04660
(207)276-5079

A carefully chosen collection of old books in a broad range of interest. Nautical, cookery, decorative & fine arts, biography, natural history, poetry & downeast Maine. Interesting ephemera & some photographica. **Pr:** $1-5,000 **Est:** 1960 **Hrs:** Jun-Oct Mon-Sat 10-5, Nov-May by appt. **Sz:** M **CC:** AX/V/MC/DIS **Assn:** MABA ESA **Dir:** Min from Arcadia National Park, near the head of Sea St in the village of Northeast Harbor on Mt Desert Island. **Own:** J Fuerst. **QC: 18 39**

Northport

Blue Dolphin Antiques

164 Atlantic Hwy (Rte 1) • 04915
(207)338-3860

Three floors of fine 18th & 19th C furniture, chandeliers, lighting fixtures, desk & table lamps, period mirrors, Oriental rugs, early glassware, estate jewelry, bronzes, clocks & distinctive art objects. $1 admission, proceeds to charity. **Hrs:** Mon-Sat 9-5, Sun by chance. **Sz:** L **CC:** V/MC **Assn:** NAWCC **Dir:** 3 mi N of Lincolnville Beach; 10 mi S of Belfast on Rte 1. **Own:** Linda Bassano & Vito Peri. **QC: 53 65 68 S1**

Ellen Katona & Bob Lutz Antiques

231 Atlantic Hwy • 04849
(207)338-1444 • (207)338-5213 (fax)
ellenbob@mint.net

Specializing in Americana, folk art, hooked rugs, painted country furniture, architectural elements & accessories. **Est:** 1985 **Hrs:** Jun 15-Oct 15 daily 10-5; Oct 15-Jun 14 by chance/appt. **Sz:** M **Assn:** MADA VADA **Dir:** Midway betw Camden & Belfast on Rte 1. **Own:** Ellen Katona & Bob Lutz. **QC: 1 34 102**

Ogunquit

Antiques Ogunquit

321 Rte 1 • 03907
(207)641-2799

A delightful collection of antiques, decorative accessories & general nostalgia. **Hrs:** Daily 10-5, Win closed Tue-Wed. **Own:** Dan Pender. **QC: 36**

Blacksmith's Antique Mall [G65+]

116 Main St (Rte 1) • 03907
(207)646-9643 • (207)646-3710 (fax)

Collectibles, decoratives, estate & costume jewelry, books & paper, sterling silver, brass, copper & iron. **Hrs:** Apr-Oct daily 9-4:50; Nov-Mar closed Wed. **Dir:** Next to PO. **Own:** David T Hutchins. **QC: 32 48**

The Pommier Collection

94 Shore Rd • 03907
(207)646-5573 • (207)646-5573 (fax)

Specializing in fine antique & estate jewelry. An unmatched selection of authentic diamond & colored gem jewelry from the Victorian era to Art Nouveau, Art Deco & Retro. Exquisite jewelry selections that withstand the test of time. **Pr:** $100-5,000 **Est:** 1993 **Hrs:** May 1-Oct 12th Thu-Mon 10-5. April & Oct 13-Dec 24 Sat-Sun 10-5. **Sz:** S **CC:** V/MC **Assn:** NAJA AAA **Dir:** Off Rte 1 halfway betw ctr of Ogunquit & Perkins Cove, at the corn of Shore Rd & Bourne Ln. **Own:** Marc & Nathalie Pommier. **QC: 64 35 78 S1 S12**

Orono

Maine Bear Antiques

293 Main St • 04473
(207)866-2367

Ephemera of all kinds: maps, prints, posters, advertising, sheet music, catalogs & historical documents. **Hrs:** Daily 10-5 or by appt. **Own:** Bob Milheron. **QC: 39 66 39**

Oxford

Meetinghouse Antiques [G8]

Rte 26 • 04270
(207)539-8480
meeting@exploremaine.com

A restored early church offering 2 floors of period & country furnishings, silver, pattern & art glass, porcelains, paintings, quilts, Shaker items, Oriental & hooked rugs & collectibles. **Pr:** $5-5,000 **Est:** 1990 **Hrs:** Jun-Col Day daily 9-4; Win Sat-Tue 9-4. **Sz:** L **CC:** V/MC **Dir:** I-495 Exit 10: Rte 26 N 20 mi from Gray to Oxford; just N of Poland at the jct with Rte 121. **Own:** Donna Johnson. **QC: 1 61 64**

Palmyra

Bane's Art & Antiques

Rte 2 • 04965
(207)938-2459

Contemporary & antique art, frames & sculpture, country & formal furniture & decoys. **Est:** 1993 **Hrs:** By chance/appt. **CC:** AX/V/MC/DIS **Own:** Douglas Bane.

Portland

Barridoff Galleries

(207)772-5011 • (207)772-5049 (fax)

Specializing in 19th & 20th C American & European paintings with annual auction held in Portland. **Est:** 1975 **Hrs:** By appt only. **Own:** Rob & Annette Elowitch. **QC: 7 S2**

Carlson & Turner Books

241 Congress St • 04101
(207)773-4200 • (207)774-8819 (fax)
(800)540-7323
swilson@maine.com

An organized collection of quality used books in all fields. Specialties include scholarly, antiquarian, fine printing, travel, Civil War, the unusual & the eccentric. 50,000 volumes. **Pr:** $3-3,000 **Est:** 1974 **Hrs:** Mon-Sat 10-5, Sun 12-5 or by chance/appt. **Sz:** L **CC:** V/MC **Assn:** MABA **Dir:** I-295 Franklin St Exit: L at 2nd light, 150 yds on L across from Eastern Cemetery. **Own:** Scott & Glenda Wilson. **QC: 18 19 74**

William Core Duffy

(207)871-8331

Early American silver for the knowledgeable collector. Exceptional silver from all periods. **Est:** 1976 **Hrs:** By appt only. **Dir:** Call for directions. **QC: 78**

Emerson Books, Maps & Prints

18 Exchange St • 04112
(207)874-2665

Maine's most extensive collection of antique maps, nautical charts & prints dating back to 17th C & earlier. Framed paintings & hand-colored antique prints. Books old & new. **Pr:** $5-3,000 **Est:** 1993 **Hrs:** Please call for hours. **Sz:** L **CC:** AX/V/MC/DIS **Assn:** MABA **Dir:** From I-295, take Franklin exit. Follow Franklin several blks to Middle St. Turn R on Middle to Exchange St. L on Exchange to #18, near bottom of hill. **Own:** Thomas & Mary Emerson. **QC: 18 66 74**

Flynn Books

466 Ocean Ave • 04103
(207)772-2685

Rare & fine press books, Americana & ephemera. **Est:** 1978 **Hrs:** By appt only. **Assn:** MABA **Own:** Robert & Anita Flynn. **QC: 18 1 39**

Heller-Washam Antiques

1235 Congress St • 04102
(207)773-8288 • (207)773-4412 (fax)
(800)464-8288

18th & early 19th C American country & formal furniture & accessories, paintings, textiles, folk art, garden furnishings & architectural elements. **Pr:** $500-50,000 **Est:** 1980 **Hrs:** By appt only. **Assn:** MADA NHADA WADA AC **Own:** Donald Heller & Kimberly Washam. **QC: 1 52 60 S1 S12**

Leif Laudamus Rare Books

534 Cumberland Ave • 04101
(207)772-9182

Eclectic & esoteric selection of early books & manuscripts. Emphasis on printed books, Americana, science & medicine, fine bindings, plate books, association copies, food & wine, foreign language. **Pr:** $50-5,000 **Est:** 1979 **Hrs:** By appt only. **Sz:** S **Assn:** MABA ABAA **Own:** Leif Laudamus. **QC: 18 S1 S9 S12**

Nelson Rarities Inc

One City Center 8th Fl • 04112
(207)775-3150

Extensive collection of estate jewelry, specializing in Art Deco, Art Nouveau & period jewelry, also stones, watches & silver. **Hrs:** Daily 9:30-5. **Assn:** MADA **Own:** Andrew Nelson & Malcolm Logan. **QC: 5 35 64**

Polly Peters Antiques

26 Brackett St • 04104
(207)774-6981

In a shingled Victorian overlooking Portland Harbor, an eclectic mix of the unusual including garden items, fun old furniture, decorator-style home ornamentation, lighting & architectural pieces. **Hrs:** Mon-Wed 10-5. **Own:** Polly Peters & Bear Blake. **QC: 60 36 3**

Portland Antique Center

221 Commercial St • 04101
(207)773-7052
(888)950-2226
info@portlandantiques.com
www.portlandantiques.com

Americana, period furniture, rare nautical items, 19th & 20th C fine art, architectural & garden elements. **Pr:** $100-20,000 **Est:** 1997 **Hrs:** Mon-Sat 10-6, Sun by appt. **Sz:** M **CC:** AX/V/MC/DIS **Assn:** MADA **Dir:** Follow signs N or S on I-95 to Portland waterfront. Shop is located in the Old Port Section of the Portland waterfront 1-1/2 hrs N of Boston on I-95. **Own:** Richard Smith. **QC: 1 9 52 S1 S8 S12**

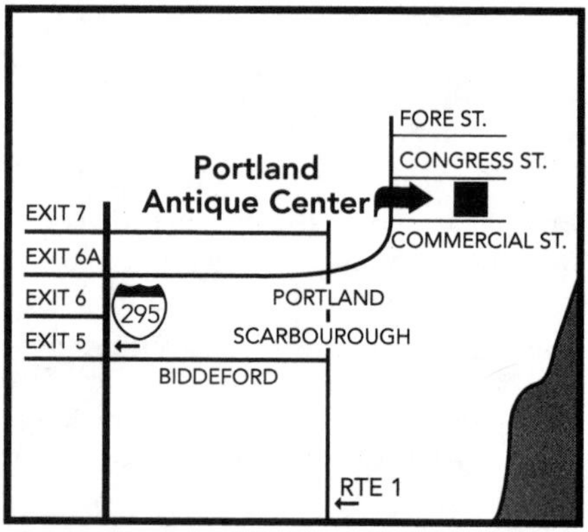

Venture Antiques

101 Exchange St • 04101
(207)773-6064

Furniture, ceramics, brass & copper, small rugs & decorative accessories. Lamps a specialty. **Hrs:** Mon-Sat 10-5. **CC:** V/MC **Assn:** MADA **Dir:** At the corn of Federal & Exchange St. **Own:** Isabel Thacher.

West Port Antiques

8 Milk St • 04101
(207)774-6747 • (207)799-5333 (fax)

Established antique shop with an accent on the decorative. Specialties are textiles & linens. Also pillows & bedspreads from old fabrics. **Pr:** $5-5,000 **Est:** 1988 **Hrs:** Tue-Sat 11-5. **Sz:** M **CC:** AX/V/MC/DIS **Dir:** In the heart of the Old Port next to the Regency Hotel. **Own:** Mary Ingalls. **QC: 36 80 81**

Wilma's Antiques & Accessories

458 Ludlow St • 04102
(207)772-9852
wilmas@javanet.com

Country pine & formal furniture, porcelain, pattern glass, hooked & braided rugs & accessories. **Est:** 1979 **Hrs:** Mar-Jan Mon-Sat 10-5, closed Feb. **Sz:** M **CC:** V/MC **Assn:** MADA **Dir:** I-95 Franklin St Exit, thru 4 sets of lights, turn L, thru 1 set of lights, diagonally across from Levinsky's. **Own:** Wilma Taliento. **QC: 102 75**

Geraldine Wolf Antiques & Estate Jewelry

26 Milk St • 04104
(207)774-8994 • (207)774-8994 (fax)

We specialize in antique & estate jewelry with a strong selection of sterling silver flatware, glassware, china & Victorian artifacts. **Pr:** $20-10,000 **Est:** 1978 **Hrs:** Jun 10-Dec 25 Tue-Sat 10-4:30; Dec 25-Jun 9 Tue-Thu 10-4, Fri-Sat 10-4:30. **Sz:** M **CC:**

AX/V/MC/DIS **Assn:** MADA **Dir:** I-95 Franklin Arterial Exit: to Middle St, go R & then L on Exchange & then L on Milk St. In the Old Port district under the peach awnings. **Own:** Geraldine Wolf. **QC: 64 78 36 S1**

Randolph

Philene's Antiques

320 Water St • 04346
(207)582-1498

Specializing in Victorian period furniture, dolls, glass & books. **Hrs:** Mon-Sat 9-5, Sun by appt. **CC:** V/MC **Own:** Phil & Arlene Carroll. **QC: 58 38 61**

Rangeley

Blueberry Hill Farm

Dallas Hill Rd • 04970
(207)864-5647

Country furniture, quilts, baskets, fishing antiques, wildlife items & limited edition prints. **Pr:** $25-800 **Est:** 1940 **Hrs:** May-Oct daily 10-5 or by chance/appt. **Assn:** MADA **Own:** Don & Stephanie Palmer. **QC: 102 37**

Gearsyl Antiques

Rte 4 • 04970
(207)864-5784

Oak, walnut, pine furniture in as-found & refinished condition. **Est:** 1981 **Hrs:** Daily 9-5. **Dir:** 4-1/2 mi from town on Rte 4 in Oquossoc. **Own:** Arthur & Sylvia Guerin.

Hayshaker Antiques

111 Main St • 04970
(207)864-3765

Pine & oak furniture, linens, kitchenwares, china, ogee mirrors & smalls. **Est:** 1981 **Hrs:** Daily 10-5 or by appt. **CC:** V/MC **Dir:** Corn of Main & Allen Sts. **Own:** Ray & Joanne Chapman.

Moose America

97 Main St • 04970
(207)864-3699

Rustic furniture including Old Hickory, twig, birch bark, Adirondack & rustic accessories including creels, pack baskets, snowshoes; country furniture in old paint; antique quilts; Indian camp blankets. **Pr:** $50-5,000 **Hrs:** May 15-Oct daily 10-5. **CC:** V/MC **Dir:** I-95 Exit 12 (Auburn) to Rte 4 & follow signs to Rangeley Lakes. **Own:** Bob Oestreicher. **QC: 1 106 79**

Rockland

Bruce Gamage Jr Antiques

467 Main St • 04841
(207)594-4963 • (207)594-0674 (fax)
(800)400-5768
bgamage@midcoast.com

Fine selection of American period furniture, paintings & rugs derived from local estates. **Hrs:** By chance/appt; Wed free appraisals. **Sz:** M **CC:** AX/V/MC/DIS **Assn:** MADA NEAA MAA **Own:** Bruce Gamage Jr. **QC: 52 7 76 S1 S2**

Haskell's Antiques

Rte 1 • 04841
(207)594-9207
fwhask@mint.net

General line of antiques, collectibles & reproduction pine country furniture. **Pr:** $15-1,200 **Est:** 1983 **Hrs:** Feb 15-Dec 31 daily 10-4; other times by chance/appt. **Sz:** M **CC:** V/MC/DIS **Dir:** Rte 1 Rockland & Thomaston line, 28 mi N of Maine State Prison Showroom, in the Pleasant Gardens section of Rockland, ME. **Own:** Franklin W Haskell Jr. **QC: 32 48 56**

Mermaid Antiques
256 Main St • 04841
(207)594-0616

Wide variety of antiques & collectibles: gold & sterling jewelry (estate, costume, old & new); vintage lamps & lighting, Roseville, Weller, Hull, Majolica, glass, china, perfume bottles, prints, furniture, linens & collectibles **Pr:** $3-2,000 **Hrs:** Jun-Dec daily 9:30-5. **Sz:** M **CC:** V/MC **Dir:** Directly in front of public landing on Main St. **Own:** Al & Claire Derosier. **QC: 101 63 64 S12 S17 S1**

Rockport

Early Times Antiques Center [G]
Rte 90 • 04856
(207)236-3001

Furniture of all periods, decorative accessories & a wide range of collectibles. Always a large selection of mirrors, spool cabinets & refurbished telephones. **Hrs:** Mon-Sat 10-4 or by appt. **Sz:** M **Assn:** MADA **Dir:** 1-1/2 mi W of Rte 1 on Rte 90. **Own:** George Martens. **QC: 36 48 68**

Joan Hartman Ellis Antique Prints
19 High St • 04856
(207)236-4524

18th & 19th C engravings, lithographs & woodcuts, including botanicals, natural history, American & European views & caricatures to the trade. **Pr:** $15-500 **Est:** 1962 **Hrs:** Appt suggested. **Dir:** In Rockport Village on Amesbury Hill. **Own:** Joan Ellis. **QC: 74**

L E Leonard
67 Pascal Ave • 04856
(207)236-0878

Antique furniture, home decor, objets d'art from China, India & the Spice Islands & jewelry. **Est:** 1992 **Hrs:** May-Dec daily 10:30-5. **Sz:** M **CC:** V/MC **Dir:** From Rte 1 take Rte 90 toward Rockport Harbor Bldg straight ahead 1/4 mi. **Own:** Linda Leonard & Philip DiGiovani. **QC: 71**

Katrin Phocas Ltd
19 Main St • 04856
(207)236-8654

Three floors of select English, American & Continental furniture, decorative accessories & fine art of the 17th, 18th & 19th centuries located at historic Rockport harbor. **Pr:** $50-12,000 **Est:** 1987 **Hrs:** Jun-Sep Mon-Sat 10-5, Sun 12-4; Oct-May by appt. **CC:** AX/V/MC **Assn:** MADA AAAA. **QC: 36 54 7**

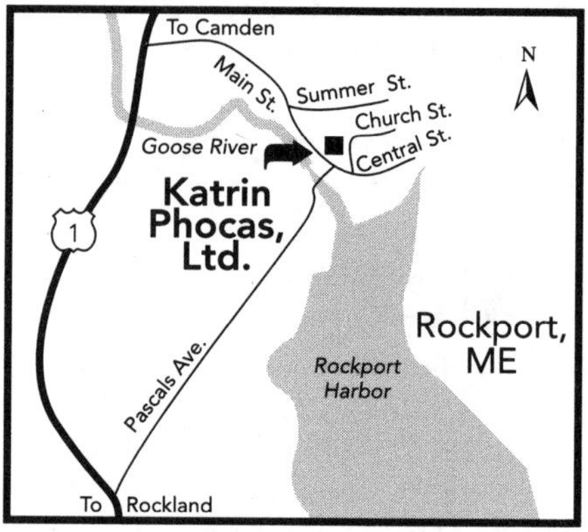

Windy Top Antiques
59 Pascal Ave • 04856
(207)236-4514

Buttons! Buying & selling to collectors & for crafts. Sewing items, soft goods, general line of smalls, Native American & jewelry. **Est:** 1970 **Hrs:** By chance/appt, call ahead suggested. **Dir:** Rte 1N to Rte 90 at Waldoboro, to dead end, shop on R, next to general store. **Own:** Marion Magee. **QC: 21**

Roxbury

Yankee Gem Corp
Rte 17 • 04275
(207)364-4458

A large barn offering glass, china, pewter,

primitives, coins, toys, furniture & paintings. **Pr:** $1-4,000 **Est:** 1954 **Hrs:** May-Nov daily 9-5, Win by chance. **CC:** V/MC **Assn:** MADA **Dir:** 9 mi N of Mexico on Rte 17. **Own:** Ann McCrillis. **QC: 48 61 41**

Rumford

Connie's Antiques

190 Lincoln Ave • 04276
(207)364-3363

Vintage clothing, linens, postcards, dolls, jewelry, glass, china, primitives, furniture, paintings, books, magazines & lamps. **Hrs:** By chance/appt, call ahead advised. **Assn:** MADA **Dir:** 1/3 mi off Rte 2, big blue house on top of hill. **Own:** Maurice & Constance Goudreau. **QC: 83 81 39**

Saco

Bay View Company

206 Main St • 04072
(207)283-0074
pngbvc@gwi.net

New England books & prints, paper, advertising, paintings & silver. **Est:** 1984 **Hrs:** Sat 10-5 or by chance/appt. **Own:** Philip Grime. **QC: 18 39**

Sargentville

Old Cove Antiques

Rte 15 • 04673
(207)359-2031

Formal & country furniture in original paint, decorative accessories, nautical antiques, paintings, hooked rugs, interesting & unusual small objects, folk art & decoys. **Hrs:** Jun-Aug daily 10-5 or by appt. **Sz:** M **CC:** V/MC **Assn:** MADA **Dir:** 9 mi from Blue Hill on Rte 15 approx 1 mi short of Deer Isle Bridge on the R. **Own:** Peg & Olney Grindall. **QC: 51 36 70**

Scarborough

Centervale Farm Antiques

200 Rte 1 at Oak Hill • 04074
(207)883-3443
(800)896-3443
www.centervale.com

Period American, country & Victorian furniture & appropriate accessories; landscapes, portraits, panel lamps, clocks, camp & sporting items, decorative smalls. **Hrs:** Nov-Jun Tue-Sun 10-5; Jul-Oct daily 10-5. **Sz:** L **Assn:** MADA **Dir:** 6 mi S of Portland via Rte 295. **Own:** Patricia & Steve Center. **QC: 48 34 41**

Cliff's Antique Market [G85]

Rte 1 • 04064
(207)883-5671
(800)230-5671 (ME only)

Oak, pine & primitive furniture; glass, china, toys, dolls, tinware, kitchenware, stoneware, jewelry & country store items. **Est:** 1984 **Hrs:** Daily 9-5. **Sz:** H **CC:** V/MC **Dir:** I-95 Exit 6: 3/10 mi N on Rte 1, just S of Portland, across from Scarborough Downs. **Own:** Joan Caton.

Top Knotch Antiques

14 Willowdale Rd • 04074
(207)883-5303

A general line of antiques, collectibles, furniture, toys, magazines, country & formal. **Hrs:** Most days and eves, knock on house door. **Dir:** Off Rte 1 diagonally across from Scarborough Downs, follow signs. **QC: 32 50 S1 S8**

The Widow's Walk

20 Black Point Rd • 04074
(207)883-8123

Oak & pine furniture, country quilts, linens, paintings, prints, country decorating items. **Est:** 1985 **Hrs:** Tue-Sat 10-5, Sun 12-4. **CC:** AX/V/MC/DIS **Dir:** Off Rte 1 on Black Point Rd, 1st house on L. **Own:** Tom & Brenda Cook. **QC: 34 55 80**

Searsport

Captain Tinkham's Emporium

34 Main St (Rte 1) • 04974
(207)548-6465
(888)528-4450
captt@mint.net
www.jonesport-wood.com

Featuring old & antique tools, old books & magazines, oil paintings, prints, collectibles, Native American folk art, ephemera. **Est:** 1995 **Hrs:** Jul-Aug daily 9-5; Sep-Jun 9-5. Call ahead in Win. **Sz:** M **CC:** V/MC **Dir:** In the ctr of town. **Own:** Skip Brack. **QC: 86 18 7 S12**

Cronin & Murphy Antiques

Rte 1 • 04974
(207)548-0073
cronmurf@ime.net

Specializing in art pottery, 19th & 20th C paintings, country painted furniture & mission furniture. **Hrs:** Thu & Sat 9:30-5, Fri 9:30-9 or by appt. **QC: 101 51 49**

Gaul's Antique Company

(207)548-0232

Sandwich, Portland & other early glass, Staffordshire & other fine china, sterling silver & whale oil lamps also a specialty. **Hrs:** By appt only. **CC:** V/MC **Own:** David & Phyllis M Gaul. **QC: 103 23 78**

Hart-Smith Antiques

190 E Main St • 04974
(207)548-2412

A small but fine selection of American period & country furniture, paintings, folk art & architectural materials. **Pr:** $25-10,000 **Est:** 1985 **Hrs:** Apr 10-Oct 31 By chance/appt. **Assn:** MADA **Own:** Scott Smith. **QC: 1 51 7**

Antiques at the Hillmans

362 E Main St • 04974
(207)548-6658

Fine china, old ivory, lamps, good bisque dolls, linens, stoneware, quilts, kitchen items, Victorian walnut, oak & country furniture. **Hrs:** May-Oct daily 9-5 or by chance/appt. **Assn:** MADA **Dir:** 2-3/4 mi N of town. **Own:** Les & Alma Hillman. **QC: 48 34**

Hobby Horse Antiques & Collectibles

Bangor Rd • 04981
(207)548-2981

Two shops full of furniture, toys, paper, jewelry, linen, kitchen, china, glass, primitives, plus many small & unusual items. Featuring Fiesta, Depression, carnival, Roseville & stoneware. **Est:** 1983 **Hrs:** May-Oct 10 daily 9-5; Jul-Aug daily 8-5. **Sz:** M **Dir:** 3 mi N of Searsport on Rte 1. **Own:** Mary Marriman & Blaine Merrill. **QC: 32 61 67**

Primrose Farm Antiques

Rte 1 • 04974
(207)548-6019 • (207)548-6524 (fax)

Country antiques, furniture, textiles, Shaker items, stoneware, baskets, tools, fine glass, china & ironstone. **Est:** 1973 **Hrs:** Apr-Nov daily 9-5; Dec-Mar by appt. **Assn:** MADA **Dir:** 3 mi N of Searsport Village. **Own:** Elizabeth Dominic. **QC: 34 61 57**

Pumpkin Patch Antique Center [G20]

Rte 1 • 04974
(207)548-6047
pumpkinpatch@acadia.net

Quality antiques from all periods emphasizing Maine antiques. Specialties include country furniture, paint decorated furniture, oak & Victorian, quilts, nautical, Native American, ephemera, art, tools, baskets, silver, jewelry & books. **Pr:** $1.00-6,800 **Est:** 1976 **Hrs:** Apr-Oct daily 9:30-5; Nov Sat-Sun 9:30-5; Dec-Mar by chance/appt. **Sz:** L **Assn:** MADA **Dir:** I-95 N to Augusta: Rte 3 E to Belfast, then Rte 1 NE 6 mi to Searsport; I-95 N to Portland Exit to Coastal Rte 1 until Searsport. Shop on Rte 1 on L. **Own:** Phyllis W Sommer. **QC: 1 51 70 S12 S19**

Red Kettle Antiques

Rte 1 • 04974
(207)548-2978

Victorian walnut & oak furniture, country furniture & accessories, dolls, toys, linen & stoneware. **Hrs:** By chance/appt. **Dir:** 3 mi N of Village on Rte 1. **Own:** Ginny & Dennis Middleswart. **QC: 34 38 50**

Searsport Antique Mall [G70+]

149 E Main St • 04974
(207)548-2640

American country, period & custom furniture as well as oak, pine & Victorian. Large selection of flow blue, Roseville, early pattern glass, Limoges, Oriental export, estate & costume jewelry, sporting collectibles, paintings, hooked rugs & folk art. **Hrs:** May-Oct 15 daily 9-5; Nov-Apr daily 10-5. **CC:** AX/V/MC/DIS. **QC: 102 22 79**

Sebago

The Gallery Shop

Jones Museum of Glass & Ceramics • 04029
(207)787-3370

Cards, decorative accessories, games, books, collectibles, cut & pressed glass, blown glass, china, porcelain & ceramics. **Est:** 1978 **Hrs:** May 7-Nov 15 Mon-Sat 10-5, Sun 1-5. **CC:** V/MC **Assn:** MADA NHADA **Dir:** I-95 Exit 8: Rte 25 to Gorham, R at lights onto Rte 114 N. Go 19 mi to E Sebago; follow signs to Rte 107 & Jones Museum. **Own:** Dr Richard Sauers. **QC: 32 36 61 S8**

Sedgwick

Thomas Hinchcliffe Antiques

Rte 176 • 04614
(207)326-9411
dhinchc@acadia.net

Early furniture, country & painted, Windsor chairs, prints, rugs, quilts, boat models, iron & other country smalls as well as hand-made furniture in the traditional manner. **Pr:** $50-2,500 **Est:** 1988 **Hrs:** May 15-Sep 15 Sat-Thu 10-5, Fri 10-12 or by chance/appt. **Sz:** M **Assn:** MADA **Dir:** Rte 176/15 from Blue Hill toward Deer Isle & Penobscot for 4 mi, R onto Rte 176 2 mi toward Penobscot. **Own:** Daphne & Thomas Hinchcliffe. **QC: 1 102 106 S17**

Sheepscot

Constance H Hurst Antiques

(207)882-7354

18th & 19th C English period furniture, porcelain, brass & copper. **Hrs:** By appt only. **Dir:** From Rte 1N, take Rte 218 from Wiscasset a little over 42 mi. Turn R Last house & barn on L before bridge. **QC: 36 54**

Sidney

Yesteryear's Treasures

2186 Summer Haven Rd • 04330
(207)622-7980
good@mint.net

Antiques, collectibles, country furniture, tintypes, advertising cards, samplers, plus country gifts & crafts. **Hrs:** Daily by chance/appt. **Own:** Gary Wood.

Skowhegan

Hilltop Antiques

55 E Front St • 04976
(207)474-3972

Victorian & country furniture, clocks, lighting & collectibles. **Hrs:** By chance/appt. **Own:** Greg Salisbury. **QC: 58 35 65**

David L Jewell Antiques

34 Turner Ave • 04976
(207)474-9676

Early American oak, pine & walnut furniture; glass, clocks, quilts, primitives, china, Oriental antiques & paintings. **Hrs:** Daily by chance/appt. **QC: 50 61**

Somesville

A V Higgins Store
Rte 102 • 04348
(207)244-5401

Small tables, stands, chests of drawers, tool chests, blue willow, flow blue, buffalo china, Staffordshire, mason bottles, calyxware, advertising, rugs, Depression glass, toys, tea sets, child-sized furniture, doll houses, jewelry & kitchen items. **Est:** 1993 **Hrs:** Mid-May to mid-Oct Mon-Sat 10-5; other times by chance. **CC:** V/MC **Own:** Elaine H Reddish. **QC: 48 34 32**

South China

Memory Lane Books
(207)968-2087
memorylane@pivot.net

Fine selection of rare, used & collectible books, prints, paintings, ephemera & paper. **Est:** 1990 **Hrs:** By appt only. **Assn:** MABA **Own:** Pamela S Drummond. **QC: 18 39 74**

Ron Reed Antiques
Rte 3 • 04358
(207)445-3551

Pine, oak, mahogany, walnut & period furniture, country smalls, paintings, trunks, mirrors, signs, lighting, sporting goods, pottery, decorative accessories & smalls. **Pr:** $5-2,500 **Est:** 1977 **Hrs:** Mon-Fri by chance/appt, Sat-Sun by appt only. Dress warmly. **Sz:** L **Dir:** 10 mi E of Augusta on Rte 3 (Belfast-Augusta Rd). **Own:** Ron Reed. **QC: 34 50 55 S1 S12**

South Portland

Mulberry Cottage
45 Western Ave • 04106
(207)775-5011

English, Irish & Continental furniture & interesting accessories. **Hrs:** By appt only. **Assn:** MADA **Own:** Mary Alice Reilley. **QC: 54 53**

Southwest Harbor

Marianne Clark Fine Antiques
Main St (Rte 102) • 04679
(207)244-9247

Authentic 18th & 19th C country & formal furniture & accessories, also paintings & folk art. **Pr:** $25-25,000 **Hrs:** Mon-Sat 10-5. **Sz:** L **Assn:** AADA MADA **Dir:** Rte 1 thru Ellsworth, to int of Rte 102, to SW Harbor, on Mt Desert Island, Acadia National Park. **QC: 102 41 52**

Springvale

Harland H Eastman Books
66 Main St (Rte 109). • 04083
(207)324-2797

General stock with emphasis on Maine town histories, Maine nonfiction & Maine authors. **Hrs:** By chance/appt **Sz:** L **Assn:** MABA. **QC: 18**

Stockton Springs

Victorian House/Book Barn
E Main St • 04981
(207)567-3351

Antiquarian books: large selection of old, out-of-print & scarce books. **Pr:** $1-100+ **Est:** 1960 **Hrs:** Apr-Dec daily 8-8; Jan-Mar by chance/appt. **Assn:** MABA **Dir:** Parallel to Rte 1. **Own:** Andrew B W MacEwen. **QC: 1 18 70**

Sullivan

Bob Havey
(207)422-3083
bobhavey@webtv.net

Specializing in early Disney, comic & cowboy character items, toys, vintage magazines & ads, paper Americana, movie items, advertising & various collectibles. **Hrs:** By chance/appt or mail order. **Dir:** E of Ellsworth. **QC: 39**

Charlotte Gray Antiques
Rte 1 • 04664
(207)422-6716

High-quality primitives, fine signed glass, furniture & silver. **Est:** 1964 **Hrs:** By chance/appt. **Dir:** Rte 1 at orange antiques sign.

Thomaston

Anchor Farm Antiques
184 Main St • 04861
(207)354-8859

Two large rooms featuring sterling silver, estate jewelry, china & tools. **Est:** 1975 **Hrs:** May-Oct, Win by chance/appt. **Sz:** L **Assn:** MADA **Dir:** Rte 1 next to ME State Prison. **Own:** Muriel Knutson. **QC: 64 78**

Brindl Fine Arts
(207)372-8523

19th & 20th C photography & folk art. **Own:** Richard & Christine Rydell. **QC: 41 73**

Ross Levett Antiques
131 Main St • 04861
(207)354-6227

American, European, Asian & Islamic antiques. **Hrs:** Wed-Sat 10-5 or by appt. **Assn:** MADA.

David C Morey American Antiques
103 Main St • 04861
(207)354-6033

17th & 18th C period American & country furniture with emphasis on original or early surface & condition as well as 18th & early 19th C American decorative & folk art, New England redware & English ceramics related to the American experience. **Hrs:** Wed & Fri-Sat 10-5 or by appt. **Assn:** ADA MADA NHADA. **QC: 52 41 23**

Wee Barn Antiques
20 Georges St • 04861
(207)354-6163

Furniture & accessories, silver, jewelry, glass & fun smalls of all kinds. **Est:** 1972 **Hrs:** Apr-Oct daily 9-4:30; Nov-Mar by chance/appt. **Dir:** Just off Rte 1. **Own:** Gwen Robinson & Lee-Ann Upham.

Topsham

Affordable Antiques [G9]
Rte 196 • 04086
(207)729-7913

Mostly smalls: china, glass, jewelry, art, books, paper goods, coins, old usables & miniatures. **Est:** 1987 **Hrs:** Mon-Sat 10-5:30; Sun 12-5. **CC:** V/MC/DIS **Dir:** I-95 Exit 24. Handicap accessible.

Eighty One Main Antiques
81 Main St (Rte 201) • 04086
(207)729-0247

Two story barn with a large selection of top quality oak, walnut & mahogany furniture; large selection of collectibles, decorator items & fountain pens. **Hrs:** Daily 9-5; Dec-Mar by chance/appt. **Own:** John & Ann Feeney. **QC: 48 50 32**

Trenton

Tiffany's Antique Center
Rte 230 • 04605
(207)667-7743

Three floors plus of quality furnishings diversely displayed. **Hrs:** Sum daily 10-5. **CC:** AX/V/MC/DIS **Dir:** 8 mi from Ellsworth on Rte 3 at Oak Point Rd. **Own:** Greg Betz.

Use the Service QuickCode indexes at the back of the book to find restorers, appraisers, refinishers, and other specialty service providers.

Troy

Bob Brennan Antiques

Mitchell Rd • 04987
(207)948-5952
bob_brennan52@hotmail.com

A barn full of antique items picked from homes in NH, VT & ME — the antiques that a "door knocker" finds. Country smalls in paint, furniture, hooked rugs, toys, architectural, campy items, signs, cupboards & birdhouse. Frequently changing stock. **Pr:** $10-1,000 **Est:** 1983 **Hrs:** By appt/chance. A call ahead is advised. **Dir:** From Belfast on the coast Rte 137 to Rte 220 N to Rtes 202 & 9 E. **Own:** Bob Brennan. **QC: 34 36 S1**

Turner

Northland Antiques & Collectibles

Rte 4 • 04282
(207)225-2466

Jewelry, dolls, sports items, glassware, furniture & tools. **Est:** 1993 **Hrs:** Mon, Wed, Fri-Sat 10-5 & Sun by chance. **CC:** V/MC **Dir:** Northland Plaza. **Own:** Joan Ricker.

Waldoboro

Central Asian Artifacts

Main & Jefferson Sts • 04572
(207)832-4003
www.midcoast.com/~caa/

Oriental carpets, Rosewood & lapis jewelry. **Hrs:** Mon-Sat 10-5. **CC:** AX/V/MC/DIS **Own:** Jeffrey Evangelos. **QC: 76**

Wink's Bottle Shop

647 Union Rd (Rte 235) • 04572
(207)832-4603

Antique bottles from the early 1800s. **Hrs:** By chance/appt. **Dir:** On Rte 235, 1 mi off Rte 1. **Own:** Robert C Winchenbach. **QC: 61**

Warren

Kenniston's "Good Old Things"

2020 Atlantic Hwy (Rte 1) • 04864
(207)273-3332
davejo@midcoast.com

20,000 children's & Maine books in stock, 75,000 postcards, paper dolls, baskets & sporting collectibles & nautical/marine antiques. **Pr:** $1-500 **Est:** 1990 **Hrs:** May 1-Oct 31 Mon-Fri 10-4, call ahead advised; Nov 1-Apr 30 by chance. **Sz:** L **CC:** V/MC/DIS **Assn:** MABA **Dir:** Located W of Rte 90 & Rte 1 int in Warren on S side of the road. **Own:** David & Joanne Kenniston. **QC: 18 32 79**

Village Antique Group Shop [G12]

Main St • 04864
(207)273-2863

Country items, glass, china, silver, jewelry, linens, furniture & collectibles. **Est:** 1987 **Hrs:** May-Oct daily 10-5. **Dir:** 1/8 mi off Rte 90 in the village. **Own:** Helen Stetson. **QC: 61 34 32**

Winslow's Antiques

Rte 1 • 04547
(207)273-2258

Furniture in as-found & restored condition (oak & pine), country items, Victorian, primitives & general line of antiques. **Pr:** $35-500 **Hrs:** Mon-Sat 10-4 by chance/appt. **Dir:** 4 mi N of Waldoboro on Rte 1. **Own:** Dana & Brenda Winslow. **QC: 32 34 55**

Washington

The Lilac Shed Antiques

Rte 17 • 04574
(207)845-2263

Antique hardware. **Est:** 1982 **Hrs:** Daily 10-5 or by chance. **Dir:** 1/3 mi W of Rte 220. **Own:** Kenneth Spahr. **QC: 62**

Wells

1774 House Antiques

1637 Post Rd (Rte 1) • 04090
(207)646-3520

Pine, country & primitive furniture, cupboards, chests, quilts, weathervanes, tables & decorative accessories, most in old paint. **Hrs:** Daily 10-5, call ahead advised. **Assn:** GSAAA **Dir:** Across from Bo-Mar Hall, Rte 1 N. **Own:** Betty Tufts. **QC: 102 106**

Bo-Mar Hall Antiques [G114]

Rte 1 • 04090
(207)646-4116

Glass, china, jewelry, books, furniture & country smalls. **Hrs:** Daily 10-5 exc Easter, Thanks, Christmas. **Sz:** L **Dir:** I-95 Exit 2: Rte 109 E, N on Rte 1, on the L. **Own:** Tim & Cathy Blair.

Peggy S Carboni Antiques

1755 Post Rd • 04090
(207)646-4551

Furniture & decorative items for home & garden. **Hrs:** Daily 10-5. **Assn:** MADA **Dir:** In the Wells Union Antique Center.

D & A Country Mouse Antiques [G35]

2077 Sanford Rd • 04090
(207)646-7334

Glass, china, lamps, clocks, advertisements, telephones, small coin-operated machines, tools, frames, prints, Oriental antiques, jewelry, baskets, crocks & country furniture. **Est:** 1990 **Hrs:** Daily 10-5; Nov-Mar closed Tue & Wed. **CC:** V/MC **Own:** Dick Rogerson & Al Hall.

Corey Daniels Antiques

Rte 1 • 04090
(207)646-5301

A large barn with Continental, American, Chinese, old paint, mahogany, architectural, garden antiques & smalls. **Est:** 1971 **Hrs:** Sum Mon-Sat 10-5, Sun by chance; Win open occasionally (best to call). **Dir:** I-95 Exit 2: N on Rte 1, R on Drakes Island Rd, R on Shady Ln. **QC: 3 52 60**

East Coast Books, Art, Autographs

Depot St • 04090
(207)646-3584 • (207)646-0416 (fax)
merv@cybertours.com

Large, eclectic collection of rare & out-of-print books, autographs & historical Americana; fine art prints, drawings, watercolors. **Hrs:** Apr-Jun daily 10-5, Jul-Oct daily 10-7, Nov-Dec by chance/appt. **Assn:** MABA **Own:** Merv & Kaye Slotnick. **QC: 18 1 7**

The Farm

294 Mildram Rd • 04090
(207)985-2656 • (207)985-1254 (fax)
dcroutha@gwi.net

Specializing in period English formal & country furniture, mirrors, lighting, prints, paintings & metalware. French country furniture & 19th C Chinese furniture, 18th & 19th C Chinese export porcelain for the discriminating collector. **Pr:** $50-30,000 **Est:** 1967 **Hrs:** Jun 15-Sep 5 Thu-Tue 10-4; Sep 5-Jun 15 Fri-Sun 10-4. **Sz:** L **CC:** V/MC **Dir:** I-95 Exit 2 (Wells): L onto Rte 109, L onto Rte 1 N, L onto Coles Hill Rd, L onto Mildram Rd, farm on R. **Own:** David & Hannah Crouthamel, Thomas & Jeannette Hackett. **QC: 54 71 20**

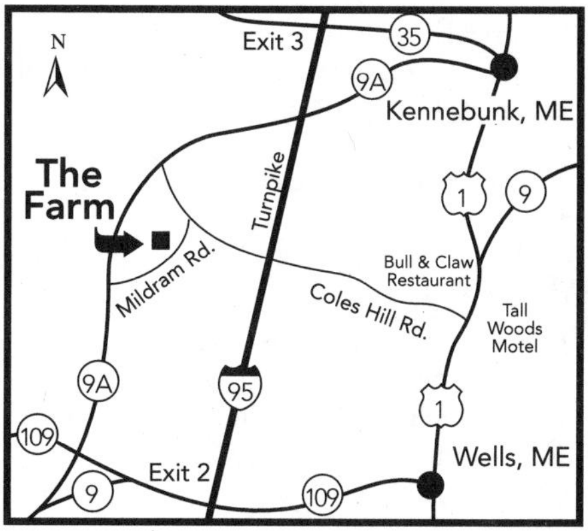

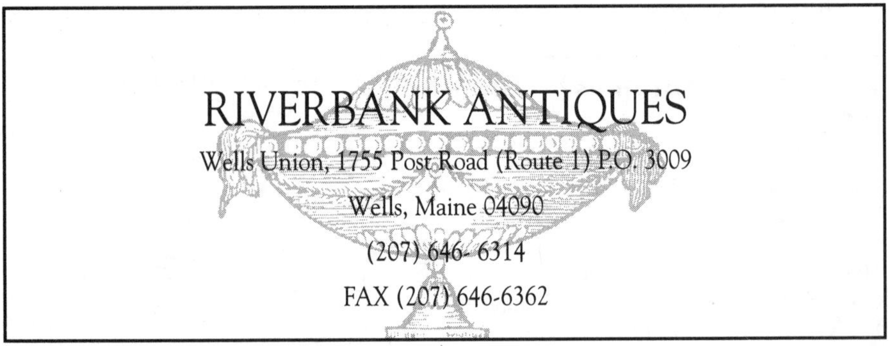

RIVERBANK ANTIQUES
Wells Union, 1755 Post Road (Route 1) P.O. 3009
Wells, Maine 04090
(207) 646- 6314
FAX (207) 646-6362

Goosefare Antiques [G4]
2232 Post Rd Rte 1 • 04072
(207)646-0505

18th, 19th & 20th C antiques. **Hrs:** Wed-Mon 10-5. **Own:** Elizabeth & John DeSimone.

Harding's Book Shop
2152 Post Rd (Rte 1) • 04090
(207)646-8785

A very large stock of quality old & rare books, fine bindings, maps & prints, Maine & New England town histories, Arctic & Antarctica, meticulously arranged. **Est:** 1980 **Hrs:** Jan-Jun daily 9-5; Jul-Aug daily 9-9; Sep-Dec daily 9-6. **CC:** AX/V/MC/DIS **Assn:** ABAA MABA **Dir:** I-95 Exit 2: E to Rte 1, N on Rte 1, beyond Drake Island Rd on the L. **Own:** Douglas N Harding. **QC: 66 74 18**

Home at Last Antiques
Rte 1 • 04090
(207)641-2476

Country furniture, accessories, smalls & mantels. **Hrs:** Daily 9-6. **Own:** Deborah Bloom. **QC: 102**

R Jorgensen Antiques
502 Post Rd (Rte 1) • 04090
(207)646-9444 • (207)646-4954 (fax)
rja@cybertours.com

Large collection of fine Americana, New England period furniture & related accessories from the 17th, 18th & 19th C as well as an extensive inventory of country & formal English & Continental tables, chairs, armoires, cupboards & smalls. **Est:** 1971 **Hrs:** Thu-Tue 10-5. **Sz:** H **Assn:** ADA MADA NHADA **Dir:** I-95 Maine Tpke Exit 2: L to Rte 1, R going S, 2-1/2 mi; large sign on the R. **Own:** Robert, Richard & Valerie Jorgenson & Pamela Higgins. **QC: 1 36 48**

MacDougall-Gionet Antiques & Associates [G60]
2104 Post Rd (Rte 1) • 04090
(207)646-3531

Wells's oldest antiques shop in an 18th C restored barn. Fine American country & formal furniture, primitives, pewter, porcelain, stoneware, earthenware, glass, Orientals, textiles, toys, rugs & paintings. **Pr:** $10-25,000 **Est:** 1965 **Hrs:** Tue-Sun 9-5. **Sz:** L **CC:** V/MC **Dir:** I-95 Exit 2: L to Rte 1, then L for 1 mi. Big red sign, house & barn on L. **Own:** Alex Gionet & Raymond MacDougall. **QC: 1 41 52**

Maine Coast Antiques
1784 Post Rd (Rte 1) • 04090
(207)641-2966
(888)641-2966

Quality antique furnishings & collectibles. "We're dealer friendly." **Hrs:** Daily 10-5.

Kenneth & Ida Manko American Folk Art
Seabreeze Dr • 04054
(207)646-2595

Offering a very choice small stock of American folk art for the advanced collector, dealer & interior designer with an emphasis on quality weathervanes, primitive paintings

& wood carvings. Select country, rustic furniture & smalls. **Est:** 1972 **Hrs:** Jun 15 - Nov 15 call ahead advised, closed Dec-May. **Assn:** NEAA **Dir:** I-95 Exit 2: Rte 109 E to Rte 1, Rte 1 S 2-1/2 mi to Eldridge Rd, E to Seabreeze, barn on R. **QC: 1 41 45 S1 S15**

Rainbow Rhino

Rte 1 • 04090
(207)641-2270

Vintage furniture & collectibles. **Hrs:** Sum Fri-Sun 11-6, Mon by chance/appt. **Dir:** Betw Exit 2 & Rte 1.

Red Barn Used Furniture & Antiques

27 Mile Rd • 04094
(207)646-2137

Quality used furniture. Mahogany, maple, cherry, pine & oak. Rugs & accessories. **Hrs:** Fri-Wed 10-5; Nov-May Fri-Tue 10-4.

Reed's Antiques & Collectibles [G103]

Rte 1 • 04090
(207)646-8010
(800)891-2017
reedtiques@cybertours.com

Fine furniture, primitives, china, pottery, porcelain, linens, jewelry, art, books, collectibles, decorator items, cut glass, pattern glass, Depression glass, art glass, silver, coins, dolls & toys. **Hrs:** Daily 10-5. **Sz:** L **CC:** AX/V/MC/DIS **Dir:** Exit 2 off Maine Tpke L on Rte 1 1/3 mi on R. **Own:** Frank & Karen Reed. **QC: 48 106 32**

Riverbank Antiques

1755 Post Rd (Rte 1) • 04090
(207)646-6314 • (207)646-6362 (fax)

Eclectic selection of 18th & 19th C American, English & Continental furniture & decorations with emphasis on garden ornaments & architectural elements. **Est:** 1974 **Hrs:** Jun-Oct Mon-Sat 10-5, Sun 12-5; May Fri-Mon 10-5. **Sz:** L **Dir:** Maine Tpke Exit 2: N on Rte 1 to the Wells Union Antique complex. **Own:** Lynn Chase. **QC: 3 36 60**

Art Smith Antiques

Rte 1 • 03902
(207)646-6996

One-of-a-kind architectural artifacts, books, decorative hardware, old fabrics, garden items, historical wallpaper, lamps & lighting, store decor, props & mirrors. **Est:** 1965 **Hrs:** Daily 10-5. **CC:** AX/V/MC/DIS **Dir:** In the Wells Union Antique complex.

Steen's Now & Then

1807 Post Rd (Rte 1) • 04090
(207)646-7563

Collectibles, toys, jewelry, paintings & crafts. **Hrs:** By chance/appt. **CC:** V/MC.

The Arringtons

1908 Post Rd • 04090
(207)646-4124

Books, prints & ephemera. **Est:** 1988 **CC:** V/MC **Assn:** MABA **Own:** Eleanor & George Arrington. **QC: 18 39**

Wells Antique Mart [G85]

Rte 1 • 04090
(207)646-8153

Furniture, decorative accessories, glass, china, quilts, metalwork, jewelry, lace & linens & quilts. **Hrs:** Daily 9-5. **Sz:** L **CC:** V/MC **Dir:** I-95 Exit 2.

Wells General Store Antiques [G]

Rte 1 • 04094
(207)646-5553

200-year-old barn with two floors of quality furniture & smalls. **Hrs:** Daily 10-5, closed Tue-Wed in Win. **Dir:** I-95 Exit 2. **QC: 48**

Wells Union Antiques

1755 Post Rd (Rte 1) • 04090
(207)646-4551

Eight individually owned shops at one location featuring New England, New York, English & Continental antiques, country & formal, decorations, accessories, glass, china, vintage clothing, linens, paintings, collectibles, architectural elements & garden. **Pr:** $1-10,000 **Est:** 1982 **Hrs:** Daily 10-5. **Sz:** H **CC:** V/MC/DIS **Dir:** I-95 Exit 2: L off Exit on Rte 109, to Rte 1, at light take L, 1/4 mi on R.

West Paris

Mollyockett Marketplace Antique Center [G12]

255 Bethel Rd (Rte 26) • 04289
(207)674-3939 • (207)674-3665 (fax)

Large two-story shop loaded with pine, oak & period furniture, toys, pedal cars, glass, china, pottery, books, paintings, prints (Parrish, Sawyer & Nutting), primitives, quilts, rugs & linens. **Pr:** $5-10,000 **Est:** 1993 **Hrs:** May 15-Oct 15 daily 10-5; Oct 16-May 14 Fri-Mon 10-4. **Sz:** L **CC:** AX/V/MC/DIS **Assn:** NFIB **Dir:** I-95 Exit 11(Gray): Rte 26N 36.5 mi from tollbooth on L just beyond junc with Rte 219. **Own:** Sandra, Ken & Kimberly Poland. **QC: 87 50 74 S12 S6 S10**

West Rockport

Antique Treasures [G]

Rte 90 • 04865
(207)596-7650

Furniture, smalls, silver, china & books. **Hrs:** Mon-Sat 9-4. **Own:** Sue Hopkins & Martha Martens

Pen Ventures Etc

Rte 17 • 04865
(207)236-3842

A medley of antiques, art, furniture, picture frames, glassware, kitchen collectibles, linens, buttons & other smalls. **Hrs:** By chance (watch for open flag). **Own:** Harold & Linda Hodgkins.

Winterport

Peter & the Baldwin Sisters
The Old County Rd • 04495
(207)223-4732

Primitive, paint-decorated country, oak & pine furniture, kitchenware, pottery & clocks: shelf, tall-case, pillar & scroll, regulators. **Est:** 1993 **Hrs:** Mon-Fri 10-4:30, Sat by chance. **Dir:** From Bangor take Rte 1A S 3.4 mi past Hampden Academy on L (riverside). Take Old County Rd to top of hill on L. **Own:** Peter & Susan Rioux. **QC: 35 102 1 S7 S1 S16**

Wiscasset

Jane Brown Antiques Unique
(207)633-6956

Early quilts, hooked rugs, sewing items, painted smalls, folk art, Victorian clothing & textiles. **Hrs:** By appt only. **Assn:** MADA. **QC: 84 41 75**

Wm Dykes Antiques
Rte 1 & Hodge St • 04578
(207)882-6381 • (207)882-6381 (fax)

18th & early 19th C American country & formal furniture, accessories, brass, iron, glass, tools, paintings & silver, early militaria. **Est:** 1974 **Hrs:** By chance/appt. **CC:** AX/V/MC **Own:** Bill Dykes. **QC: 52 34 20**

Dianne Halpern Antiques
68 Main St (Rte 1) • 04578
(207)882-8140 • (207)882-7725 (fax)
dhantiques@aol.com

Painted country furniture & accessories, folk art & toys. **Pr:** $25-10,000 **Est:** 1995 **Hrs:** May 1-Oct 15 daily 10-5; Oct 16-Apr 30 by chance/appt. **Sz:** M **Assn:** MADA NHADA. **QC: 1 41 87**

Head Tide Antiques
(207)586-6214

Country smalls, pewter, brass, copper, blue willow, ironstone, baskets & stoneware. **Hrs:** By appt only. **Assn:** MADA **Own:** Helen Keating. **QC: 34**

Elliott Healy Books
Middle St • 04578
(207)882-5446

Photography books & images, fine arts, books on antiques, illustrated & children's books, prints & maps. **Est:** 1972 **Hrs:** Jun-Oct 15 daily 10-5, rest of yr by chance/appt. **CC:** V/MC **Assn:** MABA **Dir:** Off Rte 1 in ctr Wiscasset. **QC: 18 66 73**

John M Henry
12 Summer St • 04578
(207)882-6420

18th & 19th C country furniture & accessories. **Hrs:** Daily. **QC: 34 102**

Priscilla Hutchinson Antiques
62 Pleasant St • 04578
(207)882-4200

A well-stocked shop featuring 18th & 19th C American furniture in paint & original finish, folk art, baskets, textiles & rugs. **Pr:** $100-10,000 **Est:** 1976 **Hrs:** Jun-Sep daily 10-5. **CC:** V/MC **Assn:** NHADA MADA **Dir:** 1/2 blk from Main St (Rte 1). **QC: 1 41 52**

Lilac Cottage
Rte 1 • 04578
(207)882-7059

American & English furniture, porcelain, metals & decorative items. **Est:** 1964 **Hrs:** Jun-Oct 15 Mon-Sat 10-5. **Assn:** MADA **Dir:** On the Green. **Own:** Willliam G Waters. **QC: 52 54 36**

Use the Specialty QuickCode indexes at the back of the book to find dealers who specialize in your area of interest.

Lillie Antiques & Design

Fort Hill St • 04578
(207)882-4044
lynch@wiscasset.net

18th & early 19th C country & formal American furniture, accessories, Chinese export porcelain, English & Irish Georgian silver & English garden ornaments & tools. **Hrs:** By appt only. **Assn:** VADA **Own:** Kiersten Lynch. **QC: 52 25 78**

Marston House American Antiques

Main St (Rte 1) • 04578
(207)882-6010 • (207)882-6965 (fax)
(800)852-4137
themarstonhouse@nqi.net

New England country furniture, antique textiles, quilts & homespun (wool & linens), folk art, painted accessories of the period 1800s. Garden shop. **Pr:** $100-10,000 **Est:** 1987 **Hrs:** May 1-Dec 1 Mon-Sat 10-5, Sun 12-5; other times by chance/appt. **Sz:** M **CC:** AX/V/MC **Assn:** MADA **Dir:** Rte 1 to Wiscasset, in ctr of town at corn of Main St (Rte 1) & Middle St. **Own:** Sharon Mrozinski. **QC: 51 60 80**

Meadowside Farm Antiques

(207)832-0538

Country furniture, woodenware, baskets, china, glass, primitives & decorative accessories. **Hrs:** By appt only. **Assn:** MADA **Own:** Dick & Jane Pickering. **QC: 36 17 34**

Merndale Antiques

Rte 1 • 04578
(207)882-9292

Specializing in 18th & 19th C American furniture, painted & refinished rope beds, quilts, folk art, Paris Mfg Co sleds & wagons & other decorative items. **Est:** 1972 **Hrs:** May-Oct daily 10-5. **Assn:** MADA **Dir:** Just S of the ctr of town. **Own:** Marian & Bill Merner. **QC: 51 52 41**

The Musical Wonder House

18 High St • 04578
(207)882-7163 • (207)882-6373 (fax)
(800)336-3725
music@musicalwonderhouse.com

Sell & restore all types of music boxes, wind-up phonographs & related mechanical musical devices. Oldest established full-service music box restoration company north of NYC. Branch store: The Merry Music Box in Lexington, MA. **Pr:** $1,000-150,000 **Est:** 1956 **Hrs:** May 25-Oct 30 daily 10-6; other times by appt. **Sz:** M **CC:** AX/V/MC/DIS **Assn:** MBSI **Dir:** 155 mi N of Boston on Rte 1: turn onto Lee St at Exxon in Wiscasset, go 1 blk, L onto High St, 5th bldg on L. **Own:** Donilo Konvalinka. **QC: 87 69 S16**

New England Antiques

(207)442-8000

American country furniture in original paint & decoration, wicker, accessories, hooked rugs, quilts & fine linens. **Hrs:** By appt only. **Assn:** MADA **Own:** Marion Redlon. **QC: 102 81 84**

Margaret B Ofslager

Corner of Main & Summer Sts (Rte 1) • 04578
(207)882-6082

In one of Maine's most beautiful villages, carefully selected antiques & decorative items from Maine in a late 18th C house: folk art, hooked rugs, paintings & country furniture. **Hrs:** May-Oct daily 11-5. **Dir:** At Main & Summer St. **QC: 41 102 75**

Parkers of Wiscasset [G]

Rte 1 • 04578
(207)882-5520

A quality group shop with folk art, toys, early lighting, furniture, quilts & rugs, paintings, linens, early pottery, Indian arts, country & primitives, art pottery, glass & china, costume jewelry & decorative accessories. **Est:** 1983 **Hrs:** Apr-Dec daily 10-4. **Sz:** L **CC:** V/MC **Assn:** MADA **Dir:** 1-1/2 mi S of Wiscasset. **Own:** Nancy Prince & Bette Zwicker.

Part of the Past

37 S Water St • 04578
(207)882-7908
partofpast@clinic.net

Early country furniture in original paint, early birch, cherry & tiger maple furniture in natural finish, folk art, toys, tools, hooked rugs, quilts, prints, nautical, scientific & sporting items. **Pr:** $5-75,000 **Est:** 1992 **Hrs:** Daily 9-5. **Sz:** M **CC:** V/MC **Assn:** MADA **Dir:** I-95 Exit 22: Follow Rte 1 for 21 mi past Brunswick & Bath to downtown Wiscasset. R on Water St before bridge. Shop is located in 3rd bldg on L. **Own:** Peter Pardoe. **QC: 70 75 102**

Bill Quinn Antiques

Rte 1 • 04578
(207)882-9097

Fresh, un-touched, as-found merchandise including cupboards, farm tables, garden related, folk art, architecture, birdhouses, signs, trellises & other decorative, colorful & useful items. **Hrs:** Daily. **Dir:** Corn Rte 1 & Water St in the village. **QC: 102 41 60**

Debra Schaffer

50 Water St • 04578
(207)882-8145

18th & 19th C painted furniture, samplers, silhouettes, theorems & watercolors. **Hrs:** By appt only. **Assn:** MADA NHADA **Dir:** Corn of Main St & Summer St behind Key Bank. **QC: 51 41 82**

Robert Snyder & Judy Wilson

72 Main St • 04578
(207)882-4255

American country furniture in original paint, folk art, hooked rugs, trade signs, paintings & smalls. **Hrs:** Daily. **Assn:** NHADA. **QC: 102 41 75**

Doris Stauble Antiques

Maine St • 04578
(207)882-5286

Country painted furniture, paintings, folk art, decoys & nautical items. **Pr:** $25-2,500 **Est:** 1972 **Hrs:** Daily afternoons or by chance. **Assn:** MADA **Dir:** On Rte 1 near the corn of Main & Summer. **QC: 51 7 41**

Patricia Stauble Antiques

Rte 1 • 04578
(207)882-6341

Four rooms of early country furniture in original surface & paint, appropriate accessories in a home setting. **Pr:** $40-12,000 **Est:** 1965 **Hrs:** Jul-Aug Mon-Sat 10-5 other times by chance/appt; closed Jan 1-Mar 30. **Sz:** L **CC:** V/MC **Assn:** MADA GSAAA **Dir:** Located on Rte 1 N , 1 blk before PO, at corn of Pleasant St. **QC: 1 7 51 S8 S12**

James H Welch Antiques

Main St • 04578
(207)529-5770

Country furniture in original paint, folk art & other country accessories. **Hrs:** Apr 15-Nov 1 daily 10-5. **Assn:** MADA. **QC: 102 41**

Wiscasset Bay Gallery

67 Main St • 04578
(207)882-7682 • (207)882-7682 (fax)
wbg@clinic.net
www.wiscassetbaygallery.com

Specializing in fine 19th & early 20th C American & European paintings with a focus on New England artists. **Pr:** $250-50,000 **Est:** 1985 **Hrs:** May-Oct daily 10:30-5; Nov-Dec reduced hrs. **Sz:** L **CC:** V/MC/DIS **Assn:** NEAA **Dir:** On Rte 1 in Wiscasset Village. **Own:** Keith Oehmig. **QC: 7 9 S16**

Bette Zwicker

(207)563-3897

Country furniture, smalls, hooked rugs, spongeware & yellowware, French Quimper & Christmas items a specialty. **Hrs:** By appt only. **Assn:** MADA VADA NHADA. **QC: 102**

Yarmouth

Marie Plummer & John Philbrick

68 E Main St • 04096
(207)846-1158

17th & 18th C furniture & accessories for the early American home arranged in room settings in an 18th C New England house in historic York. **Pr:** $250-5,000 **Est:** 1975 **Hrs:** By chance/appt. **Sz:** M **Assn:** MADA NHADA. **QC: 1 41 52 S1 S9**

A E Runge Oriental Rugs

108 Main St • 04096
(207)846-9000
(800)287-0009 (ME only)

Maine's largest selection of decorative & collectible & semi-antique & antique Oriental rugs. **Est:** 1986 **Hrs:** Tue-Fri 10-5, Thu til 7, Sat 10-3. **Sz:** M **CC:** AX/V/MC **Assn:** MADA VADA **Dir:** Corn of Portland & Main Sts in the old Apothecary Bldg. **Own:** "Tad" Runge. **QC: 76 S1 S16 S19**

W M Schwind Jr Antiques

51 E Main St (Rte 88) • 04096
(207)846-9458

In an 1810 Federal period house a large selection of 18th & 19th C American country & formal furniture & accessories in room settings: paintings, sculpture, prints, ceramics, glass & hooked rugs. **Est:** 1967 **Hrs:** Call ahead for hours. **Assn:** AADLA MADA. **QC: 52 61 7**

York

Bell Farm Antiques [G22]

244 Rte 1 S • 03909
(207)363-8181

Two floors of country antiques, art, silver, toys/Steiff/mechanical, Victorian furniture, china, early glass, Old Ivory china, primitives & Victoriana. **Est:** 1989 **Hrs:** Mon-Sat 10-5, Sun 12-5;Oct-Apr closed Wed. **Sz:** L **CC:** V/MC **Dir:** I-95 York Exit: 1 mi S on Rte 1. Just N of Kittery factory outlets. **Own:** Judy & Rex Lambert.

Deak's Antiques

388 Rte 1 • 03909
(207)363-4517 • (207)363-3927 (fax)

Early country furniture in oak, pine & mahogany, advertising items, pottery, garden accessories & glass. **Hrs:** Daily 10-5. **CC:** AX/V/MC/DIS **Own:** Jane & Deak Rutherford.

Rocky Mountain Quilts

130 York St (Rte 1A) • 03909
(207)363-6800 • (207)351-3381 (fax)
(800)762-5940
rockymtnquilts@cybertours.com
www.rockymountainquilts.com

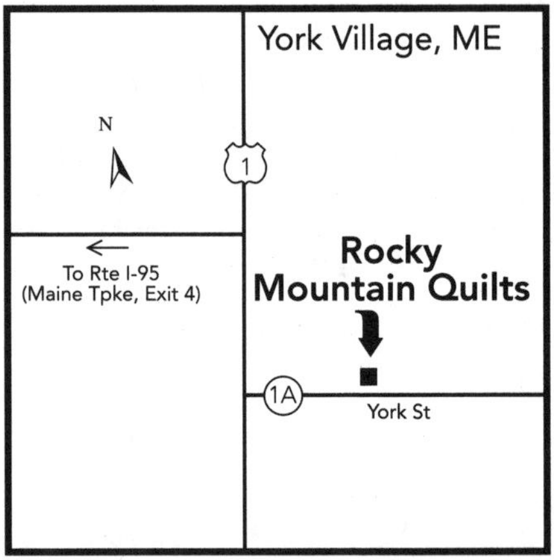

Over 400 antique quilts from 1740 to 1940 as well as quilt restoration, custom quilting & hooked rug repairs. Hundreds of quilt blocks, quilt tops, antique fabric, seed sacks, clothing & animals. **Pr:** $7.00-25,000 **Est:** 1987 **Hrs:** Mon-Sat 10-5, Sun 12-5; Nov-May Thu-Sat 10-4. **Sz:** M **CC:** AX/V/MC/DIS **Assn:** MADA NHADA **Dir:** In the village. **Own:** Betsey Telford. **QC: 84 80 S16**

Withington-Wells Antiques

191 Cider Hill Rd (Rte 91) • 03909
(207)363-7439

19th & 20th C garden furniture, accessories & decorative arts. **Hrs:** By appt only. **Assn:** NHADA MADA **Dir:** I-95 Exit 1: E to Rte 1, S to Rte 91 & W to Cider Hill Rd. **Own:** Bob & Nancy Withington. **QC: 60 34 36**

York Antiques Gallery [G]

746 Rte 1 • 03909
(207)363-5002

Quality multiple dealer shop offering a diversified selection of antiques with an emphasis on American country furniture & accessories displayed in a large restored three-story barn. **Est:** 1989 **Hrs:** Daily 10-5. **Sz:** L **Assn:** NHADA MADA **Dir:** I-95 York Ogunquit Exit: 9/10 mi N on Rte 1 (last exit before toll); 10 min from Portsmouth, NH. **Own:** Gail & Don Piatt. **QC: 1 102 34 S19**

Massachusetts

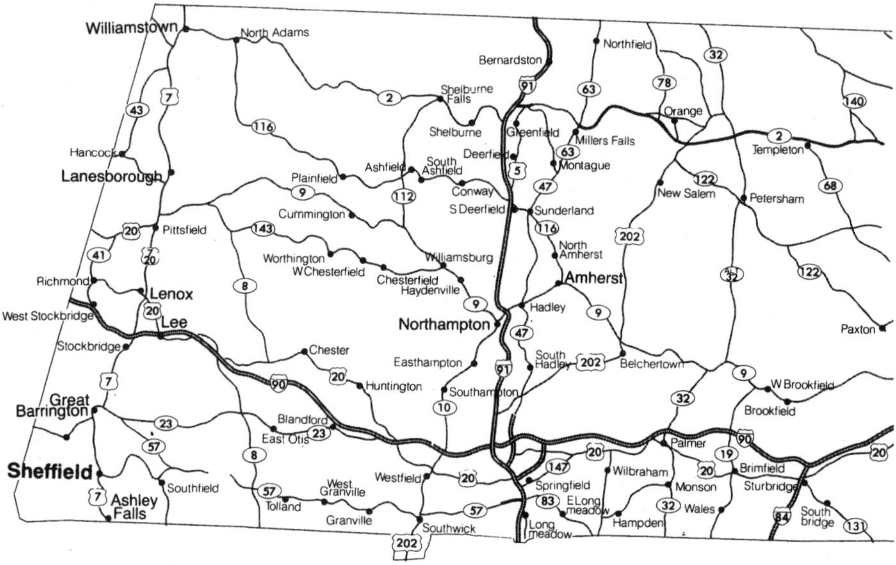

Massachusetts

LEGEND

Interstate Highway

Major U.S. and State Routes

Minor State Route

Not to Scale

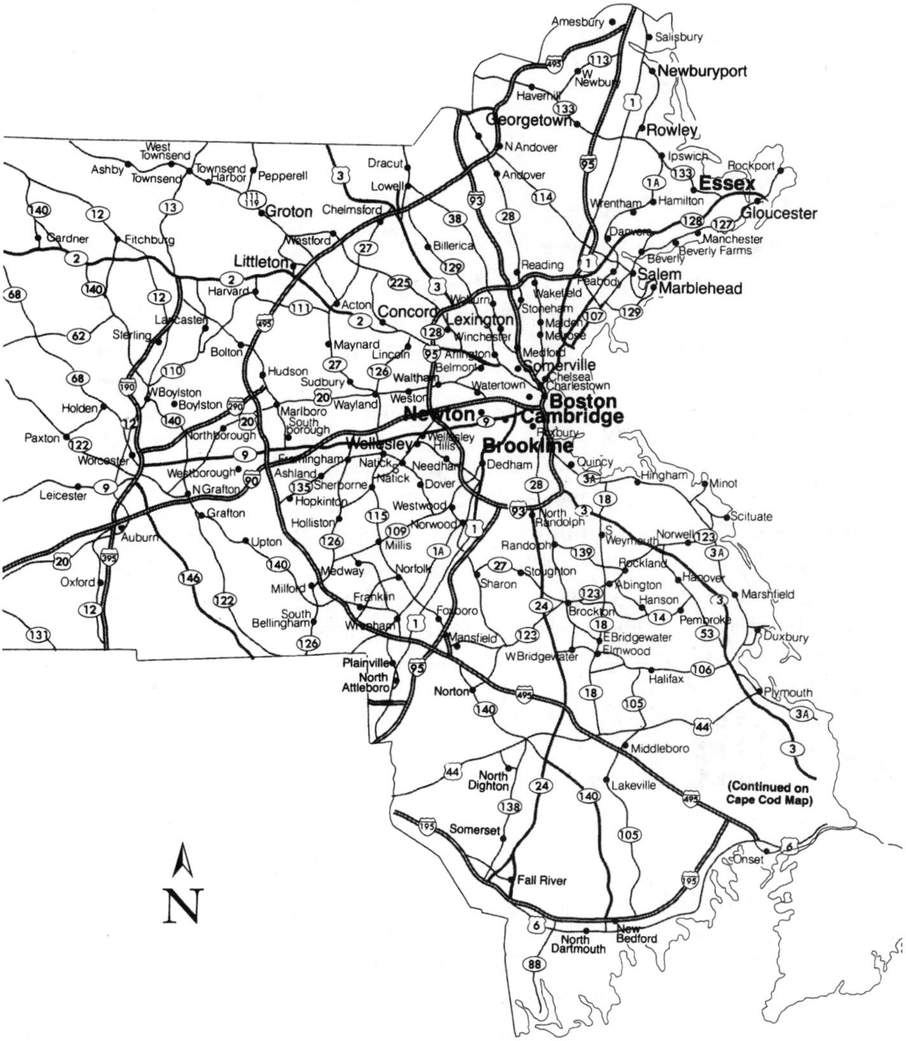

Amesbury
Salisbury
Newburyport
Haverhill
Georgetown
Rowley
N Andover
Andover
Ipswich
Rockport
Essex
Hamilton
Gloucester
Danvers
Manchester
Beverly Farms
Beverly
Salem
Marblehead
Peabody
Reading
Wakefield
Stoneham
Malden
Melrose
Medford
Somerville
Chelsea
Charlestown
Boston
Cambridge
Newton
Brookline
Dedham
Quincy
Hingham
Minot
Scituate
Norwell
Marshfield
Hanover
Pembroke
Duxbury
Plymouth
Rockland
Abington
Hanson
Brockton
E Bridgewater
Elmwood
W Bridgewater
Halifax
Middleboro
Lakeville
(Continued on Cape Cod Map)
Onset
New Bedford
North Dartmouth
Fall River
Somerset
North Dighton
Norton
Mansfield
Foxboro
Sharon
Stoughton
Randolph
North Randolph
Westwood
Norwood
Dover
Needham
Wellesley
Wellesley Hills
Natick
Framingham
Ashland
Sherborne
Hopkinton
Holliston
Millis
Medway
Norfolk
Franklin
Wrentham
Plainville
North Attleboro
Milford
South Bellingham
Upton
Grafton
N Grafton
Westborough
Northborough
Marlboro
South borough
Hudson
Sudbury
Wayland
Weston
Waltham
Watertown
Belmont
Lincoln
Maynard
Concord
Acton
Lexington
Winchester
Woburn
Billerica
Chelmsford
Lowell
Dracut
Westford
Littleton
Groton
Pepperell
Townsend
Townsend Harbor
West Townsend
Ashby
Fitchburg
Gardner
Harvard
Lancaster
Sterling
Bolton
W Boylston
Boylston
Holden
Paxton
Worcester
Leicester
Auburn
Oxford
N

Acton

The Antiquarian Scientist

(978)263-5504
antiqsci@ma.ultranet.com

16th-20th C science & medicine books, fine antique scientific instruments. **Est:** 1976 **Hrs:** By appt only. **Sz:** M **Own:** Raymond V Giordano. **QC: 18 77 S1**

Brock & Co

(978)264-4757 • (978)263-2368 (fax)
mbrock@shore.net

Original works of art from the mid-19th to early 20th C. **Hrs:** By appt only. **Own:** Mark L Brock. **QC: 7 S1 S13 S9**

Encores

174 Great Rd (Rte 2A) • 01720
(978)263-1515 • (978)263-1515 (fax)

Over 400 pieces of hand-selected European country antique furnishings: furniture, oil paintings, crocks, stoneware & copper; also featuring an outstanding collection of armoires, cupboards, sideboards, tables, chairs, dressers, desks, beds & washstands. **Pr:** $25-3,500 **Est:** 1985 **Hrs:** Mon-Sat 10-5, Sun 12:30-5. **Sz:** L **CC:** V/MC **Dir:** I-95 to Rte 2 W for 8-1/2 mi; at rotary take 2nd exit, Rte 2A/119, 1-1/2 mi on L. Rte 495 to Rte 119 E, 6.6 mi on R. **Own:** Nancy Lenicheck. **QC: 34 53 55**

Seagull Antiques

481 Great Rd • 01720
(978)263-0338

Estate treasures mostly from local homes: furniture, sterling, wicker, glass, china, militaria & accessories. **Pr:** $10-5,000 **Hrs:** Daily 10:30-4, Sun 12-5. **Sz:** M **CC:** AX/V/MC/DIS **Dir:** I-495 Exit 31: to Littleton Common, Rte 2A E, 10 min to Great Rd. Rte 128, to Rte 2W, to Rte 2A W, 15 min to Great Rd. **Own:** Al & Carole Siegal. **QC: 48 36 78 S12**

Amesbury

Deco Reflections

44 Market St • 01913
(978)388-6250

Featuring items from the 20th C including chased chrome items, Manhattan glass, small kitchen appliances, clocks, dinnerware, furniture & costume jewelry. **Hrs:** Sat-Sun 1-6 or by appt. **CC:** V/MC/DIS. **QC: 105**

Feltner Antiques

72 Haverhill Rd • 01913
(978)388-1935 • (978)388-1836 (fax)
royel@amesbury.net
www.ellroyal.com

Wholesale antiques & accessories from Early American through Art Deco. **Est:** 1976 **Hrs:** By chance/appointment. **Sz:** M **Assn:** ANS **Own:** Royal Feltner. **QC: 58 1 34 S12**

Amherst

Amherst Antiquarian Maps

McClellan St • 01004
(413)256-8900 • (413)256-6291 (fax)

Old, rare, original maps, charts & prints from the 16th through 19th C. Also publisher of Antique Map Price Record & Handbook. **Pr:** $25-3,000+ **Est:** 1978 **Hrs:** By chance/appt. **CC:** V/MC **Assn:** MARIAB **Dir:** Call for directions. **Own:** Jon Kimmel Rosenthal. **QC: 66 74 S9**

Amherst Antique Center [G70+]

308 College St (Rte 9) • 01002
(413)253-1995

Hrs: Daily 10-5.

J Austin Jeweler

31 S Pleasant St • 01002
(413)253-3986 • (413)549-0980 (fax)

Antique, estate & one-of-a-kind new jewelry & some antique furniture & accessories.

Pr: $50-5,000 **Est:** 1978 **Hrs:** Mon & Wed-Fri 10-5, closed Aug. **Sz:** M **CC:** AX/V/MC/DIS **Assn:** GIA **Dir:** On the Amherst Common betw Amherst College & U of Mass. **Own:** Joyce Austin. **QC: 5 6 64 S12 S16**

Captain's Quarters
6 Wildwood Ln • 01002
(413)549-6860

Ship models, navigational instruments, marine paintings & scientific instruments. **Hrs:** By appt only. **Assn:** VADA MADA **Dir:** 1 mi from town ctr. **Own:** Justin Cobb. **QC: 70**

Grist Mill Antiques
26 Mill Ln • 01002
(413)253-5296

In a 250-year-old grist mill, an eclectic collection of glass, ephemera, postcards, political memorabilia, kitchenware & fountain pens. **Pr:** $2-100 **Est:** 1984 **Hrs:** Thu-Sat 10-5, Sun 12-5, or by chance/appt. **Sz:** M **Assn:** PVADA **Dir:** Rte 116, 1 mi S of Amherst Commons & Amherst College. **Own:** Hill & Ronnie Boss. **QC: 39 61 67**

Andover

Andover Books & Prints
68 Park St • 01810
(978)475-1645 • (978)475-5154 (fax)
andbks@aol.com

Books, maps, prints & ephemera. **Est:** 1978 **Hrs:** Tue-Sat 11-5. **CC:** V/MC **Assn:** MARIAB ABBA **Own:** V David Rodger. **QC: 18 66 39 S1**

New England Gallery Inc
350 N Main St • 01810
(978)475-2116

Fine 18th C American furniture & accessories & 19th & 20th C paintings. **Est:** 1969 **Hrs:** Tue-Sat 9-4 appt suggested. **Dir:** I-495 Exit 41A. **Own:** Stuart Miller. **QC: 1 52 7 S1**

Arlington

Paul Klaver
5 Viking Ct #43 • 02174
(781)648-3910

Specializing in firefighting Americana & collectibles exclusively. **Pr:** $25-2,500 **Est:** 1987 **Hrs:** By appt only. **Assn:** SPNEA NEAA MAFAA. **QC: 32 67**

Lion's Head Antiques
1339 Massachusetts Ave • 02174
(781)641-9936

A general line of antiques & collectibles including paintings, prints, furniture, silver & china. **Est:** 1990 **Hrs:** Mon-Sat 11-5, Sun 1-4. Call ahead in Sum. **CC:** V/MC **Own:** Elinor McDonough. **QC: 48 7 78**

Second Tyme Around [G4]
1193A Massachusetts Ave • 02174
(781)646-5789

Small friendly group shop with a wide variety of antiques. **Est:** 1982 **Hrs:** Mon-Sat 10-5, closed Wed & Sun. **Sz:** S **CC:** V/MC **Dir:** Rte 128 Exit 29A: E on Rte 2 to Park Ave, Arlington Heights, R at Mass Ave lights, 1/4 mi on L across from St James Church. **Own:** Eleanor & Donald Chalmers.

The Way We Were Antiques
1267 Massachusetts Ave • 02174
(781)648-7016

Specializing in antique & costume jewelry; also, furniture, china, glass, quilts & collectibles. **Hrs:** Tue-Sat 11-4, Jul-Aug Tue by chance.

Ashby

Martha Perkins
(978)386-2235

Early American accessories, country smalls, early china, glass, quilts & textiles. **Hrs:** By appt only. **Assn:** NHADA. **QC: 34 61 80**

Ashland

Crawford's Yesteryear Farm

111 High St • 01721
(508)881-1589

Country & Victorian furniture, accessories, decorator items, china, silver plate, textiles & clothing all displayed in an attractive old barn setting. **Hrs:** By chance/appt, call ahead advised. **Assn:** SADA **Dir:** Off Rte 135 & Cordiville Rd; follow bird house signs. **Own:** Mavis Crawford. **QC: 102**

Ashley Falls

Don Abarbanel

E Main St (at Lewis & Wilson) • 01222
(413)229-3330

Formal furniture of the 17th, 18th & 19th C, as well as needlework, brass & metalwork, English pottery, English & Dutch delft & Chinese export porcelain. **Hrs:** Daily 10-5, call ahead in Win. **Assn:** BCADA **Dir:** Just off Rte 7A at Lewis & Wilson. **QC: 82 20 23**

Ashley Falls Antiques

Rte 7A • 01222
(413)229-8759

Extensive collection of authentic early American furniture, furnishings & carefully selected antique jewelry & old buttons, located in a picturesque brick building facing the village park in the historic (pre-Revolutionary) district of Ashley Falls. **Pr:** $2-20,000 **Est:** 1957 **Hrs:** Daily 9:30-5:30. **Sz:** M **Assn:** BCADA **Dir:** 4 mi S of Sheffield MA on Rte 7A, 1 mi N of CT border. **Own:** Jeanne, Bob & Dan Cherneff. **QC: 21 52 64**

Circa

Rte 7A • 01222
(413)229-2990

Important collections of majolica & Canton, sophisticated oddments, 18th & 19th C furniture & accessories. **Hrs:** Daily 9:30-5:30. **Assn:** BCADA **Dir:** At the int of Rte 7A & E Main St. **Own:** Frank Gabor & Jim Lawrence. **QC: 23 25 53**

Lewis & Wilson

E Main St • 01222
(413)229-3330

American, English & Continental 18th & 19th C furniture, appropriate accessories & Oriental porcelain. **Hrs:** Most days 10-5, call ahead in Win. **Assn:** BCADA **Dir:** Renovated train station, green with yellow trim, just off Rte 7A. **Own:** Don Lewis & Tom Wilson. **QC: 54 7 24**

The Vollmers

Rte 7A • 01222
(413)229-3463 • (413)229-2919 (fax)

18th & 19th C formal & country furniture & accessories, wine-related antiques, firearms, paintings & period accessories. **Est:** 1959 **Hrs:** Sat-Sun 10-5, Mon-Fri by chance/appt. **Sz:** L **CC:** AX/V/MC/DIS **Assn:** BCADA **Dir:** Just N of the CT border. **Own:** Diana B & Henry Vollmer III. **QC: 52 4 7**

Assonet

Winter Hill Antiques

46 Richmond Rd (Rte 79) • 02702
(508)644-5456
winterhill@mediaone.net

Specializing in original finish & painted pine, oak & walnut country furniture & cupboards, multi-drawer & cubbyhole cabinets, primitives, country store advertising, ephemera, collectibles & oddities all displayed on two floors of a heated barn. **Est:** 1988 **Hrs:** Mon-Fri 12-5, Sat-Sun 11-6. **Sz:** L **Dir:** Rte 24 Exit 9: 1-1/2 mi NE of Assonet

Village 4 Corners on Rte 79. **Own:** Bob & Elaine Dorsey. **QC: 34 102 106 S8 S12**

Bellingham

Oak N' Stuff Antiques

14 Stone St • 02019
(508)966-1331

Specializing in turn-of-the-century oak furniture, Phoenix Bird/Flying Turkey china with a general line of antiques. **Pr:** $5-2,000 **Est:** 1988 **Hrs:** Sat-Sun 10-5 call ahead advised or by chance/appt. **Sz:** M **Dir:** Off Rte 126 N on Medway line, 2 mi E of Rte 495 Exit 18. **Own:** Norm & Peg Swicker. **QC: 50 23 24**

Belmont

Cross & Griffin

468 Trapelo Rd • 02178
(617)484-2837

Antiques & collectibles. **Est:** 1961 **Hrs:** Wed-Sat 11-5, Sat til 4. **Dir:** Rte 128 Trapelo Rd Exit: toward Belmont, 4 mi at Waverly Sq, across from Congregational Church.

Berlin

Counting Sheep Antiques

79 Central St • 01503
(978)838-2922 • (978)838-2862 (fax)
kindredfk@aol.com

Specializing in country antiques including farm-related items, primitives & folk art. **Est:** 1999 **Hrs:** Mon-Sat 10-5, Sun 12-5. **CC:** V/MC **Dir:** Rte 495 Exit 26: follow Rte 62W. Shop 1 mi past Berlin Orchard Store. **Own:** Sally Melanson. **QC: 41 34 1**

Bernardston

Bernardston Books

219 South St (Rte 5) • 01337
(413)648-9864
bernbooks@crocker.com

Out-of-print books: history, biography, anthropology, military, natural history, Black history, fiction classics, theology & religion, philosophy of history, linguistics, sociology, art & music, poetry & literary criticism. **Pr:** $5-500 **Est:** 1986 **Hrs:** Daily 9-5 but a call ahead advised. **Sz:** L **CC:** AX/V/MC **Assn:** MARIAB **Dir:** I-91 Exit 28: Rte 10 S or I-91 Exit 27: Rte 5 N. **Own:** A Fullerton. **QC: 18 S9**

Beverly

Blair House Antiques

1 Front St • 01915
(978)921-4766

Two floors of bronze & marble sculpture, Chinese porcelain, lamps, mirrors, crystal, European & American furniture in the oldest business building in America built 1701 by Captain John Briscoe **Pr:** $25-5,000 **Hrs:** Fri-Mon 10-5. **Dir:** Rte 128 to Rte 1A: just before the Salem-Beverly bridge across from boat marina. **Own:** Louis Mangifesti. **QC: 68 71 11 S1**

PMG Antiques & Appraisals

3 Ober St • 01915
(978)927-2979

Buying, selling & providing appraisal, research & consultation to collectors, dealers & others wishing to obtain relevant recent information on decorative & fine arts, specializing in the export trade. **Hrs:** By appt only. **Assn:** AAM ISA SPNEA **Own:** Patricia Grove. **QC: 25 71 S1**

Price House Antiques
137 Cabot St • 01915
(978)927-5595

A large stock of oak, wicker, mahogany furniture, decorative accessories & collectibles. **Pr:** $5-5,000 **Est:** 1976 **Hrs:** Tue-Sat 10-5, Sun-Mon by chance/appt. **CC:** V/MC **Dir:** Rte 128 to Rte 62E 2 mi. Take R onto Cabot St, 1/2 mi on L. **QC: 48 91 S6 S1 S16**

Boston

Akin Lighting Company
28 Charles St • 02114
(617)523-1331

19th & 20th C lighting, antiques & decorative accessories. **Est:** 1991 **Hrs:** Tue-Sat 11-6. **Sz:** S **CC:** V/MC/AX **Dir:** Betw Beacon & Chestnut in the 1st blk of Charles St. **Own:** Akin Kolawole. **QC: 65**

Alberts-Langdon Inc
126 Charles St • 02114
(617)523-5954 • (617)523-7160 (fax)
albertslangdon@worldnet.att.net

Fine Far Eastern art, ceramics, paintings & furniture for the discerning collector. **Est:** 1961 **Hrs:** Mon-Fri 10-4:30, Sat 10-2 or by appt. **Sz:** M **Dir:** At the corn of Charles & Revere Sts. **Own:** Russell Alberts & Dennis Mortimer. **QC: 71 7**

Antique Revival
1 Harvard Ave • 02114
(617)787-4040

General line of antiques & collectibles. **Hrs:** Thu-Sun 10-6 other times by chance/appt. **Sz:** M **CC:** AX/V/MC/DIS **Dir:** In the Allston section of Boston.

Antiques at 80 Charles Street
80 Charles St • 02114
(617)742-8006

A shop with sterling silver, antique & estate jewelry, bronzes, pottery, porcelain, paintings, decorative accessories & furniture. **Est:** 1991 **Hrs:** Daily 10:30-6. **CC:** AX/V/MC **Dir:** 2-1/2 blks from the Public Garden. **Own:** Beverly & Robert Scholnick. **QC: 64 78**

Antiques at 99 Charles Street
99 Charles St • 02114
(617)367-8088

Continental & American furniture & elegant accessories. **Pr:** $25-2,000 **Hrs:** Mon-Sat 11-6, Sun 12-5. **Sz:** S **CC:** V/MC/AX **Dir:** Betw Pinckney & Revere Sts. **Own:** Carol Reed & R Michael Riendeau. **QC: 36 53**

Architectural Antiques
152 Warren Ave • 02116
(617)578-0095
archant@aol.com
www.archant.com

Garden pieces, architectural elements & decorative pieces of historic interest as well as aesthetic appeal. **Pr:** $300-10,000 **Hrs:** By appt only. **Own:** John Carpenter. **QC: 3 60 36**

Ars Libri
560 Harrison Ave • 02118
(617)357-5212 • (617)338-5763 (fax)
www.arslibri.com

Dealers in rare & scholarly books on the fine arts, illustrated books from 15th-20th C; stock of art reference material includes monographs, catalogues raisonne, periodicals & documents relevant to all periods & fields of art history. **Hrs:** Mon-Fri 9-6, Sat 11-5. **CC:** V/MC/AX **Assn:** ABAA **Dir:** In the South End. **Own:** Elmar Seibel. **QC: 18 S1**

Artemis
139A Newbury St • 02116
(617)867-0900 • (617)867-9723 (fax)

18th-19th C Chinese furniture & accessories. Large & small red lacquer cabinets, chairs, tables, large selection of baskets & boxes. Hand-painted wedding cabinets, tables, chairs & artifacts. **Pr:** $220-5,000 **Est:** 1996 **Hrs:** Mon-Sat 10-6, Sun 12-5. **Sz:** M **CC:** AX/V/MC/DIS **Dir:** Betw Clarendon & Dartmouth Sts. **Own:** Michelle Courie. **QC: 71**

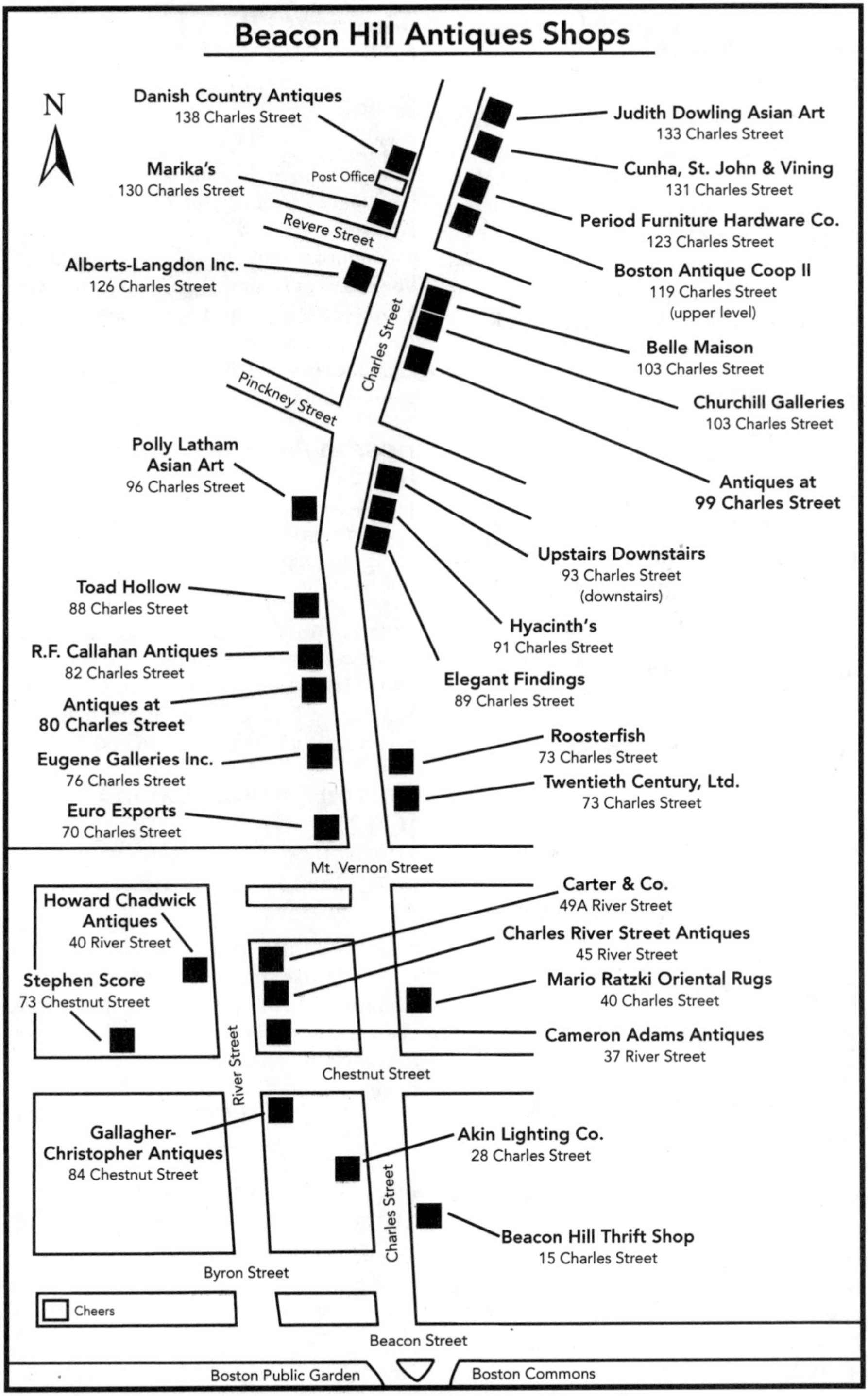
Beacon Hill Antiques Shops
N
Danish Country Antiques
138 Charles Street
Marika's
130 Charles Street
Post Office
Revere Street
Alberts-Langdon Inc.
126 Charles Street
Charles Street
Pinckney Street
Judith Dowling Asian Art
133 Charles Street
Cunha, St. John & Vining
131 Charles Street
Period Furniture Hardware Co.
123 Charles Street
Boston Antique Coop II
119 Charles Street
(upper level)
Belle Maison
103 Charles Street
Churchill Galleries
103 Charles Street
Antiques at
99 Charles Street
Polly Latham
Asian Art
96 Charles Street
Upstairs Downstairs
93 Charles Street
(downstairs)
Toad Hollow
88 Charles Street
Hyacinth's
91 Charles Street
R.F. Callahan Antiques
82 Charles Street
Elegant Findings
89 Charles Street
Antiques at
80 Charles Street
Roosterfish
73 Charles Street
Eugene Galleries Inc.
76 Charles Street
Twentieth Century, Ltd.
73 Charles Street
Euro Exports
70 Charles Street
Mt. Vernon Street
Howard Chadwick
Antiques
40 River Street
Carter & Co.
49A River Street
Charles River Street Antiques
45 River Street
Stephen Score
73 Chestnut Street
Mario Ratzki Oriental Rugs
40 Charles Street
Cameron Adams Antiques
37 River Street
River Street
Chestnut Street
Gallagher-
Christopher Antiques
84 Chestnut Street
Akin Lighting Co.
28 Charles Street
Charles Street
Beacon Hill Thrift Shop
15 Charles Street
Byron Street
Cheers
Beacon Street
Boston Public Garden
Boston Commons

Autrefois Antiques Inc

125 Newbury St • 02116
(617)424-8823 • (617)566-0113 (fax)

Antique French, English & Italian country furniture & accessories with chandeliers, lighting & Oriental porcelain. **Pr:** $300-10,000 **Est:** 1950 **Hrs:** Mon-Sat 10-5:30. **Sz:** M **CC:** AX/V/MC **Dir:** Beacon St to Clarendon (one way), go 3 blks take R on Newbury St. Shop is located on the R (Mezzanine). **Own:** Maria Francesca Rowe & Duncan Rowe. **QC: 47 53 65**

James R Bakker Antiques Inc

236 Newbury St • 02116
(617)262-8020 • (617)262-8019 (fax)

Specializing in late 19th & early 20th C American art emphasizing Boston, Provincetown & Rockport School painters. Fine arts auction & appraisal service featuring regular sales of paintings, prints & sculpture. **Hrs:** Tue-Sat 10-5 or by appt. **Sz:** M **Assn:** ADA **Dir:** Betw Exeter & Fairfield Sts. **QC: 7 74 S2 S1**

Beacon Hill Thrift Shop

15 Charles St • 02114
(617)742-2323

Antiques & collectibles from Beacon Hill & surrounding area homes including furniture, pottery, china, glass, baskets, prints & paintings. **Pr:** $1-1,000 **Est:** 1929 **Hrs:** Tue, Thu & Sat 10:30-3:30. **Sz:** S **Dir:** Betw Beacon & Chestnut Sts. **QC: 36 48**

Belle Maison

103 Charles St • 02114
(617)263-4900 • (617)263-4949 (fax)
info@belle-maison.com
www.belle-maison.com

Furnishings with a country bent emphasizing pine: American & European dining tables, chests, cupboards & coffee tables. Also painted & decorative accessories. **Hrs:** Mon-Sat 11-6, Sun 12-5. **Sz:** S **CC:** AX **Own:** Karol & Sheldon Tager. **QC: 34 47 102**

Thomas G Boss Fine Books

355 Boylston St 2nd floor • 02116
(617)421-1880 • (617)536-7072 (fax)
boss@tiac.net
www.tiac.net/users/boss

Rare & collectible books, fine bindings & bookplates. Specializing in the 1890s, Art Nouveau, Arts & Crafts, illustrated books, press books, imprints, posters, Art Deco, books about books. **Pr:** $25-50,000 **Hrs:** Mon-Sat 9-5. **Sz:** 15,000 books **CC:** AX/V/MC **Assn:** ABAA MARIAB **Dir:** Near the corn of Arlington & Boylston, next to the Arlington St Church. **QC: 18 S1**

Boston Antique Coop I [G14]

119 Charles St (lower level) • 02114
(617)227-9810
jolly26@earthlink.net

Silver, architectural & garden accessories, artifacts, arms & armor, textiles & costumes. Also jewelry, porcelain, bronze & clocks. **Est:** 1981 **Hrs:** Mon-Sat 10-6, Sun 12-6. **CC:** V/MC **Dir:** Near corn of Charles & Revere Sts across from the PO. **QC: 63 60 78**

Boston Antique Coop II [G12]

119 Charles St (Upper Level) • 02114
(617)227-9811
jolly26@earthlink.net

Showing a fine selection of antique estate merchandise from the 16th-20th C. Emphasis on 18th C Continental furniture, early textiles, American & English silver, Arts & Crafts, porcelain, books, arms, armor & objets d'art. **Est:** 1981 **Hrs:** Mon-Sat 10-5, Sun 12-5. **Sz:** M **CC:** V/MC/DIS **Own:** Lolly Chase. **QC: 18 53 78**

Brattle Book Shop

9 West St • 02111
(617)542-0210 • (617)338-1467 (fax)
(800)447-9595
brattle@tiac.net
www.brattlebookshop.com

One of Boston's oldest & largest antiquarian

bookstores housed in a three-stories: books, magazines, books on antiques, maps, prints, postcards & ephemeral items in all subjects. **Pr:** $1-25,000 **Hrs:** Mon-Sat 9-5:30. **CC:** AX/V/MC **Assn:** ABAA MARIAB **Dir:** Betw Washington & Tremont Sts downtown, 1 blk from Macy's off the Boston Common. **Own:** Kenneth Gloss. **QC: 18 S1**

Brodney Inc

145 Newbury St • 02116
(617)536-0500 • (617)536-1643 (fax)
brodneyinc@aol.com

A collection of rare antiques, jewelry, silver, collectibles, estate jewelry, European & American antiques, Oriental art, bronzes, sculptures & museum quality paintings. A shop for both the serious collector & curious shoppers. **Est:** 1939 **Hrs:** Mon-Sat 10-6, Sun 12-5. **Sz:** L **CC:** AX/V/MC **Assn:** AADLA **Dir:** Corn of Dartmouth & Newbury Sts. **Own:** Richard & Rina Brodney. **QC: 36 64 78 S1 S7 S12**

Bromer Booksellers Inc

607 Boylston St 2nd fl • 02116
(617)247-2818 • (617)247-2975 (fax)
book@bromer.com
www.bromer.com

Antiquarian books specializing in rare books of all periods, featuring literary first editions, private press & illustrated books, fine bindings, children's & miniature books. **Est:** 1975 **Hrs:** Mon-Fri 9:30-5:30. **CC:** AX/V/MC **Assn:** ABAA ILAB MARIAB **Dir:** Corn of Dartmouth & Boylston Sts in ctr of Copley Sq. 2nd floor of only office bldg at that int. On the Green Line. **Own:** Anne & David Bromer. **QC: 18**

Brookline Village Antiques Inc

One Design Center Place, Ste 325 • 02110
(617)542-2853

A diverse collection of American & European antique furniture, paintings, prints, leather books, chandeliers & accessories. **Hrs:** Mon-Fri 9-5 to the trade only. **Sz:** M **Dir:** From South Station: 1 mi S to Boston Design Center in Marine Industrial Park, on L. **Own:** Anne Hough. **QC: 52 53 65 S15**

Buddenbrooks

31 Newbury St • 02116
(617)536-4433 • (617)267-1118 (fax)
buddenbrooks@worldnet.att.net
www.bibliocity.com/home/budden

Specialties include rare books & manuscripts, early printing & incunabula, literature of all ages, travel, voyages & exploration, sciences, humanities & philosophy, illustrated & children's books & first editions. **Hrs:** Mon-Fri 9-5 & by appt. **Sz:** M **CC:** AX/V/MC/DIS **Assn:** ABAA MARIAB **Dir:** Betw Arlington & Berkeley, 4 doors down from the Ritz-Carlton Hotel. Shop is located on the 2nd floor. **Own:** Martin R Weinkle. **QC: 18 S1 S3 S16**

Bunker Hill Relics

207 Main St / Charlestown • 02129
(617)241-9534

Eclectic inventory of highly selective, unusual & hard to find decorative as well as functional quality antiques including art glass, porcelains, silverware, jewelry, clocks, music boxes, bronzes, furniture & Oriental artifacts. **Est:** 1980 **Hrs:** Mon-Fri 11-5:30, Sat 9:30-5:30 or by appt. **CC:** AX/V/MC **Dir:** In Charlestown; see map & call for directions. Also easily reached by public transportation. **Own:** Thelma Shapiro. **QC: 100 26 68 S12**

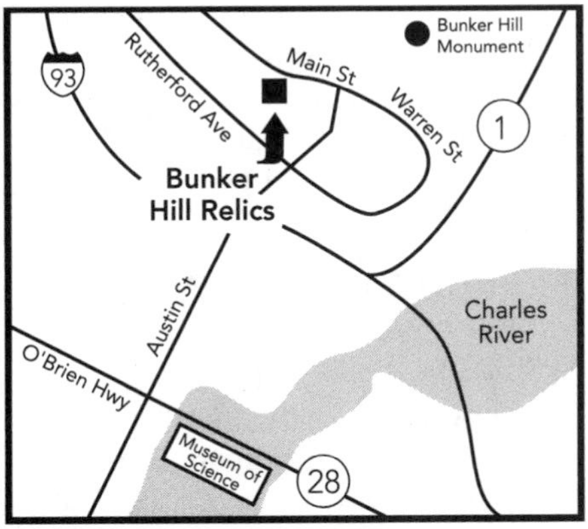

R F Callahan Antiques Arboretum [G9]

82 Charles St • 02114
(617)742-3303

Furniture, architectural pieces, fine china, glass, decorative accessories, collectibles, lighting, artwork as well as the rare & unusual from period to vintage. **Pr:** $30-5,000 **Est:** 1995 **Hrs:** Daily 10-6. **Sz:** M **CC:** V/MC **Own:** Bob Callahan. **QC: 7 48 60**

Camden Companies

211 Berkeley St • 02116
(617)421-9899

American & European antiques, custom furnishings, antique prints & accessories. **Est:** 1989 **Hrs:** Mon-Sat 10-5. **Dir:** 1 blk E of Copley Sq. **Own:** Paul Noel & Marilyn Conviser. **QC: 36 48 78**

Cameron Adams Antiques

37 River St • 02108
(617)725-1833

Fine French, English & American furniture, lighting, mirrors & fireplace equipment. **Pr:** $300-8,000 **Est:** 1992 **Hrs:** Mon-Sat 11-5. **Sz:** S **CC:** AX/V/MC **Dir:** Beacon Hill. **Own:** Stephen Sweenie & Donald Adamian. **QC: 65 68 40 S15**

Carter & Co

49A River St • 02108
(617)227-5343

Elegant English & Continental antiques. Choice selection includes period 18th C painted, giltwood & fine furniture along with decorative accessories, lamps, mirrors & sconces. **Pr:** $100-10,000 **Hrs:** Mon-Sat 10-6. **Sz:** S **Own:** Michael R Carter. **QC: 53 54 36 S15**

Howard Chadwick Antiques

40 River St • 02108
(617)227-9261

A wonderful shop on Beacon Hill filled with American & English furniture, brasses, pictures, porcelains & lamps. **Pr:** $10-10,000 **Est:** 1979 **Hrs:** Oct 15-May 15 Mon-Sat 11:30-4:30; May 15-Oct 15 Mon-Thu 11:30-4:30. Other times by chance. **Dir:** 2 short blks N of Beacon St on River St, 1/2 blk W of Charles St. **QC: 27 31 50 S9**

Charles River Street Antiques

45 River St • 02108
(617)367-3244

Tucked away on the flat of Beacon Hill, hidden treasures from the 18th & 19th C including furniture, lighting, architectural & garden antiques, paintings & decorative accessories. **Est:** 1990 **Hrs:** Mon-Sat 11-5:30. **Sz:** M **CC:** V/MC **Dir:** 1 blk W of Charles St & 1-1/2 blks N of Beacon St. **Own:** Madeline Gens. **QC: 3 60 36**

Childs Gallery Ltd

169 Newbury St • 02116
(617)266-1108 • (617)266-2381 (fax)

16th-early 20th C American & European prints, drawings, watercolors, paintings & sculpture. **Pr:** $100-1,000,000 **Est:** 1937 **Hrs:** Tue-Fri 9-6, Sat & Mon 10-5. **Sz:** M **CC:** AX/V/MC **Assn:** ABAA AC **Dir:** Betw Dartmouth & Exeter Sts. **Own:** D Roger Howlett. **QC: 7 74 41 S16**

Churchill Galleries

103 Charles St • 02114
(617)722-9490

Fine period furniture with a mix of highly decorative inventory. Good selection of mirrors, sconces, table lamps & chandeliers. Inventory provides an excellent source for the collector, casual shopper & designer. **Pr:** $200-15,000 **Est:** 1983 **Hrs:** Daily 11-6. **Sz:** M **CC:** V/MC **Own:** B Douglas Spain. **QC: 54 36 65**

> Use the Specialty QuickCode indexes at the back of the book to find dealers who specialize in your area of interest.

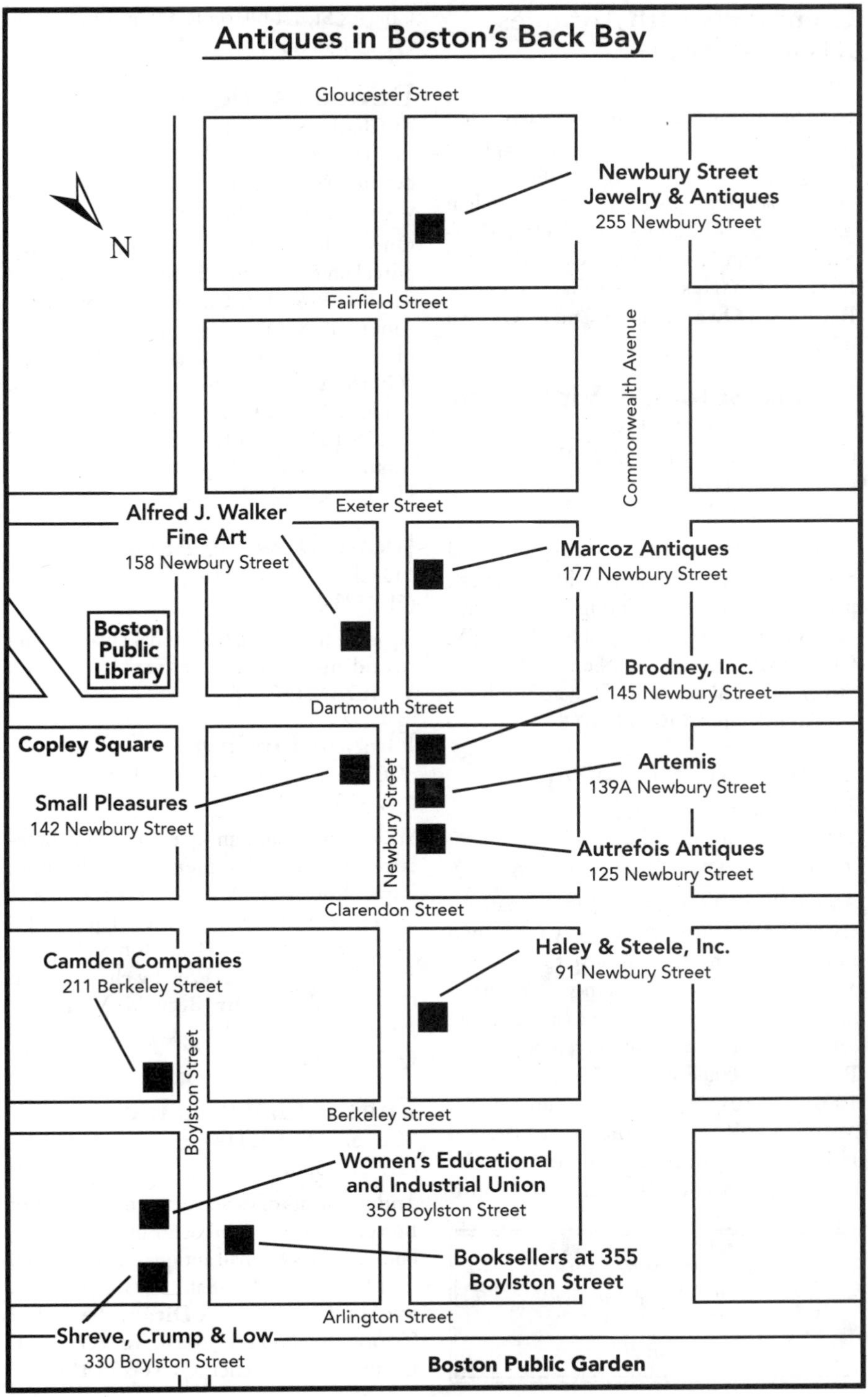
Antiques in Boston's Back Bay
Gloucester Street
N
Newbury Street Jewelry & Antiques
255 Newbury Street
Fairfield Street
Commonwealth Avenue
Exeter Street
Alfred J. Walker Fine Art
158 Newbury Street
Marcoz Antiques
177 Newbury Street
Boston Public Library
Brodney, Inc.
145 Newbury Street
Dartmouth Street
Copley Square
Small Pleasures
142 Newbury Street
Newbury Street
Artemis
139A Newbury Street
Autrefois Antiques
125 Newbury Street
Clarendon Street
Camden Companies
211 Berkeley Street
Haley & Steele, Inc.
91 Newbury Street
Boylston Street
Berkeley Street
Women's Educational and Industrial Union
356 Boylston Street
Booksellers at 355 Boylston Street
Arlington Street
Shreve, Crump & Low
330 Boylston Street
Boston Public Garden

Commonwealth Antiques

121 Charles St • 02114
(617)720-1605

Shop brimming with decorative accessories: furniture, mirrors, textiles, sconces, tole, faience, garden accessories, majolica, chandeliers, paintings, porcelain, silver & Italian glass. **Pr:** $15-3,500 **Est:** 1991 **Hrs:** Mon-Sat 10-6, Sun 12-6. **Sz:** S **CC:** V/MC/DIS **Dir:** On Charles St betw Cambridge & Revere Sts. **Own:** Jennifer Currie. **QC: 36 65 80**

Cunha, St John & Vining Ltd

131 Charles St • 02114
(617)720-7808 • (617)742-2603 (fax)
westjohn@aol.com
www.cunhastjohn.com

18th & 19th English, American, Continental & Anglo-Colonial furniture, Chinese export, period glass, lighting, paintings & decorative accessories. **Hrs:** Mon-Sat 11-5:30. **Sz:** M **CC:** V/MC **Dir:** At the N end of Charles Street. **Own:** Alan Cunha, Wayne St John & Christine Vining. **QC: 54 107 104**

Danish Country Antique Furniture

138 Charles St • 02114
(617)227-1804 • (617)227-4889 (fax)

Antique Danish & northern European country pine furniture, fine quality Chapman brass lamps, antique Chinese furniture & accessories & a scattering of painted Scandinavian pieces as well as a very large selection of Royal Copenhagen porcelain. **Pr:** $100-12,000 **Est:** 1984 **Hrs:** Mon-Wed 10-6, Thu 10-7, Fri-Sat 10-5, Sun 1-5. **Sz:** M **CC:** V/MC **Dir:** At the foot of Beacon Hill, 1 blk from Charles Circle. Govt Ctr exit from Storrow Dr, then turn R onto Charles St, 1st blk on R. **Own:** Jim Kilroy. **QC: 34 55 60**

Devonia Antiques for Dining

43 Charles St • 02114
(617)523-8313
devonia@erols.com
www.devonia-antiques.com

One of the largest collections of antique porcelain & glass for dining. Specializing in English, French & Continental porcelains, American & French stemware & centerpieces, table top services from America's "Gilded Age" & Spode decorative patterns. **Pr:** $5-20,000 **Est:** 1991 **Hrs:** Mon-Tue & Thu-Sat 11-5, Sun 12-5. **Sz:** M **CC:** V/MC **Assn:** ASA **Dir:** Upstairs. **Own:** Lori Hedtler. **QC: 23 22 104 S1**

Judith Dowling Asian Art

133 Charles St • 02114
(617)523-5211

Japanese fine arts in traditional Japanese surroundings. **Hrs:** Tue-Sat 10-5. **CC:** V/MC/AX. **QC: 36 71**

Elegant Findings

89 Charles St • 02114
(617)973-4844

Specializing in fine antique European porcelains including Meissen, KPM, Vienna, Paris, Worcester, Derby, Sevres & Limoges as well as furniture, linen, crystal, paintings, clocks & accessories. **Hrs:** Mon & Thu-Sat 11-5, Sun 12-5, Tue-Wed by chance/appt. **CC:** AX/V/MC **Dir:** Betw Mt Vernon & Pinckney Sts, upper level. **Own:** Janice Ross. **QC: 36 53 23**

Eugene Galleries Inc

76 Charles St • 02114
(617)227-3062

Antique prints of various categories; maps of Boston, New England & around the world; books, frames & small antiques. **Pr:** $1-5,000 **Est:** 1954 **Hrs:** Mon-Sat 11-5:30, Sun 12-5. **Sz:** M **CC:** V/MC/AX **Dir:** At the foot of historic Beacon Hill close to Mt Vernon St. **Own:** Barbara Fischer. **QC: 66 74 18 S13**

Euro Exports
70 Charles St • 02114
(617)720-7886 • (617)720-7883 (fax)

Fine 18th & 19th C European antiques, specializing in period Biedermeier & neoclassical furnishings & accessories. **Pr:** $500-10,000 **Est:** 1994 **Hrs:** Mon-Sat 10-6. **CC:** V/MC **Dir:** Crn Charles & Mt Vernon Sts in the Charles Street Meeting House. **Own:** Annette Wilson & Victor Bashensky. **QC: 36 53 11 S1 S8 S12**

Firestone & Parson
8 Newbury St • 02116
(617)266-1858

One of Boston's finest shops with period jewelry from the Victorian era to the present; antique English silver, early American silver & Old Sheffield plate. **Pr:** $500-100,000 **Est:** 1946 **Hrs:** Oct-May Mon-Sat 9:30-5, Jun-Sep Mon-Fri 9:30-5. **CC:** AX/V/MC **Assn:** NAADAA **Own:** Edwin & David Firestone. **QC: 64 78**

Gallagher-Christopher Antiques
84 Chestnut St • 02108
(617)523-1992

A carefully chosen selection of European, English & American antiques, 18th-20th C. Specializing in decorative & period lighting & decorative accessories including mirrors, paintings & prints. **Pr:** $100-25,000 **Est:** 1986 **Hrs:** Mon-Sat 11-6, Sun 12-5; Jun-Sep Sun by chance/appt. **Sz:** M **CC:** V/MC **Dir:** Corn of Chestnut & River Sts 1 blk from Public Garden & visible from Charles St. **Own:** Tim Gallagher & Christopher Mizeski. **QC: 53 54 65 S9**

Haley & Steele Inc
91 Newbury St • 02116
(617)536-6339 • (617)536-2298 (fax)
julien@haleysteele.com
www.haleysteele.com

Antique prints & paintings specializing in European & American prints of the 18th & 19th C including maritime, botanical, Audubon & historical. **Pr:** $1,000-10,000 **Est:** 1899 **Hrs:** Sep 2-Jun 30 Mon-Fri 10-6, Sat 10-5; Jul 1-Sep 1 Mon-Fri 9-5, Sat 10-5. **Sz:** L **CC:** AX/V/MC/DIS **Dir:** Betw Berkeley & Clarendon Sts in the Back Bay. **Own:** Julien S Tavener. **QC: 74 9 66 S13 S16**

Hilary House
86 Chestnut St • 02114
(617)523-7118

Antique furniture & decorative accessories from all over the world. **Hrs:** Mon-Fri 9:30-5. **QC: S15**

Hyacinths Antiques
91 Charles St • 02114
(617)367-0917

Lovely shop with a European flavor. 18th, 19th & 20th C furniture & decorative accessories. Wonderful selection of Canton, majolica, papier mache, tole & vintage linens. **Hrs:** Mon-Sat 11-6, Sun 12-5. **CC:** V/MC/DIS **Own:** Carol Sullivan. **QC: 53 36 80**

JMW Gallery
144 Lincoln St • 02111
(617)338-9097 • (617)338-7636 (fax)
www.jmwgallery.com

Specializing in the Arts & Crafts movement, with Mission furniture including Stickley, Limbert, Lifetime; American art pottery including Grueby, Marblehead, Dedham, art tiles & studio potters. Color wood cuts, lamps in a dramatic gallery setting. **Pr:** $100-10,000 **Est:** 1991 **Hrs:** Tue-Fri 11-6, Sat 11-5. **Sz:** 1300 sq ft **CC:** V/MC/DIS **Assn:** AAPA SPNEA **Dir:** Nr South Station 1 blk off SE Expressway. **Own:** Jim Messineo & Mike Witt. **QC: 49 101 6 S1 S8**

Kay Bee Furniture Company

1122 Boylston St • 02215
(617)266-4487

Used furniture, Oriental rugs, clocks, bronzes, paintings, china, glass & prints. **Hrs:** Mon-Sat 9-5:30, Sat til 5. **Dir:** Betw the Fenway & Massachusetts Ave. **Own:** Leonard Kadish. **QC: 48 S12**

Lame Duck Books

355 Boylston St (Second Floor) • 02116
(617)421-1880 • (617)536-7072 (fax)
lameduckbk@aol.com

American, Latin American & European literary first editions as well as primary sources in modern intellectual history. **Hrs:** Mon-Sat 9-5. **CC:** V/MC/DIS **Dir:** Near the corn of Arlington & Boylston Sts, next to the Arlington St Church. **QC: 18**

Polly Latham Asian Art

96 Charles St • 02114
(617)723-7009 • (617)723-7188 (fax)

For the serious collector, a superb collection of 17th, 18th & 19th C Chinese & Japanese porcelain & decorative arts as well as Chinese antique furniture. **Pr:** $50-20,000 **Hrs:** Mon-Sat 11-5:30. **Sz:** S **CC:** V/MC. **QC: 24 71 7**

Light Power

59A Wareham St • 02118
(617)423-9790
www.genuineantiquelighting.com

Specializing in Renaissance, Gothic revival, Victorian, inverted domes, sconces & Eastlake lighting fixtures. **Pr:** $100-3,500 **Est:** 1982 **Hrs:** Sat 10-5, Tue-Fri 8-4 by appt only. **CC:** V/MC/DIS **Dir:** In the South End. **Own:** Tom Powers. **QC: 65 S9 S16**

London Lace

215 Newbury St • 02116
(617)267-3506 • (617)267-0770 (fax)
(800)926-LACE
www.londonlace.com

The finest quality antique & reproduction laces & linens. Antique items for the home as well as antique & new furniture. Catalog available on our extensive collection of laces dating 1840-1920. **Pr:** $25-500 **Est:** 1982 **Hrs:** Mon-Thu 11-7, Fri-Sat 10-6, Sun 1-5 (Nov-Dec only). **Sz:** M **CC:** AX/V/MC **Dir:** Copley Pl subway stop in the heard of Boston's Back Bay. **Own:** Diane Jones. **QC: 81**

Marcoz Antiques & Jewelry

177 Newbury St • 02116
(617)262-0780 • (617)262-3780 (fax)
marcoz@tiac.net

Fine selection of formal English & French furniture & decorative accessories. **Est:** 1972 **Hrs:** Mon-Sat 10-6. **Sz:** M **CC:** AX/V/MC/DIS **Dir:** Betw Dartmouth & Exeter Sts. **Own:** Marc Glasberg. **QC: 36 54 47**

Marika's Antiques

130 Charles St • 02114
(617)523-4520

A broad selection of jewelry, silver, porcelain & paintings including European, Oriental & American antiques with an emphasis on wholesale trade. **Est:** 1945 **Hrs:** Tue-Sat 10-5 or by appt. **Sz:** M **CC:** AX/V/MC **Dir:** Corn of Charles & Revere Sts 1 blk from Charles MBTA. **Own:** Mathew Raisz. **QC: 7 64 78**

Mohr & McPherson

81 Arlington St • 02116
(617)3381288
www.mohr-mcpherson.com

Asian antiques. **Hrs:** Daily. **Own:** Kevin McPherson.

Native Genius Gallery

1 Lyndboro Pl • 02116
(617)350-0444 • (617)350—6744 (fax)
aglerraycarterjack@msn.com

18th-20th C American & European paintings with a specialty in American portraits. **Hrs:** By appt only. **Own:** Raymond Agler. **QC: 7 12 S9**

Newbury Street Jewelry & Antiques

255 Newbury St • 02116
(617)236-0038

Antique jewelry, silverware, ceramics, china, porcelain, modern American painting, sculpture, 19th C American art, Latin American & Oriental art, Persian rugs, precious metals & watches. **Est:** 1986 **Hrs:** Tue-Sat 10-5. **CC:** V/MC **Assn:** NEAA **Dir:** Betw Fairfield & Gloucester Sts. **Own:** Doris Nichols. **QC: 7 64 78**

The Nostalgia Factory

51 N Margin St • 02115
(617)236-8754 • (617)720-5587 (fax)
(800)479-8754
posters@nostalgia.com
www.nostalgia.com

Original posters: travel, war, 60s music & psychedelic; over 50,000 movie posters — vintage to current. **Pr:** $5-1,000 **Est:** 1970 **Hrs:** Mon-Sat 10-5. **Sz:** L **CC:** AX/V/MC **Dir:** I-93 N Station Exit: R off ramp, R onto N Washington St, 1st L at Thatcher. **Own:** Rudy & Barbara Franchi. **QC: 39 67**

David O'Neal Antiquarian Booksellers

234 Clarendon St • 02116
(617)266-5790 • (617)266-1089 (fax)
onealbks@tiac.net
www.onealbooks.com

Rare American & European books. **Hrs:** By appt only. **CC:** V/MC/DIS. **QC: 18 S1**

Mario Ratzki Oriental Rugs

40 Charles St • 02114
(617)742-7850 • (617)472-8760 (fax)

Fine Orientals, flat weaves & textiles, hooked rugs, European tapestries, Aubusson, Sauonnerie carpets, quilts & occasionally furniture. **Pr:** $500-90,000 **Est:** 1984 **Hrs:** Jan 1-Dec 30 Tue-Fri 10:30-6, Sat 10-5. **Sz:** M **CC:** V/MC. **QC: 76 80 47 S1 S16**

Restoration Resources Inc

31 Thayer St • 02118
(617)542-3033 • (617)542-3034 (fax)
www.restorationresources.com

Architectural antique warehouse store featuring mantels, hardware, doors, stained glass, pedestal sinks, claw foot tubs, bath fixtures & accessories, woodwork & ornamental plaster. **Pr:** $10-10,000 **Est:** 1987 **Hrs:** Mon-Sat 10-4. **Sz:** L **CC:** V/MC **Dir:** I-93 N: E Berkeley exit. I-93 S: Albany St exit, 2nd R onto Thayer St. **Own:** William Raymer Jr. **QC: 3 S4**

Roosterfish Home Haberdashery

73 Charles St • 02114
(617)720-2877 • (617)720-2885 (fax)
rf73@aol.com

Selectively chosen & stylishly presented furniture & accessories of all ages. Whether traditional, modern or primitive each object represents great design. Accent on antique & custom lighting, antique & modern furniture, period & decorative mirrors. **Pr:** $25-25,000 **Est:** 1995 **Hrs:** Mon-Sat 10:30-5:30, Sun by chance/appt. **Sz:** M **CC:** AX/V/MC **Dir:** Betw Mt Vernon & Pinckney Sts on Boston's historic Beacon Hill. **Own:** Ty Burks & Christopher Ridolfi. **QC: 65 68 48 S15**

Stephen Score Antiques Inc

73 Chestnut St • 02108
(617)227-9192

American country furniture, paintings, folk art & singular decorative accessories. **Est:** 1978 **Hrs:** By chance/appt. **Sz:** S **Assn:** NHADA VADA **Dir:** 1-1/2 blks W of Charles St on the flat of Beacon Hill. **QC: 41 51**

Shreve Crump & Low

330 Boylston St • 02116
(617)267-9100

Large selection of fine English, American & Chinese export, 18th & early 19th C furniture, ceramics, glass, prints & paintings. **Pr:** $50-30,000 **Est:** 1865 **Hrs:** Mon-Sat 10-5:30. **Sz:** M **CC:** AX/V/MC **Dir:** I-90 Copley Sq Exit: across from the Public Garden at Boylston & Arlington Sts. **QC: 25 61 7**

Small Pleasures

142 Newbury St • 02116
(617)267-7371

A selection of antique & estate jewelry, rare & vintage watches, art pottery & contemporary pieces. **Est:** 1981 **Hrs:** Mon-Sat 11-6. **Sz:** S **CC:** AX/V/MC **Dir:** Near the corn of Dartmouth St. **Own:** Shelley Hullar. **QC: 64 5 78**

Small Pleasures

92 State St • 02109
(617)722-9932

A selection of antique & estate jewelry, fine & vintage watches, art pottery & contemporary pieces. **Hrs:** Mon-Sat 11-6. **CC:** AX/V/MC **Own:** Shelley Hullar. **QC: 64 5 78 S16**

Peter L Stern & Co Antiquarian Booksellers

355 Boylston St 2nd Fl • 01226
(617)421-1880 • (617)536-7072 (fax)
psbook@aol.com

Antiquarian books: English & American literature, mystery & detective fiction, signed & inscribed books, rare cinema material, autographs & manuscripts. **Hrs:** Mon-Sat 9-5. **CC:** V/MC/AX **Assn:** ABAA MARIAB **Dir:** Near the int of Boylston St & the Public Garden. **QC: 18**

The Shop at the Union

356 Boylston St • 02116
(617)536-5651 • (617)247-8826 (fax)

Good selection of Oriental rugs & occasional reproduction furnishings. Purchases support the Women's Educational & Industrial Union's human service programs, including support for the elderly & battered women. **Est:** 1877 **Hrs:** Mon-Sat 10-6, Thu til 7, Sun 12-5. **CC:** AX/V/MC **Dir:** 1/2 blk W of the Public Garden on Boylston St right down the street from Shreve, Crump & Lowe. **Own:** Laurie Tellis. **QC: 76 S8**

Toad Hollow [G7]

88 Charles St • 02114
(617)367-8358

A selection of 19th & 20th C porcelain, pottery, sterling & silver objects: jewelry, vintage pens & vintage ladies boudoir items. All from local estates. **Pr:** $25-1,000 **Est:** 1990 **Hrs:** Mon-Sat 10-5:30, Sun 12-5:30. **Sz:** S **CC:** V/MC/DIS **Dir:** Middle of Charles St. **Own:** Christine Young & Jackie Lister. **QC: 64 78 36 S1 S12 S9**

Towne & Country Home

99B Charles St • 02114
(617)742-9120

Antiques & accessories — casual & elegant. **Hrs:** Mon-Sat 11-6, Sun 12-6. **CC:** V/MC.

Twentieth Century Limited

73 Charles St • 02114
(617)742-1031

20th C collectibles, vintage designer costume jewelry & estate jewelry. **Pr:** $10-1,000 **Est:** 1993 **Hrs:** Mon-Sat 11-6, Sun 12-5. **CC:** V/MC **Own:** Paul Turnberg. **QC: 32 63 64**

Upstairs Downstairs Antiques
93 Charles St • 02114
(617)367-1950 • (617)254-9377 (fax)

Four charming rooms filled with antiques & decorative furnishings for your interiors & gardens. **Pr:** $5-2,000 **Est:** 1992 **Hrs:** Mon-Sat 11-6, Sun 12-6. **Sz:** M **CC:** V/MC **Dir:** At the corn of Charles & Pinckney Sts. **Own:** Rebecca Connolly & Laren Decatur. **QC: 36 48**

Vose Galleries of Boston Inc
238 Newbury St • 02116
(617)536-6176 • (617)247-8673 (fax)
voseartgal@aol.com
www.artnet.com/vose.html

Specializing in 18th, 19th & early 20th C American paintings. Over 800 paintings in stock including Hudson River school, Boston school & Impressionist works. **Est:** 1841 **Hrs:** Mon-Fri 8-5:30, Sat 9-4. **Own:** Abbot W & Robert C Vose III. **QC: 7 8 9**

Alfred J Walker Fine Art
158 Newbury St • 02116
(617)247-1319 • (617)375-5993 (fax)
ajwalker@tiac.net

Specializing in 19th & early 20th C American paintings, drawings, watercolors & sculpture. **Pr:** $125-$125,000 **Est:** 1978 **Hrs:** Tue-Sat 10-4:30 or by appt. **Dir:** Betw Dartmouth & Exeter Sts on the 2nd floor. **Own:** Alfred J Walker. **QC: 8 9 15 S1 S8 S9**

Boxborough

Boxborough Center Antiques & Etc
61 Stow Rd • 01719
(978)264-4470
kklier2138@aol.com

Country items, furniture, glass & china. **Pr:** $2-800 **Est:** 1997 **Hrs:** Tue-Sat 10-5. **Sz:** L **CC:** V/MC/DIS **Dir:** Rte 495 to Rte 111, go E. **Own:** Kathy Klier. **QC: 1 34 36 S8**

Bridgewater

Central Market
27 Central Sq • 02324
(508)697-2121

Antiques, jewelry, reproductions & used furniture on the historic Common. **Hrs:** Daily 9-5, call ahead in Sum advised. **CC:** V/MC/AX **Assn:** HAAD **Dir:** Near the int of Rtes 18 & 28 in Bridgewater, on the Historic Common. **Own:** Rennie Cullman. **QC: 48**

Fond Memories
34 Central Sq • 02324
(508)697-5622

Early Victorian through late Art Deco: furniture, pottery, quilts, glass, linens, kitchenwares, lighting, clocks, mirrors, toys, vintage clothing, books, radios & paintings. Five showcases of vintage costume & estate jewelry. **Pr:** $2-3,000 **Est:** 1990 **Hrs:** Daily 10:30-5. **CC:** V/MC/DIS **Assn:** HAAD **Dir:** Rte 24 Exit 15 E: 3 mi on Rte 104 to Bridgewater Ctr on the R of Common. I-495 Exit 5 N: 5 mi on Rte 18/28 to Ctr. **Own:** Bob & Brenda (Varros) Ferreira. **QC: 48 64 S1 S2**

Harvest Hill Antiques
450 Plymouth St • 02324
(508)697-7160

Period & country furniture & decorative accessories, specializing in pine country dining tables over 6 feet in length & cupboards. **Est:** 1972 **Hrs:** By chance/appt. **Assn:** HAAD **Dir:** 1 mi E of Bridgewater Ctr on Plymouth St (Rte 104E); look for sign & "open" flag. **Own:** Pete & Phyllis Pike. **QC: 34 55**

Hidden Treasure
50 Central Sq • 02324
(508)697-2828

Vintage clothing, linens & jewelry. **Hrs:** Mon-Sat 10-5, Thu til 8. **Assn:** HAAD **Dir:** On Bridgewater's historic Common. **QC: 80**

Old Dutch Cottage
1 Broad St • 02324
(508)697-1586

Plain & fancy antiques. **Hrs:** Mon-Fri 12-5:30, Sun 1-5. **Assn:** HAAD. **QC: 32**

Brighton

Fusco & Four, Associates
1 Murdock Terr • 02135
(617)787-2637 • (617)782-4430 (fax)
fuscofour@aol.com

Specializing in 20th C works of art, 1900-1950, with an emphasis on art deco, WPA & modernism. **Pr:** $100-20,000 **Est:** 1979 **Hrs:** By appt only. **Sz:** M **CC:** V/MC **Dir:** Call for directions. **Own:** Anthony Fusco. **QC: 5 7 74 S1 S9**

Brimfield

Sturbridge Road Antiques [G25]
Rte 20 W • 01010
(413)245-6649

Antiques, fine furniture, collectibles & lots of art glass & china. **Est:** 1990 **Hrs:** Mon & Thu 10-5:30, Fri-Sun 12-5:30. **CC:** V/MC **Dir:** 1-1/2 mi E of Brimfield Ctr, 6 mi W of Sturbridge area shops. **Own:** Candace Perigard. **QC: 32 48 61**

Brookfield

Antiques on the Common
5 River St (Rte 148) • 01506
(508)867-3603

Furniture, smalls, pottery, elegant & Depression glass. **Hrs:** Fri-Sat 10-5, Sun 12-5 or by appt. **CC:** V/MC **Dir:** Rte 148 to Brookfield Common a few short mi from Sturbridge. **Own:** Bryant Turner & Brenda Lague. **QC: 34 22 61**

The Country Fair Antiques
11 River St (Rte 148) • 01506
(508)867-3228

Country items, furniture, glass & china & interesting collectibles. **Est:** 1974 **Hrs:** Wed-Sun 10-5. **Dir:** 8 mi N on Rte 148 from Sturbridge; 8 mi N on Brookfield Rd from Brimfield. **Own:** Irene Glass. **QC: 34 48 32**

Faxon's Antique Center [G80]
175 Brookfield Rd (Rte 148) • 01566
(508)867-2515

Glassware, porcelain, pottery, jewelry, paper & fine smalls as well as 18th C, Victorian, primitive & country furniture. **Est:** 1995 **Hrs:** Mon-Sat 10-5, Sun 11:30-5. **Sz:** H **CC:** V/MC/DIS **Dir:** From Rte 20, take Rte 148 N for 3.5 mi; from Rte 9, take Rte 148 S for 4 mi. **Own:** Tom & Lori Faxon. **QC: 48 61**

Brookline

Accents on Vieux
216 Washington St • 02445
(617)277-2700 • (617)277-2900 (fax)

One large floor of fine French 19th C architectural items, iron pieces, lamps, tapestries, Aubusson pillows, bronzes & decorative accessories. **Est:** 1998 **Hrs:** Mon-Sat 10-6. **Sz:** M **Dir:** Located 1 blk from Rte 9. **Own:** Jeffrey Diamond. **QC: 36 60 62**

The Antique Co
311 Washington St • 02445
(617)738-9476

Antique jewelry & silver, paintings, 19th & 20th C fine & decorative arts, furniture. **Pr:**

$5-15,000 **Est:** 1976 **Hrs:** Mon-Sat 10-5. **Sz:** L **CC:** V/MC **Dir:** 1 blk from Rte 9. **Own:** Tania Langderman. **QC: 36 64 78**

Antiquers III

171A Harvard St • 02146
(617)738-5555 • (617)731-9069 (fax)

Specializing in the decorative arts with an extensive collection of fine quality Art Deco & Modernism in a bright, clean, uncluttered environment. **Pr:** $75-75,000 **Est:** 1972 **Hrs:** Mon-Fri 10-5, Sat 11-5. **Sz:** M **CC:** AX/V/MC **Dir:** 15 min taxi ride from downtown Boston or 4 blk walk from T Green Line at Coolidge Corner, Brookline. **Own:** Mark Feldman. **QC: 5 65 105**

Appleton Antique Lighting Inc

195 Harvard St • 02446
(617)566-5322 • (617)566-4792 (fax)
www.appletonlighting.com

A large selection of restored antique lighting in crystal, brass, silver & iron, table lamps, floor lamps, wall sconces, chandeliers, lanterns, interior & exterior lighting. Also a selection of lamp shades. Restoration services on site. **Pr:** $20-20,000 **Est:** 1978 **Hrs:** Mon-Fri 10-6, Sat 10-5. **Sz:** M **CC:** AX/V/MC **Dir:** 1 blk from Coolidge Corner. **Own:** Jane & Loukas Diemezis. **QC: 65 S16**

Autrefois Antiques Inc

130 Harvard St • 02446
(617)424-8823 • (617)566-0113 (fax)

Antique French, English & Italian country furniture & accessories with chandeliers, lighting & Oriental porcelain. **Pr:** $300-10,000 **Est:** 1950 **Hrs:** Mon-Fri 10-4, Sat 10-5. **Sz:** M **CC:** AX/V/MC **Dir:** Huntington Ave to Rte 9 (R fork at underpass), R onto Washington & R at fork to Harvard St. White house on L with 2 stone lions. **Own:** Maria Francesca Rowe & Duncan Rowe. **QC: 47 53 65**

Cypress Trading Post

144 Cypress St • 02445
(617)566-5412

Two floors of unusual items, including porcelain, ivory & bone, bronze Oriental & European art & some furniture. **Pr:** $15-9,000 **Est:** 1970 **Hrs:** Mon-Sat 10:30-2 & 3-4:30. **Sz:** M **Dir:** Corn of Rte 9 & Cypress St in a light blue house. **Own:** Richard Maccini. **QC: 11 7 71 S12**

Dreaming of Vieux

214 Washington St • 02445
(617)277-2700 • (617)277-2900 (fax)

Four floors of French 19th & 20th C formal & country bedroom furniture: enormous selection of beds, armoires, side tables, dressers, dressing tables. **Pr:** $1,800-3,800 **Est:** 1996 **Hrs:** Mon-Sat 10-6. **Sz:** L **Dir:** Located 1 blk from Rte 9. **Own:** Jeffrey Diamond. **QC: 47 53 5 S16**

Fine Arts Rug Inc

1475 Beacon St • 02446
(617)731-3733 • (617)566-3713 (fax)
artrugs@aol.com

A family business dedicated to bringing you room-size antique & singular new rugs. A truly unique selection of antique carpets: luminous Herez, textural Oushak, subtle Serapi. Always looking to purchase or consign old rugs. **Pr:** $2,500-50,000 **Est:** 1937 **Hrs:** Mon-Sat 9-5. **Sz:** L **CC:** AX/V/MC **Own:** Roy Chatalbash. **QC: 76 S1 S12 S16**

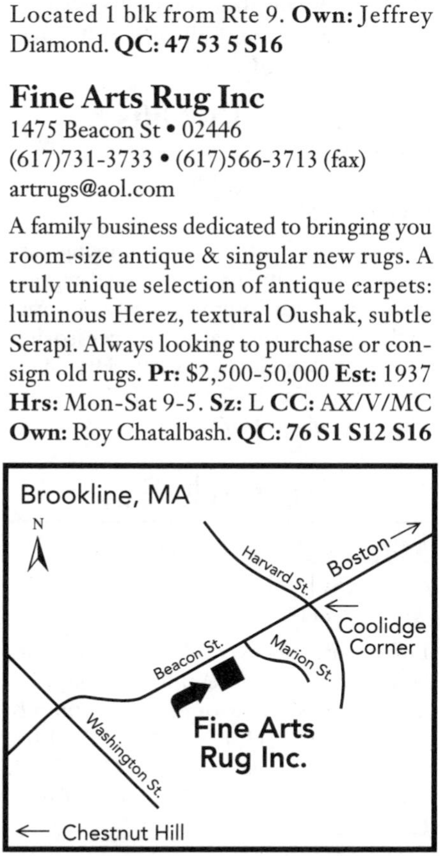

A Room with a Vieux
200 Washington St • 02445
(617)277-2700 • (617)277-2900 (fax)

Two large floors of fine French 19th C formal & country furniture & accessories: gold leaf mirrors, dining room tables, chairs, marquetry items, armoires, architectural iron pieces & decorative accessories. **Est:** 1988 **Hrs:** Mon-Sat 10-6. **Sz:** M **Dir:** 1 blk from Rte 9. **Own:** Jeffrey Diamond. **QC: 47 53 68 S9**

Towne Antiques
256 Washington St • 02146
(617)731-3326

Large selection of mahogany, cherry & walnut furniture & mirrors on two floors in the center of Brookline Village. **Pr:** $500-5,000 **Est:** 1970 **Hrs:** Mon-Sat 9-6. **Sz:** H **CC:** V/MC/DIS **Dir:** Brookline Village on the MBTA Green line, 1 blk off Rte 9. **Own:** Francis O'Boy. **QC: 48**

Vintage Jewelry, Gifts & Antiques
1382B Beacon St • 02146
(617)739-3265

Large collection of antique & contemporary jewelry, including antique diamond engagement rings. Also featuring ladies' accessories including scarves, hats, hair accessories. Antique collectibles & new gifts. **Hrs:** Mon-Sat 11-6:30, Sun 12-5. **CC:** AX/V/MC/DIS **Dir:** In Coolidge Corner. **QC: 64 83**

Buzzards Bay

Marketplace [G23]
61 Main St • 02532
(508)759-2114

Full line of antiques & collectibles including books, coins, cup plates, furniture, jewelry, military, musical instruments, paintings & more. **Est:** 1977 **Hrs:** May-Nov daily 10-5; Nov-Apr Thu-Tue 10-4. **Sz:** L **CC:** V/MC **Dir:** Across from RR station. **Own:** Charlotte Sullivan.

The Old House
294 Head of Bay Rd • 02532
(508)759-4942

Six rooms of early American pressed glass: blown & cut glass, china & porcelain. **Est:** 1936 **Hrs:** Apr-Dec Mon-Sat 9:30-5, Sun by appt only. **CC:** V/MC **Dir:** 1 mi from Belmont Cir (Shaw's Restaurant). **Own:** Pearl Henshaw. **QC: 103 104**

Byfield

International Antique Mart [G175]
12 Kent Way • 01922
(978)462-4711 • (781)273-2075 (fax)

Furniture & antique collectibles. **Est:** 1992 **Hrs:** Daily 10-5. **Sz:** H **CC:** V/MC **Dir:** I-95 Exit 55: turn L at end of ramp, cross bridge & take 2nd L into Expo Market Center. **Own:** Richard Kelly.

Cambridge

Adams Fireplace Shop
505 Concord Ave • 02138
(617)547-3100

Antique fireplace equipment & antique lighting. **Hrs:** Mon-Sat 9:30-5:30. **Sz:** M. **QC: 40 65**

Antiques on Cambridge Street [G100+]
1076 Cambridge St • 02139
(617)234-0001 • (617)234-0002 (fax)

Estate antiques & quality furniture, decorative accessories, lighting, rugs, mirrors, clocks, porcelain & glass, china, silver, estate & costume jewelry, vintage clothing, objets d'art & collectibles. **Pr:** $10-10,000 **Est:** 1997 **Hrs:** Tue-Sun 11-6, Thu til 8. **Sz:** H **CC:** V/MC **Dir:** From Boston cross Charles River at Charles River Dam. Go 1/2 mi to Lechmere T stop, bear L at fork onto Cambridge St. 1 mi to corn of Cambridge & Elm Sts. **Own:** Rob Werner, Frank Giglio & Bert Rosengarten. **QC: 36 48 11 S1 S12 S19**

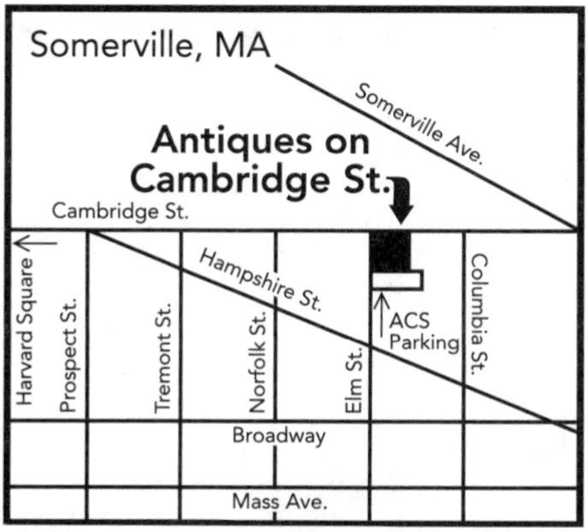

Robin Bledsoe Bookseller

1640 Massachusetts Ave • 02138
(617)576-3634
rbledsoe@world.std.com

New, used & scarce books on horses & all equestrian subjects. Out-of-print books on art history, architecture, archaeology, graphic design, photography & gardens. **Pr:** $5-200 **Est:** 1973 **Hrs:** Tue-Sat 11-6 & by appt. **CC:** AX/V/MC **Assn:** ABAA MARIAB **Dir:** Betw Harvard & Porter Sqs. **QC: 18 S1 S9**

City Lights

2226 Massachusetts Ave • 02140
(617)547-1490

Large selection of antique lighting 1850-1930, ceiling fixtures, wall sconces, table & floor lamps in many styles & periods including Georgian, European, Victorian, Mission, Eastlake, Anglo, Japanese, Aesthetic & Louis XV. **Pr:** $25-5,000 **Est:** 1976 **Hrs:** Tue-Sat 10-6, Thu til 7:30. **Sz:** M **CC:** V/MC **Dir:** 1 mi W from Harvard Sq. **QC: 65**

Easy Chairs

375 Huron Ave • 02138
(617)491-2131

Fine & funky antiques; vintage oak, wicker & rattan, brass lamps & country store items. **Pr:** $10-5,000 **Est:** 1980 **Hrs:** Mon-Sat 10-5:30. **Sz:** M **Dir:** 1 mi above Harvard Sq near Fresh Pond. **Own:** Lee Joseph. **QC: 50 65 91 S1**

Hurst Gallery

53 Mt Auburn St • 02138
(617)491-6888 • (617)661-0439 (fax)

In a sun-lit gallery 3 blocks from Harvard's Fogg Museum, antiquities & ethnographic art including African, American Indian, Oceanic, Pre-Columbian, Asian & Classical. Special exhibitions & catalog sales. **Pr:** $50-50,0000 **Est:** 1977 **Hrs:** Tue-Sat 12-6, Thu til 7. **Sz:** M **CC:** AX/V/MC/DIS **Assn:** AAA ISA **Dir:** 4 blks off JFK St Harvard Sq. **Own:** Norman Hurst. **QC: 2 10**

H L Mendelsohn Fine European Books

1640 Massachusetts Ave (rear) • 02178
(617)576-3634 • (617)661-2445 (fax)
hlm@world.std.com

Antiquarian books: architecture, decorative arts, gardening & printing history thoughtfully selected & displayed with attention to quality & condition. **Est:** 1981 **Hrs:** Tue-Sat 11-6. **Assn:** MARIAB **Dir:** Betw Harvard & Porter Sqs. **QC: 18**

Offshore Trading Company

1695 Massachusetts Ave • 02138
(617)491-8439

American, English & European antique furniture; a large selection of Mission, Arts & Crafts furniture, English & European armoires, bookcases, desks & accessories. **Est:** 1985 **Hrs:** Mon & Wed-Fri 11-6, Sat 11-5, Sun 1-5. **Sz:** M **CC:** V/MC. **QC: 48 49**

Karin J Phillips Antiques

348 Broadway • 02139
(617)547-9433

Eclectic selection of furniture & accessories ranging from early 19th C to fabulous 50s. **Est:** 1978 **Hrs:** Tue-Wed & Fri-Sat 10:30-4 or by appt. **Dir:** From Harvard, take Massachusetts Ave under the underpass & bear R on Broadway. **QC: 48 59**

Sadye & Company

182 Massachusetts Ave • 02139
(617)547-4424
sadye_co@msn.com

Furniture, collectibles, vintage timepieces, musical instruments, costume & antique jewelry & accessories. **Est:** 1988 **Hrs:** Mon-Sat 11-6, Sun 12-5. **CC:** AX/V/MC **Dir:** Betw Central Sq & MIT. **Own:** Elaine Thompson. **QC: 32 69 63**

Chesterfield

Chesterfield Antiques

Rte 143 • 01012
(413)296-4252

Specializing in American 18th & 19th C furniture & accessories, especially high country & formal American furniture circa 1780-1840. **Pr:** $200-2,000 **Hrs:** Daily by appt. **Sz:** L **CC:** V/MC **Assn:** BCADA NHADA VADA MADA **Dir:** I-91 Exit 19: betw Pittsfield & Northampton, 20 min W of Northampton on Rte 143. **Own:** Jack & Alice Geishen. **QC: 34 52**

Cohasset

Cohasset Antiques

Jonathan Livingston Sq (Rte 3A) • 02025
(781)383-6605

General line, silver, glass, lamps, fishing & militaria. **Hrs:** Mon-Sat 11-5. **Own:** Richard Ogden & Nancy Pereto.

Country House Antiques

818 Rte 3A • 02025
(781)383-1832 • (781)383-1194 (fax)

American & European country antiques, trunks, Oriental rugs & paintings. **Est:** 1979 **Hrs:** Mon-Sat 11-5, Sun by chance/appt. **CC:** V/MC **Dir:** On Rte 3A 1/2 mi S of Cushing Plaza. **QC: 34**

> Use the Service QuickCode indexes at the back of the book to find restorers, appraisers, refinishers, and other specialty service providers.

Victoria's by the Sea Antiques [G8+]

87 Elm St • 02025
(781)383-2087
vbs@gis.net
www.gis.net/~vbs/

Fine furnishings, art & decorative accessories. Featuring Victorian, country, garden & architectural elements, lighting & Howard's refinishing products. **Est:** 1994 **Hrs:** Tue-Sun 11-5, Mon by chance/appt. **Sz:** L **CC:** AX/V/MC **Dir:** See store website for map. **Own:** Victoria Chin. **QC: 48 7 36 S12 S15 S16**

Concord

The Barrow Bookstore

79 Main St • 01742
(978)369-6084

Bright friendly shop with books on many subjects. Specializing in Hawthorne, Emerson, Thoreau, the Alcotts, transcendentalism, literature & children's. **Pr:** $.95-500 **Est:** 1971 **Hrs:** Mon-Sat 9:30-5, Sun 12-5. **CC:** V/MC **Assn:** MARIAB **Dir:** Rte 2A W from Rte 128 behind Kussin's Children's Shop in Concord Ctr. Look for yellow wheelbarrow. **Own:** Pamela Fenn. **QC: 18 19**

Books with a Past

17 Walden St (2nd floor) • 01742
(978)371-0180
bwap@erols.com

A general used, antiquarian & out-of-print bookstore with books on Concord authors, Thoreau, Alcotts, Hawthorne, Concord history, transcendentalism, natural history & music. Browsers welcome. **Hrs:** Mon-Sat 10-5. **CC:** V/MC **Assn:** MARIAB **Dir:** Just off Main St. **Own:** Susan Tucker. **QC: 18**

Concord Antiques

32 Main St (Downstairs) • 01742
(978)369-8218

Specializing in American country furniture (including chests, tables, cupboards & desks) & appropriate accessories; silver, brass, copper, fireplace furnishings, porcelain, glass, lamps, paintings & prints. **Est:** 1983 **Hrs:** Wed-Sat 10-5. **Sz:** S **CC:** V/MC **Dir:** In the ctr of town. **Own:** Margaret Gilligan. **QC: 36 48 78**

Joslin Hall Rare Books

(978)371-3101 • (508)371-6445 (fax)
jhall@tiac.net
www.joslinhall.com

Specialists in out-of-print & rare books on the decorative arts & design, architecture. 16th-20th C books, with an emphasis on trade technology, illustrated books, decorative arts including furniture, silver, ceramics, glass, metals & textiles. **Pr:** $50-15,000 **Est:** 1981 **Hrs:** By appt only. **CC:** AX/V/MC **Assn:** ABAA MARIAB **Own:** Forrest & Elizabeth Proper. **QC: 19 18**

North Bridge Antiques [G10]

45 Walden St • 02176
(978)371-1442

A tasteful selection of furniture & decorative accessories from the 18th, 19th & early 20th C including country & formal furniture, accessories, mirrors, lamps, ceramics, silver, jewelry & fine art. **Hrs:** Mon-Sat 10-5, Sun 12-5. **CC:** V/MC **Assn:** SADA **Dir:** From Rte 2 or 2A follow signs to ctr of Concord. Shop is located in Tuttle's Livery 1 blk off Main St on Walden St. Across from the PO. **QC: 48 36 S1 S2 S16**

Rose-and-Crown Antiques

6 Walden St • 01742
(978)287-5130 • (508)287-5135 (fax)
broadrim@prodigy.net

Specializing in pewter. **Hrs:** By appt only. **Own:** Ian Robinson. **QC: 72**

Upstairs Antiques Etc [G14]

23 Walden St • 01742
(978)371-9095

Four rooms of antiques & collectibles at reasonable prices from primitives to Victorian to 20th C. **Est:** 1992 **Hrs:** Mon-Sat 10-5, Sun 12-5. **Sz:** M **CC:** V/MC **Dir:** Rte 95 to Rte 2 W: R at Rte 126 to Concord Ctr to Walden St, across from PO. **Own:** Carole Kitchel. **QC: 34 39 36**

Conway

Conway House

468 Ashfield Rd (Rte 116) • 01341
(413)369-4660 • (413)369-4660 (fax)

Country antiques: samplers, primitives, paintings, lighting devices, copper, brass, iron, Staffordshire, textiles & furniture. **Est:** 1963 **Hrs:** By chance/appt. **Assn:** ADA NHADA VADA MADA **Dir:** I-91N Exit 24 or I-91S Exit 25: take Rte 116 to Conway, 7-1/2 mi; 1 1/2 mi from village ctr. **Own:** Jack & Ray Van Gelder. **QC: 34 65 41**

Jan & John Maggs Antiques

2 Old Cricket Hill Rd • 01341
(413)369-4256
jmaggs@valinet.com
www.valinet.com/~jmaggs

Country furniture & accessories, 1650-1820, in room settings. Always a wide variety of interesting period smalls, hearth iron & hardware. **Hrs:** Sun & Mon by chance/appt, call ahead advised. **Assn:** VADA **Dir:** Near village ctr, 6 mi from I-91. **QC: 34 62 52**

Robert L Merriam
39 Newhall Rd • 01341
(413)369-4052
rmerriam@valinet.com

10,000 out-of-print books on a wide variety of subjects, specializing in American Revolution & colonial Americana. This bed & breakfast in an attractive country setting permits evening browsing. **Pr:** $2.50-250 **Est:** 1949 **Hrs:** By chance/appt. **Sz:** M **CC:** V/MC **Assn:** MARIAB **Dir:** From S: Rte 91 Exit 24: Rtes 5 & 10 to Rte 116 to Conway. In Conway Shelburne Falls Rd to Newhall Rd. **QC: 18 S1**

Cummington

B Shaw Antiques
Rte 9 • 01026
(413)634-2289

Large stock of furniture — oak, walnut, Victorian, wicker, early pine, primitives, desks, round tables, sets of chairs, rockers — primarily to the trade. **Pr:** $25-500 **Hrs:** By chance/appt. **Own:** Blanche & Joe Shaw. **QC: 48 50 91**

Dedham

Century Shop
626 High St • 02026
(781)326-1717

A general line of antiques, with a specialty in Dedham & Dorchester pottery. **Hrs:** Tue-Sat 10:30-4:30, Mon by chance. **CC:** AX/V/MC **Assn:** SADA **Dir:** Near Court House. **Own:** Eleanor Woodward. **QC: 22 S1 S2**

Dedham Antiques Shop
622 High St • 02026
(781)329-1114

Large stock of authentic 18th & 19th C American furniture & accessories. Fourth generation in American antiques. **Hrs:** By chance/appt, a call ahead advised. **Assn:** SADA **Dir:** In Dedham Sq. **Own:** Simon & Nathan Nager. **QC: 1 52 S1 S9**

Jim Kaufman Antiques
248 Highland St • 02026
(781)329-8070 • (781)329-9538 (fax)
(800)283-8070
dpcurator@aol.com
www.dedhampottery.com

Specializing in Dedham pottery as well Chelsea keramic artwork pottery. **Est:** 1990 **Hrs:** By appt only. **Assn:** AAPA **Own:** Jim Kaufman. **QC: 22 101 S1 S9**

Deerfield

5 & 10 Antique Gallery [G75]
Rtes 5 & 10 • 01342
(413)773-3620
chip@antiques510.com
antiques510.com

Early furniture & collectibles including glass, jewelry, prints, porcelain, pottery & ephemera. **Est:** 1980 **Hrs:** Daily 10-5. **Sz:** L **CC:** V/MC/DIS **Dir:** I-91 Exit 26: Rte 2A E toward Greenfield; R at Dunkin Donuts onto River St, 1 mi, then R at light onto Rtes 5 & 10, next to Wok Restaurant. **Own:** Lynn Breuer-Jason & Arthur N Breuer Jr.

Old Deerfield Antiques [G90]
Rtes 5 & 10 • 01342
(413)774-2954

General line in two buildings. **Est:** 1979 **Hrs:** Thu-Tue 10-5. **CC:** AX/V/MC/DIS **Dir:** 1 mi N of Historic Deerfield.

Dighton

Top of the Hill Antiques
2066 Winthrop St (Rte 44) • 02764
(508)252-3541

Old farm tools & furniture, china & glassware. **Hrs:** Tue-Sun 10-6. **Own:** Paul & Carol Hoffshire. **QC: 86 48 S16**

Dover

Karilan James Fine Arts
(508)785-0366

18th & 19th C American paintings, Arts & Crafts furniture & accessories; American furniture & decorative arts. **Pr:** $200-5,000 **Est:** 1990 **Hrs:** By appt only. **QC: 7 49 6 S12**

Whistle Stop Antiques
14 Dedham St • 02030
(508)785-1168

Restored railroad station chock-a-block full of quilts, linens, furniture, china & jewelry. **Pr:** $10-2,000 **Est:** 1991 **Hrs:** Tue-Sat 10-5:30, Sun 12-5. **Sz:** M **CC:** V/MC **Assn:** SADA **Dir:** Located at Springdale Crossing. **Own:** Gail N Albertini & Phyllis O'Leary & Barb Beausang. **QC: 34 48 80 S1 S8 S12**

Duxbury

Gordon & Genevieve Deming
125 Wadsworth Rd • 02331
(781)934-5259 • (781)934-5259 (fax)

Featuring fine New England 18th & 19th C period furniture. Specializing in early American English & Continental pewter, fireplace equipment, woodworking tools & iron. **Pr:** $25-20,000 **Hrs:** By appt only. **Sz:** M **Assn:** NHADA SADA GSAAA **Dir:** Rte 3 Exit 10: 1 mi. **QC: 52 72 62 S1**

Folk Art Antiques [G]
449 Washington St • 02331
(781)934-7132

A full line of country & formal accessories for a New England home including china, silver, furniture, paintings, decorative accessories, export porcelain & painted furniture. **Est:** 1980 **Hrs:** Mon-Sat 11-5. **CC:** V/MC **Dir:** From Rte 3A take Rte 14 E toward water; at flag pole turn R, 1 mi on L. **Own:** Lee Adams. **QC: 51 25 36**

East Bridgewater

Antiques at Forge Pond [G5]
35 N Bedford St (Rte 18) • 02333
(508)378-3057

Cup plates, glass, china, dolls, furniture & postcards. **Est:** 1974 **Hrs:** Daily 11-5. **Sz:** M **Assn:** HAAD **Dir:** On Rte 18 N of Union St. **Own:** Marie Davis. **QC: 32 39 63**

Attic Treasures
582 West St • 02333
(508)378-7510

Hrs: Wed 9-4, Thu-Sat 9-6, Sun 12-6, Mon-Tue by chance. **Assn:** HAAD **Dir:** Rte 106 at the RR crossing. **Own:** Larry & Florrie Davidson.

Hartman House Antiques
334 Bedford St • 02333
(508)378-7388
(800)461-3180 (MA only)

General line including quality mahogany, pine & refinished oak furniture, linens, china & glass. **Pr:** $1-800 **Est:** 1982 **Hrs:** Tue-Sat 10-5, Sun-Mon by chance/appt. **CC:** V/MC/DIS **Assn:** HAAD NEAA **Dir:** Rte 24 S: 106 E, 1/2 mi N on Rte 18. **Own:** Susan Hartman. **QC: 48 60 80 S1 S12 S16**

Mrs Swifts & Moore Antiques & Collectibles
741 Bedford St • 02333
(508)378-9383

Hrs: Sat-Sun 10-5 or by appt. **Assn:** HAAD.

Pepperberries
280 N Bedford St • 02333
(508)378-1411

Antiques & collectibles. **Hrs:** Mon-Sat 12-5. **Assn:** HAAD **Own:** Richard & Maryann Cannon.

Red House Antiques [G]
355 Bedford St (Rte 18) • 02333
(508)947-0344

A multi-dealer shop in a 1794 cape home with five rooms of antiques. **Hrs:** Mon-Sat 11-dark, Sun 12-4. **Assn:** HADA **Own:** Michael Hill.

East Cambridge

Cambridge Antique Market [G150]
201 O'Brien Hwy • 02141
(617)868-9655

Furniture, jewelry, books, vintage clothing, quilts, decorative accessories & porcelain. **Pr:** $1-5,000 **Est:** 1991 **Hrs:** Tue-Sun 11-6. **Sz:** H **CC:** V/MC **Dir:** Across from Lechmere T Station, 3 blks from the Museum of Science.

East Longmeadow

The Layne Gallery
260 Porter Rd • 01028
(413)525-4064

Bronzes, prints & paintings, art glass, porcelain, estate jewelry & other objets d'art. **Hrs:** By appt only. **CC:** V/MC **Own:** Evangeline & Mark Layne. **QC: 11 74 7**

Easthampton

Glaskowsky & Company
180 Main St • 01027
(413)527-2410

American 18th-19th C furniture, andirons/fenders, paintings, prints, maps, clocks, toys, cast iron door stops, bronzes, lamps, art pottery, china, glass, silver, pewter, copper, brass, wrought iron, quilts/coverlets, Baccarat paperweights, weathervanes. **Est:** 1947 **Hrs:** By chance/appt. **Assn:** AAA PVADA **Dir:** On Rte 10 4 mi S of Northampton. **Own:** Frederick Glaskowsky. **QC: 40 52 72 S1 S9**

Stevenson Antiques
52 Union St (Rte 141) • 01027
(413)527-9611

A large selection of paintings, watercolors & prints. **Est:** 1983 **Hrs:** Daily 12-6:30. **Dir:** Corn of Union & School Sts. **QC: 7 74 7**

Easton

Barbara Bailey Antiques
143 Washington St (Rte 138) • 02356
(508)238-9770

Textiles, primitives, jewelry & a general line of antiques. **Hrs:** Apr-Dec Sat 12-4 or by chance/appt. **Assn:** HAAD **Own:** John & Barbara Bailey. **QC: 64 106 80**

Orchid Antiques
593 Turnpike St (Rte 138) • 02356
(508)238-6146

Quality Victorian & period furniture & accessories, glassware & artwork. **Hrs:** Sat-Sun by chance/appt. **Assn:** HAAD. **QC: 58 61**

Elmwood

Elmwood Antiques & Country Store [G20]
734 Bedford St • 02337
(508)378-2063

Collectibles, furniture, glass & dog collectibles. **Hrs:** Daily 11-5. **Assn:** HAAD **Dir:** Rte 24 Rte 106E, E to the int of Rtes 18 & 106 in E Bridgewater. **QC: 32 48**

Essex

Americana
48 Main St • 01929
(978)768-6006
www.americanaantiques.com

Country pine & walnut furniture. Victorian oak furniture a specialty. **Pr:** $25-2,500 **Est:**

1969 **Hrs:** Daily 10-5. **CC:** AX/V/MC **Dir:** Rte 128N Exit 15: to Essex. **Own:** Kenneth & Sandy Monroe. **QC: 50 55 65**

Annex Antiques [G3]

69 Main St • 01929
(978)768-7704 • (978)768-7212 (fax)

A diversified line of antiques featuring country furniture complemented by first & second period antiques & accessories. Always striving for the unusual. **Pr:** $50-5,000 **Est:** 1958 **Hrs:** Mon-Wed & Fri-Sat 10-5, Sun 11-5. **Sz:** L **CC:** V/MC **Dir:** On Causeway (Rte 133) overlooking Essex River. **Own:** Barbara Dyer Reymond & Robert Reymond. **QC: 102 55 60**

Antiques & Elderly Things

199 Western Ave • 01929
(978)768-6328
eldthing@execelr8.net

A small shop with lots of old things including china, glass, metalware, tools, small furniture & arms. **Est:** 1976 **Hrs:** Daily 10-5. **Dir:** On the road into Essex. **Own:** Jen & Bob Cronin.

Auntie Lil's Antiques

53 John Wise Ave • 01929
(978)768-7550

Antiques, collectibles, canes & nautical items, linens & decorative accessories tastefully displayed in a Colonial farmhouse. **Est:** 1991 **Hrs:** Daily 10-5; Jan-Feb closed Mon-Tue. **Own:** Lillian Moretti. **QC: 36 70 81 S12**

Chartwell Antiques & Restoration

140 Main St (Rte 133) • 01929
(978)768-7078 • (978)768-0015 (fax)

Fine art, lighting, clocks, mirrors, upholstered seating, painted finishes & restoration. **Est:** 1996 **Hrs:** Tue-Fri 11-5, Sun 12-5. **CC:** V/MC **Dir:** On lower level. **Own:** Linda Lavery. **QC: 7 65 35 S16**

Chebacco Antiques [G8]

38 Main St (Rte 133) • 01929
(978)768-7371

American pine & country furniture & related accessories, including linens, porcelain, tools & lighting. **Pr:** $25-500 **Est:** 1981 **Hrs:** Daily 10:30-4:30. **Sz:** M **CC:** AX/V/MC **Dir:** Rte 128N Exit 15 (School St): turn L toward Essex, at int Rte 133, go L, 1 mi on R. **Own:** Roland & Jane Adams. **QC: 55 102**

R C Coviello Antiques

155 Main St (Rte 133) • 01929
(978)768-7365

Featuring 18th, 19th & 20th C furniture & decorative accessories. **Est:** 1987 **Hrs:** Daily 10-5. **CC:** AX/V/MC **Dir:** Rte 128N Exit 15 toward Essex: on Rte 133 just N of Burnham's Corner. **QC: 36 48**

The Essex Antiquarian

165 Main St (Rte 133) • 01929
(978)768-4544

Fine 18th & 19th C English & American furniture, porcelain & decorative accessories. **Hrs:** Mon-Fri 11-5, Sat-Sun 12-5. **Sz:** L **CC:** V/MC **Own:** Joseph Bevilacqua. **QC: 53 52 36 S1**

Friendship Antiques

John Wise Ave (Rte 133) • 01929
(978)768-7334

A discriminating collection of period & decorative furniture, including paintings, rugs, silver, china, glass & a library. **Pr:** $50-50,000 **Est:** 1968 **Hrs:** Wed, Sat, Sun 12-5 (appt suggested). **Dir:** 1 mi N of int of Rtes 133 & 22. **Own:** William Friend. **QC: 52 36 7**

Howard's Flying Dragon Antiques

136 Main St (Rte 133) • 01929
(978)768-7282 • (768-7730 (fax)

A general line of antiques & statuary. **Est:** 1972 **Hrs:** Daily 10:30-6. **CC:** AX/V/MC **Dir:** Rte 128N Exit 15: 4 mi in the ctr of town. **Own:** Laura & Edwin Howard. **QC: 60 61**

Joshua's Corner [G25]

4 Southern Ave • 01929
(978)768-7716

Folk, painted country furnishings & decorative accessories. Fun collectibles & serious art. **Hrs:** Daily 10-5. **CC:** V/MC **Own:** Joyce Fontaine. **QC: 41 34 1**

L A Landry Antiques

164 Main St (Rte 133) • 01929
(978)768-6233 • (978)768-6233 (fax)
pcombs@landryauctions.com
www.landryauctions.com

Buying, selling, appraising & auctioning fine antiques on the North Shore of Boston for over fifty years has made this shop one of the finest in the area. Furniture, Continental porcelain, Chinese screens, chests, porcelain & many unusual pieces. **Pr:** $25-150,000 **Est:** 1938 **Hrs:** Daily 10-5, appt suggested. **Assn:** AAA AC **Dir:** Rte 128N to Rte 133W on Burnham's Corner. **Own:** Robert Landry. **QC: 52 71 23**

Main Street Antiques

44 Main St (Rte 133) • 01929
(978)768-7039
coviello@shore.net

Antiques, furniture & collectibles specializing in a wide range of furniture, jewelry, ephemera, maps & prints, ranging from late 1700s to 20th C. **Pr:** $1-3,000 **Est:** 1981 **Hrs:** Daily 10-5. **Sz:** L **CC:** AX/V/MC **Dir:** Rte 128N Exit 15: toward Essex, 3 mi, turn L onto Main St, 1/4 mi up on R. **Own:** Robert Coviello. **QC: 48 32**

Ellen Neily Antiques

157 Main St (Rte 133) • 01929
(978)768-6436

American & Continental painted & formal furniture, silver, China trade pieces & paintings & decorative accessories. **Est:** 1985 **Hrs:** Wed-Sat 11-5, Sun 1-5, Mon-Tue by chance/appt. **Sz:** M **CC:** AX/V/MC/DIS **Assn:** NEAA **Dir:** Near Burnham's Corner in S Essex. **Own:** Ellen Neily. **QC: 78 51 71**

Neligan & Neligan

144 Main St (Rte 133) • 01929
(978)768-3910

17th-19th C English & European furniture & decorations, mirrors, paintings, objects d'art, Chinese & Japanese works of art. **Pr:** $50-20,000 **Est:** 1988 **Hrs:** Wed-Mon 11-5, Sun 12-5. **Sz:** M **Own:** Gretchen & David Neligan. **QC: 53 54 71 S1**

North Hill Antiques

155 Main St (Rte 133) • 01929
(978)768-7365

In a restored 19th C house, a collection of quality 18th & 19th C European & American formal furniture & accessories focusing on mirrors, small tables, chairs & chests, including boxes, sterling silver, inkwells & porcelain. **Pr:** $100-5,000 **Est:** 1988 **Hrs:** Daily 10-5. **Sz:** M **CC:** AX/V/MC **Dir:** Rte 128N Exit 15: toward Essex, 3 mi, turn L onto Main St, 200 yds up on L. **Own:** David & Sylvia Kaplan. **QC: 36 54 68**

Prado Antiques

163 Main St (Rte 133) • 01929
(978)768-3539

Paintings, fine furniture & Chinese export. **Hrs:** Fri 11-5, Sat by chance. **QC: 7 71**

Ro-Dan Antiques

67 Main St (Rte 133) • 01929
(978)768-3322

Oriental porcelain, 18th & 19th C American & European furniture & other accessories. **Hrs:** Mon 9-2, Thu 10-4, Fri 10-1. **Dir:** Rte 128 N Exit 15 (toward Essex): 3 mi, turn L on Main St 1/4 mi up on R. **QC: 24 52 53**

Use the Specialty QuickCode indexes at the back of the book to find dealers who specialize in your area of interest.

The Scrapbook
34 Main St (Rte 133) • 01929
(978)768-7404 • (978)768-7922 (fax)
mapman@shore.net
www.shore.net/~mapman/

One of the largest collections of antiquarian maps & prints in New England with a vast selection of American & European 16th to 19th C historical & decorative engravings. **Pr:** $15-5,000 **Est:** 1970 **Hrs:** Mon-Sat 11-5, Sun 12-5. **Sz:** M **CC:** V/MC **Assn:** ABAA **Dir:** On Rte 133 behind the White Elephant Shop. **Own:** Vincent Caravella. **QC: 66 74 S13**

South Essex Antiques [G4]
166 Eastern Ave • 01929
(978)768-6373

European & decorative accessories, fabrics, paintings, china & furniture. **Pr:** $25-7,000 **Est:** 1982 **Hrs:** Tue-Sun 11-5. **Sz:** M **Dir:** Rte 128N Exit 14: L 2-1/2 mi to Essex, on R, low white bldg surrounded by parking lot. **Own:** William Taylor. **QC: 36 60**

Andrew Spindler Antiques
143 Main St (Rte 133) • 01929
(978)768-6045 • (978)768-6065 (fax)
www.spindlerantiques.com

18th & 19th C European & American furniture, fine art & decorations; architectural drawings, engravings & photographs, ironstone china, Early Modern design & the Arts & Crafts movement. **Hrs:** Mon & Wed-Sat 11-5, Sun 12-5 or by appt. **Sz:** M **CC:** V/MC **Dir:** Rte 128 N Exit 15: L onto School St to end, then L onto Main St. Shop is located on the L. **Own:** Andrew Spindler-Roesle. **QC: 53 7 6**

Tradewinds Antiques
63 Main St (Rte 133) • 01929
(978)768-3327 • (978)526-3088 (fax)
taron@tiac.net
www.tradewindsantiques.com

The only shop in America exclusively devoted to antique canes & walking sticks. Always an inventory of 200-300 pieces. Additionally, Tradewinds conducts 2 highest-quality all-cane auctions each year since 1993. Also conducts auctions on its website. **Pr:** $50-1500 **Est:** 1980 **Hrs:** By appt or chance. **Sz:** M **CC:** V/MC **Dir:** Rte 128N Exit 15 to Main St. Essex. L on Main, shop on L. **Own:** Henry Taron **QC: S1 S2 S8**

Tuohy & Meade
1 Southern Ave • 01929
(978)768-9999
tuohyandmeade@email.msn.com

Architectural, garden & early American funky. **Hrs:** Thu-Sun 10-5 or by appt. **CC:** AX/V/MC/DIS **Own:** Crozer & Jane Fox. **QC: 3 60 S15**

Walker Creek Furniture
57 Eastern Ave (Rte 133) • 01929
(978)768-7622

Tables, chairs, chests & case pieces. Shaker furniture maker. Huge selection of antique chairs. Creates new furniture out of old materials, old painted items. **Est:** 1986 **Hrs:** Tue-Sat 11-5, Sun 1-5. **CC:** V/MC/DIS. **QC: 48 S17**

A P H Waller & Sons Antiques

140 Main St (Rte 133) • 01929
(978)768-6269

A superior collection of period Oriental pieces, bronzes, paintings, ceramics & Continental furniture. **Est:** 1975 **Hrs:** Wed-Sat 10:30-5, Sun 2:30-5. **Sz:** M **Dir:** Rte 128N Exit 15: to Burnhams Corner, just N on R. **Own:** Allen Waller. **QC: 53 7 71 S12**

Alexander Westerhoff Antiques

144 Main St (Rte 133) • 01929
(978)768-3830 • (508)768-3811 (fax)
westerhoff@nii.net
www.westerhoff.net

Specializing in chandeliers, fine dining tables, sets of chairs & sideboards, along with 18th & early 19th C English, American & Continental furniture & decorative accessories. **Pr:** $300-50,000 **Est:** 1988 **Hrs:** Wed-Mon 11-5. **Sz:** M **CC:** V/MC **Dir:** From Boston area: Rte 128N Exit 15, L at top of ramp, 3 1/2 mi, L at stop sign, go up hill, shop on R in white bldg with parking in front. **Own:** Thomas I Lang & Alexander Westerhoff. **QC: 36 53 65 S8 S12 S15**

Fairhaven

Georgian Manor Antiques

29 Centre St • 02719
(508)991-5675
www.antiquescouncil.com/georgianmanor

18th & 19th C English & Continental furniture & related accessories. **Pr:** $3,000-35,000 **Est:** 1970 **Hrs:** By appt only. **Sz:** M **Assn:** AC **Own:** Enrique Goytizolo. **QC: 48**

Fall River

Tower Antique Market [G100+]

657 Quarry St • 02723
(508)675-7940

Glass, china, linens, ephemera, jewelry & fine collectibles. **Hrs:** Mon-Sat 10-5, Sun 12-5. **CC:** V/MC **Dir:** I-95 Exit 8A: Rte 24 to Exit 2 (Brayton Ave), then L and 1st R onto Jefferson St. Follow Tower Outlet Mall signs. **QC: S8 S12**

Fitchburg

John Clement

36 Oakwood Ave • 01420-7421
(978)345-5863

American & European prints, drawings & paintings, Japanese prints. **Est:** 1985 **Hrs:** By appt only. **Dir:** Call for directions. **QC: 7 71 74 S12**

Framingham

Avery's Antiques

74 Franklin St • 01702
(508)875-4576 • (508)875-1166 (fax)

Early American furniture & accessories, beds, primitives & Victorian upholstered furniture. **Hrs:** Mon-Fri 8-5, Sat 8-12. **CC:** V/MC. **QC: 52 58**

Framingham Centre Antiques [G40]

931 Worcester Rd • 01701
(508)620-6252

Oak, country & early period furnishings & accessories, lighting, glassware, jewelry, toys, Coca Cola memorabilia & other antique advertising, baseball & vintage soda machines. **Pr:** $10-5,000 **Hrs:** Tue-Sat 10-5, Sun 12-5. **Sz:** L **CC:** AX/V/MC/DIS **Dir:** From W I-90 Exit 12: to Rte 9 E to Edgell Rd exit. L off ramp then L again on Rte 30 off ramp. On the R.

Franklin

Johnston Antiques & Appraisers

789 W Central St • 02038
(508)528-0942

Fine arts, 18th & 19th C furniture, porcelain, Orientalia, silver, pewter, prints, maps, books, stamps, coins, ephemera, formal & country antiques, glass, historical documents, folk art, theorems, samplers, quilts, export china & Staffordshire. **Pr:** $5-20,000 **Est:** 1966 **Hrs:** Jun 21-Sep 7 Mon-Sun 9-7:30; Sep 8-Jun 20 Mon-Fri 3-7:30, Sat-Sun 9-7:30. **Sz:** S **Assn:** SADA ANS **Dir:** Rte 495W Exit 17: to Rte 140. **Own:** Claire & James Johnston. **QC: 1 12 41 S1 S6 S12**

Georgetown

The Columns

5 Elm St (Rte 133) • 01833
(978)352-4891

A wide range of antiques & collectibles attractively displayed in a classic Greek revival building. Everything from formal furniture, china & accessories to country kitchen items. **Est:** 1998 **Hrs:** Mar-Dec Mon, Wed-Sat 11-5, Sun 12-5; Jan-Feb Wed-Sat 11-5, Sun 12-5. **Sz:** M **Dir:** I-95N Exit 54: 1-1/4 mi W onto Rte 133. Across from Georgetown Historical House. **Own:** Lillian Moretti. **QC: 1 25 48**

Scala's Antiques [G5+]

28 W Main St • 01833
(978)352-8614

Three floors of antiques & collectibles including a large selection of jewelry, country, formal, vintage clothing, Depression glass, dolls & more. **Hrs:** Tue-Sun 11-5. **Sz:** L **Own:** Louise & Angelo Scala **QC: S1**

Sedler's Antique Village [G30]

51 W Main St (Rte 97) • 01833
(978)352-8282

A general line of antiques including furniture, dolls, toys & estate jewelry. **Est:** 1977 **Hrs:** Daily 10-5. **CC:** V/MC/DIS **Dir:** I-95 Rte 133 exit: through town 1-1/2 mi in Georgetown.

Thomas A Edison Collection

51 W Main St • 01833
(978)352-9830

For collectors: fine phonographs, music boxes, piano rolls, cylinder & disc records, roller organs, cob organs, horns, sheet music; cylinder & record cabinets. **Pr:** $10-5,000 **Est:** 1977 **Hrs:** Tue-Wed & Fri-Sat 10-5, Sun 10-1. **Sz:** M **Assn:** AAA **Dir:** I-95 to Rte 133: W 1 mi to Georgetown Ctr. Thru lights to Sedler's Antique Village on R 1 blk. **Own:** Ralph Woodside. **QC: 69 S1 S19 S16**

Gloucester

Bananas

78 Main St • 01930
(978)283-8806

A large selection of vintage clothing, accessories & costume jewelry ranging from the turn-of-the-century to the 1970s. **Pr:** $5-150 **Est:** 1975 **Hrs:** Mon-Sat 10-5, Sun 12-5. **Sz:** M **CC:** V/MC **Dir:** Rte 128N to end, exit to downtown Gloucester. **Own:** Richard Leonard. **QC: 63 83**

Jer-Rho Antiques

352 Main St • 01930
(978)283-5066

China, glass, estate jewelry, extensive art glass, furniture, prints & paintings. **Pr:** $25-4,000 **Hrs:** Tue-Sun 10-6. **Sz:** M **CC:** AX/V/MC **Assn:** NEAA **Dir:** Rte 128 N to 2nd set of lights (end of Rte 128) turn R, go 1/4 mi shop on the R. **Own:** Jerry & Rhoda Grushka. **QC: 61 64 S1**

Main Street Arts & Antiques [G8]

124 Main St • 01930
(978)281-1531

Paintings, jewelry, ephemera, postcards, wicker, textiles, second-hand furniture, china, glass & books. **Est:** 1988 **Hrs:** Mon-Sat 10-5, Sun 1-5. **Sz:** M **Dir:** In the ctr of business district. **Own:** David Cox.

Ten Pound Island Book Co

76 Langsford St • 01930
(978)283-5299 • (978)283-5235 (fax)
tenpound@world.std.com

Old & rare books of all kinds, with specialties in maritime, local history, fine & decorative arts & antiquarian books. **Pr:** $5-5,000 **Est:** 1976 **Hrs:** Thu-Sat 12-5, Sun by appt. **Sz:** S **CC:** V/MC **Assn:** ABAA MARIAB NEAA **Dir:** Rte 128 N to 1st rotary on hwy; Rte 127 5-6 mi to Lanesville, then 1/2 mi N past Lanesville. Bldg on R with large gravel parking lot. **Own:** Gregory Gibson. **QC: 70 1 7 S1**

Great Barrington

Elise Abrams Antiques

11 Stockbridge Rd (Rte 7) • 01230
(413)528-3201 • (413)528-5350 (fax)
elise@ben.net

The largest selection of sets of antique china & stemware in the US. Specializing in dining room furniture, glass, silver, art glass & decorative & tabletop accessories. Every detail for the perfect dining experience. Custom bridal registry. **Pr:** $25-25,000 **Est:** 1986 **Hrs:** Daily 10:30-6. **Sz:** M **CC:** AX/V/MC **Assn:** BCADA **Dir:** Rtes 7 & 23 at Belcher Sq. **QC: 52 61 23 S1 S12 S15**

Bygone Days

969 Main St (Rte 7S) • 01230
(413)528-1870

A large collection of bedroom, dining room, kitchen & office furniture, antique & reproduction country pine & oak furniture. **Pr:** $5-1,000 **Est:** 1981 **Hrs:** Jul-Aug daily 12-5, otherwise closed Wed. **CC:** V/MC **Dir:** S of the fairgrounds. **Own:** Ted Portnoff. **QC: 48 50 55**

Carriage House Antiques

389 Stockbridge Rd (Rte 7) • 01230
(413)528-6045 • (413)229-6687 (fax)
m13irror@aol.com

Restored furniture from the early 19th C to the 1940s, decorative accessories & a cabinet shop. **Hrs:** Daily 9-4:30. **CC:** AX/V/MC/DIS **Assn:** BCADA **Own:** Erik, Barbara & Erik O F Schutz. **QC: 48 36 S16 S5**

The Coffman's Country Antiques Market [G108]

Stockbridge Rd (Rte 7) • 01230
(413)528-9282
ccamj@vgernet.net
www.antiquesjunction.com/coffmans

Three floors in booth settings featuring country furniture, quilts, stoneware, kitchenware, baskets & unique accessories. **Hrs:** Daily 10-5. **CC:** AX/V/MC/DIS **Dir:** On Rte 7 just S of Stockbridge in Yellow House in back of Jenifer House Commons. **Own:** Don & Joyce Coffman & John Dutilly. **QC: 48 17 60 S1 S2**

Corashire Antiques

Rte 7 (Rte 7) • 01230
(413)528-0014 • (413)528-4809 (fax)

American country furniture & accessories in the red barn. **Pr:** $25-1,000 **Hrs:** Daily 9-5. **Assn:** BCADA **Dir:** Corn Rte 7 & 23 at Belcher Sq. **Own:** Nancy & John Dinan. **QC: 34 36 102**

Map of the Members of the **BERKSHIRE COUNTY**

1 Burton Brook Farm Antiquarians
2 Buckley & Buckley
3 I. Joseph Stannard Antiques
4 The Vollmers
5 Ashley Falls Antiques
6 Circa
7 Lewis and Wilson
8 Don Abarbanel
9 Lois W. Spring
10 Kuttner Antiques
11 Cupboards and Roses
12 Howard S. Mott, Inc.
13 John Sideli Art & Antiques
14 Darr Antiques and Interiors
15 Berkshire Gilders Antiques
16 Margo Hayes Country Antiques
17 Good & Hutchinson & Associates, Inc.
18 Centuryhurst Antiques and Bed and Breakfast
19 Samuel Herrup Antiques
20 Dovetail Antiques
21 Corner House Antiques
22 David M. Weiss Antiques
23 Bradford Galleries, Ltd.
24 Saturday Sweets Antiques & Design
25 Susan Silver Antiques
26 Le Trianon
27 Falcon Antiques
28 Bill's Clock Repairs and Service
29 The Buggy Whip Factory Antique Market Place
30 Kettering Antiques
31 Dagmar's Antiques
32 Elliott and Grace Snyder
33 Howard's Antiques
34 Geffner/Schatzky Antiques
35 The Splendid Peasant, Ltd.
36 Le Périgord
37 Snyder's Store
38 McTeigue & McClelland Jewelers
39 Paul and Susan Kleinwald, Inc.
40 Mullin-Jones Antiquities
41 The Emporium Antique Center
42 Donald McGrory Oriental Rugs
43 The Kahn's Antique and Estate Jewelry
44 The Country Dining Room Antiques
45 Elise Abrams Antiques
46 Corashire Antiques
47 Carriage House Antiques
48 Reuss Audubon Galleries
49 Coffman's Country Antiques Market
50 Heirlooms Classic Jewelry
51 Sawyer Antiques
52 Aardenburg Antiques
53 Henry B. Holt
54 Lujohn's Auction Gallery
55 Stone's Throw Antiques
56 Past and Future
57 Charles L. Flint Antiques, Inc.
58 Wynn A. Sayman, Inc.
59 Berkshire Hills Coins and Antiques, Inc.
60 Pittsfield Precious Metals
61 Memory Lane Antiques
62 Chesterfield Antiques
63 Green River Gallery
64 Doyle Antiques

64 Antique Shops
For Directory
Send SASE to:
BCADA
P.O. Box 594-S
Great Barrington, MA 01230

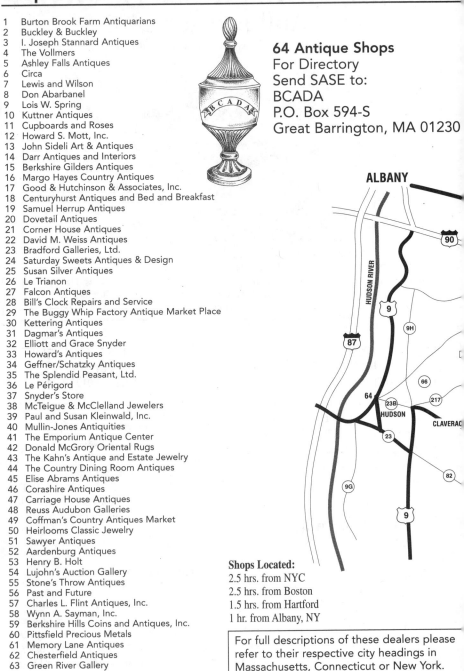

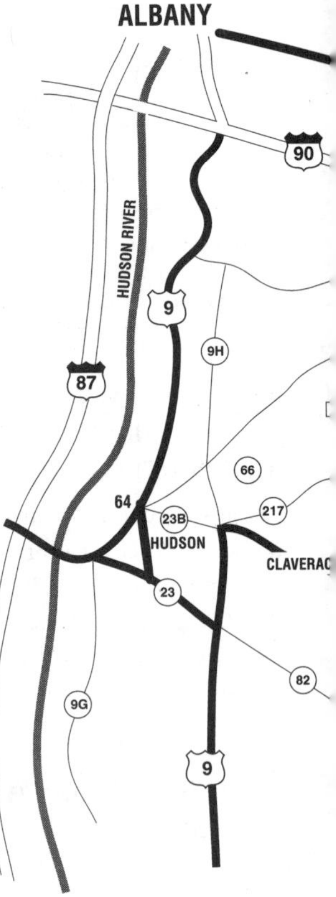

Shops Located:
2.5 hrs. from NYC
2.5 hrs. from Boston
1.5 hrs. from Hartford
1 hr. from Albany, NY

For full descriptions of these dealers please refer to their respective city headings in Massachusetts, Connecticut or New York.

MASSACHUSETTS ANTIQUES DEALERS ASSOCIATION

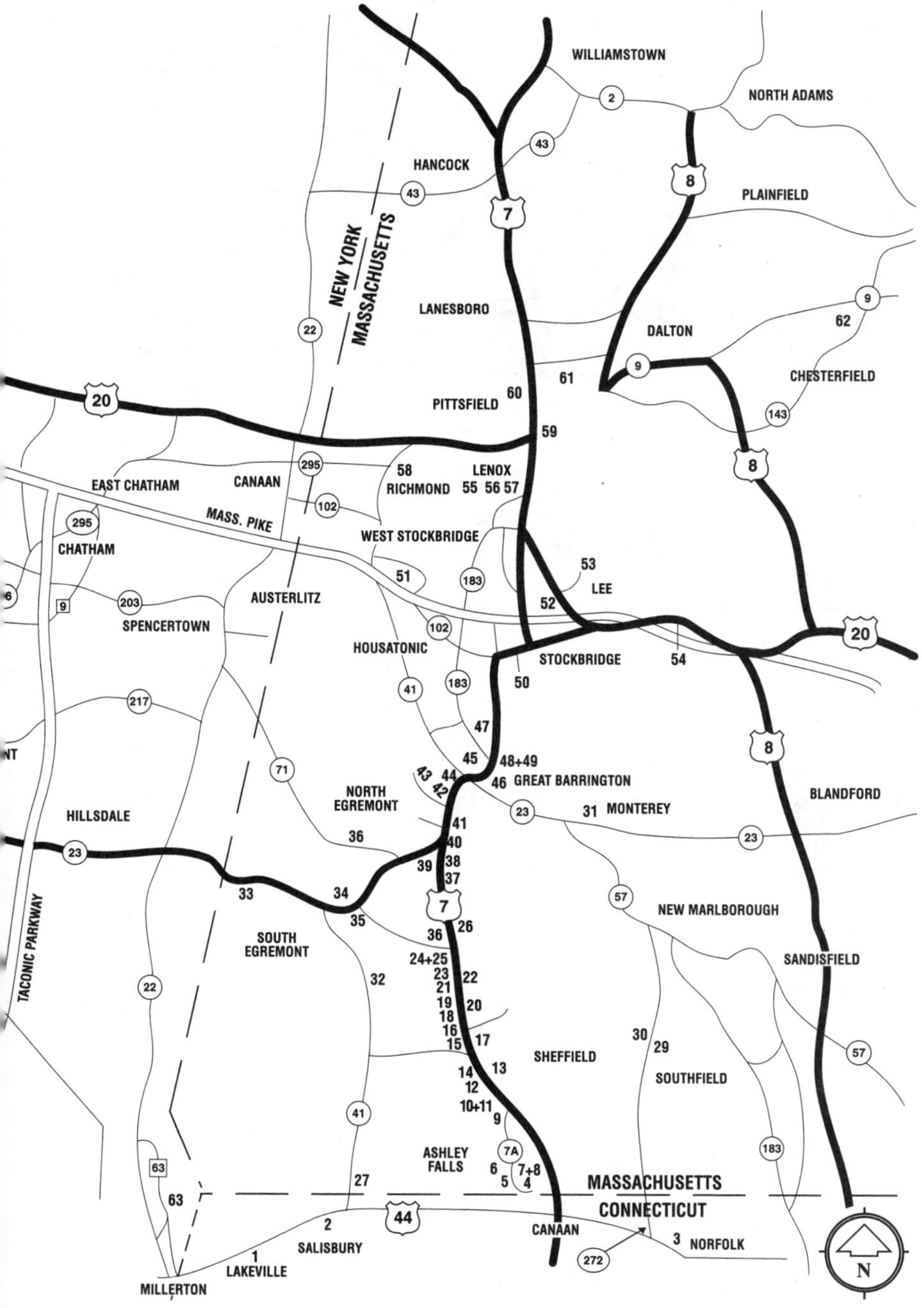

The Country Dining Room Antiques

178 Main St (Rte 7) • 01230
(413)528-5050 • (413)528-9216 (fax)
chefetz@vgernet.net
www.countrydiningroomantiq.com

The largest specialized dining room shop, featuring antique formal & country "tablescapes" on two floors, highlighting English dining furniture, porcelain, Staffordshire, Victorian silver, glasswares, linens, candleshades & the "art of dining." **Pr:** $50-10,000 **Est:** 1989 **Hrs:** Daily 10-6. **Sz:** L **CC:** AX/V/MC **Assn:** BCADA **Dir:** At the N end of town on Rte 7. **Own:** Sheila Chefetz. **QC: 23 30 54 S12 S15 S1**

The Emporium Antique Center [G25]

319 Main St (Rte 7) • 01230
(413)528-1660

The antique center in the heart of Great Barrington, offering estate jewelry, silver, art glass, fine china & a range of collectibles. **Hrs:** Mon-Sat 10-5, Sun 11-4. **CC:** V/MC **Assn:** BCADA **Own:** Arthur Greenstone & Melvin S Katz.

Kahn's Antique & Estate Jewelry

38 Railroad St • 01230
(413)528-9550

Antique & estate jewelry of all periods & silver smalls. **Pr:** $25-10,000 **Est:** 1974 **Hrs:** Mon-Sat 10-5:30, Sun by chance/appt. **Sz:** M **CC:** AX/V/MC/DIS **Assn:** BCADA **Dir:** 1 blk W of Rte 7 in the ctr of town. **Own:** Nancy & Steven Kahn. **QC: 64 78 S1 S8 S12**

Paul & Susan Kleinwald Inc

578 S Main St • 01230
(413)528-4252 • (413)528-8981 (fax)
www.bmark.com/Kleinwald.Antiques

18th & 19th C American & English furniture, paintings, silver, porcelain & other decorative accessories of excellent quality. **Pr:** $50-

50,000 **Hrs:** Wed-Mon or by chance/appt. **Assn:** BCADA. **QC: 52 53 54 S1**

Le Perigord Antiques

964 S Main St (Rte 7) • 01230
(413)528-6777

"More than French country." French furniture, leather club chairs, iron, pottery, garden & architectural elements. 18th C through Art Deco. **Hrs:** Open Sat-Sun; wkdys by chance/appt **Sz:** M **Assn:** BCADA **Own:** J D Roberts. **QC: 3 47 60**

J & J Lubrano Music Antiquarians

8 George St • 01230
(413)528-5799 • (413)528-4164 (fax)
lubrano@bcn.net
abba-booknet.com/usa/lubrano/

Rare printed music & musical literature pre-1800, autographed letters of composers, autographed musical manuscripts, rare dance books, music & dance iconography. **Pr:** $100-100,000 **Est:** 1977 **Hrs:** By appt only. **Sz:** S **CC:** V/MC **Assn:** ABAA **Dir:** Call for directions. **Own:** John & Jude Lubrano. **QC: 18 69 S1**

Donald McGrory Oriental Rugs

24 Railroad St • 01230
(413)528-9594

Antique & decorative Oriental rugs. **Est:** 1977 **Hrs:** Wed-Mon 11-5. **Sz:** M **CC:** AX/V/MC **Assn:** BCADA. **QC: 76**

McTeigue & McClelland Jewelers

597 S Main St (Rte 7) • 01230
(413)528-6262 • (413)528-6644 (fax)
(800)956-2826

Fine antique, estate & contemporary jewelry. Specializing in late 19th C-present day jewelry. Diamonds, precious stones & fine hand crafted items. Family trade since 1895. **Pr:** $100+ **Hrs:** Jul-Aug & Dec Wed-Sat 10-5, Sun 11-4; Jan-Jun & Sep-Nov Wed-Sat 10-5. **Sz:** S **CC:** AX/V/MC **Assn:** BCADA

ASJH **Dir:** 1/2 mi S of downtown Great Barrington. **Own:** Walter McTeigue & Tim McClelland. **QC: 64 S16 S12**

Memories

306 Main St (Rte 7) • 01230
(413)528-6380

Large, eclectic selection of antiques, primitives, collectibles, unusual accessories, Art Deco, books, maps, prints, lighting fixtures, phonographs, radios, old copper, old toys, sleds & bicycles, stoves & scales in a clean well lighted shop. **Pr:** $25-15,000 **Est:** 1990 **Hrs:** Wed-Mon 10-5:30. **Sz:** L **CC:** AX/V/MC **Dir:** Ctr of Great Barrington at RR station 4 mi N of Sheffield & 5 mi S of Stockbridge. **Own:** Mario & Karyn Tsakis. **QC: 6 32**

Use the Service QuickCode indexes at the back of the book to find restorers, appraisers, refinishers, and other specialty service providers.

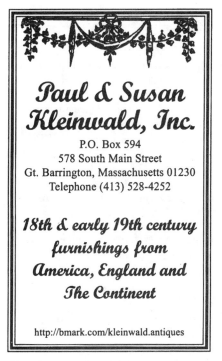

Mullin-Jones Antiquities
525 S Main St (Rte 7) • 01230
(413)528-4871

Importers of French antiques: armoires, buffets, rush-seated chairs, farm tables, extending tables, secretaries, burlwood commodes, upholstered armchairs, gilded mirrors, chandeliers, faience. "Sophisticated Provencal style, from farmhouse to chateau." **Pr:** $40-22,000 **Est:** 1986 **Hrs:** Wed-Mon call ahead advised. **Sz:** M **Assn:** BCADA **Dir:** Betw fairgrounds & S jct of Rtes 41 & 23, 1/2 mi S of downtown business district. **Own:** Patrice Mullin. **QC: 47 53 27**

Olde Antiques Market [G85]
Stockbridge Rd (Rte 7) • 01245
(413)528-1840 • (413)528-4750 (fax)

Two floors in the green house featuring quality dealers in china, glass, pottery, jewelry, furniture, books, maps, paintings, linens, lamps & more. **Pr:** $10-10,000 **Est:** 1989 **Hrs:** Daily 10-5. **Sz:** L **CC:** AX/V/MC **Dir:** At Jenifer House Commons. **Own:** Joan & Howard Basis. **QC: 36 64 60 S12**

Reuss Audubon Galleries
Stockbridge Rd (Rte 7) • 01230
(413)528-8484

Furniture & art. Specializing in Audubon & Gould prints, antique & original art. **Hrs:** Daily 11-4. **Assn:** BCADA **Dir:** At Jenifer House Commons. **QC: 74**

Snyder's Store
945 S Main St (Rte 7) • 01230
(413)528-1441

Furnishings, both functional & fanciful. Some formal but emphasis on campy, folky & architectural pieces for home & garden. Accessories include frames, jewelry, linens, tramp art & cottage craft. **Hrs:** Most Sat-Sun 12-5, wkdys by chance. **Assn:** BCADA **Own:** Shirley Snyder. **QC: 34 36 60**

Greenfield

Custom Creations
16 Chapman St • 01301
(413)775-9986

An eclectic selection of furniture, decorative accessories, art & smalls from mid-17th C to mid-20th C. Nice representation of reasonably priced Victorian & country primitive items with complementary addition of works by local artisans. **Pr:** $5-1,500 **Est:** 1998 **Hrs:** Jan 1-Nov 15 Tue-Sat 10-5; Nov 15-Dec 26 Sun-Mon 12-5, Tue-Sat 10-5. **Sz:** M **CC:** V/MC **Dir:** I-91 Exit 26: 2 mi E on Rte 2A L on Chapman St. **Own:** Vickie Hutchinson. **QC: 34 36 58 S8 S12 S15**

Nancy Stronczek Antiques
26 Bowker St • 01301
(413)774-3260
njs@crocker.com

Country & painted smalls, textiles, primitives, yellowware & decorative accessories. **Hrs:** By appt only. **Assn:** NHADA GSAAA **Dir:** From Rte 2 & I-93, 3 mi N of Historic Deerfield on Rtes 5 & 10. **QC: 80 41 36**

Groton

Pam Boynton
82 Pleasant St • 01450
(978)448-5031

Specializing in 18th & 19th C furniture & accessories in original condition. **Est:** 1948 **Hrs:** Daily by chance/appt. **Assn:** NHADA MADA **Dir:** 2 blks off Main St at int of Rtes 111 & 225. **QC: 36 52**

Groton Antiques [G40]
134 Main St (Rte 119) • 01450
(978)448-3330

Fine Americana & country including 17th & 18th C furniture, metalwork, cabinet pieces, rugs, needlework, paintings, pine & porcelain. **Est:** 1977 **Hrs:** Daily 10-5. **Dir:** On Rte 119, behind Jos Kilbridge Antiques.

Imagine

157 Main St • 01450
(978)448-5044

Glassware, artwork, furniture & ephemera **Est:** 1981 **Hrs:** Mon-Sat 10-5. **Sz:** L **CC:** AX/V/MC/DIS **Assn:** ISA **Dir:** Rte 495 to Rte 119 in Groton ctr. **Own:** Marilyn McGrath & Walter Petreyko. **QC: 7 39 61 S1 S8 S13**

Joseph Kilbridge Antiques

134 Main St (Rte 119) • 01450
(978)448-3330

18th & 19th C formal American & English furniture & fine arts at one of the largest dealers in Massachusetts. **Pr:** $100-20,000 **Est:** 1970 **Hrs:** Daily 10-5. **Sz:** L **Dir:** From I-495 take Rte 119 W 6 mi to Groton Center next to the Groton Inn. **Own:** Maurice Kilbridge. **QC: 41 52 54**

The Meadow Gallery

134 Main St (Rte 119) • 01450
(978)448-3330

Formal & country furniture & decorative accessories attractively displayed. **Est:** 1986 **Hrs:** Daily 10-5. **Sz:** L **Dir:** Behind Jos Kilbridge & Groton Antiques. **QC: 34 102**

Hadley

Hadley Antique Center [G70]

Rte 9 • 01035
(413)586-4093

Antiques & collectibles. **Est:** 1982 **Hrs:** Thu-Tue 10-5. **Sz:** L **CC:** V/MC **Dir:** I-91 N Exit 19 or I-91 S Exit 20: follow Rte 9 3 mi E, big, gray bldg on R. **Own:** Susan Allen.

Hadley Village Marketplace [G]

Rte 9 • 01035
(413)584-2306

Hrs: Daily. **Own:** Ron & Sue Sedergren.

Mountain Crest Antiques

45 Lawrence Plain Rd (Rte 47S) • 01035
(413)586-0352

Specializing in 18th & 19th C country furniture & accessories in paint, weathervanes, folk art, baskets & early textiles. **Pr:** $75-5,000 **Est:** 1980 **Hrs:** By chance/appt suggested. **Sz:** M **Dir:** I-91 N to Exit 19 (Hadley), E 1 mi on Rte 9, then 2 mi on Rte 47 S. **Own:** Marion & Ray Szala. **QC: 1 34 41**

North Hadley Antiques

399 River Dr (Rte 47) • 01035
(413)549-8776

Specializing in American blue decorated stoneware. Always a large selection. Our unheated barn is also full of an eclectic mix of antiques & collectibles. Dealers welcome. **Pr:** $5-1,000 **Est:** 1992 **Hrs:** Mar-Dec Sat-Sun 10-4; Jan-Feb Sun 10-4 or by chance/appt. **Sz:** L **Dir:** I-91 Exit 19 to Rte 9 E to Rte 47 N. 5.5 mi N on Rte 47 to shop. **Own:** John Delmolino. **QC: 31**

Westbrook House Fine Antiques & Collectibles

241 Russell St (Rte 9) • 01035
(413)586-8906

Lighting, furnishings, paintings & prints. Specializing in Art Deco, Art Nouveau & Victorian. **Est:** 1998 **Hrs:** Thu-Sat 10-5, Sun 12:30-5. **Dir:** Exit 19 off I-91. **QC: 5 89 65 S15**

Hanover Four Corners

La Petite Curiosity Shop

195 Washington St • 02339
(781)829-9599

Formal, country & Oriental furniture, Staffordshire, Dresden, Limoges, tea caddies, military, whale oil lamps, sewing items, paintings on ivory & porcelain, sterling desk & dresser accessories, iron & tin toys, jewelry & textiles. **Pr:** $50-4,500 **Est:** 1978 **Hrs:** Thu-Sat 11-5, Mon-Wed by chance/appt. **Sz:** M **Assn:** SSADA **Dir:** Rte 3 Exit 12: W on Rte 139 to Rte 53, R at Rte 53 & R on Old Washington St 1/2 mi. **Own:** Joan D Talbot. **QC: 48 36 23 S1 S12**

Harvard

Harvard Antiques Shop

1 Littleton Rd • 01451
(978)456-8729

A shop emphasizing country, Shaker, a large selection of Oriental rugs, with typical & far less common accessories. **Pr:** $25-50,000 **Hrs:** By chance/appt. **Sz:** M **Assn:** AAA **Dir:** Rte 2 or I-495 to Rte 110, 2 mi to ctr of town. **Own:** Pat Hatch. **QC: 7 34 57**

Paula Timmons McColgan Inc

170 Old Littleton Rd • 01451
(978)456-3712 • (978)456-3786 (fax)
mccolgan@bicnet.net

Quality painted furniture in original condition, artifacts & accessories. **Hrs:** By appt only. **Assn:** NHADA VADA MADA **Dir:** 1-1/2 mi from Rte 495. **QC: 34 51 36 S9 S15 S18**

Hatfield

Thomas Edward Carroll

(413)247-9767

Maps & manuscripts from 1400-1800, glass before 1930, unusual small items. **Pr:** $40-5,600 **Hrs:** By appt only. **Assn:** ADA **Dir:** I-91 Exit 21 near Northampton. Call for directions. **QC: 66 61 18**

Haverhill

Antique World [G25]

108 Washington St • 01830
(978)372-3919

A general line of antiques & collectibles. **Hrs:** Mon-Sat 10-5, Sun 12-5:30. **CC:** AX/V/MC/DIS **Own:** Cindy Tierney **QC: S12**

Greenleaf Antiques

62 Wingate St • 01832
(978)469-0017

Furniture, vintage jewelry & clothing & collectibles. **Hrs:** Tue-Sat 10-5:30. **Dir:** Behind Toula's Restaurant. **Own:** Marlene Murch.

Hingham

Pierce Galleries Inc

721 Main St (Rte 228) • 02043
(781)749-6023 • (617)749-6685 (fax)

In a large Victorian mansion, American art. Specializing in American Impressionists, Hudson River & Expressionist painters. **Est:** 1968 **Hrs:** By appt only. **Sz:** L **Assn:** AAA **Dir:** Rte 3 Exit 14: L off exit 3-1/2 mi, 3-story Victorian house set back from street with circular driveway. **Own:** Patricia Jobe Pierce. **QC: 7 11 S1 S9 S16**

Holliston

Antiques Plus [G30]

755 Washington St • 01746
(508)429-9186

Furniture, linens, Depression glass & primitives tastefully displayed in a 13-room Victorian home. **Est:** 1991 **Hrs:** Tue-Sat 10-5, Sun 1-5 (Jul-Aug til 4). **CC:** V/MC/DIS **Assn:** SADA **Dir:** Corn of Rte 16/126 & Central St. **Own:** Judy Coffey. **QC: 36 48 80**

Holliston Antiques [G35]
798 Washington St (Rte 16) • 01746
(508)429-0428

Furniture, primitives, mirrors, Fiestaware, Depression glass, jewelry & tin. **Est:** 1996 **Hrs:** Tue-Sat 10-5, Sun 1-5; Sum Tue-Sat 10-4 . **CC:** V/MC **QC: S6 S17 S7**

Wilder Shop
400 Washington St • 01746
(508)429-4836

In one of Holliston's oldest buildings, antiques, refinished furniture & accessories. Specializing in Colonial lighting fixtures, weathervanes & cupolas. **Hrs:** Tue-Sat 11-5, Sun 12-5; Sum Wed-Sat 11-5. **CC:** V/MC **Dir:** Jct of Rtes 16 & 126. **Own:** The Brighams. **QC: 48 65 45**

The Yankee Picker
86 Church St • 01746-2145
(508)429-6155
picker1@ix.netcom.com
www.tiaf.com/stores/yp

Large eclectic selection of antiques including glass & collectibles. Lots of smalls. Also some furniture. **Hrs:** Thu-Sat 10-5, Sun 12-5. **CC:** AX/V/MC **Assn:** SADA **Dir:** Corn of Church & Grove Sts. **Own:** Sylvia & Bill Stickney. **QC: 32 61**

Holyoke

Pink Swan Antiques
49 Cherry St • 01040
(413)536-SWAN

Fine New England country furniture & accessories. **Hrs:** Daily 9-5. **CC:** AX/V/MC/DIS **Dir:** I-91 Exit 16. **QC: 102 36 S1 S12**

Hopkinton

Heritage Antiques
216 Wood St (Rte 135) • 01748
(508)435-4031

Quality antiques, furniture & accessories, rugs & objets d'art. **Est:** 1959 **Hrs:** Tue-Fri 9-5; wknd eves & Mon by chance/appt. **Assn:** SADA **Own:** Clifton Gilson. **QC: 7 48 11**

Vintage Books
181 Hayden Rowe St • 01748
(508)435-3499
(800)734-7517 (MA only)
vintage@gis.net

Used, rare & out-of-print books including American history, literature, theology, illustrated books, books about collectibles, signed, limited & first edition literature. **Pr:** $4-500 **Hrs:** Tue-Sat 11-6, Fri 11-8. **CC:** V/MC/DIS **Assn:** MARIAB **Dir:** I-495 Exit 20: 3 mi N at the blinking yellow light. **Own:** Nancy & David Haines. **QC: 18**

Housatonic

Diana McGrory Oriental Rugs & Fine Textiles
410 N Plain Rd • 02136
(413)274-6532

Specializing in antique decorative Oriental carpets. **Hrs:** By appt only. **Assn:** BCADA **Dir:** 5 mi N of Great Barrington. **QC: 76**

Huntington

Barbara Paulson Antiquarian Paper
24 Allen Coit Rd • 01050
(413)667-3208

Victorian paper ephemera, antique postcards, early children's series & prints. **Est:** 1982 **Hrs:** By appt only. **QC: 39**

Indian Orchard

Patti's Antiques & Treasures

532 Main St • 01020
(413)543-8484
pixiepite@aol.com

Furniture, jewelry, collectibles & lighting, specializing in fireplace mantles, finished oak, mahogany & fine wood furniture. **Est:** 1985 **Hrs:** Wed-Sat 12-5 or by appt. **CC:** V/MC **Own:** Patti Schutte.

Lanesborough

Amber Springs Antiques

29 S Main St (Rte 7) • 01237
(413)442-1237

American furnishings large & small. Specializing in tools, pottery, advertising, country store & unusual trivia. **Est:** 1957 **Hrs:** Mar-Dec Mon-Sat 10-5, Sun 12-5; Jan-Feb wknds. **Sz:** L **Dir:** Betw Pittsfield & Williamstown. **Own:** Laurence Elfenbein. **QC: 1 39 86**

Lee

Aardenburg Antiques

144 W Park St • 01238
(413)243-0001

Furniture & accessories of the early 19th C. **Hrs:** Sat-Sun by chance or anytime by appt. **Assn:** BCADA **Own:** David Hubregsen & Douglas Howes **QC: S16**

Henry B Holt

125 Golden Hill Rd • 01240
(413)243-3184 • (413)243-9918 (fax)

Dealer in investment-quality 19th & early 20th C American paintings. Interested in purchasing or handling the disposal of individual paintings or estates on a buyout or consultant basis. **Hrs:** By appt only. **Assn:** BCADA NEAA **Dir:** I-90 Exit 2: Rte 20 through Lee, up hill to State Police on L, just before Black Swan Inn. Golden Hill Rd is on R. **Own:** Henry Holt. **QC: 41 7 S1 S9 S16**

Lenox

Charles L Flint Antiques Inc

56 Housatonic St • 01240
(413)637-1634 • (413)637-0222 (fax)
chazma@vgernet.net

19th & 20th C paintings, 19th C country furniture & accessories, Shaker, folk art, art, early glass & toys. **Pr:** $25-100,000 **Hrs:** Mon-Sat 9-5, Sun by appt. **Assn:** BCADA NEAA **Dir:** From NY: Taconic Pkwy to Rte 23 N to Rte 7 N to Lenox Ctr. Mass Pike to Rte 20 N to Lenox Ctr. From VT Rte 7 S to Lenox Ctr. **QC: 52 7 57 S1**

Past & Future Antiques

63 Church St • 01240
(413)637-2225
martiques@aol.com

19th & early 20th C fine small antiques including perfume bottles, pens & inkwells, smoking accessories, golf & tennis, sewing implements, sterling flatware, china, glass, jewelry & scientific instruments. **Pr:** $30-1,500 **Est:** 1996 **Hrs:** Jun-Sep daily 10-5, Oct-May Fri-Sun 10-5, Mon-Thu by appt. **Sz:** M **CC:** AX/V/MC **Assn:** BCADA **Dir:** From N: Rte 7 to Rte 7A into Lenox. L on Franklin St, which becomes Church St. From S: Rte 7 to Rte 183; L on 183 to Lenox, R on Church St. In the historic shopping district. **Own:** Marcy Cohen. **QC: 78 79 107**

Stone's Throw Antiques

51 Church St • 01240
(413)637-2733 • (413)637-9835 (fax)

Offering a fine selection of 18th, 19th & early 20th C furniture, china, glass, silver & decorative accessories. **Pr:** $10-10,000 **Est:** 1982 **Hrs:** Apr-Dec daily 10-5, Jan-Mar Thu-Sun 10-5. **Sz:** M **CC:** AX/V/MC **Assn:** BCADA **Dir:** In the historic shopping district. From N: Rte 7 to Rte 7A into Lenox. L on Franklin St, which becomes Church St. From S: Rte 7 to Rte 183; L on 183 to Lenox, R on Church St. **Own:** Sydelle Shapiro & Hilary Beadell. **QC: 48 60 36**

R W Wise Goldsmiths Inc
81 Church St • 01240
(413)637-1589 • (413)637-8275 (fax)
2101@polygon.net
www.polygon.net/~rwwise

Antique & estate jewelry, specializing in fine antique pieces with diamonds & colored gemstones. Dealer in fine colored gems & pearls. **Est:** 1980 **Hrs:** Tue-Sat 10-5, Jul & Aug open daily. **Sz:** M **CC:** AX/V/MC/DIS **Assn:** SJH AGTA AGA **Dir:** Mass Pike (I-90) Exit 7 (20N) to Rte 7A to Lenox Village. **Own:** Richard & Rebekah Wise. **QC: 64 S1**

Lexington

Fancy Flea Antiques
1841 Massachusetts Ave • 02173
(781)862-9650

An extensive collection of antique & fine jewelry, sterling silver, fine china, glass & decorative accessories. **Est:** 1977 **Hrs:** Sep-Jun Mon-Sat 10-5:30, Jul-Aug closed Sat. **Sz:** M **CC:** AX/V/MC/DIS **Dir:** Opp the Boston Federal Savings Bank. **QC: 64 36 78**

The Music Emporium
165 Massachusetts Ave • 02173
(781)860-0049
musicemp@tiac.net

Vintage guitars, banjos, mandolins, concertina, wooden flutes, stringed instruments & dulcimers. **Pr:** $10-15,000 **Est:** 1977 **Hrs:** Mon, Wed, Fri 11-6, Tue, Thu, Sat 11-8, Sun 12-5. **Sz:** M **CC:** V/MC. **QC: 69 S16**

Lincoln

Brown-Corbin Fine Art
Sandy Pond Rd • 01773
(781)259-1210 • (781)259-1282 (fax)
bcfa4art@earthlink.net
www.artnet.brown-corbin

Specializing in fine 19th & early 20th C American paintings, watercolors & drawings, with emphasis on Luminists, American Pre-Raphaelites & Impressionists selected with a view toward quality & importance. **Hrs:** By appt only. **Dir:** 5 mi W of Exit 28B on Rte 128. **Own:** Jeffrey Brown & Kathryn Corbin. **QC: 7 S9**

Littleton

Blue Cape Antiques
620 Great Rd (Rte 119) • 01460
(978)486-4709
curly620@aol.com

Eclectic collection from antiquities to collectibles of every sort. **Pr:** $30+ **Est:** 1964 **Hrs:** Wed-Sat 11-5, occasional Suns. **Sz:** M **Dir:** 495 Exit 31N: 1 mi W. **Own:** Norman Caron. **QC: 1 7 32 S1 S14**

Erickson's Antique Stoves
2 Taylor St • 01460
(978)486-3589

Specializing in completely restored wood & gas stoves 1890-1930s including Glenwood, Magic Chef, Crawford, Fairmount, Acorn & those made by North Dighton Stove Co. Also specializing in conversions of wood-burning kitchen ranges to gas/electric. **Pr:** $1,500-5,000 **Est:** 1980 **Hrs:** Mon-Fri 8-4; appt strongly encouraged. **Sz:** M **Assn:** SPNEA **Dir:** I-495 Exit 30: L onto Rte 110, turn L 3/4 mi after Clyde's Carwash. In Victorian RR Station behind car wash. **Own:** David Erickson. **QC: 62 S16 S17**

Littleton Antiques [G25]
476 King St • 01460
(978)952-0001

General line. **Est:** 1998 **Hrs:** Mon-Sat 10-5, Sun 12-5. **Sz:** M **CC:** V/MC **Dir:** I-495 Exit 31: toward Littleton Commons. R at the lights, located on the R. **Own:** Lally Chase.

Sunflower Antiques [G30]
537 King St • 01460
(978)486-0606
snflower@ultranet.com

Twelve rooms full of early glass, china, vintage & costume jewelry, furniture, pottery, silver, toys, 50s kitchen, primitives, tole, eglomise, bronze, lamps, textiles, early linens, vintage clothing & bedding. **Est:** 1995 **Hrs:** Tue-Sat 10-5, Sun 12-5. **Sz:** L **CC:** V/MC **Dir:** I-495 Exit 31: to Littleton Common. L at lights (Rte 110), 200 yds on R. **Own:** Catherine Halloran. **QC: 49 64 23**

Upton House Antiques
275 King St (Rte 2A-110) • 01460
(978)486-3367

Antiques in the country manner, featuring furniture & smalls in original condition, some with paint, quilts & kitchenware. **Est:** 1984 **Hrs:** Tue & Thu-Sat 10-3, Sat til 4, Sun 12-4. **CC:** V/MC **Dir:** Rte 495 Exit 30: R 1,000 ft. **Own:** Eileen Poland. **QC: 34 41**

Longmeadow

Drake Field Antiques
16 Meadowbrook Rd • 01106
(413)567-7412

Early 19th C furniture, specializing in English & American brass. **Est:** 1986 **Hrs:** By appt only. **Own:** Patricia Drake Keady. **QC: 20 52**

Lowell

Whitney House Antiques
913 Pawtucket St • 01851
(978)458-0044 • (978)458-7746 (fax)
whouse@mediaone.net
www.whouseantiques.com

Finer Victorian furniture, period American & English furniture, Tiffany lamps, fancy mirrors, oil paintings. Noted as one of the top ten antique shops north of Boston. In an 1824 house. **Hrs:** Mon-Sat 10-5, Sun 12-5. **CC:** AX/V/MC/DIS **Own:** George Guilmette.

Lunenburg

Jeffreys' Antique Mall [G200]
Rtes 2A & 13 • 01482
(978)582-7831

Glass, china, pottery, porcelain & collectibles. **Pr:** $1-500 **Est:** 1990 **Hrs:** Sun-Thu 10-5, Fri 10-6, Sat 10-5. **Sz:** H **CC:** V/MC **Dir:** Corn of Rte 2A & 13 5 mi S of West Townsend. **Own:** Jacqueline & Raymond Jeffreys. **QC: 34 48 32**

Lynn

Diamond District Antiques
9A Broad St • 01902
(781)586-8788

A large selection of furniture, collectibles, glass, pottery, china, prints, oil paintings & tapestries; specializing in the Victorian era. **Pr:** $10-1,500 **Est:** 1993 **Hrs:** Tue-Wed 10-2, Thu-Fri 10-4:30, other days by appt only. **Sz:** M **Dir:** From Boston tunnel follow Rte 1A N to signs; from Lynnway follow 1A past North Shore Comm College; shop 2 blks from College. **Own:** Karen Ring. **QC: 32 58 S9 S12**

Manchester

Susan Stella Antiques
(978)568-7371
susanstella@hotmail.com
www.susanstella.com

18th & 19th C American furniture, textiles & samplers, paintings, folk art, quilts, baskets, hooked rugs, antique garden furniture, ship models, porcelain including export & period accessories. **Est:** 1978 **Hrs:** By appt only. **CC:** V/MC **Assn:** NEAA. **QC: 1 41 80**

Marblehead

Antiquewear
82 Front St • 01945
(781)639-0070 • (781)639-1856 (fax)
(877)665-9680
antiquew@shove.net
www.shore.net/~antiquew/

Antique buttons of the 1800s fashioned to jewelry. **Pr:** $25-300 **Est:** 1970 **Hrs:** May-Dec daily or by appt. **CC:** AX/V/MC **Dir:** Across from The Landing near the harbor. **Own:** Jerry Fine. **QC: 63**

Brass Bounty
68 Front St • 01945
(781)631-3864

Nautical antiques, restored gas & electric chandeliers. **Est:** 1972 **Hrs:** Jun-Dec daily 9-5:30, Jan-May Fri-Sun 9-5:30. **Sz:** M **CC:** V/MC **Dir:** Just across from The Landing on the harbor. **Own:** Dick Dermody & Maryanne Bajackian. **QC: 65 70**

The Good Buy Antiques
120 Pleasant St • 01945
(781)631-7555

Furniture & decorative accessories. General line. **Est:** 1974 **Hrs:** Mon-Sat 10-5, Sun 1-5. **CC:** V/MC. **QC: 36 48 S2 S12**

Heeltappers Antiques
134 Washington St • 01945
(781)631-7722

19th C American country & formal furniture, silver, glass, export & English Staffordshire. **Pr:** $25-3,500 **Hrs:** Wed-Sat 11-5, Sun 1-5, Mon hols 1-5, Tue by chance/appt; closed Feb 1-Mar 15. **Sz:** M **CC:** V/MC **Dir:** In the Old Town. **Own:** Judith Scott & Anne Hosmer. **QC: 34 78 60**

Use the Specialty QuickCode indexes at the back of the book to find dealers who specialize in your area of interest.

Marblehead Antiques
118 Pleasant St • 01945
(781)631-9791

Formal & country furniture, American & Continental decorative accessories. **Est:** 1968 **Hrs:** Daily, call ahead advised. **Sz:** M **CC:** AX/V/MC/DIS **Dir:** Across from the movie theatre. **QC: 36 48**

Old Town Antique Co-op [G5]
108 Washington St • 01945
(781)631-9728

American antiques & accessories, concentrating on wicker, quilts, oak & pine furniture, prints & jewelry. **Est:** 1979 **Hrs:** Call ahead for hrs. **Sz:** M **Dir:** In the ctr of the Old Town. **Own:** Marla Bryer & Lynne Segal. **QC: 91 50 55**

Sacks Antiques
38 State St at Front St • 01945
(781)631-0770

Marblehead's oldest antique shop. Fine English furniture & china, large collection of silver objets d'art. **Pr:** $25-50,000 **Est:** 1912 **Hrs:** Tue-Sat. **CC:** AX/V/MC/DIS **Dir:** Opp the Town Landing, look for famous gold eagle. **Own:** Stanley Sacks. **QC: 48 56 78 S22**

Christine Vining Antiques
(617)631-8224

Fine period American & English furniture, glass, Chinese export porcelain & silver. **Hrs:** By appt only. **QC: 52 54 71**

Marion

The Hobby Horse
339 Front St • 02738
(508)748-0763

A varied & changing stock of 18th & 19th C furniture & decorative accessories. Buying daily from Plymouth County homes. **Pr:** $18-2,750 **Est:** 1959 **Hrs:** Mid-May to mid-

Oct Fri-Sun; after Oct 15 Sat-Sun 11-4. **Sz:** M **Assn:** SNEADA **Dir:** I-195 Exit 20 S, 3/4 mi thru Rte 6 stoplight. **Own:** Robert E Mower. **QC: 1 20 78 S1 S9 S12**

The Marion Antique Shop

335 Wareham Rd (Rte 6) • 02738
(508)748-3606 • (508)748-9968 (fax)

16th-20th C antiques including postcards, period furniture, books, Oriental rugs, silver, glass, china, paintings, prints & a great selection of antique wicker furniture. **Pr:** $1-5,000 **Est:** 1976 **Hrs:** Apr-Nov Thu-Mon 10-5; Dec-Mar Fri-Mon 10-5. **Sz:** L **CC:** AX/V/MC **Assn:** NEAA SPNEA **Dir:** Rte I-95 to Rte 105 Exit 20: L at 1st light onto Rte 6, E 1/2 mi on L. **Own:** Frank McNamee. **QC: 91 76 78 S1 S9 S12**

Marlboro

Wayside Antique Co-op [G20]

1009 Boston Post Rd • 01752
(508)481-9621

Offering a diversified selection of antiques with an emphasis on Depression glass, porcelain, linens, silver, furniture & jewelry. **Pr:** $1.00-2,500. **Est:** 1992 **Hrs:** Daily 10-5. **Sz:** M **CC:** V/MC/DIS **Assn:** SADA **Dir:** I-495 exit Rte 20 E. Rte 128 exit Rte 20 W. Co-op is next to country store near the Wayside Inn. **Own:** Buck, DJ, Linda & Ralph Maher. **QC: 48 61 80 S1 S12**

Wex Rex Collectibles

280 Worcester Rd (Rte 9) • 01702
(508)620-6181 • (508)562-1196 (fax)
wexrex@earthlink.net
www.collectingchannel.com

The emporium of popular cultural artifacts, toys, paper, music, movies & TV memorabilia, nostalgia, advertising, Disneyana, posters, Beatles & rock & roll memorabilia. **Pr:** $5-5,000 **Est:** 1984 **Hrs:** Mon-Sat 11-7, occasional Sun. **Sz:** M **CC:** V/MC **Assn:** PSMA **Dir:** Mass Pike Exit 13. In Tropic Isle Plaza. **Own:** Gary Sohmers. **QC: 87 67 39 S1 S8 S2**

Marshfield

Antiques at Springbrook

845 Union St • 02050
(781)834-7194

Large shop of quality period furniture & decorative accessories. Diverse inventory of formal, country, old paint, iron, brass, copper, fireplace accessories & garden shop. **Pr:** $25-3,000 **Est:** 1986 **Hrs:** May-Dec Thu-Sun 11-3 & always by appt. **Sz:** M **Assn:** SSADA SPNEA **Dir:** Rte 3 Exit 12: L betw Mobil & Gulf, shop is 2 mi on L. **Own:** Eleanor Hoehn. **QC: 52 34 36 S8 S9 S12**

Lord Randall Bookshop

22 Main St • 02050
(781)837-1400
lrandl@idt.net
booksonbibliofind.com

A selected general stock of antiquarian books with an emphasis on New England & literature, art & children's books, housed in a 100-year-old heated barn. **Pr:** $1-1,000 **Est:** 1972 **Hrs:** Tue-Sat 11-5, Sun by chance. **CC:** V/MC **Assn:** MARIAB **Dir:** Rte 3S from Boston, Marshfield Exit: R on Rte 139, 2-1/2 mi to 4th light, L on Rte 3A, 1st bldg on R. **Own:** Gail Wills. **QC: 18**

Mattapan

Old Mansions Co Inc

1305 Blue Hill Ave • 02126
(617)296-0445
oldmansions@earthlink.net

Diverse inventory including garden & architectural artifacts: stone fragments, columns, fountains, ironwork, colonial brick, balustrades, furniture, urns, gates, benches, paving, enclosures, colonnades & belvideres. **Est:** 1953 **Hrs:** Tue-Sat 10-5. **CC:** AX/V/MC **Own:** Frank Kaminski & Larry Richmond. **QC: 3 60**

Mattapoisett

1812 House with Antiques

35 Marion Rd • 02739
(508)758-6267

18th & 19th C furniture & accessories, primitives & the unusual. **Est:** 1960 **Hrs:** By chance/appt. **Dir:** At Bolles Corner follow signs from Rte 6. **Own:** Arlene Dexter. **QC: 36 48 106**

Jillys Antiques

87 County Rd (Rte 6) • 02739
(508)758-9755 • (508)758-6759 (fax)
nita11@mediaone.net

General line of antiques & collectibles. Specializing in architectural & garden related pieces including wrought iron furniture, unique garden statues & planters. **Est:** 1992 **Hrs:** By chance/appt. **CC:** V/MC **Dir:** Rte195 Exit 19A: L on Rte 6. Shop is 3/4 mi on L. **Own:** Jill Jarvis. **QC: 3 36 60 S8 S12 S1**

Upcellar Antiques & Aunt Sherry's [G2]

44 Main St • 02739
(508)758-6978

House full of antiques & collectibles. **Est:** 1985 **Hrs:** Wed-Sat 10-4, Sun 1-4, Mon-Tue by chance. **Dir:** Rte 6 & Main St.

Medfield

Blue Hen Antiques

2 North St • 02052
(508)359-5315 • (508)359-7093 (fax)

A general line of antiques as well as custom furniture & decorative accessories. **Pr:** $10-2,500 **Est:** 1983 **Hrs:** Tue 10-3, Wed-Sat 10-5, Sun by chance. **Sz:** M **CC:** V/MC **Assn:** SADA **Dir:** Approx 10 mi off Rte 128 on Rte 109 W, 10 mi off Rte 495 on Rte 109 E. **Own:** Judith Swanson. **QC: 48 60 36 S8 S12**

Medford

Ellen Lee Davis

43 Powder House Rd • 02155
(781)395-8717

Early country furniture & accessories in paint & original finishes, primitives, baskets, quilts & homespuns. **Est:** 1979 **Hrs:** By appt only. **Assn:** SADA. **QC: 102 106 80**

Medway

As Time Goes By [G15]

114 D Main St • 02053
(508)533-7673 • (508)533-7673 (fax)
jmen@otw.com

Largest shop of its kind in the area, featuring a large selection of Victorian, country & Deco furniture. A very nice selection of estate jewelry, glassware & the unusual. **Pr:** $25-2,500 **Est:** 1981 **Hrs:** Mon-Thu 10-4:30, Fri 10-7, Sat 10-4, Sun 12-4. **Sz:** L **CC:** V/MC **Dir:** Rte 495 to Rte 109. Approx 5 mi on Rte 109 to the Medway Shopping Plaza. **Own:** James Menize. **QC: 48 61 63**

The Red Sleigh Inn — Antiques

258 Main St • 02053
(508)533-7120
jgilliatt@aol.com

A fine assortment of Americana, primitives, cupboards, yellowware, pewter, textiles, pine tables, wooden bowls, smalls in old paint & civil war items. **Pr:** $25-4,000 **Est:** 1990 **Hrs:** Thu-Sat 10-5, Sun 12-5, Mon-Wed by chance/appt. **CC:** AX/V/MC **Dir:** I-495 Exit 18: R off ramp, 2 mi E. Shop is located in a white federal colonial house on L. **Own:** Judy Gilliatt. **QC: 106 34 1**

Mendon

Nipmuc Trading Post [G50+]

49 Uxbridge Rd (rear) (Rte 16) • 01756
(508)634-8300 • (508)478-1900 (fax)

Featuring an ever-changing variety of

antique oak, mahogany & other furniture, books, paper goods, prints, paintings, primitives, glassware, pottery, military memorabilia, hunting & fishing items, toys, vintage clothing & jewelry, lighting, rugs. **Pr:** $1-15,000 **Est:** 1992 **Hrs:** Tue 10-5, Wed 10-8, Thu-Sun 10-5. **Sz:** H **CC:** AX/V/MC **Assn:** SADA **Dir:** Across from Nipmuc Marina, on the hill. Easy to reach from Rtes 146, 495, 122, 109, 85 & the Mass Pike. **Own:** Donna Grasseschi. **QC: 48 32 36 S12 S2 S8**

Middleboro

Charles & Barbara Adams

15 Prospect St • 02346
(508)947-7277 • (508)587-5362 (fax)

Early American antiques bought & sold. Bennington Pottery a specialty; also furniture, paintings, hooked rugs, baskets, iron, redware & Indian items. **Hrs:** By appt only. **Assn:** ADA GSAAA **Dir:** Rte 495 Exit 4 to Rte 105 to Middleboro. **QC: 1 22 65 S1 S11 S14**

Ancient Art International

(508)947-6498 • (508)946-0766 (fax)
rbrockwa@ix,netcom.com
www.antiques.com/ancientart.htm

Fine art. **Hrs:** By appt only. **CC:** V/MC **Assn:** ADA. **QC: 7**

Milford

Dunbar's Gallery

76 Haven St • 01757
(508)634-8697

Vintage early American tin, cast iron & comic toys & banks, old signs & posters, folk art & Dedham pottery & Halloween items. Also automobilia & motorcycle items. **Pr:** $15-15,000 **Est:** 1970 **Hrs:** Mon-Fri 8-5, appt preferred. **Sz:** M **CC:** AX/V/MC **Assn:** SADA **Dir:** I-495 Exit 21B (W Main St & Upton): 1st L onto South St, 2-1/2 mi, L on to Haven St, 1 mi down on L side. **Own:** Howard & Leila Dunbar. **QC: 1 87 39 S1**

Milton

Earthly Possessions

10 Bassett St • 02186
(617)696-2440

Decorative china & furniture including custom iron tables & eclectic home furnishings. **Hrs:** Mon-Sat 9:30-6, Sun 11-4. **Assn:** SADA **Own:** Sandy & Ken Keohane.

Monterey

Dagmar's Antiques

Rte 23 • 01245
(413)528-6485

18th & 19th C American & Continental furniture, paintings & decorative accessories. Specializing in Biedermeier furniture. **Hrs:** By appt only. **Assn:** BCADA **Own:** Vladimir & Dagmar Kubes. **QC: 11 52 53 S16**

Needham

Esther Tuveson Books & Ephemera

30 Brookside Rd • 02492-1302
(781)444-5533

Antiquarian books: Americana, children's, fine arts, first editions, illustrated & nonfiction special interests. **Hrs:** By appt only. **Assn:** MARIAB. **QC: 18 S9**

New Bedford

Brookside Antiques — Art Glass Gallery

44 N Water St • 02741
(508)993-4944
brookside1@aol.com

Specialist in 19th C art glass including a large collection of New Bedford glass & cut glass Pairpoint products in quantity. **Est:** 1964 **Hrs:** Mon-Sat 10:30-4:30 (closed Mon in Win). **Sz:** M **CC:** V/MC **Assn:** SNEADA **Dir:** Directly E of the Whaling Museum. **Own:** Louis O St Aubin Jr. **QC: 100 S1**

Duval's Antiques
1 Johnny Cake Hill • 02740
(508)996-2320

Antique & estate jewelry, silver & other smalls. **Dir:** In New Bedford's Whaling National Historic Park. **Own:** Henry & Jean Duval. **QC: 64 78**

New Bedford Antiques Company [G260]
85 Coggeshall St • 02746
(508)993-7600

Jewelry, silver, glass, American, Victorian, oak & custom mahogany furniture, clocks & toys, Art Deco, china, pottery, ephemera, bronzes, Oriental antiques, ivories & paintings. **Pr:** $5-500 **Est:** 1986 **Hrs:** Mon-Sat 10-5, Sun 12-5. **Sz:** H **CC:** V/MC **Dir:** I-195 Exit 16E or 17W: 30 min from Providence, 50 min from Boston. **Own:** Felix Petrarca.

New Boston

Jean Campbell Antiques
185 Lyndeboro Rd • 03070
(603)487-2434

Early American primitives, country furniture, decorative accessories & collectibles. **Hrs:** By appt only. **Assn:** NHADA. **QC: 106 102 36**

Newburyport

John J Collins Jr Gallery
11 Market Sq • 01950
(978)462-7276

A handsome, large & beautifully lighted gallery of old & antique Oriental rugs; specializing in tribal & village pieces: Bidjar, Serapi, Southern Persian Tribal. **Hrs:** Mon-Fri 10-5 by chance/appt. **Assn:** ADA NHADA **Dir:** At the bottom of State St on Market Sq. **QC: 76**

Paul & Linda DeCoste
288 Merrimack St • 01950
(978)462-2138

18th & 19th C furniture & accessories, folk & nautical items with specialties in scientific instruments, dental & medical items & metal of the 17th, 18th & 19th C. **Hrs:** By appt only. **Assn:** NHADA **Dir:** Call for directions. **QC: 70 41 77**

Colette Donovan
210 Storey Ave • 01950
(978)346-0614

18th & early 19th C American country furniture in old or original surface & usual accessories with textiles: hooked yarn sewn rugs, bed coverings & other "labors of love." **Hrs:** By appt only. **Assn:** ADA MADA NHADA VADA. **QC: 102 51 80**

Peter H Eaton Antiques Inc
39 State St (2nd floor) • 01950
(978)465-2754 • (978)465-2754 (fax)
antiques@seacoast.com
www.seacoast.com/~antiques

Specializing in fine New England furniture, including Pilgrim Century & Queen Anne made between 1690-1740, primarily in original, unrestored condition. **Est:** 1970 **Hrs:** Thu-Sat 10-5 or by chance/appt. **Assn:** ADA NHADA **Dir:** Downtown near int of Essex & State St. **QC: 1 52**

Lepore Fine Arts
58 Merrimac St (Horton's Yard) • 01950
(978)462-1663 • (978)462-8847 (fax)

American & European paintings from the 19th & 20th C with a focus on the years 1870-1930. Works by such artists as Laura Hills, I Appleton Brown, Theresa Bernstein, Theodore Wendel & Gertrude Fiske in a gallery overlooking Newburyport's waterfront. **Hrs:** Tue-Sat 10-5. **Sz:** M **CC:** AX/V/MC **Own:** Sandra Lepore & Lisa Tagney. **QC: 7 9 S1 S8 S9**

Scott F Nason Antiques

12 Marlboro St • 01950
(978)462-2953
snason@mediaone.net

Printed & manuscript Americana, ephemera, 19th C photography & marine antiques. **Hrs:** By chance/appt. **QC: 18 39 70**

Olde Port Book Shop [G12]

18 State St • 01950
(978)462-0100 • (603)394-0055 (fax)
(800)870-1500

Antiquarian books & a selection of antique prints & broadsides. Specializing in culinary arts, travel, sporting & Americana. **Pr:** $5-2,500 **Est:** 1991 **Hrs:** Apr-Dec Mon-Thu 10-5:30, Fri-Sat til 6, Sun 12-5:30; Jan-Mar Mon-Fri 11-5 exc Wed, Sat 10-6, Sun12-5 **Sz:** 25,000 books **CC:** AX/V/MC **Assn:** ABAA MARIAB **Dir:** In downtown Newburyport across from Scandia Restaurant. **Own:** Philip Reynolds. **QC: 18 19 66 S1**

Newton

Belle Maison

51 Langley Rd • 02459
(617)964-6455 • (617)964-6420 (fax)
info@belle-maison.com
www.belle-maison.com

Furnishings with a country bent emphasizing pine: American & European dining tables, chests, cupboards & coffee tables. Also painted & decorative accessories. **Est:** 1994 **Hrs:** Mon-Fri 10-6, Sat 10-5, Sun 11-5. **Sz:** M **CC:** AX/V/MC **Own:** Karol & Sheldon Tager. **QC: 34 47 102**

Brass Buff Antiques

977 Chestnut St • 02464-1101
(617)964-9388

Specializing in scientific & medical instruments, nautical items, lighting, sconces, candlesticks, cannons, fireplace equipment, tools, kitchenware, copper, selected furniture, armor, corkscrews, hardware & doorknobs. **Pr:** $3-10,000 **Est:** 1973 **Hrs:** Tue-Sun 1-5, call first. **Sz:** M **Assn:** SADA **Dir:** Rte 9W Chestnut St exit: L under Rte 9, 1st shop on R at top of hill. **Own:** Mel Rosenburg. **QC: 20 40 65 S16 S12**

Edna's Attic

132 Charles St • 02466
617)969-1564

Furniture. **Est:** 1970 **Hrs:** Thu-Sat 10-4, Sun 12-4. **Dir:** I-90 Exit 14: Rte 30 E, at Mobile across from Marriott bear R onto Auburn St, 2nd R is Charles St, go thru tunnel, bear L. **QC: 48**

Art & Kathy Green

324 Ward St • 02159
(617)630-0896

Fine early glass & ceramics. **Hrs:** By appt only. **QC: 104 23 22**

Page & Parchment

375 Elliot St • 01752
(617)964-3599
vpa@world.std.com

Antiquarian books specializing in early technology, medicine, art & architecture, foreign history & travel, science, gardening & ephemera. **Est:** 1976 **Hrs:** Wed-Sat 12-6. **Sz:** S **CC:** V/MC/DIS **Dir:** Rte 9E 1/4 mi, W Newton/Waban exit: R at stop sign on Ellis St, R at stop sign up hill to Chestnut St, R at light to Elliot, 50 ft to lot. **Own:** Val Paul Auger. **QC: 18 39**

Sonia Paine Antiques

373 Boylston St • 02459
(617)566-9669 • (617)928-9806 (fax)

French & Oriental antiques, estate & period jewelry, silver, porcelain, custom-designed French & Italian furniture, Russian & French enamel. **Est:** 1968 **Hrs:** Mon-Sat 10-4 or by appt. **Assn:** AAA SADA **Dir:** On Rte 9 1 mi W of Chestnut Hill Mall & diagonally across from the Atrium. **QC: 47 64 S1 S12 S14**

Sparkle Plenty

63 Harvard St • 02159
(617)969-1193 • (617)969-1193 (fax)

Specializing in American costume jewelry from 1920-1960; large inventory of Miriam Haskell, Trifari, Pennino, Coro, Mazer, Schiaparelli & Eisenberg in addition to unsigned costume jewelry & Bakelite. **Pr:** $50-1,000 **Hrs:** By appt only. **Dir:** Call for directions. **Own:** Elizabeth Chadis. **QC: 63 S1**

Marcia & Bea Antiques [G7]

One Lincoln St • 02461
(617)332-2408

19th C American country furniture, pine, oak, wicker, bed quilts, rugs, decorative accessories, country pottery, fine silver, flatware, fine & estate jewelry, vintage costume jewelry,20th C designs from Deco to 50s, dolls, Heisey glass. **Pr:** $10-4,000 **Est:** 1974 **Hrs:** Mon-Sat 10-5, Thu til 8, Sun 1-5. **Sz:** M **CC:** V/MC/DIS **Assn:** SADA **Dir:** 1 blk from Rte 9 & Woodward St, at the int of Walnut & Lincoln. **Own:** Marcia Kohl. **QC: 48 23 64 S6 S12**

Arthur T Gregorian Inc

2284 Washington St • 02462
(617)244-2553 • (617)527-7847 (fax)
(800)272-4554
www.atgregorian.com

One of the largest & most varied collections of new, used & antique rugs. Over 6,000 Oriental rugs constantly in stock. **Hrs:** Mon-Tue & Thu-Fri 9-6, Wed 10-9, Sat 9-5, Sun 12-5. **CC:** V/MC **Dir:** Rte 95 Exit 21: near the Pillar House Restaurant. **QC: 76 S16 S1**

Norfolk

Norfolk Antiques

16 Carlson Cir • 02056
(508)528-0056

A large, constantly changing selection of country furniture & furnishings in a country setting, specializing in popular styles of oak, mahogany & cherry; collectibles, paintings, toys, rugs & the unusual. **Pr:** $50-1,500 **Hrs:** Sum Thu-Sat 10-6, Sun 12-5; Win Wed-Sat 10-6, Sun 12-5. **Sz:** L **CC:** V/MC/DIS **Dir:** Rte 128 to Rte 109 A to Rte 115, next to Norfolk commuter train depot, behind PO, in Norfolk Ctr. **Own:** Peter Kane. **QC: 34 48**

North Andover

Ruby Manor Antiques & Fine Arts

133 Main St • 01845
(978)683-4400

Porcelain, marble, bronzes, French furniture, European watercolors & oils, miniature paintings on porcelain, ivory, cloisonné & silver. Specialties include Meissen, Coalport, KPM, Minton & Mandarin porcelains. **Hrs:** Wed-Sat 10:30-5 or by appt. **Own:** Donna Lee Rubin. **QC: 23 47 10**

North Attleboro

Antiques of North Attleboro [G30]

585 E Washington St (Rte 1) • 02760
(508)643-1565
www.antiquesofna.com

Victorian & estate jewelry, Civil War & Indian artifacts, clocks, vintage clothing & fine linens, quality silver, fine china, glassware, furniture, primitives & toys. **Hrs:** Mon-Fri 10-6, Thu til 8, Sat 10-5, Sun 12-5. **Sz:** M **CC:** AX/V/MC/DIS **Dir:** I-495 Exit 14B: 4 mi S on Rte 1. I-295 Exit 1B: 4 mi N on Rte 1. **Own:** Susan Forrester, Michael LeFort & Susan Zhunga. **QC: 35 64 22 S8 S12**

North Brookfield

New England Garden Ornaments

38 Brookfield Rd • 01535
(508)867-4474 • (508)867-8409 (fax)
www.negardenornaments.com

Garden architecture & ornamentation

including sundials, garden antiques, lead statuary, decorative planters, cast-iron urns, English cast stone ornaments, plaques, cisterns, birdbaths, finials, furniture, garden seats, benches, fountains & balustrades. **Hrs:** Apr-Oct Tue-Sat 10-5:30; Nov-Mar Tue-Sat 10-4; Jan by appt only. **Sz:** L **CC:** V/MC/DIS **Dir:** Mass Pike Exit 9: to Rte 20/Charlton, 2 mi to Rte 49 N, 7 mi to T jct w/ Rte 9. Turn L on Rte 9 W 2 mi. R onto Rte 67. 2.2 mi down on R. **Own:** Nancy B Grimes. **QC: 60**

North Dighton

Walnut Hill Farm Antique Co-op [G]

2480 Winthrop St (Rte 44) • 02764
(508)252-5523

Hrs: Daily 10-5. **Dir:** 2 mi W of Taunton Flea Market.

North Scituate

The Bayfield Shop

675 Country Way • 02066
(781)545-0927

Clocks, furniture, china, lamps & glass. **Est:** 1962 **Hrs:** By appt only. **Dir:** Off Rte 3A. **Own:** Dorothy Meurch.

Village Antiques & Collectibles

143 Danielson Pike • 02857
(401)647-7780
villantq@aol.com

Furniture, china, silver, linen & collectibles. **Hrs:** Tue-Sat 10-5, Sun 11-4 (closed Sun in Jul & Aug). **Assn:** SNEADA **Own:** Karen & Charlie McCaughey.

North Weymouth

Bridge Antiques

398 Bridge St (Rte 3A) • 02191
(781)335-9264

A general line. **Est:** 1974 **Hrs:** Tue-Sat 10-4 by chance/appt. **Dir:** 1/2 mi from the Four River Bridge. **Own:** Fran Tucci.

Northampton

American Decorative Arts

3 Olive St • 01060
(413)584-6804 • (413)586-2449 (fax)
(800)366-3376
modern@decorativearts.com
www.decorativearts.com

20th C Modern decorative art & design, furniture & accessories from Art Deco to mid-century including Dunbar, Knoll, Herman Miller & Heywood-Wakefield. **Pr:** $25-2,500 **Est:** 1977 **Hrs:** Mon-Fri 9-5, Sat 1-5 by appt only. **Sz:** M **CC:** V/MC **Dir:** I-91 Exit 18: L at bottom of ramp, 1st L onto Conz, L at 1st light onto Old South, L onto South (Rte 10), Olive directly off South on L 1/2 mi down. **Own:** Chris Kennedy. **QC: 59 5 S9 S17**

Antique Center of Northampton [G40]

9-1/2 Market St • 01060
(413)584-3600

On three floors in a restored historic building: Mission furniture & accessories, Art Deco & Art Nouveau, country & formal furniture, lighting, books, 50s jewelry, American Indian items, toys, pottery & wrist watches. **Pr:** $10-10,000 **Est:** 1987 **Hrs:** Mon-Tue & Thu-Sat 10-5, Sun 12-5. **Sz:** L **CC:** V/MC **Dir:** From S: I-91 Exit 18: N on Rte 5 to 1st light, R, L at next light (Market St). From N: I-91 Exit 20: S on Rte 5, L on Market. **Own:** Stephen Whitlock. **QC: 5 49**

Family Jewels

56 Green St • 01060
(413)584-0613

Antique & period jewelry. **Hrs:** Fri-Sat 10-5 or by appt. **Dir:** I-91 W Exit 4: Rte 91 N Exit 18: L to Rte 5, L to Rte 9, L to Rte 66, 1st R Green St. **Own:** Richard Stone. **QC: 64**

Maggie Hebert
201 N Elm St • 01060
(413)586-2844

Country furniture, decorative accessories, collectibles, books & local ephemera. **Assn:** PVADA

L & M Furniture
5 Market St • 01060
(413)584-8939

Oak furniture, toys, Roseville pottery, crocks, wicker, glassware & graniteware **Hrs:** Mon-Sat 11-5. **Assn:** PVADA **Dir:** Next to Antique Ctr of Northampton. **Own:** Louis & Marge Farrick.

Memory Lane Antiques
376 Pleasant St • 01060
(413)586-7809

Used furniture, toys, collectibles. **Hrs:** Tue-Wed 10:30-6, Thu-Fri 10:30-8, Sat-Sun 9:30-6. **Dir:** I-91 Exit 18: turn L off ramp 1 mi on R.

Valley Antiques
15 Bridge St (Rte 9) • 01060
(413)584-1956

Furniture including a line of Victorian walnut items. **Hrs:** Daily 11-5 by chance, call ahead advised. **CC:** V/MC. **QC: 58**

Walters/Benisek Art & Antiques
(413)586-3909

Specializing in American folk art: watercolors, weathervanes, quilts, painted furniture, pottery & sculpture for serious collectors & museums. **Hrs:** By appt only. **Assn:** NHADA **Dir:** Call for directions. **Own:** Don Walters & Mary Benisek. **QC: 1 41 51 S12**

Use the Service QuickCode indexes at the back of the book to find restorers, appraisers, refinishers, and other specialty service providers.

Northboro

Tins and Things
28 Main St • 01532
(508)393-4647

Lamps, wicker, country furniture, linens, pine & Victorian. **Hrs:** Wed-Sat 10-4.

Norwell

Stonehouse Antiques
Rte 53 • 02061
(781)878-0172

Furniture, tools, mirrors, Oriental rugs, lamps & fireplace equipment. **Est:** 1940 **Hrs:** Mon-Tue & Thu-Sat 11-5. **CC:** V/MC **Assn:** SSADA **Dir:** 1 mi E of Rte 228 on Rte 53 on R. **Own:** Marie Anderson. **QC: 48 40 68**

Norwood

Danish Country Antique Furniture
78 Astor Ave • 02062
(781)440-0660

Antique Danish & northern European country pine furniture, fine quality Chapman brass lamps, antique Chinese furniture & accessories & a scattering of painted Scandinavian pieces as well as a very large selection of Royal Copenhagen porcelain. **Pr:** $100-12,000 **Hrs:** Sat-Sun. **CC:** V/MC. **QC: 34 55 60**

In Home Furnishings
151 Carnegie Row • 02062
(781)762-8171
mrantique@aol.com
www.inhome.com

Major retailers & importers of English & French country antiques. Three other locations: Natick at 575 Worcester Rd, Danvers on Rte 114 & Hyannis on Rte 132. **Pr:** $25-10,000 **Hrs:** Mon-Fri 10-9, Sat 10-6, Sun 12-5. **Sz:** H **CC:** AX/V/MC **Own:** Robert W Darvin. **QC: 47 107 102**

Orange

Durfee Coin-Op

57 S Main St • 01364
(978)544-3800 • (508)544-8250 (fax)
www.jukeboxparts.com

World's largest original jukebox parts supplier. Buying & selling complete jukeboxes, jukebox parts & related equipment. **Pr:** $1-5,000 **Hrs:** Sep-Apr Mon- Fri 10-4; May-Aug Mon-Thu 10-4. **Sz:** H **CC:** AX/V/MC **Dir:** Rte 2 E to Rte 122 Orange Exit: 2 mi to 1st L in Orange Ctr, bldg on R corn. **Own:** John Durfee. **QC: 1 69**

Orange Trading Company

57 S Main St • 01364
(978)544-6683 • (978)544-8250 (fax)

A general line specializing in coin-ops, signs & advertising & 60s collectibles. **Pr:** $1-1,000 **Est:** 1980 **Hrs:** By chance/appt. **Sz:** L **Dir:** Rte 2 E to Rte 122 Orange Exit: 2 mi to 1st L in Orange Ctr, bldg on R corn. **Own:** Gary Moise. **QC: 32 39 67 S12 S1**

Palmer

Quaboag Valley Antique Center [G100]

10 Knox St • 01069
(413)283-3091 • (413)283-8571 (fax)
quaboagantiques@samnet.net
www.quaboagantiques.com

Two floors of fine glass, pottery, toys, jewelry, military, sterling & decorative accessories. Largest furniture selection in area: oak, mahogany, walnut & pine. Restored or in as-found condition. **Pr:** $1-15,000 **Est:** 1983 **Hrs:** Tue-Sat 9-5, Sun 12-5, extended Brimfield hrs. **Sz:** H **CC:** V/MC/DIS **Dir:** I-90 Exit 8: 1/2 mi, R at 2nd light, R onto Rte 20, 1st R onto Knox St at Knox St Shops. From Brimfield: Rte 20 W 15 min, L at light go 1 blk, R onto Rte 20. 1st R on Knox St. **Own:** Lorraine, David & Daniel Braskie. **QC: 105 58 23 S12 S16 S1**

Peabody

Eclipse Antiques & Fine Art

eclipse@110.net
www.oldprints.com/eclipse

Decorative antiques original Currier & Ives lithographs & Audubon prints published by Havell & Bien. **Hrs:** By appt only. **Assn:** ACDA. **QC: 74 7 36**

Pembroke

Endless Antiques & Crafts [G6]

95 Church St (Rte 139) • 02359
(781)826-7177

Furniture, jewelry, linens, glass & china, cup plates, dolls & doll supplies. Three group shops at the same location. **Pr:** $2-2,000 **Est:** 1987 **Hrs:** Daily 11-5. **Sz:** M **CC:** V/MC **Assn:** HAAD SSADA **Dir:** Rte 3S Exit 12: R on Rte 139S, 1/4 mi on L. **Own:** Marie Davis. **QC: 32 63 39**

Times Past at North River Antiques Center [G22]

236 Water St (Rte 139) • 02359
(781)826-3736
timespas@gis.net

Antiquarian books, postcards, maps & ephemera. Four rooms chock full of country furniture, clocks, tools, decoys, fine art prints, photos, fine glass, china, pottery, silver, pewter, jewelry & linens. **Pr:** $1-3,000 **Est:** 1987 **Hrs:** Sun-Fri 12-5, Sat 10-5. **CC:** AX/V/MC/DIS **Assn:** MARIAB SSADA **Dir:** Rte 3 S: Exit 12, W 1/2 mi next to Taylor Rental. **Own:** Carol Franzosa. **QC: 34 32 7 S1 S8 S12**

Turner Antiques

681 Washington St • 02359
(781)826-8644

A general line of antiques with an emphasis on country. **Est:** 1986 **Hrs:** Apr-Dec most days 10-5. **QC: 34**

Petersham

Bobbi Benson Antiques
(978)724-3202

Specializing in early to mid-19th C Staffordshire. **Hrs:** By appt only. **Own:** Bobbi & Chip Benson. **QC: 30**

Pittsfield

Berkshire Hills Coins & Antiques
111 South St (Rte 7) • 01201
(413)499-1400

Small shop specializing in estate gold & costume jewelry, sterling items, oak furniture, pocket watches, antique accessories & large selection of collectible coins. **Est:** 1987 **Hrs:** Mon-Sat 10-5:30. **Sz:** S **CC:** V/MC/AX **Assn:** BCADA **Dir:** 1/2 blk N of Rte 20. **Own:** Peter Karpenski. **QC: 33 63 64**

Greystone Gardens
436 North St (Rte 7) • 01201
(413)442-9291
grestone@bcn.net
www.greystonegardens.com

A full line of ladies' & men's vintage & antique clothing & jewelry set in an environment of country ease & Victorian elegance. **Pr:** $1-500 **Est:** 1980 **Hrs:** Mon-Sat 11-6. **Sz:** M **CC:** AX/V/MC **Dir:** N of the town green. **Own:** Carla Lund. **QC: 64 39 83**

Memory Lane Antiques
446 Tyler St (Rte 8) • 01201
(413)499-2718

General line of 1850-1950 oak & mahogany furniture, costume & estate jewelry, china, glassware, books & collectibles. **Est:** 1991 **Hrs:** Mon & Wed-Sat 10-5. **CC:** V/MC **Assn:** BCADA **Own:** Beverly Martin. **QC: 48**

Pittsfield Precious Metals
93 First St • 01201
(413)443-3613
(800)243-4420

Antique & estate jewelry outlet, diamonds, pocket watches, coins, sterling silver, porcelain, art glass, decorative accessories, Bullion & art. Gemologist on premises. **Pr:** $5,000-20,000 **Est:** 1980 **Hrs:** Mon-Fri 10-5, Sat 11-2. **Sz:** S **Assn:** GIA BCADA **Dir:** Mass Pike I-90 Exit 2 (Lee/Pittsfield): Follow Rte 7 to Pittsfield. R at Park Sq onto East St, L at lights onto First St (Rte 7). 3 blks on L (corn of First & Eagle Sts). **Own:** John & Luisa Economou. **QC: 64 33 35 S1 S12**

Plainville

Briarpatch Antiques
62 Spring St • 02762
(508)695-1950

In 19th C barn, featuring country furniture & smalls, stoneware, samplers, pewter & baskets. Specializing in old paint. **Pr:** $5-5,000 **Est:** 1986 **Hrs:** Daily by chance/appt. **Dir:** I-495 Exit 15: Rte 1A to Plainville, 2-1/5 mi, L on Broad St, R on Spring St, behind fire station. **Own:** Marie Oldred. **QC: 1 34 51 S19**

Plymouth

Antiques at 108 Sandwich St
108 Sandwich St • 06479
(508)747-6968

Antique & gift shop with antique & custom furniture, decorative accessories, some silver & Oriental rugs, chandeliers, mirrors & art. Focusing on Federal period, all styles. **Pr:** $10-1,200+ **Est:** 1994 **Hrs:** Sat 11-5, Sun 12-5 or by chance/appt. **Sz:** M **CC:** AX/V/MC/DIS **Dir:** Rte 3 Exit 6: R onto

Rte 3A (Main St), which becomes Sandwich St. **Own:** June Pedalino. **QC: 36 74 78**

Dillon & Co English Country Antiques

8, 12 & 14 North St • 02360
(508)747-2242 • (508)747-2244 (fax)

A large selection of English & French antiques & some reproduction furniture & accessories including farm tables, armoires, mirrors, lamps, china & garden items. **Pr:** $10-5,000 **Est:** 1985 **Hrs:** Mon & Wed-Sat 11-5, Sun 1-5. **Sz:** L **CC:** AX/V/MC **Dir:** Rte 3 Exit 6A: R to 2nd light, then R to North St & turn L. **Own:** Gillian Dillon. **QC: 47 107 48**

Plymouth Antiques Trading Co [G125]

8 Court St • 02360
(508)746-3450

Paintings, iron, prints, glass, Oriental rugs, tools, garden, military, textiles, country, formal, jewelry, porcelain, Indian items, pottery & toys. **Hrs:** Daily 10-5. **Dir:** One blk from Plymouth Rock, in the former Buttner Bldg.

Village Braider

48 Sandwich St • 02360
(508)746-9625

Eclectic mix of American, Continental & decorative accessories. **Hrs:** Tue-Sat 11-5. **Sz:** M **Assn:** NHADA SSADA **Dir:** Across from the Green on Rte 3A S of town. **Own:** Anna & Bruce Edmond. **QC: 36**

The Yankee Book & Art Gallery

10 North St • 02360
(508)747-2691 • (508)747-1831 (fax)
yankeebk@adelphia.net

A quaint rare & out-of-print bookshop with an attached art gallery specializing in local history, fine bindings, children's books & antique & contemporary art, originals & prints. **Est:** 1981 **Hrs:** Mon-Sat 11-5; Sum Mon-Sat 11-5, Sun 12-4. **Sz:** M **CC:** AX/V/MC/DIS **Assn:** MARIAB **Dir:** SE Expressway to Rte 3S Exit 6A (Rte 44): R on Rte 44 to 3A (Court St), R at light, L on North St. **Own:** Charles Purro. **QC: 18 S1**

Raynham

Raynham Marketplace Antiques Inc [G150]

1510 New State Hwy (Rte 44) • 02767
(508)822-0500

Hrs: Mon-Wed 10-5, Thu 10-6, Fri-Sat 10-7, Sun 12-5. **Sz:** H **Dir:** Rte 495 Exit 6: Rte 44W, 2 mi on R; Rte 24 Exit 13A: Rte 44, 1 mi on L.

Rehoboth

Anawan Antiques

180 Anawan St (Rte 118) • 02769
(508)252-5204

Antiques & collectibles. **Hrs:** Thu-Sat 10-6, Sun 12-6. **Own:** Gary Jennings. **QC: 32**

Deer Run Antiques

82 Pleasant St • 02769
(508)252-9658

Books & collectibles. **Hrs:** Sat-Sun 10-5 or by chance/appt. **Own:** Edna Brunelle. **QC: 32 18**

Madeline's Antiques Inc

164 Winthrop St (Rte 44) • 02769
(508)252-3965

A dealer cooperative specializing in oak & mahogany furniture, linens & glassware. **Pr:** $1-5,000 **Est:** 1968 **Hrs:** Mon-Sat 10-5, Sun 12-5. **Sz:** H **CC:** V/MC **Dir:** I-95 Exit 16 to I-195 E Exit 4 (Rte 44E): L off exits, 3/4 mi past int of Rte 118, on the L. **Own:** Madeline Fortier. **QC: 50 61 80**

Mendes Antiques
52 Blanding Rd (Rte 44) • 02769
(508)336-7381

Large selection of antique American furniture from the 18th & early 19th C, specializing in antique four-poster rope beds in the original sizes, restored & refinished to twin, double, queen & king sizes with over 250 beds in stock. **Est:** 1959 **Hrs:** Mon-Sat 9-6, Sun 11-6, call ahead advised. **Dir:** 7 mi E of Providence, RI. **Own:** Vale & Ines Mendes. **QC: 48**

Richmond

Wynn A Sayman Inc
Old Fields • 01254
(413)698-2272 • (413)698-3282 (fax)
wynnasayman@taconic.net
www.wynnasayman.com

A comprehensive selection of fine 18th & early 19th C English pottery & porcelain primarily for collectors, connoisseurs & museums in a Federal period country home. Saltglaze, creamware & Staffordshire figures; Chelsea, Bow & Derby porcelain. **Pr:** $250-7,000 **Est:** 1978 **Hrs:** By appt only. **Sz:** M **Assn:** BCADA AC **Dir:** Call for directions. **QC: 23**

Rockland

Bayberry Antiques
925 Liberty St • 02370
(781)871-4625

American country antiques. Specializing in hooked rugs. **Hrs:** GSAAA **Own:** Laura McCarthy. **QC: 102 75**

Rockport

Rockport Quilt Shoppe
2 Ocean Ave • 01966
(978)546-1001 • (508)546-2193 (fax)
(800)456-0892
gdwhite@shore.net
www.rockportusa.com

A large collection of antique quilts from the late 18th C to 1940s cradle to king size, vintage linens & accessories from quilt scraps. **Pr:** $50-5,000 **Est:** 1994 **Hrs:** By chance/appt. **Sz:** S **CC:** V/MC **Dir:** Rte 128 N to Rte 127 to Rockport & Pigeon Cove. **Own:** Gloria White. **QC: 84 36 S17 S16**

Woodbine Antiques Ltd
35 Main St • 01966
(978)546-9694 • (978)546-2923 (fax)
woodbine@shore.net

A fine selection of 18th & 19th C English & American furniture & accessories both formal & country. **Pr:** $50-1,500 **Est:** 1976 **Hrs:** May 15-Oct Mon-Sat 10-5, Sun 12-5; Nov-May 15 Sat 10-5, Sun 12-5 or by appt. **Sz:** M **CC:** AX/V/MC **Dir:** Rte 128 to Rte 127 to Rockport. **Own:** Peter & Janice Beacham. **QC: 52 54 36 S1**

Rowley

Antiques on the Common [G12]
15 Summer St • 01969
(978)948-3932

Furniture, country, glass, porcelain, jewelry, sterling, prints, paintings & decorative accessories. **Hrs:** Thu-Tue 9:30-4:30. **CC:** V/MC/DIS.

Frank D'Angelo Inc
The Smith-Billings House • 01969
(978)948-3849

17th, 18th & 19th C American & European furniture, decorative accessories, ceramics & paintings. **Pr:** $100-25,000 **Hrs:** Tue-Sat by appt. **Assn:** NEAA SADA **Dir:** On Rowley Commons. **QC: 36 53**

Rowley Antique Center [G35]

Rtes 1A & 133 • 01969
(978)948-2591

Furniture, glass, china, quilts, jewelry & metalwork. **Hrs:** Tue-Sun 8-4 & Mon hols. **Dir:** On the grounds of Ginny's Flea Market across from Mobil Station. **Own:** James Tirani. **QC: 48**

Salt Marsh Antiques [G40]

224 Main St (Rte 1A) • 01969
(978)948-7139
www.saltmarsh-antiques.com

Full range of period antiques & decorative antique furnishings in a restored 1805 barn. **Pr:** $25-8,000 **Est:** 1985 **Hrs:** Mon-Fri 9:30-4:30, Sat-Sun 10-5. **Sz:** L **CC:** AX/V/MC/DIS **Assn:** NADA SPNEA RHC **Dir:** Rte 95N Exit Rte 133E to Rte 1A, L at lights Rte 1A, 1 mi on L. **Own:** Robert Cianfrocca. **QC: 1 7 52**

Todd Farm Antiques [G13]

Rte 1A • 01969
(978)948-2217

Thirty-one room-sized house & barn shops featuring furniture & collectibles: pine, oak, mahogany, clocks, linens, paintings, prints, glass, china, pottery, toys, primitives, antique tools, books & architectural materials. **Hrs:** House Thu-Sun 10-4 & Mon hols; Barn daily 1-4 **CC:** V/MC/DIS **Dir:** Rte 95 N to Rte 133 E to Rte 1A N.

Village Antiques [G20]

201 Main St (Rte 1A) • 01969
(978)948-7847

Furniture, glass & china. **Hrs:** Tue-Sun & Mon hols 10:30-4:30. **CC:** V/MC **Dir:** From Rte 1 to Rte 133 W to Rte 1A N.

Salem

American Marine Model Gallery Inc

12 Derby Sq • 01970
(978)745-5777 • (978)745-5778 (fax)
wall@shipmodel.com
www.shipmodel.com

Representing the finest one-of-a-kind marine models by leading professional marine model artists including antique models. Specialist in prisoner-of-war & dockyard models. **Pr:** $400-100,000 **Est:** 1982 **Hrs:** Tue-Sat 10-4 or by appt. **Sz:** M **CC:** AX/V/MC **Dir:** Rte 128 Exit 25E: Rte 114 E toward Marblehead to int of Washington St. L on Washington, R on Front 1/2 blk on L. **Own:** R Michael Wall. **QC: 70 9 S1 S16 S10**

Antiques at 285 Derby [G20]

285 Derby St (Rte 1A) • 01970
(978)741-1616

Furniture, jewelry, books, china, decorative items, sewing tools, nautical, silver, textiles, glass, rugs & art. **Pr:** $5-5,000 **Est:** 1997 **Hrs:** Daily 10-5. **Sz:** L **CC:** AX/V/MC/DIS **Dir:** Near Salem Ctr on Rte 1A, opp the wax museum. **QC: 48 64 107 S8 S12**

Antiques at Museum Place

111 Museum Place Mall • 01970
(978)745-4258

Porcelain, small furniture, jewelry, collectibles, paintings, prints, ceramics & silver. **Pr:** $25-2,500 **Est:** 1984 **Hrs:** Mon-Sat 10-6, Sun 12-6. **Sz:** S **CC:** AX/V/MC **Dir:** Across from Peabody Museum in Museum Place Mall. **Own:** Elizabeth Grader & Judith Lazdowski. **QC: 24 64 32**

Antiques Gallery [G35]

69 Wharf St • 01970
(978)741-3113
antiquesgallery@juno.com
www.plads.com/antiques

Furniture, paintings, glass, china, jewelry, silver, textiles, nautical antiques & Oriental rugs. **Pr:** $10-2,000 **Est:** 1982 **Hrs:** Daily 11-5. **Sz:** L **CC:** AX/V/MC/DIS **Dir:** Rte 1A to Derby St, R onto Union St. Shop is on the L where Union St meets Wharf St. **Own:** Bob Magro. **QC: 7 48 78 S8**

Asia House

18 Washington Sq W • 01970
(978)745-8257

Fine Oriental antiques from Japan, China & Southeast Asia & books on related subjects. **Pr:** $100-15,000 **Est:** 1977 **Hrs:** Mon-Sat 12-5. **CC:** AX/V/MC **Dir:** On Rte 1A in the Hawthorne Hotel on the Salem Common. **Own:** Emile Dubrule & V Chaicharoen. **QC: 71**

K C Clark & Associates Antiques Ltd

24 Front St • 01970
(978)741-3701 • (978)741-3928 (fax)

Specializing in fine quality 17th-19th C British formal & country furniture, 18th & 19th C British pottery with an emphasis on early creamware & Staffordshire animal & figure groups, decorative accessories & fine art all sourced directly from the UK. **Pr:** $30-25,000 **Est:** 1998 **Hrs:** Tue-Sat 10-5:30, Sun 12-5, or by appt. **Sz:** M **CC:** AX/V/MC/DIS **Dir:** Rte 28 to Rte 114 E to Front St. 2 blks W of Peabody Essex Museum. **Own:** Kevin C Clark. **QC: 107 30 26**

R A DiFillipo Antiques

131 Essex St • 01970
(978)741-0889

Featuring Continental furniture & accessories, glass, china & paintings. **Est:** 1972 **Hrs:** Tue-Sat 10-5. **CC:** AX/V/MC. **QC: 7 53**

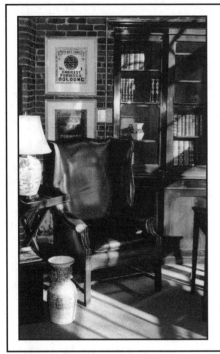

Landry & Arcari
3 Pleasant St • 01970
(978)744-5909
(800)649-5909
www.landryandarcari.com

Oriental rugs & carpeting. **Est:** 1938. **QC: 76**

Marine Arts Gallery
135 Essex St • 01970
(978)745-5000 • (978)744-0220 (fax)

Largest dealer in fine 18th & 19th C marine paintings in the Northeast. **Hrs:** Mon-Fri 9-3:30, Sat 9-3. **Sz:** L **CC:** AX/V/MC/DIS **Dir:** Directly across from the Peabody Museum. **Own:** Russell Kiernan. **QC: 9 7 S16**

Salisbury

The White Oak
27 Lafayette Rd (Rte 1) • 01950
(978)465-3635

A general line of antiques, furniture & collectibles. **Hrs:** Fri & Mon 10-4, Sat-Sun 12-4 or by chance.

Scituate

Bird-in-Hand Antiques
157 Front St • 02066
(781)545-1728

Primitives, country & garden. **Est:** 1977 **Hrs:** Tue-Sun 11-5 or by appt. **Own:** Shirley A Parkhurst & Kathleen Fortuna. **QC: 106 34 60**

Gatherings
131 Front St • 02066
(781)545-7664

Antiques, hand-painted furniture, decorating accessories & collectibles. **Hrs:** Daily 10-5. **CC:** AX/V/MC **Own:** Marsha J McNeice.

Greenhouse Antiques
182 First Parish Rd • 02066
(781)545-1964 • (781)545-2465 (fax)

Two rooms of antiques & collectibles, specializing in early lighting & clocks. **Pr:** $10-1,000 **Est:** 1987 **Hrs:** Thu-Sat 11-4:30 or by appt. **Sz:** M **CC:** V/MC **Assn:** SSADA **Dir:** Rte 3A to First Parish Rd (Town Hall & Police Station), 1/2 mi (past Common) on L. **Own:** Irving Versoy. **QC: 35 65 71 S7 S16**

The Quarter Deck
206 Front St • 02066-0075
(781)545-4303

A general line including antique postcards of Massachusetts & nautical decor. **Hrs:** Daily 9:30-6, later hrs in Sum. **CC:** AX/V/MC/DIS **Own:** Joan Noble.

Echo Lake Antiques
165 Front St • 02066
(781)545-7100

Personal owner-operated shop featuring treasure & antiques of the 18th, 19th & 20th C. **Hrs:** Tue-Sun 11-5. **Assn:** SSADA **Dir:** On Scituate Harbor. **Own:** Harry & Diane McLaughlin.

Seekonk

Antiques at Hearthstone House
15 Fall River Ave (Rte 114A) • 02771
(508)336-6273 • (508)336-6283 (fax)
hearthstone-house@worldnet.att.net

Sixteen rooms of country & formal furniture in restored & as-found condition, pewter, brass, copper & decorative accessories. **Pr:** $2-20,000 **Est:** 1974 **Hrs:** Mon-Sat 10-5, Sun 12-5. **Sz:** H **CC:** V/MC **Assn:** SNEADA **Dir:** I-95 to I-195 E to MA Exit 1: Rte 114A N across Rte 44, around bend on L. **Own:** Bob & Anne Wood. **QC: 36 102**

Country Squire Antiques [G]

1732 Fall River Ave (Rte 6) • 02771
(508)336-8442

Bohemian, cranberry & satin glass, porcelain, Limoges lamps, paintings, rugs, furniture & early American refinished country furniture. **Est:** 1991 **Hrs:** Mon & Wed-Fri 10-5, Sat-Sun 12-5. **CC:** V/MC **Assn:** SNEADA **Dir:** Betw I-195 Exits 1 & 2. **Own:** Bob & Bette Daigle. **QC: 61**

Leonard's Antiques Inc

600 Taunton Ave (Rte 44) • 02771
(508)336-8585 • (508)336-4884 (fax)
oldbeds@aol.com
www.leonardsdirect.com

Two large floors & antique barn full of fine antique furniture in as-found or restored condition. Specializing in American four poster beds. Classic reproduction furniture & decorative accessories are also available. **Pr:** $200-10,000 **Est:** 1933 **Hrs:** Mon-Sat 8-5, Sun 1-5. **Sz:** H **CC:** AX/V/MC **Assn:** NEAA SNEADA **Dir:** I-195 Exit 1 in MA: N on Rte 114A, bear R at Old Gristmill Tavern, R at next light onto Rte 44, on L at top of hill. **Own:** Jeffrey B Jenkins. **QC: 52 56 S16**

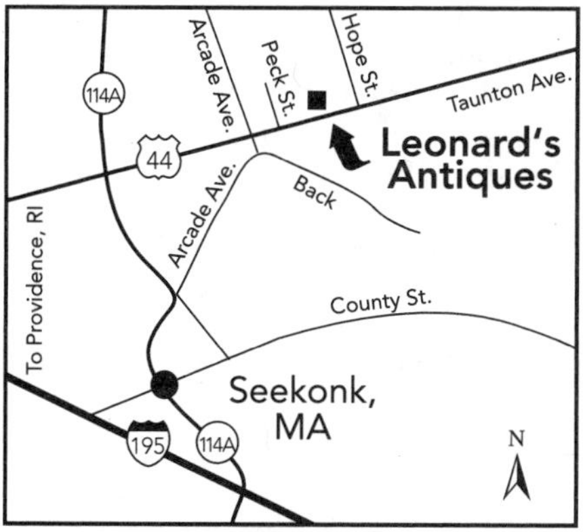

Lost Treasures Antique Center [G125]

1460 Fall River Ave (Rte 6) • 02771
(508)336-9294 • (508)336-9294 (fax)

Antiques & collectibles at reasonable prices. **Est:** 1993 **Hrs:** Mon-Tue & Thu-Sat 10-5, Fri til 7, Sun 12-5. **Sz:** M **CC:** V/MC/DIS **Assn:** SNEADA **Dir:** I-95 to I-195 E: Exit 2 to Rte 6 W, 3 mi on R. **Own:** Jake & Sue Winokur **QC: S8**

Ruth Falkinburg's Dolls & Toys

208 Taunton Ave • 02771
(508)336-6929

Antique dolls, toys & other collectibles. **Hrs:** Mon-Tue & Thu-Fri 11-3, Sat 12-4, Sun 1-4. **Assn:** SNEADA **Own:** Nancy & Dick Fredricks. **QC: 38 87 32**

Vinny's Antiques Center [G350]

380 Fall River (Rte 114A) • 02771
(508)336-0800 • (508)336-6330 (fax)

On the banks of the Runnins River, gallery room settings with fine furnishings from all periods & countless showcases filled with collectibles, jewelry & smalls. Gourmet coffee, tea, pastry, lunch & gift baskets. **Pr:** $1-30,000 **Est:** 1994 **Hrs:** Mon-Sat 10-5, Fri til 9, Sun 12-5. **Sz:** L **Dir:** From Providence: I-95 to 195 E to MA Exit 1: L on Rte 114A 1 mi. From Cape Cod: I-195 W Exit 1: R on Rte 114A 1 mi. Next to Grist Mill Restaurant **Own:** Vincent Onorato. **QC: 48 32 36 S1 S12**

Wren & Thistle Antiques

111 Taunton Ave • 02771
(508)336-0824

A small, one-owner antique store with carefully selected decorative accessories including a good array of porcelain & china tableware: flow blue, Staffordshire, Minton, Wedgwood & various Limoges pieces. Also an eclectic display of furniture, lighting. **Pr:** $10-4,000 **Hrs:** Mon-Tue & Thu-Sat 10-5. **Sz:** M **CC:** AX/V/MC **Assn:** SNEADA **Dir:** From Providence: I-95 E to Rte 44 (Taunton Ave) in E Providence. Proceed 4 mi to MA border, then 1/2 mi to int of Rtes 44 & 114A. **Own:** Jackie Williams. **QC: 23 89 30 S12**

Sharon

Gary R Sullivan Antiques Inc

15 Belcher St • 02067
(781)784-9914

Specializing in American furniture of the Federal period, with emphasis on formal furniture & grandfather clocks. **Hrs:** By appt only. **Assn:** NHADA SADA. **QC: 52 35**

Sheffield

1750 House Antiques

S Main St (Rte 7) • 01257
(413)229-6635

American, French & European clocks, music boxes & phonographs, fine glass, china, furniture & decorative accessories. **Hrs:** Always open. **Assn:** BCADA **Dir:** On Rte 7. **Own:** Frances & William Liebowitz. **QC: 35 61 69 S7**

Anthony's Antiques

S Main St (Rte 7) • 01257
(413)229-8208

In a restored Berkshire barn, a handsome collection of English furniture & ceramics of the late 18th & 19th C, English & European paintings & other works of art, Chinese porcelains (both old & new) & Chinese furniture. **Est:** 1987 **Hrs:** Daily 10-5:30. **Sz:** M **Assn:** BCADA **Own:** Anthony & Kathleen Bonadies. **QC: 54 23 24**

Antique Center of Sheffield [G]

S Main St (Rte 7) • 01257
(413)229-3400

Three buildings chock full of unusual antiques & collectibles, country furniture, folk art, signs, Shaker, cupboards, lighting, paintings, decoys, tools, architectural pieces & birdhouses. **Est:** 1982 **Hrs:** Thu-Mon 10-5 or by chance **Sz:** L **Dir:** Across from Sheffield Police Station. **Own:** Kenneth Cooper. **QC: 3 34 37**

Berkshire Gilders Antiques

15 Main St (Rte 7) • 01257
(413)229-0113 • (413)229-3396 (fax)

Period French, English & American gold leaf mirrors as well as upholstered furniture, dining tables, decorative pieces & "art de la table." Gold leaf restoration. **Est:** 1992 **Hrs:** Thu-Mon 11-4:30 in season or by appt. **Sz:** M **CC:** V/MC **Assn:** BCADA **Dir:** 1 mi S of the town ctr. **Own:** Jeffrey J Von Er. **QC: 52 68 S16**

Centuryhurst Antiques & B & B [G20]

Main St (Rte 7) • 01257
(413)229-8131

American clocks & Wedgwood, early 19th C furniture, glass, china, paintings, prints, toys & accessories to complement all furnishings. **Est:** 1980 **Hrs:** Daily 9-5. **CC:** AX/V/MC **Assn:** BCADA NAWCC **Own:** Judith & Ronald Timm. **QC: 35 52 23**

Corner House Antiques

Main St (Rte 7) • 01257
(413)229-6627

Antique wicker furniture & accessories. Traditional wicker sets as well as rare & unusual collector's items. Full line of styles in natural, original paint or custom finish. Also a diverse selection of American country furnishings & accessories. **Est:** 1977 **Hrs:** Most days 10-5, call ahead advised. **Sz:** L **Assn:** BCADA **Dir:** 1 mi N of Sheffield Ctr, on L at corn of Old Mill Pond Rd. **Own:** Thomas & Kathleen Tetro. **QC: 91 34**

Cupboards & Roses

296 S Main (Rte 7) • 01257
(413)229-3070 • (413)229-0257 (fax)

The largest selection of fine painted-decorated 17th & 18th C armoires, chests & accessories from Europe & Scandinavia, displayed in a spectacular post & beam setting in the Berkshires. **Est:** 1988 **Hrs:** Wed-Mon 10:30-5. **Sz:** L **CC:** V/MC **Assn:** BCADA **Dir:** On Rte 7 S of town ctr. **Own:** Edith Gilson. **QC: 51 41 36 S9 S17**

Darr Antiques and Interiors

28 S Main St • 01257
(413)229-7773 • (413)229-6003 (fax)

A large selection of fine formal 18th & 19th C American, English, Continental & Oriental furniture, paintings, lamps, writing tables & accessories displayed in two buildings in elegant room settings. Dining room furniture & appointments a specialty. **Pr:** $100-20,000 **Est:** 1980 **Hrs:** Jun-Oct Wed-Mon 10-5, Nov-May Fri-Mon 10-5, Tue-Thu by appt. **Sz:** L **Assn:** BCADA **Dir:** Just S of town ctr. **Own:** Donald A Cesario & Robert R Stinson. **QC: 107 54 52 S8 S15 S19**

Dovetail Antiques

440 Sheffield Plain (Rte 7) • 01257
(413)229-2628

Always a large selection of 18th & 19th C American wall, shelf & tall case clocks compatible with country or formal interiors. Country furniture mostly in old paint or finish, spongeware, redware & stoneware. No glass or china. **Pr:** $20-12,500 **Est:** 1976 **Hrs:** Wed-Mon 11-5, Tue by chance/appt. **Sz:** M **Assn:** BCADA NAWCC **Dir:** On Rte 7, 3/4 mi N of the ctr of Sheffield on E side of road. **Own:** Judith & David Steindler. **QC: 35 34 29**

Falcon Antiques

1985 S Undermountain Rd • 01257
(413)229-7745

Two floors of tools, primarily woodworking, for the collector, user & decorator. Also copper & brass household accessories. Assortment of wordworking benches. **Pr:** $10-5,000 **Est:** 1973 **Hrs:** Daily 10-5, by chance/appt. **Sz:** M **CC:** AX/V/MC **Assn:** BCADA **Dir:** Rte 41, 5 mi N of int of Rtes 41 & 44, 7 mi from Rte 7 Sheffield Ctr, follow signs at Berkshire School Rd. **Own:** Peter & Annette Habicht. **QC: 20 86**

Good & Hutchinson & Associates Inc

Main St (Rte 7) • 01034
(413)258-4555

Antiques & decorative arts of the 18th & 19th C including Chinese export porcelain; American, English & Continental furniture; prints; brass & lamps. **Est:** 1950 **Hrs:** May 15-Sep 15 Mon & Wed-Sat 10:30-4, Sun 11-4; or by chance. **Assn:** AADLA BCADA **Dir:** On the Green. **Own:** David Good & Robert Hutchinson. **QC: 25 54 74**

Jenny Hall Antiques

Rte 7 • 01257
(413)229-0277

Specializing in garden design & ornaments, architecturals, country & decorative furniture & accessories, lighting, quilts & hooked rugs. **Hrs:** Nov-May daily 10-5:30. **Assn:** BCADA. **QC: 60 3 34**

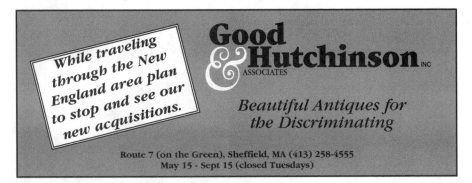

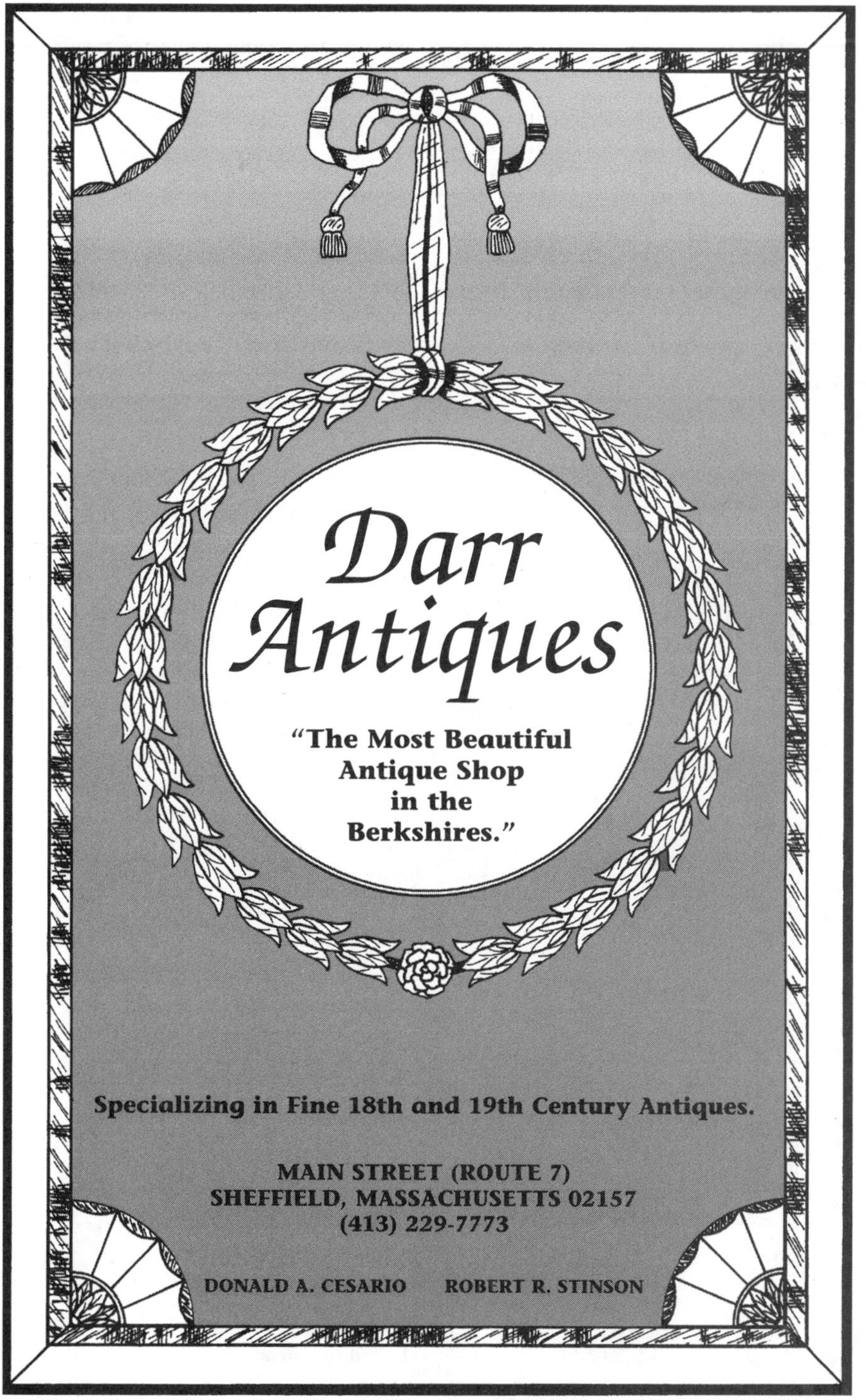
Darr
Antiques
"The Most Beautiful
Antique Shop
in the
Berkshires."
Specializing in Fine 18th and 19th Century Antiques.
MAIN STREET (ROUTE 7)
SHEFFIELD, MASSACHUSETTS 02157
(413) 229-7773
DONALD A. CESARIO
ROBERT R. STINSON

Hatfield Antiques

99 S Main St (Rte 7) • 01257
(413)229-7986

An assortment of antiques & collectibles, 18th & 19th C country & formal furniture, paintings, silver, jewelry, paper goods, architectural items, memorabilia & items from New England homes. **Est:** 1957 **Hrs:** Daily 9-5:30, Tue open at 11:30. **Dir:** 1/5 mi S of PO. **Own:** Fred & Eve Hatfield. **QC: 52 7 34**

Margo Hayes Country Antiques

27 Main St (Rte 7) • 01257
(413)229-2099

American painted cupboards, tables, blanket boxes, chairs & accessories. **Hrs:** May-Sep Web-Mon 10-4; Oct-Apr Sat-Sun 11-4 or by chance/appt. **QC: 34 51**

Samuel Herrup Antiques

435 Sheffield Plain Rd (Rte 7) • 01257
(413)229-0424 • (413)229-2829 (fax)

Choice & unusual examples of 17th-19th C American furniture, high style & country, including painted pieces; American folk art, especially portraits & sculpture; Penn & NE redware; European decorative arts including ceramics, metalwork & sculpture. **Est:** 1972 **Hrs:** By appt only. **Assn:** ADA NAADAA BCADA **Own:** Sally & Sam Herrup. **QC: 52 41 29**

Kuttner Antiques

S Main St (Rte 7) • 01257
(413)229-2955

18th & early 19th C American & English formal & country furniture, paintings (folk & academic), decorative accessories, folk art, English pottery & porcelain. **Est:** 1987 **Hrs:** Wed-Mon 10:30-5. **Sz:** L **Assn:** BCADA **Dir:** 1 mi S of Sheffield Village Green. **Own:** Kathy Immerman. **QC: 52 54 23**

Le Trianon

1854 N Main St (Rte 7) • 01257
(413)528-0775 • (413)528-3940 (fax)

Fine French, English & Continental furniture & accessories from the 17th, 18th & 19th C; a large selection of tapestries & Oriental rugs. Source for decorators, dealers & collectors. **Est:** 1983 **Hrs:** Daily 10-5:30. **Sz:** L **CC:** V/MC **Assn:** BCADA **Dir:** At the Great Barrington/Sheffield town line. **Own:** Jean Henri & Collette Sarbib. **QC: 47 53 76 S1 S8**

May's Antiques

779 N Main St (Rte 7) • 01257
(413)229-2037 • (413)229-2037 (fax)

Antique furniture, hall stands, side-by-sides, china closets, clocks & jewelry. Large selection of glassware, crystal, baby items, wicker & miniature dolls. **Est:** 1978 **Hrs:** Fri-Sun 10-5. **CC:** V/MC **Own:** May Thomas.

Howard S Mott Inc

170 S Main St (Rte 7) • 01257
(413)229-2019 • (413)229-8553 (fax)
mottinc@vgernet.net

Antiquarian book dealers in rare books & first editions, broadsides, 18th C British pamphlets, English & American literature (16th-20th C), juveniles, autographs, West Indies to 1860, golf & tennis before 1900. Located in a ca 1780 Federal house. **Est:** 1936 **Hrs:** Mon-Fri 10-6 appt highly desirable. **Sz:** L **Assn:** ABA ABAA BCADA MARIAB **Dir:** 1/2 mi S of the PO. **Own:** Donald Mott. **QC: 18 74 S1**

Ole T J's Antique Barn

S Main St (Rte 7) • 01257
(413)229-8382 • (413)229-3483 (fax)
oltjbarn@bcn.net

Two floors of antiques & collectibles from around the world: Oriental, African, New

Guinea, European & early American including jewelry, furniture, paintings, rugs, lamps & art objects. **Est:** 1985 **Hrs:** Thu-Mon 10-5, Tue-Wed by chance/appt. **Sz:** M **CC:** V/MC **Dir:** 1-1/2 mi S of Sheffield; 3-1/2 mi N of Canaan, CT. **Own:** Theodore & Grace Fuchs. **QC: 32 36 48 S9**

Saturday Sweets Antiques & Design

755A N Main St • 01257
(413)229-0026

20th C decorative arts, Art Deco, vintage costume jewelry, art pottery, art glass, silver, lamps, paintings, furniture & rugs. **Hrs:** Wed-Mon 10:30-5; Win call ahead. **Assn:** BCADA. **QC: 105 101 100**

John Sideli Art & Antiques

139 S Main St (Rte 7) • 01257
(413)229-8424

Stylish objects of the 18th, 19th & 20th C, specializing in American painted furniture & folk art, weathervanes, trade signs, architectural elements, redware, blown glass, bottles & other related smalls & accessories. **Hrs:** Jun-Oct most wknds 11-5 or by chance/appt. **Assn:** ADA NHADA BCADA. **QC: 41 45 102 S9 S15**

Bruce A Sikora — Antiquarian

549 Main St (Rte 7) • 01257
(413)229-6049 • (413)229-2584 (fax)

Specializing in 18th & early 19th C American & English furniture, 17th & 18th C delft & glassware, 15th-18th C metalware & lighting. **Hrs:** Thu-Sun 11-5. **Sz:** M **CC:** V/MC. **QC: 27 52 65**

Use the Specialty QuickCode indexes at the back of the book to find dealers who specialize in your area of interest.

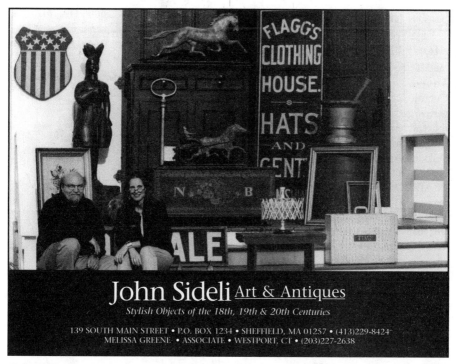

Susan Silver Antiques

N Main St (Rte 7) • 01257
(413)229-8169
ssilver@bcn.net

An important collection of English & Continental 18th & 19th C formal furniture, period gilded mirrors, chandeliers & decorative accessories. Also featuring fine furniture for the library including writing tables, desks, chairs, bookcases & ladders. **Est:** 1982 **Hrs:** Wed-Mon 10:30-5. **Sz:** L **Assn:** BCADA **Own:** Susan Silver. **QC: 54 53 68**

Lois W Spring

140 Ashley Falls Rd (Rte 7A) • 01257
(413)229-2542

18th & 19th C American high country furniture with appropriate accessories. Original paint or finish so far as possible. **Est:** 1962 **Hrs:** Daily 10-5 by chance/appt. **Assn:** BCADA. **QC: 52 51**

Robert Thayer

197 Main St (Rte 7) • 01257
(413)229-2965

Fine American antiques. **Hrs:** By appt only.

David M Weiss Antiques

Main St (Rte 7) • 01257
(413)229-2716
weissjas@vgernet.net

Quality 18th & 19th C country & formal American furniture, landscape paintings (esp Hudson River School) & select decorative accessories. **Est:** 1983 **Hrs:** By chance/appt. **Sz:** M **Assn:** BCADA GSAAA VADA **Own:** David Weiss. **QC: 1 52 8 S1**

Shelburne

Orchard Hill Antiques

108 Colrain Rd • 01370
(413)625-2433
www.angelfire.com/bizz/orchardhill/

Shop & barn annex containing a collection of country furniture, lamps, tools, brass & copper accessories. **Pr:** $5-3,000 **Hrs:** Fri 10-6, Sat-Sun 9-6, or by chance/appt. **Sz:** M **Dir:** From Greenfield: Rte 2W 4 mi, then R onto Colrain Rd, 1 mi off Rte 2 (Mohawk Trail). **Own:** Jeffrey Bishop. **QC: 1 3 10 S18**

Fair Trade Inc

(413)337-8513

Anglo-Raj furniture, Colonial British campaign pieces, English lighting, garden ornaments & architectural elements. Specializing in sales to the trade. **Hrs:** By appt only. **CC:** AX/V/MC **Own:** Bruce & Deborah Phillips.

Rainville's Trading Post

Colrain Rd (Rte 112) • 01370
(413)625-6536

Antiques, tools, furniture & collectibles. **Est:** 1981 **Hrs:** Tue-Sun 9-5. **Dir:** 1/2 mi off Rte 2. **QC: 32 48 86**

Shea Antiques

69 Bridge St • 01370
(413)625-8353
shea@sheanet.com
www.sheanet.com

Antiques, collectibles, lighting, holiday & a little bit of everything. **Hrs:** Tue-Sat 10-5, Sun 12-5. **CC:** V/MC **Dir:** In the ctr of town. **QC: 32 48 S8 S12**

Shelburne Country Shop

Mohawk Trail (Rte 2) • 01370
(413)625-2041

A country shop with glassware, oil lamps, baskets, tools, stoneware, cupboards & a selection of fine used furniture. **Hrs:** Daily 10-4. **CC:** V/MC/DIS **Dir:** I-91 Exit 26: 5 mi W on Rte 2.

Yankee Pastime Antiques

Rte 112 N • 01370
(413)625-2730

Two large floors full of refinished turn-of-the-century oak furniture: Hoosier cabinets, ice boxes, mirrored dressers, round & square tables, rolltops, lady's desks, chests, chairs &

clocks. **Hrs:** Sat-Sun 10-5, wkdys by chance/appt. **Sz:** M **Dir:** I91 Exit 26: to Rte 2 W 8 mi, follow to Rte 112 N Colrain. **Own:** Bill Bassett. **QC: 50**

Shrewsbury

Antique Center of Shrewsbury [G]

510 Boston Tpke (Rte 9) • 01545
(508)845-9600
antiquectr@mediaone.net

Furniture from Victorian through early 20th C, jewelry, china & accessories. **Est:** 1994 **Hrs:** Tue-Sat 10-5, Sun 12-5. **CC:** AX/V/MC **Own:** Elaine Davis. **QC: 48**

Somerville

Londontowne Antiques Galleries

380 Somerville Ave • 02143
(617)625-2045
londontowne@earthlink.net
www.londontowne.com

Warehouse of fine antiques, country pine, classical garden ornamentation, French country & architectural artifacts. Also Asian furniture & decorative accessories. **Est:** 1979 **Hrs:** Mon-Sat 10-5, Sun 12-5. **Sz:** L **CC:** V/MC **Assn:** NEAA **Dir:** In Union Sq, 3/4 mi from Harvard Sq. **Own:** James Herbert Sr. **QC: 3 55 60 S1 S16**

South Braintree

Antiques & Things

826 Washington St (rear) • 02184
(781)843-4196

Americana, furniture, china, Steuben, pottery, linens, prints, glass jewelry & paintings. **Est:** 1935 **Hrs:** Mon-Fri 8-4, Sat 8-12 call 1st on wknds. **Sz:** S **Dir:** Across from Town Hall. **Own:** Claire R Eason & Mary B Forlong. **QC: 48 74**

South Deerfield

House of the Ferret

221 Greenfield Rd • 01373
(413)665-0038
ferret@crocker.com

A large, eclectic inventory, dominantly American (1700-1800s) featuring quilts; samplers; maritime; tin, copper & iron; early lighting; spatter, yellow, red, stone & mochaware; folk art; Vienna bronzes & Oriental antiques. **Pr:** $50-10,000 **Est:** 1995 **Hrs:** Daily by chance/appt. **Sz:** L **CC:** AX/V/MC **Assn:** NHADA **Dir:** I-91 Exit 24: N 2 mi on Rtes 5 & 10. **Own:** Roger Perry & Rita King. **QC: 34 52 70**

Yesterday's Antique Center [G20]

226 A Greenfield Rd (Rte 5) • 01373
(413)665-7226

Ephemera, linens, china, glassware, pottery, silver, brass, prints, jewelry & furniture. **Hrs:** Wed-Mon 10-5; Sum 10-4. **Dir:** 1 mi N of Yankee Candle. **Own:** Connie Witherell & Jim Alefterakis.

South Egremont

Bird Cage Antiques

(413)528-3556

American painted country furniture & folk accessories, jewelry & silver, glass & china, toys & dolls. Emphasis on high style & country furnishings. **Pr:** $10-2,500 **Est:** 1960 **Hrs:** By appt only. **Sz:** M **CC:** AX/V/MC **Assn:** BCADA **Own:** Marilyn Baseman. **QC: 1 23 32**

> Use the Service QuickCode indexes at the back of the book to find restorers, appraisers, refinishers, and other specialty service providers.

Geffner/Schatzky Antiques

Main St • 01258
(413)528-0057

Jewelry, architectural elements, decorative furniture & accessories, 19th C to 1950s. **Hrs:** May-Aug daily 10:30-5; Sep-Apr Fri-Sun 10:30-5, by chance/appt. **CC:** AX/V/MC **Assn:** BCADA **Dir:** Rte 23 at the sign of the Juggler. **Own:** Sheldon Geffner. **QC: 3 36 64**

Bruce & Sue Gventer Books

1 Tyrrell Rd • 01258
(413)528-2327
bgventer@bcn.net
www.blaize.com

Antiquarian books. Specializing in 19th C hand-colored prints, authentic manuscript leaves from the 13th to the 15th C, rare & unique books, fashion, costume, cookbooks, calligraphy, antique reference books & a large general stock. **Pr:** $1-2,500 **Est:** 1980 **Hrs:** Jun-Oct Wed-Sun 11-5; Nov-May Sat-Sun 11-5. **Sz:** M **Assn:** BCADA MARIAB **Dir:** 1 mi E of NY state border; 2-1/2 mi W of S Egremont PO on Tyrrell Rd just off Rte 23. **Own:** Bruce & Sue Gventer. **QC: 18 19 74**

Howard's Antiques

Hillsdale Rd (Rte 23) • 01258
(413)528-1232

American country furniture including large extension tables, chairs, bookcases, chests of drawers & washstands as well as early American lighting: chandeliers, sconces, floor lamps & table lamps. **Est:** 1975 **Hrs:** Wed-Mon 10-5. **Assn:** BCADA **Dir:** 2 mi W of S Egremont, 1 mi E of New York line. **Own:** Jeff & Linda Howard. **QC: 34 102 65**

Red Barn Antiques

Rte 23 • 01258
(413)528-3230

Antique lighting from the early 1800s onward including a large selection of kerosene, gas & early electric lighting, meticulously restored by us in our shop. Antique furniture, glass & accessories. Lighting restoration & fine metal polishing. **Est:** 1967 **Hrs:** Daily 10-5. **Sz:** M **CC:** AX/V/MC/DIS **Dir:** At the int of Rtes 23 & 41. **Own:** John & Mary Walther. **QC: 65 S16 S22**

Elliott & Grace Snyder Antiques

Undermountain Rd (Rte 41) • 01258
(413)528-3581

18th & early 19th C American furniture & decorative arts with an emphasis on textiles & painted & decorated furniture in original condition. Select stock of hooked & sewn rugs, samplers, needlework pictures, early ceramics, metalware & folk art. **Hrs:** By appt only. **Assn:** ADA BCADA **Dir:** Rte 41 1/2 mi S of Rte 23. **QC: 52 80 41**

The Splendid Peasant Ltd

Rte 23 & Sheffield Rd • 01258
(413)528-5755 • (413)528-5199 (fax)
folkart@splendidpeasant.com
www.splendidpeasant.com

Two buildings overlooking a stream provide a splendid atmosphere to view an ever-changing collection of museum-quality American folk art & original-paint country furniture. Singular 18th & 19th C cupboards, armoires, tables & decorative accessories. **Pr:** $70-25,000 **Est:** 1987 **Hrs:** Daily 9:30-5:30. **CC:** V/MC **Assn:** BCADA **Dir:** 1 blk E of S Egremont Ctr. **Own:** Martin & Kitty T Jacobs. **QC: 45 41 51**

South Hadley

Victor Weinblatt

(413)533-6435 • (413)535-2303 (fax)

Gameboards, hooked rugs, architectural elements, painted furniture & folk art. **Hrs:** By appt only. **Assn:** AC. **QC: 75 41 51**

South Natick

Douglas Jenkins Antiques

21 Eliot St • 01760
(508)650-0623 • (508)650-4820 (fax)
djantiques@aol.com

Specializing in 18th & 19th C fine period American & European furniture as well as primitives & folk art sold with a guarantee from an 18th C barn in Natick Historic District. **Pr:** $200-25,000 **Est:** 1992 **Hrs:** Mon-Sat 9-5, Sun 12-5. **Sz:** L **CC:** AX/V/MC **Assn:** SPNEA **Dir:** I-95 (Rte 128) Exit 21: on Rte 16 W, 2 mi W of Wellesley Ctr. **Own:** Doug & Georgia Jenkins. **QC: 52 53 54**

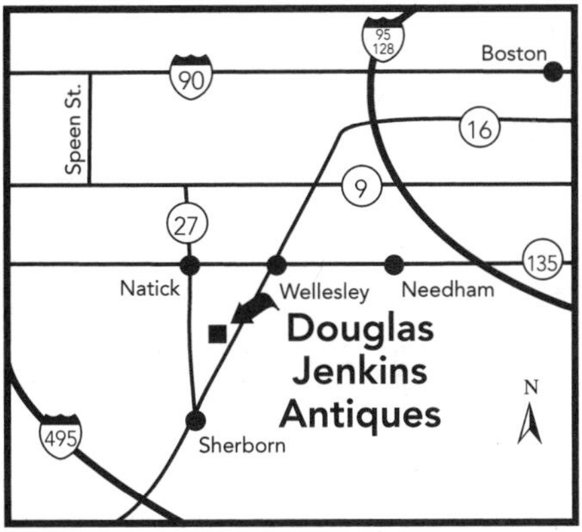

Southampton

Ester Gilbert Antiques

(413)527-8650
srkozub@crocker.com

18th-19th C furniture, decorative accessories, barometers, Civil War firearms & nautical items. **Hrs:** By appt only. **Assn:** GSAAA VADA **Own:** Sue & Bob Kozub. **QC: 77 4**

Heritage Books

College Hwy • 01073
(413)527-6200
sales@heritagebks.com
www.heritagebks.com

Old books, trade cards, postcards, sheet music. **Hrs:** Mon-Fri 9:30-4:30. **QC: 18 39**

Southampton Antiques

172 College Hwy (Rte 10) • 01073
(413)527-1022
souhantq@crocker.com
www.southamptonantiques.com

Three large barns with five floors filled with the largest selection of fine quality antique American, Victorian & turn-of-the-century oak furniture in New England. As-found & restored. Over 300 items in our on-line catalog (see URL). **Pr:** $100-50,000 **Hrs:** Sat 10-5 or by appt (closed Aug). **Sz:** L **CC:** V/MC/DIS **Dir:** From Mass Pike (I-90) Exit 3 (Westfield): L on Rte 10 N 7 mi (shop on L). From Northampton Rte 10 S 8 mi (shop on R). **Own:** Meg & Bruce Cummings. **QC: 58 50 89 S12**

Southborough

Golden Parrot

22 E Main St (Rte 30) • 01772
(508)485-5780

Baskets, tins, country & Victorian furniture, glass & collectibles. **Hrs:** Mon-Fri 1-5, Sat-Sun by chance/appt. **Assn:** SADA **Dir:** Off of Rte 85. **Own:** Glen & Gladys Urquhart **QC: S8**

Mapledale Antiques

224 Boston Rd • 01772
(508)485-5947

Furniture, accessories & collectibles. **Hrs:** Mon-Sat 2-5. **Assn:** SADA **Dir:** Rte 30 E 1/4 mi W of Framingham line. **Own:** Eleanor Hamel.

Southfield

The Buggy Whip Factory Antique Marketplace [G95]

Main St • 01259
(413)229-3576
www.buggywhip.net

Country to formal furniture, architectural pieces, kitchenware, tools, china, sterling, glassware, jewelry & books. **Hrs:** Daily 10-5; Jan-Apr closed Tue-Wed. **Assn:** BCADA. **QC: 48 3 34**

Kettering Antiques

604 Main St • 01259
(413)229-6647

Formal English & American 18th & 19th C furniture, decorative porcelain & brass. **Hrs:** Daily or by appt; Win hrs vary. **Assn:** BCADA **Own:** Ellen & David Carson. **QC: 52 54 20 S16**

Southwick

Eagle Mart Antiques & Collectibles [G23]

503 College Hwy • 01077
(413)569-3100

Hrs: Daily 9-4:30. **Dir:** Rtes 10 & 202, next to Dunkin Donuts.

Sim's Antiques

108 Congamond Rd (Rte 168) • 01077
(413)569-0450

A diversified shop of collectibles featuring postcards, books, records, glassware, games, Victorian photographs & stereoviews. **Est:** 1996 **Hrs:** Sat-Sun 10-4:30 or by chance/appt. **Own:** Simeon Pero. **QC: 73 39**

Springfield

Lady in Red Antiques

712 Sumner Ave • 01108
(413)734-6100 • (413)739-3828 (fax)

Decorative accessories, with a fine collection of antique jewelry. **Est:** 1978 **Hrs:** Mon-Sat 11-5. **CC:** AX/V/MC/DIS **Dir:** I-91 Rte 2 to Sumner Ave, Forest Park next to the Bing Movie Theatre. **QC: 36**

Stockbridge

Heirlooms Jewelry

(413)298-4436 • (413)637-8291 (fax)

Antique & estate jewelry. **Hrs:** Daily 10-6, off season closed Tue & Wed. **Assn:** BCADA **Own:** Robin Fleet. **QC: 64**

Overlee Farm Books

(413)637-2277 • (413)637-2503 (fax)

Books, maps & atlases. **Hrs:** By appt only. **Own:** Martin Torodash. **QC: 18 66**

John R Sanderson Antiquarian Bookseller

8 W Main St • 01262
(413)298-5322 • (413)298-4466 (fax)

Early, rare & fine books. **Hrs:** By appt only. **QC: 18 S1**

Sturbridge

Antique Center of Sturbridge [G25+]

426 Main St (Rte 20) • 01566
(508)347-5150
(877)347-5150

Furniture, china, glass, jewelry & metalware. **Est:** 1983 **Hrs:** Mon & Wed-Sat 10-5, Sun-12-5. **CC:** AX/V/MC/DIS **Dir:** In the ctr of town. **Own:** Beverly Sullivan.

Fairgounds Antique Center [G120]

362 Main St (Rte 20) • 01566
(508)347-3926
fairgrnds@aol.com

Antiques & collectibles. **Hrs:** Mon-Sat 10-5, Sun 12-5. **Sz:** L **CC:** AX/V/MC/DIS **Dir:** 1/4 mi W of the Mass Pike, 1/4 mi E of Old Sturbridge Village on Rte 20. **Own:** Carol Robar.

Showcase Antique Center [G100]

Rte 20 • 01566
(508)347-7190 • (508)347-5420 (fax)
showcase@hey.net
www.showcaseantiques.com

Decorative accessories, china, glass, pictures, toys & dolls, kitchenware & prints. **Est:** 1990 **Hrs:** Mon & Wed-Sat 10-5, Sun 12-5. **Dir:** Streetside to the entrance at Old Sturbridge Village. **Own:** Stuart & Karen Brody.

Sturbridge Antique Shops [G75]

200 Charlton Rd (Rte 20) • 01566
(508)347-2744

Furniture, decorative accessories, glass, china & porcelain. **Hrs:** Mon-Fri 9-5, Sat-Sun 10-5. **CC:** V/MC **Dir:** 6 mi E of Brimfield, 2 mi E of Old Sturbridge Village & 1/2 mi E of I-84 & I-90. **Own:** Robert Hopfe.

Sudbury

The Antique Exchange of Sudbury

236 Concord Rd • 01776
(978)443-8175

Two large floors of fancy American & European furniture, porcelain, estate jewelry, glass, chandeliers, tapestries, Sevres, Dresden, Wedgwood, silver, Staffordshire, flow blue & Minton. **Est:** 1987 **Hrs:** Fri-Sat 10:30-6 or by appt. **Sz:** L **Dir:** Rte 20 at Wayland Ctr to Rte 27N to Sudbury Ctr, L at lights onto Concord Rd, look for small sign; shop in barn behind house. **Own:** Jeanie Quirk. **QC: 64 48 65 S12**

Hager House Antiques

850 Boston Post Rd • 01776
(978)443-0917

A general line of 18th & 19th C furniture & interiors in a 1730 historic house. **Pr:** $20-3,000 **Est:** 1993 **Hrs:** Sat-Sun 10-5, hols Mons 10-5. **Sz:** M **Dir:** Rte 20 10 mi W of Rte 128 & 10 mi E of Rte 495. Near the Wayside Inn in Sudbury. **Own:** Dottie & Bill Schirmer. **QC: 34 52 S16**

Swansea

American Art & Antiques Inc

11 Maiden Ln • 02777
(508)678-9563 • (508)678-1470 (fax)
americanart@imaginenation.com

A diverse inventory of American paintings from early 19th to mid 20th C. **Pr:** $500-50,000 **Hrs:** By appt only. **CC:** AX/V/MC/DIS **Dir:** 15 min from Fall River or Providence. Call for directions. **Own:** Mel Davey. **QC: 7**

The Bloomin' Barn

279 Gardners Neck Rd • 02777
(508)678-4448

Primitive & country antiques & collectibles. **Hrs:** Daily. **CC:** AX/V/MC/DIS.

Taunton

Cradle Scyth Antiques

42 Orchard St • 02780
(508)942-8094
erossxncr@tmlt.com

Varied selection of vintage Victorian oak furniture, some restored, some in original condition. **Est:** 1961 **Hrs:** By appt only. **Own:** Edward G Ross. **QC: 50 58 S12 S16 S1**

Silver City Antiques & Collectibles [G]

31 Main St (Rte 44) • 02780
(508)821-1616

Hrs: Mon-Tue & Thu-Sat 10-5, Thu til 7, Wed & Sun 12-5.

Taunton Antiques Center [G300]
19 Main St (Rte 44) • 02780
(508)821-3333
antiques4u@tmlp.com

Est: 1994 **Hrs:** Mon-Sat 10-5, Thu til 7, Sun 12-5. **Sz:** H **CC:** V/MC **Dir:** I-95 N to I-195 E; Rte 24 N Exit 12 (Rte 14) to Taunton; 128 S to Rte 24 S to Rte 144 W Exit 13. **Own:** Chuck Cochrane.

Topsfield

Wenham Cross Antiques
41 Cross St • 01983
(978)887-2823 • (508)887-2711 (fax)

18th & 19th C furniture & accessories with an emphasis on country. Always a varied stock of Quimper, majolica, quilts, hooked rugs & folk art — American, French & English. **Pr:** $25-14,000 **Est:** 1980 **Hrs:** By appt only. **CC:** AX/V/MC **Assn:** NHADA MADA VADA **Own:** Emily & Irma Lampert. **QC: 34 36 60 S1 S12**

Townsend

Martha Boynton Antiques
1 Greeley Rd • 01469
(978)597-6794

18th & 19th C furniture in original paint & accessories. **Hrs:** By chance/appt. **Assn:** NHADA MADA **Dir:** Corn Rte 119 & Greeley Rd. **QC: 51 34**

Cherry Hill Antiques
67 Main St • 01469
(978)597-8903

Antiques, collectibles & advertising items. **Hrs:** Thu-Sat 10-4:30, occasional Sun 12:30-4:30. **Dir:** I-495 Littleton Exit: approx 14 mi W near the corn of Spaulding. **Own:** Ben & Joan Moran.

Harborside Antiques [G14]
Rte 119 • 01469
(978)597-8558

New stock daily from private homes including oak furniture, clocks, quilts, glass, ephemera, jewelry, dolls, lamps, books & silver. **Est:** 1982 **Hrs:** Tue-Sat 10-5. **CC:** V/MC **Dir:** I-495 to Rte 119 & corn of Spaulding St. **Own:** Gloria McCaffrey. **QC: 50 35 84**

Upton

David Rose Antiques
36 W Main St • 01568
(508)529-3838

American furniture of the 18th & 19th C, with special emphasis on American Empire & Victorian. **Pr:** $10-2,500 **Est:** 1973 **Hrs:** Daily 8-5. **Sz:** M **Dir:** I-495 Exit 21B: 4 mi to Rte 140, R on 140, approx 1 mi on L. **QC: 58**

Upton Country Store [G35+]
62 Main St (Rte 140) • 01568
(508)529-3163

Furniture, Shaker, glass, jewelry, postcards & country antiques. **Hrs:** Tue-Sat 10-5, Sun 1-5. **Own:** Judy & Ken Latimore.

Linda White Antique Clothing
2 Maple Ave • 01587
(508)529-4439

Specializing in the finest quality Victorian & Edwardian attire & accessories, beaded dresses & handbags, pre-1940s fancy wear, laces & linens & jewelry, with an emphasis on items in excellent condition. **Pr:** $20-1,500 **Est:** 1983 **Hrs:** Thu-Sat 11-4 or by appt. **Sz:** S **CC:** V/MC **Assn:** CSA **Dir:** Rte 495 Exit 21B: 5 mi to traffic light in Upton Center. Look for "old red barn" in rear of post office. **Own:** Linda White. **QC: 80 81 63 S1 S9 S12**

Waltham

Massachusetts Antiques Co-op [G100]

100 Felton St • 02154
(781)893-8893
www.massantiques.com

Antiques & collectibles in a large display gallery. **Pr:** $25-25,000 **Est:** 1991 **Hrs:** Wed-Mon 10-5, Thu til 8. **Sz:** L **CC:** V/MC **Dir:** Rte 128 Exit 26: Rte 20 E to Main St, R on Moody St. At 1st light R onto Felton St. 3 mi from int of I-90 & Rte 128. **Own:** Jerry Freidus & Staci Hartwell. **QC: 48 32 S16 S6**

Ware

Stonemill Antique Center [G100]

E Main St (Rte 9) • 01082
(413)967-5964

In a beautifully restored historic building on the National Register of Historic Places, quality antiques including furniture, glass, porcelain, silver, brass, country & architectural pieces. **Pr:** $5-35,000 **Est:** 1994 **Hrs:** Tue-Sat 10-5, Sun 12-5. **Sz:** H **Dir:** In the ctr of town 2 blks E of the jct of Rtes 9 & 32. 15 mins from Brimfield. **Own:** Joe Lotuff Sr. **QC: 32 S12 S8**

Wayland

Yankee Craftsman

357 Commonwealth Rd (Rte 30) • 01778
(508)653-0031
www.yankeecraftsman

Antique lighting & furniture, featuring one of the country's most extensive collections of antique lighting fixtures including Tiffany lamps & old fixtures for gas, oil & candles. **Est:** 1968 **Hrs:** Daily 10-5. **CC:** V/MC **Dir:** Near The Villa Restaurant. 20 mins from Boston. **Own:** Bruce, Scott & Gary Sweeney & John Lawrence. **QC: 65 S16**

Wellesley

Apple Ridge Fine Arts

(508)655-4197 • (617)345-1300 (fax)
phitt@aics.net

Fine American paintings of the 20s, 30s & 40s. American scene, figurative, regionalism, WPA & social realism & a choice inventory of baseball art (1890-current). **Pr:** $200-20,000 **Est:** 1999 **Hrs:** Wknds & eves by appt only. **Sz:** L **Dir:** Call for directions. **Own:** Arthur D Hittner. **QC: 7 12 14**

Crane Collection

564 Washington St (Rte 16) • 02482-6409
(781)235-1166 • (781)235-4181 (fax)
cranecolec@aol.com
www.artnet.com/crane.html

Fine oil paintings by 19th C American & European artists as well as early 20th C works. Large selection of small paintings & some period sculpture. **Pr:** $1,000-100,000 **Est:** 1983 **Hrs:** Mon-Sat 10-5. **Sz:** M **CC:** AX/V/MC **Assn:** NEAA **Dir:** Mass Pike W Exit 16: Thru Newton Lower Falls past Town Hall & library on L, 1st commercial blk is Wellesley Sq. **Own:** Bonnie & Loyd Crane. **QC: 7 8 15 S1 S8 S12**

Prado Antiques

12 Church St • 02482
(781)237-5140

A beautiful collection of original period oil paintings, fine furniture, European & Chinese export porcelain for the discerning collector. **Est:** 1978 **Hrs:** By chance/appt. **Dir:** Mass Pike exit Rte 16: to lights at Wellesley Sq. Bear L on Rte 16 300 ft to Treadway Inn & go R onto Church St. **QC: 7 53 25**

Spivack's Antiques
54 Washington St (Rte 16) • 02181
(781)235-1700

One of New England oldest & largest shops, direct importers of European furniture & accessories; also carry American furniture & accessories. **Pr:** $100-15,000 **Est:** 1936 **Hrs:** Sep-May Mon-Fri 8:30-5:30, Sat-Sun 10-4; Jun-Aug closed Sat-Sun. **Sz:** H **CC:** AX/V/MC **Dir:** I-90 to Rte 128S to Rte 16 W, 1/2 mi on Rte 16 to Washington St, on the L. **Own:** Bob & Joan O'Leary. **QC: 54 52 48**

D B Stock Antique Carpets
464 Washington St (Rte 16) • 02482
(781)237-5859

19th & early 20th C Persian village & Caucasian rugs & carpets in very good to excellent condition. Specializing in Bidjar, Fereghan Sarouks & NW Persian carpets, including serapis & other Herez weavings. Search service. **Pr:** $1000-50,000 **Hrs:** Wed-Sat 12-6 & by appt. **Sz:** M **Assn:** AADLA ADA **Dir:** I-95 (Rte 128) to Rte 16 W approx 3 mi on the L across from Haskins Oldsmobile. Park in front or in the back lot. **Own:** Douglas & Helen Stock. **QC: 76 S1 S18**

Antique Time Machines
339 Washington St (Rte 16) • 02181
(781)431-1174

One of the largest selections of fine antique clocks in the Boston area, as well as 17th, 18th & 19th C furnishings & accessories. **Est:** 1988 **Hrs:** Wed-Sat 10-5 or by appt. **CC:** AX/V/MC **Assn:** NAWCC **Dir:** Rte 128 to Rte 16 W or Rte 9 W to Wellesley Hills. On Rte 16 next to the PO in the Old Train Station. **Own:** Stephen Carter. **QC: 35 52 54 S7**

Ernest Kramer Fine Arts & Prints
(781)237-3635 • (781)235-0112 (fax)

Specializing in late 19th & 20th C American & European prints & drawings: Benson, Benton, Cadmus, Chamberlain, Clark, Hassam, Kent, Landacre, Landeck, Lozowick, Lewis, Markham, Marsh, Nason, Pennell, Ripley, Riggs, Schaldach, Sloan, Tissot, Wood & Zorn. **Pr:** $150-7,500 **Est:** 1984 **Hrs:** By appt only. **CC:** AX/V/MC/DIS **Dir:** Call for directions. **QC: 14 7 74 S1 S8 S12**

Wenham

Aachen Books
300 Main St • 01982
(978)468-4066

Antiquarian & out of print books, prints & ephemera. **Est:** 1990 **Hrs:** Tue-Wed & Fri-Sat 12-5. **Sz:** M **Assn:** MARIAB **Dir:** Rte 1A N 3 mi from int with Rte 128 in North Beverly. **Own:** Cheever Cressy. **QC: 18 39 74**

Firehouse Antiques
148 Main St (Rte 1A) • 01984
(978)468-9532

Fine furniture & antiques, including a large selection of brass & iron beds. **Est:** 1980 **Hrs:** Daily 10-5 or by appt. **CC:** V/MC **Own:** Palmer Bromley. **QC: 48**

West Boylston

The Deacon's Bench [G14]
18 N Main St (Rte 140) • 01564
(508)835-3858

Est: 1973 **Hrs:** Apr 15-Oct 15 Wed-Sat 11-5, Sun 12-5; Oct 15-Apr 15 Wed-Sat 10:30-4:30, Sun 12-5. **Sz:** L **Dir:** I-190 Exit 5: S on Rte 140. **Own:** Judith Miracle.

Obadiah Pine Antiques
160 W Boylston St (Rte 12) • 01583
(508)835-4656

Country oak & walnut furniture, baskets, lighting, clocks, jewelry & glass. **Hrs:** By chance/appt. **Dir:** Rte 190 Exit 4: to Rte 12,

L on W Boylston 3/4 mi. **Own:** Linda Toppin. **QC: 35 50 65**

Robert Antiques [G23]
271 W Boylston St (Rte 12) • 01583
(508)835-6550

Eclectic mix of antiques & collectibles. **Est:** 1990 **Hrs:** Tue-Sat 11-5, Sun 12-5. **CC:** V/MC **Dir:** I-190 Exit 4: N on Rte 12 1 mi on L. **Own:** Gert Robert. **QC: 36 48 7**

Wayside Furniture & Antiques [G38]
Rtes 12 & 140 • 01583
(508)835-4690

Furniture, paintings, clocks, prints, jewelry, glass, lamps, rugs & linens in an old organ factory. **Est:** 1991 **Hrs:** Tue-Sat 10-5, Sun 12-5. **CC:** V/MC **Dir:** At the RR underpass. **Own:** David Vendreau.

Yankee Heritage Antiques
44 Sterling St • 01583
(508)835-2010

A general line including oak furniture, old prints, clocks, collectibles & glassware. **Hrs:** Sun-Fri 10-5:30. **Dir:** At jct Rtes 12 & 110. **Own:** Rod & June Reams. **QC: 50 61**

West Bridgewater

America's Attic
221 W Center St (Rte 106) • 02379
(508)584-5281

Furniture, paintings, rugs, clocks, figurines, garden decorations & architectural elements. **Est:** 1988 **Hrs:** Mon-Fri 9:30-2. **Sz:** M **Assn:** HAAD **Own:** Manny & Lois de Castro. **QC: 32**

Antiques Now
223 W Center St (Rte 106) • 02379
(508)580-1464

Fine silver, jewelry, glass & china. **Hrs:** Daily 10-4. **Assn:** HAAD **Own:** Laura Oppenheim & Armen Amerigian. **QC: 61 63 78**

Carriage House Antiques
102 W Center St (Rte 106) • 02379
(508)584-3008

Quality furnishings & accessories, antique jewelry a specialty. **Hrs:** Fri-Sun 12-5 or call ahead. **Assn:** HAAD **Dir:** Across from the High School. **Own:** Diana C Lathrop. **QC: 64 36**

More Fond Memories
168 S Main St (Rte 28) • 02379
(508)583-1919

Family owned & operated antiques shop, second for the Ferreiras, with six rooms full of treasures from the early 19th C through the nifty sixties. Furniture, artwork, jewelry, lighting, china & old toys. **Pr:** $2-3,000 **Hrs:** Daily 11-5. **Sz:** L **CC:** V/MC/DIS **Assn:** HAAD SPNEA **Dir:** From Rte 24 N or S Exit 16A (Rte 106E) 2 mi, then bear R onto Rte 28 S. Shop is 1/2 mi on L. **Own:** Bob & Brenda Ferreira. **QC: 48 18 63 S1 S12 S8**

One Horse Shay Antiques
194 S Main St (Rte 28) • 02379
(508)587-8185

Ever-changing variety of antiques & collectibles at affordable prices purchased from South Shore homes. **Pr:** $1-1,000 **Est:** 1992 **Hrs:** Sep 15-Jun 30 Thu-Sat 11-5, Sun 12-5; Jul 7-Sep 14 Thu-Sat 11-5. **Sz:** M **Assn:** HADA **Dir:** Next to West Bridgewater Antique & Artisans Ctr. **Own:** Nancy Nevens. **QC: 32 63 48**

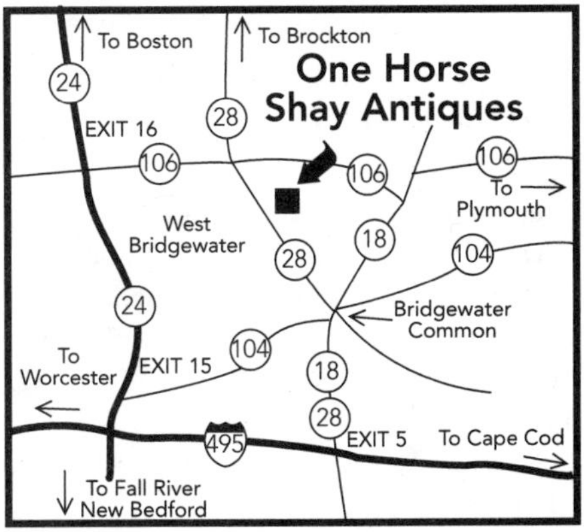

Antique Associates
at West Townsend
America's Finest Multiple Dealer Shop
473 Main St. P.O. Box 129W, West Townsend, MA 01474 • (978) 597-8084 • drh@aaawt.com

Upstairs-Downstairs Antiques 2

118 S Main St (Rte 28) • 02379
(508)586-2880

Depression & 1950s collectibles, jewelry, linens & antiques. **Hrs:** Mon-Sat 11-4:30, Wed & Sun by chance. **Assn:** HAAD **Own:** Jane Wood & Pamela Collins & Holly Carruthers. **QC: 32 63 39**

West Bridgewater Antique & Artisan Center [G200]

220 S Main St (Rte 28) • 02379
(508)580-5533

Quality antiques & collectibles including furniture, paintings & prints, art pottery, glass, china, silver, jewelry, toys, dolls, quilts, primitives, sports memorabilia & ephemera. **Est:** 1993 **Hrs:** Mon-Sat 10-5, Sun 12-5. **Sz:** H **CC:** V/MC/DIS **Assn:** HAAD **Dir:** Rte 24 Exit 16A: Rte 106 E to Rte 28 S I mi. **Own:** William Bassett.

Westbridge Antiques

165 W Center St (Rte 106) • 02379
(508)584-9111

Dolls, jewelry, primitives & furniture. **Hrs:** By chance/appt. **Assn:** HAAD **Own:** Sherryl W Bently.

West Stockbridge

Sawyer Antiques at Shaker Mill

One Depot St • 01266
(413)232-7062
stopper@bcn.net
www.bcn.net/~stopper

Early American furniture & accessories, formal, Shaker & country on two floors of a Shaker-built mill. **Est:** 1974 **Hrs:** By chance/appt. **Sz:** M **CC:** V/MC **Assn:** ASA BCADA **Dir:** Mass Pike exit 1. **Own:** Edward S Sawyer & Scott W Sawyer. **QC: 1 7 51 S1 S2 S12**

West Townsend

Antique Associates at West Townsend [G80]

473 Main St • 01474
(978)597-8084 • (978)597-6704 (fax)
drh@aaawt.com
www.aaawt.com

High-quality country & formal furniture, folk art, glass, ceramics, earthenware, pewter, silver, iron, decorative accessories, autographs & textiles. All items period, all guaranteed. Shipping services available. **Pr:** $25-25,000 **Est:** 1983 **Hrs:** Daily 10-5. **Sz:** L **CC:** V/MC **Dir:** I-495 Exit 31: Rte 119 W in West Townsend. **Own:** David & Lynn Hillier. **QC: 1 4 41 S1 S8**

Delaney Antique Clocks

435 Main St • 01474
(978)597-2231

In a classic red New England barn, the largest selection of antique American tall clocks in the country. Over 300 clocks on display along with antique furniture. Tall clocks are guaranteed. **Pr:** $150-100,000 **Est:** 1968 **Hrs:** Sat-Sun 9-5, Mon-Fri by chance/appt. **Sz:** L **Assn:** NAWCC **Dir:** Rte 2 from Boston or Rte 128 to Rte 119 to West Townsend; shop is on R, 2 mi from 2nd light in Townsend. **Own:** John & Barbara Delaney. **QC: 35**

Hobart Village Antique Mall [G80]

445 Main St • 01474
(978)597-0332 • (508)597-0332 (fax)
hobartvill@net1plus.com
www.hobartvillage.com

Rooms of furniture & cases of porcelain, sterling silver, clocks & glassware. Also Bradford Antiques, featuring country antiques, Staffordshire, clocks & accessories. **Est:** 1995 **Hrs:** Wed-Mon 10-5. **Sz:** L **CC:** AX/V/MC/DIS **Dir:** From Boston: Rte 2 W to Rte 119 W. Shop on corn of Rte 119 & Canal St (NH Rte 124). From Worcester: Rte 290 to I-495 N Exit 31: Rte 119 W 16 mi. **Own:** Anthony Silva. **QC: 48 78 64 S10 S12 S19**

West Upton

Rose's Antiques

36 W Main St • 01568
(508)529-3838

Quality Victorian, walnut, rosewood, mahogany, oak, wicker & early furniture, glass, china, lamps, silver & ephemera. **Hrs:** Daily 10-5 or by appt. **Assn:** SADA. **QC: 48 89**

West Whately

The Miller's Daughter

21 Poplar Hill Rd • 01039
(413)665-4464

The latest price guides & reference books on art, china, glass, jewelry, country, tools, toys & dolls. **Assn:** PVADA **Own:** Cecil & Grace Miller Dickinson & David Dickinson.

Westborough

Maynard House

11 Maynard St • 01581
(508)366-2073

Country shop featuring cupboards, tables, baskets, herb loft & exclusive line of upholstered country sofas & wing chairs representing 1750-1820. **Hrs:** Thu-Sun 11-4 or by appt. **Assn:** SADA **Dir:** Off Rte 135. **Own:** Betty Urquhart. **QC: 34 56**

Salt-Box House Antiques

9 Maynard St • 01581
(508)366-4951
cpgure@banet.net

19th & early 19th C American antiques in original paint & also choice smalls including lighting, textiles, folk art & treen. **Hrs:** By chance/appt. **Assn:** NHADA **Dir:** I-495 Exit 23B: W to Rte 9W to Rte 135E, R on Rte 135, 3rd R is Maynard St. **Own:** Margaret M Gure. **QC: 65 88 51**

David Wheatcroft
220 E Main St • 01581
(508)366-1723

Quilts, American painted furniture, folk art, Fraktur, sculpture & Native American pieces for serious collectors. **Hrs:** By appt only. **Assn:** NHADA **Own:** David Wheatcroft. **QC: 80 51 41**

Westfield

Ashley Antiques
(413)562-3188

Fine general line with emphasis on American coin silver & paintings. **Est:** 1971 **Hrs:** By appt only. **Assn:** PVADA MADA **Own:** Fred & Janice Pugliano. **QC: 78 7 S1**

Paula Patterson
(413)568-0317

Country furniture & accessories. **Hrs:** By appt only. **Assn:** GSAAA **Own:** Paula Patterson. **QC: 102 34**

Westford

Antiques
301 Littleton Rd (Rte 110) • 01886
(978)392-9944

A selection of American furniture & accessories. **Pr:** $5-5,000 **Est:** 1972 **Hrs:** Wed-Mon 10-5, Sun 12-4:30. **CC:** V/MC **Dir:** I-495 Exit 32: Boston Rd to lights, turn R on Rte 110. **Own:** Brian & Deborah Orr.

Wolf's Den Antiques
139 Concord Rd • 01886
(978)692-3911 • (781)862-0312 (fax)
(800)479-3913
bettewolf@aol.com
www.westford.com/wolfsden

Full line of Victorian walnut, oak, old wicker, custom mahogany, hanging lamps, panel lamps, good clocks, china & glass, sterling & a vast variety of antique items. **Pr:** $100-10,000 **Est:** 1976 **Hrs:** Sat-Sun 12-5, or by chance/appt. **Sz:** L **CC:** AX **Assn:** SADA **Dir:** I-495 Exit 31: E 1/4 mi then take R at 1st traffic light. On Rte 110 go 1-1/2 mi, then R onto Concord Rd (Rte 225). Go under Rte 495 overpass. Barn is on L 500 yds. **Own:** Bette Wolf. **QC: 58 50 65 S1 S12 S19**

Westhampton

Joseph Hunt Marshall
254 Reservoir Rd • 01027
(413)529-9995

18th & 19th C New England furniture, early blown glass & appropriate accessories. **Hrs:** By appt only. **Assn:** ADA. **QC: 52 104**

Westport

Westport Antiques Center [G178]
522 American Legion Hwy • 02790
(508)636-2373

Porcelain, glassware, textiles & toys. **Pr:** $1-1,200 **Est:** 1992 **Hrs:** Mon-Sat 10-5, Sun 12-5. **Sz:** L **CC:** V/MC **Assn:** SNEADA **Dir:** I-195 Exit 10: Rte 88 to Rte 177 turn R. **Own:** Carol Bryden.

Whately

Whately Antiquarian Book Center [G50]
25 West St (Rte 5) • 01066
(413)247-3272
whatebks@crocker.com

In a turn-of-the-century brick schoolhouse, out-of-print, rare & collectible books, posters & prints in the fields of art, photography, Americana, local history, military, literature, mysteries, children's, social studies **Est:** 1991 **Hrs:** Mon-Tue & Thu-Sat 10-

5:30, Sun 12-5. **Assn:** MARIAB **Dir:** I-91 Exit 23N: R onto Rte 5. 3 mi N on L. I-91 S: Exit 25, turn R on Rte 5, S for 1 mi. Shop is in brick schoolhouse **Own:** Barbara Smith & Eugene Povirk. **QC: 18 74 39**

Williamstown

The Amber Fox
622A Main St (Rte 2) • 01267
(413)458-8519

China (Shelly, Belleek, Wedgwood, Lenox, Nippon, Noritake), art pottery, Victorian & oak furniture, prints, paintings & glass. **Est:** 1996 **Hrs:** Wed-Sat 10-5, Sun-Tue by appt only. **Sz:** M **CC:** AX/V/MC/DIS **Own:** Tracie Fisk. **QC: 1 101 89 S12**

Collector's Warehouse
105 North St • 01267
(413)458-9686

Literally a warehouse of every kind of antique including furniture, glassware, jewelry, linen, books, frames & dolls. **Est:** 1985 **Hrs:** Wed-Sat 12-5 or by appt. **CC:** V/MC **Dir:** Off Rte 7 next to Le Country Restaurant in the McClelland Press Bldg. **Own:** Deborah Elder.

The Library Antiques
70 Spring St • 01267
(413)458-3436
(800)294-4798

Early American & Oriental furniture, lamps, china, prints, Victoriana, books, jewelry, porcelain & collectibles **Est:** 1992 **Hrs:** Jun-Oct Mon-Sat 10-6, Sun 11-5; Nov-May Mon-Fri 10-5:30, Sat 10-6, Sun 11-5. **Sz:** L **Dir:** Just past the PO. **Own:** Edgar Fauteok

John Robinson
(413)458-3589
jrobinson@taconic.net

American country furniture & accessories, historical Staffordshire & porcelains, architectural elements/dismantled bldgs, Oriental rugs & fireplace equipment. **Hrs:** By appt only. **QC: 34 30 3**

Saddleback Antiques [G]
1395 Cold Springs Rd (Rte 7) • 01267
(413)458-5852

An array of antiques from primitive American, Victorian & wicker furniture to a large collection of smalls. **Hrs:** Mon-Tue & Thu-Sat 10-5, Sun 12-5. **CC:** V/MC **Own:** Dan Rhodes.

Winchester

Koko Boodakian & Sons
1026 Main St • 01890
(781)729-5566 • (781)729-5595 (fax)
www.kokorugs.com

Experts in Oriental rugs offering fine quality rugs for sale or trade to the discriminating collector. Complete restoration a specialty. **Est:** 1938 **Hrs:** Tue-Sat 9:30-5, Thu til 9. **CC:** AX/V/MC/DIS. **QC: 76 S9 S16**

Lee Gallery
One Mt Vernon St • 01890
(781)729-7445 • (617)729-4592 (fax)
www.leegallery.com

Fine 19th & 20th C vintage photographs. **Pr:** $500-25,000 **Est:** 1981 **Hrs:** Tue-Fri 11-5. **Sz:** M **CC:** V/MC **Assn:** AIPAD **Dir:** Next to Book Ends at Main & Mt Vernon St. **Own:** Mack Lee. **QC: 73**

Worcester

Brickyard Place Antiques & Collectibles [G40]
65 Water St • 01604
(508)755-4500

Diverse inventory of art, pottery, china, silver, jewelry, furniture, lamps, lighting, copper, brass, toys, sporting collectibles, linens, tools, daguerreotypes, ambrotypes, tintypes, postcards, ledgers & old books. **Pr:** $1-5,000 **Est:** 1998 **Hrs:** Wed-Sun 10-4 closed major hols. **Sz:** L **Dir:** I-290 Exit 13: Kelly Sq to Water St. **Own:** James Komenos. **QC: 7 64 65 S8 S6 S9**

Wrentham

Bittersweet Boutique

715 East St • 02093
(508)384-3173
mary@bittersweetboutique.com
www.bittersweetboutique.com

1800-1970s vintage clothing, jewelry & accessories. **Pr:** $5.00-500 **Est:** 1989 **Hrs:** Wed-Fri 11-5, Sat 10-5. **Sz:** M **CC:** V/MC **Dir:** I-495 to Rte 140. **Own:** Mary Penza. **QC: 83**

His & Hers Antiques

121 East St • 02093
(508)384-3894

Flow blue, dinner services, Heisey, elegant Depression glass, banks, toys, kitchenware, furniture & oil lamps. **Pr:** $25-3,000 **Hrs:** By chance/appt. **Dir:** From int of Rte 1 & Rte 140 go 1/4 mi E to antique red colonial on L. **Own:** Cynthia Veilleux. **QC: 61 23 S1 S9 S12**

Wrentham Antiques Marketplace Inc [G65]

513 South St (Rte 1A) • 02093
(508)384-2811 • (508)285-4350 (fax)

Fine china, glass, pottery, estate & antique jewelry, ephemera, mirrors & lamps. Specializing in restored furniture from the mid-1800s through 1940s including bedroom & dining room sets. Reproduction harvest tables & Warren chairs. **Pr:** $40-4,000 **Est:** 1990 **Hrs:** Tue-Fri 10-6, Thu til 8, Sat 10-5, Sun 12-5. **Sz:** L **CC:** AX/V/MC **Dir:** I-495 Exit 15: Rte 1A N to Wrentham (2 min). **Own:** Chuck & Kathy McStay. **QC: 36 48 76 S16 S8 S10**

Cape Cod, Martha's Vineyard, and Nantucket

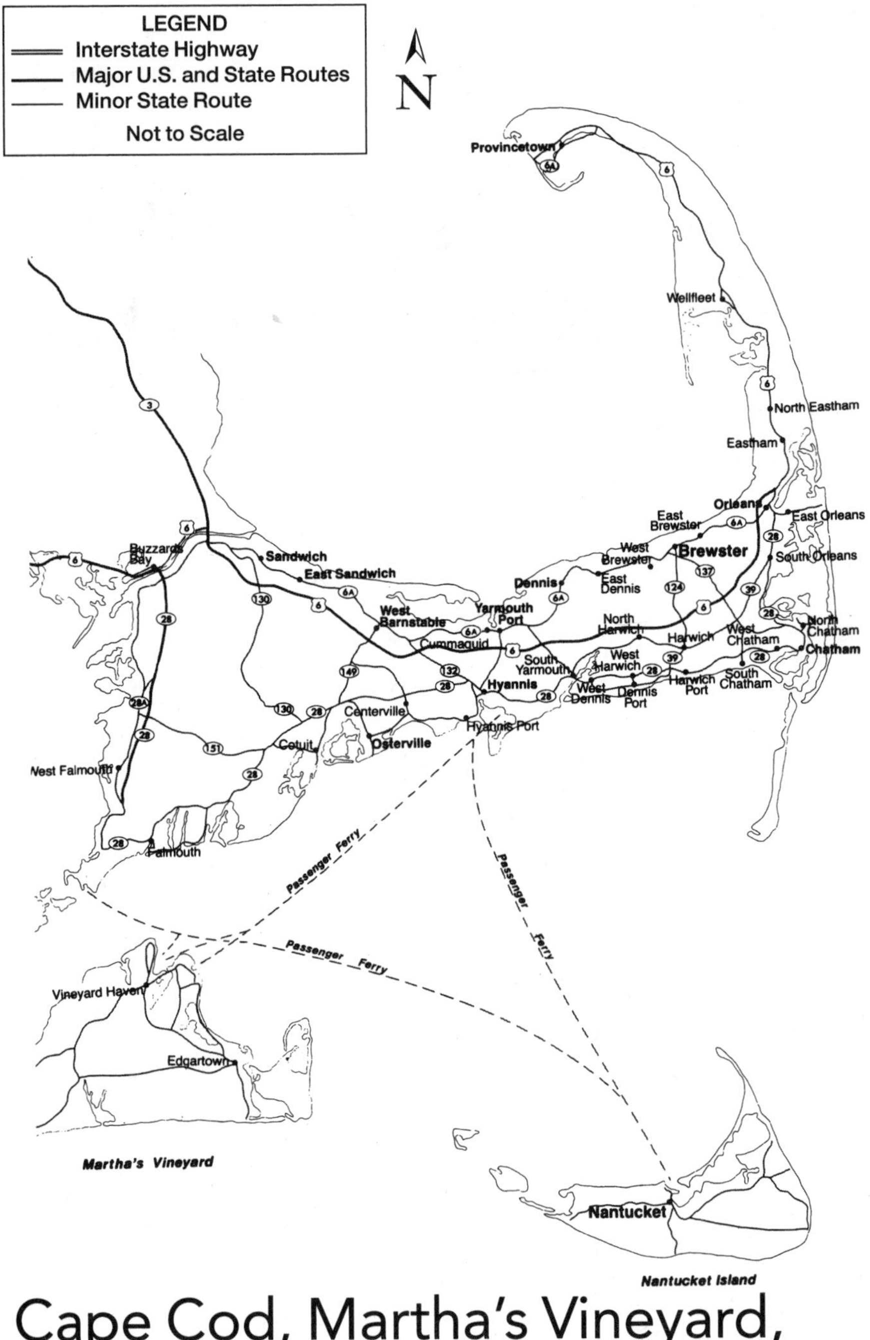

Cape Cod, Martha's Vineyard, and Nantucket

Barnstable

Esprit Decor

3941 Rte 6A • 02630
(508)362-2480
suzannck@yahoo.com

From folk to Federal: furniture & all manner of accessories including silver, rugs & porcelain. **Est:** 1972 **Hrs:** Mem Day-Oct 31 Mon-Sat 10-5, Sun 12-5; Spr/Fall by appt. **Sz:** M **Assn:** CCADA **Dir:** 1.3 mi E of traffic light in Barnstable Village on R betw Mary Dunn Rd & the Cummaquid PO. **Own:** Suzanne C Kelly. **QC: 48 36 78**

Harden Studios

3264 Main St (Rte 6A) • 02630
(508)362-7711 • (508)362-0217 (fax)

In the Deacon Robert Davis House, c 1719, a collection of early American antiques, complemented by fine upholstered furniture, fabrics, lighting & decorative accessories. Also a small gallery of original etchings, paintings & sporting prints. **Pr:** $25-15,000 **Hrs:** Mon & Wed-Sat 9:30-5, Sun 10-4. **Sz:** L **CC:** V/MC **Assn:** SPNEA ASID **Dir:** In the ctr of the Barnstable Village business district. **Own:** Charles M Harden. **QC: 7 34 52 S9 S15 S12**

Village Antiques

3267 Main St (Rte 6A) • 02675
(508)362-6633
npantiques1@aolcom

18th & 19th C furniture, Belleek, Wedgewood, Rookwood, primitives, china, paintings & sterling. **Hrs:** Sum daily 10:30-4:30; call ahead in Win. **Assn:** CCADA **Own:** Nancy L Perry. **QC: 48 23 106**

Brewster

Breton House

1222 Stoney Brook Rd • 02631
(508)896-3974

Eclectic selection focusing on children's toys, opera, theater & film memorabilia, sports & professional memorabilia as well as furniture. **Est:** 1956 **Hrs:** Daily 11:30-5. **CC:** V/MC **Dir:** At jct of Stoney Brook Rd & Rte 6A. **Own:** Jack Saggsser & Bernard Diamond. **QC: 87 67 79**

William Brewster Antiques

73 Fox Meadow Dr • 02631
(508)896-4816

A fine selection of antiques including mirrors, furniture, glass, Royal Doulton & select smalls. **Est:** 1990 **Hrs:** By appt only. **Assn:** CCADA **Own:** Don & Marge Wilks. **QC: 36 61 68**

Captain Freeman Perry House

1531 Main St (Rte 6A) • 02631
(508)896-5323

Brass, copper, treen & decorative accessories. **Est:** 1969 **Hrs:** Jan-Feb & Apr-Nov daily 9-5, closed Dec & Mar. **Sz:** M **Own:** Victor Cohen. **QC: 20 36 88**

Eve's Place

564 Main St (Rte 6A) • 02631
(508)896-4914

Estate jewelry including pearls, Victorian clothing, china, silver, glass, furniture & primitives. **Hrs:** Daily 10-5; Sep-Mar closed Tue. **Assn:** CCADA **Own:** Eve Roulier. **QC: 61 64 89**

Barbara Grant Antiques & Books

1793 Main St (Rte 6A) • 02631
(508)896-7198

Old & out-of-print books, furniture, primitives, old kitchenware, glass, porcelain, prints, linen, decorative accessories, jewelry, collectibles & nostalgia. **Pr:** $1-1,000 **Est:** 1980 **Hrs:** May-Oct daily 10-5; other times by chance/appt. **Sz:** M **Assn:** CCADA **Dir:** On Rte 6A betw Rte 137 & Rte 124. **Own:** Barbara Grant. **QC: 18 34 36**

Donald B Howes Antiques & Fine Art

1424 Main St (Rte 6A) • 02631
(508)896-3502

Folk & fine art, paintings, prints, books, documents & furniture. **Hrs:** By chance/appt. **Assn:** CCADA **Dir:** Almost opp Fire Museum. **QC: 7 41 74**

Huckleberry's Antiques

2271 Main St (Rte 6A) • 02631
(508)896-2670

Quaint Victorian cottage featuring restored pine trunks, small tables & furniture, linens, hooked rugs, Americana, primitives & collectibles. **Pr:** $1-500 **Hrs:** Daily 10-4. **Sz:** S **CC:** AX **Assn:** CCADA **Dir:** 1 mi E of the Brewster General Store. **Own:** Robert & Linda Bugle. **QC: 34 81 75**

B D Hutchinson Watchmaker

1274 Long Pond Rd (Rte 137) • 02631
(508)896-6395

Specializing in antique clocks & watches. **Est:** 1970 **Hrs:** Mon, Wed, Fri-Sat 9-5 or by chance/appt. **Assn:** NAWCC **Dir:** On Rte 137. **QC: 35 S7**

Kings Way Books & Antiques

774 Main St (Rte 6A) • 02631
(508)896-3639

Old, rare & out-of-print books. **Hrs:** Apr-Dec Thu-Sun 10-6; Jul-Sep daily 10-6. **Assn:** CCADA **Own:** Richard & Ella Socky. **QC: 18**

Mark Lawrence Fine Antiques

1050 Main St (Rte 6A) • 02631
(508)896-8381

Fine 18th & early 19th C American, English & Continental antiques with an emphasis on porcelain, furniture, paintings & silver. **Est:** 1971 **Hrs:** May-Nov daily 9-5; Dec-Apr by chance/appt. **Sz:** M **CC:** AX/V/MC **Assn:** NEAA CCADA **Dir:** Across from the Lemon Tree. **Own:** Robert L Barry. **QC: 36 53 7 S1**

Monomoy Antiques

3425 Main St (Rte 6A) • 02631
(508)896-6570
email@monomoyantiques.com
www.monomoyantiques.com

Fine furniture, china, paintings, clocks, rugs, books, tools, country accents, old iron, early lighting, sterling silver, Sandwich glass & vintage fishing tackle. **Est:** 1994 **Hrs:** Daily 10-5. **Assn:** CCADA **Own:** Rob & Mary Beth Bergh. **QC: 48 34 65**

The Pflocks

598 Main St (Rte 6A) • 02631
(508)896-3457

A nice selection of quality copper & brass metalwork, fireplace equipment, nautical, furniture, primitives & metal restorations. **Hrs:** Apr-Oct Mon-Sat 10-5, Sun 1-5; Nov-Mar Mon-Sat 10-4:30, Sun 1-4:30, call ahead advised. **Sz:** M **Assn:** CCADA **Dir:** On the S side of Rte 6A. **Own:** Anne Pflock. **QC: 20 40 70 S9 S16**

Pink Cadillac Antiques

3140 Main St (Rte 6A) • 02631
(508)896-4651

Collectibles from the 1920s-1950s. Specializing in Depression glass & novelty salt & peppers, china, pottery. **Hrs:** Jul-Lab Day daily 11-5. **Assn:** CCADA **Own:** Anne Milzoff. **QC: 61 32**

The Punkhorn Bookshop

672 Main St (Rte 6A) • 02631
(508)896-2114

Antiquarian books: American literature, history, limited editions, natural history, prints, publishers' covers & first editions. Exceptional selections in the fields of natural history, classics & Americana. **Hrs:** Jun-Oct Tue-Sun 10-5; Nov-May by appt. **Assn:** MARIAB CCADA **Dir:** 2 mi E of the Brewster Town Marker going E on 6A. **Own:** David & Irene Luebke. **QC: 18 74 S1**

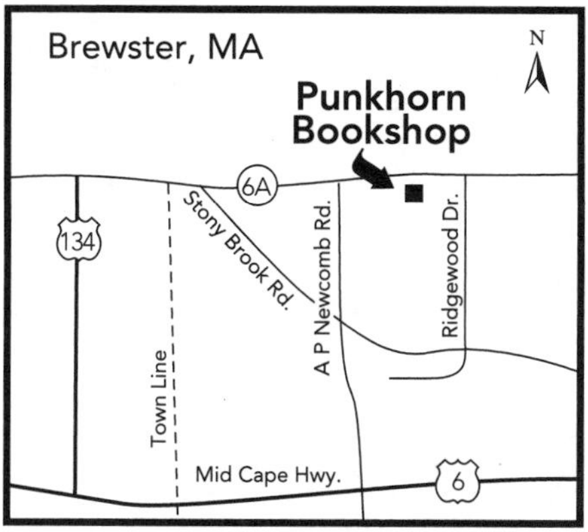

Shirley Smith & Friends [G5]

2926 Main St (Rte 6A) • 02631
(508)896-4632

Featuring 18th to early 20th C antiques including furniture, primitives, silver, glass, pottery, porcelain, miniatures, prints, rugs, Oriental & decorative items. **Pr:** $15-2,000 **Est:** 1993 **Hrs:** May-Oct 12 daily; Nov-Apr by chance. **Sz:** M **CC:** V/MC **Assn:** CCADA **Dir:** Mid-Cape Hwy Exit 10: N to Rte 6A, R on 6A 2 mi. **QC: 78 48 1 S1 S12**

Spyglass Antiques

2257 Main St (Rte 6A) • 02631
(508)896-4423

Period American 18th & 19th C furniture & accessories. **Est:** 1981 **Hrs:** Mon-Sat 10-5, Sun by chance. **Assn:** CCADA **Own:** Brad & Dusty Finch. **QC: 52 70 36**

Tymeless Antiques & Art Gallery

3811 Main St (Rte 6A) • 02631
(508)255-9404

Country pine furniture & accessories including cupboards, tavern tables, farm tables, blanket chests, baskets, treenware & American art pottery. Watercolors by award-winning Cape artist Tom Stringe. **Hrs:** May-Sep daily 10-6; Oct-Apr Thu-Mon 10-4. **CC:** AX/V/MC **Assn:** CCADA **Own:** Jim Kostulias & Tom Stringe. **QC: 55 17 101**

Wisteria Antiques

1199 Main St (Rte 6A) • 02631
(508)896-8650
buckster@capecod.net

Gorgeous Victorian on Old King's Highway filled to the brim with glass, Limoges, fine porcelain, mirrors, pottery & a fabulous collection of costume jewelry & perfume bottles. A lavender home that invites people to go back in time to the Victorian era. **Pr:** $10-2,500 **Est:** 1986 **Hrs:** Daily 12-5 or by chance/appt. **Sz:** M **CC:** AX/V/MC/DIS **Dir:** 2 mi from Drummer Boy Windmill, 1 mi from Museum of Natural History, 1/4 mi from Lemon Tree Village. **Own:** Ken DiCarlo & Clay O'Connor. **QC: 68 23 89 S15**

Works of Art Antiques

3799 Main St (Rte 6A) • 02631
(508)255-0589

18th & 19th C country furniture (much in old paint or surface), folk art, fine art & period accessories. **Hrs:** Jun-Sep daily 10-5; Oct-May wknds or by chance/appt. **Assn:** CCADA **Own:** Richard & Edith Broderick. **QC: 34 41 7**

Centerville

Cape Cod Clockwork
1694 Falmouth Rd (Rte 28) • 02632
(508)771-1082 • (508)775-4599 (fax)
ccclocks@capecod.net
www.capecod.net/clocks

Antique & new clocks. **Est:** 1992 **Hrs:** Mon-Sat 10-5. **CC:** V/MC **Dir:** At Centerville Shopping Plaza. **Own:** Wendell Sharp. **QC: 35**

For Olde Time's Sake
168 Longview Dr • 02632
(508)771-2089

Americana, primitives, country smalls, furniture & Oriental rugs. **Hrs:** By appt only. **Assn:** CCADA SNEADA **Own:** Belle & Herb Dienes. **QC: 1 41 48**

Chatham

Aquitaine Antiques
35 Cross St • 02633
(508)945-9746

Exceptional antiques including furniture, china, silver, fine quilts, linen, crocks, jewelry, decorative arts, rugs & paintings, marine items & ship models. **Hrs:** Apr-Dec 22 Thu-Sat 1-4, Dec 23-Mar by chance/appt. **Assn:** CCADA **Own:** Sallie D Mazzur. **QC: 48 70 78**

Estate Fare
741 Main St • 02633
(508)945-2509

Diverse offering of American antiques & collectibles including works of art, china, glass, pottery, bottles & photographica. Specializing in old porcelain view china souvenirs & shaving mugs. **Hrs:** By appt only. **Assn:** CCADA **Own:** Laurence W Williams. **QC: 22 61 73**

House on the Hill
17 Seaview St • 02633
(508)945-2290 • (508)945-2819 (fax)

Attractive shop of small collectibles & small furniture, inclusive of old memorabilia, old advertising items, ephemera, books, postcards, interesting china & glass, baskets & primitives. **Pr:** $5-2,000 **Hrs:** Jun 15-Sep 15 daily 11 to dusk; other times pls call ahead. **CC:** AX/V/MC/DIS **Assn:** CCADA **Dir:** From Rtes 3 & 495: Rte 6 Exit 11 S to Rte 28 to downtown Chatham. Shop on Seaview St at Main St. **Own:** Richard & Marie Soffey. **QC: 1 39 67**

The Spyglass
618 Main St • 02633
(508)945-9686

Antique nautical instruments: mounted & hand-held telescopes, mercurial & aneroid barometers, charts, half-models, lap desks, captain's desks, shadow boxes, old sea charts & maps. **Est:** 1981 **Hrs:** Mon-Sat 10-5, Sun by chance. **Assn:** CCADA **Own:** Bradley C Finch. **QC: 70 77 66**

Cotuit

Acorn Acres Antiques
4339 Falmouth Rd (Rte 28) • 02635
(508)428-3787

General line including American country & oak furniture, white, mulberry & gaudy ironstone, cast iron doorstops, glass & metal fluid & electric lamps & lighting devices, quilts, coverlets & many other fine antiques. No collectibles. **Pr:** $25-3,500 **Est:** 1976 **Hrs:** Apr-Dec Mon, Thu-Sat 10-5, Sun 12-5. **Sz:** M **Assn:** CADA CCADA NAWCC WICA APS **Dir:** 1/2 mi N of Rte 130. **Own:** Frank H Twyeffort Jr. **QC: 30 50 65 S1**

Cotuit Antiques
4404 Falmouth Rd (Rte 28) • 02635
(508)420-1234

Large old Cape home & oversized barn full of furniture, advertising, memorabilia, collectibles & vintage toys. **Hrs:** Wed-Mon 10-5. **Assn:** CCADA **Own:** Henry A Frongillo. **QC: 39**

Sow's Ear Antique Co

4698 Falmouth Rd (Rte 28) • 02635
(508)428-4931

Antiques & vintage furnishings, country pieces & garden accessories, folk art, decorated furniture & Oriental rugs displayed in an 18th C setting. **Hrs:** Tue-Sun 10-5. **CC:** V/MC **Assn:** CCADA **Own:** Stephen & Laurie Hayes. **QC: 34 36 48**

Isaiah Thomas Books & Prints

4632 Falmouth Rd (Rte 28) • 02635
(508)428-2752 • (508)428-2752 (fax)
isthomas@aol.com

Used & rare books in all fields, including Americana, first editions, local history, miniature books & prints. 60,000 volumes. **Est:** 1969 **Hrs:** Sum Mon-Sat 10-6, Sun 10-5; Jan-Mar Sat-Sun only; otherwise Tue-Sat 10-5, Sun 12-5. **CC:** AX/V/MC/DIS **Assn:** ABAA MARIAB **Dir:** On Cape Cod, approx 10 mi from the bridge; Jct 130 on Rte 28. **Own:** James Visbeck. **QC: 18 19 74 S1**

Cummaquid

The Picket Fence

4225 Main St (Rte 6A) • 02637
(508)362-4865
www.thepicketfence.com

Furniture, primitives, glassware, pottery, porcelain, tools, prints, paintings, linens & quilts & a year-round Christmas room in a 19th C barn. **Est:** 1987 **Hrs:** Daily 10-5, reduced hrs in Win. **CC:** V/MC **Dir:** 1-1/4 mi from Barnstable Village lights. **Own:** Raymond & Cathy Leonardi. **QC: 52 61 74**

Dennis

Antiques 608

608 Main St (Rte 6A) • 02631
(508)385-2755

Americana, rare books, collectibles, sports memorabilia & ephemera from the 19th & 20th C. **Hrs:** By appt only. **Dir:** Rte 6 Exit 8: L on Station Ave, R on Rte 6A, 4 mi down. **Own:** Tom Cardaropoli. **QC: 32 39 79**

Antiques Center of Cape Cod [G265]

243 Main St (Rte 6A) • 02638
(508)385-6400 • (508)385-3798 (fax)

Fine furniture, clocks, antique dolls, paintings, prints, jewelry & watches, antique books, ephemera, primitives, Oriental porcelain, antique toys, glass, china, Art Noveau & Art Deco. **Est:** 1991 **Hrs:** Mon-Sat 10-5, Sun 11-5. **Sz:** H **CC:** V/MC **Dir:** Rte 6 Exit 8: N to Rte 6A, R on Rte 6A to shop. Near the Cape Cod playhouse. **Own:** Michael Power. **QC: 36 48 7 S12 S1 S8**

Audrey's Antiques

766 Main St (Rte 6A) • 02638
(508)385-4996

18th C furniture: cherry, mahogany, pine, chestnut, camphorwood, country & painted including cupboards, benches, sea chests, tables & chests of drawers; flow blue, early ironstone as well as porcelain, mirrors, lamps, silver, cut glass & quilts. **Pr:** $10-3,500 **Est:** 1991 **Hrs:** Sum Wed-Mon 12-5: Win Thu-Tue 12-5. **Sz:** S **CC:** V/MC/DIS **Dir:** Rte 6 E across Bourne Bridge to Exit 8: L off ramp to 6A. Turn R heading E to Dennis. Shop is on corn of Hope Ln & Main St. **Own:** Audrey Flanagan. **QC: 34 48 22**

Boston Brass Works

804 Main St (Rte 6A) • 02638
(508)385-7188

Custom & antique lighting & chandeliers including dining room chandeliers, wall sconces, wall lamps, desk, table & floor lamps, some Victorian, some French country & some pieces from the 1920s. **Est:** 1975 **Hrs:** Thu-Sat 12-4 or by appt. **CC:** V/MC/DIS **Dir:** Next to the PO. **QC: 65**

Liz Broadrick

(508)385-8912

Early American folk art, primitives, antique baskets, quilts & old Shoenhut toys. **Hrs:** By appt only. **Assn:** CCADA. **QC: 41 84**

Leslie Curtis Antiques & Design

838 Main St (Rte 6A) • 02638
(508)385-2921

Distinctive early wicker & Victorian furniture, lovely accessories, pre-World War II Quimper pottery & imaginative objets d'art. **Hrs:** Mem Day-Col Day daily 10-5 or by appt. **Assn:** CCADA **Dir:** Rte 6A at Corporation Rd. **QC: 91 58 11**

Dennis Antiques

437 Main St (Rte 6A) • 02638
(508)385-8091

Quality glassware, porcelain, china & pottery: Belleek, Waterford, Lenox, Royal Copenhagen, Doulton, Heisey, Depression glass, early Hall, Fiesta, Russel Wright, Roseville & Blue Ridge. **Pr:** $10-1,000 **Est:** 1971 **Hrs:** May 15-Oct 15 11-5. **Assn:** CCADA **Dir:** Mid-Cape Hwy: Exit 8 or 9 from Rte 6 to Rte 6A. **Own:** James J Scott. **QC: 101 61 23**

Dovetail Antiques

543 Main St (Rte 6A) • 02638
(508)385-2478

Old woodworking & machinist's tools & country furniture. **Est:** 1984 **Hrs:** Fri-Sun 10-5. **Dir:** 1/4 mi from Dennis PO. **Own:** Dale Lumsden. **QC: 102 86**

Lilac Hedge Antiques

620 Main St (Rte 6A) • 02638
(508)385-0800 • (508)385-0842 (fax)
(888)38-LILAC
www.lilachedge.com

Vintage & Victorian antiques. **Est:** 1997 **Hrs:** Mon & Wed-Sat 10-5, Sun 12-5; Jul-Aug Mon-Sat 10-5, Sun 12-5. **CC:** AX/V/MC **Dir:** Directly across the street from the Armchair Bookstore. **Own:** Priscilla & Roy Dreier.

Barbara Tamasi — Antique Jewelry

2 Farm Hill Rd (Rte 6A) • 02638
(508)385-8774

Distinctive jewelry designs: gemstones & antiques. **Pr:** $100-6,000 **Est:** 1989 **Hrs:** By appt only. **Sz:** S **Assn:** CCADA. **QC: 64**

Dove Cottage

43 Mill St • 02639
(508)394-6739

Fine china, glass, country items, toys, linens, furniture & estate jewelry. **Hrs:** Wed-Sun 12-7. **Assn:** CCADA **Dir:** 1 blk S off Rte 28 at Depot St. **QC: 64 34 61**

Main Street Antique Center [G120]

691 Rte 28 • 02639
(508)760-5700
msac@capecod.net

Upscale & diversified multi-dealer shop. Emphasis on Americana. Furniture includes formal, Shaker & rustic. Glass includes Sandwich, pattern & Depression. Textiles, porcelains, art pottery, clocks & watches, silver, art, redware & primitives. **Est:** 1986 **Hrs:** Mon-Sat 10-5, Sun 12-5. **Sz:** L **CC:** V/MC **Assn:** CCADA NEAA **Dir:** Rte 6 Exit 9: R on Rte 134. 2 mi to Rte 28, then L 1.3 mi on Rte 28. **Own:** Richard White & Vince Hinman. **QC: 1 32 52**

The Side Door

103 Main St (Rte 28) • 02639
(508)394-7715

Large selection of paper collectibles, postcards, sheet music, photographs, books, china & glass. **Pr:** $1-500 **Est:** 1997 **Hrs:** Sum Tue-Sat 10-5; Win Fri-Sat 10-5. **CC:** AX/V/MC **Own:** Irma Lewy. **QC: 39 73 18**

East Dennis

East Dennis Antiques

1514 Main St (Rte 6A) • 02641
(508)385-7651
edantiques@aol.com

Well-established shop with a high-quality inventory primarily consisting of American furniture & related decorative accessories from the 18th to early 20th C including choice pieces of wicker. **Pr:** $75-10,000 **Est:** 1973 **Hrs:** Daily 10-5. **Sz:** M **CC:** AX/V/MC/DIS **Assn:** CCADA **Dir:** Rte 6 (Mid Cape Hwy) Exit 9: L on Rte 134 to Rte 6A, next L shop is 2nd bldg on R. **Own:** Thomas Buto & Frederick DiMaio. **QC: 1 36 91 S8 S9 S12**

Webfoot Farm Antiques

1475 Main St (Rte 6A) • 02641
(508)385-2334

In a lovely 19th C Captain's house on the historic north side of Cape Cod, a large selection of fine antiques & decorative accessories. Furniture, silver & Oriental antiques. **Pr:** $10-25,000 **Est:** 1990 **Hrs:** Daily 10-5; mid-Sep-mid-Jun closed Wed. **Sz:** L **CC:** V/MC **Assn:** CCADA **Dir:** Rte 6 Exit 9: L onto Rte 134, to int of Rte 6A, turn L again, 1/4 mi on L. **Own:** George & Diane King. **QC: 36 48 71**

East Falmouth

Thomas Slaman Antiques

13 Farview Ln • 02536
(508)548-6799

Late 18th & early 19th C furniture & period accessories & American folk art. **Hrs:** By appt only. **Assn:** CCADA. **QC: 52 41**

East Orleans

Countryside Antiques

6 Lewis Rd • 02643
(508)240-0525 • (508)255-8399 (fax)

Antique furniture from Scandinavia & mainland China & delightfully appointed British Colonial pieces along with European & English pine. **Pr:** $40-5000 **Est:** 1984 **Hrs:** Jun-Aug Mon-Sat 10-5, Sun 12-4. **Sz:** L **CC:** AX/V/MC **Dir:** Rte 6 Exit 12 (Orleans): R at light, thru next light, R at 3rd light, approx 1-1/5 mi to Lewis Rd (on R), 1st driveway on R. **Own:** Deborah R Rita. **QC: 107 55 70 S15**

East Orleans Art & Antiques Gallery

204 Main St • 02643
(508)255-7799

Estate jewelry, decorative antiques & glassware. **Hrs:** May-Sep Tue-Sat 10-5 or by appt. **Assn:** CCADA **Own:** Katherine Fox. **QC: 64**

East Sandwich

Henry Thomas Callan Fine Antiques

162 Quaker Meeting House Rd • 02537-1312
(508)888-5372

Specializing in American & English samplers, Chinese export porcelain, Staffordshire & soft paste. **Pr:** $100-3,000 **Est:** 1969 **Hrs:** By appt only. **Assn:** CCADA MADA NEAA GSAAA **Dir:** Rte 6 (Mid Cape Hwy) Exit 3: Quaker Meeting House Rd. **QC: 82 25 30 S1 S9**

Horsefeathers Antiques
454 Rte 6A • 02537
(508)888-5298

Specializing in linens & lace, christening gowns, floral vintage china, decorative accessories & Victoriana. **Est:** 1983 **Hrs:** Call ahead advised. **CC:** V/MC **Assn:** CCADA **Dir:** Next to East Sandwich Fire Station. **Own:** Jeanne Gresham. **QC: 80 81 89**

Old Time Shop
379 Rte 6A • 02537
(508)888-2368

Small shop with large stock of Americana, Sandwich glass, china, clocks, jewelry, fabrics, nautical, baskets & interesting collectibles. **Est:** 1957 **Hrs:** By chance/appt. **Assn:** CCADA **Own:** Rosanna Cullity. **QC: 1 103 36**

Eastham

Antiques Warehouse of Cape Cod
3700 Rte 6 • 02642
(508)255-1437

Antique toys, pressed steel, pedal cars, balloon tire bikes, automobilia, petroliana, tin litho, porcelain & advertising. **Pr:** $50-5,000 **Est:** 1970 **Hrs:** May-Oct daily 9-6; Oct-May by appt only. **Sz:** S **CC:** V/MC/DIS **Assn:** CCADA **Dir:** 1/2 mi N of Cape Cod National Seashore entrance on Rte 6 at Atlantic Oaks Camp. **QC: 87 32 90 S1**

The Birches Antiques
60 Depot Rd • 02642
(508)240-1936

Country items, furniture & small accessories. **Hrs:** By chance/appt. **Assn:** CCADA **Dir:** Across from Windmill Green. **Own:** Dawn Carlson. **QC: 34**

Falmouth

Aurora Borealis Antiques
104 Palmer Ave • 02540
(508)540-3385

Specializing in English ceramics, Oriental antiques, maritime, prints, furniture, lamps, glass, ephemera & books. **Est:** 1972 **Hrs:** In season Thu-Sat & Mon; off season by chance/appt. **Sz:** M **Assn:** CCADA **Dir:** Rte 28 to ctr of Falmouth. **Own:** Maureen & Cliff Northern. **QC: 23 71 70**

Harwich

The Barn at Windsong [G5]
245 Bank St • 02645
(508)432-8281

A large barn with a good selection of primitives, country, linen, lace, brass, glass, china, jewelry, silver & collectibles. **Est:** 1988 **Hrs:** May-Oct Mon-Sat 10-5, Sun 12-5. **Dir:** In Harwich betw Rte 28 & Rte 39. **QC: 34 32 106**

A London Bridge Antiques
9 Pleasant Lake Ave (Rte 124) • 02645
(508)432-6142

Specializing in English furniture, paintings, prints, glass, china & small collectibles direct from the United Kingdom. **Hrs:** Apr-Dec daily 10-5; off season by chance/appt. **Assn:** CCADA **Own:** Anthea Throup. **QC: 107**

Patti Smith Antiques
51 Parallel St • 02645
(508)432-3927

Specializing in antique decorated blue stoneware. **Pr:** $200-2,000 **Est:** 1979 **Hrs:** By appt only. **Assn:** CCADA. **QC: 31**

Syd's A & J
338 Bank St • 02645
(508)432-3007

Depression era glasswares, pottery, costume jewelry, cast iron, china & smalls. **Hrs:** Thu-Tue 10:30-4:30 or by appt. **Assn:** CCADA **Own:** Sydney & Harold Mercer. **QC: 61**

The Bradford Trust

66 Miles St • 02646
(508)430-1482 • (508)430-1482 (fax)
mennell@capecod.net
www.capecod.net/bradford

Fine arts, silver, furniture, decorative antiques, American & European art. **Est:** 1987 **Hrs:** By appt only. **CC:** V/MC **Assn:** CCADA NEAA **Own:** Roy Mennell. **QC: 7 36**

The Mews at Harwichport [G5]

Rte 28 • 02646
(508)432-6397

Early American pattern glass, majolica, Staffordshire, ironstone, country furniture, primitives, ogee mirrors, fluid lamps, children's glass dishes, chocolate, butter & jelly molds, hooked rugs, Dorchester & Dedham pottery & antique decorated stoneware. **Est:** 1992 **Hrs:** May-Jun 15 Thu-Sun 11-4; Jun 16-Oct 13 Mon-Sat 10-5, Sun 12-5. **Assn:** CCADA **Dir:** At Ayer Ln across from Port O Call Gift Shop & diagonally across from Augustus Snow House Inn; entrance at rear parking lot off Rte 28. **Own:** Betsy Hewlett. **QC: 34 103 23**

Seven South Street Antiques

7 South St • 02646
(508)432-4366

Silver, jewelry, china & glass. **Est:** 1976 **Hrs:** Sum Mon-Sat 10-5:30, Sun 12-5; Win Mon-Sat 12-5:30 or by appt. **Sz:** M **Dir:** Around the corn from the PO, just off Rte 28. **Own:** Philip Marsh. **QC: 64 78**

Hyannis

Columbia Trading Co Nautical Books & Antiques

1 Barnstable Rd • 02601
(508)778-2929 • (508)778-2922 (fax)
nautical@capecod.net
www.columbiatrading.com

New England's largest selection of out-of-print nautical books with a large collection of nautical & marine antiques, ship models, navigational instruments, marine art, brass reproductions & scrimshaw. **Pr:** $1-5,000 **Est:** 1983 **Hrs:** Mon-Fri 9-5, Sat 10-5. **Sz:** M **CC:** AX/V/MC/DIS **Dir:** Rte 6 Exit 6 to Rte 132. Follow signs to Hyannis Ctr. 2nd R off airport rotary to Barnstable Rd. **Own:** Bob & Ed Glick. **QC: 9 18 70 S1 S12 S17**

William R Davis Fine Art

(508)778-0009 • (508)385-6101 (fax)
wdavis@mailhost.capecod.net
www.capecod.net/davisart/

Fine 19th & 20th C American paintings; reproduction tiger maple furniture. **Pr:** $200-20,000 **Est:** 1992 **Hrs:** By appt only. **CC:** AX/V/MC **Assn:** CCADA **Own:** William & Judith Davis. **QC: 7 9 56 S1 S8 S16**

Hyannis Antique Center [G60]

500 Main St • 02601
(508)778-0512 • (508)775-4043 (fax)
moedelaney@capecod.net

Collectibles, furniture, oriental rugs, china, Depression glass, jewelry, silver, paintings, dolls & toys, military & nautical antiques. **Pr:** $1.00-3,000 **Est:** 1991 **Hrs:** Wed-Mon 10-5. **Sz:** L **CC:** V/MC **Dir:** Rte 6 (Mid-Cape Hwy) to Exit 6 (Hyannis). Follow signs to downtown waterfront district. **Own:** Maureen Delaney. **QC: 48 63 76 S15 S17 S8**

Precious Past

315 Iyanough Rd (Rte 28) • 02601
(508)771-1741

Nippon, Fiesta, Noritake, Limoges, Depression, Pairpoint, cut glass & early American pattern glass. Linens, old dolls & accessories, collectibles, ephemera, toys & furniture. **Hrs:** Mon-Sat 10-4, Sat til 3. **Dir:** Behind Mr Donut. **QC: 23 103 61**

Use the Specialty QuickCode indexes at the back of the book to find dealers who specialize in your area of interest.

Stone's Antique Shop
659 Main St • 02601
(508)775-3913

One of the oldest antiques shops on Cape Cod. English & American period furniture, Sandwich glass & cut crystal. **Est:** 1919 **Hrs:** Mon-Sat 9-5. **Sz:** L **CC:** V/MC **Dir:** W end of Main St. **QC: 53 54 103 S1**

Hyland Granby Antiques
(508)771-3070 • (508)778-4842 (fax)

A large inventory of museum-quality 18th & 19th C nautical antiques. Specializing in ship models, navigational instruments, marine paintings & scrimshaw. **Hrs:** By appt only. **Own:** Janice Hyland & Alan Granby. **QC: 70 9**

Marston Mills

Crocker Farm [G5]
1210 Race Ln • 02648
(508)428-3326

A barn full of interesting old things: primitives, folk art, iron, wood & tin. Also featuring antiques for children. **Hrs:** By chance/appt. **Assn:** CCADA **Dir:** Rte 6 (Mid-Cape Hwy) to Exit 5: Rte 149 to Marstons Mills, R at light onto Race Lane. Shop is 7/10 mi on R. **Own:** Bunny Warner. **QC: 41 62 85**

Martha's Vineyard

The Book Den East
71 New York Ave / Oak Bluffs • 02557
(508)693-3946

In a turn-of-the-century carriage barn, a large stock of carefully selected books on Martha's Vineyard, New England, sea & naval history, travel, world history, biography, 1st editions, fine bindings, prints, maps, charts & manuscripts. **Est:** 1977 **Hrs:** Jun-Oct Mon-Sat 10-5, Sun 1-5; Nov-May Thu-Sun 11-4. **Sz:** L **CC:** V/MC **Dir:** 1/2 mi from Oak Bluffs Ctr on the rd to Vineyard Haven on Martha's Vineyard. **Own:** Cynthia Meisner. **QC: 18 74 66**

Bramhall & Dunn
Main St / Vineyard Haven • 02568
(508)693-6437 • (508)693-0653 (fax)
bramdun@vineyard.net

English, Irish & French country furniture, dressers, linen presses, dining tables, counters & sideboards often in original paint & smalls. **Pr:** $140-7,800 **Est:** 1982 **Hrs:** Jun-Sep daily 9:30-10; Oct-May daily 10-5:30. **Sz:** L **CC:** AX/V/MC **Own:** Emily Bramhall. **QC: 55 102 36**

Chartreuse
State Rd / Vineyard Haven • 02568
(508)696-0500 • (508)696-0500 (fax)

European antiques, Maine cottage furniture, Skona hem art furniture & unique decorative accessories. **Est:** 1995 **Hrs:** Apr-Oct daily 10-5:30; Nov-Dec some wknds or by appt. **CC:** AX/V/MC **Dir:** At Woodland Ctr. **Own:** Laura Joseph & Neal Matticks. **QC: 51 36**

Clocktower Antiques
Nevins Sq / Edgartown • 02539
(508)627-8006

Large collection of sterling flatware & hollowware, jewelry, porcelain, paintings, prints, dolls, Orientals & bronzes. Large selection of ephemera, cut crystal, pattern, art glass & paperweights. **Pr:** $25-1,800 **Hrs:** May 15-Oct daily 10-5. **Sz:** M **CC:** AX/V/MC **Own:** Renita Stern & Fran Fischer. **QC: 36 78**

Early Spring Farm Antiques
201 Lagoon Pond Rd / Vineyard Haven • 02568
(508)693-9141

Small barn & cottage full of 18th & 19th C country furniture, quilts, hooked rugs, folk art, iron, copper, woodenware, children's items, nautical & architectural fragments. **Pr:** $5-3,000 **Est:** 1984 **Hrs:** Sum daily 10-6,

Wed & Sat 2-6; Win, Spr & Fall: daily 11-5. **Sz:** M **Assn:** CCADA **Dir:** Boat to Vineyard Haven, Lagoon Pond Rd at 5 Corners to Hine's Point, on R. **Own:** Allen Hanson. **QC: 34 51 80 S1**

The Granary Gallery

Old County Rd / West Tisbury • 02575
(508)693-0455
granary@vineyard.net
www.granarygallery.com

Mostly country furniture & interesting pieces in a barn devoted mainly to original realistic Island-oriented art. **Est:** 1954 **Hrs:** Sum Mon-Sat 10-5, Sun 11-4; otherwise by appt. **CC:** AX/V/MC/DIS **Dir:** 1/2 mi N of Edgartown-West Tisbury Rd on Old County Rd. **Own:** Sheila Morse. **QC: 7 34**

Hull Antiques

574 Edgartown Rd / West Tisbury • 02568
(508)693-5713
bhrant@vineyard.net

18th & 19th C American furniture & accessories, folk art, Victorian sterling silver, porcelain, glass, pottery, garden ornamentation, woodware, cast iron, decoys, prints, paintings & the unusual. **Pr:** $20-2,500 **Est:** 1988 **Hrs:** May 1-Nov 1 Thu-Mon 10-5. **Sz:** M **CC:** V/MC/DIS **Assn:** NEAA **Dir:** Betw the firehouse & the mill pond. **Own:** Richard & Barbara Hull. **QC: 52 60 78 S1**

C W Morgan Marine Antiques

Beach Rd / Vineyard Haven • 02568
(508)693-3622

A museum-quality marine antiques shop consisting of fine oil paintings, watercolors, lithographs, prints & engravings. Also navigation instruments, ship models, whaling gear, Eskimo art, porcelain, glass & pottery. **Hrs:** Apr-Dec daily 10-5, Jan-Mar by appt only. **CC:** V/MC **Own:** Frank Rapoza. **QC: 70 77 9**

The Old Barn Antiques

Lagoon Pond Rd / Vineyard Haven • 02568
(508)693-3425

The island's oldest antique business. Furniture, china & jewelry. **Hrs:** May-Christmas Mon-Sat 12-3. **Dir:** One blk past Vineyard Haven PO. **QC: 32 34 S1**

Past & Presents

37 Main St & 42 Main St / Edgartown • 02539
(508)627-3992

Two shops of carefully chosen eclectic antiques & accessories in two historical buildings. **Pr:** $10-5,000 **Hrs:** Jun 15-Sep 15 daily 10-10; Sep 16-Jun 14 Mon-Sat 10-5; Jan-Feb wknds only. **Sz:** M **CC:** AX/V/MC **Own:** Jane Norton & Beverly Feary. **QC: 36**

M M Stone Fine Art & Antiques

527 State Rd / North Tisbury • 02568
(508)693-0396
mmstone@vineyard.net

Featuring 18th & 19th C American furniture & decorative accessories of the period. Specializing in early lighting, folk art, marine items, paintings, metalware, export porcelain, woodenware, stained glass & baskets. Vineyard art, antiques & memorabilia. **Pr:** $100-15,000 **Est:** 1970 **Hrs:** Mem Day-Lab Day daily 10-6; Spr & Fall wknds only. **Sz:** L **Dir:** Towards Gay Head on State Rd 1 mi past Cronig's Market on the R. **Own:** Michael Stone. **QC: 41 36 52**

Vintage Jewelry

66 Main St / Edgartown • 02539
(508)627-5409 • (508)627-3259 (fax)
www.vintagejewelryco.com

Collection of estate jewelry, antique gold & gemstone, silver & costume jewelry; vintage glass & china from the Victorian era to the 50s; antique crystal necklaces & earrings, collectible designer jewelry, English pot lids & old ice fishing decoys. **Pr:** $25-2,000 **Est:** 1984 **Hrs:** Jun-Sep daily 10-10, Oct-Jan daily 10-5, Jan-May wknds only. **Sz:** S **CC:** AX/V/MC **Dir:** In Edgartown on R in yellow house with the bookstore. At corn of Main & S Summer Sts. **Own:** Susan Pacheco. **QC: 64 63 32 S12 S16 S1**

Vivian Wolfe Antique Jewelry

33 Winter St / Edgartown • 02539
(508)627-5822 • (508)627-5822 (fax)

Specializing in a superb assortment of antique jewelry. Also old silver, stones & old American Indian jewelry. **Est:** 1959 **Hrs:** Jul-Aug daily 9:30 AM-10 PM; Jun & Sep daily 10-5; off season by chance. **CC:** AX/V/MC **Dir:** In the ctr of town, one blk from Harbor. **QC: 64 78**

Mashpee

Mashpee Antiques & Collectibles

538 Mashpee Rotary (Rtes 28/151) • 02649
(508)539-0000 • (508)539-0000 (fax)
3dantiques@capecod.net
3dantiques.baweb.com

Antiques & collectibles of all kinds dating from the early 1800s to 1950s. Large selection of "room-ready" furniture in oak, mahogany & walnut. All are displayed in a clean, bright & uncluttered showroom. Mirror resilvering service available. **Pr:** $0.50-3,000 **Est:** 1994 **Hrs:** Tue-Sun call ahead for hrs or check our website. **Sz:** L **CC:** AX/V/MC/DIS **Dir:** From Bourne Bridge: Rte 28 to Rte 151 (turn R) toward Mashpee; from Sagamore Bridge: Rte 6E Exit 2: Rte 130S to Rte 28, Rte 28 N to Mashpee Rotary. **QC: 48 32 36 S12 S1 S16**

Nantucket

Janis Aldridge Inc

50 Main St • 02554
(508)228-6673

17th-19th C decorative engravings, botanical, architectural & natural history. English & Continental furnishings & accessories. **Hrs:** May-Oct. **CC:** AX/V/MC **Dir:** 2 doors down from Main St on Centre. **QC: 74 36**

Antiques Depot

14 Easy St • 02554
(508)228-1287

Furniture, decorative accessories, paintings & prints, tribal art, folk art & an extensive collection of duck & fish decoys, all well displayed in an old Nantucket building overlooking the harbor. **Est:** 1972 **Hrs:** May 22-Oct 10 Mon-Sat 10-4, Sun 12-4, Daffodil Wknd & Xmas Stroll or by appt. **Sz:** M **CC:** V/MC **Dir:** Just a few feet from Steamboat Wharf & a few steps from Main St. **Own:** Howard Chadwick & Jack Fritsch. **QC: 9 54 37 S1 S8**

Belle Maison

5 S Water St • 02554
(508)228-2450 • (508)228-2306 (fax)
info@belle-maison.com
www.belle-maison.com

Furnishings with a country bent. Emphasizing American & European dining tables, chests, cupboards, coffee tables. Painted & decorative accessories. **Est:** 1997 **Hrs:** Apr 15-Dec 15 Mon-Sat 10-6, Sun 10-5; Jan 1-Apr 14 Thu-Sat 10-5, Sun 11-4; Mon hols 10-3. **Sz:** M **CC:** AX/V/MC **Own:** Karol & Sheldon Tager. **QC: 34 47 102**

Celtic Pine
118 Lower Orange St • 02554
(508)228-6866 • (508)228-0170 (fax)

Country furniture. **Hrs:** Open all year. **Dir:** Near Marine home center. **QC: 102**

East End Gallery
3 Old North Wharf • 02554
(508)228-4515

19th & 20th C European & American art & furnishings. **Hrs:** Mar-Dec 25. **QC: 36 7**

European Traditions
54 Union St • 02554
(508)325-0038

European antiques. **Hrs:** Daffodil wknd-Dec 25.

Forager House Collection
20 Centre St • 02554
(508)228-5977 • (508)228-7067 (fax)

Folk art, Americana, rugs, quilts, whirligigs, toys, marine, Nantucketiana, painted furniture, decorative & American master prints. **Pr:** $50-10,000 **Est:** 1975 **Hrs:** May-Dec Mon-Sun 10-6, Jan-Apr Sat-Sun 10-6. **CC:** AX/V/MC **Dir:** In the ctr of the Historic District. **Own:** Richard Kemble & George Korn. **QC: 1 41 74**

Four Winds Craft Guild Inc
6 Ray's Court • 02554
(508)228-9623 • (508)228-8958 (fax)
sylvias@nantucket.net
www.nantucket.net/antiques/baskets

Nantucket lightship baskets, scrimshaw, marine items & island memorabilia. **Est:** 1948 **Hrs:** Mon-Sat 9-5, Sun 10-1, shorter hrs in Win. **CC:** AX/V/MC/DIS **Dir:** Near the Thomas Macy Museum, only yellow bldg on the blk. **QC: 70 41 17**

The Gallery at Four India Street
4 India St • 02554
(508)228-8509 • (508)228-8509 (fax)
gallery@nantucket.net

Fine art & antiques from the 18th, 19th & 20th C: paintings, sculpture, sporting art, decoys, pond models, estate jewelry & unusual collectibles. **Est:** 1989 **Hrs:** Feb-Dec 24 daily 10-5. **CC:** AX/V/MC/DIS **Own:** Kathleen Knight. **QC: 7 37 70**

Nina Hellman Marine Antiques
48 Centre St • 02554
(508)228-4677 • (508)228-1934 (fax)

Fine selection of nautical antiques: ship models, navigational instruments, scrimshaw, marine paintings, whaling items, Nantucket memorabilia, Americana & folk art. **Pr:** $10-10,000 **Hrs:** May-Dec daily; Jan-Apr wknds & by appt. **CC:** AX/V/MC **Dir:** Near the int of Gay & Centre Sts. **QC: 1 71 41**

Hollycroft Antiques
50 Main St • 02554
(508)325-9518

19th & 20th C antiques, collectibles & decorative accessories. **Hrs:** Daffodil wknd to mid-Oct, also Stroll.

Island House Gallery & Antiques
8 Washington St • 02554
(508)228-6640

Primitive & painted country antiques, wicker, folk art, hooked rugs, quilts & lighting, Nantucket memorabilia, 18th C reproductions, chandeliers & lighting. **Hrs:** By appt only. **Own:** Deborah Timmermann. **QC: 41 65 84**

Paul La Paglia Gallery
38 Centre St • 02554
(508)228-8760

Antique print gallery specializing in Nantucket & whaling memorabilia. **Hrs:** Daily 10-5. **Sz:** S **CC:** AX/V/MC **Dir:** Near the corn of Quince St. **QC: 74 S13**

Leonard's Antiques
31 Washington St • 02771
(508)228-0620 • (508)228-8056 (fax)

Large inventory of antique furniture, specializing in antique four-poster beds. **Hrs:** Open Late Apr-Dec. Please call for hrs. **Sz:** M **CC:** AX/V/MC **Assn:** SNEADA **Dir:** A short walk from Main St, adjacent to town parking lot. **Own:** Jeffrey B Jenkins. **QC: 52**

Letitia Lundeen Antiques
34 Centre St • 02554
(508)228-8566

18th & 19th C English & Continental furniture & decorative accessories. Featuring a fine collection of Georgian & Regency porcelain. **Hrs:** Seasonally 10-10. **CC:** V/MC **Assn:** AADLA **Own:** Letitia Lundeen. **QC: 53 54 23**

Val Maitino Antiques
31 N Liberty St • 02554
(508)228-2747

English & American furniture, marine items, old hooked rugs, lighting fixtures, weathervanes, Nantucket lightship baskets & decorative accessories. **Est:** 1958 **Hrs:** Year round. **CC:** AX/V/MC **Dir:** N Liberty St opp Franklin St. **QC: 54 65 70**

Modern Arts
67 Old South Rd • 02554
(508)228-6711

Vintage furniture, pottery & glassware & accessories. **Hrs:** Year round.

Nantucket Country
38 Centre St • 02554
(508)228-8868 • (508)228-0266 (fax)

19th & 20th C country furniture, folk art, primitives paintings, vintage books, textiles & kitchen items. Specializing in period quilts. **Own:** Catherine Dunton. **QC: 84 102**

Nantucket House Antiques & Interior Design Studio, Inc
2 S Beach St • 02554
(508)228-7648 • (508)228-7421 (fax)
www.nantuckethouse.com

American, English & French country furniture & decorative accessories & folk art. **Est:** 1973 **Hrs:** Apr 1-Dec 10 Mon-Sat 9:30-5:30; Dec 10-Mar 30 by appt. **Sz:** L **CC:** AX/V/MC **Dir:** Next to the Whaling Museum, across from Nantucket Yacht Club. **Own:** Sandra Ray Holland. **QC: 36 41 52 S1 S16**

Nantucket Lightship Baskets
9 Old South Wharf • 02584
(508)228-2326

Lightship baskets in traditional oak construction. **Est:** 1964 **Hrs:** May-Oct daily 10-5 & 7-10 or by appt. **CC:** AX/V/MC **Dir:** 1 blk over from Main St. **QC: 17**

David L Place Antiques & Estate Jewelry
17 Correia Ln • 02554
(508)228-6000

Accessories from the US, Canada, England & France, as well as jewelry, paintings, scrimshaw, ivory canes, marine items, sterling & fine porcelains. **Pr:** $1-5,000 **Est:** 1974 **Hrs:** By appt only. **Sz:** S **CC:** AX/V/MC/DIS **Dir:** Across from the Museum on the way to Surfside Beach. **Own:** David & Francine Place. **QC: 36 7 78 S19**

Wayne Pratt Inc
28 Main St • 02554
(508)228-8788 • (508)228-8137 (fax)

Fine American 18th & early 19th C furniture with an emphasis on original condition & patina. **Hrs:** Daily 10-9 Daffodil Wknd to Christmas Stroll. **Dir:** Main St across from Federal St. **QC: 52**

Sylvia Antiques
6 Ray's Ct • 02554
(508)228-0960 • (508)228-8958 (fax)

New England & Island antiques in an old Nantucket barn: furniture, paintings, silver, porcelains, scrimshaw & maritime pieces. **Est:** 1927 **Hrs:** Open year round. Sum 9-5. **CC:** AX/V/MC **Dir:** 1 blk from int of Fair & Main Sts, behind Fair Street Museum. **Own:** Richard Sylvia. **QC: 41 52 78**

Frank Sylvia Jr Art & Antiques
0 Washington St at Main • 02554
(508)228-2926

American & European paintings, prints, furniture, porcelain, silver, brass, estate jewelry, marine items & collectibles. **Hrs:** May-Oct. **QC: 7 74 64**

Tonkin of Nantucket
33 Main St • 02554
(508)228-9697 • (508)228-9511 (fax)
tonkinatq@capecod.net
www.tonkin-of-nantucket.com

English furniture with a large selection of silver, Staffordshire, marine & scientific instruments, long case clocks, brass & copper accessories, marine paintings & English prints, ship models & fishing equipment. **Est:** 1971 **Hrs:** Sum Mon-Sat 9:30-1 & 2-5; Win Mon & Wed-Sat 10-5; mid-Feb to mid-Mar closed. **Sz:** L **CC:** AX/V/MC/DIS **Dir:** Near the int of Main & Federal. **Own:** Robert & Dorothy Tonkin. **QC: 107 54 78**

Vis-a-Vis Ltd
34 Main St • 02554
(508)228-5527

Quilts, hooked rugs, furniture, bed & house linens, silver, china, decorative accessories & antique jewelry. **Hrs:** Mar-Dec 10-6 by chance/appt; Jan-Feb wknds. **CC:** AX/V/MC **Dir:** In the ctr of town on Main St. **Own:** Avis Skinner. **QC: 84 75 36**

> Use the Service QuickCode indexes at the back of the book to find restorers, appraisers, refinishers, and other specialty service providers.

Weeds
14 Centre St • 02554
(508)228-5200 • (508)228-5202 (fax)

19th C English & French furniture, specializing in marine objects, pond yachts & garden items. **Hrs:** Daily 9-7, shorter hrs in Win. **Sz:** M **CC:** AX/V/MC **QC: 60 70**

Wicker Porch Antiques
13 N Water St • 02554
(508)228-1052

American wicker furniture, cast iron doorstops, baskets & ephemera. **Hrs:** Mid-May-mid Oct. **QC: 91 17**

Lynda Willauer Antiques
2 India St • 06612
(508)228-3631

An exceptional collection of English & American furniture, Chinese export porcelain, paintings & watercolors, tortoise & wooden boxes, samplers, quilts & majolica. **Est:** 1974 **Hrs:** Mid-May-mid-Oct Mon-Sat 10-6. **CC:** AX **Dir:** 1 blk from Main St, corn of India & Federal. **QC: 52 25 7**

North Chatham

Bayberry Antiques
300 Orleans Rd (Rte 28) • 02650
(508)945-9060

Excellent selection of Americana, smalls, furniture, gunning decoys, ephemera, holiday collectibles, postcards, paper dolls, ice cream & chocolate molds. Early painted items a specialty. **Pr:** $1-2,500 **Est:** 1986 **Hrs:** Jun-Sep 15 Mon-Sat 10-5, Sun & Wed by chance; Sep-May by chance/appt. **Sz:** M **CC:** V/MC/DIS **Assn:** CCADA **Dir:** On Rte 28 betw Chatham & Orleans. **Own:** Dick & Carolyn Thompson. **QC: 1 37 51 S19**

Orleans

Continuum
7 Rte 28 • 02653
(508)255-8513 • (508)255-8515 (fax)
www.oldlamp.com

A small shop specializing in restored electric lighting. Approximately 400 old lamps of all types, original lead crystal shades by Holophane & others are featured; folk art & Americana including old wooden fish decoys. Annual sale on New Year's Day. **Pr:** $10-3,000 **Est:** 1982 **Hrs:** Call for hrs or appt. **Sz:** M **CC:** AX/V/MC **Dir:** Across from the Christmas Tree Shop. **Own:** Dan Johnson. **QC: 37 41 65**

Frank H Hogan Fine Arts Inc
9 Herringbrook Rd • 02653
(508)255-2676 • (508)255-3743 (fax)
fhogan@capecod.net
www.frankhoganart.com

Fine arts dealer specializing in paintings & prints of the Rockport & Provincetown Schools. **Pr:** $500-15,000 **Est:** 1963 **Hrs:** By appt only. **Assn:** ISA **Dir:** Mid-Cape Hwy Exit 12: to ctr of Orleans, then call for directions. **QC: 7 74 S1**

Lilli's Antique Emporium [G]
225 Rte 6A • 02653
(508)255-8300 • (508)255-5040 (fax)
lillis@capecod.net
www.lillisantiques.com

Primitives, ephemera, glassware, china, pottery, books, jewelry, lighting, vintage linens, tools & furniture. **Pr:** $10-10,000 **Est:** 1994 **Hrs:** May-Sep Mon-Sat 10-5; Oct-Apr Tue-Sat 10-5. **Sz:** L **Dir:** Rte 6 (Mid-Cape Hwy) to Exit 12: L onto Rte 6A W, 1/4 mi to traffic light, shop on L at light. **QC: 48 61 S12 S8 S9**

Osterville

The Farmhouse Antiques
1340 Main St • 02655
(508)420-2400

Unique seven-room shop full of antique, old & decorative furniture & accessories. Specializing in old iron, lamps, mirrors, architectural elements & the unusual. **Est:** 1988 **Hrs:** Mon-Sat 10-5, Sun 12-4. **Assn:** CCADA **Own:** Barry & Carolyn Crawford. **QC: 48 62 3**

A Stanley Wheelock Antiques
870 Main St • 02655
(508)420-3170

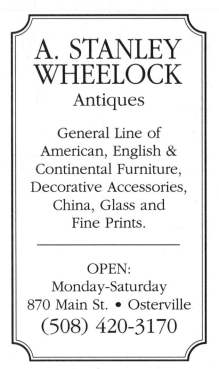

General line of American, English & Continental furniture & decorative accessories, china, China trade items, glass & fine prints. **Hrs:** Mon-Sat 10-12 & 1-5; Jan-Mar closed Mon. **Assn:** CCADA **Dir:** Behind the Eldred Wheeler store. **QC: 52 53 71**

Provincetown

Clifford-Williams Antiques

225 Commercial St • 02657
(508)487-4174

A full selection of English pine & oak furniture including dressers, chairs, cabinets, servers & decorative accessories. **Est:** 1977 **Hrs:** Daily 11-5. **CC:** AX/V/MC **Dir:** Next to Seaman's Savings Bank above the Cheese Shop. **Own:** Bill Hoontis & Clifford Cowgill. **QC: 54 36**

Julie Heller Gallery

2 Gosnold St • 02657
(508)487-2169 • (508)487-6205 (fax)
www.juliehellergallery.com

Fine art by early Provincetown artists, fine estate jewelry, museum caliber folk art, Americana & 19th & 20th C decorative arts. **Est:** 1980 **Hrs:** May-Oct daily 10-11 PM; Nov-Apr daily 12-4. **CC:** AX/V/MC/DIS **Assn:** CCADA **Dir:** On the beach Town Landing across from Adams Pharmacy. **QC: 1 41 7**

Robert M Kaminski

(508)487-7293

Specializing in quality hand-painted china, Limoges & other European manufacturers, some RS/Nippon, roses, florals, fruit, portraits plus serving pieces but not a replacement service. Photos available for all items for sale. **Hrs:** By appt only. **Assn:** CCADA **QC: 23**

Remembrances of Things Past

376 Commercial St • 02657
(508)487-9443 • (508)487-2629 (fax)
roftpast@capcod.net
www.ptown.com/ptown/rotp

An unusual shop of remembrances, both old & new, from turn-of-the-century to 1950s with emphasis on nostalgia from the 20s & 30s, including celebrity memorabilia, World's Fair & Josephine Baker, Art Deco, jewelry, especially Bakelite & neon. **Pr:** $25-5,000 **Hrs:** Apr 15-Oct 31 daily; Nov 1-Apr 14 Sat-Sun. **Sz:** L **CC:** AX/V/MC **Dir:** Corn of Pearl & Commercial Sts at the end of Rte 6. **Own:** Helene Lyons. **QC: 5 63 67**

September Morn

385 Commercial St • 02657
(508)487-9092

Featuring estate jewelry including numerous gold pocket & wristwatches, a collection of art glass, saltcellars & spoons, bronzes & Chinese snuff bottles. **Hrs:** Daily 11-10 in season or by chance/appt. **CC:** AX/V/MC/DIS **Dir:** E of the town ctr. **Own:** Ronnie Szeszler. **QC: 35 61 64**

Small Pleasures

359 Commercial St • 02657
(508)487-3712

In art deco display cases, an exciting collection of gold jewelry, mostly Victorian, as well as a comprehensive selection of gentlemen's jewelry. **Est:** 1972 **Hrs:** Sum daily 11-11, all yr, always wknds. **CC:** AX/V/MC **Dir:** Across from the Heritage Museum. **Own:** Virginia McKenna. **QC: 35 64**

Sagamore

The Crystal Workshop

794 Sandwich Rd • 02561
(508)888-1621 • (508)888-9298 (fax)
(888)869-0867
crystalw@capecod.net

Cut glass, engraved glass, cranberry glass, Victorian art glass, stemware, pottery & porcelain. Glass repair shop on the premises. **Est:** 1980 **Hrs:** Apr-Dec Mon-Fri 9-5, Sat-Sun 12-5; Jan-Mar Sat-Sun by appt. **Own:** Edward & James Poore. **QC: 61 100 S16**

Brian Cullity
18 Pleasant St • 02561
(508)888-8409
bcullity@capecod.net

Specializing in early American ceramics including redware & other stoneware as well as specialty reference works on American ceramics. **Hrs:** By appt only. **QC: 22 31 29 S1 S9**

Just Like Home
Rte 6A • 02561
(508)888-5186

Specializing in restored antique brass & iron beds complimented by antique furniture, textiles & accessories. **Hrs:** Feb-Dec Wed-Sun 11-5. **Sz:** M **CC:** AX/V/MC **Assn:** CCADA **Dir:** Exit 1 after Sagamore Bridge, R at lights, 1/4 mi on R, corn Rte 6A & Westdale Pk. **Own:** Peg Wilson. **QC: 36 48 80**

Sandwich

The Brown Jug
155 Main St • 02563
(508)833-1088

Antique glass: Art Nouveau, Tiffany, Sandwich & Cameo. **Est:** 1935 **Hrs:** Daily 9:30-5:30. **Dir:** 3 doors from Daniel Webster Inn. **Own:** Audrey O'Toole. **QC: 5 100 103**

Keepers of the Past Antiques
198 Old King's Hwy • 02563
(508)888-8278

Specializing in hand-painted china, Limoges, Shelley, chintzware, teacups, Dedham, Dorchester, art pottery, English, French & German porcelain, furniture, lamps, books, art, linens, silver, glass & rugs. **Hrs:** Daily in season; most Fall wknds. **Assn:** CCADA **Own:** Frank & Jackie Nuccio. **QC: 23 22 101**

Paul Madden Antiques
16 Jarves St • 02563
(508)888-6434
(888)888-1938
madden@antiquescrimshaw.com

Americana in great variety. **Pr:** $25-25,000 **Hrs:** By chance/appt. **Sz:** M **CC:** V/MC/DIS **Assn:** CCADA **Dir:** Around the corn from Daniel Webster Inn on Jarves St at only stop light on Rte 6A in Sandwich. **Own:** Paul Madden. **QC: 1 70 41 S1 S9 S14**

May Pop Lane [G10]
161 Old King's Hwy (Rte 6A) • 02563
(508)888-1230

Estate jewelry, silver & silverplate, brass, china, glass, furniture, decoys, pond boats & more. **Hrs:** Daily 10-5. **CC:** V/MC **Dir:** At int of Rte 6A & Main St.

Sandwich Antiques Center [G150+]
131 Rte 6A • 02563
(508)833-8580

In the historic village of Sandwich, in 85 well-light cases & 75 warm spaces: excellent glass, porcelain, silver, jewelry, primitives, toys, tools, books; 18th, 19th & 20th C furniture, clocks, art, pewter, stoneware. **Pr:** $15-5,000 **Est:** 1995 **Hrs:** Daily 10-5. **Sz:** L **CC:** V/MC/DIS **Dir:** Light at corn of Rte 6A & Jarves St. **Own:** Russell Johnson. **QC: 48 61 32 S1 S8 S12**

Shawme Pond Antiques
13 Water St (Rte 130) • 02563
(508)888-2603

Sandwich glass, fine linens, framed fashion prints, accessories & a general line. **Hrs:** Year round by chance/appt. **Assn:** CCADA **Own:** Beverly & James Turnbull. **QC: 103 81 74**

H Richard Strand Antiques

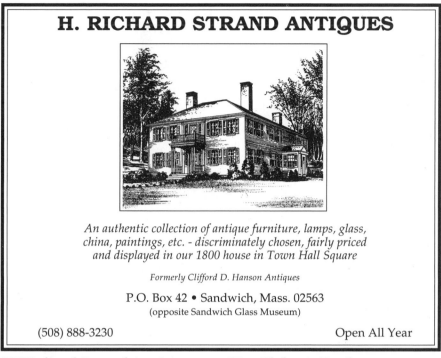

2 Grove St • 02563
(508)888-3230

An authentic collection of antique furniture, lamps, china, paintings including an outstanding selection of American glass shown in period room settings in an 1800 house in Town Hall Square. Lighting is a specialty. **Hrs:** Daily 9-5. **Sz:** M **Assn:** CCADA NEAA **Dir:** Opp the Sandwich Glass Museum. **QC: 61 65 52**

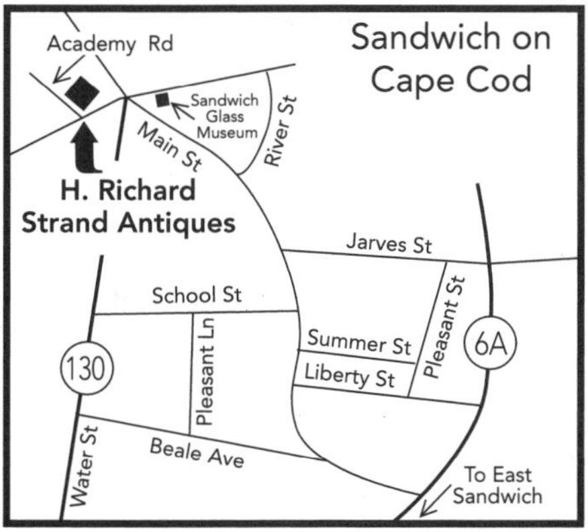

Van Slyke & Bagby

127A Main St • 02563
(508)833-3777

Period case furniture & appropriate accessories. **Hrs:** By appt only. **Assn:** CCADA **Own:** Virginia Shaw & Kim Collins. **QC: 52**

The Weather Store

146 Main St • 02563
(508)888-1200 • (508)888-6398 (fax)
(800)646-1203
pmadden@wxstore.com
www.wxstore.com

Interesting & unusual weather instruments including barometers, thermometers, maps, globes, weathervanes, whirligigs & weather books. **Pr:** $5-10,000 **Est:** 1992 **Hrs:** Apr-Dec Mon-Sat 10-5; Jan-Mar by chance/appt. **CC:** V/MC/DIS **Dir:** Across from Daniel Webster Inn. **Own:** Parke & Paul Madden. **QC: 70 77 45 S8 S16**

Santuit

Etcetera Antiques
Rtes 28 • 02635
(508)428-5374

Antiques & collectibles, brass & sterling belt buckles, miniatures & decorative accessories. **Est:** 1981 **Hrs:** Daily 9:30-5:30. **CC:** V/MC **Dir:** At the end of Rte 130. **Own:** Ann & Joe Barrett. **QC: 32**

South Harwich

Old Cape Antiques
1006 Main St (Rte 28) • 02666
(508)432-8885

Small shop in an antique three-quarter Cape. Mostly 19th C antiques. Specializing in early American pattern glass, especially flint. **Hrs:** By chance/appt. **Assn:** CCADA **Own:** Barry Knowles. **QC: 103 104**

South Orleans

Pleasant Bay Antiques
540 Chatham Rd (Rte 28) • 02662
(508)255-0930

Large house & barn filled with 18th & 19th C American furniture & decorative accessories, decoys & paintings. **Pr:** $10-25,000 **Est:** 1966 **Hrs:** Mon-Sat 9-5. **Sz:** M **CC:** V/MC **Assn:** CCADA **Dir:** 4 mi S of int of Rtes 6 & 28. **Own:** Steve Tyng. **QC: 37 52**

South Yarmouth

Lillian Colford Antiques
Lily Pond Apts, Country Club Dr • 02664
(508)398-1193

American furniture, pewter, Chinese export, Staffordshire, glass, primitives & early related American accessories. **Est:** 1981 **Hrs:** By appt only. **CC:** V/MC **Assn:** CCADA. **QC: 52 72 25**

Kay Wignot
142 Astor Way • 02664
(508)398-0174

Variety of antiques & collectibles including Royal Bayreuth & Shelley china. **Hrs:** By appt only. **Assn:** CCADA **Own:** Katherine M Wignot. **QC: 32 23**

Truro

Trifles & Treasures
11 Truro Center Rd • 02666
(508)349-9509

American country pine furniture & accessories, contemporary folk art, antique boxes, chests, mirrors & some china & glassware. **Hrs:** Jun-Oct 12 daily 11-5; Spr/Fall wknds. **Assn:** CCADA **Own:** Judy Perry & Mary Kelley. **QC: 55 34**

Wellfleet

The Farmhouse Antiques Etc [G12+]
20 Village Ln • 02667
(508)349-1708
farmhouse@c4.net
www.farmhouseantiques.com

Antique & collectible furniture, lighting, glass, Oriental antiques, books & ephemera, **Pr:** $1-5,000 **Est:** 1988 **Hrs:** Daily 10-5. **Sz:** L **CC:** AX/V/MC **Dir:** 5 mi N of Orleans Rotary, Rte 6, opp Wellfleet Drive-In. **Own:** Judy Leckey & Donna Cansdale. **QC: 32 39 65 S1 S12**

The Wellfleet Collection
355 Main St • 02667
(508)349-0900 • (508)349-0901 (fax)
wellcoll@capecod.net

An 1850s Greek Revival house filled with fine art by outstanding American artists, folk art, Americana, antique rugs, decoys & art glass. **Pr:** $25-1,500 **Est:** 1989 **Hrs:** May-Sep 9:30-6 & some eves, wknds rest of year. **Sz:** M **CC:** V/MC/DIS **Dir:** Rte 6 to

Wellfleet Ctr sign: go L to ctr of town, R on Main St, next to Cape Cod 5 Cent Savings Bank. **Own:** Lorraine Rosenbaum. **QC: 41 61 1**

West Barnstable

Barnstable Stove Shop

Rte 149 • 02668
(508)362-9913

Large inventory of almost 500 stoves, ranges, parlor heaters from early 1800s to 1930s; antique coal, wood & gas stoves. **Est:** 1976 **Hrs:** Sep-Apr Thu-Tue 9-5, Sat 10-4, or by chance/appt. **Dir:** Rte 6 Exit 5: Rte 149 N 1 mi up on L on traintracks. **Own:** Doug Pacheco **QC: S17**

The Bird Cage Inc

1064 Main St • 02668
(508)362-5559 • (508)362-5559 (fax)

Sport collectibles by Winchester, Remington, Denson, Bishop & Clark as well as ice cream scoops from many eras. **Est:** 1994 **Hrs:** Fri-Mon 10-5 or by chance. **CC:** V/MC **Dir:** Next to Packet Landing Iron. **Own:** James Dow III & James Dow IV. **QC: 79**

Maps of Antiquity

1022 Rte 6A • 02668
(508)362-7169

A large selection of antique maps from the 16th to 19th C covering all continents, most countries, many cities & some townships; also coastal charts & prints of places. **Pr:** $20-5,000 **Est:** 1989 **Hrs:** May 15-Oct 15 10-5 daily; mail-order year round. **CC:** AX/V/MC **Assn:** CCADA MARIAB **Dir:** Rte 6 Exit 5: Rte 149 N. At end turn R on 6A, first corner on L. **Own:** Lynn Vigeant. **QC: 66 74 S1 S13**

Paxton Antiques

1996 Rte 6A • 02668
(508)362-4913

Country antiques, brass/copper, furniture, folk art, primitives & decorative accessories. **Hrs:** Daily 10-5. **Sz:** S **Dir:** Mid-Cape Hwy Exit 6: to Rte 6A, 200 ft E on Rte 6A. **Own:** Rita & Don Paxton. **QC: 34 20 41**

West Barnstable Antiques

625 Main St (Rte 6A) • 02668
(508)362-2047

Antiques & period articles: china, glass, pottery, paintings, prints, furniture, nautical & surveying instruments. Harpsichords, melodeons, seraphines & cabinet organs. **Hrs:** Apr-Nov daily 10-5; Nov-Mar by chance. **CC:** V/MC **Assn:** CCADA **Dir:** 1/2 mi from the int of Rte 6A & 149 heading W. **Own:** Cynthia A Munday. **QC: 69 69 70**

West Chatham

1736 House Antiques

1731 Main St (Rte 28) • 02669
(508)945-5690

Glass, china, furniture, primitives, toys, postcards, paper, political pins, Cape Cod memorabilia, old advertising items, baseball cards & sports memorabilia. **Hrs:** Sum daily til dusk; off season, please call. **Assn:** CCADA **Own:** John & Judith Miller. **QC: 61 39**

Chatham Antiques

1409 Main St (Rte 28) • 02670
(508)945-1660

Set in a charming ca 1674 Cape farmhouse featuring period & quality custom furniture, clocks, paintings, pewter, silver, glass, china & collectibles. **Pr:** $25-5,000 **Est:** 1980 **Hrs:** Daily 11-4; off season by chance/appt. **Sz:** M **Assn:** CCADA NEAA **Dir:** Rte 6 Exit 11 to Rte 137 S to Rte 28, L to W Chatham after Chatham Motel. **Own:** Ruth & Daniel Rubin. **QC: 48 35 52 S1**

West Dennis

Central Market II

292 Main St • 02670
(508)760-1028

Antiques, reproductions, collectibles & country. **Est:** 1996 **Hrs:** Tue & Thu-Sun 11-4. **Own:** Virginia Blaikie

Rumford Antique Treasures

218 Main St • 02670
(508)394-3683

Antique lighting, Depression & pressed pattern glass, china, decorative arts. **Hrs:** Sum daily 10-5 or by chance/appt. **Assn:** SNEADA **Own:** Lowell & Edna Anness. **QC: 65 103**

West Falmouth

Antiques in West Falmouth [G5]

634 W Falmouth Hwy (Rte 28A) • 02574
(508)540-2540

Located in the quaint & historic village of West Falmouth, early American & 19th C furniture, decorative accessories, majolica, paintings & prints, Oriental porcelain, carpets & antique country selections tastefully displayed in five rooms. **Pr:** $25-5,000 **Est:** 1995 **Hrs:** Jun-Sep Mon-Sat 10-5, Sun 11-5 or by appt. Call for off-season hrs. **Sz:** M **CC:** AX/V/MC **Assn:** CCADA **Dir:** From the Bourne Bridge: S on Rte 28 to Thomas Landers Rd exit; R off exit to Rte 28A, L on Rte 28A 1.3 mi, shop on R. **Own:** Joan & Gene Marchand & Bob Mola. **QC: 1 36 48 S8 S12 S15**

The Village Barn Antique Coop [G10]

606 Rte 28A • 02574
(508)540-3215

Antiques & collectibles including furniture, paintings & prints, china, silver, jewelry & country accessories in a Cape Cod barn. **Hrs:** Daily 10-5, Win wknds or by appt. **CC:** V/MC.

West Harwich

Carriage Barn Antiques

27 Main St (Rte 28) • 02671
(508)430-9878

Art & cameo glass, art pottery, Rookwood, Weller, Roseville, Dedham, Royal Bayreuth, Royal Doulton & costume jewelry. **Hrs:** Daily. **Assn:** CCADA **Own:** Bill & Shirley Godbout. **QC: 100 101 63**

Diamond Antiques & Fine Art

103 Main St (Rte 28) • 02671
(508)432-0634

19th & early 20th C American oil & watercolor paintings specializing in New England artists including Enneking, Cahoon, Gifford, Eldred, Chapin, Batcheler, Leavitt, McKnight. Also frames, bronze & marble sculpture, silver & Oriental rugs. **Hrs:** By appt only. **Assn:** CCADA NEAA **Dir:** Rte 6 Exit 9: S to Rte 28. **Own:** Ralph Diamond. **QC: 7 11 S1**

Harwich Antiques Center [G]

10 Main St (Rte 28) • 02671
(508)432-4220
antiques@cape.com
www.comml.com/capecod/antique

Fine country furniture, jewelry, primitives, toys, tools, Art Deco, old radios, paintings, prints, porcelains, glass, china, majolica, Orientals, coins, clocks, silver & Native American. **Hrs:** Daily 10-5. **QC: 102 106 5**

Yarmouth Port

The Cobweb Corner [G5]

153 Main St (Rte 6A) • 02675-1403
(508)362-3138

China, glass, silver, brass & copper, quilts, small furniture, toys & accessories. **Pr:** $10.00-300 **Est:** 1980 **Hrs:** May 15-Oct 15 Mon-Sat 10-5; Oct 16-May 14 closed. **Assn:**

CCADA **Dir:** Cross Sagamore Bridge: follow Scenic 6A to middle of Yarmouth Port. Shop is "Town Crier" on Rte 6A beyond bank bldgs. **Own:** Marge Ruppert. **QC: 61 102 34**

Ryan M Cooper Maritime Antiques

161 Main St (Rte 6A) • 02675
(508)362-0190

Nautical items including scrimshaw, models, paintings, bells, photography, Americana, military & Civil War, early American flags. **Hrs:** Apr-Oct Tue-Sun 11-5, Nov-Mar by chance/appt. **Assn:** CCADA. **QC: 70 S1**

Crook'Jaw Antiques

186 Main St (Rte 6A) • 02675
(508)362-6111 • (508)362-2002 (fax)
jdowcett@capecod.net

Chinese country furniture & accessories, woodworking tools & smalls. **Est:** 1994 **Hrs:** Daily in season & by appt year round. **CC:** AX/V/MC/DIS **Assn:** CCADA **Own:** Karen Dowcett.

Design Works

159 Main St (Rte 6A) • 02675
(508)362-9698 • (508)362-1710 (fax)

Scandinavian country antiques & accessories with a scattering of American & Continental majolica & fine linens. **Pr:** $5-25,000 **Hrs:** Mon-Sat 10-5, Sun 12-5. **Sz:** L **CC:** AX/V/MC/DIS **Dir:** Rte 6 Exit 7N: to Rte 6A, 3/4 mi on R. **Own:** Jack Hill. **QC: 51 55**

Emerald House Antiques

(508)362-9508

18th & 19th C formal furniture, clocks, fireplace items & decorative accessories. **Hrs:** By appt only. **Assn:** CCADA **Own:** Majorie Alter. **QC: 52 35 40**

Stephen H Garner Antiques

169 Main St (Rte 6A) • 02675
(508)362-8424

18th & early 19th c American furniture, paintings & decorative accessories. **Hrs:** By chance/appt, call ahead advised. **Assn:** CCADA ADA. **QC: 36 52 7**

Constance Goff Antiques

161 Main St (Rte 6A) • 02675
(508)362-9540

Late 19th C furniture & related accessories, sterling, flatware, English white ironstone a specialty, oriental & hooked rugs, textiles, china & glass. Chair caning service available. **Pr:** $20-2,500 **Est:** 1977 **Hrs:** May 1-Nov 1 Mon-Sat 11-5; Nov 2-Apr 30 Wed-Thu 12-4:30, Fri 12-5, Sat 11-5. **Sz:** M **CC:** V/MC/DIS **Assn:** CCADA **Dir:** Rte 6 (Mid Cape Hwy) Exit 7: N 1 1/2 mi to shop on Rte 6A. **QC: 52 60 80 S6**

King's Row Antiques

175A Minden Ln (Rear) • 02675
(508)362-3573

Featuring 18th & early 19th C furniture, primitives, paintings, Oriental rugs, china & authentic accessories. **Est:** 1995 **Hrs:** Daily 11-5 or by appt. **Assn:** CCADA **Own:** Lore Garner. **QC: 52 106 7**

Lil-Bud Antiques

142 Main St (Rte 6A) • 02675
(508)362-8984

A well-established specialist in early American pattern glass including flint, non-flint, colored & ruby-stained. Over 7,500 pieces in stock; also fine china & silver & related books. **Est:** 1968 **Hrs:** May-Oct by chance/appt. **Assn:** CCADA SADA **Own:** Lillian & Bud. **QC: 61 103 78**

Minden Lane Antiques

175 Main St (Rte 6A) • 02675
(508)362-0220

A small shop with great style featuring American & Continental decorative furnishings along with garden & architectural elements. **Hrs:** Year round. **Assn:** CCADA **Own:** Donald Gray. **QC: 36 3 60**

Nickerson's Antiques

162 Main St (Rte 6A) • 02675
(508)362-6426

Country, mahogany & formal furniture, china, period paintings, metalware & decorative accessories. **Est:** 1961 **Hrs:** Mon-Sat 10-5, Sun 12-5. **Own:** Mary Nickerson. **QC: 34 36 48**

John C Weld Antiques

(508)394-7376

Specializing in Victorian Majolica & early Americana with emphasis on original surface & paint, folk art, 18th & 19th C engravings, prints & watercolors. **Hrs:** By appt only. **Assn:** CCADA. **QC: 1 41 74**

Yarmouth Port Antiques

431 Main St (Rte 6A) • 02675
(508)362-3599

Early American furniture, country & formal, as well as Chinese export porcelain, Staffordshire, flow blue, pewter, Americana, fine paintings, lamps, fireplace items, silhouettes, pottery, decoys & related accessories. **Hrs:** Daily in season 10-5. **Assn:** CCADA **Own:** Lillian McKinney. **QC: 25 30 36**

New Hampshire

New Hampshire

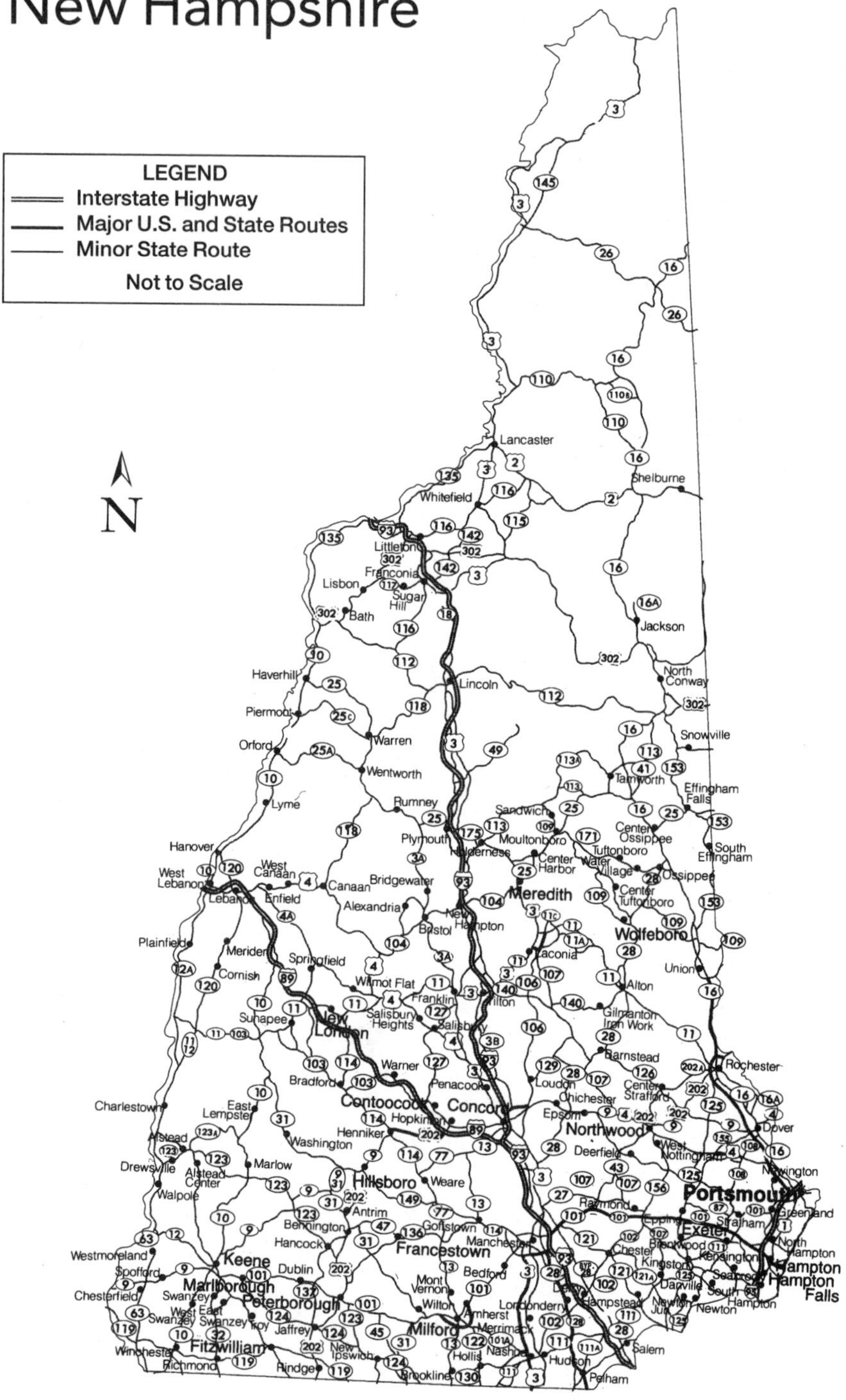

Acworth

Antique Apparel

(603)835-2295 • (603)835-2295 (fax)

Wide range of antique & vintage clothing, accessories & related items. **Pr:** $1-500 **Hrs:** Open to the trade anytime by chance/appt. **Assn:** CSA **Dir:** Rte 123A to South Acworth, then 2 mi up hill to Acworth Town. **Own:** Fay Knicely. **QC: 83**

Alstead

The Alstead Group [G8]

1793 Mechanic St • 03602
(603)835-7810 • (603)446-7334 (fax)

Located on two floors of an 18th C grist mill featuring period country f[illegible]rniture, Americana, histori[illegible]ilitaria, boo[illegible]l rugs, quil[illegible]alls & ephe[illegible]teed. **Pr:** $[illegible]-Dec Thu-[illegible]ue 10-5. **Sz:** M **Ass**[illegible]ADA GSAAA **Dir:** From Keene, NH: Court St N to Rte 12 A to Rte 123. L on Rte 123 W. In Mill opposite Vilas School. **Own:** Horace Howland. **QC: 1 52 4 S8 S9 S19**

Closed

Richard C Kyllo

(603)835-2851

Period & primitive American antiques & accessories. **Est:** 1967 **Hrs:** By appt only. **QC: 52 106**

Alton

Fleur-De-Lis Antiques

Rte 11 • 03809
(603)875-6555

Quality general line: glass, Chinese pottery, primitives, paintings. **Hrs:** Mem Day-Lab Day Wed-Sun 10-4, wknds in Sep. **Assn:** NHADA **Own:** Audrey Ritchie. **QC: 61 106**

Amherst

101A Antique & Collectible Center [G175]

141 Rte 101A • 03031
(603)880-8422
www.nhantiquetrail.com

A general line of antiques, collectibles & furniture. **Hrs:** Mon-Sat 10-5, Sun 9-5. **Assn:** NHADA.

Mark & Marjorie Allen Antiques

6 Highland Dr • 03031
(603)672-8989
www.antiquedelft.com

American period & high style country furniture & appropriate period accessories. Specializing in Delft, Chinese export porcelain & early metalwork, especially brass. **Hrs:** Appt suggested. **Assn:** ADA NHADA. **QC: 52 27 20**

Antiques at Mayfair [G]

119 Rte 101A • 03031
(603)595-7531 • (603)598-9244 (fax)
www.cinemagraphics.com/antiquetrail/

Hrs: Mon-Fri 10-5, Thu til 8, Sat 9-5, Sun 8-5. **Sz:** H **CC:** V/MC **Dir:** 1/4 mi from Howland's. **Own:** Linda May & Can Blais.

Carriage Shed Antiques

35 Walnut Hill Rd • 03031
(603)673-2944

Country furniture & quality accessories. **Est:** 1955 **Hrs:** By appt only. **Assn:** NHADA **Dir:** Off Rte 101, stay R for 1 mi up Walnut Hill Rd. **Own:** Arlene Smith. **QC: 34**

Damon House Antiques

79 Horace Greeley Rd • 03031
(603)673-4071

In a charming c 1815 Federal farmhouse displaying American country & formal furniture & accessories. Pine, birch, maple, walnut, cherry, mahogany in original & restored finishes including paint; china, crystal, pottery, prints, paintings & linens. **Pr:** $25-2,500 **Est:** 1991 **Hrs:** Sat-Sun 11-5; or by appt. **Sz:** M **Assn:** GSAAA **Dir:** From Rte 101: Turn N on Horace Greeley Rd at the Cider Mill General Store. Stay R, 1-1/2 mi past Damon Pond to shop. **Own:** Susan Averill. **QC: 34 51 22 S8 S12 S19**

Constance Greer Antiques

158 Mack Hill Rd • 03031
(603)673-5717
nhada@un.ultranet.com

Early painted American furniture, baskets, hooked rugs, quilts, painted smalls, folk art, early textile items, homespuns & decorative accessories. **Est:** 1990 **Hrs:** By chance/appt. **Sz:** M **Assn:** GSAAA MADA NHADA **Dir:** Rte 101 or 101A to Rte 122 to Amherst Ctr. R to Town Hall to Manchester St 1/10 mi. Stay L on Mack Hill Rd 2 mi, then R again on Mack Hill 8 mi on L. **Own:** Constance Greer. **QC: 41 51 80**

Hamilton's Antique Gallery [G]

Rte 101A • 03031
(603)578-3334
hagspl@aol.com **Hrs:** Daily 10-5. **Sz:** L **Dir:** 1/4 mi W of Mayfair. **Own:** Chuck & Cindy Hamilton.

His & Hers Antiques

96 Rte 101A • 03031
(603)881-7722 • (603)883-0077 (fax)
(888)465-3489

Sports memorabilia. **Hrs:** Thu-Mon. **CC:** V/MC **Own:** Meryl Pelletier. **QC: 79**

Hubbard & Co Ltd

(603)673-7304

Finely bound antiquarian books & related library furniture & accessories from the 18th & 19th C. **Pr:** $45-7,500 **Est:** 1990 **Hrs:** By appt only. **Sz:** S **Assn:** GSAAA **Dir:** Rte 101. **Own:** Leslie & Ro Anne Hubbard. **QC: 18 36 48 S8 S12 S15**

Needful Things Antiques & Collectibles [G185]

112 Rte 101-A • 03031
(603)889-1232
www.nhantiquetrail.com

Furniture, primitives, art, rugs, quilts, toys, folk art, glass, china, advertising, coins & stamps. **Hrs:** Mon-Sat 10-5, Sun 8-4. **CC:** V/MC **Assn:** NHADA **Dir:** Across from Dexter Shoe. **Own:** Bill & Nancy Day.

Jason Samuel Antiques

(603)672-8220 • (603)672-5314 (fax)

Period American & English furniture & appropriate accessories. Quality 19th & 20th C American & Continental paintings. Quality export & Continental porcelain & silver. **Hrs:** By appt only. **Assn:** NHADA **Dir:** Call for directions. **Own:** Jason Hackler. **QC: 52 54 7**

Treasures Antiques & Collectibles [G20]

106 Ponemah Rd (Rte 122) • 03031
(603)672-2535 • (603)672-4232 (fax)
(888)777-0430
www.nhantiquetrail.com

Victorian & country furniture, estate & costume jewelry, china, pottery, paintings, prints, lighting, kitchen collectibles all nestled in a c 1750 farmhouse & barn. **Pr:** $1-2,000 **Est:** 1991 **Hrs:** Daily 10-5, closed Thanks & Christmas only. **Sz:** L **CC:** AX/V/MC/DIS **Dir:** From Rte 101, take Rte 101-A E 1/4 mi, then Rte 122 S for 2/10 mi. **Own:** Rick & Sherry Tobin. **QC: 48 34 89 S22**

Tricorn Antiques
50 Rte 101A • 03031
(603)672-2268

Fine china, porcelain & furniture including a quality selection of early 20th C walnut & oak tables, desks & dressers. **Hrs:** Mon-Sat 10-5, Sun 8-4. **Dir:** Next to Galli Tile. **Own:** Sande & Alan Beede.

Antrim

Backward Look Antiques
Rte 9 • 03440
(603)588-2751

In a 14-room Federal inn, a general line of primitives, tools, early lighting, furniture in paint & horsedrawn vehicles. **Hrs:** May-Dec daily 10:30-4:30; Jan-Apr Thu-Mon 10:30-4:30. **Sz:** L **Assn:** GSAAA NHADA **Dir:** On the Keene-Concord Rd at entrance to Hawthorne College. **Own:** Bob & Gay McNeil. **QC: 51 106 90**

Court's Cupboard Antiques
Rtes 202 & 31 • 03440
(603)588-2455

General line of as-found & refinished pine, Victorian oak & accessories. **Hrs:** Usually open, Win by chance. **CC:** V/MC **Assn:** NHADA **Dir:** Rte 202 just S of Antrim. **Own:** Dick & Carol Court. **QC: 50 55 58**

Bedford

Bedford Center Antiques
7 Meetinghouse Rd • 03102
(603)472-3557

Furniture, glass, china, silver, paintings & country antiques. **Hrs:** By appt only; closed Jan-Feb. **Assn:** NEAA NHADA **Own:** M Elaine Tefft. **QC: 34 48 61 S1**

> Visiting one of our advertisers? Please remember to tell them that you "found them in the Green Guide."

Bell Hill Antiques [G20]
155 Rte 101 • 03110
(603)472-5580 • (603)669-2910 (fax)

Furniture & decorative accessories in room-like settings. Emphasis on American country, folk art & primitives. **Est:** 1973 **Hrs:** Daily 10-5. **CC:** V/MC **Dir:** In Houck Realty Bldg; halfway betw Townsend, MA & Rte 4 in NH; 2 mi W of Manchester. **Own:** Donna Welch. **QC: 34 41**

Drummer Boy Antiques
278 Wallace Rd • 03102
(603)472-3172 • (603)472-3706 (fax)

Primitives, Americana, general antiques, Civil War, military & early photography. **Hrs:** By appt only. **Assn:** NHADA GSAAA **Own:** Hank Ford. **QC: 1 4 73**

Belmont

Hoffman's Antiques
532 Union Rd • 03220
(603)528-2792
glogeo@landmarknet.net

Specializing in 18th C American painted furniture & accessories in a 200-year-old barn. Pewter, textiles, early ironware. **Est:** 1978 **Hrs:** By appt only. **Sz:** M **Dir:** I-93 Exit 20: 5-1/3 mi N on Rte 3, R on Union Rd at Double Decker Restaurant, 2-1/2 mi on R. **Own:** George & Gloria Hoffman. **QC: 51 80 62**

Bethlehem

Checkered Past [G10]
154 GuiderRd • 03574
(603)444-6628
kscope@connriver.net
www.simplegifts.com

Antiques & collectibles in a 1920s barn. **Est:** 1995 **Hrs:** July-Oct Mon-Sat 10-5, Sun 12-4; Nov-Jun closed Wed. **Sz:** L **CC:** V/MC **Assn:** GSAAA **Dir:** I-93 Exit 40 or Rte 302: turn at Adar Country Inn sign & follow Guider Ln 4/10 mi to end. **Own:** Doug Clickenger. **QC: 32 48**

The Dancing Bear [G6]

2055 Main St (Rte 302) • 03574
(603)869-5781

Ephemera, silver, books, china, dolls & glass. **Hrs:** May-Oct daily 9:30-5:30; Nov-Apr Thu-Mon 9-5. **Assn:** GSAAA **Dir:** On Rte 302 betw Montreal & Portland. **Own:** Nancy & Judy Wallace.

Bow

Bowfront Antiques & Interiors

(603)228-1886

American country furniture in original surface & condition, paintings, garden, architectural & decorative accessories. **Assn:** NHADA **Own:** Mary Carmen Labrie. **QC: 102 60 36**

Bradford

Jef & Terri Steingrebe

Hogg Hill Rd • 03221
(603)938-2748

Country furniture & accessories. **Hrs:** By appt only. **Assn:** NHADA. **QC: 34**

Brentwood

Brentwood Antiques [G120]

Rte 101 • 03833
(603)679-1500

Fine furniture & quality smalls in a medieval-style shopping village with castle towers & stone walls. Old world charm in a European village setting. **Est:** 1991 **Hrs:** Daily 10-5. **Sz:** L **Assn:** NHADA GSAAA **Dir:** On Rte 101 near the int of Rte 27 betw Rtes 125 & 95. **Own:** Margaret & Richard Ridolfo.

Crawley Falls Antiques [G35]

159 Crawley Falls Rd • 03833
(603)642-3417 • (603)642-6529 (fax)

18th C homestead featuring a barn filled with antique furniture, primitive & vintage decorative accessories, jewelry, linens, china, ephemera, smalls & hand tools. **Pr:** $1.00-3,000 **Est:** 1984 **Hrs:** Mon-Sat 10-5, Sun 12-5. **Sz:** L **CC:** AX/V/MC **Assn:** NHADA **Dir:** I-495 Exit 51B: Rte 125 to Rte 111A. R at light, shop is 1st L. From Rte 101 exit Rte 125S to Rte 111A. **Own:** Donna Judah. **QC: 34 39 102 S6 S8 S19**

Bristol

Pedigree Antiques

61 W Shore Rd • 03222
(603)744-5346 • (603)744-5346 (fax)
pedigree1@usa.net
www.angelfire.com/nh/pedigreeantiques

Large selection of flow blue china (English & American), majolica, Limoges, Roseville, Lundberg Studios art glass & other American art pottery, vintage jewelry, art. **Pr:** $15-4,000 **Est:** 1982 **Hrs:** May 15-Oct 15 Thu-Sun 9-5 (call ahead advised), or by appt. **Sz:** M **Dir:** 8 mi off I-93, 1000 ft off Rte 3A, 2 mi N of Bristol on Newfound Lake. **Own:** John Bove. **QC: 23 30 101 S19 S12**

Remember When Antiques & Collectibles

355 Summer St • 03222
(603)744-2191 • (603)744-6730 (fax)
rewhen@earthlink.net
www.tias.com/stores/rewhen/

Vintage jewelry, books & ephemera. **Est:** 1993 **Hrs:** Fri-Sat 11-5 or by appt. **CC:** AX/V/MC/DIS **Dir:** Rte 93 Exit 23: continue 5 mi W on Rte 104. **Own:** Rita Perloff. **QC: 63 18 39**

The Tin Shoppe [G41]
18 Central Sq • 03222
(603)744-5723 **Hrs:** May-Nov daily 9-5. **Own:** John Taylor.

Brookfield

White Manor Gallery
Rte 109 • 03872
(603)522-9748

Sporting & angling antiques & art. **Hrs:** By chance/appt.

Canaan

American Decorative Arts
Off Canaan St Rd • 03741
(603)523-4276 • (603)523-4888 (fax)
amr_dec_arts@endor.com

Shaker furniture & smalls, American & English accessories, Stevengraphs, maritime trade silks. **Pr:** $25-5,000 **Hrs:** By appt only. **Sz:** M **Dir:** Rte 4 to Canaan St Rd. Signs at Fernwood Farms Rd; follow to shop. **Own:** Richard Vandall & Wayne Adams. **QC: 1 70 57 S13**

Candia

Antiquarian Associates
451 High St • 03034
(603)483-8428

American country art & antiques. **Hrs:** By appt only. **Assn:** GSAAA **Own:** Eric Brown. **QC: 34**

Center Harbor

June's Junqtiques & Jack's Rejuvenations
36 Bean Rd • 03226
(603)253-7794

Depression-era collectibles, Fiestaware, kitchen, toys, prints & quality smalls. **Hrs:** Mem Day-Col Day Fri-Sun 11-6; Mon-Thu & Win by chance/appt. **Assn:** NHADA **Own:** Jack Ranes. **QC: 32 61 60**

Center Ossipee

Grant Hill Antiques

Grant Hill Rd • 03814
(603)539-2431

Two large floors of furniture & collectibles. **Pr:** $25-500 **Est:** 1980 **Hrs:** Daily 10-5, closed Mon in Win. **Sz:** L **CC:** V/MC/DIS **Assn:** NHADA **Dir:** Follow signs from Rte 16 2 mi N of Green Mtn Furniture & next to the Town Hall. **Own:** Marion & Bruce Rines. **QC: 32 48 S16**

John's Records

Village Square • 03814
(603)539-2431

Antiques & collectibles. **Hrs:** May-Oct daily 10:30-4:30. **QC: S16**

Kelley Wingate Shop

Village Sq • 03814
(603)539-6047

Quaint little shop of vintage fashions, collectibles & memorabilia. **Hrs:** May-Oct Wed-Sat 11-4. **QC: 83**

Rita Nevins

Village Sq • 03814
(603)539-4257

Glass, china, Wedgewood, Rose Medallion, contemporary Quimper, teddy bears & theorems. **Hrs:** Sum Tue-Sat 10-5 or by appt.

Center Strafford

Bert Savage — Larch Lodge

Rte 126 • 03815
(603)269-7411
rustic@worldpath.net

Rustic antique furniture & related accessories including Adirondack, Old Hickory, sample & full-size canoes, 19th C fish paintings & other old camp art. **Hrs:** By appt only. **Sz:** L **Assn:** NHADA **Dir:** 30 mi from Portsmouth or Concord NH. **QC: 1 52 79**

Chester

Hayloft Barn Antiques

161 Derry Rd (Rte 102) • 03036
(603)887-3616

Specializing in flow blue. **Hrs:** By appt only. **Assn:** NHADA GSAAA **Own:** Dottie & Dan Dwyer. **QC: 22**

Hemlock Hill Antiques

Cross Rd • 03466
(603)256-3281

Country pine & Shaker furniture, sewing, crocks, decoys, pewter & accessories. **Hrs:**

In the Fireplace

Bottle-jack: A spring-driven mechanism for turning the spit introduced at the end of the 18th century. Named for its bottle-shaped case, which was usually made of brass. The mechanisms of spit-jacks and bottle-jacks were larger versions of those used in long-case clocks.

Chimney fan: A fan, fitted horizontally in the chimney that was turned by the rising heat. It turned the spit via a system of pulleys.

Chimney crane: A bracket of wrought iron or brass used to suspend a pot or tea kettle over an open fire. Originally from Scotland, where it is known as a swey, the crane is fixed to the wall and may come in a variety of sizes or with a device to raise, lower, or swing the pot to any position over the fire.

Trammel: A device for adjusting the height at which a pot hung over the fire. The adjustment was effected by either a peg fitting into a series of holes, or by a latch moved up and down a saw-toothed bar.

Wed-Mon 10-5:30; Win call ahead suggested. **Assn:** NHADA SNEADA **Dir:** I-91 Exit 3: E on Rte 9, turn onto Cross Rd. **Own:** John & Sheila Kinnare. **QC: 55 57**

Stone House Antiques & Books

Jct Rtes 9 & 63 • 03443
(603)363-4866 • (603)363-4245 (fax)
stonehou@sover.net

In an historic stage coach inn, 18th & 19th C American, English & Continental furniture, paintings, prints, silver, porcelain & antiquarian books displayed in 6 large rooms. Quality formal & country decorative accessories. **Pr:** $25-5,000 **Est:** 1995 **Hrs:** Wed-Sun 10-5, Mon-Tue by appt; Win call ahead advised. **Sz:** M **Assn:** AAA NHADA VADA **Dir:** Rte 91 N Exit 3: Rte 9 E 5 mi. At int of Rtes 9 & 63. **Own:** Constantine Broutsas. **QC: 52 54 36 S1 S12**

Chichester

Austin's Antiques [G60]

Rte 4 • 03236
(603)798-3116

Primitives, textiles, glassware, early blown bottles, country furniture & accessories. **Hrs:** Daily 9-5. **Assn:** NHADA **Dir:** 2.2 mi W of Epsom Circle at Chichester Commons. **Own:** Peter & Lorna Austin. **QC: 102 104 106**

Douglas Hamel Antiques

56 Staniels Rd • 03234
(603)798-5912 • (603)798-5447 (fax)
dhamel7@chi.tds.net

Specializing in Shaker furniture & accessories, country furniture & folk art. **Est:** 1969 **Hrs:** Call ahead advised. **Assn:** NHADA. **QC: 57 102**

Teacher's Antiques at Thunder Bridge

11 Depot Rd • 03234
(603)798-4314

Country furniture & accessories in original finish, flow blue, Shaker & a general line. **Hrs:** Daily but a call ahead advised. **Assn:** NHADA MADA GSAAA **Dir:** 2 mi N of Epsom Circle: Depot Rd off Rte 28. **Own:** Fred & Maureen Fenton. **QC: 34 51 57**

Chocorua

Chocorua View Farm Antiques

Rte 16 • 03817
(603)323-8041

Antique furniture, collectibles, paintings & prints. **Hrs:** Jul-Oct 10-5, Nov-Jun by chance.

Michael Daum Bookseller

Rte 16 at Chocorua View Farm • 03817
(603)323-2332

A constantly changing selection of fine old books, books on antiques, prints, maps, photographs in a 1840s farmhouse with an adjacent antique shop in the barn **Pr:** $1-2,500 **Est:** 1989 **Hrs:** Jul-Oct daily 10-5; Nov-Jun by chance. **Sz:** M **Dir:** Rte 16: 300 yds S of Rte 113 int in Chocorua Village; 4 mi N of int with Rte 25 W. **QC: 18 74 66 S1**

Lucky Acres

Rte 16 • 03817
(603)323-8502

Antiques, collectibles, furniture, militaria, tools. **Hrs:** May-Oct daily 9-5 or by appt.

Claremont

The Scottish Bear's Antiques Inc

54 Pleasant St • 03743
(603)543-1978

New England antiquities, furniture, boxes, baskets, metal items, textiles, folk art, glassware & woodenware. **Hrs:** By chance/appt. **Own:** Charles & Joan Hutcheon.

Concord

Concord Antique Gallery Inc [G120]

Storr & Depot Sts • 03301
(603)225-2070 • (603)223-0902 (fax)
concordantiquesnh.com

19th C furniture (country & Victorian), kitchen collectibles, 20th C paper, vintage clothing, linens, silver & copper. **Hrs:** Mon-Sat 10-6, Sun 12-4. **Sz:** L **CC:** AX/V/MC/DIS **Dir:** I-93 Exit 13: Manchester St to S Main St, R on Storrs, shop is on L after Pleasant St. **Own:** Jay Haines. **QC: 32 102**

Kimberly's House of Dolls

9 Warren St • 03301
(603)228-3022

Fine collectibles. **Hrs:** Mon-Fri 10-5, Sat 10-3 or by appt. **CC:** V/MC **Own:** Sherry & Kimberly Fish.

Contoocook

Antiques & Findings

835 Main St • 03229
(603)746-5788
agardner@nh.ultranet.com

Old-style shop with a selection of early furniture & decorative accessories. An interesting, ever-changing selection. **Est:** 1986 **Hrs:** Daily 10-5 or by appt. Call ahead suggested. **Assn:** NHADA **Own:** Audrey & Bruce Gardner. **QC: 48 36**

Piatt's Copper Cow

1221 Briar Hill Rd • 03229
(603)746-4568

Country furniture, cupboards, early accessories & textiles. **Hrs:** By appt only. **Assn:** NHADA **Own:** Gail & Don Piatt. **QC: 102 80**

Danville

F Russack Books Inc

(603)642-7718 • (603)642-7718 (fax)
rick@antiquesbooks.com
www.antiquesbooks.com

Out-of-print reference material about the American decorative arts. Specializing in books about objects used or displayed in American homes of the 17th-19th C. Wide selection of hard-to-find books. Mail order available. **Hrs:** By appt only. **CC:** AX/V/MC/DIS **Assn:** MADA NHADA **Own:** Richard & Francine Russack. **QC: 19**

Deering

David Gallery

East Deering Rd • 03244
(603)529-4725

18th & early 19th C American antiques, furniture, paintings, Chinese export porcelain, Canton & redware. **Hrs:** Jun-Nov by appt only. **Assn:** NHADA **Own:** Sally David.

Peter Wood Hill Antiques

Peter Wood Hill Rd • 03244
(603)529-2441

General line including early ironstone, Limoges, Heisey, Dresden, "Italian Building" flow blue, crystal & silver. **Hrs:** Thu-Sat 10-5; Sun 1-5 or by chance/appt. **Assn:** NHADA **Dir:** From Weare or Hillsboro take Rte 149 to East Deering Rd. 3.7 mi to Peter Wood Hill Rd, shop located 1/4 mi on R. **Own:** Thomas J Copadis. **QC: 23**

Visit our web site at www.antiquesource.com for more information about antiquing in New England and the Midwest.

Derry

Derry Depot
1 E Broadway • 03038
(603)434-7588

Est: 1995 **Hrs:** Tue-Sat 10-5, Sun 12-5. **Sz:** M **CC:** V/MC **Dir:** I-93 Exit 4: Rte 102 E, 2 mi on R. **Own:** Priscilla Cox.

Derry Exchange
13-1/2 W Broadway • 03038
(603)437-8771

Furniture, smalls, glassware & collectibles. **Hrs:** Mon-Fri 9-5, Sat-Sun 10-3. **Own:** Gregory Mann.

GR's Trading Post
108 Chester Rd (Rte 102) • 03038
(603)434-0220 • (603)425-2199 (fax)
grtrde@aol.com

Armoires, desks, chests of drawers, corner cupboards, painted items, dry sinks, chairs, tables, china cabinets. Wholesale or retail. **Hrs:** Mon-Fri 10-4, Sat-Sun 10-5. **Dir:** I-93 Exit 4 approx 5 mi E.

Dover

Peddler's Wagon
394 Central Ave • 03820
(603)740-9494

Furniture & decorative accessories from formal to folk. **Est:** 1996 **Hrs:** Mon-Sat 10-5:30, Sun 11-5. **CC:** AX/V/MC **Own:** Cheryl Murphy & Wayne Miller. **QC: 48 36**

Timeless Appeal
83 Washington St • 03820
(603)749-7044

Furniture, lamps, country items, glass, china & jewelry. **Hrs:** Mon-Sat 10-5, Sun 10-4.

Traders of the Lost Art [G12]
453 Central Ave • 03820
(603)742-2000 • (603)742-2000 (fax)

Pottery, glass, china, collectibles, primitives, Japanese glassware, costume & estate jewlery & local hand-crafted gifts. **Pr:** $1-2,000 **Est:** 1996 **Hrs:** Jun-Sep Mon-Sat 10-6, Sun 11-5; Oct-May Mon-Tue & Thu-Fri 10-6, Sat 10-5, Sun 12-4. **Sz:** M **CC:** AX/V/MC/DIS **Dir:** I-95 Exit 7 (Rte 16, Spaulding Tpke): to Central Ave. Across from Riveis camera shop. **Own:** Sondra J Sweeney. **QC: 7 39 106 S9 S16 S6**

Ubiquitous Antiques I & II
284- 286 Central Ave • 03820
(603)749-9093

Range of antiques including architectural. **Hrs:** Tue-Sun 11-5. **CC:** V/MC.

Dublin

William Lary Antiques
Gold Mine Rd • 03458
(603)563-8603

Early furniture & accessories including decoys, Shaker, paint & folk. **Hrs:** Tue-Wed 10-5 or by chance/appt. **Assn:** GSAAA NHADA **Dir:** 3 mi W of Peterborough off Rte 101 at entrance to Gold Mine Rd, 1st house on R. **QC: 37 41 57**

Peter Pap Oriental Rugs Inc
Main St (Rte 101) • 03444
(603)563-8717 • (603)563-7158 (fax)
ppordub@top.monad.net

An internationally recognized gallery featuring antique rugs, textiles & tribal weavings. Summer seminars conducted regularly. **Pr:** $200-100,000 **Est:** 1976 **Hrs:** Mon-Sat 10-5. **Sz:** L **CC:** V/MC **Assn:** NHADA **Dir:** 13 mi E of Keene on Rte 101. **QC: 76 80 S16 S1 S9**

Seaver & McLellan Antiques Inc
Rte 101 • 03444
(603)563-7144

Antiques, fine & decorative arts from a wide variety of cultural traditions. **Hrs:** Tue-Sat 10-5. **Assn:** NHADA GSAAA **Dir:** On Rte 101 at corn of Rte 137. **QC: 36 7**

Nancy Sevatson Country Antiques
163B Gold Mine Rd • 03458
(603)563-8422

Early country & painted furniture, textiles, folk art & appropriate accessories. **Hrs:** By chance/appt. **Assn:** NHADA GSAAA **Dir:** 3 mi W of Peterborough on Rte 101, R on Gold Mine Rd, 1/2 mi on R. **QC: 34 41 51**

Durham

Wiswall House Antiques
28 Wiswall Rd • 03824
(603)659-5106

On a tree-lined back country road, a two-story barn with a selection of American furniture & accessories. Specializing in restored American antique furniture, lighting, linens & decorative accessories. **Est:** 1975 **Hrs:** Mar-Dec Wed-Sat 10-5. **Assn:** GSAAA NHADA **Dir:** Rte 108 S from Durham toward Newmarket 1.1 mi, R on Bennett Rd to end, R then next L. **Own:** Joan & Frank Carter. **QC: 52 65 36**

East Andover

Behind the Times Antiques
110 B Maple St • 03231
(603)735-5086

Victorian furniture, glass, china, metalware & collectibles of the period. **Est:** 1960 **Hrs:** By appt only. **Assn:** NHADA **Dir:** 1/2 mi W of Rte 11 on Maple St. **Own:** Robert G Larsen. **QC: 89 58**

Use the Specialty QuickCode indexes at the back of the book to find dealers who specialize in your area of interest.

East Swanzey

O'Brien's Antiques & Collectibles [G8]
320 Monadnock Hwy (Rte 12) • 03446
(603)358-3799

Est: 1997 **Hrs:** Daily 9-5. **CC:** V/MC/DIS **Own:** Scott O'Brien.

Effingham Falls

Chicken Coop Antiques
Rte 153 N • 03864
(603)539-2411
skeat@landmarknet.net

General line. **Hrs:** Daily 10-5. **CC:** V/MC **Own:** Doug & Marie Brown.

Enfield

Goslar-Rock Antiques
195 Shaker Hill Rd • 03748
(603)632-7461

Clocks, furniture & accessories. **Hrs:** May 15-Nov 30 by chance/appt. **Assn:** NHADA **Dir:** 1-1/2 mi off Rte 4. **Own:** Geraldine Goslar & June Rock. **QC: 35 48**

Epsom

The Betty House
105 North Rd • 03234
(603)736-9087

Four barns full of a general assortment of antiques including furniture, household items of wood, tin & iron & a large collection of tools. **Pr:** $1-200 **Est:** 1969 **Hrs:** By chance/appt. **Sz:** L **Assn:** NADA NHADA **Dir:** 1/2 mi off Rte 4 on North Rd. **Own:** Charles Yeaton. **QC: 86 85 62**

Woodward Antiques
1217 Suncook Valley Hwy • 03234
(603)798-4225

Country collectibles, Depression glass, 19th & 20th C furniture, tools, ephemera, textiles, prints, brass & iron. **Pr:** $1-1,800 **Est:** 1990 **Hrs:** Mon-Sat 10-5. **CC:** V/MC **Dir:** I-93 Exit 15E to Epsom: 1.3 mi N of Epsom traffic cir. **Own:** Mim Woodward. **QC: 34 61 48**

Exeter

Decor Antiques
11 Jady Hill Cir • 03833
(603)772-4538
decorant@hh.ultranet.com

18th, 19th & early 20th C antique gilded frames, oil paintings, watercolors, prints & mirrors. **Pr:** $10-5,000 **Est:** 1980 **Hrs:** Daily 9-5 call ahead advised. **Sz:** S **Assn:** NHADA **Dir:** From 108 S (Portsmouth Ave) in Exeter, take R at lights onto Green Hill Rd, then next L. Around the corn from Walgreen Drug. **Own:** Leo DesRoches. **QC: 7 68 74 S13 S16 S17**

Lily Rose Curiosity Shop Ltd [G22]
48 Lincoln St • 03833
(603)772-1444

General line. **Hrs:** Mon-Sat 10-5. **Dir:** At Exeter Handkerchief Co. **Own:** Marie Doan & Debbie Hayes.

Trisha McElroy
(603)778-8842

Early New England decorative arts & accessories, iron hearth equipment, lighting, 18th C ceramics, delft, mezzotints, bottles, textiles & American furniture. **Hrs:** Call ahead appreciated. **Assn:** NHADA SPNEA. **QC: 1 65 62 S9**

Peter Sawyer Antiques
17 Court St • 03833
(603)772-5279

Specializing in important American clocks, particularly those from New England; 18th & 19th C New England furniture emphasizing original state of preservation; American paintings, watercolors, drawings & folk art. **Est:** 1979 **Hrs:** By chance/appt. **Assn:** NHADA **Dir:** 1 hr N of Boston, 6 mi from I-95 on Rte 108. **QC: 35 52 7**

Shared Treasures
142 Front St • 03833
(603)778-1943 • (603)427-0613 (fax)

18th & 19th C furniture, smalls, rugs, jewelry & clocks. **Pr:** $5-2,000 **Est:** 1969 **Hrs:** Sep 1-Jul 31 Thu-Sat 10-5 (closed Aug). **CC:** V/MC **Dir:** Rte 495N to Rte 125N to Rte 111 E. **Own:** Carol L Callahan. **QC: 34 48 106 S1 S8 S12**

Farmington

Side of the Road Shoppe
Rte 11W • 03855
(603)755-2868 **Hrs:** Wed-Sun 10-5. **Own:** Ruth Harding.

Ye Olde Brush Factory
1 Spring St • 03835
(603)755-3654 • (603)755-4433 (fax)

In a large heated 1840s wire brush factory, a large selection of furniture, glass, lighting, Victoriana & a large selection of old frames & prints. **Est:** 1970 **Hrs:** Thu-Sat 10-5, Sun 12-4. **Sz:** L **Assn:** NHADA **Dir:** Near PO. **Own:** Lorraine Meyer. **QC: 48 61 89**

Fitzwilliam

Bloomin' Antiques [G35]
Rte 12 • 03447
(603)585-6688

A quality group shop of professional dealers offering 18th & 19th C furniture & accessories, art, clocks, toys, Orientalia, rugs, country paint & lighting. **Hrs:** Daily 10-5. **Assn:** MADA NHADA GSAAA **Dir:** 3 mi S of junc Rtes 12 & 119. **Own:** Gary Taylor & Robert Camara. **QC: 34 52**

Claire Borowski
(603)585-6837

18th & 19th C country goods in original surface, early ceramics, textiles & quality accessories. **Hrs:** By appt only.

Clocks on the Common

Village Common • 03447
(603)585-3321

Specializing in antique clocks. **Hrs:** Call ahead advised. **Assn:** NHADA NAWCC **Dir:** Yellow house on Village Common, driveway on Rte 119. **Own:** John Fitzwilliam. **QC: 35 S7**

Dennis & Dad Antiques

Rte 119 • 03447
(603)585-9479

Specializing in 18th & 19th C English ceramics including transferware, pearlware, lustres, Staffordshire figures, mocha, ABC children's plates, Gaudy Welsh, spatter, salt glaze & creamware. **Pr:** $5-5,000 **Hrs:** By chance/appt. **Assn:** NHADA **Dir:** Off Rte 12 heading E on Rte 119, 5th house on L. No business sign. **Own:** Dennis & Ann Berard. **QC: 23 26 30**

Fitzwilliam Antiques Center [G40]

Jct Rtes 12 & 119 • 03447
(603)585-9092

A group shop with quality 19th C furniture, rugs, paintings, glass, china & country accessories. **Hrs:** Mar-Oct Mon-Sat 10-5, Sun 12-5; Nov-Feb Mon-Sat 10-4, Sun 12-4. **Sz:** L **Assn:** GSAAA NHADA **Dir:** Just S of the int of Rtes 12 & 119. **Own:** Warren & Marion Legsdin. **QC: 48 34**

Bob Jessen/Jim Hohnwald — Antiques

(603)585-9188

Country furniture in solid colors & paint decoration, treenware, painted pantry boxes, bowls, plates, candle boxes & game boards, textiles, painted baskets, redware, early lighting & portraits. **Pr:** $35-3,500 **Est:** 1981 **Hrs:** By chance/appt, call ahead advised. **Sz:** S **Assn:** NHADA **Dir:** From Keene, NH take Rte 12 S off Rte 101 through Troy to flashing light in Fitzwilliam. Call for directions from the gas station. **QC: 51 88 82 S4**

William Lewan Antiques

Old Troy Rd • 03447
(603)585-3365

Actively changing inventory of early & country furniture, assorted primitives, art, folk art & other quality accessories. **Pr:** $25-5,000 **Est:** 1972 **Hrs:** All year by chance/appt. **Sz:** M **Assn:** NHADA **Dir:** 4-1/2 mi from Fitzwilliam Village, W on Rte 119. Look for sign for turn. **QC: 34 41 48**

Old England Enterprises

2A Upper Troy Rd (Rte 119) • 03447
(603)585-7198 • (603)585-6919 (fax)

English & European pine furniture & smalls. Also a B&B. **Hrs:** Thu-Tue 10-6. **Own:** David & Tina Ashton.

Pregent's Antique Center & Oriental Rug Gallery [G]

Rte 12 • 03447
(603)585-7766
antqiues@top.monad.net

Period furniture, accessories, collectibles & hand-knotted carpets. **Hrs:** Mon-Sat 9-5, Sun 10-4. **Assn:** NHADA **Dir:** 200 yds S of int of Rtes 119 & 12.

Red Barn Antiques

58 Richmond Rd • 03447
(603)585-3134

An eclectic shop of New England country furniture in original paint & refinished surfaces, decorative accessories including paintings, mirrors, architectural & unusual items in a cozy, heated barn shop. **Pr:** $20-4,000 **Est:** 1987 **Hrs:** Daily 10-4 by chance/appt. **Sz:** L **CC:** V/MC **Assn:** GSAAA NHADA **Dir:** 14 mi S of Keene, NH, off Rte 12 & Rte 119 in SW corner of NH. From Fitzwilliam Inn parking lot 1/5 mi. **Own:** Arlene Rich. **QC: 1 36 48 S8 S12**

Francestown

Thomas C Clark

82 Clarkville Rd • 03043
(603)547-9955

18th, 19th & 20th C Americana & decorative objects, furniture, folk art & garden objects. **Hrs:** By appt only. **Assn:** NHADA. **QC: 1 60 41**

The Francestown Gallery

101 Main St • 03043
(603)547-6635

Late 18th & early 19th C New England antiques, folk art & textiles. **Pr:** $25-3,500 **Est:** 1986 **Hrs:** Yr round by chance/appt. **Sz:** S **Own:** Ann & Dave Stewart. **QC: 41 80**

Mill Village Antiques

New Boston Rd (Rte 136E) • 03043
(603)547-2050

Duck & fish decoys, clocks, country furniture, ice cream & chocolate molds, primitives, glass & china. **Est:** 1982 **Hrs:** By chance/appt, call ahead advised. **CC:** V/MC **Assn:** GSAAA NHADA **Dir:** 1/2 mi E of Francestown Town Hall. **Own:** Barbara Radtke. **QC: 35 34 37**

Stonewall Antiques

532 New Boston Rd (Rte 136E) • 03043
(603)547-3485

Selected formal, country & painted furniture, glass, china, paintings, primitives, decorator & collector items. **Hrs:** May-Dec by chance/appt. **Assn:** GSAAA NHADA **Dir:** 1 mi E of Francestown Village going toward New Boston. **Own:** Elsie E Mikula. **QC: 51 61**

Woodbury Homestead Antiques

1 Main St • 03043
(603)547-2929

Specializing in kerosene lamps, Victorian & estate jewelry. **Pr:** $25-5,000 **Est:** 1983 **Hrs:** By appt only. **Assn:** GIA GSAAA NHADA **Dir:** On the Town Common at Jct of Rtes 136 & 47. **Own:** Barbara & Alan Thulander. **QC: 64 65**

Franconia

Lawrence & Barbara Forlano

(603)823-8852

Antique & old Oriental rugs, garden antiques & selected smalls. **Hrs:** By appt only. **Assn:** NHADA. **QC: 76**

Franklin

Antiques by Judy A Davis

(603)934-5545

General line. **Hrs:** By appt only. **Assn:** GSAAA NHADA.

Freedom

Freedom Bookshop

Old Portland Rd • 03836
(603)539-7265

Over 10,000 antiquarian books of the 19th & 20th C with emphasis on literature, poetry, history, the Arts, books on books & 20th C history. Literary magazines seen by appt. Small gallery of 19th & 20th C American paintings, watercolors & prints. **Pr:** $5-1,000 **Est:** 1987 **Hrs:** Jul-Sep Tue-Sun 11-5 or by chance/appt. **CC:** V/MC **Assn:** MABA NHADA **Dir:** From int of Rte 16 & 25, approx 5 mi E then 1/2 mi N on Rte 153; follow signs to village 1/4 mi E of bridge in village ctr. **Own:** George Wrenn & Bill Gordon. **QC: 18 7 74**

Fremont

Jeremiah Benfield's Antiques & Collectibles

41 Scribner Rd • 03044
(603)895-3923

Glassware, primitives, photos, small furniture & linens. **Est:** 1996 **Hrs:** Fri-Sat & Mon 10-5, Sun 12-6, Wed by chance/appt. **Dir:** 4-1/2 mi from Carriage Town Plaza off Rte 125 at Rte 107N or Rte 125 to 111A approx 2-1/2 mi from Crawley Falls Antiques. **Own:** Cynthia Salois. **QC: 61 106**

Georges Mills

Prospect Hill Antiques

Prospect Hill Rd
(603)763-9676

Furniture from England, Ireland, Europe, New England, including Victorian, country pine & Mission oak. **Hrs:** Daily 10-5. **Dir:** Located at N end of Lake Sunapee off Rte 11, 1 mi up Prospect Hill Rd.

Gilmanton

E S Lamprey Antiques

(603)267-7788

Photographs, prints & historical documents. **Hrs:** By appt only. **Assn:** GSAAA **Own:** Evelyn Lamprey. **QC: 73 74**

Goffstown

Goffstown Village Antiques

9 N Mast St • 03045
(603)497-5238
gvantiques@aol.com

All varieties of antiques, with a special focus on American art pottery; thirteen showcases, floor display & picture & frame gallery; estate furniture from country to formal arriving daily. **Est:** 1996 **Hrs:** Wed-Sat & Mon 10-5, Sun 11-5, Tues by chance/appt. **Sz:** L **CC:** V/MC **Dir:** Across from Sully's Superette on Rte 114 in Goffstown. **Own:** Jim Campbell. **QC: 22 23 60 S8 S12 S1**

Robert & Karen Vincent Antiques

(603)774-4376

Country furniture & accessories. Specializing in early dolls: china, papier mache, bisque & cloth, including early Raggedy Annes & teddy bears. **Hrs:** By appt only. **Assn:** NHADA. **QC: 38 87**

Gorham

Tara

60 Glen Rd • 03581
(603)466-2624
tory@ncia.net

Specializing in 19th C prints & maps of the White Mountains; Currier & Ives, Oakes, Hinton's History, Jackson's Geology, Prang, Bufford, Sabatier, town Bird's-Eyes, Ladies Repository, Winslow Homer, Barlett, Boardman, Bond, Leavitt & others. **Est:** 1987 **Hrs:** By chance/appt. **Assn:** NHABA **Dir:** Call for directions. **Own:** Douglas & Andrea Philbrook. **QC: 66 74**

Grantham

Falcon's Roost & Reminiscenence

Sawyer Brook Plaza • 03753
(603)863-8100

Period American furniture, including Queen Anne, Chippendale, Hepplewhite & Sheraton, as well as tall clocks & appropriate accessories. **Pr:** $100-10,000 **Est:** 1985 **Hrs:** May-Oct Wed-Sun 10:30-4:30; Nov-Apr Thu-Sun 10:30-4:30. Call ahead advised or by appt. **Sz:** M **CC:** V/MC **Assn:** CADA MADA NHADA VADA GSAAA **Dir:** I-89 Exit 13: 500 ft to Sawyer Brook Plaza. **Own:** Edmund & Marilyn Bierylo & Tony & Michele Robinson. **QC: 52 36 35 S1 S12 S15**

Greenfield

Blue Barn Antiques
Sawmill Rd (Rte 31) • 03047
(603)547-3583

Antiques & collectibles with special interest in linens & jewelry. **Hrs:** By chance. **Assn:** GSAAA **Dir:** Behind Greenfield Meeting House. **Own:** Ann Geisel. **QC: 81 63**

Greenville

Brooksmeet II Antiques
Livingston Rd • 03048
(603)878-3693

General line. **Assn:** GSAAA **Dir:** Off Rte 31 S on Livingston Rd, 8 mi S of Rte 101, 5 mi N of Rte 119 from Townsend, MA.

Hampstead

Nattibunco Antiques Ltd
406 Emerson Ave • 03841
(603)329-7201 • (603)329-5472 (fax)
mmcquaid@shore.net

Fine furniture, jewelry, china & custom furnishings. **Est:** 1998 **Hrs:** Wed-Sun 10-6. **CC:** V/MC **Own:** Margaret McQuaid **QC: S12**

Hampton

Russ & Karen Goldberger / RJG Antiques
PO Box 2033 • 03843
(603)926-1770 • (603)929-4267 (fax)
antiques@rjgantiques.com
decoys@rjgantiques.com
www.rjgantiques.com

Specializing in original painted surfaces including 18th & early 19th C American furniture, appropriate smalls, quality decoys & folk art. **Hrs:** By appt only. **CC:** AX/V/MC **Assn:** ADA MADA NHADA VADA **Dir:** On the seacoast, 1 hr N of Boston. **QC: 37 41 51**

H G Webber Antiques
495 Lafayette Rd • 03842
(603)926-3349

Large barn filled with variety of merchandise, featuring furniture, Oriental rugs, music boxes, clocks, china & glass. **Pr:** $25-16,000 **Est:** 1950 **Hrs:** Tue-Sat 9-5, Sun 1-5. **Assn:** NAA NAWCC NHADA **Dir:** I-95 Exit 2: follow Rte 51E to Rte 1, turn L, 1 block on R. **Own:** Robert Webber. **QC: 76 35 48**

Antiques at Hampton Falls [G50]
Lafayette Rd (Rte 1) • 03844
(603)926-1971

Fine furniture, primitives, smalls & collectibles in a three-story barn. **Est:** 1987 **Hrs:** Mon-Sat 10-5, Sun 12-5. **Sz:** L **Dir:** I-95 Exit 1: 2 mi N, corn of Rtes 1 & 88 on Hampton Falls Green. **Own:** William Low & Ann Smith.

Antiques New Hampshire [G40]

Rte 1 • 03844
(603)926-9603

Antiques in a large restored late Victorian house & barn. Furniture & accessories from all periods with an emphasis on New Hampshire found items. **Est:** 1987 **Hrs:** Daily 10-5. **Sz:** L **Assn:** NHADA **Dir:** I-95 Exit 1 or 2: On Rte 1 betw Rtes 51 & 107. **Own:** Bob Hudson.

Antiques One [G50]

80 Lafayette Rd (Rte 1) • 03844
(603)926-5332

A large two-story barn with books, ephemera, postcards, graphics & art. **Hrs:** Fri-Sun 12-5. **Dir:** I-95 Exit 1: Rte 1N, 2 mi, just S of int with Rte 88. **Own:** Alma Libby & Susan Fisher.

The Barn Antiques at Hampton Falls [G]

44 Lafayette Rd (Rte 1) • 03844
(603)926-9003 • (603)926-0741 (fax)
barn1@tiac.com
www.barnantiques.com

Specializing in fine American & European antique furniture & accessories including wardrobes, dining sets, bedroom furniture, upholstered furniture, office furnishings & estate jewelry. Also carry a large line of reproductions. **Est:** 1977 **Hrs:** Daily 10-5. **Sz:** H **CC:** V/MC **Dir:** I-95 Exit 1: N of Rte 107 & S of Rte 88. **Own:** Norier Avakien. **QC: 48 56**

Richard A Kenney

189 Exeter Rd • 03844
(603)778-2891

18th & early 19th C formal & country furniture & accessories. **Hrs:** By appt only. **Assn:** NHADA. **QC: 102 52**

Hancock

The Barn of Hancock Village

Main St • 03449
(603)525-3529

19th C country pine, porcelain, china, glass, accessories, kerosene lamps, silverware, kitchen utensils & cookware. **Pr:** $21-2,500 **Est:** 1983 **Hrs:** May 15-Nov 2 Tue-Sat 10-5, Sun 11-3; Nov 3-May 14 by appt only. **Sz:** M **Assn:** NHADA **Dir:** Across from John Hancock Inn. **Own:** Helen & Ray Pierce. **QC: 34 36 48**

Hardings of Hancock

2 Depot St • 03449
(603)525-3518

Country furniture, hearth equipment, early lighting, period iron, brass, copper, some pewter, small woodenware. **Pr:** $50+ **Est:** 1965 **Hrs:** By chance/appt; call ahead advised (closed in Win). **Assn:** GSAAA NHADA **Dir:** 1/4 mi W from the John Hancock Inn on Rte 123 bear R at fork; red house on the point overlooking Norway Pond. **Own:** Eileen Harding. **QC: 20 62 65**

Haverhill

The Victorian on Main Street

Rte 10 • 03765
(603)989-3380

Linens, lace, quilts, vintage clothing, textiles & accessories. **Hrs:** Jun-Oct Thu-Mon 12-5. **QC: 81 83**

Henniker

Corn Crib Antiques

20 Old Concord Rd • 03242
(603)428-7385

Furniture, accessories & collectibles **Hrs:** By chance/appt. **Assn:** NHADA **Dir:** 1/2 mi W of int of Rte 9/202 & Old Concord Rd. **Own:** Peter & Jan Hale. **QC: 32**

Henniker Kennel Company Antiques
(603)428-7136

A shop totally devoted to dog enthusiasts. Featuring bronzes, china, jewelry, prints, toys & books. **Hrs:** Wed-Sat 10:30-4 or by chance/appt. **Dir:** Follow signs off Rtes 202/9 or 114S.

Young at Heart [G]
7 Maple St (Rte 114) • 03242
(603)428-8201

Antiques & collectibles in an 1830s home. **Hrs:** Wed-Sun 10-5. **Own:** Reid & Colleen Trevaskis.

Hillsboro

Gondola Antiques & Collectibles
118 W Main St • 03244
(603)464-2795
canctil@contik.net

Eclectic mix of Victorian & oak furniture, paper, Depression glass, vintage clothing, collectibles & cookie jars. **Est:** 1998 **Hrs:** Closed Tue. **CC:** V/MC **Own:** Armand & Cheryl Anctil. **QC: 58 39 61**

Parkside Gallery
17-19 W Main St • 03244
(603)464-3322

Blending an interesting mix of country primitives, textiles, tools, hearth iron, china, art pottery, Stoddard glass, furniture, paintings, frames & decorative accessories. **Hrs:** Daily 10-5. **Sz:** S. **QC: 106 80 86**

Cheryl & Paul Scott Antiques
232 Bear Hill Rd • 03244
(603)464-3617 • (603)464-5837 (fax)

19th & 19th C country & formal furniture & appropriate accessories & decorative objects. **Est:** 1980 **Hrs:** By appt only. **Assn:** ADA NHADA MADA VADA. **QC: 36 52 102**

Tatewell Gallery
Jct Rtes 9 & 31 N • 03244
(603)478-5755 • (603)478-5756 (fax)
(888)TATEWELL
tatewell@juno.com

A wide selection of art, furniture, lighting, glass & china. Quality framing available. **Pr:** $25-5,000 **Est:** 1982 **Hrs:** By chance/appt. Call ahead advised. **Sz:** M **CC:** AX/V/MC **Assn:** NHADA **Dir:** Next to the Franklin Pierce homestead. **Own:** Jack Tate & Don Boxwell. **QC: 7 61 65 S8 S13**

Timeless Pieces
246 W Main St (Rte 9) • 03244
(603)464-6747
timeless@conknet.com

Victorian & Edwardian clothes, accessories, linens, furniture, dolls, toys, children's & adult vintage clothes, country textiles, kitchen accessories & folk art. **Pr:** $1-2,000 **Est:** 1996 **Hrs:** Mon & Wed-Sat 10-5, Sun 12-4. **CC:** V/MC/DIS **Dir:** Rte 9 (Main St) halfway betw Keene & Concord. **Own:** Karl & Linda Dalenberg. **QC: 34 38 41 S1 S11 S12**

Wyndhurst Farm Antiques
552 Center Rd • 03244
(603)464-5377

A general line of glass, china, furniture & accessories, specializing in early pattern glass. **Hrs:** May 15-Oct 15 by chance/appt. **Assn:** NHADA **Own:** David & Rosa Webb. **QC: 48 103**

Hooksett

Worldwide Gallery
1878 Hooksett Rd • 03106
(603)485-2718 • (603)425-2199 (fax)
grtrde@aol.com
www.tradingpostantiques.com

Antiques & replicas. **Est:** 1992 **Hrs:** Wed-Fri 10-4, Sat-Sun 10-5. **Sz:** H **CC:** V/MC **Dir:** DW Hwy at Rtes 3 & 28. **Own:** Nora Routhier.

Hopkinton

Anderson's Antiques Inc

South Rd • 03229
(603)746-3364

Fine 18th C & Federal furniture, overlay & whale oil lamps, export, Canton & English porcelains & decorative accessories for the discriminating & knowledgeable collector **Est:** 1934 **Hrs:** Daily 9-5. **Sz:** M **Assn:** NHADA **Dir:** Rte 89 Exit 4: to ctr of village, L at gas pumps, 2nd house on R. **QC: 52 23 25**

Roland & Joyce Barnard

558 Beech Hill Rd • 03229
(602)224-6889

Specializing in early American furniture & clocks. **Hrs:** By chance/appt. **Assn:** NHADA. **QC: 52 35**

Shirley D Quinn

371 Putney Hill Rd • 03229
(603)746-5030
sdquinn_98@yahoo.com

Textiles, especially quilts, country antiques & childhood treasures. **Pr:** $10-1,500 **Hrs:** By chance/appt. **CC:** V/MC **Assn:** GSAAA VADA. **QC: 34 38 80 S12**

Hudson

Colonial Shoppe

20 Old Derry Rd • 03051
(603)882-2959

Country & primitive furniture, kitchen & hearth accessories, treen & early iron. **Hrs:** By chance/appt. **Assn:** NHADA GSAAA **Dir:** From Rte 102, turn onto Old Derry Rd at Hudson Motor Inn. **Own:** Carol & Bill Murray **QC: S6**

Intervale

Christopher Noonan Oriental Rugs

Dundee Rd • 03845
(603)356-2309
cjnoonan@ncia.net

Old & antique Oriental rugs. **Hrs:** By appt only. **Assn:** NHADA **Dir:** In the heart of New Hampshire's White Mountains. **QC: 76**

Some Furniture Parts

Astragal: A plain, semi-circular molding often applied to cabinets but most commonly used to face the mullions on the glass doors of cabinets and bookcases.

Pilaster: A flat-faced column protruding from a wall or other surface. Placed for decorative effect rather than as a support.

Apron: The lower front edge of a piece of furniture, sometimes elaborately shaped.

Mullion: A thin strip of wood holding and separating the panes of glass in a glazed door or window. Sometimes confused with....

Muntin: A vertical piece of wood holding and separating panels, sometimes confused with....

Stile: A vertical member, often load-bearing, that frames a paneled door or chest, or a chair back. Stiles often extend downward to form legs, as on a paneled chest, or the back of a chair.

Rail: A horizontal member, often used with stiles to frame a panel. Also used for seat rails and crest rails on chairs.

Stretcher: Rail joining the legs of tables or chairs to strengthen them.

Jaffrey

Sir Richard's
(603)532-7945
astra@paladin.mv.com

A general line. Specializing in walking sticks. **Est:** 1995 **Hrs:** By appt only. **Own:** Richard Wagner.

The Towne House
9 Ellison St • 03452
(603)532-7118

Antiques & a large collection of early lamps, replacement shades & parts. **Hrs:** Mon-Fri 10-5, Sat 10-4, Sun by appt. **Sz:** M **CC:** V/MC **Assn:** NHADA **Dir:** Rte 119: Rte 124 from Townsend; Rte 101: Rte 124 from Keene; Rte 202: Rte 124 from Rindge NH. **Own:** Tat & Charlotte Duval. **QC: 65 S16**

Keene

The Anderson Gallery
(603)352-6422 • (603)352-4449 (fax)

A sophisticated collection of 19th C silver & very fine linens. **Hrs:** By appt only. **CC:** AX/V/MC/DIS **Assn:** AAA GSAAA **Own:** Thelma Anderson. **QC: 78 81**

Antiques at Colony Mill [G175+]
222 West St • 03431
(603)358-6343

An array of high quality antiques elegantly displayed in a historic woolen mill. Featuring Staffordshire, early primitives, Coca Cola & Pepsi memorabilia, furniture, art & jewelry amidst a vast variety of other high end & accessible antiques. **Pr:** $1-6,000 **Est:** 1991 **Hrs:** Dec 25-Nov 30 Mon-Sat 10-9, Sun 11-6; Dec 1-Dec 24 Mon-Sat 9-10, Sun 10-6. **Sz:** L **CC:** AX/V/MC/DIS **Assn:** NHADA GSAAA **Dir:** Located 10 min from I-91 (Exit 3) via Rte 9E; 1-1/2 hrs from Boston, Rte 2 W to Rte 12 N. **Own:** Emile Legere. **QC: 19 48 S8 S1**

Cohen & Son Oriental Rugs
443 Winchester St • 03431
(603)357-5152
(800)339-5122
info@cohenrugs.com
www.cohenrugs.com

Collection of over 3000 new decorative & antique rugs. Cleaning, handwashing, repairs, restoration & appraisal. **Est:** 1986 **Hrs:** Daily 9-5. Eves by appt. **Sz:** L **CC:** V/MC **Assn:** VADA NHADA **Own:** Menashe Cohen. **QC: 76 S16**

Anne M Piper
(603)352-0005

Appointments in silver including sterling, Sheffield plate, English & American plate. **Hrs:** By appt only. **Assn:** NHADA GSAAA. **QC: 78**

Washington Street Gallery
117 Washington St • 03431
(603)352-2194

Antique furniture, quilts, paintings, prints & small accessories. **Hrs:** By chance/appt. **Assn:** NHADA. **QC: 7 74 S13**

Kingston

A Well Kept Secret
3 Newton Jct Rd • 03848
(603)642-5279
secrets@mva.com

Ephemera & collectibles. **Hrs:** Mon & Thu-Sat 10-5, Sun 12-5. **CC:** V/MC/DIS **Dir:** Corn Rte 125 & Newton Jct Rd. Turn at Citgo Station. **Own:** Pam Mastroianni. **QC: 32**

Old Teahouse Antiques
24 Scotland Rd • 03848
(603)642-5290
qkdraw@nh.ultranet.com

Small furnishings & glassware. **Est:** 1994 **Hrs:** Thu-Tue 10-5. **Own:** Evelyn Nathan.

Red Bell Antiques Co-op [G30]

Rte 125 • 03848
(603)642-5641

Limoges & Carnival glass, Wallace Nutting & milk bottles as well as furniture, paper goods, jewelry, china, toys & collectibles. **Hrs:** Daily 10-5. **CC:** V/MC **Dir:** On Rte 125 near int of Rte 107A. **Own:** Robert Hughes.

Laconia

Agora Collectibles

373 Court St • 03246
(603)524-0129

Specializing in dolls & furniture; also antiques, collectibles & new dolls. **Hrs:** By chance/appt. **Assn:** NHADA **Own:** Alice & John Ortakales. **QC: 32 38 S11**

Almost All Antiques [G50]

100 New Salem St • 03246
(603)527-0043

Hrs: Daily 10-5, Nov-Apr closed Mon. **Assn:** NHADA **Dir:** 100 yds down the tracks from the Old Train Station. **Own:** Dick & Martha Mitchell.

Country Tyme Antiques & Collectibles Inc [G150+]

Rte 3 • 03246
(603)524-2686

Antiques & collectibles. **Est:** 1992 **Hrs:** Daily 9:30-5. **Assn:** NHADA **Dir:** I-93 Exit 20 toward Laconia. In Major Brands Plaza. **Own:** Cliff & Leah Ernst.

Lancaster

Israel River Trading Post

69 Main St • 03584
(603)788-2880
(800)290-2880

Antiques & collectibles. **Hrs:** Tue-Sat 10-4.

Lancaster Traditions

73 Main St • 03584
(603)788-2446

Antiques & collectibles. **Hrs:** Mon-Sat 10-4.

Twin Maples B & B and Antiques

185 Main St (Rtes 2/3) • 03584
(603)788-3936
twinmapl@ncia.net
www.greatnorthwoods.org/twinmaples

Specializing in vintage kitchenware, pottery & glassware, both elegant & Depression. Including Hall, Homer, Laughlin, Franciscan, Roseville, Heisey, Cambridge & Fostoria. **Pr:** $5-1,000 **Est:** 1997 **Hrs:** May-Oct Wed-Sat 11-5; Nov-Apr by chance/appt. **Sz:** S **CC:** V/MC **Dir:** From VT: Rte 2 E. From ME: Rte 2 W. From I-93 Exit 35 to Rte 3 N. From I-91 Exit 19 (I-93): Turn L then R onto Rte 2 E. Main St is both Rtes 2 & 3. **Own:** Sandra Hegyi & Barbara Mastriano. **QC: 61 22 32**

Lee

Lee Circle Antiques [G]

Rte 125 • 03824
(603)868-3424

Hrs: Daily 9-6. **Dir:** Just N of Lee Cir. **Own:** Robert & Barbara Callioras.

Lincoln

Gionet's Antiques & Collectibles [G]

Rte 112 — The Depot • 03251
(603)745-3131 • (603)745-3131 (fax)
gionetsantiques@yahoo.com

General line. **Hrs:** Wed-Mon 10-5. **Own:** Edmond Gionet.

Littleton

Titles & Tales
73 Main St • 03561
(603)444-1345 • (603)444-6625 (fax)
titles&tales@anotchabove.com
www.titlesandtales.com

Two floors with 80,000+ volumes for all readers as well as collectors: specializing in nautical, militaria, aviation, New Hampshire & White Mountains literature. **Pr:** $2-500 **Est:** 1989 **Hrs:** Sun-Thu 10-6, Fri-Sat 10-8. **CC:** V/MC **Assn:** NHADA **Dir:** I-93 Exit 41. 10 mi N of Franconia Notch. **Own:** Bob & Florence Cook. **QC: 70 4 18 S1 S12 S3**

Londonderry

The Cranberry House [G20+]
3 Crosby Ln • 03053
(603)432-8729

Antiques & collectibles. **Hrs:** Mon-Sat 10-5, Sun 12-5. **CC:** V/MC/DIS **Dir:** 2.2 mi W on Rte 102 from Rte 93. **Own:** Leslie & Doug Pease.

Joan & Virginia Dahlfred
3 Twin Isles Rd • 03053
(603)437-1139

Early Americana, fireplace accessories, architectural items & early metals. **Hrs:** By appt only. **Assn:** NHADA GSAAA. **QC: 1 3 40**

Log Cabin Antiques & Collectibles [G]
182 Rockingham Rd • 03053
(603)434-7068
Hrs: Tue & Thu-Fri 10-5, Sat-Sun 11-4. **Dir:** Rte 93 Exit 5: to Rte 28, 1/2 mi on R.

The Tates Antiques
449 Mammoth Rd (Rte 128) • 03053
(603)434-0449

Specializing in 18th & 19th C New England country furniture & accessories, old & new finishes, lighting, hearth equipment, textiles, art & early glass in a 1752 cape. **Est:** 1980 **Hrs:** By chance/appt. **Assn:** NHADA **Dir:** I-93 Exit 5: 2 mi. **Own:** Linda & Mike Tate. **QC: 34 102 40**

Loudon

Joann Cadarette Antiques
Rte 129 • 03301
(603)435-6615

Authentic period formal & country furniture in paint & old surface as well as lighting, portraits, pottery, folk art, rugs, toys & fabrics. **Pr:** $50-20,000 **Hrs:** By appt only. **Assn:** NHADA **Dir:** Rte 129 E off Rte 106, N 4 mi, black house on R. **QC: 52 51 41**

Lyme

Lyme Creamery Antiques
Creamery Ln • 03768
(603)795-4204

In the historic Lyme Creamery, a fine collection of American & English antique furniture & accessories including silver, crystal, china & boxes galore as well as rugs, lamps, garden items & soft goods, antique to contemporary prints, watercolors & oils. **Pr:** $3-6,000 **Est:** 1996 **Hrs:** May -Nov Wed-Sun 12-6. **Sz:** M **CC:** AX/V/MC **Assn:** NHADA **Dir:** I-91 N Exit 14: 3 mi to Lyme, then 1/2 mi N of Lyme Common on Rte 10.10 mi N of Hanover, NH (Dartmouth College). **Own:** Marcia & John Armstrong. **QC: 52 53 36 S8**

Madison

1790 House Antiques
31 Rte 113W • 03849
(603)367-8440

Antique furniture, Buffalo pottery, Shelley, china, glass, art, primitives, silver & jewelry. **Hrs:** May-Oct Wed-Sun 11-4 or by chance/appt. **Assn:** NHADA **Dir:** 4-1/2 mi E of Rte 16. **Own:** Laurence & Dolores Messner. **QC: 48**

Manchester

Bijoux Extraordinaire
N Elm St • 03104
(603)624-8672

Fine quality antique, estate & custom-designed jewelry. **Hrs:** By appt only. **Assn:** NHADA ISA **Dir:** Call for directions. **Own:** Judi & Arthur Anderson. **QC: 63 64 S1**

From Out of the Woods Antique Coop [G40]
394 Second St • 03101
(603)624-8668

Antiques and country collectibles, primitives, ephemera, pottery, oil paintings & fine furniture. **Hrs:** Mon-Sat 9-5, Sun 11-4.

Kotekas Fine Arts
406 Chestnut St • 03101
(603)669-5028

A small but refined gallery of American 19th & 20th C art & Japanese woodblocks — both 19th & 20th C — & Oriental rugs. **Pr:** $5,000-25,000 **Est:** 1988 **Hrs:** Most morns & by appt. **Dir:** I-93 Wellington Rd/Bridge St exit: R to town. From I-293: exit Granite St to center of town. **Own:** Lewis Julian Kotekas. **QC: 7 71**

The Exchange
710 Somerville St • 03103
(603)634-4114
ccexchange@aol.com

Fine home furnishings, antiques & collectibles. **Est:** 1997 **Hrs:** Win Tue-Fri 10-6, Sat 10-5, Sun 12-5; Mem-Lab Day Tue-Fri 10-6, Sat 10-5. **CC:** AX/V/MC/DIS **Own:** Bob & Oral Foster. **QC: 48**

Marlborough

Thomas R Longacre
726 Jaffrey Rd (Rte 124) • 03455
(603)876-4080

American country & formal furniture including early New England pieces, paintings & appropriate accessories for dealers & collectors. **Est:** 1971 **Hrs:** By chance/appt, call ahead advised. **Assn:** NEAA NHADA VADA **Dir:** 3-1/2 mi E on Rte 124, off Rte 101. **QC: 1 52 7**

Betty Willis Antiques Inc
509 Jaffrey Rd (Rte 124) • 03455
(603)876-3983

American, English & European formal & country furniture & accessories of the 18th & 19th C. **Pr:** $500-50,000 **Hrs:** By chance/appt. **Sz:** L **Assn:** NHADA **Dir:** From Keene, NH: E on Rte 101 to Marlborough. At int of Rtes 10, 1 & 24, turn R on Rte 24, 2-1/2 mi to shop. **Own:** Nancy Willis. **QC: 52 53 54**

Woodward's Antiques
166 Main St (Rte 101) • 03455
(603)876-3360

Country furniture refinished & in the rough: beds, tables, chairs, boxes, chests, stands, desks, cupboards & some accessories. **Pr:** $25-2500 **Est:** 1968 **Hrs:** All year by chance/appt. **Sz:** M **Assn:** NHADA **Dir:** On Rte 101 downtown. **Own:** Terry Woodward. **QC: 34 102 S16**

Marlow

Peace Barn Antiques
Forest Rd (Rte 123N) • 03456
(603)446-7161

A country home, barn & herb garden offering early furniture, decorative accessories & garden furnishings. **Est:** 1982 **Hrs:** May-Nov by chance/appt. **Assn:** GSAAA NHADA **Dir:** Red barn & Cape at edge of village. **Own:** Gen Ells. **QC: 1 34 36**

Meredith

Alexandria Lamp Shop

62 Main St • 03253
(603)279-4234

Restored antique kerosene, gas & electric lighting, lamp supplies, shades, chimneys, fabric shades, refinished pine & oak furniture, prints, jewelry, glassware, tools, reference books & collectibles. **Pr:** $5-1000 **Hrs:** Mon-Sat 10-6, Sun 1-5; closed Wed exc in Sum. **Sz:** M **CC:** V/MC **Assn:** NHADA **Dir:** From int of Rtes 3 & 25 go S on Main St. 3rd bldg on the L. Entrance on the side of the bldg. **Own:** Fran & Tony Governanti. **QC: 34 55 65**

Burlwood Antique Center [G170]

Rte 3 • 03253
(603)279-6387

A full line of antiques on three floors of a large, converted 18th C barn. **Est:** 1983 **Hrs:** May-Oct daily 10-5. **Sz:** H **CC:** V/MC **Assn:** NHADA **Dir:** I-93 Exit 23 to Rte 104 E. Go 9 mi to jct with Rte 3, turn R, 100 yds up on R. **Own:** Tom & Nancy Lindsey.

Chi'-lin Asian Arts & Antiques

Main & Lake Sts • 03246
(603)527-1115 • (603)528-4688 (fax)

Fine Oriental "country" antiques, including baskets, pottery & furniture. Specializing in custom mirrors & occasional tables using antique carvings, tile or stone with exotic woods. Large selection of contemporary Asian prints & paintings. **Pr:** $6.50-12,000 **Est:** 1982 **Hrs:** Jun-Aug Tue-Sun 11-4; Sep-May Thu-Sun or by appt. **Sz:** L **CC:** V/MC **Assn:** NHADA **Dir:** I-93 Exit 21 (Meredith): Rte 104E to Rte 3, L at light into Meredith. At bottom of hill, across from town docks, go L on Lake St. Top house on R at corner of Main. **Own:** Suzanne & Terry Lee. **QC: 34 71 74 S5 S10 S15**

Gordon's Antiques

45 Daniel Webster Highway • 03253
(603)279-5458 • (603)279-5458 (fax)
mcgordon@cyberportal.net

Turn-of-the-century antiques including porcelains (Meissen, Limoges), pottery (Buffalo to Dedham), art glass, sterling silver, linens, lamps, clocks, furniture, jewelry & decorative objects. **Pr:** $2-5,000 **Est:** 1980 **Hrs:** Mon-Sat 10-5, Sun 11-4. **Sz:** M **CC:** AX/V/DIS **Assn:** NHADA NHAA **Dir:** Rte 93 N Exit 23: to Rte 104 E to end, R on Rte 3, 1-1/2 mi S on L from Harts Restaurant. **Own:** Marlene & Charles Gordon. **QC: 36 60 48 S1 S2**

The Old Print Barn

1008 Winona Rd • 03253
(603)279-6479 • (603)279-1337 (fax)
www.nhada.org/prints.htm

Largest print gallery in northern New England. Specializing in six centuries of rare prints, etchings, engravings, lithographs, scrigraphs, photographs, oils & watercolors from international, national & local artists. **Pr:** $25-20,000 **Est:** 1976 **Hrs:** Mem Day-Col Day & Day after Thanks-Mem Day daily 10-5 (closed Christmas & New Year's). **Sz:** L **CC:** V/MC **Assn:** NHADA **Dir:** Turn onto Winona Rd at double blinkers on Rte 104. 7 mi from Exit 23 off I-93, 2 mi from Hart's Turkey Farm on Rte 3 in Meredith. **Own:** Charles & Sophia Lane. **QC: 7 8 14 S1 S13 S16**

Parkledge Antiques & Collectibles

30C Main St • 03253
(603)279-3393

Furniture, collectibles, books, ephemera & glass. **Hrs:** May-Oct daily 9-8; Nov-Apr daily 9-6. **QC: 48 39**

Use the Specialty QuickCode indexes at the back of the book to find dealers who specialize in your area of interest.

Merrimack

Jeannine Dobbs: Country/Folk/Antiques

(603)424-7617

Early furniture & accessories, mostly with original paint. **Hrs:** By appt only. **Assn:** NHADA. **QC: 51 34**

Milford

The Alphabet Soup Co

263 Union Sq • 03055
(603)673-1033

Primitive & French country & painted cottage furniture, architectural pieces, fine reproductions & decorative accessories, including linens, lighting, mirrors & florals. Garden items a specialty: twig & iron furniture, statuary, planters & urns. **Pr:** $25-3,500 **Est:** 1978 **Hrs:** Wed-Sat 10-4, Sun 12-4. **Sz:** M **CC:** V/MC/DIS **Dir:** Convenient to Rtes 3, 101, 101A & 93 (45 mins N of Boston). **Own:** Marge McGann. **QC: 34 36 60 S15**

Candlewick Antiques

112 Amherst St • 03055
(603)673-1941

Country & period furniture, early china & glass, Christmas items, toys & textiles. **Hrs:** By chance/appt. **Assn:** NHADA GSAAA **Own:** Jessie Anderson-Erwin & John Anderson. **QC: 34 52**

Centurywood Antiques Coop [G]

571 Elm St (Rte 101A) • 03055
(603)672-2264

Quality furniture & smalls at affordable prices in a charming antique building. **Hrs:** Mon-Sat 10-5:30, Sun 11-5. **Own:** Suzy McLaren.

Golden Opportunities

326 Nashua St (Rte 101A) • 03055
(603)672-1223

Antiques, coins, jewelry, paintings & Oriental rugs. **Hrs:** Mon-Sat 10-5, Sun 12-5.

Milford Antiques

40 Nashua St • 03055
(603)672-2311

Jewelry, oak furniture, china, religious items, coins & medals & paintings. **Est:** 1955 **Hrs:** Thu-Tue 10-5. **Dir:** Near the rotary, across from the library. **Own:** Mary & Frank Dugan. **QC: 50 64 33**

New Hampshire Antique Co-op Inc [G288]

Rte 101-A • 03055
(603)673-8499 • (603)672-5314 (fax)

A professionally run group shop featuring period furniture, pottery & porcelain, glass & collectibles. **Est:** 1983 **Hrs:** Daily 10-5. **Sz:** H **CC:** V/MC/DIS **Assn:** GSAAA NHADA **Dir:** Rte 3 Exit 7W: Rte 101A into Milford 1-1/2 mi W of ctr of Milford. **Own:** Sam Hackler. **QC: 32 48 60**

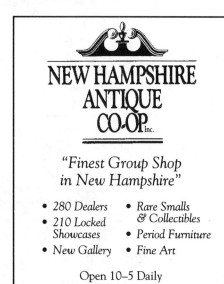

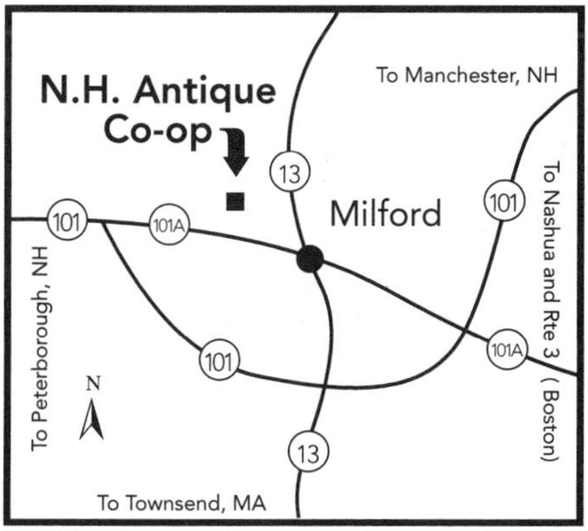

Pine Shed Antiques
287 Elm St (Rte 101A) • 03055
(603)673-2167

Glass, jewelry, china dolls, silver, linens, kerosene lamps, Oriental rugs, trunks, beds & stained glass. **Est:** 1959 **Hrs:** Daily 10-4 by chance/appt. **Dir:** W of the Milford Rotary. **Own:** Jim & Cynthia Forsyth. **QC: 61 64 78**

This Olde Stuff Antiques & Collectibles [G200+]
180 Elm St • 03055
(603)673-5454
www.nhantiquetrail.com

General line. **Hrs:** Daily 10-5. **CC:** AX/V/MC **Dir:** Next to McDonalds. **Own:** Bill & Nancy Day.

Mirror Lake

Apple Hill Antiques
Rte 109 • 03853
(603)569-8220
bogannan@worldpath.net

Charming shop filled with furnishings & accessories for the country home. Variety of vintage & antique treasures, folk art, furniture & garden accents. **Pr:** $1-2,000 **Est:** 1998 **Hrs:** May-Dec Tue-Sat 9:30-4:30, Sun 12-5; Jan-Apr Sat 9:30-4:30, Sun 12-5. **Sz:** M **CC:** V/MC **Dir:** Rte 16 or Rte 28 to Rte 109N. 4-1/2 mi N of downtown Wolfeboro at the int of Rte 109 & Tuftonboro Neck Rd. **Own:** Suzanne Bogannan. **QC: 34 36 102**

Moultonboro

Antiques at Moultonboro
26 Old Rte 109 • 03254
(603)476-8863
(800)573-8863
mayarts@lr.net

An active general line shop featuring everything from early American to modern design & collectibles. Good selection & turnover. **Pr:** $10-3,000 **Est:** 1985 **Hrs:** May-Oct daily 10-5; other times by chance/appt. **Sz:** M **CC:** V/MC **Assn:** NHADA GSAAA **Dir:** Just off Rte 25, on Old Rte 109 S, Moultonboro Ctr. **Own:** Cheryl & Tom May. **QC: 48 60 32 S12**

Nashua

AAA Antiques & Memorabilia [G40]
214 Daniel Webster Hwy • 03060
(603)888-3222 **Pr:** $2-2,000 **Est:** 1986 **Hrs:** Mon-Thu 10-6, Fri-Sun 11-5. **Sz:** L **CC:** AX/V/MC **Dir:** Rte 3 Exit 1: 1 mi N of Pheasant Lane Mall. **Own:** Bradley Heath.

Guerette Cosgrove
85 W Pearl St • 03060
(603)598-3647
gcantiks@aol.com

Furniture, silver, paintings, lighting, prints & porcelain. **Est:** 1997 **Hrs:** Mon-Sat 10-6, Thu til 8. **CC:** V/MC/DIS **Dir:** Downtown Nashua. **Own:** Michael Cosgrove & Richard Guerette.

House of Josephs Antiques [G35]
523 Broad St (Rte 130) • 01463
(603)882-4118

Furniture, china, glass, collectibles, ephemera, toys & crafts. **Est:** 1989 **Hrs:** Tue-Sun 10-5. **CC:** AX/V/MC/DIS **Dir:** Rte 3 Exit 6: Rte 130 W 2 mi. **Own:** Linda & Barry Williams.

Rustic Accents Inc
43 Ayer Rd • 03060
(603)882-3367

Selected general line, emphasis on country furniture & distinctive smalls in original paint. **Hrs:** By appt only. **Assn:** NHADA GSAAA **Own:** Ken & Robin Pike. **QC: 102 41**

New Boston

Jane Workman Antiques
129 Thornton Rd • 03070
(603)487-2315

18th & 19th C furniture & accessories in paint & old surfaces, folk art, smalls, hooked rugs, school girl art & textiles. Quality Americana for dealers & collectors. **Hrs:** By chance/appt. **Sz:** S **Assn:** NHADA GSAAA **Dir:** Off Rte 136 W, New Boston. Call for directions. **QC: 1 41 51**

New Castle

Compass Rose Antiques
38 Laurel Lane • 03854-0157
(603)436-3642

Diverse selection of general antiques, with accent on country smalls, Staffordshire, period lighting & early glass. **Pr:** $10-5,000 **Est:** 1981 **Hrs:** By appt only. **Sz:** M **Assn:** GSAAA NHADA **Dir:** From Portsmouth: Rte 1B (Portsmouth Ave), across 2 bridges & 1 causeway onto island of New Castle. Take 1st R onto Laurel Ln, 5th place on R. **Own:** Charles & Laurie Clark. **QC: 65 23 61 S1 S12 S19**

New Hampton

New Hampton Antique Center [G75]
Rte 104 • 03256
(603)744-5652

General line of antiques & collectibles. **Hrs:** Daily 10-5; Jan-Mar closed Tue. **CC:** V/MC **Assn:** NHADA **Dir:** I-93 Exit 23.

New Ipswich

Estelle M Glavey Inc
Rte 124 • 03071
(603)878-1200

Two brick Colonials with rooms of quality stock including country & formal furniture, paintings, rugs, porcelains & garden ornaments. **Est:** 1964 **Hrs:** All year; Win by chance/appt. **Assn:** NHADA. **QC: 1 7 48**

Jim & Ellen Hicks Antiques
Ashby Rd • 03071
(603)878-3807

Country furniture, accessories, lighting, scales & primitives. **Hrs:** By appt only. **Assn:** GSAAA ISASC. **QC: 65 77 102**

Richard J Riley Antiques
21 Main St • 03071
(603)878-2261 • (603)878-0604 (fax)

Antique & collectible tools of all types; kitchen & domestic artifacts. Scientific, medical, dental & apothecary items. **Pr:** $1-999 **Hrs:** By appt only. **Assn:** GSAAA **Dir:** Call for directions. **Own:** Dick Riley. **QC: 86 77**

New London

Lee Burgess Antiques
208 Little Sunapee Rd • 03257
(603)526-4657

18th & 19th C fine American country furniture, folk art & Canton. **Hrs:** By appt only. **Assn:** NHADA. **QC: 41 34 52**

Colonial Farm Antiques

Rte 11 • 03257
(603)526-6121 • (603)641-0314 (fax)

Eclectic selection of furniture, collectibles, lamps, rustics, decoys, glass & china. **Hrs:** Mem Day-Oct daily 10-5. **CC:** AX/V/MC/DIS **Assn:** NHADA **Dir:** 2 mi E of I-89 Exit 11. **Own:** Kathryn & Robert Joseph.

Priscilla Drake Antiques

33 Main St • 03257
(603)526-2151

A barn full of furniture, glassware, china & accessories. **Hrs:** Mem Day-Oct 12 daily 10-4. **Assn:** NHADA. **QC: 48 61**

Pear Tree Hill Antiques

Shaker Rd • 03257
(603)526-9339

Specializing in country & formal period furniture & accessories. **Hrs:** By appt only. **Assn:** GSAAA. **QC: 102**

John H Rogers Antiques

(603)526-6778

Early American country furniture, refinished & painted. Early woodenware & accessories. **Hrs:** By appt only. **Assn:** NHADA. **QC: 34 51**

Newbury

Susie Burmann Antiques

29 Longview Dr • 03255
(603)763-3058

Select American rural & period furniture with compatible accessories such as textiles, folk art & appropriate smalls. **Pr:** $200-10,000 **Est:** 1974 **Hrs:** By appt only. **Assn:** NHADA **Dir:** Off Rte 103 at the southern tip of Lake Sunapee. **Own:** Susie & Rich Burmann. **QC: 1 41**

Newton

Steven J Rowe

One N Main St • 03858
(603)382-4618

Fresh stock of high country & classical furniture, period accessories & decorative arts. **Hrs:** By appt only. **Assn:** NHADA **Dir:** I-495 Exit 53: 4 mi. **QC: 52 36**

Drinking Glasses I

Cordial glass: A small glass made in the late 17th and throughout the 18th centuries for drinking sweet liqueurs, or cordials. In the 18th century, cordials were commonly drunk with tea.

Surfeit water glass: Surfeit water was a very strong 18th century brandy, so the glasses from which to drink it were small, about three-quarters of an inch in diameter, and usually flute shaped.

Toasting glass or firing glass: A short, stubby glass made strong enough to be knocked loudly on the table when toasts were drunk. As toasts tended to be numerous, and the rapping increased in volume as they progressed, the glasses had to be strong indeed. Another type of toasting glass was made with a slender stem that could easily be snapped to mark a special occasion. Predictably, these are difficult to collect.

Dram: Today a measure of liquid, an eighth of a fluid ounce. Our forefathers were untroubled by such precision and used the word more loosely as a measure of the smallest amount of liquor that was worth drinking.

North Conway

Antiques & Collectibles Barn [G25]

3425 Main St • 03860
(603)356-7118
antiquesnh@aol.com

A wonderful blend of antiques & collectibles including jewelry, paper, glass, silver, pottery, porcelain, postcards & furniture. **Est:** 1983 **Hrs:** Daily 10-5. **Sz:** L **CC:** AX/V/MC/DIS **Assn:** NHADA **Dir:** 1-1/2 mi N of the center of town or 1-1/2 mi N of RR station on Rte 16 & Rte 302. **Own:** Mardy Friary. **QC: 1 7 100**

North Conway Antiques & Collectibles [G80]

Rte 16 • 03860
(603)356-6661

A wide range of quality & affordable antiques & collectibles. **Hrs:** Daily 10-5. **CC:** V/MC **Assn:** NHADA **Dir:** At junc Rtes 16 & 302 1-1/2 mi N of N Conway Village.

Richard M Plusch Antiques

Main St • 03860
(603)356-3333
rmp@landmarknet.net

Period furniture, paintings, prints, glass, china, Oriental antiques, silver, jewlery, rugs, clocks & folk art. **Pr:** $5-10,000 **Est:** 1970 **Hrs:** Jun 1-Oct 31 Mon-Sat 10-5, Sun 12-5; Nov 1-May 30 Sat 10-5, Sun 12-5 or by chance/appt. **Sz:** L **CC:** V/MC **Assn:** NHADA **Dir:** Rte 16 & Rte 302 in the center of the White Mtns of NH. **QC: 1 52 61 S1 S12**

North Hampton

Drake Farm Antiques & Gallery

148 Lafayette Rd (US Rte 1) • 03862
(603)964-4868

Fine arts, furniture, smalls, antiques, collectibles, books, prints, country things, games, sporting equipment on two floors in a c 1850s barn & connecting General Store. **Hrs:** Mon-Sat 10-6, Sun 12-6. **Sz:** M **Dir:** 7 mi S of Portsmouth traffic circle on US Rte 1. 3 mi N of Hampton Center at Rte 27 on US Rte 1. **Own:** Marica Van Dyke & Robert Gross. **QC: 32 34 52**

North Hampton Antique Center [G12+]

One Lafayette Rd • 03862
(603)964-6615

General line of antiques & collectibles. **Hrs:** Sum Mon-Sat 10-4; Win Tue-Sat 10-4. **Assn:** NHADA **Dir:** 1 mi N of Hampton Ctr on Rte 1; 6 mi N of Exit 1.

George & Debbie Spiecker Fine Americana

(603)964-4738

Specializing in 18th & early 19th C American furniture, weathervanes & New England paintings. **Hrs:** By appt only. **Assn:** ADA MADA NHADA **Dir:** On the seacoast, 1 hr from Boston. **QC: 52 45 7**

Northfield

Thomas M Thompson

585 Concord Rd • 03276
(603)286-4908

Children's items, country accessories, garden & architectural elements & folk art. **Pr:**

$25-3,000 **Hrs:** By appt only. **Assn:** NHADA VADA. **QC: 34 41 60**

Northumberland

Potato Barn Antiques Center Ltd [G70]

Rte 3 • 03584
(603)636-2611

Est: 1988 **Hrs:** Jan-Mar Fri-Sun 10-4; Apr-Jun Thu-Mon 9-5; Jul-Sep Thu-Tue 9-5; Oct-Dec Thu-Mon 9-5. **Sz:** L **CC:** V/MC **Assn:** NHADA **Dir:** 4-1/2 mi N of Lancaster, NH, fairgrounds on Rte 3. **Own:** Ernie & Janice Yelle.

Northwood

R S Butler Trading

Rte 4 • 03261
(603)942-5249

Antiques, furnishings, collectibles, records & quilts. **Hrs:** Fri, Sat & Mon 10-5, Sun 12-5. **QC: 48 32 84**

Country Tavern Antiques [G40]

Rte 4 • 03261
(603)942-7630

Room settings in 18th C tavern & barn. Country furniture, smalls, rugs & toys. **Hrs:** Mon-Sat 10-5, Sun 12-5.

Coveway Corner Antiques

Rte 4 • 03261
(603)942-7500 • (603)942-7500 (fax)

Furniture, smalls & unusual antiques. **Hrs:** Sat-Thu 10-5, Fri by appt. **Dir:** Rte 4, 1/8 mi W of Hudson's Restaurant in the Benjamin Bldg.

Drake's Hill Antiques

Rte 202A • 03261
(603)942-5958

English china 1820-1860, country furniture & accessories for the country home. **Hrs:** By chance/appt. **Assn:** NHADA **Own:** James & Nancy Boyd. **QC: 34 23**

Fern Eldridge & Friends [G20]

800 Rte 4 • 03261
(603)942-5602
fern27@tiac.net
www.tiac.net./users/fern27

In an 18th C house & barn in room settings, fine country furniture with original paint & surface, hooked rugs, folk art, primitives & related smalls. **Hrs:** Daily 10-5. **Sz:** L **Assn:** NHADA **Dir:** In the Bradbury Newell House, next to Town Hall. **QC: 34 48 41**

The Hayloft Antique Center [G80+]

1190 First NH Tpke (Rte 4) • 03261
(603)942-5153 • (603)942-7126 (fax)
lpguevin@together.net
www.hayloft.net

Large variety of antiques & collectibles, military, toys, glass, ceramics, linens, jewelry, ephemera, sports, art pottery, glass, tools & cameras. We also have an art gallery, furniture gallery & a book corner. **Pr:** $1-5,000 **Est:** 1986 **Hrs:** Daily 10-5. **Sz:** L **CC:** V/MC **Assn:** NHADA **Dir:** I-93 to Concord, NH, to Rte 4 E. Approximately 15 mi shop on L. **Own:** Louis & Patty Guevin. **QC: 7 23 49 S2 S8 S12**

Northwood Cordwainer House

Rte 4 • 03261
(603)942-8111

Jewlery, glass, porcelain, cameras, books, games, prints & decorative pieces. **Dir:** Blue barn near the int of Rte 152.

Nostalgia Antiques
Rte 4 • 03261
(603)942-7748

Specializing in carpenter's hand tools, fishing tackle & related items, smalls, glassware & furniture. **QC: 86 79**

Ole Parsonage Antiques
Rte 4 • 03261
(603)942-5749

Tools, primitives & collectibles. **Dir:** Located on Northwood Ridge. **QC: 86 106**

On the Hill Collectables
Rte 4 • 03261
(603)942-8169
georgelsh@aol.com

Postcards, paper, glass, coins, toys, collectibles & political. **Est:** 1996 **Hrs:** Fri-Sun 10-5. **CC:** V/MC **Own:** George Shattuck. **QC: 39 33 32**

Parker-French Antique Center [G135]
1182 First NH Tpke (Rte 4) • 03261
(603)942-8852

A quality group shop with a full range of antiques from primitives to jewelry & silver. **Est:** 1974 **Hrs:** Daily 10-5. **Sz:** H **Dir:** Midway betw Concord & Portsmouth, 12 mi W of Lee traffic circle, 6 mi E of Epsom traffic circle. **Own:** Richard Bojko & John Mullen.

Pioneer America
Rte 4 • 03261
(603)942-8588

Country antiques, primitives, Victoriana, glass, china & kitchenware. **Hrs:** Daily 10-5.

Ringing Anvil
Rte 4 • 03261
(603)942-5272

Antique barn filled with glass, china, tools, books, toys, furniture & collectibles.

Sleigh Bell Antiques [G]
Rte 4 • 03261
(603)942-9988 **Hrs:** Daily 10-5 or by appt. **Sz:** S **Own:** Cam Brisard.

George & Donna Thomas
152 Olde Canterbuy Rd • 03261
(603)942-7801
george@neantiques.com
www.neanitques.com

18th & 19th C furniture & quality accessories. **Hrs:** By appt only. **Assn:** NHADA. **QC: 36 48**

Town Pump Antiques [G75]
295 First NH Tpke • 03261
(603)942-5515 **Hrs:** Mon-Sat 9-5, Sun 10-5. **Own:** Joanne Swallow.

White House Antique Center
180 First NH Tpke (Rte 4) • 03261
(603)942-8994
picker47@aol.com

Advertising, bottles, country, collectibles, furniture, primitives & Victoriana. **Hrs:** By chance/appt. **Dir:** Just W of Rte 202. **Own:** Joe & Muriel Trovato. **QC: 34 106 89**

Willow Hollow Antiques [G20]
Rte 4 • 03261
(603)942-5739

In an apothecary shop setting, country primitives, toys, paper Americana, Shaker items, old iron & metals. **Hrs:** Daily 10:30-4:30. **CC:** V/MC **Assn:** NHADA **Dir:** Betw Rte 202 & 107 on Rte 4 beyond Town Hall. **Own:** Nancy Winston.

Wonderful Things
94 Rte 4 • 03291
(603)942-8832

Offering wonderful furniture of all periods, estate jewelry & general antiques & decorative items in a green house and barn setting. **Pr:** $25-2,500 **Est:** 1997 **Hrs:** Thu 12-5, Fri-Mon 10-5 or by chance/appt. **Sz:** S **CC:**

V/MC **Assn:** GIA NAWCC **Dir:** 10 mi W of Lee traffic cir on Rte 4 next to R S Butler. **Own:** Elizabeth Norton. **QC: 48 64 S12 S19**

Orfordville

Dame Hill Nostalgia

Dame Hill Rd • 03777
(603)353-4717

Specializing in Amish quilts. **Hrs:** By appt only. **Own:** Judy Siemons. **QC: 84**

Ossipee

The Baron Antiques

(603)539-2717

General line of English smalls. **Hrs:** By appt only. **Assn:** NHADA **Dir:** . **Own:** Frank de Ramer.

Lakewood Station Antiques [G50+]

Rte 16 • 03890
(603)539-7414

Est: 1992 **Hrs:** Daily 10-5 except major hols. **Sz:** M **Assn:** NHADA **Dir:** 1 hour N on Rte 16 from Portsmouth NH traffic circle; 4 mi S of Rte 25E. **Own:** David DeJager. **QC: 34 61 60**

The Stuff Shop

25 Water Village Rd • 03864
(603)539-7715

Diverse selection of antiques & collectibles, primarily country with a large selection of clocks & watches. **Pr:** $10-1,000 **Est:** 1960 **Hrs:** Apr-Oct 12 daily 9-5. **Sz:** M **Assn:** AAA **Dir:** Rte 16 to Rte 28W on Rte 171, 6th house on L from Rte 28. **Own:** Len Wenant. **QC: 35 34**

Treasure Hunt Antiques [G100+]

465 Rte 16 • 03864
(603)539-7877
antiques@worldpath.net

Advertising, collectibles, books, china, copper, dolls, ephemera, glass, gold, Indian artifacts, lace, linens, souvenirs, toys, paper, pewter, pottery, silver, stoneware & Victorian items. **Pr:** $1-1,000 **Est:** 1997 **Hrs:** Mon-Sat 9:30-5, Sun 10:30-5. **Sz:** H **CC:** V/MC **Dir:** Rte 16 2 mi S of the jct of Rtes 16 & 28. **Own:** Al & Maggie Ricci. **QC: 32 48 67 S2 S8**

Peterborough

Brennans Antiques

130 Hunt Rd • 03458
(603)924-3445

Country furniture, primitives, textiles, treen, tin, iron & decorative accessories. **Hrs:** By chance/appt. **Assn:** GSAAA NHADA **Dir:** Call for directions. **Own:** Judy Brennan. **QC: 34 40 36**

The Cobbs Antiques & Auctioneers

83 Grove St • 03458
(603)924-6361
www.thecobbs.com

Quality primitive, country, formal & painted furniture, paintings, rugs, fabrics, folk art, porcelains, glass & silver for the serious collector. **Hrs:** Mon-Sat by chance/appt. **Assn:** NHADA **Dir:** 1 block N of lights at the int of Rtes 202 & 101. **Own:** Charles Cobb. **QC: 34 41 51 S2**

Old Town Farm Antiques

1218 Old Town Farm Rd • 03458
(603)924-3523

Period & country furniture, Oriental rugs, decorative accessories, paintings & smalls. **Est:** 1970 **Hrs:** Daily 12-4 or by appt. **Sz:** L **Assn:** NHADA **Dir:** From Rte 101W, S on Rte 202 1 mi. R on Old Jaffrey Rd, R on Old Town Farm Rd, big red barn on R. **Own:**

> Use the Service QuickCode indexes at the back of the book to find restorers, appraisers, refinishers, and other specialty service providers.

Robert Taylor. **QC: 7 34 52**

Peterborough Fine Art

Depot Square • 03458
(609)924-7558 • (603)924-7409 (fax)
info@peterboroughfineart.com
www.peterboroughfineart.com

A broad selection of 19th & early 20th C academic paintings with emphasis on American art. New England painters, particularly those who worked in the Monadnock region of New Hampshire. **Pr:** $500-45,000 **Est:** 1995 **Hrs:** May 1-Oct 30 Wed-Sat 11-4, Sun 1-4, or by appt; Nov 1-Apr 30 Wed-Fri 1-4, Sat 11-5, Sun 1-5. **Sz:** M **CC:** V/MC **Assn:** ASA NHADA **Dir:** Midway betw Manchester & Keene on Rte 101 in downtown Peterborough. Depot Sq is at the end of Depot St off Main. **QC: 8 9 12 S1 S9 S16**

Tom & Barbara Tripp

(603)924-6106
nhattic@aol.com

Large inventory of antique (1880-1930) souvenir china & glass from New England towns. Business is primarily mail-order. **Pr:** $35-200 **Est:** 1988 **Hrs:** By appt only. **Own:** Tom & Barbara Tripp. **QC: 1 67**

Pike

Brown Farmhouse

Jeffers Hill Rd • 03780
(603)989-5543

General line. **Hrs:** By chance/appt.**QC: S7**

Plainfield

Richard Miller

1106 Rte 12A • 03781
(603)675-9112
rpmiller@sover.net

American folk painting, sculpture, textiles, pottery & painted furniture. **Hrs:** By appt only. **Own:** Richard Miller. **QC: 1 41 52 S9 S12 S8**

Plaistow

Plaistow Commons Antiques [G200]

160 Plaistow Rd (Rte 125) • 03865
(603)382-3621
www.plaistowcommons.com

Huge selection of furniture, glass & collectibles. **Hrs:** Mon-Sat 9-6, Sun 12-6. **Sz:** H **Assn:** NHADA **Dir:** Rte 495N Exit 51B to Rte 125 Plaistow.1/2 hr from Boston, Nashua & Portsmouth.

Plymouth

Pauline Gatz Antiques

1009 Texas Hill Rd • 03264
(603)968-7975

Country furniture & primitives. **Assn:** NHADA. **QC: 102 106**

Portsmouth

Antiques & A.R.T.

116 State St • 03801
(603)431-3931

Period country & formal furniture, architectural elements & period decorative accessories. **Hrs:** Apr-Dec Tue-Sat 11-5; Jan-Mar by chance/appt. **Assn:** NHADA VADA **Own:** Richard Costa & David Currier. **QC: 36 52 3**

Hollis E Brodrick

(603)433-7075

Specializing in decorative arts & artifacts of early America. **Hrs:** By appt only. **Assn:** NHADA. **QC: 1**

M S Carter Inc

175 Market St • 03801
(603)436-1781

Large selection of quality furnishings & accessories. Specializing in 18th & 19th C samplers, pottery, apothecary items & an entire floor of fine & functional woodworking tools in a pleasant little shop near the harbor. **Est:** 1976 **Hrs:** Mon-Sat 9:30-5, Sun 12-5. **CC:** V/MC **Assn:** NHADA **Dir:** I-95 Exit 7: 1/2 mi toward historic district. **Own:** Margaret S Carter. **QC: 82 36**

The Doll Connection

117 Market St • 03801
(603)431-5030

Dolls ranging from 1820-1950, doll accessories including clothes, doll house furniture. **Est:** 1973 **Hrs:** Mon-Sat 10-4. **Dir:** I-95N Exit 7: 3/4 mi. **Own:** Helen Jarvis. **QC: 38**

Portsmouth Bookshop

1 Islington St • 03801
(603)433-4406 • (603)433-0901 (fax)
oldbooksmaps@fcgnetworks.net

Buy & sell antiquarian, used, rare & out-of-print books of all types. Deal in old & rare maps as well. **Pr:** $3-5,000 **Est:** 1988 **Hrs:** Mon-Fri 9:30-5:30, Sat 9:30-6, Sun 12-5:30. **Sz:** L **CC:** AX/V/MC/DIS **Assn:** NHABA **Dir:** From downtown thru 2 sets of lights on R in large yellow house (c 1720), diagonally across from library. **Own:** Brian DiMambro. **QC: 18 66 74 S1 S19**

Thanas Galleries

249 Islington St • 03907
(603)436-5900

Fine arts purchased & appraised. **Hrs:** By appt only. **Own:** Philip & Michele Thanas. **QC: 7 S1**

The Trunk Shop

23 Ceres St • 03801
(603)431-4399
www.trunk.com

On Portsmouth Harbor, a long-established dealer in fine old trunks. **Est:** 1978 **Hrs:** Oct-Jun Thu & Sun 12-6, Fri-Sat 12-8; Jul-Sep Sun-Thu 12-5, Fri-Sat 12-8. **CC:** V/MC **Dir:** 1/2 block off Bow St. **Own:** Linda Edelstein. **QC: 48 S16**

The Victory Antiques [G30]

96 State St • 03801
(603)431-3046
www.thevictory.com

Specializing in European & American country pine & formal furnishings, old woodworking tools, collectible clothing & jewelry. **Pr:** $25-5,000 **Est:** 1988 **Hrs:** Mon-Sat 10-5, Sun 12-6. **CC:** AX/V/MC/DIS **Assn:** NEAA **Dir:** In the heart of historic Portsmouth across from the Strawbery Banke Guild. **QC: 34 86 S1**

Blue-and-White Porcelain

Flow blue, originally called "flowing blue": Transferware produced in numerous patterns in which the cobalt blue ink flowed, or smeared, during firing. The resulting out-of-focus look was colorful and popular, and flow blue was widely produced in England and the Netherlands from 1830 to 1900. Its popularity was welcomed by the manufacturers, because the flowing disguised the smudges that were made if the transfer was moved slightly as it was laid on the item: this enabled them to deskill the decorating process even more, and thus to pay even lower wages to the women and girls who did the job.

Historical blue: A blue-and-white china made in Staffordshire for the American market from about 1820 to 1840. The pattern shows American scenes or historical events surrounded by a flowered border. Each factory had its own border, but the same scenes were copied by many factories. English scenes were also produced, but it is the American ones that are most eagerly collected. "Second period" historical blue was popular from about 1850 to 1920. It showed a greater number of scenes, many of which were specially printed as souvenirs for the growing tourist trade. It is often printed in a lighter blue than the deep cobalt of the first period, is easier to find, cheaper, and widely collected.

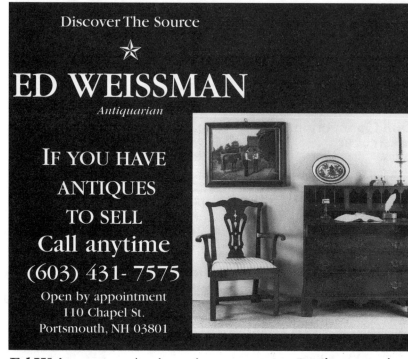

Ed Weissman — Antiquarian

110 Chapel St • 03801

(603)431-7575

Fine period American furniture; American, European & Oriental 15th-early 19th C accessories concentrating on metalware; & paintings & folk art located in a charming 19th C ship captain's home. **Est:** 1956 **Hrs:** By appt only in summer only. **Assn:** ISA NHADA **Dir:** I-95 Exit 7 to Market St to first major L (Bow St). **QC: 36 52 7**

Raymond

Al Martin Antiques

65 Chester Rd (Rte 102) • 03077

(603)895-4532

almartin@mediaone.net

Large barn full of American oak & Victorian furniture & accessories. Wholesale to dealers. **Hrs:** By appt only. **Dir:** I-93 Exit 4: Rte 102 E 14 mi or Rte 101 Exit 5: Rte 102 W 2 mi. **QC: 50 58**

Richmond

John D Wahl Antiques

135 Old Homestead Hwy • 03470

(603)239-7200

Selected line of American country furniture & related accessories including folk art, treen, signs, baskets & cupboards. Special emphasis on painted or original surfaces. **Pr:** $10-5,000 **Est:** 1990 **Hrs:** By chance/appt. **Sz:** M **Assn:** GSAAA NHADA **Dir:** On Rte 32 7/10 mi N of Rte 119 (Richmond Four Corners), 20 min S of Keene. **Own:** Danny Wahl. **QC: 1 34 51**

The Yankee Smuggler Antiques

122 Fitzwilliam Rd (Rte 119) • 03470

(603)239-4188 • (603)239-4653 (fax)

smuggler@cheshire.net

www.nhada.org/yankee.htm

Specializing in early American country & painted furniture, folk art & unusual quality accessories located in two rooms in the house & a full barn. **Pr:** $5-5,000 **Hrs:** Yr round daily by chance/appt. **Assn:** NHADA NEAA MADA VADA **Dir:** On Rte 119 12 mi S of Keene or 7 mi W of Fitzwilliam & 1/2 mi E of Rte 32. 6th house on L going E from Four Corner Store. **Own:** Carole & Ted Hayward. **QC: 1 34 51**

Rindge

Scott Bassoff/Sandy Jacobs

200 Robbins Rd • 03461
(603)899-3373
jetbass@top.monad.net

Early American high style country & formal furniture with an emphasis on old surface & original paint. Accessories comprise a selection of quality redware, choice treen, samplers, hooked rugs, decorated tin, folk art, weathervanes & paintings. **Hrs:** By appt only. **Assn:** ADA NHADA **Dir:** Rte 202 to Thomas Rd, 3 mi, brown Cape with red picket fence. **QC: 29 52 88**

Rochester

Peter Carswell Antiques

293 Pond Hill Rd • 03867
(603)332-4264
pacart@worldpath.net

Wide selection from New England homes with emphasis on country & formal furniture & accessories in as-found condition. **Pr:** $25-10,000 **Est:** 1964 **Hrs:** Daily by chance/appt. **Sz:** M **Assn:** NHADA **Dir:** W of Rochester approx 3 mi off Rte 202A (corn of Pond Hill Rd). **Own:** Peter Carswell. **QC: 34 52 102**

Equine Antiques

256 Meaderboro Rd • 03867
(603)330-0944
horse@acornworld.net

Specializing in antiques, collectibles & decorating accessories with a horse use or motif. **Est:** 1997 **Hrs:** By chance/appt. **Dir:** 3 mi off Rte 202-A. **Own:** Fredricka B Olsen.

Rye

Antiques at Rye Center

655 Wallis Rd • 03870
(603)964-8999

Honesty, quality & diversity. Fine & whimsical antiques. Hand-painted porcelains, art, china, crystal & art glass, select furniture, Victorian jewelry, silver, toys, French & Continental antiques, decorative accessories, objects of virtue. **Pr:** $25.00-15,000 **Est:** 1997 **Hrs:** Daily 10:30-6. **Sz:** L **CC:** AX/V/MC/DIS **Assn:** NHADA, GSAAA **Dir:** 1 hr N of Boston. Just 10 mins S of Portsmouth by Rte 1 or 1A. Take Washington Rd to Wallis Rd. **QC: 23 87 89 S12**

Salem

R O Schmitt Antiques

(603)893-5915

American & European clocks; beginner through advanced level. **Hrs:** By appt only. **Assn:** NHADA **Dir:** Call for directions. **QC: 35**

Sanbornville

Richard & Patricia Lewis

222 Witchtrot Rd • 03872
(603)522-6177

Huge barn shop, largest in area. Furniture, glass, architectural & decor. **Hrs:** Mid May-Oct Thu-Sun 10-4 or by appt.

Shelburne

Crow Mountain Farm Antiques

North Rd • 03581
(603)466-2509

Two rooms of carefully selected items from New England, including primitives, folk art, tools, paintings, prints, furniture & a wide variety of general items. **Pr:** $50-2,500 **Est:** 1972 **Hrs:** May-Oct daily 9-5, Nov-Apr by chance/appt. **Sz:** M **Assn:** NHADA **Dir:** 1 mi E of Philbrook Farm Inn on North Rd, 2-1/2 mi off Rte 2. **Own:** Ben Werner. **QC: 1 41 52**

Snowville

Sleigh Mill Antiques

Snow Rd • 03832
(603)447-6791 • (603)447-6791 (fax)
sleigh@landmarknet.net
www.tias.com/stores/sm

An authentic sleigh mill full of antiques, accessories & authentic 19th C lighting. **Est:** 1982 **Hrs:** Daily 10-5 or by chance/appt. **Sz:** M **CC:** V/MC **Dir:** 6 mi S of Conway NH off Rte 153. 1 mi from Rte 153 Crystal Lake to Snowville. **Own:** Donald & Edith Dashnau. **QC: 35 52 65**

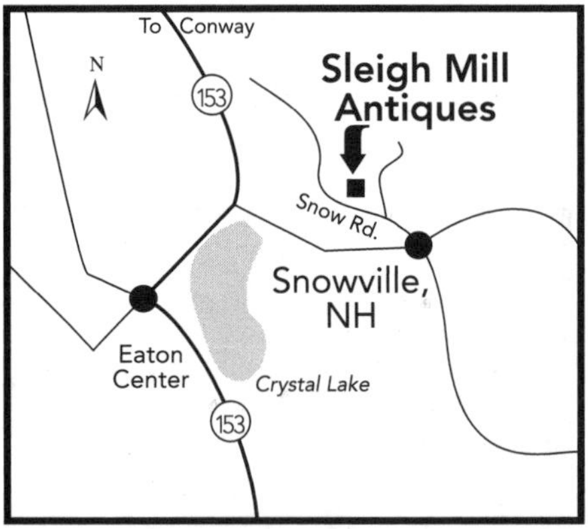

Springfield

Lazy Fox Antiques et Gallerie

(603)763-2122

English, European & American furniture; porcelains, attic treasures, dolls & child-related items. **Hrs:** Jun-Oct most days 10-5 or by appt. **Assn:** NHADA **Own:** Jacki Beam.

Stratham

The Olde Tannery Antiques & Rare Books

249 Portsmouth Ave (Rte 33) • 03885
(603)772-4997

Early 18th & 19th C American furniture, lighting, iron hearth equipment & accessories. **Hrs:** By chance/appt. **Assn:** NHADA **Dir:** On Rte 33 (formerly Rte 101). **Own:** Esther & Michael Flanagan. **QC: 52 65 62**

John Piper House Antiques

10 Sandy Point Rd • 03885
(603)778-1347
babsi@nh.ultranet.com

Early American, country furniture, early glass, silver, coverlets, mirrors & andirons — a good general selection in a barn. **Pr:** $25-8,000 **Est:** 1971 **Hrs:** By chance/appt. **Sz:** M **Assn:** NHADA **Dir:** I-95 to Rte 101W to Rte 108 E to Rte 33 to Stratham approx 5-1/2 mi, L onto Sandy Pt Rd opp Stratham Hill Rd. 1st house on R. **Own:** Barbara & Graeme Mann. **QC: 34 52 78**

The Wingate Collection

94 Portsmouth Ave (Rte 108) • 03885
(603)778-4849

A large selection of French Canadian & American country furniture, architectural mirrors, framed prints & decorative accessories. Specializing in farmhouse & butterfly tables; cupboards; meeting house, buggy seat & garden benches; desks & blanket boxes.

Pr: $50-5,000 **Est:** 1983 **Hrs:** Mon-Sat 9-5, Sun 12-5. **Sz:** L **CC:** V/MC **Dir:** From N: I-95 Exit 3A: Rte 33W to Rte 108S approx 10 mi from exit. From S: I-95 Exit 2: Rte 101W to Rte 108 N approx 6-1/2 mi from exit. **Own:** Norman MacLean. **QC: 34 36 51**

Sugar Hill

Colonial Cottage

720 Blake Rd • 03585
(603)823-5614

A charming six-room cape cottage brimming with early New England furniture & formal decorative accessories including brass, copper, pottery & porcelain; specializing in early American glass, lamps & lighting fixtures. **Est:** 1955 **Hrs:** Daily 9-4 by chance/appt. **Sz:** M **CC:** V/MC/DIS **Dir:** 1-1/2 mi up Blake Rd off Rte 117. **Own:** Lauren & Eleanor Howard. **QC: 52 104 65**

Sunapee

John Melby Antiques

28 Bradford Rd • 03782
(603)863-2137

Early painted furniture, folk art & other country accessories. **Hrs:** By chance/appt. **Assn:** NHADA. **QC: 51 34 41**

Frank & Barbara Pollack

Box 344 • 60035
(603)763-2403
fpollack@compuserve.com
www.maineantiquedigest.com/adimg/pollack.htm

American primitive paintings, furniture in original finish & paint, folk art & textiles of the 18th & 19th C & decorative arts & jewelry of the 20th C. Sep-May: 1214 Green Bay Rd, Highland Park, IL 60035; (708)433-2213. **Hrs:** Jun-Aug by appt only. **Assn:** ADA NHADA **Dir:** Call for directions. **QC: 1 51 41 S1**

Swanzey

Fairgrounds Antique Market [G75]

Rte 12 • 03446
(603)352-4420

Hrs: Daily 9-5. **Dir:** 3 mi S of Keene on Cheshire Fair Grounds. **Own:** Jim & Audrey O'Brien.

Secords Antique Center

Rte 10W • 03469
(603)352-9009

Oak furniture, Wallace Nuttings, postcards, Roseville, toys & carnival glass. **Hrs:** Daily 9-5. **Sz:** H **Own:** Bob Secord.

Tuftonboro Center

The Ewings

65 Federal Corner Rd • 03816
(603)569-3861 • (603)569-3861 (fax)
jewing@worldpath.net

Diverse stock of New England antiques. Emphasis on 18th & 19th C furniture & related accessories with good form & original surface, 19th & early 20th C art & folk art. All items guaranteed authentic & as represented. **Pr:** $50-3,500 **Est:** 1974 **Hrs:** May 1-Oct 31 Mon-Sat 10-4; Nov 1-Apr 30 by chance/appt. **Sz:** M **Assn:** NHADA **Dir:** NH Rte 109A to Tuftonboro General Store & PO; turn onto Federal Corner Rd. Shop is 3/4 mi on R, look for sign. **Own:** Joe & Cecelia Ewing. **QC: 34 80 41 S19 S15**

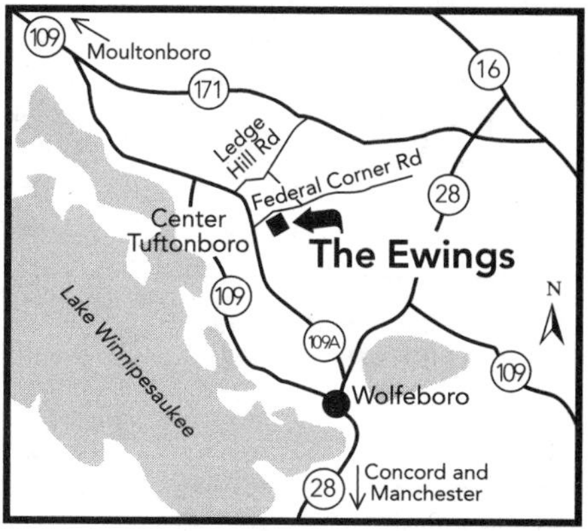

Golden Past Antiques [G8]
Rte 109A • 03816
(603)569-4249

Specializing in country smalls with a wide selection of advertising, kitchen, linens, tools, glass & china. **Hrs:** May-Oct daily 10-5. **Assn:** NHADA **Dir:** Betw General Store & school. **Own:** Elaine Miller.

Log Cabin Antique Shop
Rte 109A & Ledge Hill Rd • 03816
(603)569-1909

Small shop off the beaten path with a general line of antiques & collectibles including antique buttons & postcards. **Pr:** $5-250 **Est:** 1968 **Hrs:** May 22-Oct 12 Fri-Sun 10-5, Mon-Thu by chance/appt. **Sz:** M **Assn:** NHADA **Dir:** From Wolfeboro, Rte 109A, 6 mi to int of 109A & Ledge Hill Rd, on corn opposite Center Tuftonboro School. **Own:** Betty & Harold Holmquist. **QC: 21 32 39**

Tuftonboro Corner

Dow's Corner Shop
Rte 171 & Ledge Hill Rd • 03864
(603)539-4790

An old-fashioned single-owner shop in a large & extraordinarily well-stocked barn. An immense range of inventory from furniture, clocks & porcelain to metalwork & silver supplied by the owners' "fearless buying." Well worth the trip. Dealers welcome. **Est:** 1948 **Hrs:** May 1-Oct 15 daily 10-5; Oct 15-Apr 30 by chance/appt. Call Tue-Wed in advance. **Sz:** H **Assn:** NHADA **Dir:** On Rte 171 betw Rtes 16 or 28 & 25. **Own:** Marjorie & Albert Dow. **QC: 52 34 78**

Union

Carswell's Antiques
203 Wakefield Rd • 03887
(603)473-2304

Two floors in an interesting old barn with country & period furniture, primitives, smalls, folk art & some oak, linens & vintage clothing. **Est:** 1947 **Hrs:** By chance or appt. **Sz:** M **Assn:** NEAA NHADA **Dir:** From Rochester take Rte 16 to Rte 153, turn R, 3/10 mi on L. **Own:** Kippy & Diana Carswell. **QC: 34 41 81 S1 S12**

Walpole

The Golden Past of Walpole
N River Rd • 03608
(603)756-3974

A spacious, heated private showroom offering a wide variety of American furniture & accessories, paintings, fine china & glass. **Est:** 1980 **Hrs:** Apr 20-Dec 15 daily 10-5 by chance/appt. **Sz:** L **Assn:** NADA NHADA **Dir:** 16 mi N of Keene, turn R at blinking light (1st exit into Walpole) & R onto River Rd. 1st house. **Own:** Harwood & Judith Boynton. **QC: 35 52 7**

Warner

Kate A Alex & Co
Beaver Bog Rd • 03278
(603)456-3267

Eccentric furniture & accessories for home & garden. Architectural elements, folk & outsider art & the whimsical. **Hrs:** By appt only. **Assn:** NHADA. **QC: 3 60 41**

Washington

Tintagel Antiques
Rte 31 • 03280
(603)495-3429

Country furniture & accessories, flow blue china, tools, frames, quilts & hooked rugs. Pewter repair services. **Hrs:** Daily 10-5. **Assn:** NHADA **Dir:** 1 mi N of village on Rte 31. **Own:** Sally & Ralph Krone. **QC: 34 55 S16**

Waterville Valley

Adornments

1 Town Sq • 03215
(603)236-4355

Jewelry. **Hrs:** Sun-Thu 10-6, Fri-Sat 10-9. **Assn:** NHADA **Own:** Gloria Gardner Moore. **QC: 63**

Weare

Sykes & Flanders Antiquarian Booksellers

99 Woodbury Rd • 03281
(603)529-7432

Old & rare books & manuscripts. **Hrs:** By appt only. **Assn:** NHADA **Own:** Dick & Mary Sykes. **QC: 18 S1**

West Lebanon

Colonial Antique Markets [G100]

Colonial Plaza • 03784
(603)298-8132

General line. **Hrs:** Daily 9-5. **Sz:** H **CC:** V/MC.

West Nottingham

Merry Hill Farm [G]

Rte 4 & Merry Hill Rd • 03291
(603)942-5370

Specializing in country furniture, folk art, oak & Victorian furniture & decorative accessories. **Hrs:** Mon-Sat 10-5, Sun 12-5. **Dir:** W of the Lee Traffic circle. **Own:** Rebecca Demisch.

West Swanzey

Knotty Pine Antique Market [G300]

Rte 10 • 03469
(603)352-5252 • (603)352-5019 (fax)
(800)352-5251
www.knottypineantiques.com

Antiques & collectibles: glass, silver, jewelry, iron, pottery, furniture, primitives, rugs, quilts, art glass, china, pewter, dishes, toys & advertising **Est:** 1973 **Hrs:** Daily 9-5 exc Thanks & Christmas. **Sz:** H **CC:** V/MC/DIS **Dir:** 5 mi S of Keene. **Own:** Stephen & Joan Pappas. **QC: 30 103 S1 S2 S12**

Drinking Glasses II

Dram glass: A short drinking glass for strong drink, whose conical bowl often had a solid lower part.

Sham dram: A dram glass with a bowl that looks as though it holds more than it does. Often used by innkeepers who had to drink with each customer but also remain competent through a long evening.

Toastmaster glass: A finer version of the sham dram designed to ensure that the final toast was (almost) as clearly articulated as the first.

Rummer: A general name for a large, stemmed glass, usually with the rim narrower than the bowl. Used mainly in taverns.

Toddy Rummer: The largest of all 18th century glasses, often with a finely engraved bowl, used for drinking hot toddy.

Toddy: A drink made with liquor and hot water, often sweetened and spiced with cloves. Well suited to a New England winter.

Westmoreland

The Antique Shops at Jingle's [G40]

Rte 12 • 03467
(603)399-7039

Hrs: Daily 10-5. **Dir:** 7 mi N of Keene.

The Antiques Shops [G40]

1024 Rte 12 • 03467
(603)399-7039 • (603)399-7039 (fax)

Est: 1987 **Hrs:** Daily 10-5. **Sz:** L **CC:** V/MC/DIS **Dir:** Rte 12N, 7 mi N of Keene. **Own:** Larry Muchmore.

Lucienne Elshout Prints & Books

1835 Rte 12 • 03467
(603)399-4883 • (603)399-4883 (fax)
elshoutbks@monad.net

Rare books, non-fiction, prints, ephemera, postcards, paintings, furniture & smalls. **Hrs:** Mon-Sun 10-5. **CC:** V/MC **Assn:** VADA VABA **Dir:** From VT: I-91 Exit 5: Rte 5S 1/4 mi to Rte 123. Cross the Connecticut River at Rte 12, go R toward Keene 5 mi, bldg on R. From Boston: Rte 2W to Rte 12, 9 mi on Rte 12 on L. **QC: 18 7 39**

Whitefield

The Fairweather Shop

65 Jefferson Rd (Rte 116) • 03598
(603)837-9806

Specializing in glass & china with an emphasis on quality antiques only. **Hrs:** By chance/appt. **Assn:** NHADA **Dir:** 1/4 mi from blinking light in Whitefield. **Own:** Mary Fairweather. **QC: 61**

Nee-Mo's Nook Antiques & Collectibles

Rte 3 • 03598
(603)837-2396

General line of country antiques & collectibles, glass, china, advertising & postcards. **Hrs:** All year by chance/appt (not heated). **Assn:** NHADA **Dir:** 8/10 mi N of Whitefield Common on Rte 3. **QC: 39 61**

Wilmot

Kearsarge Lodge Antiques [G]

Kearsarge Valley Rd • 03287
(603)927-4594

Specializing in Americana, primitives, folk art, painted items, rustic, garden, formal &

Samplers I

Sampler: A piece of needlework in various patterns with examples of letters and figures for use as a "sample" in marking household linens and textiles. Many included lines of verse, figures and houses.

The earliest samplers from the 17th and early 18th centuries were references of stitches and patterns. They were ongoing projects, to which a woman would add a band as she learned another design or stitch. These long narrow samplers, without borders, were not for display, but were rolled up and put away when not in use.

In the 18th century, samplers became the learning and reference tools of girls aged eight to sixteen. Most girls produced two: the earlier was a simple one, in which she learned the letters and figures to mark initials on linen and clothing; the second was fancier and more decorative and prepared her to make needlework pictures. Most were signed and dated. Samplers grew squarer as the century passed until by its end some were wider than they were deep. Most had borders and were designed to be framed for display. The period from 1785 to 1810 saw the most intricate samplers which took even the most industrious girl many months to complete.

architectural, as well as smalls. **Hrs:** Daily 10-5; Win Tue-Sun 10-5. **Assn:** NHADA **Dir:** Near the base of Mt Kearsarge & Winslow State Park. **QC: 106 41 3**

Wilton

Frye's Measure Mill

12 Frye Mill Rd • 03086
(603)654-6581

Folk art, antiques & collectibles with a country focus. **Hrs:** Tue-Sat 10-5, Sun 12-5. **Assn:** GSAAA **Dir:** From the Wilton business district follow Rte 31 N 1.5 mi. L after RR crossing, shop is located 1.5 mi on R. **QC: 41 34**

Here Today

Main St • 03086
(603)654-5295

Furniture, textiles, china, glass & decorative accessories. **Hrs:** Wed-Fri 10-5, Sat 10-4, Sun 9:30-2. **Dir:** Downtown beside the P.O.

Noah's Ark Antiques Center [G234]

604 Gibbons Hwy (Rte 101) • 03086
(603)654-2595

Furniture, decorative accessories including primitives, advertising items, Depression glass, jewelry, children's toys, bottles, pins & military items, with fresh merchandise coming in daily. **Est:** 1984 **Hrs:** Mon-Sat 10-5, Sun 9-5. **Assn:** GSAAA NHADA **Dir:** On Rte 101 betw Milford & Peterborough. **Own:** Rod & Penny Sanders.

Winchester

Fat Chance Antiques

102 N Main St • 03470
(603)239-6423

Postcards, books, maps, prints, sheet music, ephemera, wicker, coins, stamps, furniture & glassware. **Est:** 1979 **Hrs:** May-Thanks Mon & Wed 10-3, Sat 11-4; Win by chance. **Dir:** 1/2 mi N of town on Rte 10. **Own:** Robert Evans. **QC: 39 33 74**

The Halloween Queen

4 Lawrence St & Rte 10 • 03470
(603)239-8875

Over 1 million old postcards, posters, sheet music, prints, toys, advertising, glass, china & books. Specializing in Halloween & holiday collectibles. **Hrs:** By chance/appt. **Assn:** GSAAA **Dir:** On Rte 10. **Own:** Chris Russell & Pamela E Apkarian-Russell. **QC: 39 32**

Hearthside Antiques & Collectibles [G]

858 Keene Rd (Rte 10) • 03470
(603)239-8697
hearthantiques@cheshire.net

Hrs: Thu-Tue 10-5. **CC:** V/MC **Dir:** 7 mi S of Keene.

Wolfeboro

1810 House Antiques

458 Center St • 03894
(603)569-8093

Unusual antiques, collectibles, memorabilia. Fresh additions weekly. **Hrs:** May-Dec Thu-Tue 10-4; off season by chance/appt. **Dir:** Rte 28 across from Allen "A" Motel.

The Architectural Attic

Rte 28 Clark Plaza • 03896
(603)569-8989 • (603)569-8920 (fax)
netec@worldpath.net
www.architecturalattic.com

Antiques, decorative painted furniture, accessories & architectural. **Pr:** $1-600 **Est:** 1997 **Hrs:** Sum Mon-Wed & Fri-Sat 10-5, Thu 1—6:30, Sun 11-3. Call for other times. **Sz:** M **CC:** V/MC **Dir:** Approx 1/2 mi N on Rte 28 from int of Rte 109 & Rte 28 & South Main St in Wolfeboro. **Own:** Julie Fergus. **QC: 48 3 S15 S18**

Barbara's Corner Shop
67 N Main St • 03894
(603)569-3839

Collectibles, glass, china, linens & jewelry. **Hrs:** Daily 11-6, some eves til 8; Win by appt. **QC: 32 61**

Hutchins Antiques
68 Center St • 03894
(603)569-3203

Barn overflowing with antique furniture, china & tools. Pattern glass a specialty. **Hrs:** May-Oct Mon-Sat 10-5. **QC: 103 48 86**

Richard G Marden
59 Elm St • 03894
(603)569-3209
rmarden@landmarknet.net

Staffordshire historical china, Leeds & other early china for the American market, small folk art items & early American glass. **Pr:** $10-10,000 **Hrs:** Strictly by appt. **Dir:** 100 mi N of Boston. **QC: 23 41 104**

Monique's Antiques
5 Brummitt Ct • 03894
(603)569-4642

General line of china, glass, textiles, silver, small furniture. **Pr:** $25-500 **Est:** 1982 **Hrs:** Sat-Sun 12-4 or by chance/appt. **Sz:** M **Assn:** NHADA **Dir:** 1 blk S of Town Hall, 1st house on R off Main St. **Own:** Jean Radetzky. **QC: 61 80**

New England Gallery
367 Governor Wentworth Hwy • 03894
(603)569-3501 • (603)569-3358 (fax)
scollysq@aol.com

Antiques, fine art, blacklights. **Pr:** $100-5,000 **Est:** 1959 **Hrs:** By appt only. **CC:** AX/V/MC **Own:** Arthur & Patti Fraumeni. **QC: 7 6 89 S1 S2 S9**

Out of the Past
38 Glendon St • 03894
(603)569-4774

China, glass, linens, metals, furniture & collectibles. **Hrs:** Wed-Sun 10-5, Apr-Dec by appt. **QC: 61 48 81**

Ralph K Reed Antiques
Pleasant Valley Rd • 03894
(603)569-1897

Furniture: mainly English campaign chests, boxes & sea chests in camphorwood, teak, mahogany & pine. Stick & wheel type mercury barometers a specialty. **Pr:** $50-5,000 **Est:** 1965 **Hrs:** All year by chance/appt. **Assn:** NHADA **Dir:** 3 mi off Rte 28 on Pleasant Valley Rd, 2 mi S of Wolfeboro. **Own:** Ralph Reed. **QC: 71 54 70**

Frank & Cathy Sykes
320 Pork Hill Rd • 03894
(603)569-0000
neevents@worldpath.net

Dealers in Americana, early painted furniture & folk art. **Pr:** $1-5,000 **Est:** 1958 **Hrs:** By appt only. **QC: 41 48 60 S2 S12**

New York
(Upstate)

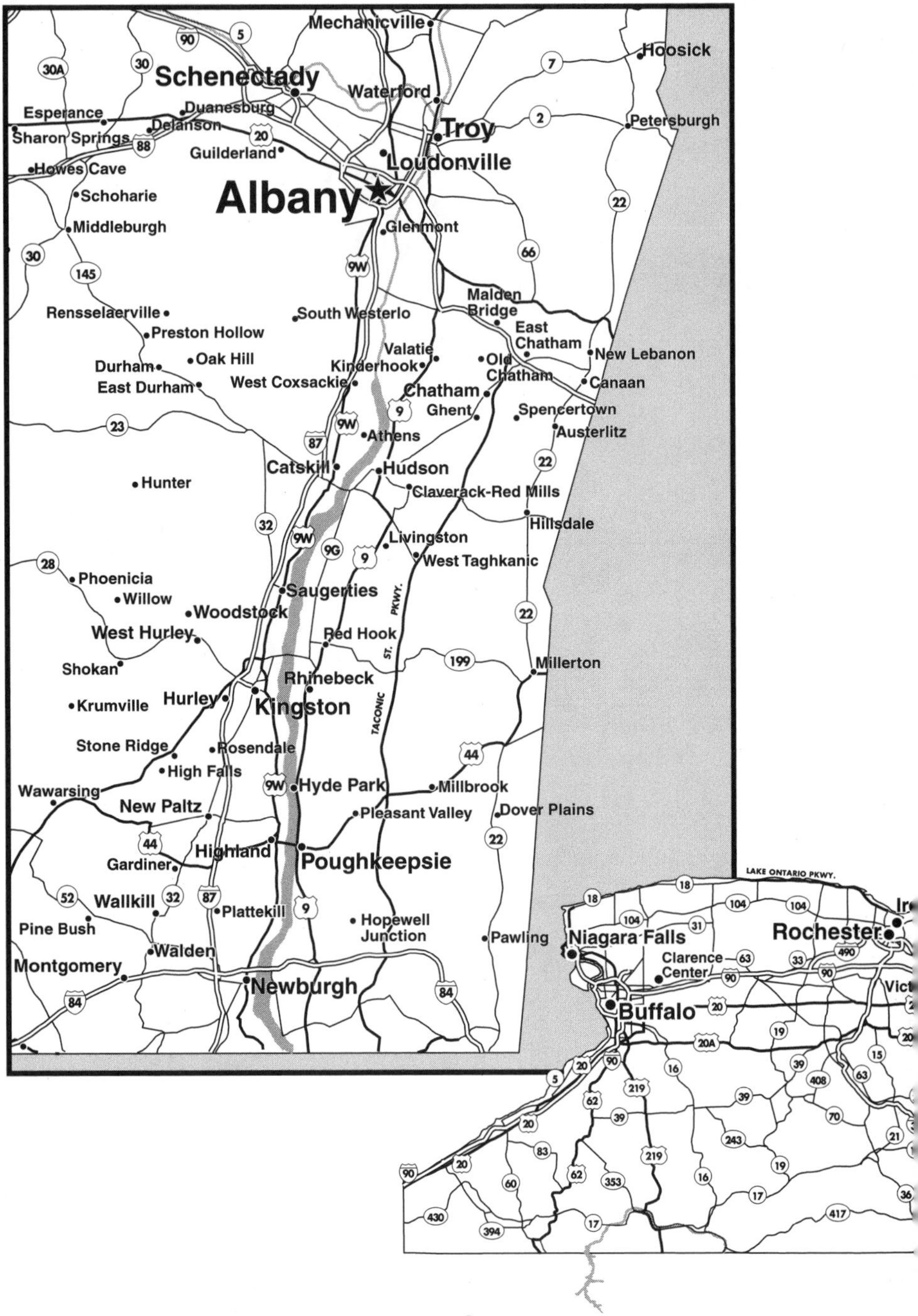

Upstate New York

LEGEND

Interstate Highway

Major U.S. and State Routes

Minor State Routes

Not to Scale

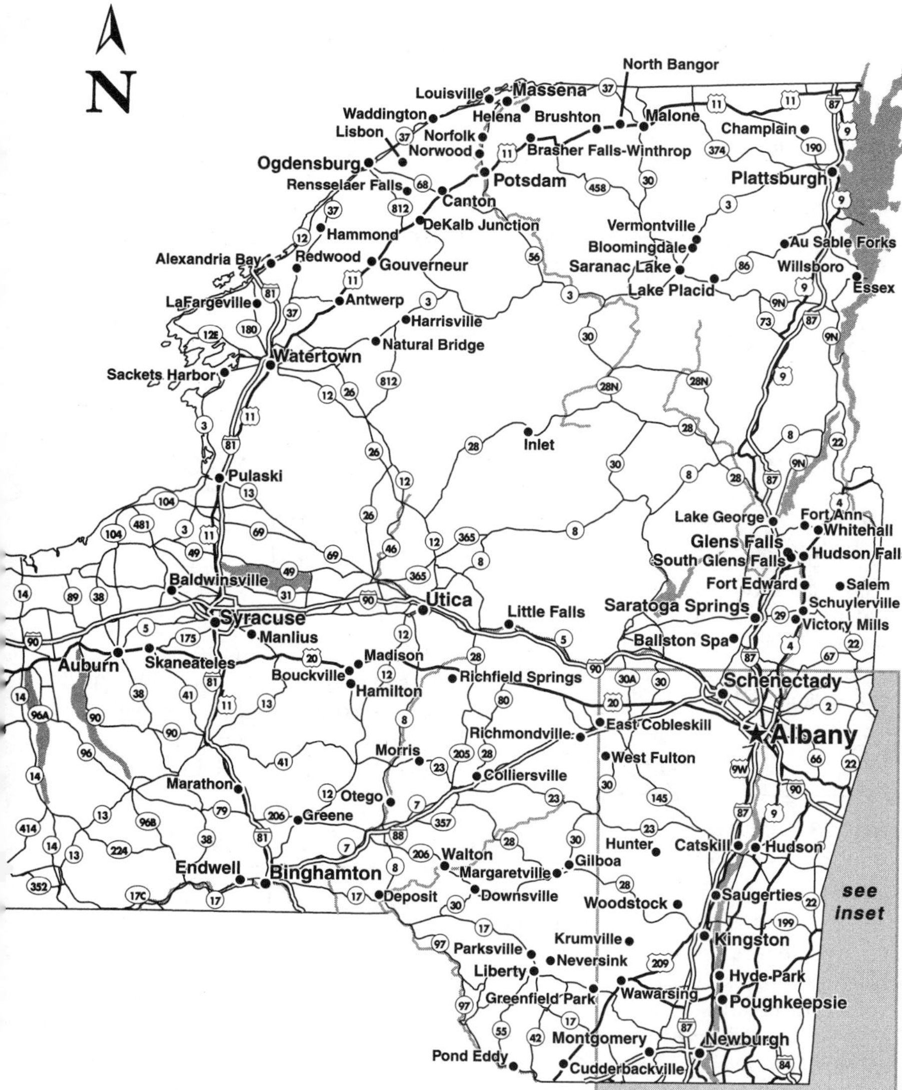

Albany

Architectural Parts Warehouse

83-89 Lexington Ave • 12206
(518)465-2987 • (518)465-2987 (fax)

Architectural antiques. Historic preservation organization that accepts donations of architectural salvage & sells it to fund operations. **Hrs:** Wed-Fri 12-5, Sat 9-5. **Own:** Jeff Dembowski. **QC: 3 S4**

Alexandria Bay

Linda's Little House

22995 Shoulette Rd • 13607
(315)482-5658
lovely@gisco.net

A rustic shop in a beautiful country setting with an ever-changing inventory of affordable collectibles, small antiques & treasures. **Hrs:** By chance or appt. **Dir:** 2 mi from the Alex Bay Drive-In, 1st L off Bailey Settlement Rd, 1st house on L. **Own:** Linda M LaRock.

Port of Call

65 Church St • 13607
(315)482-6544
fberge@gisco.net

Antiquities, tribal art, ethnographics. Historic & prehistoric Native American, stone age, Egyptian & other classical, Oriental & pre-Columbian antiquities **Hrs:** By chance/appt. **QC: 2 42**

Antwerp

Finders Keepers [G]

38515 Rte 11 N • 13608
(315)659-8028

Antiques, collectibles & memorabilia. Extensive general line of merchandise includes glassware, smalls, books, tools, pottery, furniture, household, jewelry. **Hrs:** May-Oct daily 7-7; Nov-Apr by chance/appt. **Own:** Kim Crowner. **QC: 48 61 S6**

Athens

Opera House Antique Center [G50]

21 Second St • 12015
(518)945-3224
operahouseantiques@worldnet.att.net
www.mycommunitynetwork.com

General line. **Hrs:** Tue-Sun 11-5, Sat til 6. **CC:** V/MC/DIS **Dir:** From Hudson: Rip Van Winkle bridge R onto Rte385 N for 5 mi.L onto 2nd St. From Albany: NYS Thruway Exit 21B to Rte 9W S then L onto Schoharie Tpke for 4 mi, turn L onto 2nd St. **Own:** Don Fontaine.

Auburn

Ward's Antiques

Rte 20 • 13021
(315)252-7703

American, Oriental & European antiques. **Est:** 1943 **Hrs:** Mon-Sat 10-6, Sun 1-6. **QC: S1**

Ausable Forks

Don's Antiques

25 N Main St • 12912
(518)647-8422
blaisdell1@KVV1.net

Furniture, Depression, pattern & carnival glass, collectibles, clocks, stoneware, quilts, general line of ancestral paraphernalia. **Hrs:** By chance/appt. **Own:** Rick & Dawn Denette Blaisdell. **QC: 61 35 S7**

Austerlitz

Suzanne Courcier/Robert Wilkins

11463 Rte 22 • 12017
(518)392-5754 • (518)392-5754 (fax)

American antique furnishings. Specializing in furniture & accessories of the Shakers.

Painted & decorated furniture in original condition as well as a good selection of textiles. **Est:** 1974 **Hrs:** By appt only. **Assn:** ADA NHADA **QC: 34 51 57**

Baldwinsville

James William Lowery

30 Canton St • 13027
(518)638-1329

18th & early 19th C furniture, artwork & appropriate accessories. **Hrs:** By appt only. **Assn:** NHADA **Dir:** NY Thruway Exit 39. **QC: 52 7 36**

Ballston Spa

Ballston Spa Antique Center [G18]

217-221 Milton Ave • 12020
(518)885-6746 **Est:** 1989 **Hrs:** Daily 10-5. **Sz:** H **CC:** V/MC/DIS.

Binghamton

Pages of History

(607)724-4983 • (607)724-0120 (fax)

Autographs. **Est:** 1983 **Hrs:** By appt only. **Own:** Jerry Docteur. **QC: 67 39**

Bloomingdale

Buyer's Paradise

Rte 3 • 12913
(518)891-4242

General line including oak & Victorian furniture, glass, china, paintings, lamps, primitives, tools. **Hrs:** Mon-Sat (Sun in Sum & Fall) **Dir:** 5 mi from Saranac Lake on Rte 3 going N toward Plattsburgh. **Own:** Gerald & Barbara Yelle. **QC: 50 58 61**

Sign of the Fish Studio & Gallery

State St & Winter Pl (Rte 3) • 12913
(518)891-2510

Pictures, books, glass, furniture, china, old things for sale. Antiques & art of any moment. **Hrs:** Call for hrs. **Own:** Henry & Virginia Jakobe.

Bouckville

Bittersweet Bazaar

Rte 20 • 13310
(315)893-7229

Country accessories, Old Village paint & tin lighting. **Hrs:** Thu-Tue; Win by chance. **Assn:** MBADA **Dir:** Next to Landmark Tavern. **Own:** Laura Thayer.

Around the Fire

Fireboard: A decorated board used to hide the fireplace opening in summer.

Fireback: Cast iron plate standing behind the fire to protect the brick or stone and to throw the heat forward into the room.

Firescreen: A small screen, usually of fine needlework in a frame, that can be moved up and down a pole rising from a tripod base. Firescreens were used to protect ladies' faces from the direct heat of the fire in order to preserve their fine complexions. As only the complexions of the upper classes appeared to be susceptible to such damage, firescreens are invariably high-quality pieces of furniture.

Fireboards, firebacks, and firescreens were all beautifully decorated and are thus very collectible today.

Bouckville Antique Corner [G20]
Rte 20 • 13310
(315)893-1828

Antiques, books & collectibles. **Hrs:** Daily 10-5. **Sz:** H **CC:** V/MC/DIS.

Brick House Antiques
Rte 20 • 13402
(315)893-7352

18th & 19th C furniture & accessories. **Hrs:** By chance/appt. **Assn:** MBADA **Own:** Kathleen Carney.

The Depot Antique Gallery [G40]
Rte 20 • 13310
(315)893-7676 **Hrs:** Daily 10-5. **Sz:** L **CC:** V/MC/DIS.

The Gallery Co-Op [G20]
Rte 20 • 13310
(315)893-7752

Antique furniture, accessories & collectibles. **Hrs:** Mar-Dec daily 10-5. **Assn:** MBADA **Own:** Lori Rifenburg.

Indian Opening Antique Center [G20]
Rte 20 • 13310
(315)893-7303

Two floors of an 1800s barn filled with furniture, lamps, glass, china, tools, linens, cast iron, primitives & accessories. **Hrs:** Apr 15-Nov 15 daily 10-5. **Assn:** MBADA **Own:** Jim & Pat Gerow.

Jackie's Place
Rte 20 • 13310
(315)893-7457

Vintage jewelry & art deco. **Hrs:** By appt only. **Assn:** MBADA **Own:** Jackie Carrese. **QC: 63 5**

Old Bottle Shop
Rte 20 • 13310
(315)893-7541

Old phones, musical items & bottles. **Assn:** MBADA **Own:** Stewart & Maxine Barber.

Elvira Stanton Antiques
Rte 20 • 13310
(315)893-7479

Dolls, miniatures & toys. **Hrs:** By appt only. **Assn:** MBADA **Own:** Elvira Stanton. **QC: 38 87**

Stone Lodge Antiques
Rte 20 • 13310
(315)893-7263

Oak, trunks, tins, toys, military, Indian, bottles & kitchen collectibles. **Hrs:** Daily 10-5. **Assn:** MBADA.

Veranda Antiques & Art [G20]
Rtes 20 & 12B • 13310
(315)893-7270
verandatq@aol.com

Furniture & accessories. **Hrs:** Daily 10-5 or by appt. **Dir:** Centrally located betw Bouckville & Madison on Rte 20 off Rte 12B S. **Own:** Susan McKee. **QC: 48**

Brasher Falls

Triple R Antiques & Collectibles
Rte 53 • 13613
(315)389-4783

General line. **Hrs:** Thu-Sat 10-4 & by appt. **Dir:** 2 mi betw Brasher Falls & Brasher Center. **Own:** Louise Jenkins.

Brushton

Dizzy Izzy's Antiques
Rte 11 • 12916
(518)529-0424

Antiques, primitives, glass, used furniture, books, paintings. **Hrs:** Open wknds, closed Nov-Apr. **Dir:** Behind the Bank. **Own:** Isabelle Dorey. **QC: 106**

Buffalo

Dana E Tillou Fine Arts & Antiques
417 Franklin St • 14202
(716)854-5285

Period American & English 17th, 18th & 19th C furniture & appropriate accessories. Wide range of paintings. **Est:** 1965 **Hrs:** Wed-Sat 11-5, Tue by appt. **QC: 52 54 7 S1**

Canaan

Iris Cottage Antiques
2068 Rte 295 • 12029
(518)781-4379
akoppel@taconic.net

Early American pattern glass & related glass objects. **Hrs:** May-Sep Sat-Sun 10-5 or by appt. **Dir:** At the blinking light. **QC: 103 61**

Canton

Country Rose Collectibles
31 Plains Rd • 13617
(315)386-1122

General line of antiques, including linens, kitchen items, primitives & small collectibles. **Hrs:** By chance/appt. **Dir:** 10 mi from Canton & minutes from the heart of Crary Mills. **Own:** Sherry Rose.

The Glass Bubble
1278 Old DeKalb Rd • 13617
(315)386-3228

Old & new collectibles, bisque, china, Depression, satin, cranberry & cobalt glass, redware, Heisey, ironstone, crocks, baskets, cookie jars, evening purses, furniture, jewelry. **Hrs:** Open year-round, eves, Sun. Please call in advance. **Dir:** Turn off Rte 68 at Coakley's True-Value Hardware in Canton; 3 mi out on Old Dekalb Rd. **Own:** Terry Faucher. **QC: 61 31 29**

House Portraits & Quilts
12 E Main St • 13617
(315)386-1487 • (315)379-0684 (fax)
ckolson@northnet.org

Artwork, antiques & uniques. **QC: 84**

North Country Bottle Shop
PO Box 417 • 13617
(315)386-8715

Antique bottles, canning jars, insulators, stoneware, general line of antiques. **Hrs:** By appt only. **Own:** John Crary. **QC: 61 31**

Pineapple Place
77 E Main St (Rte 11) • 13617
(315)386-4996

Antiques & traditional crafts. **Dir:** On Rte 11 across from SLU entrance. **Own:** Sheila Hobbs. **QC: S1**

Catskill

Philip & Kathleen Seibel Antiques
40 N Jefferson Ave • 12414
(518)943-2256
seibel@mhonline.net

Early painted country furniture 17th-19th C, early fabrics, folk art & pottery. **Pr:** $50-20,000 **Est:** 1974 **Hrs:** By appt only. **Sz:** M **Dir:** NY Thruway Exit 21: L off ramp, continue 1 mi to N Jefferson Ave, then turn L. Last house on R. **QC: 1 29 34**

Townhouse Antiques
375 Main St • 12414
(518)943-7400

Furniture, pottery, collectibles, toys & postcards. **Hrs:** Call ahead for hrs.

Champlain

Border Antiques

Rte 276 • 12919
(518)298-3791

General line including china, glass, furniture, primitives. **Hrs:** By chance/appt. **Dir:** 2 mi N of Rte 11 on Rte 276. **Own:** Lilah Stiles.

Chatham

Mark Feder & Sons

161 Hudson Ave • 12037
(518)392-3738 • (518)392-7276 (fax)
silverspon@aol.com
www.markfeder.com

Antique sterling silver, flatware & hollowware. Bridal registry. **Est:** 1970 **Hrs:** Mar 1-Nov 30 Tue-Sun 10-5, by chance/appt. **Sz:** S **CC:** AX/V/MC/DIS **Dir:** 1 blk S on Rte 66 on R near intersection with Rte 203. **QC: 78 58 60 S1**

Green Willow Farm

Raup Rd • 12037
(518)392-9654

Furniture & accessories, chrome, glass & leather furnishings, kitchen items, mirrors, tables, chairs, clocks, radios, lighting from 1930s-1950s. **Est:** 1971 **Hrs:** By appt only. **QC: 105**

Sarris Quilts

15 Elm St • 12037
(518)392-6323 • (518)392-6498 (fax)
melissa@sarrisquilts
www.sarrisquilts.com

Quilts, pillows, wall hangings, tote bags. **Est:** 1991 **Hrs:** By chance/appt. **CC:** AX/V/MC **Dir:** Above Crandell Theatre. **Own:** Melissa Sarris. **QC: 84**

Skevington-Back Antiques

1555 County Rte 9 • 12037
(518)392-9056

Period English & Continental furniture, prints & appropriate accessories. **Hrs:** By chance/appt. **Own:** Ruth Back. **QC: 53 54 74**

Beds Great and Small I

In 1430 the Duke of Burgundy had a bed made for his wedding to Princess Isabella of Portugal. It was 19 feet long and 12 feet 6 inches wide. The Duke was presumably able to consummate his marriage and then take his dog for a walk before getting dressed. The Great Bed of Ware, now in the Victoria and Albert Museum, London, is, by comparison, a mere 10 feet 8 inches square. It was made c. 1590 for Sir Henry Fanshaw of Ware, but by 1612 it had been bought by the local inn, the White Hart. Here it must have been a good money maker — in 1700, for instance, Sir Henry Chauncey records that "six citizens and their wives came from London and slept in it." Hopefully these marriages had already been consummated, otherwise the crowding might have led to regrettable errors.

In this country master beds were not confined to private bedrooms until late in the 18th century. Before then they were commonly set in the parlor where the richness of their hangings could be admired by guests.

Tester: The canopy over a four-poster bed, originally of wood, but, by the 18th century, of fabric.

Bed hangings: Curtains surrounding a four-poster bed that not only ensured warmth and privacy but also displayed the family's wealth and good taste. Bed hangings were among the most expensive linens in a colonial household.

Yesteryears
3 Railroad Ave • 12037
(518)392-3949

Furniture & accessories. **Hrs:** Mon-Sat 11-5, Sun 12-5. **Sz:** S **CC:** V/MC.

Clarence

Muleskinner Antiques
10626 Main St • 14031
(716)759-2661 • (716)759-0724 (fax)
www.muleskinnerantiques.com

Painted furniture, folk art, redware & Americana. **Est:** 1973 **Hrs:** Mon-Fri 10-5, Sat-Sun 12-5. **Sz:** L **CC:** V/MC **Own:** Ronald Korman. **QC: 41 1 51 S1**

Claverack

The Dutch House
179 Rte 23 • 12513
(518)851-2011

A high-quality general line specializing in early treenware, baskets, textiles & country antiques. **Est:** 1960 **Hrs:** Apr-Dec 9-6; Jan-Mar by appt only. **Own:** Nellie Ptaszek. **QC: 88 17 80**

Colliersville

Colliersville Cottage Antiques [G11+]
Rte 7 • 13747
(607)432-7427
mrsflew@wpe.com **Hrs:** Daily 11-5. **CC:** AX/V/MC/DIS.

Corning

Margaret S King
10 E First St • 14830
(607)962-0876

18th & 19th C antiques. **Hrs:** By appt only.

Crary Mills

Crary Mills Mighty Mall [G]
(315)386-3483

Antiques, furniture, glassware. **Hrs:** Thu-Sat 10-4. **Dir:** 6 mi from Canton & 7 mi from Potsdam. **Own:** Roger Huntley.

Cudderbackville

Old Red Barn
37 Rte 211 • 12729
(914)754-7122

Turn-of-the-century oak & Victorian furniture. Auctions held on the 1st Sat of the month at 6. **Hrs:** Sat-Sun 9-5, Mon-Fri by appt. **CC:** V/MC/DIS **Own:** Vincent Bambina. **QC: 50 58 S2**

DeKalb Junction

B & W Collectibles
4370 US Hwy 11 • 13630
(315)347-3772

Two buildings containing a large collection of furniture, Depression glass, carnival glass, old tools, primitives, cast iron, cupboards, jewelry, baskets, plus a multitude of collectibles. **Hrs:** Win Sat-Sun 10-5; Sum Thu-Mon 10-5. **Own:** Bob & Wanda Law. **QC: 61 48**

Northern Antiques
Rte 11 • 13630
(315)347-3797

Three buildings filled with furniture, glassware, china, cupboards, primitives, oak, pine. One of the largest dealers in the North Country. New merchandise daily. **Hrs:** Daily 8-4. **Dir:** 3 mi S of DeKalb Jct & 2 mi N of Richville. **Own:** Glenn & Lynn Davis. **QC: 48 61 106 S12**

Delanson

The Attic Antiques
13818 Duanesburg Rd • 12053
(518)875-6635

Furniture, tools, lamps, glass, linens & primitives. **Hrs:** By chance/appt. **Dir:** Rte 7 betw Central Bridge & Quaker St. **Own:** Paul & Barbara Munson.

The Dapper Frog Antiques Center [G]
Rte 7 & Junction Rd • 12053
(518)868-4228

Furniture & smalls. **Hrs:** Wed-Mon 10-5, Sun 12-5; Jan-Feb closed Tue & Wed. **Dir:** I-88 exit 23 (Schoharie/Central Bridge): W 1/2 mi on Rte 7 to corner of Junction Rd.

The Junction Shop
Rte 7 • 12053
(518)295-8987

Furniture, accessories & farm relics. **Hrs:** Sat-Sun 12-5:30, Fri by appt. **Sz:** M **Dir:** I-88 Cloverleaf: 23 E on Rte 7 2 mi.

Middlefield Antiques
1583 Eaton's Corners Rd • 12053
(518)875-6542 • (518)875-6542 (fax)
kdtlasher@aol.com

18th & 19th C American country furniture, primitives & accessories. **Hrs:** By appt only. **Own:** Kathryn Thomas & David Lasher. **QC: 102 106**

Deposit

Axtell Antiques
1 River St • 13754
(607)467-2353 • (607)467-4316 (fax)
rsaxtell@aol.com

Seven rooms filled with American country furniture, cupboards, treenware, early lighting, redware, folk art, baskets, hearth accessories & stoneware. **Hrs:** Mon-Sat 10-4, Sun 12-4. Call ahead advised. **CC:** AX/V/MC/DIS **Own:** Richard Axtell. **QC: 65 102 41**

Dover Plains

Coach House Shop
Old Rte 22 • 12522
(914)832-9532

American Indian jewelry, blown & pattern glass, candlesticks, coin silver, ironstone, lustre, primitives & vinaigrettes. **Hrs:** Sat-Sun 12-8 or by appt. **QC: 42 61**

Downsville

Covered Bridge Gifts & Antiques
Main St (Rtes 30 & 206) • 13755
(607)363-7712 • (607)363-7712 (fax)

Furniture, prints, glass, primitives, tools, quilts. **Hrs:** Mon-Sat 9-5, Sun 10-4; Win by chance/appt. **CC:** V/MC **Dir:** Located at the covered bridge. **Own:** Gary, Carol & Michellee Hood.

Duanesburg

Black Sheep Antique Center [G70]
US Rte 20 • 12056
(518)895-2983

In an early 19th C Dutch barn, late 18th through early 20th C antiques, decorative accessories, jewelry, toys & collectibles. **Hrs:** Daily 10-5. **Sz:** L **CC:** V/MC **Dir:** I-88 Exit 24: 3-1/2 mi W on Rte 20. **Own:** Mary Jane Breedlove. **QC: 1 34 36**

Things
Rte 20 • 12056
(518)462-3436
www.albany.net/~things

Art deco, pottery, Depression glass, furniture, linens & toys. **Hrs:** Fri-Mon 12-4 or by appt. **QC: 5 61**

Durham

Mulberry Bush Antiques

Susquehanna Tpke (Rte 22) • 12422
(518)239-4563

Specializing in country furniture & smalls. **Hrs:** Wed-Mon 9-5. **Own:** Clayton & Shirley Reynolds. **QC: 102**

East Chatham

Anderson American Antiques

Rte 295 • 12060
(518)392-3956

American Federal, neoclassical & country furniture, mirrors, paintings & decorative accessories of the late 18th & early 19th C. **Hrs:** Sat-Sun afternoons or by appt. **Assn:** BCADA **Dir:** 1/4 mi W of Taconic Pkwy. **Own:** Steven & Susan Anderson. **QC: 52 68 36**

Antiques at Peaceable Farm

983 Rte 295 • 12060
(518)392-5157

Primitives, dolls, country furniture & glassware. **Hrs:** Daily. **Dir:** Corn of Rte 295 & Rock City Rd. **QC: 38 61 102**

Richard & Betty Ann Rasso

Village Square (Rte 9) • 12060
(518)392-4501

American antiques, folk art & Shaker furniture & accessories. **Est:** 1952 **Hrs:** By appt only. **Assn:** ADA. **QC: 41 57 1**

East Cobleskill

The Patent Antique Emporium [G]

Rte 145 • 12043
(518)296-8000 **Hrs:** Jan-Jun daily 10-5, Jul-Dec daily 10-6. **Dir:** I-88 Exit 22: 1 mi S on Rte 145.

East Durham

Mooney's Antique & Mercantile [G20]

Rte 145 • 12423
(518)634-2300 • (518)634-2969 (fax)

General line. **Hrs:** Daily 10-5. **Own:** Theresa Cochran. **QC: S2**

Endwell

Fran-Tiques

3300 E Main St • 13760
(607)748-4422

Fine china, chintz, Shelley, jewelry, paper, vintage clothing, prints & Victorian & country furniture. **Est:** 1990 **Hrs:** Thu-Sat 11-6, Mon-Wed & Sun by chance/appt. **CC:** AX/V/MC/DIS **Own:** Fran Marsh. **QC: 102 22 39**

Esperance

Esperance Antique Gallery

19 Main St (Rte 20) • 12066
(518)875-6080

Furniture & accessories. **Hrs:** Wed-Sun 11-6. **CC:** V/MC **Dir:** 1/2 mi off Rte 30 junc. **Own:** Alan Gusse.

Hickory Hill Antiques

3256 State Rte 30 • 12066
(518)875-6133 • (518)875-9141 (fax)
oldquilt@albany.net
www.hickoryhillquilts.com

Antique quilts, tops, blocks, vintage fabric, reproduction fabric, batting & notions. **Hrs:** Wed-Sun 10-7. **CC:** AX/V/MC/DIS **Own:** John & Chris Driessen. **QC: 84**

Essex

Colin & Elizabeth Ducolon

(518)963-7921

Early textiles, flint glass & rural paint. **Hrs:** Sum by appt only. **Assn:** VADA. **QC: 51 80**

Margaret Sayward Antiques

Main St • 12936
(518)963-7828

Charming 1810 Federal house filled with furniture of all styles, clocks, linens, clothing, prints, glass, china & collectibles. **Hrs:** May 22-Oct 19 daily 10-5; Oct-Dec Fri-Sun 10-5 or by chance/appt. **Dir:** Next to Post Office. **QC: 48 35 80 S12**

Fort Ann

Fort Ann Antiques [G8]

Intersection Rtes 4 & 149 • 12827
(518)639-8806

Victorian to country primitive. **Est:** 1997 **Hrs:** Wed-Mon 10-4. **CC:** V/MC **Own:** Stephanie Safka.

George St Antiques

Rtes 4 & 149 • 12827
(518)639-4006

Furniture, glassware, smalls & cookie jars. **Hrs:** Mar 1-Dec 1 Wed-Mon 9-4. **Own:** Anna K Tierney.

Towpath Antiques

Rtes 4 & 149 • 12827
(518)639-8923

Located in an 1839 canal store, offering a variety of antiques & collectibles. **Hrs:** Apr 1-Nov 1 Wed-Mon 9-4. **Own:** Joe & Sally Brillon.

Fort Edward

Weber Antiques

46 East St • 12828
(518)747-8233 • (518)747-2241 (fax)

Furniture, memorabilia, advertisements, artwork, pottery, toys, estate jewelry & clocks. **Hrs:** Daily 8-4:30. **Own:** John Weber. **QC: 48 67 39**

Beds Great and Small II

Four-poster: A bed with four tall corner posts, that may, or may not, support a tester.

Campaign bed: A four poster bed, easily demountable, for use by military officers in the field.

Trundle bed or truckle bed: A low bed on wheels that was kept under a large bed and trundled out at night for use, probably by a child.

Hired man's bed: A narrow slatted bed, often spool turned, produced in quantity by factories in the Midwest and New England between about 1840 and 1890. Despite its name, it was designed as cottage furniture, not for servants.

Bed bench or bed settle: A wooden bench or settle whose box-like seat opened out to form a bed.

Sleigh bed: Bed with curved head- and foot-boards resembling a sleigh. An Empire period design, showing the French influence whose popularity at the time reflected the belief that the French Revolution and the American Revolution were twins.

Gardiner

The Country Store Antique Center [G20]

Rtes 44 & 55 • 12525
(914)255-1123

Antiques, collectibles, furniture, primitives in a delightful country store setting. **Est:** 1987 **Hrs:** Mon-Tue & Thu-Sat 10-5, Sun 11-5. **CC:** AX/V/MC **Assn:** UCADA **Dir:** In the village of Gardiner **Own:** Paul Osgood. **QC: 48 106**

Guilford Station

Rtes 44 & 55 • 12525
(914)255-4349

Country, primitive, Victorian furniture & accessories. **Hrs:** Thu-Sat & Mon-Tue 10-5; Sun 11-5. **Dir:** At Station Sq. **QC: 58 34**

Ghent

Ghent Center Antiques [G]

2237 Rte 66 • 12075
(518)392-9681

Oak furniture, glassware & dolls. **Est:** 1996 **Hrs:** Thu-Mon 10-5, Sun 11-4. **CC:** AX/V/MC/DIS **Own:** Max & Yvonne Slominski & Ron Moore. **QC: 50 38 61**

Gilboa

Day-Barb Antiques

Rte 145/81 • 12076
(607)588-9435

Furniture, glassware, china & lamps. **Hrs:** By chance/appt. **Own:** Barbara DeWitt.

Glenmont

Charles F Breuel Antiques

(518)439-6717
cfbclock@aol.com

American timepieces, 19th C American furniture & appropriate accessories including paintings, baskets & boxes. **Hrs:** By appt only. **CC:** V/MC **Assn:** NHADA VADA GSAAA **Own:** Charles & Lori Breuel. **QC: 35 34 36**

Glens Falls

Glenwood Manor Antiques [G35]

60 Glenwood Ave • 12801
(518)798-4747

General line. **Hrs:** Mon-Sat 10-5, Sun 12-5; Jul-Aug Mon-Sat 10-6, Sun 12-6. **Dir:** 20 min N of Saratoga & 10 min S of Lake George outlets. **Own:** Paul McMore

Gouverneur

JW Antiques

157 W Main St • 13642
(315)287-1745

Furniture (refinished & rough), primitives, collectibles, glassware & refinished trunks. **Hrs:** Open Fri-Sun. Mon-Thu by chance/appt. **Own:** Don & Gloria Walker. **QC: 48 106 32**

Smith Antiques

151 W Main St • 13642
(315)287-2271

Refinished furniture, lamps, pottery, flow blue. Signed art & cut glass & various collectibles. **QC: 48 32 100**

Greene

Grandma Kate's Antiques

41 Genesee St • 13778
(607)656-9877

Furniture & decorative accessories. **Hrs:** Daily 10-5. **CC:** V/MC **Own:** George Rood.

Pheasant Farm [G50]

7 Foundry St • 13778
(607)656-9188

Turn-of-the-century furnishings, pottery, glassware, artwork, toys, books, prints, collectibles. **Est:** 1990 **Hrs:** Daily 10-5 (closed New Year's). **Sz:** H **CC:** V/MC **Own:** Nels & Margaret Buchanan.

Greenfield Park

Apple Tree Antiques

Caston Rd Ext • 12435
(914)647-7651

Depression glass, furniture, carnival glass, pottery & miscellaneous smalls. **Hrs:** Fri-Sun 11-5, by chance/appt. Jan-Mar by appt only. **Assn:** UCADA **Dir:** Rte 52 W from Ellenville to Caston Rd, Exit 2. **Own:** Elma Reider.

Guilderland

Hamilton House Antique Center [G40+]

2261 Western Ave • 12084
(518)862-0001

Fine furniture, artwork, glass, linens, lighting, vintage toys & sports. **Hrs:** Wed-Fri 10-6, Thu til 10-8, Sat-Sun 10-5. **CC:** V/MC/DIS **Dir:** 1/4 mi W of Rte 155 on Rte 20; mins from the Northway. **Own:** Steve Farina.

Hamilton

The Gin Mill Antique Center [G20]

Rte 12B S & Middleport Rd • 13346
(315)824-4911

Quilts, linens, sports, fishing lures, Victorian lighting, custom shades, pottery, kitchenware, dolls, games, jewelry, furniture, glassware & reproductions. **Hrs:** Wed-Sun 10-5. **CC:** V/MC/DIS **Dir:** 10 min S of Bouckville.

Hammond

McWharf's Country Treasures

Black Lake Rd • 13646
(315)375-4460

Depression & carnival glass. **Hrs:** By chance/appt. **Dir:** Between Hammond & Edwardsville. **Own:** Don & Sue McWharf. **QC: 61**

TLC Antiques

St Lawrence Ave • 13646
(315)324-5383

Furniture, clocks, crocks, decoys, china, fishing lures, lamps, vintage clothing, postcards, books, prints, tools, toys, small collectibles. **Dir:** In center of village, turn at light on Rte 37 onto St Lawrence Ave. Hammond is 21 mi S of Odgensburg, 15 mi N of Alexandria Bay & 37 mi N of Watertown. **Own:** Tom & Betty Chapman. **QC: S12**

Harrisville

Antiques by the Lake

Rte 3 • 13648
(315)543-7535

Antiques, collectibles, glassware, kerosene lamps, crocks, jugs, linens, furniture, gifts. **Hrs:** By chance/appt. **Dir:** 2 mi W of

Harrisville on Rte 3. **Own:** Mel & Leanna Trombley.

Atkinson Enterprises
Rte 3 • 13648
(315)543-2474

Pressed back chairs & early oak. 200+ refinished chairs in stock in singles & sets. Also collectibles, old tools & other antiques. **Hrs:** By chance/appt. **Dir:** 1 mi E of Harrisville on Rte 3 by the Rte 812 turn-off. **Own:** Richard Atkinson. **QC: 50**

Helena

Gray's Millstream
15 Main St • 13649
(315)764-1564

Specializing in stoneware, woodenware & tools. General line of antiques & collectibles including furniture, glass, Art Deco, paintings, prints, ceramics, textiles, toys, cast iron & paper. **Hrs:** Nov-May Wed. Other times by chance/appt. **Own:** Madeline Gray. **QC: 31 86**

Lantry's Antiques
Depot St • 13649
(315)769-5641

General line of early country furniture, refinished & as found. Also some china, paintings, primitives, Ironstone, hooked rugs, postcards & collectibles. **Hrs:** By chance/appt. **QC: 102 106**

High Falls

Linger Corner Gift Company
8 Second St • 12440
(914)687-7907 • (914)687-7907 (fax)

Antiques & gifts for the home & garden. **Hrs:** Wed-Thu 11-5, Fri-Sat 11-6, Sun 10-5; call for Win hrs. **CC:** V/MC **Own:** Michelle Lay. **QC: 48**

Marilyn's Yesteryear
Leggett Rd • 12440
(914)687-9344

Porcelain, silver, fine arts, furniture & collectibles. **Hrs:** By chance/appt.

Highland

Highland Antique & Art Center
Rtes 44 & 55 • 12525
(914)691-5577

Furniture, clocks & country in an historic bank building. **Hrs:** Mon-Tue & Thu-Fri 11-5, Sat 10-5, Sun 12-5. **Dir:** Off Rte 9 at junc with Rtes 44 & 55.

Hillsdale

Pax Antiques
Rte 23 • 12529
(518)325-3974

Victoriana, Noveau, Deco, jewelry, advertising items. **Est:** 1972 **Hrs:** Daily 11-6. **Dir:** E of Rte 22. **Own:** Nickie & Jerry Frankel. **QC: 89 5 39**

Red Fox Antiques
9315 State Rte 22 • 12529
(518)325-3841 • (518)325-3841 (fax)

Americana, including country & high-style furniture, fine art, porcelain & appropriate decorative accessories. **Hrs:** Fri-Mon 11-5 or by appt. **Own:** Marilyn R Simon & Carlos Justiniano. **QC: 1 52 7**

Hoosick

Hoosick Antiques Center [G65]

NY Rte 7 • 12089
(518)686-4700

General line. **Est:** 1987 **Hrs:** Mon-Sat 10-5, Sun 12-5. **CC:** V/MC/DIS **Own:** Joe & Anita Hervieux.

Hopewell Junction

Hopewell Antique Center [G24]

Jct Rtes 82 & 376 • 12533
(914)221-3055

Four floors of furniture, glass, linens, fine jewelry, coins, baseball cards, books, paintings. Fine jewelry repair & porcelain restoration. **Est:** 1984 **Hrs:** Daily 11-5. **Dir:** 3 mi S of Taconic Pwy. **Own:** Douglas McHoul. **QC: 48 61 39 S16**

Wiccopee Antiques

Old Grange Rd • 12533
(914)896-7956
wicctiques@aol.com

Antique wicker, furniture, glassware, records, books, prints, tools, pottery. **Pr:** $0.50-1,000 **Est:** 1969 **Hrs:** May 1-Oct 31 Fri-Sun 11-5 or by appt. **Sz:** S **Dir:** On Rte 52 5 mi E of Fishkill. **Own:** Ed & Dianne Hickman. **QC: 48 32 60**

Howes Cave

Cavern View Antiques

Barnerville Rd • 12092
(518)296-8052

19th C furniture & decorative items. **Hrs:** By chance/appt. **Own:** Jim & Mara Kerr. **QC: S1 S12**

Hudson

20th Century

556 Warren St • 12534
(518)822-8907 • (518)822-0946 (fax)
centuryfr@aol.com

1920s-1950s furniture & decorations. **Hrs:** Mem Day-Lab Day Thu-Tue 11-5; Win Thu-Mon 11-5. **CC:** V/MC **Own:** Frank Rosa. **QC: 105**

Abyssinia Antiques

524 Warren St • 12534
(518)828-5163 • (518)822-0377 (fax)

Fine 18th-20th C furniture & decorations. **Hrs:** Wknds & by appt. **Sz:** L **Own:** Gene Hovis. **QC: 48 36**

Antiques at 601

601 Warren St • 12534
(518)822-0201

18th, 19th & 20th C American & Continental furniture, decorative arts & industrial objects. **Hrs:** Thu-Mon 11:30-5, Tue by chance/appt. **Own:** David Petrovsky. **QC: 52 36 53**

Arenskjold Antiques & Art

537 Warren St • 12534
(518)828-2800

European antiques, paintings, decorative objects. **Hrs:** Thu-Tue 11-5. **Own:** Kim & Jennifer Arenskjold. **QC: 7 53 65**

The Armory Art & Antiques Gallery [G70+]

State & N Fifth Sts • 12534
(518)822-1477
www.hvareaweb.com/armory.htm

Furniture, lighting, architectural items & paintings. **Hrs:** Thu-Mon 11-5. **Own:** Edward Keegan.

The Benson House [G14]

306 Warren St • 12534
(518)822-0277 • (518)822-0874 (fax)
ber01544@berk.com

www.hvareaweb.com/benson.htm

Antique, art & design center. Also a B & B. **Hrs:** Thu-Mon 11-6. **CC:** AX/V/MC/DIS **Own:** Charles & Marlene Berlt.

Botanicus Antiques

446 Warren St • 12534
(518)828-0520 • (518)828-0971 (fax)

Fine period 18th & 19th C antiques for home & garden set in a beautifully restored c 1790 Federal townhouse & gardens. **Hrs:** Fri-Mon 11-5, Tue & Thu by chance/appt. **Own:** Philip Alavare & Edwin Geissler. **QC: 60 53 25**

The British Accent

537 Warren St • 12534
(518)828-2800

19th & 20th C English & American furniture & accessories. **Hrs:** Thu-Tue 11-5. **Own:** Rosalind Ashford. **QC: 54 52**

Bryant Farms Antiques & Auctions

5498 Rte 9H • 12534
(518)851-9061

Antiques & collectibles. Auctions 1st Tue of month. **Hrs:** Sat-Sun 9-5. **Sz:** H **Own:** Del Delaurentis.

Carriage House Antiques

454 Union St • 12534
(518)828-0365

19th & 20th C furniture, accessories & artwork. **Hrs:** Thu-Mon 11-5. **Dir:** Just off the corn of S 5th & Warren fronting Cherry Alley. **QC: 59 36 7**

Davis & Hall

362 1/2 Warren St • 12534
(518)822-8258
gallery@mhonline.net

Contemporary painting, sculpture & country furniture. **Hrs:** Fri-Mon 11-5. Thu by appt only. **CC:** AX/V/MC **Own:** John Davis. **QC: 7 102**

Howard Dawson

701 Warren St • 12534
(518)822-9775 • (607)369-2708 (fax)

18th & 19th C Continental furniture, English & Continental porcelain, lamps & accessories. **Hrs:** Thu-Mon 12-5, Tue-Wed by chance/appt. **QC: 53 36**

Doyle Antiques

711 Warren St • 12534
(518)828-3929 • (518)828-3929 (fax)
doyle@mhonline.net

Fine quality Continental, American & English furniture & decorative accessories. Dining tables, chairs, desks, sofas, mirrors, paintings, clocks, architectural items & garden urns. **Hrs:** Thu-Tue 11-5, Wed by chance/appt. **Sz:** M **CC:** AX/V/MC **Assn:** BCADA HADA **Own:** Timothy Doyle & Sarah Lipsky. **QC: 53 52 54**

Eustace & Zamus Antiques

422-1/2 Warren St • 12534
(518)822-9200 • (518)822-8354 (fax)

Country & formal furniture, folk art to fancy, all in premium condition set in a beautiful historic Victorian townhouse. **Pr:** $200-3,500 **Est:** 1997 **Hrs:** Mon & Thu-Fri 12-5, Sat-Sun 11-5:30. **Sz:** M **CC:** AX/V/MC **Own:** Susanne Davino. **QC: 52 41 34 S15 S16**

Fern

554 Warren St • 12534
(518)828-2886

Primitives & folk art, industrial objects, garden accessories. **QC: 41 60**

Foxfire Ltd

538 Warren St • 12534
(518)828-6281

Oriental art & English porcelain through 19th C; Sheffield silver, furniture & paintings. **Est:** 1974 **Hrs:** Thu-Tue 11-5, call ahead off season. **CC:** V/MC **Own:** John Anderson. **QC: 71 78 23**

Glenbrook Antiques

433 Warren St • 12534
(518)822-9782
mingus@ulster.net

American classical furniture, English & Continental furniture, silver, decorative accessories & 19th & early 20th C paintings. **Est:** 1980 **Hrs:** Fri-Mon 12-5 or by chance/appt. **Own:** Jason Komyathy. **QC: 52 78 36**

Hallam & Swope

415 Warren St • 12534
(518)822-0326

American Empire, early 19th C European, Roman antiquities. **Hrs:** Thu-Tue 11-5. **Own:** Jonathan Hallam. **QC: 52 53 2**

Judith Harris Antiques

608 Warren St • 12534
(518)822-1371

Early 19th to mid-20th C English & American pottery & porcelain, textiles, paintings, furniture. Decorative accents & surprises of two centuries. **Est:** 1993 **Hrs:** Sun-Mon & Thu-Fri 11-5, Sat 10:30-5:30, Tue by appt. **Sz:** M. **QC: 52 23 36**

Antiques by John Hicks

725 Warren St • 12534
(518)822-0449

Fine 18th & 19th C American, Continental & English furniture, clocks, small curiosities, accessories & garden architecture. **Hrs:** Thu-Mon 10:30-6. **CC:** V/MC. **QC: 52 53 35**

Hudson Antiques Associates [G4]

357 Warren St • 12534
(518)828-6982 • (518)828-7134 (fax)
haa@berk.com

17th-19th C American period furnishings, paintings, prints, folk art & accessories. Decorative, European & Asian antiques of

Beds Great and Small III

Bedstead-washstand: A piece of furniture resembling a secretary, in which the "desk" opened to a washstand, and the "bookcase" to a bed. An extreme example of Victorian ingenuity, but there were many like it, showing that even by the end of the 19th century, living rooms were still slept in.

Bedmoss: A fibrous growth on trees, sometimes called Spanish moss, used for bed stuffing.

Bed warmer: A long-handled brass or copper pan that held hot coals for warming the bed. Called a "warming pan" in England.

Bed pole: Either the poles running between the tops of the bed posts to support the hangings, or a long-handled paddle used for smoothing the sheets when making a bed kept in the corner of a room.

Bed steps: A set of two or three steps, sometimes with a compartment for a chamber pot, to help the elderly, the delicate, and the short-legged get in and out of high beds.

Bedding-down candle: A short candle that burned for only 15 or 20 minutes and extinguished itself after one had gone to bed. The stub ends of regular candles were often used in this way.

N.B. Period beds often need to be lengthened to accommodate today's taller people: this is an acceptable reconfiguration.

all periods. **Pr:** $100-50,000 **Est:** 1997 **Hrs:** Fri-Mon 11-5, Tue-Thu by appt. **Sz:** L **CC:** AX/V/MC **Own:** Ralph Leed, Dolores Murphy, Roderic Blackburn & Michael Black. **QC: 1 8 12 S1 S8 S18**

Hudson House American Antiques

415 Warren St • 12534
(518)828-1024 • (518)828-1024 (fax)
bahh@capital.net

19th & 20th C American paintings, sculpture, folk art & furniture. **Hrs:** Thu-Tue 11-5, Wed by chance/appt. **Own:** Bonnie Andretta. **QC: 7 41**

Hudson Photographic Center

611 Warren St • 12534
(518)828-2178

Antique cameras, vintage prints & any photographic related material, garden antiques & furniture. **Pr:** $1.00-5,000 **Est:** 1987 **Hrs:** Mon-Fri 9-5, Sat 10-5. **Sz:** M **CC:** AX/V/MC/DIS **Own:** Scott Neven. **QC: 73 3 102 S8**

Hulsey-Kelter Antiques

421 Warren St • 12534
(518)822-1927

Antiques from a diverse range of cultures chosen for uniqueness & graphic, sculptural or textural appeal. **Hrs:** Thu-Mon 11-5, Tue-Wed by appt.

Peter Jung Art & Antiques

537 Warren St • 12534
(518)828-2698
pjthecj@capital.net

Fine American & European art from 1850-1950. **Hrs:** Thu-Tue 11-5. **Dir:** On the mezzanine level of Arenskjold Antiques Art. **QC: 7**

Kendon

508 Warren St • 12534
(518)822-8627 • (518) 822-0398

Americana, tramp art, folk art & vintage toys. **Hrs:** Thu-Tue 11-5:30. **QC: 1 41 87**

Kermani Oriental Rugs

348-1/2 Warren St • 12534
(518)828-4804 • (518)828-1640 (fax)
kermani@taconic.net

Affordable classic textiles, vintage & modern, featuring exemplary pieces from select current productions. **Hrs:** By appt only.

Keystone

746-750 Warren St • 12534
(518)822-1019 • (518)822-1018 (fax)
keystone@berk.com

Architectural, lighting & plumbing fixtures, decorative & garden objects. **Hrs:** Thu-Mon 9-5. **Own:** James R Godman Jr. **QC: 3 65 36**

Lawrence P Kohn

624 Warren St • 12534
(518)822-1924

Eclectic antiques. **Hrs:** Thu-Sun 11-5.

Larry's Back Room Antiques

612 Warren St • 12534
(518)477-2643
lforman@nycap.rr.com

Ephemera, postcards, sheet music, books, furniture, collectibles. **Est:** 1991 **Hrs:** Fri-Sun 11-5. **Own:** Larry Forman. **QC: 39 18**

Michael Phillip Law & Jacqueline & Frank Donegan

409 Warren St • 12534
(518)822-0880

American classical furniture, period accessories & unusual pieces from the 20th C. **Hrs:** Thu-Tue 11-5:30. **QC: 1 52 65 S1 S9**

Mark's Antiques
612 Warren St • 12534
(518)766-3937

Specializing in all categories. Look & surface our specialties. **Est:** 1989 **Hrs:** Thu-Mon 11-5. **QC: 3 7 48**

David & Bonnie Montgomery Antiques
526 Warren St • 12534
(518)822-0267 • (518)822-0267 (fax)

French & European antiques & decorative accessories, mirrors, lamps, sconces, screens, garden accents & architectural elements. **Pr:** $500-5,000 **Hrs:** Thu-Mon 11-5 or by appt. **Sz:** M **Own:** David & Bonnie Montgomery. **QC: 47 3 60 S12**

Vincent R Mulford
711 Warren St • 12115
(518)828-5489

Objects & furnishings from America & beyond. **Hrs:** Fri-Sun 11-5, Mon-Thu by appt.

9 Pieces
621 Warren St • 12534
(518)822-8131

Country, primitive & painted furniture & art. **QC: 34 51**

Noonan Antiques
551 Warren St • 12534
(518)828-5779

18th-20th C American & Continental furniture, decorations & eccentricities. **Est:** 1989 **Hrs:** Thu-Mon 11-5, Sat til 6, Tue-Wed by chance/appt. **Own:** Tom Noonan. **QC: 52 53 36**

Northstar Antiques
502 Warren St • 12534
(518)822-1563

Antiques, decorative objects & artwork from the 18th-20th C. Specializing in Hudson Valley antiques, mirrors, paintings, textiles, folk art, architectural items & decorative objects from witty to formal. **Hrs:** Fri-Mon 11-5, Tue & Thu by chance. **Own:** William Lohrman. **QC: 102 36 41**

Alain Pioton Antiques
536 Warren St • 12534
(518)828-9920 • (518)822-8351 (fax)

18th-20th C French & Continental furniture & accessories. **Est:** 1985 **Hrs:** Thu-Fri & Sun-Tue 11-5, Sat 10-6. **CC:** AX/V/MC. **QC: 53 47 36**

Portobello Antiques
441 Warren St • 12534
(518)828-2035 • (518)828-2035 (fax)

18th & 19th C European & English furniture. **Hrs:** Thu-Sun 12-5:30. **CC:** AX/V/MC **Own:** Ben Izett. **QC: 53 54**

Quartermoon
528 Warren St • 12534
(518)828-0728

20th C furniture & decorative accessories. **Est:** 1993 **Hrs:** Thu-Mon 11-5. **CC:** V/MC **Own:** Kay Bradshaw. **QC: 59 105**

Thurley Randolph Antiques
434 Warren St • 12534
(518)822-1376
thurley@epix.net
www.trandolphantiques.com

19th & 20th C furnishings for home & garden (American, Continental & Asian), decorative accessories & lighting. **Pr:** $800-5,000 **Est:** 1997 **Hrs:** May-Dec Thu-Tue 11-5; Jan-Apr Thu-Mon 11-5. **Sz:** M. **QC: 52 59 36**

Relics
448 Warren St • 12534
(518)828-4247

19th & 20th C decorative furniture & objets d'art. **Hrs:** Thu-Mon 11-5, Sun 12-5. **Sz:** L **CC:** V/MC **Own:** Kathy Pakay. **QC: 59 11**

Florence Sack Ltd

602 Warren St • 12534
(518)822-0363

Period 17th through early 20th C furniture. An eclectic selection plus accessories & lamps. **Pr:** $300-10,000+ **Est:** 1979 **Hrs:** Fri-Sun 11-5. **Sz:** L. **QC: 48 53 54**

Savannah Antiques

535 Warren St • 12534
(518)822-1343 • (518)822-1343 (fax)

Quality architectural & garden elements, formal & country furnishings. **Pr:** $1-25,000 **Est:** 1992 **Hrs:** Sat-Sun 11-5, Mon-Tue & Thu-Fri by chance/appt. **Sz:** L **CC:** AX **Own:** Anita & Phil Boyd. **QC: 3 60 48**

K Stair Antiques

621 Warren St • 12534
(518)828-3351 • (518)828-3351 (fax)

17th, 18th & 19th C English & Continental furniture & decoration. **Pr:** $30-10,500 **Est:** 1998 **Hrs:** Mon & Thu-Sat 11-5, Sun 12-5 or by appt. **Own:** Katrina Stair. **QC: 54 53**

A Sutter Antiques

556 Warren St • 12534
(518)822-0729 • (518)822-0946 (fax)
asutter@aol.com

18th & 19th C furniture & decorations. **Hrs:** Thu-Tue 11-5, call ahead off season. **CC:** V/MC **Own:** Frank Rosa & Alfons Sutter. **QC: 48**

Frank Swim Antiques

430 Warren St • 12534
(518)822-0411

Eclectic late 19th & early 20th C furniture, lighting, glass, decorative accessories. **Est:** 1995 **Hrs:** Thu-Mon 11-5, Sat til 6. **QC: 65 59 105**

Theron Ware Antiques

548 Warren St • 12534
(518)828-9744

17th-19th C American & Continental furniture, garden & architectural objects. **Hrs:** Fri-Mon 11-5, Tue & Thu 12-5. **Own:** Michael Egan & Christopher Boslet. **QC: 48 60 3**

Uncle Sam Antiques

545 Warren St • 12534
(518)828-2341

Furniture, smalls & glassware. **Hrs:** By chance/appt. **Own:** Tom Barron & Bruce Kalbacher. **QC: 48 61 S16**

Kevin Walker Antiques

18 N Fifth St • 12534
(518)822-1812

New York furniture, art, lighting & decorative objects. **Hrs:** By appt only. **QC: 48 7 65**

Walker's Mill Antiques

549 Warren St • 12534
(518)822-8016 • (518)822-8543 (fax)

Continental furnishings; specializing in Biedermeier, Swedish & Danish. **Est:** 1997 **Hrs:** Mon-Sat 11-5, Sun 12-5. **Sz:** H **CC:** AX/V/MC/DIS **Own:** Jozef Anvin. **QC: 53**

K West Antiques

715 Warren St • 12534
(518)822-1960

Furniture, Arts & Crafts, art pottery, lamps, artwork. Comfortable, affordable, easy to live with. **Hrs:** Thu-Fri & Mon 11-4, Sat & Sun 11-5. **QC: 6 91 101**

Whatnot Shop & Auction Service

525 Warren St • 12534
(518)822-1413

Oak, walnut, mahogany, cherry, pine, old quilts, cut & Depression glass, sterling & silver plate, cupboards, stoneware. Country auction in Columbiaville, 5 mi N of Hudson. **Hrs:** Mon-Sat 10-4. **Own:** Richard & Lois Tanner. **QC: S2**

Hannah Williamson Antiques
438-1/2 Warren St • 12534
(518)822-8512 • (518)822-8512 (fax)

Diversity & delight: decorative, serious & whimsical objects of earlier times. **Pr:** $30-4,000 **Est:** 1997 **Hrs:** Thu-Mon 11-5. **Sz:** M **CC:** V/MC **Own:** Hannah Williamson & George Cornaccio. **QC:** **54 1 41**

Benjamin Wilson House Antiques
513 Warren St • 12534
(518)822-0866

Unique American urban & country furniture & decorations. **Hrs:** Thu-Tue 11-5 or by appt. **QC:** **48 36**

Anna's
221 Main St • 12839
(518)747-2662

Collectibles, jewelry, glassware & kitchen items. **Hrs:** Mon-Sat 10-5. **CC:** V/MC **Own:** Shirley Miller. **QC:** **32 61**

Hunter

American Gothic Antiques
Main St • 12442
(518)263-4836

19th & 20th C lighting, custom mica shades. **Hrs:** Thu-Sun 11-5. **Own:** Joe Valerio. **QC:** **65**

Hurley

Van Deusen House Antiques
11 Main St • 12443
(914)331-8852

Country & formal furnishings, early porcelain, glass, Orientals, tools, paper ephemera in 18th C Landmark District. **Est:** 1960 **Hrs:** Daily 10-5 by chance/appt **Sz:** M **CC:** AX/V/MC **Assn:** UCADA **Dir:** NYS Thruway Exit 19: 2-1/2 mi S of Kingston, 2 blks off Rte 209 S. **Own:** Jonathan & Iris Oseas. **QC:** **39 34 23 S1**

Hyde Park

Hyde Park Antiques Center [G50]
544 Albany Post Rd (Rte 9) • 12538
(914)229-8200

Period furniture, silver, porcelain, art pottery, glassware, estate & costume jewelry, commemoratives, toys, dolls, antique prints & paintings, fishing lures & art deco. **Est:** 1980 **Hrs:** Daily 10-5. **Sz:** H.

The Village Antique Center at Hyde Park [G35]
597 Albany Post Rd (Rte 9) • 12538
(914)229-6600

General line. **Hrs:** Daily 10-5. **CC:** AX/V/MC/DIS **Own:** Rose Gaches.

Inlet

Parkwood Farm Antiques
(315)357-2973

18th & early 19th C American furniture, accessories & textiles. **Est:** 1970 **Hrs:** By appt only. **Own:** Jane T Reilly. **QC:** **52 80**

Kinderhook

Kinderhook Antiques Center [G]
Rte 9H • 12106
(518)758-7939

American antiques & decorative arts. **Est:** 1980 **Hrs:** Win Mon-Fri 9-4, Sat-Sun 9-5; Sum daily 9-5. **CC:** V/MC **Dir:** 7 mi S of I-90.

R H Blackburn & Associates — The Pavilion Gallery

17 Broad St • 12106
(518)758-1788 • (518)758-6211 (fax)
blackburn@berk.com
www.b6.com

18th & 19th C American paintings & period furnishings, related decorative arts, antique firearms, historical medals, antiquarian & regional books. **Pr:** $100-50,000 **Est:** 1995 **Hrs:** Sat 11-6, Sun 12-6 or by chance/appt. **Sz:** M **CC:** AX/V/MC **Dir:** On Rte 9 in village. 20 mi from Albany, 12 mi from Hudson. **Own:** Roderic H Blackburn. **QC: 1 4 7 S1 S16 S18**

Kingston

Bear Antiques

Rte 32 S • 12401
(914)338-8737

Bears, dolls, Steiff animals, porcelain & glass as well as 19th C furniture & accessories. **Hrs:** Thu-Sun 11-5. **Own:** G Lowe & J Fairclough. **QC: 87**

Catskill Mountain Antique Center [G30]

Rte 28 • 12401
(914)331-0880 **Est:** 1984 **Hrs:** Mon-Tues & Thu-Sat 10-5, Sun 11-5. **Dir:** NY Thruway Exit 19: 2 mi W of Kingston traffic circle.

Cedar Hill Antiques

552 Lucas Ave • 12401
(914)331-3979

18th C American furniture & accessories. **Hrs:** By appt only. **Own:** Robert Slater. **QC: 52**

Holiday Hill Antiques & Restoration Services

66 Holiday Ln • 12401
(914)340-9090

Specializing in country furnishings, paper, 18th-20th C items. **Hrs:** By appt only. **Dir:** Fifth R off Miller's Ln. **QC: S16**

Home Antiques & Furnishings

45 N Front St • 12401
(914)331-6463

Offering fine country & formal antiques, distinctive furnishings & accessories. **Hrs:** Daily 11-6 or by appt. **Dir:** NYS Thruway Exit 19.

N & L's Emporium [G]

25 Broadway • 12401
(914)331-8709

Antiques & collectibles. **Hrs:** Sat-Sun 11-4.

Outback Antiques

72 Hurley Ave • 12401
(914)331-4481

Antique & vintage clothing, textiles, hats, linens, bedding & costume jewelry. **Hrs:** Wed-Mon 10-5. **QC: 63 80 83**

Skillypot Antique Center [G21]

41 Broadway • 12401
(914)338-6779

Furniture, glass/china, jewelry, clothes, Americana, gifts, collectibles. **Est:** 1980 **Hrs:** Thu-Tue; Jan-Mar closed Tue-Thu. **Sz:** L **CC:** AX/V/MC/DIS.

Velsani Arts & Antiques Inc

334 Wall St • 12401
(914)340-0409 • (914)340-0408 (fax)

17th, 18th, 19th, 20th C decorative arts. **Hrs:** By appt only.

Jack & Mary Ellen Whistance

288 Rte 28 • 12401
(914)338-4397

18th & 19th C country furniture, paintings, glass, bottles, marbles & other decorative objects. **Hrs:** By chance/appt. **Dir:** NY Thruway Exit 19: 1 mi W on Rte 28. **QC: 52 61**

Widow Davis Tavern Antiques

2906 Rte 209 • 12401
(914)339-0600 • (914)339-0660 (fax)

The old, the new, the classic & the eccentric wrapped in an exquisite 17th C stone house. **Hrs:** Thu-Mon 11-6. **CC:** V/MC **Dir:** On Rte 209 N of the village of Stone Ridge. **Own:** Alan Brasington & Rita Lutsky. **QC: 48**

Zaborski Emporium

27 Hoffman St • 12401
(914)338-6465 • (914)331-8608 (fax)
nytn@ulster.net

Architectural details, lighting fixtures, antiques hardware, iron fencing, doors, antique plumbing fixtures, pedestal sinks, clawfoot tubs, housewares, advertising, Lionel trains, restaurant equipment, wood stoves. **Pr:** $1-20,000 **Hrs:** Wed-Sat 11-5, Sun 1-5. **Sz:** H **Assn:** UCADA **Dir:** NYS Thruway Exit 19: To Rte 587 off traffic circle to Broadway. Continue to 2nd R after RR underpass to Hoffman St. 1st bldg on R. **Own:** Stanley Zaborski. **QC: 3 48 86**

Krumville

Old Mill Antiques

Sahler Mill Rd • 12447
(914)657-8235

Five houses full of oak, walnut & primitive furniture, grandfather clocks, bric-a-brac. **Est:** 1970 **Hrs:** Fri-Mon 12-5, Win by appt. **Own:** Steve & Vicky Livanos.

LaFargeville

Kindred Spirits Antiques & Collectibles

Main & Maple St • 13656
(315)658-4243

Antique shop in an old Baptist church, filled with furniture, glassware, kitchenware, books, records, tools, jewelry, lighting, toys & more. **Hrs:** Apr-May & Oct-Dec: Fri-Sun 11-4; Jun-Sep: Daily 10-6 or by appt. **CC:** V/MC.

Lake George

Ralph Kylloe Gallery

Lake Luzerne Rd (Rte 9N) • 12845
(518)696-4100 • (518)696-3555 (fax)
rkylloe@capital.net

Specializing in rustic furniture & accessories including Old Hickory, Adirondack, twig, antler & root furnishings. **Hrs:** By appt only. **CC:** V/MC **Dir:** I-87 Exit 21: S toward Lake Luzerne on 9N, 2.7 mi on L. **QC: 1 48 52**

Red Wheel Antiques

One Lake Ave • 12845
(518)668-2401

18th & 19th C furniture, primitives, folk art & accessories. **Assn:** VADA **Own:** Joe Ferrone. **QC: 52 106 41**

Lake Placid

Grammy's Antiques & Dolls

9 Sentinel Rd • 12946
(518)523-1783
grammy@northnet.org

Dolls a specialty. **QC: 38**

Log Cabin Antiques
86 Main St • 12946
(518)523-3047

General line. **Hrs:** Daily 10-5. **Dir:** In center of village. **Own:** Gregory Peacock. **QC: S12**

Reflections Antiques & Accessories
7 Main St • 12946
(518)523-8115

Adirondack, English, country & Victorian furniture. Equestrian memorabilia, small antiques & accessories. **Own:** Mary Pat Ormsby.

With Pipe & Book
91 Main St • 12946
(518)523-9096

Large general stock of old, used & rare books. Specialties include Adirondacks, tobacco, Olympics, skating & sporting. Antique prints of the Northeastern US & Canada. Adirondack pack baskets, canoes, guideboats & other sporting equipment. **Est:** 1977 **Hrs:** Most wknds 9:30-6. Call ahead advised. **Sz:** L **CC:** AX/V/MC/DIS **Dir:** Ctr of Main St business district. **Own:** Breck Turner. **QC: 18 74 79**

Liberty

Liberty Antiques Center [G9]
120 Mill St • 12754
(914)292-3319

Dir: Rte 17E Exit 100: R 0.2 mi; Rte 17W Exit 101: L to light, then L 0.8 mi.

Lisbon

Country Garden at Iroquois Farm
Rte 37 • 13658
(315)393-6252

Fine china, crystal, sterling silver, copper & brass. Amish quilts. **Dir:** On Rte 37 betw Ogdensburg & Waddington NY.

Little Falls

Antique Center of Little Falls [G]
25 W Mill St • 13365
(315)823-4309
(888)762-4309

Antiques, decorative arts, furniture, glassware, art & books. **Hrs:** Daily 10-5. **Dir:** Located in Historic Canal Place. Midway betw Albany & Syracuse, mins from NYS Thruway Exit 29A.

Livingston

Howard Frisch Antiquarian Books
116 County Rte 19 • 12541
(518)851-7493 • (518)851-3540 (fax)
hfhbooks@capital.net

Antiquarian book shop with books on art, architecture, archaeology, books on books, illustrated books, performing arts, history , literature & science. **Hrs:** May-Dec Fri-Sun 11-4 or by appt. **CC:** V/MC. **QC: 18 19**

Loudonville

Loudonville Folk Art
32 Maria Dr • 12211
(518)438-0333 • (518)438-2234 (fax)
wthrvanes@aol.com
members.aol.com/wthrvanes

Specializing in American folk art in the form of weathervanes, trade signs, carvings, architectural elements, American painted furniture, shaker & garden accessories. **Pr:** $500-16,000 **Est:** 1994 **Hrs:** By appt only. **Sz:** S **Dir:** 1 mi from I-87 Exit 4, 1-1/2 mins from N end of Wolf Rd in Colonie, NY. **Own:** Mike White. **QC: 44 45 51**

Louisville

Wyman's Totem Pole Antiques & Collectibles

Willard Rd • 13662
(315)769-6650

Primitives, china, glass & carnival. Military items, duck decoys, small furniture. **Hrs:** By chance/appt. Closed Jan-Mar. **Dir:** Off Rte 37, W of Massena, turn at G & C Country Store on Willard Rd.

Madison

Grasshopper Antique Center [G]

Rte 20 • 13402
(315)893-7664

Antiques, paintings, African art, fish decoys, graniteware & American Indian. **Hrs:** By chance/appt. **Assn:** MBADA.

Madison Inn Antiques [G25]

7417 Rte 20 • 13402
(315)893-7639

Antiques & collectibles. **Hrs:** Mar-Dec daily 10-5; Jan-Feb Fri-Mon 10-5. **CC:** V/MC/DIS **Assn:** MBADA **Own:** Larry Spooner.

Three Owls/1840s House

Rte 20 • 13402
(315)684-9401

Dolls, home furnishings, tools, music & art objects. Specializing in children's books, illustrated, agricultural, reference books & Americana. **Hrs:** By appt only. **Assn:** MBADA **Dir:** Across from Dawn to Dark Mini Mart. **Own:** Charles & Barbara Bostic. **QC: 18 38 69**

Willow Hollow Antiques

7585 Rte 20 • 13402
(315)893-7696

Restored oak & country furniture, accessories, lamps, graniteware & kitchen collectibles. **Hrs:** By chance/appt. **CC:** V/MC/DIS **Assn:** MBADA.

Malden Bridge

Willard Vine Clerk — Wonderful Things

Rte 66 @ Shaker Museum Rd • 12115
(518)766-4650

American & European decorative arts & antiques. **Hrs:** Daily 10-5.

Malone

The Market Barn [G85]

E Main St (Rte 11) • 12953
(518)483-9341

Antiques, crafts & gifts. **Hrs:** Jul-Dec Mon-Sat 10-5, Sun 12-5; Jan-Jun Tue-Sat 10-5, Sun 12-5. **Sz:** L.

Ken & Susan Scott Antiques

Rte 11B • 12953
(518)483-1868

Country furniture, quilts, hooked rugs, samplers, folk art & country accents. **Hrs:** By chance/appt. **Assn:** GSAAA VADA **Own:** Ken & Susan Scott. **QC: 102 84 82**

Manlius

The Caldwell Gallery

4574 Meadowridge Rd • 13104
(315)682-6551 • (315)682-4032 (fax)
(800)331-1278

American, European & modern art. **Hrs:** By appt only. **Own:** Joseph Caldwell. **QC: 7**

Marathon

Cross's Antiques [G30]

Rte 11 • 13794
(607)849-6605

General line. **Hrs:** Daily 10-5. **CC:** AX/V/MC/DIS **Own:** Jo Cross.

Margaretville

Margaretville Antique Center [G20+]

Main St., Theater Bldg • 12455
(914)586-2424
(888)825-8211
mrtoad2@catskill.net
www.antique-center.com

Country, Victorian & eclectic antiques. **Est:** 1983 **Hrs:** Daily 10-5. **Sz:** L **CC:** AX/V/MC/DIS **Dir:** Junc Rtes 28 & 30. **Own:** Jack Goth. **QC: S1 S12 S8**

Massena

A & B Collectibles

154 Dennison Rd • 13662
(315)769-7527

Glass, furniture, primitives, stemware, sterling. Watt pottery a specialty. **Hrs:** By appt only. **Own:** Alice & Bob Dishaw. **QC: 22**

Elizabeth's Antiques & Collectibles

56 Woodlawn Ave • 13662
(315)769-6978 • (315)769-8130 (fax)

Flow blue, Carnival, Nippon, RS Prussia, Heisey, art glass, cut glass, furniture, old toys, jewelry, dolls, books, sterling silver. **Hrs:** Thu-Sat 10-5, Mon-Wed by appt. **QC: 61 100**

North Racquette Antiques

924 N Racquette River Rd • 13662
(315)769-5697

Furniture, glassware, picture frames, smalls. **Hrs:** Daily 10-6. **Dir:** 2 mi E of Massena Airport & 2 mi from the St Lawrence Centre Mall. **Own:** Carol & Fred Hartle.

South Raquette River Antiques & Collectibles

(315)769-5426
williams@slic.com

Primitives & fanciful antiques: woodenware, tin, baskets, whimsey, Americana, yellowware, folk art, Adirondack, garden & painted items. **Hrs:** By chance/appt. **Dir:** From Rte 37 turn onto Rte 37C at Mobil Gas/Country Store. Cross bridge, turn R onto County Rte 46, 4th house on L.

Mechanicville

Hudson River Trading Company

38 N Main St • 12118
(518)664-9743 • (518)664-9743 (fax)

Antique & collectible firearms, militaria, Americana & Adirondack art. **Hrs:** Daily 10-6. **Sz:** L. **QC: 1 4**

Middleburgh

Antique Center of Preston Hollow [G40]

Rte 145 • 12122
(518)239-4251

Furniture, glassware, china, linens, quilts, primitives, advertising, military, toys, tools, art, costume jewelry, kitchenware & lamps. **Hrs:** Apr-Oct Fri-Wed 10-5, year round by appt. **Sz:** L **Own:** Dottie & Skip Como.

Jacqueline Donegan Antiques

107 River St • 12122
(518)827-5224

Specializing in American classical furniture, accessories & period lighting with a barn full of unusual selections from many periods. **Hrs:** By appt only. **Assn:** ADA **Dir:** On Rte 30 in Middleburgh Village across from Schoharie Creek. **QC: 36 52 65 S1**

Good Earth [G]

65 Main St • 12122
(518)827-4619 • (518)827-4621 (fax)
www.telnet.net/commercial/dollsale

Dolls, estate jewelry, glass & collectibles. **Hrs:** Mon-Thu 10-7, Fri-Sat 10-8, Sun 12-5. **QC: 38 61 64**

Memories [G]
138-140 Main St • 12122
(518)827-7040

Depression glass, oak furniture, kitchen collectibles & coins. **Hrs:** Mon-Sat 7-3, Sun 7-12. **QC: 61 33**

Millbrook

Millbrook Antiques Mall [G]
Franklin Ave (Rte 44) • 12545
(914)677-3921

18th & 19th C furnishings & accessories. **Hrs:** May-Oct daily 12-6; Nov-Apr 11-5; Sun & hols 1-5. **Own:** Malcolm Mokotoff.

Village Antique Center [G44]
Franklin Ave (Rte 44) • 12545
(914)677-5160

Country & formal furniture, American & European silver, fine china, estate jewelry, watches, pottery, quilts, paintings, glass, stamps, coins & ephemera. **Hrs:** Mon-Sat 11-5, Sun 1-5:30. **Own:** Jeffrey A Lark.

Millerton

Green River Gallery
Boston Corners Rd (Rte 63) • 12546
(518)789-3311

A pre-1775 Colonial displaying 19th & 20th C American art with emphasis on art of the American West. Paintings, bronze sculpture & Navajo weavings. Appraisals, consulting, framing & restoration services available. **Pr:** $25-25,000 **Est:** 1975 **Hrs:** Sat 10-5, Sun 12-5 or by appt. **Sz:** L **Assn:** BCADA **Dir:** Off Rte 22, 10 mi S of Hillsdale & 6 mi N of Millerton. **Own:** Arthur Kerber. **QC: 7 28 52 S1 S8 S13**

Millerton Center for Antiques [G40]
Main St • 12546
(518)789-6004

Antique center, art promenade & shoppers arcade. **Hrs:** Thu-Tue 10-5. **Dir:** At the crossroads of NY, CT, MA (Rtes 22, 44 & 199).

Montgomery

Black Scottie Antiques [G8]
165 Ward St (Rte 17K) • 12549
(914)457-9343

Four levels of antiques, collectibles & furnishings. Silverplate, sterling, children's antiques, primitive & Victorian furniture, pottery, estate jewelry & costume jewelry. **Pr:** $1-2,500 **Est:** 1997 **Hrs:** Thu-Tue 11-5. **Sz:** M **CC:** V/MC/DIS **Dir:** NY Thruway Exit 17 (Newburgh/Montgomery): to 17K W for 15 min. **QC: 78 32 48 S9**

Clinton Shops Antique Center [G14]
84 Clinton St • 12549
(914)457-5392

Jewelry, primitives, furniture, glass, china, country furniture & accessories, vintage jewelry. **Hrs:** Thu-Tue 11-5. **Dir:** 1 block from int of Rte 211 & 17K. **Own:** Joyce Fogelman.

Country Corner Antiques [G10]
Bridge St & Rte 17K • 12549
(914)457-5581

Country antiques, oak furniture, jewelry & a general line. **Hrs:** Thu-Tue 11-5. **Own:** Carol Devine.

Guns & Collectibles
1092 Rte 17K • 12549
(914)457-9062

Guns & collectibles. **Hrs:** Daily 11-5. **CC:** V/MC **Own:** Glenn & Barbara Doty. **QC: 4**

Lamplighter Antiques
70 Union St • 12549
(914)457-5228

Folk art, quilts, country pieces & decorative accessories. **Hrs:** Daily 10-5. **Own:** Marilyn Quigley.

Montgomery Antiques Mall [G14]
40 Railroad Ave • 12549
(914)457-9339

Country furniture, Americana, Art Deco, oak & mahogany furniture, glassware, china & jewelry. **Hrs:** Thu-Tue 11-5. **Own:** Linda Boyle & Mary Arlotta.

Olde Towne Antiques
136 Clinton St • 12549
(914)457-5770 • (914)457-5770 (fax)

Furniture, decorative items, Americana & architectural. **Hrs:** Daily 10-5. **CC:** AX/V/MC/DIS **Own:** Nancy DeWitt.

22 Railroad Avenue
Railroad Ave & Charles St • 12549
(914)457-9213

General line. **Hrs:** Thu-Tue 11-5, Wed by chance. **Own:** Harold Barger.

Red Rooster Antiques
63 Clinton St • 12549
(914)457-4023 **Hrs:** Thu-Tue 11-5, Wed by chance.

Morris

The Gatehouse
4 W Main St • 13808
(607)263-5855

18th-19th C lighting & antique furnishings. **Est:** 1966 **Hrs:** Wed-Sat 10-4, Jan-Mar Fri-Sat 10-4. **Sz:** M **Dir:** I-88 Exit 13: 13 mi W on SR 23. **Own:** Peter & Audrey Gregory. **QC: 65 48**

Natural Bridge

Lane's End Antiques
Rte 3 • 13665
(315)644-4097

Good old furniture in original paint & condition, refinished furniture, good early smalls. **Hrs:** May-Oct 15 by chance/appt. **QC: 51 34**

Neversink

Hamilton's Antique Shoppe
Rte 55 • 12765
(914)985-2671

Furniture to antique jewelry, glassware. **Hrs:** Daily 10-5. **Own:** Regina Hamilton.

New Lebanon

Golden Eagle Antiques
Rte 20 & County Rte 5 • 12125
(518)794-9809

Furniture, glass, china & primitives. **Hrs:** Wknds or by chance/appt.

Hulmes Fine Art & Antiques
Rtes 20 & 22 • 12125
(518)794-7496

Dolls, brass, copper & silver. **Hrs:** Jun-Nov 15 Fri-Mon 10-5.

New Paltz

Marna Anderson
2 Wawarsing Rd • 12561
(914)255-1132 • (914)255-2341 (fax)

Quality American folk art specializing in weathervanes, textiles & 19th C decorative arts. **Hrs:** By appt only. **Assn:** ADA **Dir:** NY Thruway Exit 18. **QC: 41 80 45**

Broome & Allen
6 Church St • 12561
(914)255-5144

Linens & vintage fabric, furnishings & ephemera. **Hrs:** Thu-Tue 11-5. **QC: 81 39 S16**

Country Charm Antiques
201 DuBois Rd • 12561
(914)255-4321 • (914)255-4321 (fax)

Specializing in primitives, tinware & the unusual. **Hrs:** By chance/appt. **Dir:** 1/4 mi off Rte 32.

Fred Hansen Antiques Inc
27 N Chestnut St (Rte 32N) • 12561
(914)255-1333 • (914)255-0928 (fax)
fred@fredhansen.com
www.fredhansen.com

American & European furniture, clocks & barometers a specialty. **Pr:** $20-5,000 **Hrs:** Mon & Thu-Sat 9-5, Sun 11-6. **Sz:** L **CC:** V/MC **Assn:** UCADA **Dir:** NY Thruway Exit 18: L at light onto Main St, R at the 4th light on N Chestnut St. Shop is located on the L. **QC: 35 77**

Warren F Hartmann
5 Paradies Ln • 12561
(914)895-3627 • (914)895-3627 (fax)
whartmann1@aol.com

Early American stoneware. **QC: 31**

Jenkinstown Antiques
520 Rte 32 S • 12561
(914)255-8135

Country & formal furniture, paintings, accessories. **Est:** 1974 **Hrs:** Fri-Mon 11-5 or by appt. **Dir:** 4 mi S of town. **Own:** Sanford Levy & Charles Glasner. **QC: 36 102 7 S9 S15 S18**

Candles I

In the 17th and 18th centuries candles were costly, either in cash, on the rare occasions when they were bought, or in labor, where candlemaking was yet one more slow and repetitive task for the colonial woman. Common candles were made of tallow, finer ones of wax.

Tallow was made by boiling animal fat in water until it rose to the top where it was skimmed off, only to be boiled up again and again until all impurities were gone. Then a large kettle of pure tallow was hung over the fire.

Candles were made from this tallow either by dipping or molding. For dipping, long poles with short, removable cross pieces were laid across two chair backs in front of the fire. A wick of flax or cotton was hung from each cross piece and dipped in the hot tallow. By the time the last crosspiece had been dipped, the first would have hardened enough to be dipped again, and process was repeated until the candles were thick enough to use. Great skill was needed to keep the tallow at the right temperature: too hot and it would melt the tallow off the wick, too cold and it congealed unevenly and lumpily. Not surprisingly colonial housewives took great pride in well-made, even-burning candles.

Making candles in molds was quicker, but the molds had to be bought, whereas the equipment for dipping was all home-made. Tin or, more rarely, pewter candle molds for making between two and twenty-four candles at a time were common domestic utensils.

Bees wax and bayberry wax were prepared in much the same way as tallow. Spermiceti, a fatty substance from the head of the sperm whale, was popular from the 1730s onward because its candles were about twice as bright as tallow ones.

New Paltz Antique Center [G]
256 Main St • 12561
(914)255-1880

Antiques & collectibles, including jewelry & vintage clothing. **Hrs:** Mon-Wed 11-5:30, Thu-Sun 11-7; Nov-Mar Thu-Sun 11-6, Mon-Tue by chance. **Dir:** NY Thruway Exit 18: 1 mi W. **QC: 83 63**

North Front Antiques
7 N Front St • 12561
(914)255-5144

Victorian to 1950s. Cozy furnishings, playful housewares, vintage ephemera. **Hrs:** Mon-Sat 11:30-5, Wed by chance/appt. **QC: S1**

Newburgh

Antiques Are Us
5455 Rte 9W N • 12550
(914)562-1506

Furniture, jewelry, collectibles, artwork, porcelain. **Hrs:** Mon-Fri 11-6, Sat-Sun 10-6. **Dir:** 4 mi N of Newburgh/Beacon Bridge I-84. Across from Cedar Hill Cemetary. **QC: 48**

Grandpa Charlie's Attic
476 Broadway • 12550
(914)568-5789
grantman@warwick.net

Victorian through modern art, furniture, oils, prints, collectibles & a large selection of costume jewelry. **Hrs:** Mon & Wed-Fri 11-4, Sat 12-4 or by appt. **Own:** Ed, Edward & Diane Novak. **QC: 7 48 63**

Newburgh Antique Gallery
394 Broadway • 12550
(914)565-1041 • (914)565-1061 (fax)
vcollens@aol.com

Antique books, furnishings, collectibles, primitives & art. Mostly American items, some European. Also modern art & folk art representing the estate of Brooklyn NY artist Elijah Silverman, 1910-1994. **Est:** 1998 **Hrs:** Mon-Fri 11-4:30, Sat 10-4. **Sz:** M **CC:** AX/V/MC **Dir:** From I-84, Newburgh Exit, Rte 32 S. From NYS Thruway, head E on Rte 17K. **Own:** Vivien Abrams Collens. **QC: 1 7 48 S12 S8 S9**

The Now & Then Shop
115 Liberty St • 12550
(914)352-8232

Antiques, lamps, china, books, jewelry & collectibles. **Hrs:** Wed-Sat by chance/appt. **Own:** Mary Scully. **QC: 63 65**

Norfolk

Norfolk Antiques
1 W Main St • 13667
(315)384-3534

Furniture from the 1800s to early 1900. Tables, dressers, commodes & primitive pieces. Glassware, collectibles & unusual knick-knacks. **Hrs:** Daily 9-6. **QC: 48**

North Bangor

Split Rail Antiques
Taylor Rd • 12966
(518)483-4112

Old carpenter, cobbler, blacksmith & farrier tools, saws including ice saws, old hand tools, corn shellers, DeLaval, cast iron, old kitchen & house items, milk bottles, horse-drawn plows, cultivators & milk cans. **Hrs:** By chance/appt. **Dir:** 1 mi from Rte 11 or Rte 11 B. **Own:** Beverly Griffin. **QC: 86**

Norwood

Ashley House Antiques & Gifts [G]
1 Park St • 13668
(518)353-4609

Furniture, antiques, collectibles & gifts. **Hrs:** Tue-Sat 10:30-4:30, Sun 12:30-4:30.

Mac's Place Antiques & Collectibles
18 N Main St • 13668
(315)353-3511

Pottery, glassware, prints, frames, kitchenware & smalls. **Hrs:** Fri 3-5, Sat-Sun 10-5. Daily in Sum, otherwise by appt.

Oak Hill

The Assemblage
Rte 81 • 12460
(518)239-6231

Antiques, prints, ephemera. **Hrs:** Fri-Mon by chance/appt.

Cheritree Antiques of Oak Hill
Rte 81 • 12460
(518)239-4081

Furniture, accessories, architectural & jewelry. **Hrs:** May-Nov Thu-Mon; Dec-Apr Sat-Sun. **Dir:** In center of Oak Hill.

Country Kitchen Antiques
Durham Rd (Rte 22) • 12460
(518)239-4076

Kitchenware, china, linen, jewelry & collectibles. **Hrs:** By chance/appt. **QC: 81 32**

DeWitt Hotel Antiques [G]
Rte 81 • 12460
(518)239-6960

Furniture, quilts, linens, brass, silver, iron, porcelains, lamps, crystal, jewelry, books & collectibles. **Hrs:** May-Nov Fri-Wed 10-5; Dec-Apr Fri-Sun 10-4. **Dir:** Rte 81, 3 mi E off Rte 145.

Ogdensburg

Johnson Antiques
513 Ogden St • 13669
(315)393-2905

Specializing in oak furniture including tables, chairs, buffets, china cabinets, bookcases, glassware. **Hrs:** Thu-Sat 12-5 or by appt. **Dir:** From Rte 37 to New York Ave, L to Ogden. **QC: 50**

O'Donoghue's Antiques
Arnold Rd (Rte 28A) • 13669
(315)393-1505

Country furniture, primitives, quilts, lighting, woodenware, baskets. **Dir:** 1 mi from Rte 68, brown house on L. **Own:** Bob & Stephanie O'Donoghue.

Old Chatham

Turnpike Antiques
1057 Albany Tpke • 12136
(518)794-8667

Fine early primitives. **Hrs:** Daily. **QC: 106**

Otego

John & Lynn Gallo Antiques
75 Main St • 13825
(607)988-9963
jlgallo@dmcom.net

18th & 19th C painted country furnishings, braided & hooked rugs, yellowware, pottery, folk art & early advertising. **Hrs:** By chance/appt. **Assn:** NHADA VADA **Dir:** I-88 Exit 12: R at Big M, shop is located 1 mi on R. **Own:** John & Lynn Gallo. **QC: 102 75 29**

Parksville

Antique Cellar
2198 State Rd 17 • 12768
(914)292-8612
dawne@catskill.net

Three rooms filled with turn of the century Americana, glass, china, Depression, paper, jewelry, clothing, kitchenware, tools & collectibles. **Est:** 1968 **Hrs:** Sat-Sun 10-5 or by chance/appt. **CC:** V/MC/DIS **Own:** Dawne & Lester Norris.

Pawling

Antique Center [G20]

248 Rte 22 • 12564
(914)855-3611

Early American & Victorian furniture, toys, games, rugs, oil paintings, art glass, Roseville & jewelry. **Hrs:** Daily 11-5. **Dir:** Follow the rd to the bright yellow house.

Petersburgh

The New Meeting House Antiques [G]

Rte 22 & Rte 2 • 12138
(518)658-2099

18th, 19th & 20th C formal & country furniture, paintings, folk art, toys, early glass, pottery, quilts, textiles, clocks. Shaker, early lighting, books, china, silver & pewter. **QC: 1 52 41**

Phoenicia

A Country Gallery

46 Rte 214 • 12464
(914)688-7604 • (914)688-7604 (fax)

Country antiques, folk art, crafts, quilts, rugs & Christmas. **Hrs:** Wknds or by chance. **CC:** V/MC **Own:** Lynn Parker. **QC: 34**

The Acorn

59 Main St • 12464
(914)688-9896

Mission (1895-1920) oak, art pottery, lighting, paintings, original & custom furniture in the Arts & Crafts style. **Est:** 1977 **Hrs:** Win Fri-Mon 11-5; Sum Thu-Mon 10-6 or by chance/appt. **QC: 6 59 101 S16 S17**

Craftsmen's Gallery — Mission Oak

48 Rte 214 • 12464
(914)688-2100

Specializing in American Arts & Crafts, art pottery, paintings, lighting & decorative arts. **Hrs:** By appt only. **QC: 6 105 101 S16**

Phoenicia Antique Center [G]

Rte 28 • 12464
(914)688-2095
www.antiques-pac.com

Largest multi-dealer shop in the Catskills. Antiques, collectibles, furniture, books, 1950s-1960s, toys. **Hrs:** Daily.

Pine Bush

The Coffee Grinder Farmhouse Antiques

70 Main St • 12566
(914)744-3946
coffee@warwick.net

Antiques & collectibles. **Hrs:** Tue-Sat 10-5. **CC:** AX/V/MC/DIS **Own:** Carlos Ingraisci.

Country Heritage Antiques Center [G]

Rte 302 • 12566
(914)744-3792

One of the largest inventories in the Hudson Valley. Specializing in high quality Victorian & Federal oak furniture. **Hrs:** Thu-Sun 11-5:30 or by appt. **CC:** V/MC/DIS **Dir:** Off Main St. **Own:** Richard Triggiani. **QC: 58 50**

Plattekill

Fox Den at Red Top Farm

695 Plattekill-Ardonia Rd • 12568
(914)564-0336

Antiques, collectibles, good used furniture, costume jewelry. **Hrs:** 12-6 most days or by appt. **QC: 32**

Plattsburgh

Antique & Variety Mall [G20+]
12 Margaret St • 12901
(518)563-7750

Antiques, furniture, coins, glassware, china.

Bushey's Antiques
Rte 22 • 12901
(518)563-5716

Glass, china, furniture, decoys, picture frames, crocks & jugs. **Dir:** 3 mi N of Plattsburgh on Rte 22. **Own:** Randy & Richard Bushey. **QC: 61 37**

Philip & Shirley Gordon
119 Prospect Ave • 12901
(518)561-3383 • (518)561-4740 (fax)

Fine jewelry, sterling silver, art glass, art pottery, fine porcelains, bronzes, lamps & works of art. **Hrs:** By chance/appt. **Own:** Philip & Shirley Gordon. **QC: 100 101 11**

Town & Country Antique Shop
Rte 22 • 12901
(518)561-4658

Oak & Victorian furniture, wicker, pine, primitives, crocks & collectibles. **Hrs:** Mon-Fri 11-5, Sat 10-4. **Dir:** Northway Exit 38N: 4 mi N of Plattsburgh in the village of Beekmantown. **Own:** Wayne & Sheila Dumont. **QC: 50 58**

Yankee Peddler
579 Irish Settlement Rd • 12901
(518)563-1089

Antiques & collectibles. **Own:** Jeff Pescia.

Pleasant Valley

A Beckwith Antiques
Rte 44 • 12569
(914)635-3217

An open shop antique business offering a diverse selection of antiques from estates & private purchases. **Est:** 1953 **Hrs:** Tue-Sat 12-5. **Sz:** M **Dir:** 6 mi E of Poughkeepsie on Rte 44. **Own:** Asa Beckwith.

Tomorrow's Treasures [G8]
Rte 44 • 12569
(914)635-8402
joeyoneantiques@msn.com

General line. **Hrs:** Wed-Sun 10-5 or by chance/appt. **Dir:** 2 mi E of Pleasant Valley. **Own:** Judith Krimmer.

Pond Eddy

Anthony S Werneke
Hollow Rd • 12770
(914)856-1037 • (914)856-1037 (fax)

Period 17th & 18th C American furniture, English delft, glass, brass & 18th C accessories. **Hrs:** By appt only. **QC: 52 27 20**

Potsdam

Eben Hill Antiques
Rte 11 • 13676
(315)265-3627

North Country antiques, Adirondack, folk art, paintings, prints, tiger maple furniture & primitives. Specializing in flow blue china, Fenton, Burmese & Mary Gregory. **Hrs:** Daily. **Dir:** On scenic Rte 11 betw Potsdam & Canton. **Own:** Jim & Mary Mundy. **QC: 22 41 48**

Memory Lane
34 Market St • 13676
(315)265-6032

Antiques, vintage clothing, Victorian decor, primitives, quilts, postcards, books, lamps & jewelry. **Hrs:** Mon-Sat 10-5. **Own:** Karen Osoway. **QC: 83 89 106**

Rainbow Antiques
226 May Rd • 13676
(315)265-4012

Furniture, collectibles, primitives, Amish quilts, Amish rockers, dolls, Wade miniature nursery rhyme figures, hats & clothing. **Hrs:** By chance/appt. **Dir:** 1 mi from Rte 56. Turn off Market St at Burger King. **Own:** Bob & Laura Moore.

Poughkeepsie

Rood's Antiques & Collectibles
584 South Rd (Rte 9) • 12601
(914)454-8465 • (914)454-2339 (fax)
judyyih@yahoo.com

Asian fine arts, specializing in classical Chinese furniture, Ming & Qing Dynasty from the 16th-19th C. Restore original antique pieces directly from remote villages in China. Most of the pieces are made of Jama or Elm. **Hrs:** Mon-Sat 10-5. **Sz:** M **Own:** Judy Yih. **QC: 2 11 71 S2 S15 S18**

Preston Hollow

Barbara's Antiques
3084 Rte 145 • 12469
(518)239-6224

Furniture, lighting, vintage clothing, quilts, linens, jewelry, tools & dolls. **Hrs:** By chance/appt. **Sz:** M **Dir:** Corn of Main St & Schoolhouse Ln.

By Chance Antiques
3053 Rte 145 • 12469
(518)239-8073

18th & 19th C American country furniture, primitives, architectural elements & fine art. Garden furniture, cast iron & decorative elements a specialty. **Hrs:** Apr-Oct Fri-Mon 10-5 or by chance/appt. **QC: 60 36 102**

Pulaski

The Unicorn Antique Shop
19 Bridge St • 13142
(315)298-4581

Depression glass, collectibles, pressed glass, Nippon, glass kitchenware & pottery. **Hrs:** By chance/appt. **Dir:** Rte 81 Exit 36 to ctr of village. **Own:** C H (Larry) Carney. **QC: 103 61 32**

Red Hook

Annex Antiques Center [G]
23 E Market St • 12571
(914)758-2843

Depression glass, toys, jewelry & oak furniture. **Hrs:** Daily 11-5.

Attic Memories [G18]
18 E Market St • 12571
(914)758-9283

General line. **Hrs:** Daily 11-5. **CC:** V/MC **Own:** William & Elizabeth Norton & Susan Maywalt.

Broadway Antiques & Collectibles
30 N Broadway (Rte 9) • 12571
(914)876-1444

Antiques in a home setting. **Est:** 1993 **Hrs:** Daily 11-5. **CC:** V/MC/DIS.

La Vie en Rose
85 S Broadway • 12571
(914)758-4211

Fine vintage clothing, apparel & accessories. **Hrs:** Wed-Sun 11-5, Mon by chance/appt. **CC:** V/MC/DIS **Own:** Joanne Capalbo-Flachs. **QC: 83**

Redwood

DJ Old World Emporium

43508 Main St • 13679
(315)482-2417

Victorian, gothic & Renaissance antiques, primitives, collectibles, artwork & statues. **Hrs:** Apr 15-Dec daily 10-5 or by appt. **Dir:** Rte 37 to 43508 Main St. Look for Amish wagon in front. **QC: 89 106**

Rensselaer Falls

Vintage Paper

(315)344-8882 • (315)344-7247 (fax)

Paper memorabilia. **Hrs:** By appt only. **QC: 67 39**

Rensselaerville

Rensselaerville Antiques

5000 Delaware Tpk (Rte 85) • 12147
(518)797-3499
g.elk@worldnet.att.net
www.home.att.net/~g.elk

Antiques in a restored historic church. Full line of quality merchandise including Americana, English & Continental porcelains & pottery, paintings, prints, furniture, quilts, silver, glassware & decorative items. **Pr:** $75-1,500 **Est:** 1974 **Hrs:** By chance/appt. **Sz:** M **CC:** AX/V/MC **Dir:** From Hudson: W on Rte 23, cross Rip van Winkle bridge, then R on Rte 32 through Greenville. L on County Rte 405, L on Rte 402, then R onto Rte 351, R on Rte 85. **Own:** George & Hedda Elk. **QC: 7 48 23**

Rhinebeck

Dennis & Valerie Bakoledis

109 E Market St • 12572
(914)876-7944

American furniture, folk art, garden furniture, architectural elements, paintings & decorative items of interest. **Hrs:** By appt only. **Sz:** M. **QC: 1 3 60**

Candles II

Taper: A thin candle, sometimes rigid, and sometimes a thinly waxed multi-thread wick that could be coiled up. Tapers were rarely used as lighting, but rather to light candles or to melt sealing wax.

Candlebox: A long, narrow, lidded box used for storing candles horizontally. Most were made of wood or tin, but brass, pewter, and even silver ones may be found. They may be wall-hung or free-standing. Lids may be sliding or hinged. Wooden ones are usually square in section, but those made out of metal are often cylindrical.

Rushlights were the cheapest "candles" of all. They were made by soaking the pith of the cat o' nine tails reed in tallow. If short, they were burned directly in a rushlight holder, but longer ones were loosely coiled and moved up in the holder as they burned down.

Grisset: An iron implement for soaking reeds in hot tallow to make rushlights. It resembled a ladle with a long, narrow, shallow bowl.

Candlewood: A resinous pitch pine common along the New England coast. When cut and split into pieces about the size of a candle it gave a good light, but smoked and dropped a pitchy substance. For poorer households its cheapness and easy availability overcame these drawbacks, and it was widely used.

Beekman Arms Antique Market [G3+]

Behind Beekman Arms Hotel • 12572
(914)876-3477

Americana, country, primitives, period decorative furniture, jewelry, books & accessories. **Est:** 1986 **Hrs:** Daily 11-5. **CC:** V/MC **Dir:** Behind Historic Beekman Arms Hotel.

Old Mill House Antiques

144 Rte 9 N • 12572
(914)876-3636

Primitives to deco, architectural, folk art, pottery, glass, jewelry, ephemera & lamps. **Hrs:** Daily 11-5, Oct-Mar closed Wed. **Dir:** 1 mi N of int of Rte 9 & 9G.

Rhinebeck Antique Center [G40]

7 W Market St • 12572
(914)876-8168

Fine antiques from the 18th C to the 1950s: ceramics, glassware, silver, bronzes, artwork, photos, textiles, lace, collectibles, games, toys & jewelry. **Hrs:** Thu-Tue 11-5. **Dir:** Ctr of village.

Richfield Springs

Rick Worden's Antiques [G12]

120 W Main St • 13439
(315)858-9354
rwordenjr@mvip.net

General line. **Hrs:** Fri-Wed 10-5 or by appt. **CC:** V/MC/DIS.

Richmondville

The Bear Gulch Shoppe

Rte 7 • 12149
(518)294-6567

Furniture, collectibles, glassware & linens. **Hrs:** May-Oct Sat-Sun 12-5 or by appt.

Rochester

Miriam Rogachefsky Antiques

1905 Westfall Rd • 14618
(716)256-3426

Orientalia & fine Oriental porcelain. Native American arts. **Hrs:** By appt only. **Own:** Miriam Rogachefsky & Jack Williams. **QC: 25 71 42**

Rosendale

Rural Delivery Antiques

407 Main St (Rte 213) • 12472
(914)658-3485

Rustic, Mission, Art Deco, painted country & outdoor furniture. Folk art, textiles, braided rugs, pottery, advertising, sporting, architectural & 200 lamps. **Pr:** $5-750 **Est:** 1987 **Hrs:** Fri-Sun 12-7, Mon 12-5 or by appt. **Sz:** M **CC:** AX/V/MC/DIS **Dir:** In the middle of historic Rosendale, midway betw New Paltz & Kingston. **Own:** Gary Schwartz. **QC: 49 51 65**

Sackets Harbor

Sackets Harbor Antiques

221 W Main St • 13685
(315)646-2185
www.cbridge@imcnet.net/

Specializing in postcards, photographs & paper. **Hrs:** Sum Fri-Sun 11-4; Win by appt. **Own:** Charles & Marcia Bridge. **QC: 39**

Salem

Fitch House Antiques

(518)854-7544

Fine period & early country painted furniture, accessories, samplers, early dolls. **Hrs:** By appt only. **Assn:** VADA **Dir:** Rte 29 1 mi W of Rte 22; 35 mi from Dorset/Manchester, VT. **Own:** Maryann Boyter. **QC: 102 82 38**

Hebron Hills Antiques

(518)854-7544

19th C Americana, specializing in spatterware & spongeware, redware & textiles. **Hrs:** By appt only. **Assn:** VADA **Own:** James S Lawrence. **QC: 1 22 80**

Salem Art & Antique Center [G35]

Rte 22 • 12865
(518)854-7320 • (518)854-3196 (fax)
edowling@ix.netcom.com

Largest multi-dealer shop in Washington County offering a selection of 19th & 20th C furniture, jewelry, collectibles, fishing & more at country prices. **Pr:** $1-1,000 **Est:** 1994 **Hrs:** Mon-Sat 10-5, Sun 12-5. **CC:** AX/V/MC **Dir:** Just S of the village of Salem on Rte 22. **Own:** Jane Dowling. **QC: 34 S1 S8 S17**

Zweig Fine Arts & Antiques

(518)854-7844

Period American furniture, paintings, silver & accessories. **Hrs:** By appt only. **Dir:** Washington County on VT border, a few minutes from Dorset, VT. **Own:** Felice Zweig. **QC: 52 78 7 S1**

Saranac Lake

Germaine Miller

Bloomingdale Rd (Rte 3) • 12983
(518)891-1306

Majolica, Quimper, country & small Adirondack furniture, painted cupboards, fine china, glassware, sterling, local artwork. **Hrs:** By chance/appt. **QC: 23 34 61**

Saratoga Springs

Broadway Antiques Gallery

484 Broadway • 12866
(518)581-8348 **Hrs:** Mon-Sat 10-6, Sun 12-5. **CC:** AX/V/MC/DIS.

Regent Street Antique Center [G22]

153 Regent St • 12866
(518)584-0107

General line. **Hrs:** Daily 10-5. **CC:** V/MC **Own:** Willard Grande.

Saugerties

Central Hotel Antiques [G]

83 Partition St • 12477
(914)246-8183

Hrs: Daily 11-5. **Own:** Harold Swart.

Dust & Rust Antiques

Rte 32 • 12477
(914)246-7728

Tools, primitives, art, furniture, books, jewelry, architecturals & collectibles. **Hrs:** Sat-Sun or by appt. **Dir:** 1 mi N of NY Thruway Exit 20. **Own:** Lou Parisi. **QC: 86 48 3**

Fed-On Antiques

Market & Livingston Sts • 12477
(914)246-8444

Specializing in lighting fixtures (19th & 20th C); footed tubs & sinks, architectural artifacts, furniture & glassware on two floors. **Est:** 1978 **Hrs:** Thu-Mon 12-5:30. **Sz:** L **Dir:** NY Thruway Exit 20: 100 mi N of New York City, 40 mi S of Albany. **Own:** Don & Anne Curry. **QC: 65 48 60 S12**

Ed & Sharon Finney Antiques

106 Partition St • 12477
(914)247-0765

Furniture, lighting, clocks, paintings & toys. **Hrs:** Wed-Mon 10:30-5 or by appt. **QC: 48 65 35**

Graphic Collectibles
22 Blue Hill Dr • 12477
(914)246-0952 • (914)246-1025 (fax)
graphcoll@codexx.com
www.graphiccollectibles.com

Specializing in original American illustration art & comic art. **Est:** 1976 **Hrs:** Mon-Fri 9-6; Sat-Sun by appt. **CC:** AX/V/MC/DIS. **QC: 39 7**

Old & New Clock Shop
88 Market St • 12477
(914)246-5707 • (914)246-8226 (fax)
www.oldandnew.com

Specializing in antique clocks with a good selection. All sales/repairs guaranteed. **Pr:** $25-4,000 **Est:** 1994 **Hrs:** Mon-Tue & Thu-Fri 9-5, Sat 9-3, Wed by appt. **Sz:** M **CC:** AX/V/MC/DIS **Assn:** NAWCC AWI **Own:** Mike Loebbaka. **QC: 35 S7**

Partition Street Antiques [G]
114 Partition St • 12477
(914)246-1802 • (914)247-0932 (fax)
(800)948-8567

Fine furniture from Victorian to 1950s. Also delightful selection of Arts & Crafts furniture from Gustave Stickley, glass, pottery, jewelry & always unique smalls. **Hrs:** Mon-Tue & Thu-Sun 10-5. **Sz:** L **CC:** V/MC. **QC: 6 48 101 S1**

Piggy Wig Antiques
407 Phillips Rd • 12477
(914)246-2452

Country things: furniture, kitchen items, glass, china, toys & miscellaneous collectibles. **Hrs:** By chance/appt. **Dir:** Between Glasco Tpke & Rte 212.

Saugerties Antique Center & Annex [G18]
220 Main St • 12477
(914)246-4363

Furniture, jewelry, china, toys, glass, Deco, Mission, Victorian, primitive. Affordable prices. **Pr:** $5-5,000 **Est:** 1975 **Hrs:** Mon-Sat 10-5, Sun 12-5. **Sz:** L **Dir:** NY Thruway: Exit 20, 1 mi to village. **Own:** Lee & Chris Schackne. **QC: 6 7 10**

Saugerties Antiques Gallery
104 Partition St • 12477
(914)246-2323

An eclectic collection of fine antiques from Chippendale to Art Moderne, paintings, bronzes & an ever-changing variety of the unusual & wonderful. All merchandise guaranteed. **Hrs:** Daily.

Schoolhouse Emporium
Rte 32 N & Harry Wells Rd • 12477
(914)247-0191

19th C schoolhouse filled with collectibles, jewelry & antiques. **Hrs:** Sat-Sun 10-6. **Own:** Dorothy Dodig.

Stone House Gallery
102 Partition St • 12477
(914)247-0827

Primitives to Deco. Something special of any period. Estate jewelry, furniture, architectural & art objects, garden antiques. Things of charm or for serious investment. **Est:** 1973 **Hrs:** Fri-Mon 10-5, or by chance/appt. **Sz:** M **CC:** V/MC **Own:** Natalia Pohrebinska. **QC: 64 48 3**

Schoharie

Ginny's Hutch
Rte 30 • 12157
(518)295-7470

Art glass, primitives, art nouveau, furniture, jewelry & decorator items. **Hrs:** Daily 10-5; Oct-Jun closed Mon. **CC:** V/MC **Dir:** 1/2 mi S of village of Schoharie. **Own:** Virginia Kintz. **QC: 5 48**

Saltbox Antiques
Stony Brook Rd • 12157
(518)295-7408

American country furniture, textiles, toys, stoneware, jewelry & early glass. **Hrs:** Apr-Dec Wed-Sun 11-5. **Dir:** 1 mi S of Schoharie Village, just off Rte 30. **Own:** Ruth Anne Keese. **QC: 102 80 87**

Tinker's Shop Antiques
Rte 30 • 12157
(518)827-4970

Furniture, iron, tin & kitchen collectibles. **Hrs:** By chance/appt. **Own:** Helen Moltzen-Wright.

Schuylerville

The Barking Frog/Olympia Hall [G]
76 Broad St • 12871
(518)695-1028

General line. **Hrs:** Daily. **Sz:** L **CC:** V/MC/DIS.

Birdsnest [G]
74A Broad St • 12871
(518)695-5608

Paper, glassware, collectibles, movie posters, books, tools, prints, photos & jewelry. **Hrs:** Jul-Aug Mon-Sat 10-5, Sun 12-5; Sep-Jun Tue-Sat 10-5, Sun 12-5.

Miss Daisy's Teacarte
65 Broad St • 12871

Collectibles, artwork, china, teapots & tinware. **Hrs:** Mon-Sat.

Now & Then Antiques
Louden Rd • 12871
(518)581-0618

18th & 19th C furniture, silver, Depression glass, linen, crystal & sterling. **Dir:** 1/2 mi on Louden Rd from Rte 29.

Schuyler Antique Center [G]
106-110 Broad St • 12871
(518)695-4246

General line. **Hrs:** Daily 10-5. **Sz:** L **QC: S16 S1**

Stan's
122 Broad St • 12871
(518)695-5237

Oak, mahogany & red cherry furniture, collectibles, kitchenware & country pieces. **Hrs:** Sun-Thu 10-5, Fri-Sat 10-7. **QC: 48**

Sharon Springs

Little Bit O'Country
Rte 20 • 13459
(518)284-2150

Furniture, smalls, glassware, advertising memorabilia & stoneware. **Hrs:** Mon, Fri & Sat 10-4 by chance/appt.

Skaneateles

Skaneateles Antique Center [G30+]
12 E Genesee St • 13152
(315)685-0752

Early American, mission & 20th C furniture, estate & Victorian jewelry, china, glass, silver, pottery, books, art, clocks, textiles, lighting, primitives, militaria, advertising & decorative accessories, Arts & Crafts. Quality antiques. **Est:** 1992 **Hrs:** Mon-Sat 10-5:30, Sun 12-5. **CC:** AX/V/MC/DIS.

White & White Antiques & Interiors Inc

18 E Genesee St • 13152
(315)685-7733

Americana from 1690 to 1960. Specializing in early paint & paintings. **Est:** 1965 **Hrs:** Mon-Sat 10-5. **CC:** AX/V/MC/DIS **Assn:** ADA **Own:** Stephen & Beverly White. **QC:** **51 7 41 S15 S1**

Skokan

Winchell's Corners Antiques [G20]

Rte 28 & Reservoir Rd • 12481
(914)657-2177

In a turn-of-the-century meeting hall. **Hrs:** Call for hrs.

South Glens Falls

Route 9 Antiques

Rte 9 • 12803
(518)798-8971

Primitives, rustic & Adirondack furniture, lamps, topographical maps & post cards. **Hrs:** Daily 11-5. **Dir:** I-87 Exit 17: 2 mi N on Saratoga Rd. **Own:** Harold Fuller. **QC:** **106 66**

Village Antiques [G6]

162 Saratoga Ave • 12803
(518)792-9645
b3888@together.net

Furniture, radios, glassware, advertising, hunting & fishing, tools, toys & brass lights. **Hrs:** Daily 11-4. **Own:** Bill Tranowicz.

South Westerlo

The Country Gentlemen Antiques

Rte 401/405 • 12083
(518)966-5574

Furniture, collectibles, glass & paintings. **Est:** 1990 **Hrs:** Thu-Sat 10-5, Sun 11-4:30. **Dir:** 1/4 mi off Rte 32. **Own:** Galbreath E Palmer.

Taking Tea III

Mote spoon: A small spoon, usually made of silver, with a decoratively pierced bowl and a long, pointed handle. The bowls were used to skim tea leaves off the surface of the cup of tea, and the handles for clearing leaves that clogged the spout of the teapot. Most were made between 1725 and 1800 and are superbly crafted.

Tea strainer: A small strainer that fit over the cup to catch tea leaves. Made from about 1750 onwards

Spencertown

Spencertown Art & Antiques Company
Rte 203 • 12165
(518)392-4442
mpart@taconic.net

In a restored Greek Revival church, a large stock of fine paintings, sculpture, prints, Americana, jewelry, 18th & 19th C furniture, Oriental rugs, antique firearms, Shaker & folk art, all from local homes & estates. **Pr:** $500-10,000 **Est:** 1984 **Hrs:** By appt only. **Sz:** L **CC:** AX **Dir:** I-90 Austerlitz Exit: Rte 22 to Taconic Pkwy. Exit Spencertown/Rte 203, Rte 22 N or S to Rte 203 W 4 mi. **Own:** Martin Parker. **QC: 4 7 74 S1 S9 S16**

Stone Ridge

Antiques at Marbletown Square [G]
Rte 209 • 12484
(914)687-7229

Collectibles & furniture in ten rooms packed with treasures. **Hrs:** Daily 11-5.

Stone Ridge Antiques [G12]
Main St (Rte 209) • 12484
(914)687-7400

Three floors in an 1860s building filled with primitives, jewelry, furniture, prints, toys. **Hrs:** Wed-Mon 11-5, Tue by appt. **Own:** Bruce Alter.

Things Antique
Rte 209 S • 12484
(914)687-4577

Large barn packed full with country furniture, architectural elements, outdoor (lawn, garden, patio) furnishings & lighting. **Pr:** $50-1,000 **Hrs:** Fri-Mon 10-5 or by appt. **Sz:** M **Dir:** NYS Thruway: Exit at Kingston, Rte 209 S to Stone Ridge, 2 mi S of village. **Own:** Joel Wolf. **QC: 3 102 65**

Thumbprint Antiques
209 Tongore Rd • 12484
(914)687-9318

A huge barn full of china, glass, silver, furniture & lighting. **Est:** 1966 **Hrs:** Tue-Sun 12-5. **Sz:** H **CC:** AX/V/MC **Dir:** 1/4 mi off Rte 209. **Own:** Bob Palmatier. **QC: S1**

Tomfoolery Antiques
3829 Main St • 12484
(914)687-4943

An eclectic mix from elegant to primitive, furniture, lamps, mirrors, pottery. Moderately priced. **Hrs:** Wed-Mon 12-5. **Dir:** I-87 Kingston Exit: 15 min S on Rte 209 at Rte 213 E. **Own:** Tom Blake.

Syracuse

Lilac House Antiques & Galleries [G30+]
1415 W Genesee St • 13204
(315)471-3866

General line. **Hrs:** Mon-Sat 10-6, Sun 11-5. **CC:** V/MC/DIS **Own:** Mark Carfagno.

Syracuse Antiques Exchange [G60]
1629 N Salina St • 13204
(315)471-1841

Antiques & collectibles. No reproductions. **Hrs:** Mon-Sat 10:30-5, Sun 12-4 (except Jul-Aug). **Sz:** H **CC:** AX/V/MC/DIS **Dir:** Near the Carousel Ctr & Regional market. **Own:** David Jenks.

Thousand Island Park

Park Antiques
Rainbow St • 13692
(315)482-6907

Fine antiques, art glass, art pottery, china, furniture, estate & vintage jewelry, country kitchen corner with primitives & collectibles. **Hrs:** May 15-Oct 15 daily 10-5. **Dir:** 4 mi W of Thousand Island bridge (I-81). **Own:** Sharon & Carl Castro. **QC: 100 101 64**

Valatie

The Millstone Trading Co

3037 Main St • 12184
(518)758-7004

Formal & country furniture, textiles & pottery. **Hrs:** Sat-Sun 12-5 or by appt. **QC: 80 S12**

The White Goose

317 Reed Rd • 12184
(518)766-3909

Antiques & collectibles. **Hrs:** Sat-Sun 9-4, by chance/appt. **Dir:** Off Rte 66 betw Malden Bridge & Chatham Ctr. **Own:** Carolyn M Allen.

Vermontville

Forest Murmurs Studio/Antiques

(518)327-9373

Specializing in rustic interiors, furniture, paintings, prints, books, hunting & fishing items, old boats & canoes, taxidermy & unique lighting. **Hrs:** May-Oct daily 11-5 or by appt. **Dir:** On Rte 3 just a short ride from Saranac Lake. **Own:** Glenn Bauer. **QC: 79 74**

Victor

Traditions

7834 North Rd • 14564
(716)924-7826 • (716)271-4305 (fax)

19th C American Indian antiques & beaded bags. **Hrs:** By appt only. **Own:** Martin Gingras. **QC: 42**

The Black Shutters

86 Gates Ave • 12884
(518)695-9225
hook@global200.net

Four floors in two large buildings: eclectic general line emphasizing country furniture, better china & glass, textiles. **Pr:** $2-2,000 **Est:** 1964 **Hrs:** Mar 1-Dec 31 Fri-Sun12-5. **Sz:** L **Assn:** NEAA **Dir:** 12 mi E of Saratoga Springs; 1 mi S of Schuylerville on Rte 32. **Own:** George Kahnle & Richard LaBarge. **QC: 34 52 57 S1**

Waddington

A Place in Tyme

153 McGinnis Rd • 13694
(315)388-4070

Furniture & collectibles. **Hrs:** By chance/appt. **Dir:** Rte 37 W past Coles Creek State Pk, over bridge. Take 1st L onto McGinnis Rd. Sign on crnr of Rte 37 & McGinnis Rd. Shop is located 1 mi on R. **Own:** Sharon Baker. **QC: S16**

Walden

Wallkill Antique Center aka "The Barn" [G25+]

2660 Rte 208N • 12586
(914)778-5822
anteq1@aol.com

General line. **Hrs:** Daily 10-5. **Sz:** H **CC:** V/MC **Own:** Linda Horton. **QC: S8**

Wallkill

Wallkill River House [G4]

38 Wallkill Ave • 12586
(914)895-1410
flydutch@frontiernet.net

Country & Victorian antiques, primitives, jewelry & gifts. **Hrs:** Mon & Wed-Sat 10:30-5, Sun 12-4. **CC:** V/MC **Own:** Freda Fenn, Lisa Stoker, Nancy Glassen & Hazel Terwilliger. **QC: 89 34**

Walton

TJ's Wagon Wheel Antiques

Marvin Hollow Rd • 13856
(607)865-7165

General line. **Hrs:** By chance/appt. **Dir:** 3 mi off Rte 10 across from Agway Petroleum.

Waterford

Blanchet's Antiques & Uniques

57 Broad St • 12188
(518)235-2235

Furniture, accessories, smalls, china, glass, architectural & decorative accessories. **Hrs:** Daily. **QC: 48 36 3**

Watertown

The Antique Shop [G4]

122 Court St • 13601
(315)782-5200

Country to oak furniture, primitives, paintings, china, baskets, glass & quilts. **Hrs:** Mon-Sat 9:30-5. **Dir:** In the Empsall bldg in downtown Watertown. **QC: 102 106**

Curtis Antiques

19705 Hillside Dr • 13601
(315)782-3617
bcurtis@northnet.org

Specializing in old woodworking tools with an emphasis on 19th C planes. **Hrs:** By appt only. **Own:** Bill Curtis. **QC: 86**

Wawarsing

Old Mine Road Antiques

Rte 209 • 12489
(914)647-6771

Fine general line. Specializing in unusual jewelry, silver, china & small items. **Hrs:** By chance/appt. **Own:** Nadia Shepard.

West Coxsackie

Coxsackie Antique Center [G55]

Crnr Rte 9W & Rte 81 • 12192
(518)731-8888 • (518)731-8888 (fax)
antiques@coxsackie.com
www.coxsackie.com

General line. **Hrs:** Mon-Tue, Thu & Sat 10-5, Wed 10-8, Fri 10-6, Sun 11-5. **CC:** AX/V/MC/DIS **Dir:** Crnr Rte 9W & Rte 81. **Own:** Bill Johns.

West Fulton

The Chicken Coop

W Fulton Rd • 12194
(518)827-7222

General line. **Hrs:** By chance/appt.

West Hurley

Elusive Butterfly Antiques

Rte 28 • 12491
(914)679-2521

American turn-of-the-century oak & Victorian walnut furniture, period lighting & decorative accessories. **Hrs:** By chance/appt. **QC: 89 50 65 S1**

Goosewing Antiques

51 Nissen Ln • 12491
(914)679-9206

Specializing in antique woodworking tools & decorated stoneware. **Hrs:** By chance/appt. **Own:** Cliff Yaun. **QC: 86 31**

West Taghkanic

Rural Provisioner Ltd

(518)851-6934
(888)876-3084

Formal & country antique & collectible furniture, glass, china & linens. **Hrs:** Thu-Sun 10-6 or by appt.

Whitehall

Jami's Second Impressions [G3]

114 Main St • 12887
(518)499-1390
dukefly1@aol.com

Victorian furniture to 1960s bedroom sets, gold, diamonds, sterling jewelry, costume jewelry, glassware, etched vases, wine glasses, decanters, carnival glass, Depression, milk glass & Victorian clothing. **Pr:** $5-1,400 **Est:** 1996 **Hrs:** May 1-Dec 31 Mon-Thu 10-5, Fri-Sat 10-7, Sun 12-4; Jan 1-Apr 30 Mon-Sat 10-5, Sun 12-4. **Sz:** L **CC:** AX/MC **Dir:** I-87 Exit 20: Rte 149 N to Rte 22 E into Whitehall. R at 2nd light, shop is located on crnr of Saunders & Main Sts. **Own:** JoAnn Ingalls. **QC: 48 61 33 S1 S8 S12**

Whitehall Antique Center [G]

Rte 4 • 12887
(518)499-2501 • (518)499-2557 (fax)

General line. **Hrs:** Mon-Thu 10-5, Fri-Sat 9-5. **Sz:** L.

Willow

James Cox Gallery

4666 Rte 212 • 12495
(914)679-7608 • (914)679-7627 (fax)
jcoxgal@ulster.net

20th C artwork. Specializing in Woodstock art. **Est:** 1990 **Hrs:** Mon-Fri 10-5. **CC:** V/MC **Dir:** 7 mi from Woodstock Village Green. **QC: 7 S1 S16**

Willsboro

Brown House Antiques

Main St (Rte 22) • 12996
(518)963-7352

Furniture, wicker, Cambridge, Fostoria, Heisey, white ironstone, holiday collectibles, prints, books, watercolors, kitchen items, Fiestaware, dolls, sewing items, Shelley, flow blue, Victorian silverplate, quilts, vintage clothing & linens. **Hrs:** Jul 1-Sep 2 Tue-Sat 10-4:30. **Dir:** Rte 22 across from the Methodist Church. **QC: 91 80 29**

Woodstock

Ivy on Mill

94 Mill Hill Rd • 12498
(914)679-4378

Rural American farm furniture, ironstone, art pottery, architectural, decorative & lighting. **Hrs:** Thu-Tue 11-6.

New York
(Long Island plus Westchester, Rockland, Orange, and Putnam Counties)

Long Island and Westchester, Rockland, Orange, and Putnam Counties

LEGEND
Interstate Highway
Major U.S. and State Routes
Minor State Routes
Not to Scale

Albertson

Robert Lloyd Inc

(516)625-5794

Fine antique silver. **Hrs:** By appt only. **QC: 77**

Bedford

Antiques II Ltd

656 Rte 22 • 10506
(914)234-6521 • (914)234-4089 (fax)

Lighting, furniture, garden ornaments, fireplace equipment, mirrors, leather books & decorative accessories. **Hrs:** Tue-Thu 10:30-5:30, Fri-Sat 10-5, Sun-Mon by chance/appt. **Sz:** M **CC:** AX/V/MC **Dir:** I-684 Exit 4 to Rte 22. **QC: 36 60 65**

Aunty Faye's Antiques & Collectibles

Bedford Village Green • 10506
(914)234-7789 • (914)234-7789 (fax)
ntyfaye@aol.com
www.magicgate.com/auntyfayes/

American country furniture, glassware, quilts, books, American pottery. **Est:** 1997 **Hrs:** Tue-Fri 11-5, Sat 10-5, Sun 1-5. **CC:** V/MC **Own:** Fayette M Wester. **QC: 102**

Voss Beringer Ltd

(914)241-4687 • (914)241-1265 (fax)
slk431@aol.com

Fine American antiques. **Hrs:** By appt only. **Own:** Gregory Palitz. **QC: 1**

Brewster

There's No Place Like Home

90 Main St • 10509
(914)278-9228 • (914)278-9228 (fax)
cdavern@aol.com

Antiques, lampshades, framing. **Est:** 1992 **Hrs:** Tue-Fri 10-4, Sat 10-5, Sun 1-5. **Sz:** M **CC:** V/MC/DIS **Own:** Cynthia Davern. **QC: S13 S15**

Bridgehampton

Nancy S Boyd

Main St • 11937
(516)537-3838 • (516)329-3241 (fax)

Carefully selected 18th & 19th C American furniture: paint decorated, sophisticated country or higher style & decorative arts including folk carvings, weathervanes, blown glass, unusual hooked rugs & paintings, as well as iron garden accessories. **Hrs:** By appt only. **CC:** AX/V/MC **Assn:** ADA AC. **QC: 1 52 45**

Kinnaman & Ramaekers

2466 Main St • 11975
(516)537-3838 • (516)537-0779 (fax)
ramaekers@earthlink.net

Fine American antiques with emphasis on painted furniture in original finish, folk art, American Indian artifacts, paintings, textiles & early glass. **Pr:** $100-25,000 **Est:** 1969 **Hrs:** May-Oct 15 Thu-Tue 11-5; Oct 16-Apr Fri-Sun 11-5; closed Feb. **Sz:** M **CC:** AX/V/MC **Assn:** NAADAA **Dir:** Montauk Hwy (Rte 27) in center of village, three doors W of the library. **Own:** Robert Kinnaman & Brian Ramaekers. **QC: 1 41 52**

Sterling & Hunt

42 Butter Ln • 11932
(516)537-1096

American art & antiques, weathervanes, folk art. **Est:** 1972 **Hrs:** Daily 12-5. **Dir:** On the N side of Montauk Hwy at Butter Lane. 2nd house on L turning N. **QC: 41 45 1**

Chappaqua

Crown House

297 King St • 10514
(914)238-3949 • (914)238-0307 (fax)

Furniture, brass, china & glass. **Hrs:** Tue-Sat 10-5 or by appt.

Chester

M G Galleries & Cafe [G22]
55 Main St • 10918
(914)469-2115 • (914)469-6011 (fax)

Three floors of antiques, fine arts, Victorian glass, collectibles & decoys. **Est:** 1986 **Hrs:** Wed-Sun 11-5. **Sz:** M **CC:** V/MC/DIS **Own:** Mike Farrow. **QC: 7 32 61**

Village Gallery & Auction Hall [G7]
3 Howland St • 10918
(914)469-6979 • (914)469-8480 (fax)

An eclectic mix of antiques & vintage collectibles. **Est:** 1998 **Hrs:** Wed-Sun 11-5. **Sz:** L **CC:** AX/V/MC/DIS **Own:** Glynnis & Alan Jorgensen.

Cold Spring

Bijou Galleries Ltd [G20]
50 Main St • 10516
(914)265-4337
bijou@bestweb.net
www.bijougalleries.com

Antiques, art & collectibles in a bright & cheerful atmosphere. **Hrs:** Daily. **Own:** Jane & Michael Timm.

Dew Drop Inn Antique Center [G40]
Rte 9 • 10516
(914)265-4358

Antiques & collectibles. **Hrs:** Wed-Mon 11-6. **Dir:** 1 mi N of Rte 301, 5 mi S of I-84 Exit 13.

Once Upon a Time Antiques
101 Main St • 10516
(914)265-4339

Oak furniture, antique dolls & toys, holiday collectibles. **Hrs:** Mon-Tue & Thu-Fri 10:30-4, Sat-Sun 10-6. **Own:** Bob & Barbara Wade. **QC: 50 38 87**

Other's Oldies
169 Main St • 10516
(914)265-2323

Estate jewelry, watches, oak furniture. **Hrs:** Daily 10-6. **Own:** Tom Valentino. **QC: 64 50 35**

Taca-Tiques
109 Main St • 10516
(914)265-2655
tacatiques@aol.com

Alcoholic Antiques I

Cellaret: An 18th century lidded case for wine bottles, often of the highest craftsmanship, usually on casters. Cellarets were fitted with locks to keep bibulous servants at bay and were typically kept under serving tables in the dining room. Sideboards, introduced at the end of the century, included cupboards for storing bottles. They rapidly replaced cellarets.

Wine cistern: An elaborate tub of silver, pewter or, most often, of wood lined with lead for cooling wine in ice.

Wine coaster: Originally, in the 18th century, a small wagon on wheels used for circulating wine around a large dining table. Often a coaster would be fitted with decanters for port, claret, and madeira. Coasters were made of silver or mahogany and later were made to slide on baize rather than roll on wheels. It is this form that evolved into the modern coaster.

Tantalus: A lockable liquor rack, usually holding three cut-glass decanters, that allowed the liquor to be seen but not drunk. A Victorian invention designed to ensure that the master of the house controlled its alcohol.

American Victorian sterling silver & beveled glass mirrors as well as furniture, porcelain, glass, restored trunks, telephones & costume jewelry. **Pr:** $3-12,000 **Est:** 1981 **Hrs:** Wed-Sun & hol Mons 12-5. **Sz:** L **CC:** AX/V/MC/DIS **Dir:** Rte 84W Exit 13 (Poughkeepsie/Fishkill): Rte 9 S to light. At Rtes 9 & 301 turn R onto Rte 301. 3 mi on L. **Own:** Sarita & Lew Osterman. **QC: 48 68 78**

Cold Spring Harbor

Huntington Antiques Center [G20]

129 Main St • 11724
(516)549-0105

18th & 19th C furniture, ceramics, silver, glass, jewelry, fireplace equipment, decoys, Long Island maps, art & decorative accessories. **Pr:** $50-10,000 **Est:** 1986 **Hrs:** Tue-Sat 10:30-5, Sun 12-5. **Sz:** L **CC:** V/MC **Dir:** Rte 25 A (Main St) in Cold Spring Harbor across from Municipal Parking Lot. **Own:** Kathy Sapio. **QC: 23 48 78 S6 S12 S19**

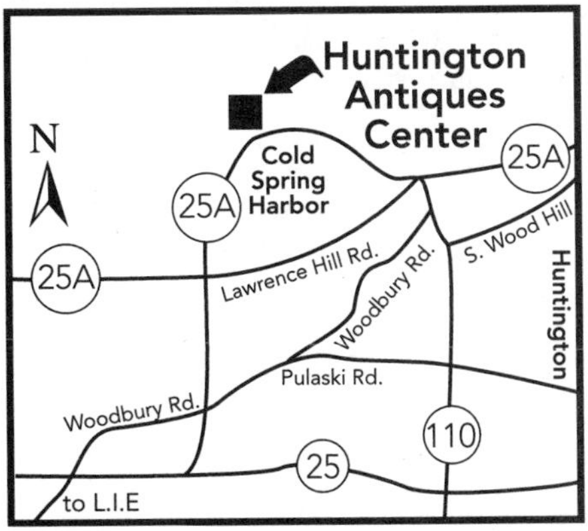

Cortlandt Manor

Timothy Trace Booksellers

144 Red Mill Rd • 10566
(914)528-4074

Books on antique American decorative arts. **Hrs:** By appt only. **QC: 18 19**

Cross River

Yellow Monkey Antiques

Rte 35 • 10518
(914)763-5848 • (914)763-8832 (fax)
www.yellowmonkey.com

English pine country furniture, accessories & garden accessories. **Hrs:** Tue-Sun 10-6. **Sz:** L **CC:** AX/V/MC **Dir:** I-684 Exit 6 (Rte 35) or Saw Mill River Pkwy to I-684: E on Rte 35 4 mi to entrance on L. **Own:** Richard Pickett. **QC: 34 54 60**

Croton-on-Hudson

Patricia A Vaillancourt

143 Grand St • 10520
(914)271-2082 • (914)271-5857 (fax)

Dolls, painting's, folk art, accessories. **Hrs:** By appt/chance. **CC:** V/MC. **QC: 38**

East Hampton

Architrove

Red Horse Plaza • 11937
(516)329-2229 • (516)329-1155 (fax)

Antique lighting (sconces & chandeliers), American & European furniture, bath accessories. **Pr:** $18-15,000 **Est:** 1993 **Hrs:** Mon & Thu-Fri 10-6, Sat 9-6, Sun 10-5. **Sz:** M **Dir:** Across from Hampton Bowling in the Red Horse Plaza. **Own:** Gary Kephart & Susan Allen. **QC: 65 48 70**

Faces Antiques

251 Montauk Hwy • 11937
(516)324-9510 • (516)324-9510 (fax)

Art Noveau, Tiffany lamps, American art pottery, sterling silver & decorative items. **Hrs:** Call for hrs. **Sz:** M **CC:** AX/V/MC **Own:** Bonny & Mel Aarons. **QC: 65 5 101**

Florida

Antique Center of Orange County [G]

2 N Main St • 10921
(914)651-2711 • (914)651-6102 (fax)
www.antiquescenteroc.com

Toys, games, Roseville pottery, glass, china, furniture, cookbooks, World's Fair, jewelry, artwork, advertising, automobilia, sports. **Hrs:** Wed-Sat 10-5, Sun 11-4. **Sz:** L **CC:** AX/V/MC/DIS **Dir:** 4 mi from Goshen on Rte 17A, Exit 124. 15 min from Rte 17 & Rte 84 (1 hr from NYC). **Own:** Lenny Rifkin. **QC: 87 101 32**

Randallville Mill Antiques

65 Randall St (Rte 94) • 10921
(914)651-7466

Country pine & oak furniture & accessories. **Hrs:** Sat-Sun 1:30-5. **Own:** Gary & Kathy Randall. **QC: 34 50**

Goshen

Remington's

65 Phillipsburg Rd • 10924
(914)291-1277 • (914)291-7193 (fax)
remington@pioneeris.net

Stickley, Lifetime, Tiffany, Mettlach, Muller Freres, Steuben, Heisey, Nemethy, fiestaware, Gorham, Wallace, Noritake, Haviland. **Hrs:** Wed-Fri 10-5, Sat-Sun 11-6. **Sz:** H **CC:** AX/V/MC/DIS **Dir:** Rte 17 Exit 22A (Goshen). From 17 W go R, from 17 E go L to end of Exit (Burke High School) then R on Fletcher St, L on Minisink Trail to 1st stop sign, L on Phillipsburg Rd. **Own:** Karina M Ariola.

John P Spencer Antiques

36 St John St • 10992
(914)497-7193
jspeant@warwick.net

American Federal furniture. **Est:** 1984 **Hrs:** By appt only. **QC: 52**

Great Neck

Cutlery Specialties

22 Morris Ln • 11024
(516)829-5899 • (516)773-8076 (fax)
dennis13@aol.com
www.silversmithing.com/cutleryspecialties

Antique factorymade, handmade & custom-made knives & related cutlery items & cutlery ephemera. **Est:** 1993 **Hrs:** By appt only. **CC:** AX/V/MC/DIS **Dir:** Call for directions. **Own:** Dennis Blaine. **QC: S9 S16**

Highland Falls

The Old Stock Exchange

312 Main St • 10928
(914)446-5500

An eclectic mix of antiques & collectibles. **Hrs:** Thu-Sat 11-5, Sun 12-3 or by appt. **CC:** V/MC **Own:** Joanne Devereaux. **QC: S8**

Katonah

Garden Antiques

296 Mt Holly Rd • 10536
(914)232-4271 • (212)744-2188 (fax)

19th C statuary, cast iron & wrought iron for the formal garden. Specializing in classical themes & offering figural statues, animal statues, sundials, birdbaths, urns, benches, chairs, tables & decorative accessories for the garden. **Hrs:** By chance/appt. **Assn:** ADA **Own:** Barbara Israel. **QC: 60**

Larchmont

Arti Antiques Inc
2070 Boston Post Rd • 10538
(914)833-1794

Antique furniture & accessories direct from France, Belgium & Holland including Art Deco, Arts & Crafts & Art Nouveau. **Hrs:** Mon-Fri 10-5:30, Sat 10-5, Sun 12-5. **Dir:** I-95 Exit 17 from S or Exit 18A from N, 30 min from Manhattan. **QC: 53 56**

Briggs House Antiques
2100 Boston Post Rd • 10538
(914)833-3087

A large variety of imported furniture: country French, Irish pine & English; mirrors, lamps, prints & decorative accessories. **Hrs:** Mon-Sat 10-5:30. **Sz:** L. **QC: 36 53 54**

Post Road Gallery
2128 Boston Post Rd • 10538
(914)834-7568 • (914)834-9245 (fax)
staff@postroadgallery.com
www.postroadgallery.com

Specializing in 19th C American paintings, sculpture & decorative arts. **Hrs:** Tue-Sat 10-5. **Own:** Robert, David & Jennifer Bahssin. **QC: 7**

Thomas K Salese Antiques
2372 Boston Post Rd • 10538
(914)834-0222 • (914)834-2632 (fax)
(877)250-2634

18th-19th C English & Continental furniture & accessories. **Hrs:** Mon-Sat 10-5. **Sz:** L **CC:** V/MC. **QC: 36 54 53**

Woolf's Den Antiques
2130 Boston Post Rd • 10538
(914)834-0066

Furniture, paintings, silver, gold, clocks, ivory & jewelry. **Hrs:** Mon-Sat 10-5, Sun 12-4. **QC: 48 7**

Mahopac

Elaine's Antiques & Collectibles
441 Rte 6 • 10541
(914)621-0993

American pottery, sterling. **Hrs:** Wed-Sat 11-5. **CC:** AX/V/MC.

Yellow Shed Antiques
571 Rte 6 • 10541
(914)628-0362

Oak, walnut, pine & mahogany furniture, unique jewelry, coins, stamps, collectibles & memorabilia. **Est:** 1970 **Hrs:** Tue-Sun 10-5; Jul-Aug closed Mon & Tue. **Sz:** L **CC:** AX/V/MC/DIS **Dir:** Taconic State Pkwy Rte 6 Exit: toward Mahopac 5.7 mi. I-84W Exit 19: R on Rte 312, R on Rte 6 to Mahopac. **Own:** Mark Liff. **QC: 48 71 32**

Mamaroneck

Cavendish Gallery
400 Mamaroneck Ave • 10543
(914)698-7192 • (914)698-4320 (fax)

Fine 18th & 19th C French, English & American furniture, porcelains, bronzes, paintings, Oriental rugs, statuary & objects d'art. **Pr:** $200-75,000 **Hrs:** Mon-Fri 8:30-5, Sat 8:30-2; Jun 1-Aug 31 Mon-Thu 8:30-5, Fri 8:30-3. **Dir:** 20 mi N of NYC. I-95N Exit 18: R on Fenemore Rd, 3rd L on Hoyt, R on Mamaroneck Ave. I-95S Exit 18: toward Mamaroneck. **Own:** F Rotondo. **QC: 11 36 53 S1**

Den of Antiquity
219 Mamaroneck Ave • 10543
(914)698-6280

Bronzes, marble statues, pictures, Tiffany style lamps, antique & reproduction furniture. **Hrs:** Mon-Fri 12-5 **Dir:** Next to the Bank of New York **Own:** Elliot Shapiro.

Mt Kisco

Antiques Etc

145 Lexington Ave • 10549
(914)666-2599

17th-20th C boxes, furniture, arts, crafts, chintz & Art Nouveau. **QC: 48 6 5**

Antiques on the Mall [G5]

195 N Bedford Rd (Rte 117) • 10549
(914)242-3522

Coins & jewelry, artwork, country to formal furniture, glassware. **Hrs:** Mon-Sat 10-9, Sun 12-6. **CC:** AX/V/MC/DIS **Dir:** I-684 Exit 4 or Saw Mill Pkwy Exit 37: L to traffic sign, L to Outlet Center (upstairs).

The Last Detail

84 Lexington Ave • 10549
(914)666-3620

Oak furniture & art pottery. **QC: 50 101**

New Hampton

Four Winds Antique Center [G3+]

Rte 17M • 10958
(914)374-7272

Furniture, dolls, toys, silver, lamps, pottery, glass, antiques, postcards & paper. **Hrs:** Daily 11-5. **Dir:** I-84 Exit 3E: 1/2 mi on Rte 17M, shop is located on R.

Steve's Antiques

Rte 17M • 10958
(914)374-6111 **Hrs:** Daily 11-5. **Dir:** Between Middletown & Goshen. **Own:** Steve Tava.

North Salem

Artemis Gallery

Wallace Rd • 10560
(914)669-5971 • (914)669-8604 (fax)
artemis@bestweb.net

Alcoholic Antiques II

Monteith: A bowl used to cool drinking glasses in iced water. Its rim had notches into which stemmed glasses were slotted. Named after the 17th century Earl of Monteith, a court fop noted for the elaborately scalloped hems on his cloaks which the rim of the monteith resembled, the first British examples date to around 1680, while the first American one was made about 1700 by the Boston silversmith John Coney. Later monteiths were also made of porcelain and glass, sometimes with a removeable silver rim, in which case the bowl doubled as a punch bowl.

Wine stand: A small stand with a dish or tray top. It resembles a candlestand, but is two or three inches lower, making it a convenient height for a wine glass when placed at the arm of one's easy chair.

Toddy table: An 18th century name, now fallen into disuse, for a side table for holding drinks. Its alliterative aptness makes it a term worth reviving. The interior design guru David Hicks advises readers of *Antique Interiors International* that drinks should always be served on a marble- or stone-topped table and never from a cocktail cabinet, which he disdains as suitable only for the outer reaches of suburbia.

Can or wine can: A small handleless cup of silver or porcelain, usually a straight-sided or slightly flared cylinder, used for drinking wine in the 18th century.

Specializing in American Federal period furniture & American paintings. Furniture includes Hepplewhite, Sheraton & neoclassical pieces. Paintings cover all major schools from 1800 to 1940s. **Pr:** $500-50,000 **Est:** 1977 **Hrs:** Best to call ahead. **Sz:** M **Assn:** ADA **Dir:** Just off I-84 at the CT-NY border. **Own:** Carol & Jesse Goldberg. **QC: 52 7 S1 S9 S15**

The Guv'nor & Mrs A
Rte 116 • 10560
(914)669-8101

English & French furniture, paintings, clocks & accessories. **Hrs:** Wed-Sun 11-5 & by appt. **CC:** AX/V/MC/DIS. **QC: 54 35 36**

Kathy Schoemer American Antiques
12 McMorrow Ln • 10560
(914)277-8464 • (914)277-8464 (fax)

American informal antiques of the 19th C in original surface & appropriate accessories including textiles, basketry, pottery, folk art & children's antiques. **Pr:** $25-5,000 **Est:** 1971 **Hrs:** By appt only. **Sz:** M **CC:** AX **Assn:** ADA **Dir:** Rte 684 Exit 8. **QC: 1 36 52**

Nyack

LeVesque
170-2 Main St • 10960
(914)353-1900 • (914)353-1909 (fax)

French antiques including the largest selection of antique beds in the tri-state area: Louis XV, Louis XVI, Louis Phillipe, Deco, Empire, country French, day & sleigh. **Hrs:** Mon-Sat 10:30-6, Sun 12-5. **Sz:** H **CC:** V/MC/DIS **Own:** Eric Le Vesque. **QC: 47**

Old Business Antiques [G25]
142 Main St • 10960
(914)358-7008 • (201)986-0943 (fax)
76072.621@compuserve.com
www.ourworld.compuserve.com/homepages/ptalis2antiques

Victoriana, chintz, Shelley, Limoges, flow blue, furniture, paintings, vintage beaded purses, sterling silver, dolls, lamps, dresser sets, chandeliers, boxes, tins, Nippon, toys, linens, laces, mirrors & hat pins & holders. **Est:** 1990 **Hrs:** Wed-Sun 11-5. **Sz:** M **CC:** AX/V/MC/DIS **Dir:** NY State Thruway Exit 11 to Main St. **Own:** Sandy & Don Ptalis. **QC: 89 7 48 S12**

Old Brookville

Eugene L Oakes
(516)671-7512

A wonderful selection of 18th C American furniture & 19th C American paintings & English sporting paintings. **Hrs:** By appt only. **Assn:** ADA. **QC: 52 7 79 S16**

Pawling

Chez Genevieve
11 E Main St • 10564
(914)855-0079

Antiques & collectibles. **Hrs:** Tue-Sat 10-5, Sun 10-3.

Pelham

Accents on Antiques [G9]
125 Wolfs Ln • 10803
(914)637-1195 • (914)738-0075 (fax)

Period & antique furnishings, home accessories, collectibles. **Hrs:** Mon & Fri-Sat 9-5, Tue-Thu 9-7:30. **CC:** AX/V/MC/DIS. **QC: S8**

Bill Eayrs Antiques
656 Boulevard W • 10803
(914)738-1162

General line of antiques & collectibles. **Pr:** $1.00-$2000 **Est:** 1995 **Hrs:** Daily 11-6. **Sz:** M **Dir:** Hutchinson River Pwy Exit 10S & 9N.

Top Drawer Antiques
84 Lincoln Ave • 10803
(914)738-2254

Furniture, lighting, porcelain, kitchenware & musical objects. **Hrs:** Sat-Sun 8-10. **Own:** Joseph Spinelli.

Port Chester

Greenberg's Antiques Mall [G]
27 S Main St (Rte 1) • 10573
(914)937-4800

Furniture, collectibles & jewelry. **Hrs:** Mon-Sat 11:30-5:30, Sun 1-5. **Own:** Frank Greenberg.

Port Washington

Patricia V Giles Antiques
287 Main St • 11050
(516)883-1104

18th & 19th C country furniture & accessories. **Hrs:** By chance/appt.

Port Antique Center [G]
289 Main St • 11050
(516)767-3313

A quality group shop with a range of antiques. **Hrs:** Tue-Sat 11-5, Sun 12-5. **Own:** Judy Bergman.

Pound Ridge

Antiques & Tools of Business & Kitchen [G]
65 Westchester Ave • 10576
(914)764-0015

Tools of the chef, doctor, cabinetmaker, farmer, office, kitchenware, advertising, tools. 2nd Sunday outdoor markets. **Hrs:** Daily 11-5. **Sz:** M **CC:** V/MC **Own:** Joan Silbersher. **QC: 39 86 39**

Antiques & Interiors Inc
67 Westchester Ave • 10576
(914)764-4400

Furniture, rugs, vintage costume jewelry, accessories & lighting.

Purple Cornucopia
69 Westchester Ave • 10576
(914)764-5427 **Hrs:** Tue-Sat 11-5, Sun 11-3.

Rockville Centre

Joan Bogart Antiques
(516)764-5712 • (516)764-0529 (fax)
joanbogart@aol.com
www.joanbogart.com

High-style 19th C American classical & Victorian furniture with an emphasis on Belter, Meeks, Quervelle, Horner & Jelliff. Also gas chandeliers, argand & astral lamps, parian, majolica, Victorian silverplate & epergnes. **Est:** 1975 **Hrs:** By chance/appt. **Sz:** M **Assn:** AAA **Own:** Joan Bogart. **QC: 52 58 65**

Sag Harbor

Sage Street Antiques
Sage St & Rte 114 • 11963
(516)725-4036

Country antiques, kitchenware, botanicals, framed antique prints & local scenes; separate bldg with lower priced items. **Est:** 1979 **Hrs:** Sat 11-5, Sun 1-5. **Sz:** M **Own:** Eliza Werner. **QC: 34 74**

Scarsdale

Nana's Attic
414 Central Park Ave • 10583
(914)472-3806
www.nanasattic.com

Chandeliers, furniture & decorative accessories. **Hrs:** Wed-Sun 12-5; Jun-Aug closed Sun. **Own:** Cindy & Bradford Cromwell. **QC: 65 36**

South Salem

John Keith Russell Antiques Inc
110 Spring St • 10590
(914)763-8144 • (914)763-3553 (fax)
jkrantique@aol.com

American country furniture, Shaker & related antique items of decorative or artistic merit. **Est:** 1979 **Hrs:** Tue-Sun 10-5:30. **Assn:** ADA **Dir:** 55 mi NE of New York City. **QC: 1 34 57**

Janice F Strauss American Antiques
399 Poundridge Rd (Rte 124) • 10590
(914)763-5933 • (914)763-5933 (fax)
janicestrauss@eartthlink.net
home.earthlink.net/~janicestrauss

A gallery of authentic 18th & early 19th C formal & country American furniture, andirons & accessories; all items sold with a written guarantee. **Pr:** $100-50,000 **Est:** 1977 **Hrs:** By appt only. **Sz:** S **Assn:** NHADA **Dir:** I-684 Exit 6: 7 mi E on Rte 35, 1 mi S on Rte 124. **QC: 52 40 51 S8**

Southampton

Croft Antiques
11 S Main St • 11968
(516)283-6445

18th & 19th C English furniture, accessories, pottery & upholstered 19th C English & French chairs. **Pr:** $50-10,000 **Est:** 1978 **Hrs:** Fri-Mon 11-5 or by appt. **Sz:** M. **QC: 54 36**

Morgan MacWhinnie American Antiques
1411 N Sea Rd • 11968
(516)283-3366 • (516)283-7876 (fax)

Large selection of 18th & 19th C American furniture (some English), furnishings & accessories. Large selection of period andirons. **Est:** 1970 **Hrs:** Mon-Tue & Thu-Sun 11-6. **Sz:** L **Dir:** I-495 (Long Island Expressway) Exit 70: Rte 27 E 12 mi to Exit 9 (Mobile Station on L), turn L, go N 2 mi to shop. **QC: 52 53 54**

North Sea House Antiques
848 N Sea Rd • 11968
(516)283-3614

Furniture & painted accessories. **Hrs:** Daily by chance. **Dir:** 1-1/4 mi N of 7-11. **Own:** Monica Asche.

Suffern

North Hill Antiques
(914)357-4484

Early American silver. **Hrs:** By appt only. **QC: 78**

Tarrytown

Sam Said Antiques
80 S Broadway (Rte 9) • 10591
(914)631-3368

Specializing in textiles, folk art, decorative accessories & painted furniture. **Hrs:** Wed-Sun 12-5 or by appt. **Own:** Stephanie Leggio. **QC: 36 41 80**

Tarrytown Antique Center [G28]
25 Main St • 10591
(914)366-4613 • (914)366-4615 (fax)

Antiques & collectibles, including French Limoges, Irish lace, Celtic stained glass, vintage jewelry & clothing, collectibles. **Hrs:** Tue-Sun 11-5, call for extended hrs. **Sz:** L **Own:** Patrick McEntegrat.

Tuxedo

Tuxedo Antique Center
Rte 17N • 10987
(914)351-4466

Vintage jewelry, silver, crystal, lamps, furniture, paintings, prints. **Hrs:** Thu-Mon 11:30-5 **Sz:** M **CC:** AX/V/MC **Dir:** NYS Thruway Exit 15A: Rte 17 N 1 mi N of village of Tuxedo Park. **Own:** Vera Peterkin Johnson. **QC: 63 78 48**

Wainscott

Georgica Creek Antiques
Montauk Hwy • 11975
(516)537-0333 • (516)537-0333 (fax)
antiqueshows@hamptons.com
www.georgicacreek.com

European & American furniture, formal to country. Architectural & garden antiques, decorative accessories. **Est:** 1970 **Hrs:** Mon-Sat 11-5, Sun 12-5. **Sz:** L **CC:** AX/V/MC **Dir:** LIE E Exit 70: Rte 111S to Rte 27E to Montauk Hwy. Follow E to Wainscott. **Own:** Jean R Sinenberg. **QC: 53 3 36 S1 S12**

Yorktown Heights

John D Gould
(914)245-2481

American formal & country furniture in cherry, tiger maple, walnut, pine & birch; 19th C gilt frames, quilts & textiles. **Hrs:** By appt only. **Assn:** VADA. **QC: 102**

Rhode Island

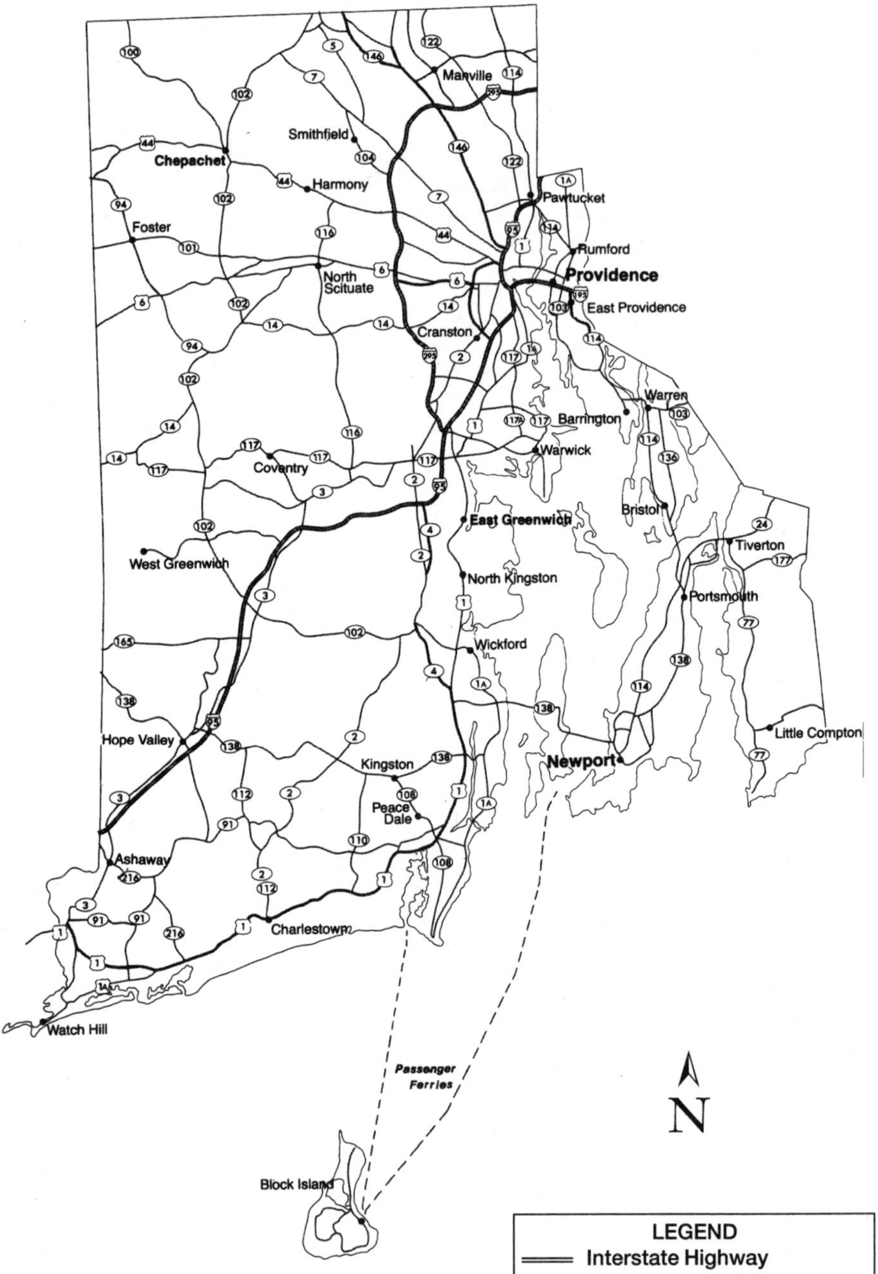

Rhode Island

LEGEND
Interstate Highway
Major U.S. and State Routes
Minor State Route
Not to Scale

Barrington

Antique Depot
40 Maple Ave • 02806
(401)247-2006

Antiques & collectibles, quality furniture, paintings, jewelry (antique & costume), Victoriana. **Hrs:** Mon-Sat 10-4:30, Sun 1-4:30. **Sz:** M.

Barrington Place Antiques
70 Maple Ave • 02806
(401)245-4510

Eclectic collection of formal Victorian, mahogany & oak furniture, fine china, silverware, prints, estate jewelry, costume jewelry & textiles. **Est:** 1993 **Hrs:** Tue-Sat 11-4. **CC:** AX/V/MC/DIS **Own:** Denise Loiselle. **QC: 50 64 78**

Robert J Doherty Gallery
10 George St • 02806
(401)431-1320

A small collection of antique & vintage Oriental rugs & weavings. **Pr:** $50-10,000 **Hrs:** By appt only. **Dir:** Call for directions. **QC: 76 S1**

House of Windsor
233 Waseca Ave • 02806
(401)245-7540

European, antique & estate jewelry; gold, diamonds, pearls & gemstones of high caliber. Gemologist on premises. **Hrs:** Tue-Sat 10-5. **Assn:** SNEADA **Own:** Karen & Glen St Pierre. **QC: 64 S1**

Stock Exchange
57 Maple Ave • 02806
(401)245-4170 • (401)247-1801 (fax)

Fine quality used home furnishings: china, crystal, jewelry, sterling, glassware & good quality furniture on three floors. **Hrs:** Tue-Sat 10-4, Thu til 7, Sun 12-4. **Sz:** L **CC:** AX/V/MC/DIS **Dir:** From I-95, Rte 114S to Barrington: R at red light at Town Hall, 5 bldgs down on R. **Own:** Jennifer LaFrance. **QC: 48 64 78**

Block Island

Lazy Fish
Water St • 02807
(401)466-2990

A wonderful collection of vintage home accessories, lamps, ceramics & small furnishings as well as unique estate jewelry. Also offering a collection of K C Perry photographs, posters & postcards. **Pr:** $5-300 **Est:** 1996 **Hrs:** Mem Day-Col Day Mon-Sun 10-8;Win please call. **Sz:** S **CC:** V/MC **Dir:** Block Island Ferry from Point Judith, RI. Shop is located under the National Hotel on Water St across from the ferry landing. **Own:** KC Perry & Carolyn Collins-Perry. **QC: 36 64 65**

Bristol

Alfred's
327-331 Hope St • 02809
(401)253-3465

A general line: furniture, glass, china, flow blue, postcards, lamps, shades & silver. **Est:** 1971 **Hrs:** Daily 10-5. **CC:** AX/V/MC/DIS **Assn:** SNEADA **Own:** Alfred Brazil. **QC: 48 61**

The Center Chimney
39 State St • 02809
(401)253-8010 • (401)253-1570 (fax)

Glass, estate jewelry, linens, furniture, Bristol postcards & maps. **Hrs:** Tue-Sat 1:30-4:30. **Assn:** SNEADA **Own:** John & Lee White. **QC: 61 64 81**

Chesterfield's Antiques
500 Metacom Ave (Rte 136) • 02809
(401)254-6184 • (781)934-0843 (fax)
chesterfields-antiques@celticweb.com

English pine country furniture & decorative accessories. All buying done in England. **Est:** 1998 **Hrs:** Tue-Sat 11-5, Sun 12-4. **Sz:** M **CC:** AX/V/MC **Own:** Rebecca & Mavis Hemsley. **QC: 54 55**

Dantiques
676 Hope St • 02809
(401)253-1122

Furniture, glassware & accessories. **Hrs:** Tue-Sat 10-4 or by appt. **Assn:** SNEADA **Own:** Chris & Dan Manchester. **QC: 48 61 S12**

Charlestown

Artist's Guild & Gallery
5429 Post Rd (Rte 1) • 02813
(401)322-0506

Specializing in 19th & 20th C RI art. **Hrs:** Sat-Sun 10-5 or by appt. **Dir:** Across from Ninigret Pond. **Own:** Ruth Gulliver. **QC: 7**

Chepachet

Chestnut Hill Antiques
One Victory Hwy • 02814
(401)568-4365
egrasso456@aol.com

Furniture, glass & china. Specializing in postcards, watches, sterling & country. **Hrs:** Wed-Sat 10-5, Sun 12-5, closed Dec 15-Mar 15 & Sun in Sum. **CC:** AX/V/MC **Dir:** 1 blk N of Chepachet Ctr on Rte 102. **Own:** Edward Grasso. **QC: 50 39**

Coventry

Indigo Moon
192 Pilgrim Ave • 02816
(401)823-7471

A small shop specializing in antique buttons, Victorian era smalls, tea cups, vases, trays, linens, framed trade cards & lace. **Pr:** $2-150 **Est:** 1987 **Hrs:** Wed-Sat 10-5. **Sz:** M **CC:** AX/V/MC/DIS **Dir:** I-95 S Exit 7: R off ramp, L at stop sign, 2 mi to Rte 3, go R 3/4 mi, on L at corn of Pilgrim Ave. **QC: 21 89 81**

Cranston

Village Art & Antiques
2145 Broad St • 02905
(401)461-4733 • (401)461-4733 (fax)
PS02822@aol.com

Fine art, collectibles & a general line. **Hrs:** Tue-Sat 10-5 or by appt. **Assn:** SNEADA **Own:** Pamela Sheridan & Lil Mangan. **QC: 7 S12**

East Greenwich

Antique Common of East Greenwich [G60+]
461 Main St • 02818
(401)885-4300 • (401)885-5657 (fax)

Located in an historic RI village, antiques, collectibles & jewelry. **Hrs:** Tue-Sat 10-5, Thu til 7, Sun 12-5, Mon by chance. **Sz:** H **CC:** AX/V/MC/DIS.

Botanica
37 Main St • 02818
(401)884-8800

Vases, teapots, garden accessories & botanical prints. **Hrs:** Tue-Fri 9:30-6, Sat 9:30-4. **CC:** AX/V/MC **Dir:** Across the street from EG Armory. **Own:** Jolli. **QC: 60 74**

Country Squire Antiques
86 Main St • 02818
(401)885-1044

Antique furniture & accessories. **Hrs:** Tue-Sat 10:30-4:30, Sun 12-3, Mon by chance. **Sz:** L **CC:** V/MC **Own:** Karen Stewart.

Shadows of Yesteryear Ltd
307 Main St • 02818
(401)885-3666

Fine glass, Irish & American Belleek & fine

furniture. **Hrs:** Daily. **Assn:** SNEADA **Own:** Richard R Heroux. **QC: 61 48 23**

Stevens Oriental Rugs Inc

88 Main St • 02819
(401)885-6066

Handwoven Oriental rugs & European tapestries. Cleaning & repair. **Hrs:** Mon-Sat 10-6. **Assn:** SNEADA **Own:** David Stevens. **QC: 76 S16**

Greenville

Greenville Antique Center [G]

711 Putnam Pike • 02828
(401)949-4999

Antiques & collectibles. **Dir:** On Rte 44 near Waterman's Lake.

Hope Valley

Hope Valley Antiques

1081 Main St • 02832
(401)539-0250

In an 1864 red brick building, two floors of quality furniture & decorative accessories: Governor Winthrop desks & secretaries, grandfather clocks, marble top tables, highboys, china cabinets, brass, iron beds, rope beds, trunks & wingbacks. **Est:** 1990 **Hrs:** Wed-Sun 10-4. **Sz:** H **CC:** V/MC **Dir:** I-95 N Exit 2 (Rte 3):Go R 2 mi to a red brick bldg with flag pole. I-95 S Exit 3B to Rte 138 W: 1 mi. Red brick bldg with flag pole & stone in front on R. **Own:** Sandra Avery. **QC: 36 48 S9**

Wood River Antiques

1017 Main St • 02832
(401)539-0070
basker13@aol.com

19th & 20th C furniture & smalls, mahogany to country. Paintings & unusual artifacts. **Est:** 1993 **Hrs:** Tue-Sun 10-5. **Sz:** L **Dir:** Rte 95 Exit 3. **Own:** Robert Block & Charles Duksta. **QC: 48 7**

Kingston

Kingston Hill Store

2528 Kingstown Rd (Rte 138) • 02881
(401)792-8662 • (401)789-9923 (fax)
allison@riconnect.com

General antiquarian books, maps, postcards. 20,000 volumes in all subjects. Quaint bookshop in old country store in historic Kingston Village. **Pr:** $1.00-2,000 **Est:** 1997 **Hrs:** Daily 10-6. **Sz:** M **Assn:** MARIAB SNEADA **Dir:** Rte 95 Exit 3: Rte 138 in Village of Kingston at the University of RI. **Own:** Allison B Goodsell. **QC: 18 19 1**

Little Compton

Blue Flag Antiques

601 W Main Rd • 02837
(401)635-8707

Paintings, drawings, 19th C furniture, photographs & a broad range of curious & unusual things, from primitives to industrial design. **Pr:** $5.00-2,500 **Est:** 1983 **Hrs:** May 15-Oct 15 1-5 daily; Win wknds by chance/appt. **Sz:** M **Assn:** SNEADA **Dir:** Rte 77 2 mi below turn off to Little Compton Ctr & 2 mi above harbor on R. **Own:** Sarah Harkness & John Nelson. **QC: 3 52 11**

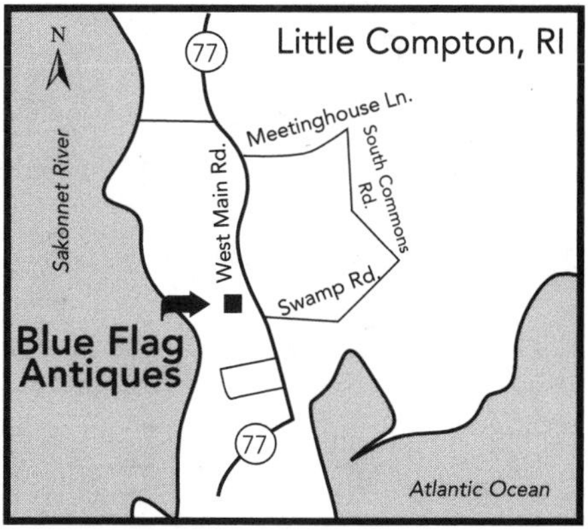

Newport

Aardvark Antiques

475 Thames St • 02840
(401)849-7233
(800)446-1052

Architectural antiques, garden statuary, ornaments, iron fences, gates, stained glass & decorative lighting. Indoor & outdoor showrooms. **Est:** 1967 **Hrs:** Mon-Sat 10-5. **CC:** V/MC **Own:** Arthur Grover. **QC: 60 61 65**

Armchair Sailor — Seabrooks

543 Thames St • 02840
(401)847-4252 • (401)847-4252 (fax)
armchair@seabrooks.com
www.seabrooks.com

Nautical books, charts & gifts. **Hrs:** Mon-Sat 10-5, Sun 12-5. **Sz:** L **CC:** AX/V/MC/DIS **Own:** Susan Dye. **QC: 70**

The Armory Antiques & Fine Art [G125]

365 Thames St • 02840
(401)848-2398

All facets of antiques & fine arts. **Hrs:** Wed-Sat 10-9, Sun-Tue 10-6. **CC:** V/MC.

Bellevue Antiques

121 Bellevue Ave • 02840
(401)846-7898

Furniture & decorative objects for house & garden. **Hrs:** Daily 12-5. **QC: 48 60**

The Burbank Rose

111 Memorial Blvd W • 02840
(401)849-9457 • (401)848-9827 (fax)
(888)297-5800
jmcn1122@aol.com
www.burbankrose.com

Collectibles, sports memorabilia & ephemera. **Est:** 1992 **Hrs:** Daily 10-5. **Sz:** M **CC:** AX/V/MC **Dir:** I-95 Exit 3-A: Follow

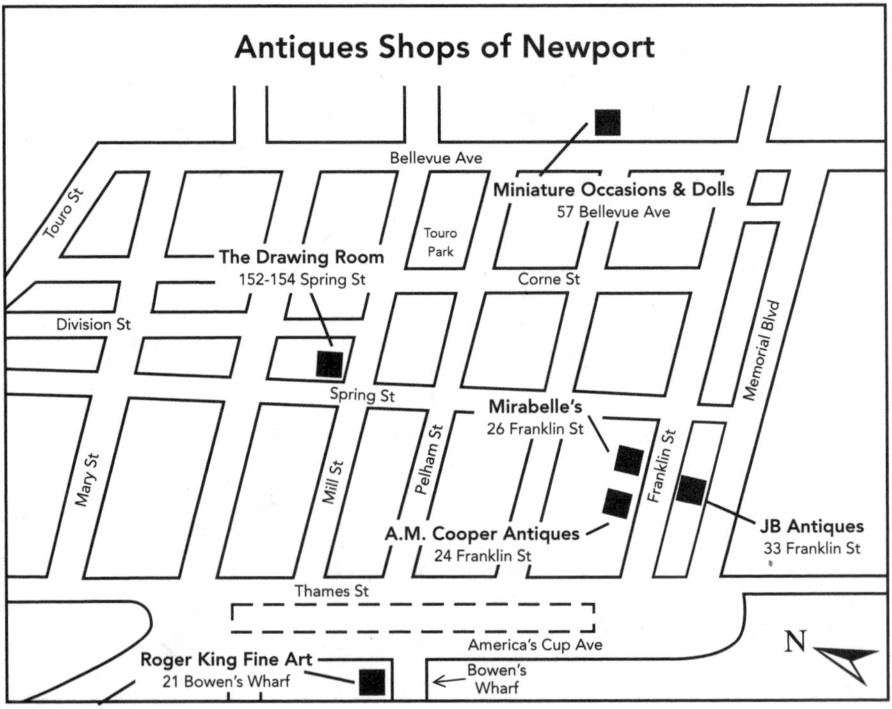

signs to Newport. On Memorial Blvd betw Spring & Thames Sts. **Own:** John & Bonnie McNeely. **QC: 67 16 32 S8**

A M Cooper Antiques

24 Franklin St • 02840
(401)849-3707
amcantique@aol.com

18th & 19th C furniture & decorative arts, lamps, mirrors, paintings & prints & silver. **Hrs:** Mon-Sat 11-4 or by appt. Hrs reduced in Win. **Sz:** M **CC:** AX/V/MC **Own:** Alletta Cooper. **QC: 52 53 36**

Courtyard Antiques

142 Bellevue Ave • 02840
(401)849-4554

Unique collection of art glass, silver, antique jewelry, furniture, paintings, musical instruments & collectibles. **Hrs:** Thu-Tue 11-5. **QC: 100 64 69**

The Doll Museum

520 Thames St • 02840
(401)849-0405 • (401)847-0068 (fax)
dollmuseum@aol.com
www.dollmuseum.com

A fine collection of antique & modern dolls. **Pr:** $50-5,000 **Est:** 1987 **Hrs:** Mon & Wed-Fri 11-5, Sat 10-5. **CC:** AX/V/MC **Own:** Linda Edward. **QC: 38**

The Drawing Room of Newport

152-154 Spring St • 02840
(401)841-5060 • (401)848-0953 (fax)
drawingroom@drawrm.com
www.drawrm.com

Furnishings from Newport's Gilded Age: period 19th C lighting, fine European porcelain & glass, high style furniture, 19th C French, aesthetic & Eastern European art pottery, Amphora to Zsolnay. Selling to advanced collectors, museums & the trade. **Pr:** $100-25,000 **Est:** 1972 **Hrs:** Daily 11-5, appt suggested. **Sz:** M **CC:** AX/V/MC **Dir:** Across from Trinity Church. **Own:** Federico Santi & John Gacher. **QC: 65 23 101**

Eclectics
5 Lee's Wharf • 02840
(401)849-8786

An eclectic selection of books, collectibles, Victoriana, cottage chests & chairs & paintings. **Hrs:** Daily 10-4. **Own:** Jean Smith. **QC: 32 48 89**

Euphoria
429 Thames St • 02840
(401)846-2290

Estate & American Indian jewelry, amber set in sterling & 14 K, amber sculptures, Reuge music boxes, vintage crystal, porcelain & silver. **Est:** 1995 **Hrs:** Mon-Thu 10-6, Fri-Sat 10-11, Sun 10-8; reduced hrs in Win. **CC:** AX/V/MC/DIS **Own:** Barbara Samra. **QC: 64 42 10**

Exotic Treasures
622 Lower Thames St • 02840
(401)842-0044

Victorian, Edwardian & Oriental silver, porcelain, bronze & crystal. **QC: 78 11**

Farewell 2 Broadway
2 Broadway • 02840
(401)848-0401

Antiques & art. **Hrs:** Thu & Sat-Mon 10-4, Fri 11-6. **QC: S8**

Forever Yours Inc
220 Spring St • 02840
(401)841-5290
www.foreveryoursinc.com

Early Victorian & French antiques, unique silk & dried floral arrangements, chandeliers & decorative designs. **Hrs:** Daily 9-6. **Sz:** M **Dir:** Thames to Franklin St to Spring St. **Own:** Patrick Doyle. **QC: 36 47 89**

A & A Gaines Antiques
40 Franklin St • 02840
(401)849-6844
info@aagaines.com
www.aagains.com

18th & 19th C antiques, furniture, clocks, China trade artifacts & nautical antiques. **Hrs:** Tue-Sat 11-5 or by appt. **CC:** V/MC **Dir:** Just off Thames St on Antique Row. **Own:** Alan & Amy Gaines. **QC: 35 52 71**

Alan David Golash
42 Spring St, Ste 1 • 02840
(401)847-4300 • (401)847-8669 (fax)

Antique estate & fine jewelry. Restoration in platinum, gold & silver. Ship miniatures in gold & silver. **Est:** 1997 **Hrs:** Daily 10-5. **CC:** AX/V/MC/DIS. **QC: 64 10 S16**

Harbor Antiques
134 Spring St • 02840
(401)848-9711
morris@edgenet.net

Furniture, glass, prints, mirrors, jewelry, linens & architectural pieces. **Pr:** $20-8,000 **Est:** 1994 **Hrs:** May-Oct Mon-Thu 10-6, Fri-Sat 10-7, Sun 10-5; Nov-Apr Sun-Fri 12-5, Sat 10-5. **Sz:** M **CC:** AX/V/MC **Dir:** Crn Church & Spring Sts & kittycorner to Trinity Church in historic Newport. **Own:** Betty Ann Morris. **QC: 3 48 S12**

J B Antiques
33 Franklin St • 02840
(401)849-0450

Fine period antique furniture, pottery & porcelain, paintings & prints, inkstands, lamps, mirrors, Sheffield & toleware. **Hrs:** Daily 10:30-5. **CC:** AX/V/MC **Dir:** 1/2 blk E of Thames St. **Own:** Jacqueline Barratt. **QC: 11 7 60**

Roger King Fine Arts
21 Bowen's Wharf • 02840
(401)847-4359 • (401)846-4096 (fax)
rkinggal@mail.bbsnet.com
www.rkingfinearts.com

Nationally recognized fine arts gallery specializing in important American, marine, early African-American & New England regional paintings of the 19th & early 20th C. Newport's oldest fine arts gallery. **Pr:** $200+ **Est:** 1973 **Hrs:** Mem Day-Sep 30 daily 10-10; Oct-Apr daily 10-5. **Sz:** M **CC:** AX/V/MC **Assn:** NEAA **Dir:** Opposite the Clarke Cooke House & Black Pearl restaurants on the 2nd fl. **QC: 7 8 9 S1 S8 S9**

Lamplighter Antiques

42 Spring St • 02840
(401)849-4179

American furniture, clocks, Currier & Ives prints, oil lamps, dolls, silver & accessories. **Est:** 1976 **Hrs:** Mon-Sat 11-5. **Own:** Al Lozito. **QC: 35 74 57**

Miniature Occasions & Dolls

57 Bellevue Ave • 02840
(401)849-5440 • (401)849-7575 (fax)
(800)358-4285
dolls@necw.com
www.necw.com/minidolls

Full-service doll repairs & restoration, custom dollhouses & miniatures. **Hrs:** May-Dec Mon-Sat 10-5, Sun 1-4, eves by chance. **CC:** V/MC/DIS. **QC: 38 S11**

Mirabelle's

26 Franklin St • 02840
(401)841-9669 • (401)841-9669 (fax)

Distinctive mix of Continental antiques & decorative accessories. **Hrs:** Daily 11-5. **Sz:** S **Own:** Bernadette Lirakis. **QC: 36**

New England Antiques

60 Spring St • 02840
(401)849-6646
woodmansee@efortress.com
www.antiques-arts.com

19th & 20th C American art, pattern glass, early glass, Staffordshire plates, country antiques, iron, photography & china. **Est:** 1981 **Hrs:** Daily 11-5. **Sz:** S **CC:** AX/V/MC **Dir:** Int of Spring & Touro Sts in the heart of the Newport Historic District across from Touro Synagogue. **Own:** Jack Woodmansee. **QC: 7 103 30**

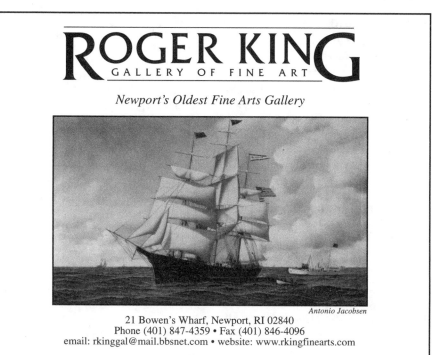

New England Architectural Center

22 Franklin St • 02840
(401)845-9233 • (401)847-2431 (fax)

Fireplace mantles, stained & bevelled glass, chandeliers & sconces, columns, entryways, garden fountains & elements, iron gates & fencing, granite cobblestones & curbing. **Est:** 1998 **Hrs:** Mon-Sat 10-5, Sun 12-5. **Sz:** L **CC:** AX/V/MC **Own:** Ann M Fiore. **QC: 3 60 65 S4**

Newport Book Store

116 Bellevue Ave • 02840
(401)847-3400 • (401)847-1948 (fax)
nptbks@wsii.com
www.nptbooks.com

Important, fine & rare books, military & naval history, Newport & RI specialties. **Hrs:** Daily 11-6. **Own:** Donald Magee. **QC: 18 S1**

Newport China Trade Company

8 Franklin St • 02840
(401)841-5267

18th & 19th C China trade porcelain, furniture, mirrors, silver & lamps. **Est:** 1988 **Hrs:** Daily 11-5 or by appt. **Dir:** Near the corn of Franklin & Thames Sts. **Own:** Blair Simmons. **QC: 65 71 24**

Oriental Arts Ltd

Brick Market Place • 02840
(401)846-0655

Antique chests & porcelains, reproductions, screens, framed art, lamps, decorative accessories, collectibles & stands. **Hrs:** Sum daily 10-9, Win daily 10-6. **QC: 60 71**

Patina

35 Franklin St • 02840
(401)846-4666

Continental country & Americana, period pieces, garden & architectural items. **Est:** 1991 **Hrs:** May-Oct daily Mon-Sat 11-5, Sun 12-5; Nov-Apr Fri-Sun only. **Sz:** M **CC:** AX/V/MC/DIS **Own:** Bob Arrick. **QC: 1 3 60**

Petteruti Antiques

105 Memorial Blvd W • 02840
(401)849-5117

Antique wicker, fine paintings, 19th C bronzes, quality furniture & objets d'art. **Hrs:** Mon-Sat 10-5, Sun 12-5. **CC:** AX/V/MC **Dir:** Below int of Memorial Blvd & Spring St. **Own:** Carmine Petteruti Jr. **QC: 11 7 91**

Prince Albert's

61 Kay St • 02840
(401)848-5372

Victorian furniture & furnishings, armoires, tables, desks, lamps, clocks, paintings, china, mirrors, cut glass, carnival glass & silver. **Pr:** $20-5,000 **Est:** 1989 **Hrs:** By chance/appt. **Sz:** M **Own:** Judith Paul. **QC: 58 89 61**

Ramson House Antiques

36 Franklin St • 02840
(401)847-0555

Furniture, lamps, shades, custom lamp fittings, candleshades, decorative accessories & period reproductions. **Est:** 1976 **Hrs:** Mon-Sat 11-5, Sun by chance. **CC:** V/MC **Own:** Joan DeDionisio. **QC: 56 65**

Renaissance Antiques

42 Spring St, No 6 • 02840
(401)849-8515
(800)850-8515
www.antique_lighting.com

Antique lighting 1820-1920, replacement glass shades, restoration & consultants for historic lighting. **Pr:** $50-10,000 **Est:** 1989 **Hrs:** Tue-Sat 10-4. **Sz:** M **CC:** AX/V/MC/DIS **Dir:** Rte 95 S or 24 S to Rte

Use the Specialty QuickCode indexes at the back of the book to find dealers who specialize in your area of interest.

114 or Rte 138 S to Newport. **Own:** John DeAngelo. **QC: 65 S16 S17**

Candida Simmons Gallery
221-223 Spring St • 02840
(401)848-0339
candida@edgenet.net

Decorative antique prints, maps, ads, paper theaters, books & original artwork. **Hrs:** Mon, Wed, Fri & Sat-Sun 11-4. **QC: 39 66 74**

Alice Simpson Antiques
40-1/2 Franklin St • 02840
(401)849-4252

Victorian silver plate, textiles & jewelry. **Hrs:** Mon-Sat 11-5. **CC:** V/MC **Dir:** 1/2 blk from Newport PO. **QC: 64 78 80**

Smith-Marble Ltd
44 Franklin St • 02840
(401)846-7689

English & European antique furniture, works of art, porcelains, bronzes, silver & Oriental antiques. **Est:** 1970 **Hrs:** Daily 10-5. **CC:** AX/V/MC **Dir:** Crnr of Franklin & Spring. **Own:** Ada Smith & Enrica Marble. **QC: 48 11**

Stetson & Sons
138 Spring St • 02840
(401)848-8484

Painted country furniture & architectural antiques. A continually changing selection of antiques & decorative items. **Pr:** $5-2,500 **Est:** 1997 **Hrs:** Jun-Sep Mon-Sat 11-5, Sun 12-5 or by appt. **Sz:** M **CC:** AX/V/MC **Dir:** Opp Trinity Church on Spring St. **Own:** Elizabeth Stetson. **QC: 3 34 36 S12**

Tyme Flies
365 Thames St • 02840
(401)847-8807

Arts & Crafts period furniture, pottery & lighting. Stickley, Limbert, Harden. **Hrs:** Call for hrs/appt. **QC: 6 49 22**

William Vareika Fine Arts
212 Bellevue Ave • 02840
(401)849-6149

18th, 19th & early 20th C American paintings, drawings & prints by important artists including Bierstadt, Church, Gifford & Kensett. Two large floors in a museum-like setting, located on Newport's historic Bellevue Avenue. **Pr:** $500-500,000 **Est:** 1987 **Hrs:** Mon-Sat 10-6, Sun 1-6 or by appt. **Sz:** L **CC:** AX/V/MC **Assn:** NEAA **Dir:** From N: Rte 124 S to Rte 114 to central Newport. From W: Rte 138 & Newport Bridge, 1 blk S of Intl Tennis Hall of Fame. **QC: 7 74**

Michael Westman Fine Arts
135 Spring St • 02840
(401)847-3091

Antiques of all periods. **Hrs:** By appt. **QC: S1**

North Kingstown

Apple Antiques
11 Burnt Cedar Dr • 02852
(401)295-8840
kmac@ios.net

General line including period furniture & folk art, 1700-1950. **Est:** 1977 **Hrs:** By appt. **Assn:** SNEADA **Own:** Roberta & Ken MacDonald.

Cottage Treasures
629 Boston Neck Rd (Rte 1A) • 02852
(401)294-7511

Furniture, glass, porcelain & linens as well as local artists & artisans. **Hrs:** Tue-Sat 10-5, Sun 12-5. **CC:** AX/V/MC **Own:** Ernestine Bash.

Lillian's Antiques

7442 Post Rd (Rte 1) • 02852
(401)885-2512

Antique jewelry, china, glass, paintings, furniture & linens. **Hrs:** Thu-Sat 1-5 or by appt. **Assn:** SNEADA **Own:** Lillian Anderson. **QC: 61 64**

Mentor Antiques

7512 Post Rd (Rte 1) • 02852
(401)294-9412

Carefully selected English furnishings & decorative accessories: armoires, wardrobes, linen presses, tables, cupboards, sideboards, & hallstands. **Est:** 1984 **Hrs:** Tue-Sat 10-5, Sun-Mon 12-5. **CC:** V/MC **Assn:** SNEADA **Dir:** I-95 to Rte 1 in North Kingstown: at the bright red English telephone box. **Own:** Marry Gormally. **QC: 36 54**

South County Antiques Center [G30]

7444 Post Rd (Rte 1) • 02852
(401)294-0855

General line. **Est:** 1997 **Hrs:** Tue-Sat 10-5, Sun 12-5. **Sz:** L **CC:** AX/V/MC/DIS **Assn:** SNEADA **Dir:** I-95 S to Rte 403, follow signs to Wickford (Rte 1). 1 mi S of the old Quonset Point naval air station. **Own:** Robert & Beth Bennett. **QC: 32 67 S8 S12**

In the Library

The earliest bookcases date to the late 17th century, but these are very rare. In England few houses had enough books to warrant furniture or a room dedicated to them until the middle of the next century. In America, bookcases and library furniture are less common and later.

Library steps: A step ladder on casters to enable readers to reach the topmost shelves of bookcases. As only the wealthiest households had large quantities of books, library steps are always of the highest quality design and craftsmanship. They were introduced in the Chippendale period and were made until the Victorian. Presumably the books on the upper shelves were the least often consulted, so library steps were not heavily used pieces of furniture. These expensive pieces were often made more useful by being made metamorphic (see below).

Library chair: A metamorphic chair that through ingenious design could be unfolded and transformed into a set of library steps. Stools and side tables were also designed to metamorphose into steps when necessary. Some of these pieces are so elaborate that we have to suspect that their owner's pleasure in their ingenuity outweighed their usefulness as dual-purpose furniture. Today, we assume too, that while they might maintain their primary use as chairs or tables, their secondary use would be as conversation pieces.

Library table: A table for writing and reading in the library, usually designed to stand in the center of the room and to be used from at least two sides. Library tables were made in three forms. (1) A large writing surface supported on two pedestals that were fitted with drawers and/or cupboards. This form was typically massive, ornate, and often architectural. (2) A comparatively simple rectangular table, with shallow drawers, raised on four legs, or, in the Regency and Federal periods, on lyre-shaped ends. (3) An octagonal table on a central pedestal, usually fitted with shallow drawers, and sometimes with sloped surfaces. Today the term sometimes refers to drop-leaf tables on a central pedestal: this is inaccurate, as libraries were large rooms whose furniture did not need to fold up when not in use.

Rent table: A library table of the third form (see above) whose drawers were fitted with small compartments for money and bills, at which the land agent sat to collect rent from tenants.

Pawtucket

My Three Sons
201 Pine St • 02862-1892
(401)722-4488

General line. **Hrs:** Tue-Fri 10-6, Sat 10-4. **Sz:** L **Own:** Frank & Pauline Lefebvre.

Portsmouth

Benjamin Fish House Antiques
934 E Main Rd • 02871
(401)683-0099

Early furniture, primitives, clocks, paintings, pewter, dolls, Dedham, Dorchester, Oriental porcelain. **Est:** 1980 **Hrs:** Mon-Sat 10-4. **Assn:** SNEADA **Dir:** On Rte 138 2 doors from Portsmouth Historical Society. **Own:** Charles & Caroline Crouch. **QC: 52 71 106**

Eagles Nest Antique Center [G125]
3101 E Main Rd • 02871
(401)683-3500

Antiques, furniture, jewelry, toys, fine glassware, silver & collectibles. **Hrs:** Mon-Sat 10-5, Sun 12-5. **Dir:** Call for directions.

Providence

125 Benefit Street Antiques
125 Benefit St • 02903
(401)274-1232 • (401)454-4651 (fax)
benefit125@aol.com

A large collection of 18th & 19th C collectibles, furnishings & decorative accessories located in an 1851 townhouse on historic Benefit Street, most imported from the UK. Brass, porcelain, glass, majolica, custom lamps, inkwells, prints & Staffordshire. **Pr:** $25-2,500 **Est:** 1985 **Hrs:** Mon, Wed, Fri 11-5. **CC:** V/MC **Dir:** I-95 E to Wickenden St Exit: follow signs to Benefit St, shop 1 mi from int of Benefit & Wickenden on R. **Own:** Courtney Taylor. **QC: 107 23 S15**

A.C.M.E. Antiques
460 Wickenden St • 02903
(401)751-6085

20th C furniture, collectibles & decorative accessories. **Est:** 1999 **Own:** Kevin Regan & Al Hughes. **QC: 59 105**

Acquisitions
405 Wickenden St • 02906
(401)276-6000

18th-20th C European & American antiques, architectural & garden. **Hrs:** By chance/appt. **Sz:** M **CC:** AX/V/MC/DIS **Own:** Steven Fusco.

The Alaimo Gallery
301 Wickenden St • 02903
(401)421-5360

Hundreds of 19th & early 20th C prints, posters, ephemera & photos in three cozy rooms. **Hrs:** Mon-Sat 9:30-5. **CC:** AX/V/MC **Dir:** 2 blks E of Benefit St betw Brook & Hope Sts. **Own:** Matthew Alaimo. **QC: 39 74 S13**

Ancient Objects
395 Wickenden St • 02903
(401)455-3538 • (401)455-3538 (fax)
tayo@ids.net

Carefully chosen classical pottery, ancient stone & bronze sculpture & objects, important dinosaur material, early Persian & Islamic artifacts, European objects medieval through Renaissance. Interesting old tribal pieces. Metal a specialty. **Pr:** $50-10,000 **Est:** 1999 **Hrs:** Tue-Sat 11-5, Sun by chance. **Sz:** M **Dir:** I-95 to I-195 E: Wickenden St exit. L on Wickenden to corn of Hope. **Own:** Jeffrey Shore. **QC: 2**

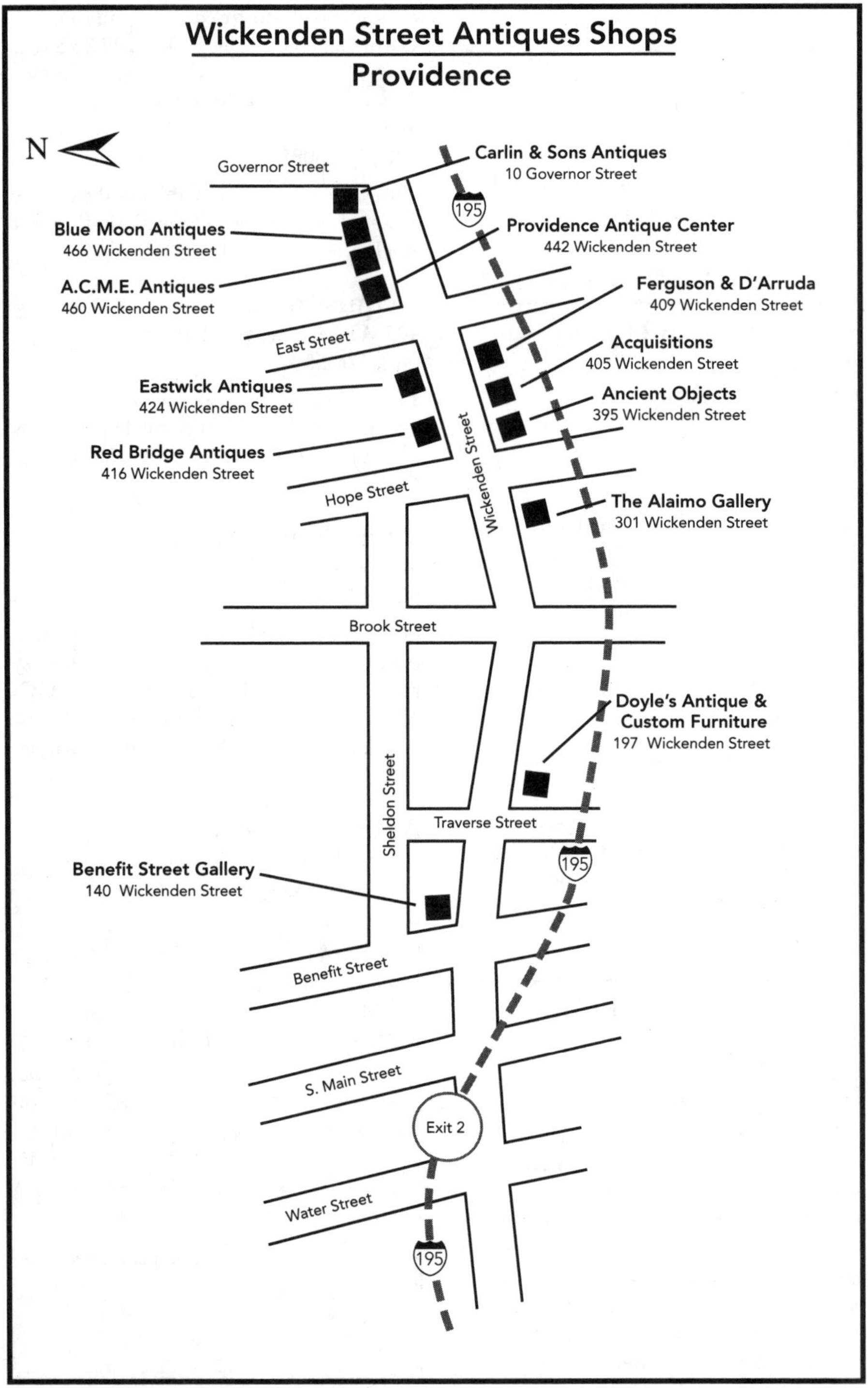
Wickenden Street Antiques Shops
Providence
N
Governor Street
Carlin & Sons Antiques
10 Governor Street
195
Blue Moon Antiques
466 Wickenden Street
Providence Antique Center
442 Wickenden Street
A.C.M.E. Antiques
460 Wickenden Street
Ferguson & D'Arruda
409 Wickenden Street
East Street
Acquisitions
405 Wickenden Street
Eastwick Antiques
424 Wickenden Street
Ancient Objects
395 Wickenden Street
Red Bridge Antiques
416 Wickenden Street
Wickenden Street
Hope Street
The Alaimo Gallery
301 Wickenden Street
Brook Street
Doyle's Antique &
Custom Furniture
197 Wickenden Street
Sheldon Street
Traverse Street
195
Benefit Street Gallery
140 Wickenden Street
Benefit Street
S. Main Street
Exit 2
Water Street
195

Antiques & Artifacts

436 Wickenden St • 02903
(401)421-8334 • (401)331-2742 (fax)
artifacts1@aol.com

18th-20th C items of interest, art, furnishings, pottery, Arts & Crafts & Moderne. **Hrs:** By appt. **CC:** V/MC **Dir:** Wickenden St at corn of East St. **Own:** Dennis Devona. **QC: 6 105**

Benefit Street Gallery

140 Wickenden St • 02903
(401)751-9109

A carefully selected inventory of furniture, glass, pottery, sculpture, porcelain & paintings by New England artists in an attractive shop at the foot of Benefit Street. **Est:** 1975 **Hrs:** Tue-Wed & Fri-Sat 10-5, Thu 1-7, Sun-Mon by appt. **Sz:** M **Assn:** SNEADA **Dir:** I-95 Exit 2 E: 2 stop lights on L. I-95 Exit 2 W: 1st R off ramp, turn R at top of street onto Benefit, 2 blks on L. **Own:** Alice K Miles & Marian L Clark. **QC: 36 48 7 S1 S16**

Bert Gallery Inc

540 S Water St • 02901
(401)751-2628 • (401)854-0599 (fax)

On the Providence waterfront, a spacious gallery featuring American painting of the 19th & 20th C from the New England region, contemporary realists & early 20th C printmakers. **Pr:** $200-10,000 **Est:** 1985 **Hrs:** Mon-Sat 11-5. **Sz:** M **CC:** V/MC **Dir:** I-195 E Exit 2 (India Point): Thru traffic light to 1st stop sign, R onto Tockwotton St, then R on S Water St. **Own:** Catherine Bert. **QC: 7 74 S1 S16**

Blue Moon Antiques

466 Wickenden St • 02903
(401)331-1336

20th C American cultural artifacts from boudoir bureaus to bawdy baubles, kitchen to deco & fabulous fifties. **Pr:** $2.00-2,000 **Est:** 1998 **Hrs:** Mon & Wed-Sat 11-5, Sun 12-5. **Sz:** S **CC:** AX/V/MC/DIS **Dir:** I-195 Exit 2: L onto Wickenden St thru 2 traffic lights. Continue 4.5 blks, shop is on L at top of hill across from elementary school. **Own:** Kristi Agniel & Sara Agniel. **QC: 105 59 63**

Carlin & Sons Antiques

10 Governor St • 02906
(401)421-0190

Formal French, English & Italian lighting & decorative accessories. **Est:** 1990 **Hrs:** Wed-Sun 12-5. **Sz:** M **CC:** V/MC **Own:** Skip Carlin. **QC: 48 65 68**

Cellar Stories Books

111 Mathewson St • 02903
(401)521-2665 • (401)454-7143 (fax)
cellarstor@ids.net

Antiquarian books: first editions, literature, RI history, science fiction & fantasy, theatre. **Pr:** $1.00-2,000 **Hrs:** Sum Mon-Sat 10-6. **Sz:** M **CC:** V/MC/DIS **Assn:** MARIAB **Dir:** I-95 N Exit 21 (Broadway): R off exit ramp on Empire St thru 4 lights, L at Weybosset St, 2 blks, then L on Mathewson. **Own:** Michael Chandley. **QC: 18**

Doyle's Antique & Custom Furniture

197 Wickenden St • 02903
(401)272-3202

Period & custom 18th, 19th & 20th C mahogany, walnut & cherry furniture, mirrors & wrought iron. **Est:** 1991 **Hrs:** Mon-Fri 10-4:30, Sat 11-4 (closed Sat in Sum). **Sz:** M **CC:** V/MC **Own:** Beverly, Stephen & Jonathan Doyle. **QC: 48 60 68**

Eastwick Antiques [G8]

424 Wickenden St • 02903
(401)621-6021 • (401)455-1720 (fax)
eastwix@aol.com

Hrs: Tue-Sat 11-5, Sun 12-4. **Sz:** M **CC:** AX/V/MC/DIS **Own:** Steven M Fusco.

Ferguson & D'Arruda Antiques at India Point

409 S Wickenden St • 02093
(401)273-5550

A diverse & ever-changing selection of antique furnishings & decorative objects for use inside & outside the home, from furniture, lighting, textiles & decorations to architectural materials & artifications for restoration or the pleasure of owning. **Pr:** $50-10,000 **Hrs:** Tue-Sat 11-5. **Sz:** M **Assn:** NHADA **Dir:** From I-95 take I-195 E to Wickenden St, India Point exit, on Providence's east side. **Own:** Brian Ferguson & Thomas D'Arruda. **QC: 3 48 60**

Edward J Lefkowicz Inc

500 Angell St • 02906
(401)277-0787 • (401)277-1459 (fax)
(800)201-7901
seabooks@saltbooks.com
www.saltbooks.com

Rare books & manuscripts relating to the sea & islands & nautical science, including voyages & exploration by sea including Pacific basin & polar regions. Naval history & tactics, navigation, shipbuilding, seamanship, whaling, sailing & sea charts. **Pr:** $50-20,000 **Est:** 1974 **Hrs:** By appt. **Sz:** M **CC:** AX/V/MC **Assn:** ABAA ILAB MARIAB **Dir:** Rte 195 to Gano St. Exit on Providence's East Side N on Gano to Waterman St, R onto Waterman to Wayland Ave. Office entrance is at 225 Wayland Ave. **Own:** Ed Lefkowicz. **QC: 18 70 S1**

M & S Rare Books Inc

245 Waterman St, Ste 303 • 02906
(401)421-1050 • (401)272-0831 (fax)
dsiegel@msrarebooks.com

Rare 18th & 19th C American imprints. **Hrs:** By appt. **Assn:** ABAA MARIAB **Own:** Daniel Siegel. **QC: 18 S1**

Providence Antique Center

442 Wickenden St • 02903
(401)274-5820

A quality selection of 20th C furniture & decorative accessories attractively displayed on two floors: Art Deco, American Art Pottery, Arts & Craft furniture, rugs, chrome bar accessories, vintage telephones. **Pr:** $10-1,200 **Est:** 1993 **Hrs:** Mon-Fri 11-6, Sat 10-6, Sun 12-5. **Sz:** L **CC:** V/MC **Dir:** Betw East & Governor Sts at Fox Point. **Own:** Keith Redman. **QC: 5 6 59 S1 S9**

Red Bridge Antiques

416 Wickenden St • 02903
(401)453-3377 • (401)453-3388 (fax)
rredbridge@aol.com

Eclectic selection of fine art, antiques & curious objects. **Est:** 1998 **Hrs:** Mon-Sat 11-5, Sun by chance. **Sz:** M **CC:** AX/V/MC/DIS **Own:** Richard Kahan. **QC: 7 22 48**

This & That Shoppe [G50]

236 Wickendon St • 02906
(401)861-1394

Antique furnishings, glassware, pottery, china, paintings, jewelry, primitives, advertising, collectibles, wicker & baskets. **Pr:** $5-500 **Hrs:** Mon-Sat 10-5, Sun 12-5. **Sz:** M **Dir:** Rte 95 Exit 20: Rte 195 1/2 mi to exit 2 (Wickenden St). **QC: 32 48 91**

Tyson's Old & Rare Books

334 Westminster St • 02903
(401)421-3939 • (401)421-3939 (fax)
tysonbks@aol.com
www.abebooks.com

Americana, American history & literature. **Hrs:** Mon-Fri 11-5, most Sat 11-4 or by appt. **Sz:** M **CC:** V/MC **Assn:** MARIAB **Dir:** 5 min from I-95. **Own:** Mariette Bedard. **QC: 18 S1**

The Stanley Weiss Collection at the Tilden-Thurber Company

292 Westminster St • 02903
(401)272-3200 • (401)454-5919 (fax)
(888)884-5336
www.stanleyweiss.com

A large selection of fine antiques including an extensive collection of antique furniture on three floors in an historic bldg. Specialists in American furniture especially from the Neo-Classical period, with a good collection of estate jewelry. **Est:** 1993 **Hrs:** Tue-Fri 11-5, Sat 10-5. **Sz:** L **CC:** AX/V/MC/DIS **Assn:** SPNEA **Dir:** I-95 to downtown Providence Exit: Exit onto Memorial Blvd, then R on Westminster. At corn of Westminster & Mathewson Sts. **Own:** Stanley Weiss. **QC: 52 54 64 S12 S19**

Zuzu's Petals

288 Thayer St • 02906
(401)331-9846

Antique jewelry reconstruction using 1920s glass & moldings. **Est:** 1989 **Hrs:** Mon-Thu 11-6, Fri 11-9, Sat 10-6, Sun 12-5. **CC:** AX/V/MC/DIS **Dir:** On the E side of Providence near Brown University. **Own:** Lois Hollingsworth. **QC: 63 83**

Rumford

Camera Obscura

7 Centre St • 02940
(401)438-1828 • (401)438-1828 (fax)

Specializing in 19th & 20th C photography, in particular daguerreotypes, as well as antique posters, ephemera, prints, art, antiques & books. **Pr:** $1.00-10,000 **Est:** 1995 **Hrs:** By chance/appt. **Sz:** S **CC:** V/MC **Dir:** I-195 Exit 6: N on N Broadway to Centre St. E on Centre St. **Own:** David Chow. **QC: 73 39 74 S1 S8 S16**

Purple Opal

36 Hood Ave • 02916
(401)438-5240
tjgomes@worldnet.att.net

China, glass, collectibles & jewelry. **Hrs:** By chance/appt. **Assn:** SNEADA **Own:** Joyce & Tony Gomes.

Zexter Antiques

9 Newman Ave • 02916
(401)438-2368

A selection of 18th & 19th C American & European furniture including tables, chests & dressers. **Est:** 1977 **Hrs:** By appt. **Sz:** S **Own:** Philip Zexter. **QC: 52 53 S16**

Tiverton

The Cottage at Four Corners

3847 Main Rd • 02878
(401)625-5814 • (401)624-4960 (fax)

A gallery specializing in country antiques & reproductions, home & garden accessories, furniture & unique gift items. **Pr:** $5.00-5,000 **Est:** 1992 **Hrs:** Mon-Sat 10-5, Sun 12-5; Jan-Feb closed Mon. **Sz:** M **CC:** AX/V/MC **Dir:** From Fall River, Rte 195 Exit 8A: Rte 24 to Tiverton, Rte 77 S 6 mi to Four Corners, large barn on R. **Own:** Nancy Hemenway. **QC: 34 36**

Wakefield

Dove & Distaff Antiques

365 Main St • 02879
(401)783-5714

Early American furniture & accessories. **Hrs:** Mon-Fri 8-5, Sat 9-12. **Sz:** L **Dir:** Rte 1 Wakefield Exit: take Main St into Old Wakefield. **Own:** Caleb Davis. **QC: 52 S16 S22**

Helen C Ferris

135 Whitford St • 02879
(401)783-7389

Early American clocks, country furniture, primitives & a general line of country accessories. **Hrs:** By appt. **Assn:** SNEADA. **QC: 35 34 106 S1 S12**

The Rathbun Gallery

Rose Hill Farm • 02879
(401)789-2033

Shaker furniture & accessories, painted country furniture & accessories primarily 19th C. **Pr:** $35.00-70,000 **Est:** 1987 **Hrs:** By appt only. **Sz:** M **Assn:** VADA GSAAA **Dir:** Please call for directions. **Own:** Richard Schneider. **QC: 1 57 102 S1 S8 S9**

Warren

Behind the Times

4 Turner St • 02885
(401)245-8357

Furniture, silver, linens, glassware, costume jewelry & collectibles. **Hrs:** Fri-Sat 10-4 or by appt. **Assn:** SNEADA **Own:** Barbara & Franklin Faris.

Warren Antique Center [G100]

5 Miller St • 02885
(401)245-5461 • (401)245-4571 (fax)
jmr650@aol.com
www.antiquecenter.com

In an old renovated theater building, furniture, art pottery, paintings & prints, garden architectural, porcelain & pottery & collectibles. Cafè on premises. **Hrs:** Sat-Thu 10-5, Fri 10-9. **CC:** AX/V/MC/DIS **Assn:** SNEADA **Dir:** I-195 E to Exit 2: Rte 136 S, R at fork to end of street. R at end of the street shop is on the L. **Own:** Jane Ryan & Gail Morris. **QC: 48 32 S8**

Warwick

The Emporium
1629 Warwick Ave • 02889
(401)738-8824

Fine jewelry, costume jewelry, kitchen collectibles, glassware, furniture, silver, paintings, china & postcards. **Est:** 1983 **Hrs:** Wed-Thu 11-5, Sat 12-5. **CC:** V/MC **Dir:** In back of Green Airport.

Golden Heart Antiques & Collectibles
1627 Warwick Ave • 02889
(401)738-2243

Vintage linens, fine china, glassware, dolls, books & jewelry, furniture & novelties, all in an owner-operated shop. **Est:** 1984 **Hrs:** Wed-Sat 10-5. **Sz:** M **CC:** V/MC **Own:** Estelle & Sonny Goldman.

The Schoolmaster's Wife
598 Warwick Neck Ave • 02889
(401)737-4366

Country furniture & accessories. **Hrs:** By chance/appt. **Assn:** SNEADA GSAAA **Own:** Nancy & Carl Johnson. **QC: 34 102**

West Kingston

Peter Pots Authentic Americana
494 Glen Rock Rd • 02892
(401)783-2350

Stoneware, period furniture, decorative & collectible items. **Hrs:** Mon-Sat 10-4, Sun 1-4. **CC:** AX/V/MC/DIS **Dir:** I-95 to Rte 138 W, approx 5 or 6 mi, watch for signs. **Own:** Oliver & Elizabeth Greene. **QC: 1 31 52**

West Warwick

Rosewood Antiques
1630 Main St • 02893
(401)823-3196

Antiques, collectibles, jewelry, old books, comics, dolls & postcards. **Hrs:** By appt. **Assn:** SNEADA **Own:** Mae Childs.

Westerly

The Book & Tackle Shop
(401)596-0700 • (617)965-0459 (fax)

Rare & out-of-print books, old photographs & postcards. **Pr:** $0.25-3,000 **Est:** 1953 **Hrs:** Jun 10-Sep 10 daily 9-9. **Sz:** M **CC:** V/MC **Assn:** MARIAB SADA ABAA **Dir:** I-95 Exit 92 in CT/I-95 Exit 1 in RI, in the Watch Hill section of Westerly. **Own:** Bernie Gordon. **QC: 19 39 74 S1 S8 S12**

Lilly's Place [G60]
5 Canal St • 02891
(401)348-2838
lilly@riconnect.com

General line. **Est:** 1998 **Hrs:** Mon-Wed & Sun 10-6, Thu-Sat 10-9. **Sz:** L **CC:** AX/V/MC/DIS **Dir:** Across from Dylan's Restaurant. **Own:** Camille Tine.

Riverside Antiques [G30+]
8 Broad St • 02891
(401)596-0266 • (401)596-0409 (fax)

Antiques & collectibles. **Hrs:** Daily 10-5. **Sz:** L **CC:** V/MC **Dir:** On the bridge along the Pawcatuck River (formerly the McCormick's Bldg). **Own:** Martha Vacca.

Woonsocket

Vaznaian's Antique Market Place
291 High St • 02895
(401)762-9661

Antique toys. **Pr:** $10-20,000 **Hrs:** Dec 1-Apr 19 Wed-Fri & Sun-Mon 12-5, Sat 10-5; Apr 20-Nov 30 by appt. **CC:** V/MC/DIS **Own:** Matthew Vaznaian. **QC: 19 32 87**

Vermont

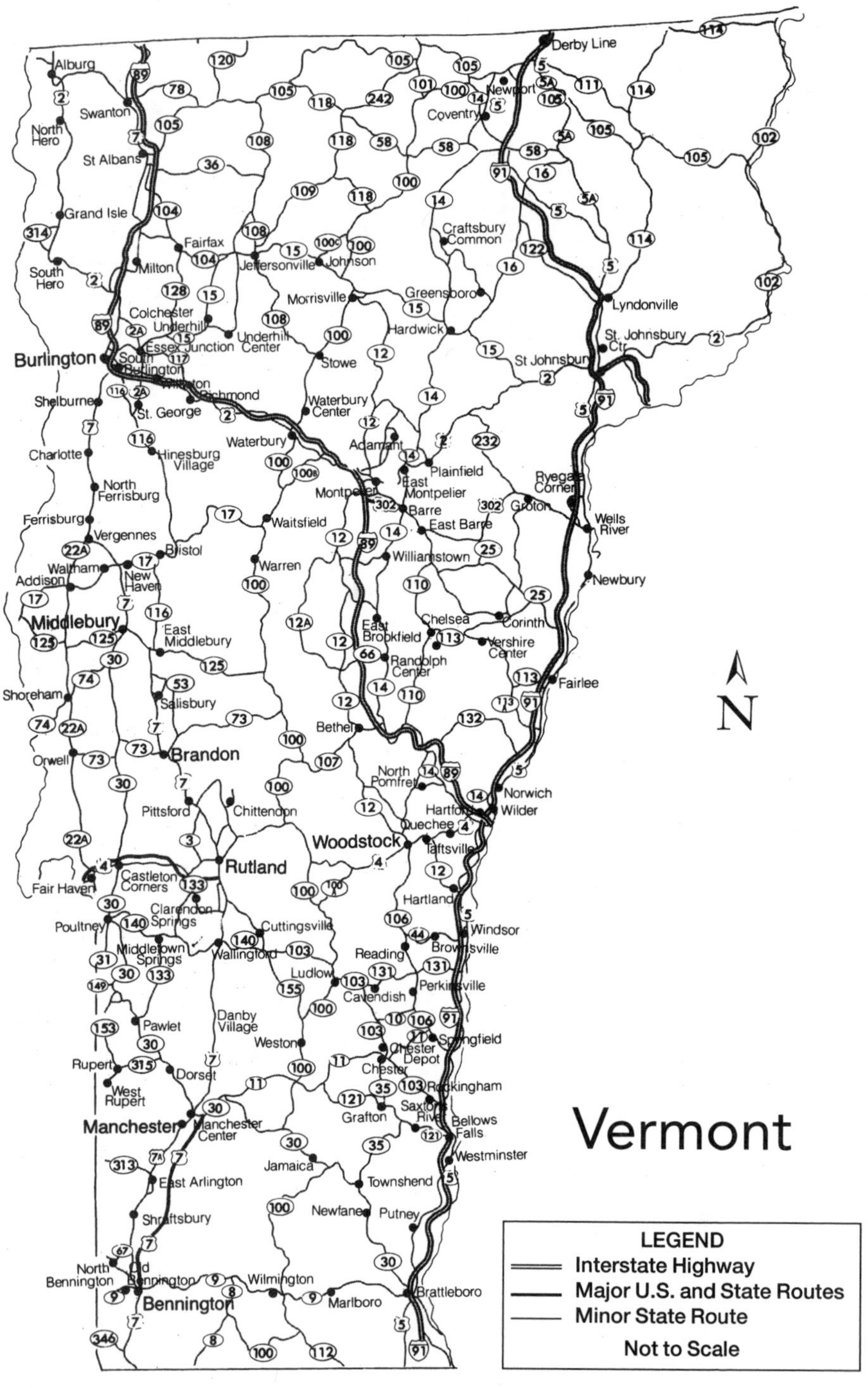
Vermont
LEGEND
Interstate Highway
Major U.S. and State Routes
Minor State Route
Not to Scale
N
Derby Line
Alburg
Swanton
North Hero
St Albans
Grand Isle
South Hero
Newport
Coventry
Craftsbury Common
Fairfax
Milton
Jeffersonville
Johnson
Morrisville
Greensboro
Hardwick
Lyndonville
St. Johnsbury Ctr
St Johnsbury
Colchester
Underhill
Essex Junction
Underhill Center
Burlington
South Burlington
Williston
Richmond
Stowe
Shelburne
St. George
Waterbury Center
Waterbury
Charlotte
Hinesburg Village
Adamant
Plainfield
East Montpelier
Montpelier
Barre
East Barre
Groton
Ryegate Corner
Wells River
North Ferrisburg
Ferrisburg
Vergennes
Waitsfield
Bristol
Williamstown
Waltham
Addison
New Haven
Warren
Newbury
Middlebury
East Middlebury
East Brookfield
Chelsea
Corinth
Vershire Center
Randolph Center
Fairlee
Shoreham
Salisbury
Bethel
Orwell
Brandon
North Pomfret
Norwich
Hartford
Wilder
Pittsford
Chittenden
Quechee
Woodstock
Taftsville
Rutland
Castleton Corners
Fair Haven
Hartland
Clarendon Springs
Poultney
Cuttingsville
Windsor
Middletown Springs
Wallingford
Reading
Brownsville
Ludlow
Cavendish
Perkinsville
Pawlet
Danby Village
Weston
Springfield
Chester Depot
Chester
Rupert
West Rupert
Dorset
Rockingham
Grafton
Saxtons River
Bellows Falls
Manchester
Manchester Center
Westminster
Jamaica
Townshend
East Arlington
Newfane
Putney
Shaftsbury
North Bennington
Old Bennington
Wilmington
Bennington
Marlboro
Brattleboro

Alburg

Personal Touch Antiques & Collectibles

55 S Main St (Rte 2) • 05440
(802)796-3948
lcetatro@together.net

Antiques, collectibles, furniture, primitives, kitchen tools, woodenware, prints & children's items. **Hrs:** By chance/appt. **Own:** Lance & Cathy Tatro. **QC: 106 74 87**

Arlington

The Farm Antiques

Historic Rte 7A • 05250
(802)375-6302

Fine Americana, 18th & 19th C formal & country furniture & accoutrements; folk art. **Hrs:** By appt only. **Assn:** VADA **Dir:** From Rte 7A W on VT 313 for 3.4 mi. **Own:** Jean G & Gedeon LaCroix. **QC: 1 52 41**

Ascutney

P Gerard Mazzei Art, Antiques & Reproductions

(802)674-2116 • (802)674-2262 (fax)
mazzei@sover.net
www.pgerardmazzei.com

18th, 19th & early 20th C American, English & Continental art, antiques & fine handmade reproductions in the manner of the 18th & early 19th C. **Est:** 1964 **Own:** P Gerard Mazzei. **QC: 1 54 56 S17**

John Waite Rare Books

Rte 5 • 05030
(802)674-2665 • (802)674-2665 (fax)

Rare & unusual books. **Hrs:** By appt only. **Assn:** VABA. **QC: 18**

Barnard

Wayne M Ridley Oriental Rugs

North Rd • 05031
(802)234-6907

Specializing in old & antique Oriental carpets, tribal & village rugs. Handwashing, repair, appraisal & padding. **Hrs:** By appt only. **Assn:** VADA **Dir:** N of Woodstock up Rte 12. **QC: 76 S1 S16**

Barton

The Wee Shop

63 Pleasant St • 05822
(802)525-6534

General line in an old red barn. **Hrs:** Mon-Sat by chance/appt. **Assn:** VADA **Own:** Elizabeth G Lewis.

Bellows Falls

The Depot Antiques & Collectibles [G24]

17 Depot St • 05101
(802)463-3455 • (802)463-4678 (fax)

Hrs: Mon-Sat 10-5, Sun 12-5. **CC:** V/MC **Dir:** Across from the Green Mtn RR station.

Belmont

Fiske & Freeman

4841 VT Rte 155 • 05730
(802)259-2579 • (802)259-3615 (fax)
lfreeman@antiquesource.com
www.antiquesource.com/fiske

Distinctive high country & period formal furniture, American & English, from the Pilgrim Century through the Federal period as well as New England country furniture. Delft, early English ceramics, mirrors, pewter & appropriate quality smalls. **Pr:** $100-15,000 **Est:** 1994 **Hrs:** Jun-Oct daily, call ahead advised. **Assn:** VADA **Dir:** Rte

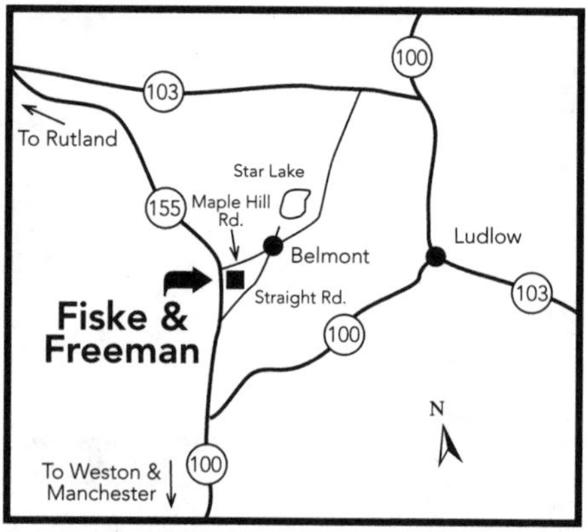

155 8 mi N of Weston at the corn of Maple Hill Rd. **Own:** John Fiske & Lisa Freeman. **QC: 52 54 27**

Bennington

Antique Center at Camelot Village [G126]

60 West Rd (Rte 9) • 05201
(802)447-0039 • (802)447-0039 (fax)
camelot1@sover.net
www.antiquesatcamelot.com

Furniture, china, glass, paintings, pottery, porcelain, brass, primitives & folk art. Also estate jewelry & ephemera. **Est:** 1987 **Hrs:** Daily 9:30-5:30. **CC:** AX/V/MC/DIS **Dir:** On Rte 9 W 1 mi from Bennington Museum at Camelot Village. **Own:** Brian Lewis. **QC: 61 48 22 S8**

Fonda's Antiques

Pownal Bennington Rd (Rte 7) • 05201
(802)442-5985

A family-owned & operated business with an interesting & expanding collection of period & country furniture, English & American glass & china, stoneware, ceramics, old Bennington pottery & collectibles. **Pr:** $2.00-5,000 **Est:** 1927 **Hrs:** Mon-Sun 10-5, closed Christmas & New Years. **Sz:** L **Dir:** 1-1/2 mi S on Rte 7 from int of US Rte 7 & VT Rte 9. **Own:** Susan Church & Richard Bump. **QC: 34 103 22 S1 S6 S12**

Four Corners East Inc
307 North St • 05201
(802)442-2612

Large, varied & constantly changing stock of fine American antiques, including furniture, paintings, rugs & accessories attractively displayed. **Est:** 1973 **Hrs:** Wed-Mon 10-5. **CC:** AX/V/MC **Assn:** VADA **Dir:** On Rte 7 going N from the ctr of town. **Own:** Russell Bagley. **QC: 52 53 7**

New Englandiana
121 Benmont Ave • 05201
(802)447-1695

Antiquarian books: Americana, biography & autobiography, genealogies, history, religion. **Pr:** $1.00-100 **Est:** 1961 **Hrs:** Mon 8-4:30, other days by chance . **Assn:** VADA **Dir:** From US Rte 7 take River St betw Brooks Drug & Mazda dealer 2 blks to shop on corn of Benmont Ave. **Own:** Roger Harris. **QC: 18**

Now & Then Books
439 Main St • 05201
(802)447-1470

General stock of used & out-of-print books. **Hrs:** Tue-Sat 10-5, Fri 10-8, Sun by chance. **Assn:** VABA **Own:** Paul Lamontagne. **QC: 18**

Stonewalls Antiques
136 Monument Ave Ext • 05201
(802)447-1628

High country furniture in cherry & pine. Lamps, flow blue, Staffordshire, cranberry, amberina, Chinese export, early Windsor chairs & many unusual decorative accessories. **Est:** 1987 **Hrs:** May-Dec daily 10-5 or by chance/appt. **Sz:** L **Assn:** VADA **Dir:** 4/10 mi S of Old First Church in Old Bennington. **Own:** Gloria & James Lernihan. **QC: 55 65 22**

Berlin

Stephen Jones Antiques
66 Barre-Montpelier Rd • 05641
(802)476-3223 • (802)883-9398 (fax)

Large selection of folk art, toys, furniture & paper items. Smalls from local Vermont estates. **Hrs:** Mon-Fri 12-5, Sat by chance. **Sz:** M **CC:** V/MC **Assn:** VADA **Dir:** I-89 Exit 7 (Berlin) 1.2 mi to W, then 1.1 mi to bottom of hill, then R 1.4 mi on R. **QC: 102 87 41 S1 S8 S12**

Bradford

Bradford 4 Corners Antiques
Rtes 25 & 5 • 05033

Glass, primitives, collectibles, advertising, tools, jewelry, clothing & books. **Hrs:** Daily. **Dir:** I-91 Exit 16.

Brandon

Gloria D's Antiques & Collectibles
57 Park St (Rte 73E) • 05733
(802)247-5648

A shop attached to an 1830 home on historic Park St with a selection of stoneware, glassware, jewelry, furniture, primitives, toys & general antiques. **Hrs:** Wed-Sat 11-5; May-Oct by chance. **Own:** Gloria Darmstadt. **QC: 61 48 106**

James W McCullough Antiques
(802)247-8634

Authentic early American & English decor. Estate liquidation service. **Est:** 1946 **Hrs:** Apr-Nov by appt. **Assn:** AAA VADA **QC: S1**

Nutting House Antiques [G]
22 Center St (Rte 7) • 05733
(802)247-3302
(800)870-9866

18th, 19th & 20th C country to formal furniture with emphasis on quality smalls & decorative accessories. **Pr:** $60-3,000 **Est:** 1984 **Hrs:** Wed-Mon 10-5. **CC:** V/MC **Assn:** VADA **Own:** Pamela & David Laubscher. **QC: 34 36**

Lee B Pirkey

27 Center St • 05733
(802)247-3277

Art, formal & country furniture & accessories, lighting & mirrors. **Hrs:** Daily 10-5, off season Fri-Tue 10-4 or by appt. **CC:** V/MC. **QC: 36 48**

Brattleboro

Black Mountain Antique Center [G100]

Rte 30 • 05302
(802)254-3848

Furniture, glassware, china, stoneware, milk bottles, books, ephemera, tools & jewelry. **Hrs:** Mon-Thu 10-5, Fri-Sun 10-6. **Sz:** H **CC:** V/MC **Dir:** I-91 Exit 2: 1-1/2 mi N of downtown Brattleboro on Rte 30. **Own:** Charles Stokes.

Cornucopia

34 Myrtle St • 05301
(802)254-2198
cornucop@sover.net

Books on 19th C to 1940 social & domestic history, cookery, etiquette, needlework & pastimes. **Hrs:** By chance/appt. **Assn:** VABA **Own:** Carol Greenberg. **QC: 18**

A Richter Gallery

111 Main St • 05301
(802)254-1110
oldlabel@sover.net
www.sover.net/~oldlabel

Antique prints including botanicals, etchings & illustrative art, antique labels, as well as original contemporary oil paintings, contemporary arts & crafts. **Est:** 1982 **Hrs:** Mon-Sat 10-5:30, Sun 12-5. **CC:** V/MC/AX/DIS **Own:** Allison Richter. **QC: 74**

Candleholders I

Candles shed faint light and thus needed to be a close as possible to what their user wanted to see. Apart from sconces and chandeliers, the devices for holding them, then, were portable, sometimes adjustable, and often equipped with hooks, spikes, or other means of placing them where they were needed.

Candlestick or candleholder: A device to hold a candle, made of metal, porcelain, or wood in many forms.

Chamberstick: A candleholder with a handle, designed for carrying from room to room, particularly to the bedroom.

Taper stick: A holder for a rigid taper, like a small candlestick.

Taper jack or wax jack: A small, footed reel on which a flexible taper was coiled. Fitted with a pincer device for holding the end that was lit. An 18th century desk implement that was often highly elaborate, especially when made of silver.

Hogscraper: A simple iron candlestick on a circular base. Its shape and strength enabled farmers to use it for scraping the hair off pigskin.

Candelabra: A multiple-branched candleholder, often very ornate.

Sconce: A wall-mounted candleholder.

Bridgewater

Bridgewater Mill Antique Center [G150]

Rte 4 • 05034
(802)672-3049

Antiques, collectibles & antique furniture housed in an old mill. **Hrs:** Daily 10-6. **Dir:** Betw Killington & Woodstock at the Old Mill Marketplace.

The Red Horse

Rte 4 • 05034
(802)672-3220

In a converted carriage house overlooking the river, a selection of country furniture, quilts, early prints, appropriate accessories & unusual garden accents. **Hrs:** Thu-Sat 10-5, Sun 11-2, Wed by chance. **Sz:** M **CC:** V/MC **Assn:** VADA **Dir:** Approx 8 mi W of Woodstock in Bridgewater Village opposite church. **Own:** Sue Lilly. **QC: 34 60 74 S13**

Bridport

Wayside Antiques

415 Lake St • 05734
(802)758-2565
waysideant@aol.com

Furniture, smalls & collectibles. **Hrs:** Mar-Dec Mon & Fri-Sat 10-5, Sun 12-4 or by appt. **CC:** V/MC/DIS/AX **Dir:** Rte 125 W to Lake St. **Own:** Kathie Anderson.

Brookline

River's Edge Antiques

Grassy Brook Rd • 05735
(802)365-4401

Specializing in oak furniture. Country & Victorian furniture & accessories. **Hrs:** Daily. **QC: 50 58**

Brownington

Joseph & Marilyn Martin

(802)754-6659
mmartin@together.net

Early painted & decorated furniture, folk art & decorative arts. **Hrs:** By appt only. **Assn:** NHADA VADA **Dir:** Phone for directions. **QC: 51 41**

Burlington

Architectural Salvage Warehouse

212 Battery St • 05401
(802)658-5011
salvage@together.net
www.architecturalsalvagevt.com

Specializing in architectural antiques: stained glass, fireplace mantels, pillars, early hardware, clawfoot bathtubs, French doors, art deco lighting, marble & pedestal sinks & fretwork. **Pr:** $25-10,000 **Hrs:** Mon-Sat 10-5, Sun 12-5 in season. **Dir:** On the Burlington waterfront - entrance on Maple St side. **Own:** David Ackerman. **QC: 3 S18 S4**

Phil & Vera Brothers Antiques

North Ave • 05401
(802)862-8014

Specializing in sterling silver, cut glass, jewelry, china, crystal & art glass. **Hrs:** By appt only. **Assn:** VADA **Dir:** Just off Rte 127, 2.5 mi from ctr of town. **QC: 100 64 78**

Conant Custom Brass Inc

270 Pine St • 05402
(802)658-4482 • (802)864-5914 (fax)
(800)832-4482

A mix of fine brass & copper antiques & unusual one-of-a-kind treasures all set in a bustling workshop. 300 restored antique light fixtures & hundreds of glass shades in stock. **Pr:** $5-5,000 **Est:** 1979 **Hrs:** Mon-Fri

8:30-5, Fri til 7, Sat 10-5. **Sz:** L **CC:** V/MC/DIS **Dir:** Rte 89N Exit 14W: W on Rte 2 into Burlington, cross Church St, St Paul St & turn L on Pine St, 2 blks down. **Own:** Stephen Conant. **QC: 20 65 S16**

North Country Books
2 Church St • 05401
(802)862-6413 • (802)862-0828 (fax)
norbooks@together.net

Out-of-print collectible & rare books, maps & a broad range of prints. **Hrs:** Mon-Thu 9:30-7, Fri-Sat 9:30-9, Sun 11-6. **Own:** Mark Ciufo. **QC: 18 66 74**

Rte 7 Antiques & Treasures [G30]
388 Shelburne Rd • 05401
(802)859-0917
sevene@together.net

Constantly changing inventory of walnut, mahogany & oak furniture, paper collectibles, glassware, paintings, prints, pottery, old books, linens, postcards, sterling, jewelry, coins, clocks, watches, dolls, porcelain. **Pr:** $10-2,000 **Est:** 1998 **Hrs:** Mon-Thu & Sat 9-5, Fri 9-6, Sun 12-5. **Sz:** L **CC:** V/MC **Dir:** I-89 Exit 13: Rte 7 N 1/2 mi on R. **Own:** Valerie Sevene. **QC: 48 39 78**

Somewear in Time
96 Church St • 05401
(802)864-5183

Specializing in high-style & designer fashion from this millenium — for the next one — with vintage clothing & accessories in wearable, fun styles. Featuring day & evening wear, hats, purses, lingerie, jewelry, vintage riding apparel & jewelry. **Hrs:** Daily, call for hrs. **Own:** Barbara Ann Curcio. **QC: 83**

Three Old Bats
207 Flynn Ave • 05401
(802)860-1488

Hrs: Tue-Sat 10-6, Sun 1-5. **CC:** V/MC **Dir:** 1/2 mi from Rte 7 by the tracks. **Own:** Virginia Winn & Kathy Valloch.

Cavendish

Sigourney's Antiques
Rte 131 • 05142
(802)226-7713

General line including small country furniture, primitives, kitchenware, bottles, ephemera, advertising, tobacco cards, prints, children's & other books, toy soldiers & other toys. **Hrs:** May-Oct by chance/appt. **Assn:** VADA **Dir:** 3/4 E of Cavendish on Rte 131. **Own:** Henry & Doris Sigourney. **QC: 34 106 39**

Chester

1828 House Antiques
5227 VT Rte 103 N • 05143
(802)875-3075 • (802)875-6362 (fax)

Wide selection of quality 18th & 19th C English & French country furniture enhanced by 19th C bird's eye frames, prints, lamps, glass & ceramics attractively displayed in an 18th C carriage shed. **Pr:** $25-5,000 **Est:** 1985 **Hrs:** May 15-Oct 15 daily 10-5. **Sz:** M **CC:** AX/V/DIS **Assn:** VADA **Dir:** I-91 Exit 6: Rte 103 N. **Own:** Jane Thraikill. **QC: 107 23 47**

William Austin's Antiques
Maple St (Rte 103) • 05143
(802)875-3032
(877)447-5268

Over 300 pieces of quality country furniture in all woods. **Hrs:** Daily 9-5, Fri til 9. **CC:** V/MC/DIS **Dir:** Int of Rtes 103N & 11. **QC: 48 102**

Stone House Antiques & Crafts Center [G250]
Rte 103 S • 05143
(802)875-4477

Large group shop with quality antiques & collectibles. **Est:** 1990 **Hrs:** Daily 10-5. **Dir:** I-91 Exit 6: 6 mi S of Chester on Rte 103. **Own:** Bob Warner & Kathy King.

Clarendon Springs

Clarendon House Antiques Inc

Clarendon Springs Rd • 05777
(802)438-2449 • (802)438-2030 (fax)
user766668@aol.com

In a lovely Vermont country village, a diverse & ever-changing inventory of unusual country, Victorian & formal furniture, folk art, paintings, rugs, toys, stoneware, china, silver & vintage clothing. In the historic former Clarendon Springs Hotel. **Pr:** $25-35,000 **Est:** 1973 **Hrs:** By chance/appt. **Sz:** H **Assn:** VADA **Dir:** 3 mi S of West Rutland off Rte 133. **Own:** Bonnie & Tony Costantino. **QC: 52 41 7 S12**

Danby

The Barn Antiques

286 S Main St • 05739
(802)293-5512
bbmartin@sover.net

A general line of furniture & accessories. **Est:** 1976 **Hrs:** By chance/appt. **Own:** Barbara & Brian Martin. **QC: 48 34**

Danby Antiques Center [G25]

S Main St • 05739
(802)293-5990

18th & 19th C American furniture & antique accessories in spacious room settings in an 11-room Federal house plus a large barn with furniture in-the-rough & accessories. Emphasis on Americana. Some funk too! **Pr:** $25-5,000 **Est:** 1983 **Hrs:** Daily 10-5, Jan-Mar call ahead for Tue-Wed. **Sz:** L **CC:** AX/V/MC **Assn:** VADA **Dir:** 12 mi N of Manchester, 1/8 mi off Rte 7 (watch for state signs). **Own:** Agnes Franks. **QC: 1 41 52**

> Use the Specialty QuickCode indexes at the back of the book to find dealers who specialize in your area of interest.

Tabor Mountain Marketplace [G20]

Rte 7 • 05739
(802)293-5333

Antiques, furniture, glassware, china, sleighs, clocks & prints. **Est:** 1996 **Hrs:** May-Dec daily 10-5, Jan-Apr wknds only. **Sz:** L **CC:** AX/V/MC/DIS **Own:** John Carr.

Danville

Farr's Antiques

Peacham Rd • 05828
(802)684-3333

An old-fashioned country store with three levels of New England antiques: furniture, glass, china, clocks, primitives & old tools. **Pr:** $25-3,500 **Est:** 1968 **Hrs:** Daily 10-4. **Sz:** L **Assn:** VADA **Dir:** 1/4 mi S of Rte 2 on the Peacham Rd; 15 min from I-91 & 93. **Own:** Edward Farr. **QC: 48 60 106**

Derby Center

Canterbury House

N Main St • 05829
(802)766-2158
cantbarb@together.net

Glassware, china, prints, primitives, furniture. **Hrs:** Open all year. **Own:** Barb Frawley. **QC: 48 106 61**

Dorset

Phyllis Carlson Antiques

3390 Rte 30 • 05251
(802)867-4510

Eight rooms of fine period & country furniture, textiles, antique quilts, hand painted porcelain, sterling silver, needlepoint footstools & pillows, books & appropriate antique accessories in a 19th C shop on the Green in picturesque Dorset. **Pr:** $25-8,000

Est: 1989 **Hrs:** Daily 10-5; Win Tue-Wed by appt. **Sz:** L **CC:** V/MC **Assn:** VADA NHADA MADA **Dir:** 6 mi N of Manchester on Rte 30. **Own:** Phyllis Carlson. **QC: 1 52 80 S1 S12**

Geranium Antiques

Upper Dorset Hollow Rd • 05251
(802)867-5588

American Historical Staffordshire, early Bennington pottery, spatter & spongeware, 18th & early 19th C English ceramics & pottery, Currier & Ives prints. **Hrs:** By appt only. **Assn:** VADA **Own:** Bill & Marcia King. **QC: 23 30 31**

Peg & Judd Gregory

(802)867-4407

Fine period antiques. Specializing in 18th C furniture from New England as well as early English furniture, delftware & decorative accessories. Early portraits always on hand. **Pr:** $50-20,000 **Hrs:** By appt only. **Sz:** M **Assn:** VADA **Dir:** Call for directions. **QC: 1 52 7 S1 S8 S9**

Middlestone Antiques

(802)867-4448

Fine & folk art, antiques, country furniture & furnishings, treenware, grenfells, hooks & tribal Oriental rugs. **Hrs:** Wed-Sat 11-5 or by appt. **Dir:** At the Green Gate next to the PO in Dorset. **Own:** Anne & Bob August.

Marie Miller American Quilts

1489 Route 30 • 05251
(802)867-5969 • (802)867-0324 (fax)
quiltslr@vermontel.com
www.antiquequilts.com

19th & early 20th C quilts in pristine condition, pillows, samplers & hooked rugs. **Hrs:** Daily 10-5. **Sz:** M **CC:** AX/V/MC **Assn:** VADA GSAAA **Dir:** 4-1/2 mi N of Manchester Ctr (opposite J K Adams). **Own:** Marie Miller. **QC: 80 S16**

The Old Cow's Tail Antiques

Rte 30 • 05251
(802)362-3363 • (802)362-3372 (fax)
cowstail@sover.net
www.oldcowtailantiques.com

Featuring 18th & 19th C country furniture & accessories, English, American sterling silver, early pattern glassware, fine china, porcelain, linens, oil lamps, primitives & tools. **Est:** 1997 **Hrs:** Mon-Sun 10-5. **Sz:** M **CC:** V/MC **Dir:** 4 mi N of Manchester Ctr at corn of Stonewall Ln. **Own:** Mark & Wendy Putnam. **QC: 34 65 36**

East Arlington

East Arlington Antique Center [G125]

Old Mill Rd & Maple St • 05252
(802)375-9607

Country & formal furniture, primitives, Oriental rugs, paintings, jewelry, china, glass & early 20th C kitchenware, located in two separate historic bldgs nestled in the Currier & Ives style village of East Arlington. **Est:** 1987 **Hrs:** Daily 9-5. **Sz:** H **CC:** V/MC **Dir:** In the PO bldg across from the Candle Mill Village betw Rtes 7 & 7A. **Own:** Phil Elwell.

Gebelein Silversmiths

(802)375-6307

Antique silver including American 18th C, Arts & Crafts & Chinese export. **Hrs:** By appt only. **Assn:** VADA **Own:** Dave & Pat Thomas. **QC: 6 78**

East Barre

East Barre Antique Mall [G300]

133 Mill St • 05649-0308
(802)479-5190

General line of antiques with some collectibles & the largest assortment of furniture in the area tastefully arranged in an old furniture store. Reasonable prices. **Est:** 1994 **Hrs:** Tue-Sun 10-5. **Sz:** H **CC:** V/MC **Dir:** From Barre Rte 302 E to jct Rte 110, cross brook, turn R at fork, mall at top of hill on L. **Own:** Robert Somaini. **QC: 7 22 34 S8 S16 S6**

East Cornith

Easter Hill Antiques

(802)439-6400

Furniture & accessories. **Hrs:** By chance/appt. **Own:** Tom O'Hara. **QC: 48 34**

East Middlebury

Middlebury Antique Center [G50]

Rtes 7 & 116 • 05740
(802)388-6229 • (802)388-6224 (fax)
(800)339-6229 (VT only)
www.middantiques.com

A wide variety of high-quality antiques including country furniture & a diverse range of smalls. **Est:** 1987 **Hrs:** Daily 9-6 or by appt. **Sz:** L **CC:** V/MC/DIS **Assn:** VADA **Dir:** Halfway betw Rutland & Burlington, on corn of Rtes 7 & 116. **Own:** Francis & Dianne Stevens. **QC: 34 36 52**

Enosburg

Ragged Island Books, Maps & Prints

(802)933-6248
raggedis@together.net

Antiquarian books, images & paper, especially industrial Americana (mines, factories, mills, railroads). **Est:** 1991 **Hrs:** By appt only. **Assn:** VABA **Own:** Joanne & Richard Gumpert. **QC: 18 1 74**

Fair Haven

Foundation Antiques

148 N Main St • 05743
(802)265-4544

Strong accent on primitive accessories & furniture. Specializing in Quimper, graniteware, kitchenware, early hearth & lighting, corkscrews, art pottery, violins, books, ephemera & milk bottles. **Pr:** $1.00-20,000 **Est:** 1975 **Hrs:** Apr 1-Jan 15 Mon-Sun 9:30-5. **Sz:** L **Assn:** VADA VABA **Dir:** 16 mi W of Rte 7; approx 300 yds N of Village Green. **Own:** Stephen Smith. **QC: 27 101 47**

Fairfax

Buck Hollow Farm

Buck Hollow Rd • 05454
(802)849-2400
inn@buckhollow.com
www.buckhollow.com

Country furniture, clocks, quilts & coverlets, yellowware, primitives, folk art & doorstops as well as other interesting items. **Hrs:** Most days 9-5. **CC:** AX/V/MC/DIS **Assn:** VADA **Dir:** 6 mi N of Rte 104. **Own:** Brad Schwartz. **QC: 102 35 41**

Country Charm Antiques

1144 Main St (Rte 104) • 05454
(802)849-2920

In our quaint 19th C house we have items for the outdoorsperson (old lanterns, lure, decoys, knives, snowshoes, backpacks) as well as a constantly changing variety of antique furniture & decorative accessories. **Hrs:** By chance/appt. **Own:** Walt & Kathi Lattrell.

Fairfield

Fairfield Country Store

Rte 36 • 05455
(802)827-6160
(800)639-7190

Original 1800s country store with a wide variety of antiques & collectibles. **Hrs:** Mon-Fri 9-6, Sat-Sun 10-4. **CC:** AX/V/MC/DIS **Own:** Russell & Patty Esden.

Fairlee

Edith M Ackerman

4 Woodland Terr • 05045
(802)333-4457

Over 3,000 pieces of Depression era glassware, Royal Doulton figurines, Roseville pottery & other collectibles from that era. **Pr:** $25-500 **Est:** 1970 **Hrs:** By chance/appt. **Sz:** S **Dir:** Off Lake Morey Rd. **QC: 61 62**

Chapman's

Rte 5 • 05045
(802)333-9709

Used & antiquarian books. **Hrs:** Mon-Sat 8-6, Sun 8-5. **Sz:** M **CC:** V/MC **Own:** Will Chapman. **QC: 18**

Gryphon Antiques

On The Green • 05045
(802)222-4488

Art, furnishings, smalls, glass & china. **Hrs:** Wed-Mon 10-5, by appt. **Own:** Paul Clemens Naughton. **QC: 61 48**

Larson's

Rte 5 • 05045
(802)333-4784

Ephemera, linens, lace, postcards & books. **Hrs:** Thu-Mon 10-4, or by chance/appt. **QC: 39 81**

Old Book Store at Chapmans

Rte 5 • 05045
(802)333-9709

Rare books. **Hrs:** Daily. **QC: 18**

Vollbrecht Antiques

Main St (Rte 5) • 05045
(802)333-4223

Furniture, glass, china & stained glass. **Hrs:** Daily 10-5. **CC:** V/MC **Dir:** I-91 Exit 15. **Own:** Ruth Klein & Bill Vollbrecht. **QC: 48 61**

Felchville

Black Horse Farm

13 Rte 106 • 05062
(802)484-3539

Offering affordable country furniture & collectibles. Also in-shop folk art painting on vintage pieces, handmade Nantucket baskets & commissioned work. **Hrs:** Daily in season, off season by chance. **Dir:** 1 mi S of Reading. **Own:** Holly Martin. **QC: 41 34 48**

Ferrisburgh

Eighth Elm Farm Antiques

Rte 7 • 05456
(802)877-3218 • (802)877-0091 (fax)
eightelm@together.net

Oak, country pine & Victorian furniture, refinished & as found, as well as a full line of antiques & collectibles & decorative accessories. Large selection of iron & brass beds. **Hrs:** By chance/appt. **Sz:** L **CC:** V/MC **Dir:** On Rte 7 N of jct Rte 7 & Rte 22A in Ferrisburgh. **Own:** Paulette & Bob McNary. **QC: 61 63 32**

Georgia

Weeds n' Things

Georgia Plain Rd • 05468
(802)524-2826

Featuring an extensive array of both country & Victorian treasures. **Hrs:** Mon-Sat 9-5. **Dir:** Georgia Plain Rd 1/2 mi off Rte 7. **Own:** Pauline Nye & Sara Nye Vester.

Grafton

Grafton Gathering Place Antiques

Eastman/Sylvan Rd • 05146
(802)875-2309

A two-story country barn with period 18th & 19th C formal & country furniture, fine & interesting quilts & coverlets, blown & pattern glass, hooked rugs, Staffordshire & other period decorative smalls. **Hrs:** Wed-Mon 10-4. **Sz:** L **CC:** V/MC **Assn:** VADA **Dir:** I-91 Exit 6: Rte 103 N to Chester, Rte 35 W toward Grafton; L off Rte 35 onto Eastman Rd (follow signs). **Own:** Mary & Peter Pill. **QC: 1 104 52**

Sylvan Hill Antiques

Eastman/Sylvan Rd • 05146
(802)875-3954 • (802) 875-3956 (fax)

American & English period furniture, small decorative antiques & paintings & children's antique furniture. **Pr:** $50-10,000 **Hrs:** Daily 10-5 by chance/appt, call ahead advised. **Assn:** VADA **Dir:** I-91 Exit 6: Rte 103 N to Chester, Rte 35 W toward Grafton 4 mi. Follow State Rd signs. Betw Grafton & Chester. **Own:** Thelma & Albin Zak. **QC: 107 36 54**

Grand Isle

Vallees Den of Antiquity

Rte 2 • 05458
(802)372-8324

Formal & country furniture, glass, pottery, silver, costume jewelry, decoys, folk art, farm implements, tools, paper memorabilia, sports antiques, toys & auto related items. **Est:** 1949 **Hrs:** May-Nov daily 10:30-5:30. **Sz:** L. **QC: 102 78 37**

Greensboro

Mabel Wilson Fine Antiques

745 Edson Hill Rd • 05841
(802)533-2478

Fine American furniture of the 18th C & 19th C, primitives, tall clocks, portraits & folk art. Specializing in Vermont & New England pieces. **Pr:** $500-100,000 **Est:** 1991 **Hrs:** By appt only. **CC:** V/MC **Assn:** VADA **Dir:** Call for directions. **Own:** Trish & Bill Alley. **QC: 35 41 52**

Hartland

Hartland Antique Center [G60]

Rte 4 • 05073
(802)457-4745
hartland@sover.net
www.antiquesnet.com

Antiques, collectibles & furniture. **Est:** 1994 **Hrs:** Daily 10-5. **CC:** V/MC **Dir:** I-89: 7 mi W on Rte 4, 4 mi W of Quechee Gorge. **Own:** Josiah Lupton.

John Nichols

250 Rte 5 • 05089
(802)674-5477

Large inventory of exceptionally fine period American furniture & accessories, including slant-lid desks, highboys, chests-on-chests, card tables, small stands, paintings & folk art. **Hrs:** By appt only. **Dir:** Exit 9S from I-91. **QC: 52**

Hinesburg

Hawk's Nest Antiques & Decoys

Silver St • 05461
(802)482-2076

Specializing in fine decoys by well-known carvers, early & paint-decorated furniture, country accessories, quilts & folk art. **Hrs:** By chance/appt. **Assn:** NHADA **Dir:** 1 mi S of village. **Own:** Loy & Rae Reynolds Harrell. **QC: 34 37 51**

Walker Antiques

Rte 116 & Charlotte Rd • 05461
(802)482-3410

Country furniture, accessories, primitives & collectibles fill a small barn at the setting of President Chester A Arthur's boyhood home. **Hrs:** May15-Oct by chance/appt. **Dir:** Across from Lantman's IGA. **Own:** Dona Walker.

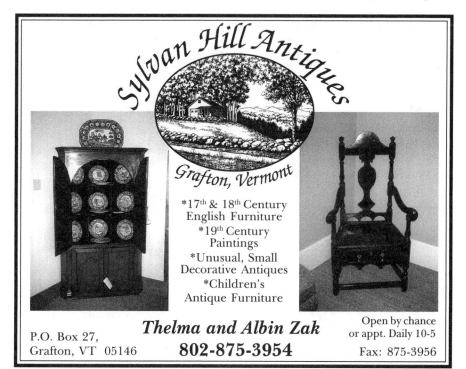

Jacksonville

Marilla's Antiques & Country Goods [G8]

Rtes 100 & 112 • 05342
(802)368-7725

Furniture & decorative accessories, oil paintings, prints, early glass, china & porcelain, cupboards, Victorian in an 1840 house. **Est:** 1995 **Hrs:** Thu-Mon 10-5. **CC:** V/MC **Own:** Suzanne Strattner.

Jamaica

Antiques Anonymous

Rte 30 • 05343
(802)874-4207

A small shop in a barn with furniture, quilts, advertising, accessories, political, coins, sports, memorabilia & toys. **Est:** 1979 **Hrs:** Early Spr to late Fall by chance/appt. **Assn:** VADA **Dir:** 2 houses S of bank. **Own:** Andrew & Fiona Avery. **QC: 48 84 39**

Old Corkers Antiques

Rte 30 • 05343
(802)874-4172

A general line. **Hrs:** May-Oct daily 10-5.

Jay

The Tickle Trunk

Jay Village • 05859
(802)988-4731 • (802)988-4731 (fax)

Country & Victorian antiques, clocks, books, whatnots, gifts, crafts, vintage clothing, furniture, jewelry. **Hrs:** Thu-Mon 10-5. **QC: 34 35 83**

Jeffersonville

1829 House Antiques [G40]

Rte 15 • 05464
(802)644-2912
hover1859@aol.com

Country antiques in a turn-of-the-century barn, heated in the winter, specializing in country furniture & Victorian lighting. **Est:** 1976 **Hrs:** Mon-Sat 9-5. **Sz:** L **CC:** AX/V/MC/DIS **Dir:** 2-1/2 mi E of Jeffersonville on Rte 15. **Own:** Dick & Carolyn Hover. **QC: 34 61 65 S19**

Mary's Glass & Collectibles

139 Rte 109 • 05464
(802)644-8878

Small shop featuring Depression & collectible glass, kitchen collectibles, linens, old books, tinware & some small furniture. **Hrs:** By chance/appt. **Dir:** Int Rtes 15 & 108: N on Rte 108 1/2 mi, Rte 109, 1st house on L. **Own:** Mary Edwards. **QC: 61 32**

Smuggler's Notch Antique Center [G35]

Rte 108S • 05464
(802)644-8321
r.s.v.p@mannsview.com

Antiques, collectibles, country furniture & primitives in a restored dairy barn. **Pr:** $5-2,000 **Est:** 1989 **Hrs:** May-Oct daily 10-5; Nov-Apr Sat-Sun 10-5. **Sz:** H **CC:** AX/V/MC **Dir:** Rte 108 S of Jct with Rte 15 2 mi before the village, next to Mannsview Inn. **Own:** Kelley & Bette Mann. **QC: 32 34 48 S1**

Johnson

The Buggy Man Antiques

Rte 15 • 05656
(802)635-2110

Horse-drawn vehicles & country primitives. Specializing in anything you'd find on the farm. **Pr:** $2.00-10,000 **Est:** 1980 **Hrs:** Daily

9-5. **Sz:** L **CC:** V/MC **Dir:** Rte 15 W of Johnson Village. **Own:** Edward Barnes. **QC: 37 34 48 S17 S12 S15**

Mel Siegel Antiques
Rte 15 • 05656
(802)635-2000

Country antiques in a pretty rural setting. Refinished furniture (mostly pine) primitives, majolica, mocha, Quimper, jewelry, glass, china, tools, flow blue. **Pr:** $10.00-35,000 **Est:** 1959 **Hrs:** May-Oct daily 9:30-5. **Sz:** M **Assn:** VADA **Dir:** From Burlington: E on Rte 15. **QC: 55 106 23 S1**

Victorian House Antiques [G15]
325 Lower Main W • 05656
(802)635-9549 • (802)635-3692 (fax)
vhouseant@pwshift.com

Antiques & collectibles. **Est:** 1994 **Hrs:** Daily 9:30-5. **Sz:** M **CC:** V/MC/DIS **Own:** Gordon & Janice Goodwin **QC: S8 S16.**

Ludlow

Cool-Edge Collection
1235 Rte 100N • 05149
(802)228-4168

Antiques & collectibles. **Hrs:** Thu-Sun 11:30-4:30, or by appt. **Own:** Charlotte Sumner & Jane Wallace.

Lunenberg

Attic Shop Antiques
S Lunenberg Rd • 05906
(802)892-5907

Country antiques, furniture & smalls. **Hrs:** May-Nov by chance/appt. **Dir:** Just off Rte 2, L at PO if headed W; R if from E. 23 mi E of St Johnsbury. **Own:** Pat Briggs. **QC: 34**

Lyndonville

Suzanne Bruckner Antiques
(802)626-4019

Country furniture, folk art & appropriate accessories. Emphasis on original paint & decoration. **Hrs:** By appt only. **Assn:** NHADA VADA. **QC: 102 41 51**

Rte 5 Antiques & Collectables Plus [G]
Rte 5 • 05851
(802)626-5430

Hrs: Wed-Mon 10-5. **Dir:** I-91 Exit 23. **Own:** Wayne & Pam Comeau.

Manchester Center

Brewster Antiques
152 Bonnet St • 05255
(802)362-1579

Antique & estate jewelry, sterling flatware & hollowware, bronze, mirrors, glass, paintings, small furniture & lamps. **Est:** 1940 **Hrs:** Mon-Sat 10-5, call ahead advised. **Sz:** S **Assn:** VADA **Dir:** VT Rte 7 to Rte 7A to Rte 30N. 1 blk on R. **Own:** Barbara M. Brewster. **QC: 61 64 78**

The Cachet Collection
Rtes 11 & 30 • 05255
(802)362-0058

Linen, textiles, furniture & decorative arts as well as antique china & accessories. **Hrs:** Daily 10-5. **Assn:** VADA **Own:** Judy Roseley ASID. **QC: 36 80 48 S15**

Carriage Trade Antiques Center [G31]

Rte 7A N • 05255
(802)362-1125

A constantly changing selection of quality antiques including country & formal furniture, accessories, quilts, rugs, dolls, glass & porcelain in a restored 18th C barn. **Hrs:** Apr-Dec daily 10-5; Jan-Mar Thu-Mon 10-5 & by appt. **CC:** V/MC **Dir:** 2-1/2 mi N of Manchester Ctr on Rte 7. **Own:** Tom & Carmen Kingery.

Center Hill Past & Present [G23]

Center Hill • 05255
(802)362-3211

Country antiques & furniture (pine, oak, painted), folk art, collectibles, quilts & quality crafts. **Pr:** $2.00-5,000 **Est:** 1980 **Hrs:** Mon-Sat 10-5, Sun 11-5. **Sz:** L **CC:** V/MC **Dir:** On Center Hill, just off Rtes 11/30 & Rte 7. **Own:** Jeffrey & Kathy Metzger. **QC: 1 34 41 S8 S5 S17**

Comollo Antiques & Auctions [G5]

4686 Main St • 05253
(802)362-7188 • (802)362-4794 (fax)
comollo@sover.net

From early NE furniture to Eames designs, coins, silver, Jensen, early Christmas ornaments, toys, stoneware, faience, sandwich, Steuben, fine art & photography. **Pr:** $10.00-40,000 **Est:** 1989 **Hrs:** Jan 8-Jun 30 Mon-Tue & Thu-Sat 10-5, Sun 11-5; Jul 1-Jan 7 Mon-Sat 10-5, Sun 11-5. **Sz:** M **CC:** V/MC **Dir:** Rte 7A S of Rte 11/30 & Rte 7A int: 250 yds S of light (next to Gooseberry Shop). **Own:** Clarke & Barbara Comollo. **QC: 22 102 105 S1 S2 S19**

> Use the Service QuickCode indexes at the back of the book to find restorers, appraisers, refinishers, and other specialty service providers.

Dave Kutchukian Photographer

(802)362-4216
kooch@vermontel.net

Fine art & antiques. **Hrs:** By appt only.

Meander Bookshop

Elm St • 05255
(802)362-0700

Five rooms of old & antiquarian books in a Victorian house. From scarce 1st editions to ephemera, prints, maps including New Englandiana, travel & exploration, history, biography, art, antiques, cookbooks, fiction, children's, leatherbound & nature. **Hrs:** Thu-Mon 10-6, Tue-Wed by chance/appt. **Own:** Neil Landres. **QC: 18 74 39**

Judy Pascal Antiques

Le Depot at Elm St • 05761
(802)362-2004

An eclectic mix of country furniture & furnishings, vintage textiles, architectural elements, tole, painted furniture & garden accents. **Pr:** $50-3,500 **Est:** 1975 **Hrs:** Mon & Wed-Sat 10-5, Sun 12-3. **Sz:** M **CC:** AX/V/MC **Assn:** VADA **Dir:** Turn off Rtes 11/30 at Tilting at Windmills Gallery, 1 blk up Highland Ave to Elm St **Own:** Judy Pascal. **QC: 3 36 102 S15 S8 S22**

Mark Richard Reinfurt — Equinox Antiques

5036 Historic Main St • 05254
(802)362-3540 • (802)362-0806 (fax)
markreinfurt@equinoxantiques.com
www.equinoxantiques.com

Quality 18th & early 19th C American formal furniture, painted country, Shaker, Chinese export porcelain, Oriental rugs, fine art & ivory portrait miniatures. **Pr:** $100.00-150,000 **Est:** 1984 **Hrs:** Mon-Sat 10-5 or by appt. **Sz:** M **CC:** AX/V/MC/DIS **Assn:** VADA NHADA **Dir:** Located in the heart of Manchester shopping district. 2 1/2 blks

N of Ralph Lauren int on Rte 7A. Shop is on the R just before Manchester Chamber of Commerce bldg. **Own:** Mark Reinfurt. **QC: 52 7 25 S1 S9 S12**

Stevenson Gallery

Rte 7 N • 05255
(802)362-3668

Fine art: specializing in American artists & American folk art. Representing area artists as Jay H Connaway, Bernadine Custer, Elsa Bley, Robert Daley & Arthur Jones. Also painted country furniture of the 19th C. **Hrs:** Thu-Mon 10-5 exc lunch hr. **CC:** V/MC **Dir:** 2-1/2 mi N of Manchester Ctr next to Carriage Trade Antique Center. **Own:** Timothy Stevenson. **QC: 41 7**

Trotting Park Antiques

Rte 7A N • 05255
(802)362-2374

Country furniture, stoneware, handmade jointed teddy bears. Country accessories made in our shop. **Hrs:** By chance/appt **Dir:** Behind Ye Old Tavern. **Own:** Susan & Peter Palmer. **QC: 34**

Manchester Village

Antiques by J K Meiers

Historic Rte 7A • 05254
(802)362-3721

An array of interesting & unusual antiques, jewelry, silver, bronzes, Oriental antiques, art glass & paintings. **Hrs:** Daily by chance/appt. **Assn:** VADA **Dir:** Just N of the Equinox Hotel. **Own:** Judith Meiers. **QC: 36 52 78**

Ex Libris

Equinox Village Shops (Rte 7A) • 05254
(802)362-7363 • (802)362-1261 (fax)
johnhelm@vermontel.com

A place for readers & writers. Antique library furnishings & writing accoutrements. Fine pens; signed, special edition & antiquarian books; handcrafted stationery, albums & journals. **Pr:** $5-5,000 **Est:** 1995 **Hrs:** Daily 10-5. **Sz:** M **CC:** AX/V/MC **Assn:** VADA **Dir:** From Rte 7, Rtes 11/30 W to Historic Rte 7A. L on 7A in Manchester Center. Shop 1 mi S across from Equinox Hotel in Manchester Village. **Own:** John Helm. **QC: 18 36 48 S8**

Paraphernalia Antiques

Historic Rte 7A • 05254
(802)362-2421

Collectibles & decorative antiques, furniture, jewelry, silver, bronzes, Oriental, art glass & paintings. **Pr:** $10-10,000 **Est:** 1967 **Hrs:** May 20-Oct 31 10-6 by chance/appt. **Sz:** L **Assn:** VADA **Dir:** 1-1/4 mi S of Manchester Village. **Own:** Anne Alenick. **QC: 32 78 100**

Marlboro

The Bear Bookshop

Butterfield Rd • 05301
(802)464-2260

General line of used & rare books, especially strong in scholarly & academic areas, music, art & literature. **Pr:** $1.00-500 **Est:** 1975 **Hrs:** Generally Spr-Lab Day daily 10-5. **CC:** V/MC **Assn:** VABA **Dir:** 1/2 mi S of Rte 9, 1 mi E of Hogback Mtn, turn is approx 13 mi W of int of I-91 & Rte 9 in Brattleboro (Exit 2). **Own:** John Greenberg. **QC: 18**

Mendon

The Gallery of Antiques [G40]

Rte 4 E • 05701
(802)773-4940

Antiques & collectibles from furniture to glassware. **Hrs:** Daily 10-5. **CC:** V/MC **Dir:** On Rte 4 E betw Killington/Pico area & Rutland. **Own:** Mary Ann Stickney.

Middlebury

BeJewelled

4 Frog Hollow Alley • 05753
(802)388-2799
csjm@sover.net
www.bejewelled.com

Vermont's largest single collection of antique & collectible jewelry beautifully displayed in antique cases. Also featuring vintage clothing & accessories, small antiques, collectibles, pottery, buttons & lace. **Pr:** $3-2,000 **Hrs:** May-Dec Mon-Sat 10:30-5, Sun 11-4; Jan 2 - Apr 30 closed Sun. **Sz:** S **CC:** V/MC **Dir:** Across from Vermont State Craft Center in downtown Middlebury. **Own:** Clarisse Shechter. **QC: 63 64 83 S16**

Bix Restoration & Antiques

Rte 116 • 05753
(802)388-2277
(800)486-4355(VT)

Specializing in country & Victorian with large tables & four poster beds in as-found & refinished condition. Some china, linens, woodenware, tools & the unusual. **Hrs:** Mon-Sat 8-5. **CC:** AX/V/MC/DIS **Dir:** 1-1/2 mi N of East Middlebury on Rte 116. **Own:** John & Laurie Wetmore. **QC: 34 86 S16**

Dr Tom's Antiques

Rte 7 • 05753
(802)388-0153

Specializing in furniture cured from functional & apprearance disorders. Will refinish to your liking or sell as found. **Hrs:** Fri-Mon or by appt. **Dir:** 1 mi N of Middlebury Antique Center. **Own:** Tom Comes. **QC: 48 S16**

Weybridge Antiques • 05753

(802)545-2454

Specializing in 18th & 19th C ceramics, small paintings & accessories of small proportions. **Hrs:** By appt only. **Assn:** VADA **Own:** Betty S Ellovich. **QC: 23 10 36**

Candleholders II

Chandelier: Candelabra hung from the ceiling.

Candle slide: A small pull-out slide, usually in a secretary or gaming table, designed to hold a candlestick.

Candlestand: A small, easily portable table, typically on a tripod base, for a candlestick or lamp. Forms range from primitive through country to formal. Some have built in candleholders whose height is adjustable by means of a central post threaded like a screw.

Torchere: A tall candlestand, always formal, often very sophisticated, and usually in pairs.

Floor candleholder: A tall iron candleholder on a tripod base, usually for two or more candles whose height could be adjusted by a spring or screw devise.

Sticking Tommy: A simple iron candleholder mounted on a horizontal spike that could be stuck into a beam or wall crevice. Used in mines as well as in houses.

Loom light: An iron candleholder shaped like an elongated "S" that could be hung on the top bar of a loom.

Rushlight holder: A hinged iron device for holding a rushlight at about a forty-five degree angle, at which it burnt most cleanly and efficiently.

Middletown Springs

The Clock Doctor Inc
41 South St (Rte 133) • 05757
(802)235-2440

European & American mechanical clocks, all restored & in good running order; mixture of tall clocks, wall clocks & shelf clocks. **Est:** 1976 **Hrs:** By chance/appt. **Assn:** VADA **Dir:** 1/4 mi from int of Rtes 133 & 140. **Own:** Alan Grace. **QC: 35 S7**

The Lamplighter
57 South St • 05757
(802)235-2306

Early lighting from 1700-1900; hundreds of old oil lamps & a good selection of hanging lamps. **Est:** 1980 **Hrs:** Daily 10-5 by appt. **Sz:** S **Assn:** VADA **Own:** James & Janet Webber. **QC: 65**

Nimmo & Hart Antiques
53 South St • 05757
(802)235-2388

17th & 18th C furniture & decorations, pottery & porcelains, oak, walnut, fruitwoods, nice selection of drop-leaf tables, chests & chairs. **Est:** 1965 **Hrs:** By chance/appt. **Assn:** VADA **Dir:** 1 blk from crossroads of village. **Own:** Robert Nimmo & John Hart. **QC: 52 53 23 S1**

Old Spa Shop Antiques
On Village Green • 05757
(802)235-2366
bene3@together.net

Specializing in the Victorian styles & 19th C formal furniture & diverse accessories. **Est:** 1978 **Hrs:** By chance/appt. **Sz:** M **Assn:** VADA **Dir:** From Rutland: Rte 4 to W Rutland then Rte 133W into Middletown Springs. **Own:** Janna Tornabene Rupprecht. **QC: 89 52 10**

Milton

Calico Countrie Antiques
309 Rte 7 S • 05468
(802)893-6694

Antiques, collectibles, hardware, tools, furniture, kitchen items, toys, trains, primitives, postcards, books & glassware. **Hrs:** Apr-Dec Wed-Sat 9-5 or by appt. **Dir:** I-89 Exit 16. **QC: 86 87 39**

Morrisville

Carwin's Antiques
45 Bridge St (Rte 100) • 05661
(802)888-3100
rlarose@pwshift.com
www.pwshift.com/carwins

Two floors of refinished oak, pine, walnut, cherry & mahogany furniture & appropriate accessories: fine glass, china,mirrors, primitives, advertising, quilts, paintings, prints, linens, mirrors, decorative accessories. **Hrs:** Mon-Fri 10-5, Sat 10-3. **Sz:** L **CC:** AX/V/MC **Own:** Dick & Winona Larose. **QC: 34 48 61 S16 S12**

New Haven

Black Hawk Farm Antiques
Twitchel Hill Rd • 05472
(802)545-2216

Fine 18th & 19th C American country & country-formal furniture. Early painted bowls, trenchers, frames, lighting, garden & architectural pieces & art pottery. **Hrs:** By chance/appt. **Assn:** VADA **Dir:** Rte 17W at New Haven Jct to Field Days. R, then 2 mi S turn L on Twitchel Hill Rd. Sign at 1st drive on R. **Own:** Jeanne Peech. **QC: 1 34 3 S15**

Collectors Emporium Antique Center [G]
Rte 7 • 05491
(802)877-2853

Furniture, primitives, baskets & collectibles. **Est:** 1985 **Hrs:** Daily 10-5. **Sz:** M **Dir:** 2 mi S of Vergennes on Rte 7. **Own:** Dick & Joyce Adams.

Newfane

The British Clockmaker
49 West St • 05345
(802)365-7770

Sales & restoration of antique clocks, music boxes & automata. **Hrs:** By appt only. **Own:** Joseph Bates. **QC: 35 S7**

Fritzingers Antiques
West St • 05345
(802)365-9312

Early American country antiques & pre-Civil War militaria. **Est:** 1994 **Hrs:** May-Oct by chance/appt. **Own:** Joseph Fritzinger. **QC: 4 34**

Hall & Winter Ltd
Main St (Rte 30) • 05345
(802)365-4810

Fine American, English & Continental antiques of the 18th & early 19th C. Specializing in dining furniture: banquet & farm tables, large sets of chairs. **Pr:** $100-50,000 **Hrs:** May 24-Jun 30 daily 10-5; July 1-May 23 daily by chance/appt. **Assn:** VADA **Dir:** On Rte 30 in historic Newfane Village. **Own:** Richard Hall. **QC: 1 52 54 S12 S15 S8**

Photographic Discovery
49 West St • 05345
(802)365-7770

Fine art photography, vintage prints, books, posters & magazines. **Hrs:** May-Oct Thu-Mon 10-6.

Schommer Antiques
Main St (Rte 30) • 05345
(802)365-7777
www.southvermont.com/newfane/schommer

19th C furniture, china, glass, prints, table settings & paintings, displayed in a white Victorian listed in the National Register of Historic Houses. **Est:** 1967 **Hrs:** May-Oct daily, Win/Spr by chance/appt. **Sz:** L **Assn:** VADA **Dir:** N of Village Commons next to Vermont National Bank & across from Newfane Country Store. **Own:** Shirley & William Schommer. **QC: 54 36 7**

Village Workshop
143 Rte 30 • 05345
(802)365-4653

Fine classic & country antiques, featuring tin of the 1800s. **Pr:** $25-500 **Est:** 1982 **Hrs:** Daily 10:30-4:30. **Sz:** M **CC:** V/MC **Dir:** 2 mi S of Newfane Village on Rte 30. **QC: 34 85**

Jack Winner Antiques
505 Rte 30 • 05345
(802)365-7215 • (802)365-7215 (fax)

18th & 19th C formal & country furniture & accessories. Gallery of prints including botanical, historical & equestrian. Tin, brass, iron, folk art. **Est:** 1984 **Hrs:** Thur-Mon 10-5 or by appt. **Sz:** M **CC:** V/MC/DIS **Assn:** VADA **Dir:** 1/2 mi S of Newfane Common. **Own:** Jack & Gill Winner. **QC: 52 74 41**

North Dorset

School House Folk Art & Antiques
Rte 7 • 05253
(802)362-2180

American folk art & country accessories. **Hrs:** Daily, call ahead advised. **CC:** V/MC **Dir:** 8 mi N of Manchester Center, beyond Emerald Lake. **Own:** Marge Cook.

North Ferrisburg

Champlin Hill Antiques

Champlin Hill Rd • 05473
(802)425-3383

Quality country & primitive furniture at affordable prices plus small treasures in a lovely country setting. For dealers, collectors & people seeking something special. **Hrs:** Sun 11-5 or by chance/appt. **Assn:** VADA **Dir:** 2nd L off Hollow Rd, 0.7 mi E of Rte 7. **Own:** Marna & Steve Tulin. **QC: 34 41**

Martin House Antique Center [G15]

Corner of Rte 7 & Hollow Rd • 05473
(802)425-2874

18th & 19th C country & formal furniture, country Irish pine furniture, linens, jewelry, collectibles, advertising items & a large selection of antique wicker. Barn full of pieces in the rough. Eleven rooms & two barns. **Hrs:** May-Oct daily 10-6; Nov-Apr daily 10-5. **Sz:** H **CC:** V/MC **Dir:** 4 mi N of Vergennes, 12 mi S of Shelburne. **Own:** Tyler Anderson & Cheryl O'Bryan.

North Hero

Simply Country Antiques

1091 US Rte 2 • 05474
(802)372-3301

Quality restored furniture, specializing in oak & wicker. Great accessories from floor lamps to mirrors, country decorating & linens. **Pr:** $1.00-3,500 **Est:** 1995 **Hrs:** May 15-Oct 15 Mon-Sat 10-5, Sun 12-5; Oct 16-Dec 31 Fri-Sat 10-4, Sun 12-4; Jan 1-May 15 by appt. **Sz:** M **CC:** V/MC **Dir:** I-89 Exit 17: N on Rte 2 approx 20 mi to drawbridge. Shop is 1 mi N of bridge. **Own:** Audrey & John Lambert. **QC: 50 102 65**

North Pomfret

Jane & Richard Adelson Antiquarian Booksellers

1162 Galaxy Hill Rd • 05053-5013
(802)457-2608 • (802)457-5157 (fax)

Specializing in Americana, rare voyages, travels, juveniles & minature books. **Hrs:** By appt only. **Assn:** VABA. **QC: 18 1 S1 S2**

North Westminster

Karen Augusta Antique Lace & Fashion

Gage St • 05101
(802)463-3333
(800)OLD-LACE
www.antique-fashion.com

Museum-quality & couture clothing, fine laces & linens from the 18th C to 1950s. **Hrs:** By appt only. **Assn:** VADA. **QC: 81 80 S1**

Norwich

G B Manasek Inc

(802)649-1722 • (802)649-2256 (fax)

Authentic maps & prints, pre-1900, as well as books about cartography. **Hrs:** Daily 10-5. **CC:** AX/V/MC/DIS **Assn:** ABAA **Dir:** I-89 Exit Rte 4 (Queechee), 3 mi W. **Own:** Francis Manasek. **QC: 66 74**

Old Bennington

Karafinn Oriental Rugs

Rte 9 • 05201
(802)447-3424
jgavagan@wsg.net

In a red one-room schoolhouse, old & antique Oriental rugs. **Hrs:** Mon-Sat 10-5, Sun by chance/appt. **Assn:** VADA **Dir:** On Rte 9 1/4 mi W of historic Old First Church. **Own:** Suzy & James Gavagan. **QC: 76 S1**

Orwell

Brookside Antiques & Country Collectibles

Rte 22A • 05760
(802)948-2727 • (802)948-2800 (fax)
hbfinnvt@aol.com
www.brooksideinnvt.com

Fine period & country furnishings c 1700-1870. Folk art, early lighting, pewter, stoneware, quilts, china, paintings & prints. Appropriate 17th, 18th & early 19th C accessories & collectibles. **Est:** 1983 **Hrs:** Daily. **Assn:** VADA **Dir:** 1-1/4 mi S of Rte 73. **Own:** The Korda Family. **QC: 34 54 41**

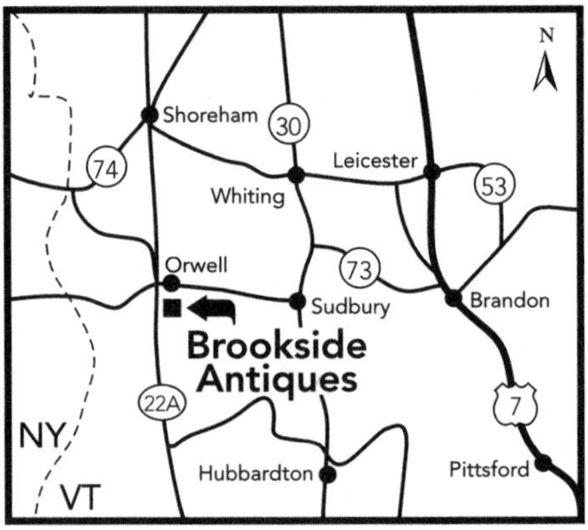

Peru

Dick & Heila Everard

Hapgood Pond Rd • 29803
(802)824-8406

18th & 19th C American country antiques & appropriate accessories. **Hrs:** Mid-Jun to late Oct by chance/appt. **Sz:** S **Assn:** VADA **Dir:** Just off Rte 12, 1/2 mi E of Peru village center. **QC: 52 41**

Peru Village Barn Antiques

Main St • 05152
(802)824-6336

Antique & vintage country things: furniture, accessories, folk art, lamps, paintings, architectural, china, glass, silver, primitives, linens, jewelry, plant & garden accents. **Hrs:** Daily 10-5, Win 10-4:30. **Sz:** M **Dir:** 10 mi E of Manchester on Main St (Rte 11) in Peru Village. **Own:** Margaret Hussey. **QC: 34 1 106**

Pittsford

Brookside Antiques [G70]

Rte 7 • 05763
(802)483-2822

Hrs: Daily. **CC:** V/MC **Dir:** Rte 7, 8 mi N of Rutland, 8 mi S of Brandon, in Furnace Brook Marketplace. **Own:** Al & Colleen Maxham.

Mitchell's Sugarhouse & Antiques

Rte 7 • 05763
(802)483-9405

Hrs: Daily 10-6. **CC:** V/MC.

Rutland Antiques

2025 Rte 7 • 05763
(802)483-6434
antinfo@sover.net
www.sover.net/~antinfo

18th, 19th & 20th C furniture, paintings, folk art, smalls, country to formal in as-found condition. Stock changes daily. Picked from local homes & auctions. Emphasis is on wholesale to the trade. **Pr:** $5-25,000 **Est:** 1982 **Hrs:** By chance/appt. **Sz:** M **CC:** V/MC **Assn:** NHADA VADA GSAAA **Dir:** Betw Rutland & Pittsford on Rte 7 6-1/2 mi N of Rte 4E. **Own:** Michael Seward. **QC: 1 34 7 S1 S9 S12**

Lucinda Seward Antiques

2025 Rte 7 • 05763
(802)483-6434

Hooked rugs, country furniture in old or original surface, primitive paintings, early quilts, country pottery, early needlework & theorems. **Hrs:** By chance/appt. **Assn:** VADA **Dir:** Betw Rutland & Pittsford on Rte 7 6-1/2 mi N of Rte 4E. **QC: 1 75 84**

Tuffy's Antiques Center [G50]

Rte 7 • 05763
(802)483-6610

Baseball cards, ephemera, postcards, paper, military, advertising & unusual smalls. **Est:** 1986 **Hrs:** Apr-Nov daily 10-5; Nov-Mar daily 10-4. **CC:** AX/V/MC/DIS **Own:** Kayce Ann Dimond. **QC: 32 67 39**

Poultney

Picture Window Antiques

150 Main St • 05764
(802)287-2050

Vintage clothing, textiles, quilts & antique pocket watches. **Hrs:** Mon-Sat 10-4. **Own:** Joyce G McGreevy. **QC: 80**

Sankanac Antiques

8 Granville St • 05764
(802)287-4030

General line. **Hrs:** Daily. **Own:** Thomas Snyder.

Putney

The Unique Antique

71 Main St (Rte 5) • 05346
(802)387-4488

Specializing in 19th C art, books, photographs, maps & ephemera. **Hrs:** By chance/appt. **Assn:** VADA VABA **Dir:** I-91 Exit 4. **Own:** Jonathan Flaccus. **QC: 7 18 73**

Quechee

Antiques at the Sign of the Ordinary

1830 Main St • 05059
(802)295-0058

American country furniture, accessories & oddities, including items in old finish. **Est:** 1998 **Hrs:** Wed-Sun 10-5. **Sz:** M **CC:** V/MC **Assn:** VADA **Dir:** 1/4 mi off Rte 4 in the Village of Quechee. **Own:** Kenneth Reid & Robert Hamilton. **QC: 102 36 1**

Antiques Collaborative Inc [G160]

Rte 4 (Waterman Place) • 05059
(802)296-5858 • (802)296-2577 (fax)
collab@sover.net

Converted farmhouse filled with three floors of period European & American country & formal furnishings, silver, porcelain, glassware, Oriental rugs, quilts, estate jewelry, books, paintings, prints, stained glass, toy soldiers & decorative accessories. **Pr:** $1.00-10,000 **Est:** 1990 **Hrs:** Daily 10-5. **Sz:** H **CC:** AX/V/MC/DIS **Assn:** NHADA VADA **Dir:** I-89 Exit 1: W 4 mi on Rte 4 at blinker light in Quechee; 3/4 mi W of Quechee Gorge. **Own:** Bill & Isabelle Bradley. **QC: 78 48 7 S8**

Quechee Gorge Village Antiques Center [G450]

Rte 4 • 05059
(802)295-1550 • (802)295-6759 (fax)
(800)438-5565

Antiques, collectibles, furniture, glass, china, porcelain, primitives, paintings, prints & quilts. **Pr:** $1.00-5,000 **Est:** 1985 **Hrs:** Sum daily 9:30-5:30, Fri & Sat til 8; Win daily 10-5. **CC:** AX/V/MC **Dir:** I-91 Exit 10: 6 mi on Rte 4. I-89 Quechee Exit: 2 mi on Rte 4. **Own:** Nancy Connolley.

Randolph Center

Page Jackson Antique Gallery

Ridge Rd • 05061
(802)728-5303

Country & formal furniture & accessories, original prints, Navajo rugs, American Art Pottery & selected ephemera. **Hrs:** By chance/appt. **Assn:** VADA **Dir:** I-89 Exit 4: 2 mi N of Randolph Ctr on Ridge Rd, on way to floating bridge. **QC: 101 102 74**

Charlie Sjobeck's Antique Clocks

Harvey Rd • 05061
(802)728-3056
(800)390-9903 (VT only)
zrt600@sover.net
www.vermontsite.com

Hundreds of antique clocks in many styles & prices. **Hrs:** By chance/appt suggested. **Assn:** VADA **Dir:** I-89 Exit 4: Harvey Rd betw interstate & Rinker's Mobil. **QC: 35**

Reading

Atelier Gallery

Rte 106 • 05062
(802)484-3718

Antiques & collectibles featuring glassware, pottery & small furniture. Many folk art painted items, both old & new. **Hrs:** Mon-Fri 9-5, Sat-Sun 10-7. **Dir:** On Rte 106 in Reading next to Indian Stone Monument. **Own:** Katherine Gionet-Kloszewski. **QC: 41 61**

Liberty Hill Antiques

Rte 106 • 05062
(802)484-7710

Country furniture refinished & as found; accessories, woodworking tools & molding planes for craftsperson & collector. **Hrs:** May-Oct; off season by appt. **Assn:** VADA **Dir:** 11 mi S of Woodstock & just S of Mill Brook Antiques. **Own:** James & Suzan Mulder. **QC: 34 86**

Mill Brook Antiques

Rte 106 • 05062
(802)484-5942

Country shop & 200-year-old barn filled with as-found & refinished early American furniture, decorated stoneware, primitives, china, quilts, coin silver, baskets & country store collectibles. **Est:** 1960 **Hrs:** By chance/appt, call ahead advised Nov-Apr. **Assn:** VADA **Dir:** 11 mi S of Woodstock, 2 mi N of Reading. **Own:** Nancy & John Stahura. **QC: 34 31 106**

Yellow House Antiques

Rte 106 • 05062
(802)484-7799
antmac@sover.net
www.antweb.com/yellowhouse

A small shop of fine Shaker, 18th & early 19th C American furniture, decorative & folk art, with an emphasis on provincial New England forms & museum-quality community Shaker pieces. **Hrs:** Generally 10-5 daily or by appt. **Sz:** M **Assn:** NHADA VADA **Dir:** 10 mi S of the Woodstock Green, on the E side of Rte 106. **Own:** James & Elizabeth Harley. **QC: 1 52 57**

Richmond

Isaac's Antiques

Round Church Rd • 05477
(802)434-3235 • (802)434-3237 (fax)

A friendly shop specializing in New England country furniture & accessories, glass, china, jewelry, toys & ephemera. **Pr:** $18-4,000 **Est:** 1986 **Hrs:** May-Dec Mon-Sat 10-4, Sun 12-4. **CC:** V/MC **Dir:** I-89 Exit 11: Rte 2 for 2 mi, near historic round church. **Own:** Phyllis Sherman. **QC: 34 102 64**

Rockingham Village

Stephen-Douglas Antiques

Meetinghouse Rd • 05101
(802)463-4296

A carefully selected inventory of 18th & early 19th C Americana displayed in a historic setting; furniture, ceramics, textiles, paintings, folk art & metalwares. **Hrs:** By chance/appt suggested. **Assn:** NHADA ADA **Dir:** I-91 Exit 6: 1 mi W in Old Rockingham Village. **Own:** Stephen Corrigan & Douglas Jackman. **QC: 1 41 52**

Rupert

The Country Gallery

Rte 315 • 05768
(802)394-7753 • (802)394-0076 (fax)
antiques@countrygallery.com
www.countrygallery.com

Scandinavian antique scrubbed pine in 3 stuffed barns. Always 50 armoires in stock, many suitable for entertainment centers; wonderful old beds, dressers, mirrors, coffee & dining tables, vintage brass sconces & chandeliers, old shades & rag rugs. **Pr:** $2.00-3,000 **Est:** 1986 **Hrs:** All year by chance/appt (hrs on answering machine). **Sz:** L **CC:** V/MC **Assn:** VADA **Dir:** From Manchester, N on Rte 30, L on Rte 315, 4.1 mi. **Own:** Janet Fram & Borge Hermansen. **QC: 55 65 29**

Rutland

Bargain Country

209 N Main St (Rte 7) • 05701
(802)775-1109

Victorian, oak, mahogany & country furniture, paintings, primitives, collectibles, china & glass. **Hrs:** Mon-Sat 9-5. **CC:** V/MC **Own:** Robert J & Robert M Prozzo.

Conway's Antiques & Decor

90 Center St • 05701
(802)775-5153

American, Chinese & English furniture from country to formal plus countless smalls. Specialties are Oriental rugs & porcelain, Rose Medallion & Imari, silver, glassware, old prints & paintings, folk art, hooked rugs, quilts & wicker. **Est:** 1956 **Hrs:** Mon-Fri 9:30-5, Sat 9:30-12. **CC:** V/MC **Assn:** NEAA VADA **Dir:** 1 blk W of Rte 7. **Own:** Thomas D Conway. **QC: 76 24 78**

Eagle's Nest Antiques

53 Prospect St • 05701-5013
(802)773-2418

Selection of primitives, fine china, glass (pressed, flint, Sandwich, cut), dolls, kettles, jewelry, silver, bottles, copper & miniatures. **Est:** 1950 **Hrs:** By chance/appt. **Assn:** NEAA VADA **Dir:** Beyond white marble church on Rte 7, turn onto Madison St. At 3rd blk turn R onto Prospect St. **Own:** James & Angeline Lemmo. **QC: 65 60 41**

Freeman Jewelers

76 Merchants Row • 05701
(802)773-2792 • (802)773-1685 (fax)

An extensive antique & estate jewelry & vintage watch department, featuring many one-of-a-kind & collectible items. Repairs & restorations done on premises. **Pr:** $25-25,000 **Est:** 1890 **Hrs:** Mon-Wed & Sat 9:30-5:30, Thu til 6:30, Fri til 8. **CC:** AX/V/MC/DIS **Assn:** AGS GIA. **QC: 64 35 S16**

New England Visions Antiques

27 Woodstock Ave • 05701
(802)775-2619

Ephemera, pottery, teapots, military, sporting, artwork, photos, books, jewelry, glass, furniture, toys, country furnishings, tools, lighting & rugs. **Hrs:** By appt only.

Tuttle Antiquarian Books Inc

28 S Main St (Rte 7) • 05702
(802)773-8229 • (802)773-1493 (fax)
tuttbook@interloc.com
www:tuttlebooks.com

Antiquarian books: Americana & general second-hand stock, genealogies & miniature books. **Hrs:** Mon-Fri 9-5, Sat 9-4. **Assn:** ABAA VABA **Own:** Jon Mayo. **QC: 18**

> Use the Service QuickCode indexes at the back of the book to find restorers, appraisers, refinishers, and other specialty service providers.

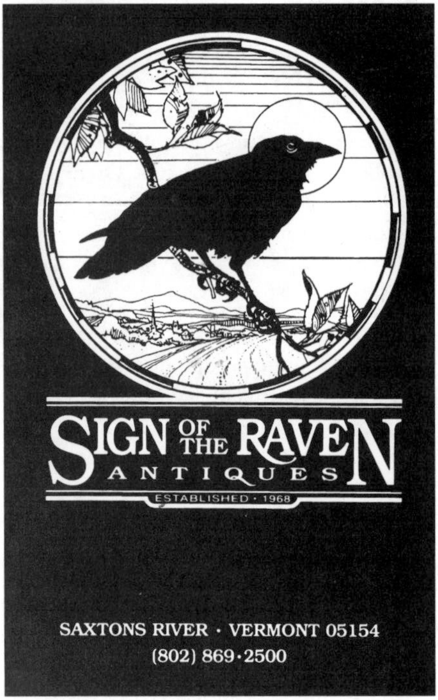

Ryegate Corner

Ryegate Corner Antiques

(802)584-3538

Fine china & glass: early American pattern, colored & fine cut glass. Some prints & paintings. **Hrs:** By chance/appt. **Assn:** VADA **Dir:** 2 mi W of Rte 5 or 3 mi N off Rte 302. **Own:** Melve & Ed Zuccaro. **QC: 61 74**

Salisbury

Blue Willow Antiques

Smead Rd • 05769
(802)352-1000

In an old country store plus two-story barn, a wide selection of blue willow, books, advertising items, Depression glass, kitchen collectibles, furniture, primitives, toys, lamps & pottery **Hrs:** Wed-Mon 10-5. **CC:** V/MC **Dir:** 3/4 mi from Rte 7 in Salisbury Village. **Own:** Jon & Connie Needham. **QC: 60**

Saxtons River

Schoolhouse Antiques

Rte 121 • 05154
(802)869-2332

Two floors of country furniture, paint & refinished, & a wide selection of carefully selected accessories. **Pr:** $10-5,000 **Est:** 1972 **Hrs:** All year by chance. **Sz:** M **Assn:** VADA **Dir:** 2.2 mi W of Saxtons River on Rte 121 or 4.8 mi E of Grafton. Turn at the blue mailbox. **Own:** Faith Boone & Sandy Saunders. **QC: 1 51 52**

Sign of the Raven

Main St (Rte 121) • 05154
(802)869-2500

Large barn full of quality early American antiques, lots of glass, china, silver, primitives, painted furniture in original finish, pewter, rugs, paintings & Oriental antiques. **Pr:** $25-25,000 **Est:** 1968 **Hrs:** May-Nov daily by chance/appt. **Sz:** L **CC:** AX/V/MC **Assn:** VADA GSAAA **Dir:** 6 mi W of I-91 from Bellows Falls on Rte 121 in Saxton's River. **Own:** Bob & Mary Ellen Warner. **QC: 1 34 36 S1 S12 S2**

Shaftsbury

The Chocolate Barn Antiques

Rte 7A • 05262
(802)375-6928

Two floors of antiques, furniture & decorative accessories in period room settings in an 1842 sheep barn as well as 500 antique chocolate molds used to form Swiss chocolate figures. **Est:** 1976 **Hrs:** Daily 9:30-5:30. **CC:** V/MC **Dir:** 8 mi N of Bennington on historic Rte 7A. **Own:** Lucinda Gregory. **QC: 1 48 68**

Norman Gronning Antiques

6645 Rte 7A • 05262
(802)375-6376
egronnin@erols.com
www.erols.com/egronnin

17th, 18th & early 19th C American furniture, formal & country. Some Continental furniture. Art, bronzes, early caligraphy, paintings, landscapes, stilllifes, portraits. Early American hearth cooking iron, andirons, cranes & firebacks. Folk art. **Pr:** $100-50,000 **Hrs:** By appt only. **Assn:** VADA AAAA **Dir:** On Rte 7A, 4 mi S of Arlington. **Own:** Norman & Mary Gronning. **QC: 52 7 41 S1 S9 S12**

Shelburne

Burlington Centre for Antiques [G80+]

3093 Shelburne Rd (Rte 7) • 05482
(802)985-4911 • (802)985-1123 (fax)

Glass (Tiffany to Depression), furniture, decoys, jewelry, sterling, clocks. **Est:** 1993 **Hrs:** Sun-Thu 10-5, Fri-Sat 10-6. **Sz:** H **CC:** V/MC **Dir:** 3 mi N of Shelburne Museum betw Ben & Jerry's & the Christmas Loft.

Champlain Valley Antique Center [G25]

3426 Shelburne Rd (Rte 7) • 05482
(802)985-8116

Country & oak furniture, folk art, tools, fine china, glass, kitchen & dining room accessories, linens, quilts. **Hrs:** Daily 10-5. **Sz:** L **CC:** V/MC **Own:** Thomas Cross.

Vincent J Fernandez Oriental Rugs

Rte 7 • 05482
(802)985-2275

New, used & semi-antique rugs: Persian, Turkish, Caucasian, Turkoman, Pakistani, Indian & Chinese. Cleaning, restoration, appraisals. Also a general line of antiques. **Pr:** $25-25,000 **Est:** 1976 **Hrs:** Mon-Fri 10-5, Sat 10-3. **Sz:** L **CC:** V/MC **Assn:** NEAA VADA ORRA **Dir:** Opposite the Shelburne Museum on Rte 7. **QC: 76 S1 S9 S8**

It's About Time Ltd

3 Webster Rd, Ste 1 • 05482
(802)985-5772

Antique clocks, pocket watches & vintage wrist watches. All repairs done on premises & warranteed for two years. **Hrs:** Wed-Mon 10-5. **Dir:** Off Rte 7 in old "Copytek" bldg. **Own:** Gary J LaPan. **QC: 35 S7**

Shelburne Village Antiques

Rte 7 • 05482
(802)985-1447

New England country furniture & decorative accessories. A complete line featuring Americana, folk art & primitives. **Est:** 1990 **Hrs:** Mon-Sat 10-5, most Sun. **CC:** V/MC **Assn:** VADA GSAAA **Dir:** 1/4 mi N of the Shelburne Museum. **Own:** Deborah Loveitt. **QC: 102 41 106**

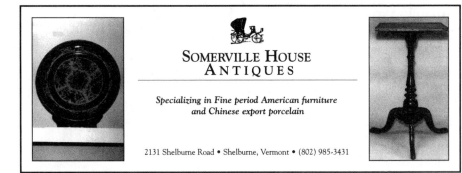

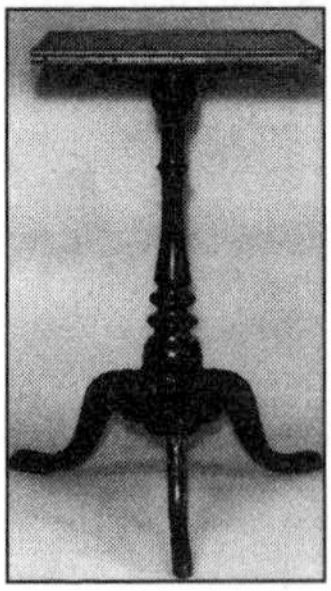

Somerville House Antiques
2131 Shelburne Rd (Rte 7) • 05482
(802)985-3431

Fine period American furniture, both formal & country, Chinese export porcelain & Currier & Ives prints as well as other quality smalls including Bennington stoneware, Sandwich glass & Staffordshire figures. **Hrs:** Wed-Sat 10-5, Sun 11:30-3:30 (call ahead advised). **Sz:** M **CC:** AX/V/MC **Own:** George S Colpitts Jr. **QC: 52 25 74**

Shoreham

Lapham & Dibble Gallery Inc
410 Main St • 05770
(802)897-5531

19th & early 20th C American paintings, prints & maps. **Hrs:** By chance or appt. **Dir:** 3/10 mi from the int of Rte 22 & 74 W. **Own:** Rick & Martha Lapham. **QC: 66 7 74**

South Barre

The Country Loft Antiques
Middle Rd • 05641
(802)476-8439

Country furnishings & accessories in as-found or refinished condition attractively displayed in loft. **Est:** 1984 **Hrs:** Daily 9-4 by chance or call ahead. **Dir:** 2-1/4 mi S on Rte 14 from Barre, follow sign to Granite Quarries. **Own:** Marilyn & Lionel Carbonneau. **QC: 34**

South Burlington

Brady Galleries Inc
(802)475-2534

American paintings of the 19th & early 20th C as well as period American furniture, formal & country, plus accessories. **Hrs:** By appt only. **Assn:** VADA **Dir:** Call for directions. **Own:** Rosemary & Ed Brady. **QC: 7 52 36**

Ethan Allen Antique Shop Inc
1625 Williston Rd (Rte 2) • 05403
(802)863-3764

Large stock of early American furniture & accessories, china, prints & primitives. **Est:** 1938 **Hrs:** Tue-Sat by chance/appt. **Assn:** VADA **Dir:** I-89 Exit 14E: On Rte 2 E of Burlington. **Own:** Duane Merrill. **QC: 34 48**

South Dorset

Dorset Antiques Center [G10]
Rte 30 • 05251
(802)362-0292 • (802)362-2660 (fax)
eichelpc@together.net

In a 200-year-old farmhouse with furniture, books, fishing tackle, sporting, china, advertising, cigar-related items, prints, artwork & smalls. **Pr:** $10-2,500 **Est:** 1996 **Hrs:** May 1-Dec 1 Mon & Fri 10-5, Sat 10-5:30, Sun 11-5; Dec 1-May 1 Sat 10-5:30, Sun 12-4. **Sz:** L **CC:** V/MC **Dir:** 3 mi N on Rte 30 from main int in Manchester Center. **Own:** Buzz Eichel & Annaick Travis. **QC: 79 18 39**

South Woodstock

South Road Country Barn

Rte 106 • 05701
(802)457-2376

Antiques for all pocketbooks: furniture, glassware, pottery, country items. **Hrs:** Apr-Nov Sat-Sun & hols 10-5. **CC:** V/MC **Dir:** 4.2 mi S on Rte 106 from Woodstock Green on R before Kedron Valley Horse Stables.

Springfield

Bittersweet Antiques

64 Elm St • 05156
(802)885-3705 • (802)885-2573 (fax)
antiques@vermontel.com
www.vermontel.com/~antiques

1780-1880 C English & American transferware, period Staffordshire earthenware & figures, English & American silhouettes & a selection of soft paste & Goudy Welsh. **Pr:** $50-3,000 **Est:** 1989 **Hrs:** Eves & wknds by chance/appt. **Sz:** S **CC:** V **Assn:** VADA GSAAA **Dir:** I-91 Exit 7: Rte 11 N thru center of town. Go up steep hill on R as you leave the center. Go beyond Miller Art Center, shop is 4th house on L after Parker & Ankuda Law office **Own:** James & Elizabeth Dunn. **QC: 30 23 74 S1**

Murray's Antiques

10 Royal St • 05156
(802)885-3046

General line of antiques. **Hrs:** Daily 10-5 by chance/appt. **Own:** Gordon Murray.

St Albans

Hodge-Podge Antiques

(802)524-2650

Depression glass, stoneware, primitives & furniture. **Hrs:** Daily by chance/appt. **Dir:** On Rte 104 to Fairfax, 2 mi S of Exit 19 off Interstate. **Own:** Richard & Shirley Shores.

Paulette's Antiques

Fairfield Hill • 05478
(802)524-5664

Large, constantly changing variety of restored furniture, mostly Victorian but country too. Specializing in oak. Also cut glass, china, lamps, brass, iron, clocks, art, quilts & linens. Heated shop. **Hrs:** Mon-Sat 9-5, Sun a.m., Sun afternoon by appt. **Dir:** I-89 Exit 19: Rte 36E. **Own:** Harry & Marge Paulette.

Sugar Mill Antique Mall [G70+]

50 N Main St • 05478
(802)527-0042

Furniture, glass, china, advertising & toys. **Hrs:** Daily exc hols. **CC:** V/MC/DIS **Own:** Stephen McDonald.

Trader's Way

Lake Rd • 05481
(802)527-9647

Antiques, collectibles, treasures, linens, estate jewelry. **QC: 80 64**

St Johnsbury

Moose River Lake & Lodge Store

69 Railroad St • 05819
(802)748-2423

Specializing in treasures from the northwoods: old taxidermy; moose, deer, elk & caribou antlers; skulls; snowshoes, creels, packbaskets, sporting prints & paintings, rustic furniture & accessories. **Pr:** $2-2,000 **Hrs:** Jun-Dec Mon-Sat 9:30-5:30, Fri til 8, Sun 11-4; Jan-May Mon-Sat 9:30-5, Fri til 6, Sun 11-4. **Sz:** M **CC:** AX/V/MC **Dir:** I-91 N Exit 20 (St. Johnsbury): Rte 5 N to store. **Own:** Bob Hoffman. **QC: 14 79 34 S15**

Stockbridge

Old Hotel Antiques

Rte 100 • 05772
(802)746-8418

Eclectic antiques. **Est:** 1981 **Hrs:** Jun-Oct daily 10-5. **Sz:** M **Dir:** At the jct of Rtes 100 & 107, across the road from Ted Green Ford. **Own:** Barbara Green.

Stowe

Belle Maison

1799 Mountain Rd • 05672
(802)253-8248 • (802)253-2926 (fax)
info@belle-miason.com
www.belle-maison.com

Presented in handsomely merchandised settings Belle Maison is an unusual collection of wonderful furnishings with a country bent. An emphasis on pine: American & European dining tables, chests, cupboards, coffee tables, painted & decorative accessories. **Est:** 1994 **Hrs:** Jun 25-Oct 15 Mon-Fri 10-6, Sat 10-5:30, Sun 11-5; Oct 16-Dec 10 Mon-Tue & Thu-Sat 10-5, Sun 11-5. **Dir:** I-89 Exit 10: Rte 100 N to Rte 108 (Mountain Rd). Located in the Red Barn Shops. **Own:** Karol & Sheldon Tager. **QC: 34 47 102**

Rosebud Antiques at Houston Farm

Mountain Rd • 05672
(802)253-2333

Children's folk art sleds, chocolate & ice cream molds. Small country furniture, accessories & unusual decorative pieces. **Hrs:** Wed-Sun 10-5, Mon-Tue by chance/appt. **Assn:** VADA **Dir:** 3 mi N of village of Stowe. **Own:** Ed & Jean Baldassarre. **QC: 36 102**

Stowe Antiques Center

51 S Main St • 05672
(802)253-9875 • (802)253-7162 (fax)
stoweantiq@aol.com

Superior tiger maple & cherry furniture,

Turnings

The lathe was the first piece of woodworking machinery. It was used in ancient Egypt, Greece, and Rome. A limited number of designs could be produced on a lathe, but their combinations were many and varied.

In the Pilgrim and William and Mary periods, turners and joiners were the only woodworkers. In the Queen Anne and Chippendale periods, turning went out of fashion, and turners were largely confined to producing Windsor chairs and the standards of tripod tables. Hepplewhite and Sheraton reintroduced turned legs for chairs, tables, and four-legged stands.

Ring, baluster, bobbin, ball, and sausage: Turnings characteristic of the Pilgrim and William and Mary periods. They decorate the legs and stretchers of tables, chairs, and case pieces.

Block: A square length left on an otherwise turned leg or stretcher, especially on William and Mary furniture, to receive a mortice-and-tenon joint. Such legs and stretchers are called "block and turned."

Cannon barrel: A plain, slightly tapering shaft, sometimes found on early tripod stands. More common in England than America.

Vase and flattened ball: Turnings introduced in the Queen Anne and Chippendale periods. The vase was often surmounted by a plain shaft. They decorate the standards of tripod stands and tables.

quality country furniture, linens, quilts, art, folk art, toys, dolls, glass, china, advertising, jewelry, pottery & primitives. Period reproductions. **Pr:** $5-15,000 **Est:** 1985 **Hrs:** Daily 10-5 or by appt. **Sz:** M **CC:** AX/V/MC **Dir:** I-89 Exit 10: 10 mi to Stowe on Rte 100 In the Masonic Hall across from Stowe Woolens. **Own:** Fred Paulette. **QC: 34 50 41**

Sudbury

Juniper Hill Antiques

909 Rte 73 E • 05733
(802)623-8550 • (802)623-6309 (fax)

Wide & diverse selection of distinctive, sensibly priced country & formal antique furniture & accessories from Vermont homes, beautifully displayed in a two-story barn near the Champlain River Valley. Paintings, unusual smalls. **Pr:** $10-3,000 **Est:** 1991 **Hrs:** Apr 1-Dec 1 Mon-Sun 9-6; Dec 1-Apr 1 Sat-Sun 9-6, Mon-Fri by chance/appt. **Sz:** M **Assn:** VADA **Dir:** 4-1/2 mi W of Rte 7 in Brandon. **Own:** Cliff Alexander. **QC: 34 36 102 S12 S15**

Sunderland

Equinox Mountain Antiques Center [G35]

Historic Rte 7A • 05250
(802)362-5459
emac@tias.com
www.tias.com/stores/EMAC

Displayed on two floors of the historic Gideon Bronson home (c 1790) at the foot of Equinox Mountain, country & period furniture, silver, jewelry, clocks, porcelain, rugs, unusual toys & decorative accessories. **Hrs:** Daily 10-5. **Sz:** M **CC:** V/MC **Dir:** Midway betw Manchester Village & Arlington on Historic Rte 7A. **Own:** John Maynard. **QC: 48 78 60 S15 S1 S13**

Swanton

Squirrel Haven Antiques & Collectibles

Monument Rd • 05488
(802)868-7221
www.tias.com/stores/squirrel

Furniture, Victoriana, dolls & glass. **Hrs:** By chance/appt. **Assn:** VADA **Dir:** Rte 7 N from Swanton to Monument Rd. **Own:** Marcia & Robert Brown. **QC: 48 38**

Tansy Farm Antiques

Rte 7 • 05488
(802)868-2340

Pine, oak, primitives, quilts & folk art. Custom pine furniture reproductions. **Hrs:** By chance/appt. **Dir:** On Rte 7, 1 mi S of Swanton. **Own:** Lorraine Raleigh. **QC: 34 48 41 S16 S17**

Taftsville

Fraser's Antiques

Happy Valley Rd • 05073
(802)457-3437

Village barn filled with country antiques including baskets, country furniture, quilts, coverlets, samplers, books, wrought & cast iron, folk art, soft paste, stoneware, yellowware, woodenware, hooked & woven rugs. **Pr:** $25-2,500 **Hrs:** All year by chance/appt. **Sz:** M **Assn:** VADA NHADA **Dir:** 3 mi E of Woodstock, just off Rte 4, turn at Taftsville Country Store 1/10 mi. **Own:** Bob & Mary Fraser. **QC: 1 19 34**

Thetford Center

William & Susan Gault

42 Grove Hill Rd • 05075
(802)785-2805
sbg@valley.net

Pre-1850s American furniture, accessories & folk art. **Hrs:** By appt only. **Assn:** GSAAA VADA. **QC: 34 41**

Townshend

Angel Fire East Antiques
Rte 35 • 05353
(802)365-7276

Furniture, decorative accessories, garden antiques, old iron, old signs & weathered architectural fragments. **Hrs:** Sat-Sun or by chance. **QC: 60 3**

The Colt Barn Antiques
Rte 35 • 05353
(802)365-7574 • (802)365-7577 (fax)
coltbarn@juno.com

A small shop, filled with country furniture & accessories, cupboards, drop-leaf tables, chairs, mirrors, unusual folk art & iron. **Hrs:** By chance (call ahead advised). **Sz:** M **Assn:** NHADA VADA MADA **Dir:** 1 mi N of Townshend toward Grafton on Rte 35. **Own:** Howard Graff. **QC: 34 41 52**

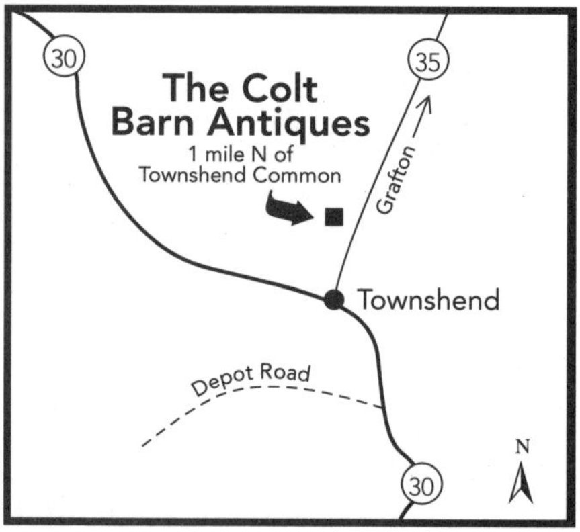

Harmonyville Antiques
Rte 30 • 05353
(802)365-7679

Country furniture & accessories, china, glass, silver & quilts. **Hrs:** Daily.

Barrett Menson Antiques
Rte 30 • 05353
(802)365-7020

Country furniture, folk art, period frames plus framed works including sandpaper/pastel drawings, calligraphy, primitive oils. **Hrs:** By chance/appt, call ahead advised. Open most wknds. **Assn:** VADA **Dir:** 1/4 mi N of the Townshend Green on Rte 30. **QC: 34 41 7**

Riverdale Antiques & Collectibles [G65]
Rte 30 • 05353
(802)365-4616

Antiques & collectibles. **Hrs:** Daily 10-5, except hols. **Dir:** Rte 30 2.6 mi N of Newfane Flea Market. **Own:** Janet Puglisi & Vickie Beattie.

Taft Hill Collection
Rte 30
(802)365-4200 • (802)365-4420 (fax)

Tables, cupboards, photography equipment, benches. **QC: 102 52**

Warle Antiques
Rte 35 • 05353
(802)365-4339

European & Oriental antiques, porcelain, faience, glass, paintings, engravings & decorative accessories. **Hrs:** By appt only. **QC: 71**

Vergennes

Factory Marketplace Antiques [G150+]
11 Main St (Rte 22A) • 05491
(802)877-2975
www.kennedy-brothers.com

Large restored creamery building housing a multi-dealer shop featuring furniture, silver, glass, china, paintings, prints, coins as well as crafts & food. **Pr:** $10-1,000 **Est:** 1987 **Hrs:** Daily 10-6. **Sz:** H **CC:** AX/V/MC/DIS **Dir:** 22 mi S of Burlington. Rte 7 to Rte 22A, 1/2 mi S on Rte 22A to Kennedy Bros on L.

Own: Win Grant & Tom Murray.

Fitz-Geralds' Antiques

Rte 7 • 05491
(802)877-2539

Shop with pre-1900 furniture, clocks & tools; barn with furniture-as-found. No glass or china. **Hrs:** Mon-Sat open at 8 am. **Sz:** L **Assn:** NAWCC **Dir:** 1 mi S of Vergennes on Rte 7. **Own:** Barbara & GM Fitz-Gerald. **QC: 35 48 86**

Stone Block Antiques

219 Main St • 05491
(802)877-3359
gah@together.net

Silver, books, furniture & marbles. **Pr:** $10-3,000 **Est:** 1998 **Hrs:** May 15-Nov 15 Mon-Sat 11-5, Sun 11:30-4; Nov 16-May 14 Wed-Sat 11-5, Sun 11:30-4. **Sz:** M **CC:** V/MC **Dir:** Approx 1 mi from Rte 7 on Rte 22A in downtown Vergennes. **Own:** Greg Hamilton. **QC: 78 48 32 S12**

Waitsfield

Alba Antiques

(802)496-2213

Importers & dealers in Scottish antiques. Extensive inventory lists & pictures: oil paintings, engravings, jewelry, tartanware, Scottish objets d'art & militaria. **Pr:** $100-25,000 **Est:** 1990 **Hrs:** By appt only. **CC:** V/MC **Own:** Marguerite Munro. **QC: 4 11 64 S1 S9**

Forgotten Furnishings

Rte 100 • 05673
(802)496-9744
forgottn@wcvt.com

American country, Victorian & oak furniture as well as a large selection of decorative accessories. **Hrs:** Daily; closed or by chance midweek off season. **Assn:** VADA **Dir:** In Waitsfield Village. **Own:** Arthur Bennett. **QC: 58 50 102**

Step Back In Tyme Antiques

Rte 100 • 05673
(802)496-9744

Furniture, lamps, dishes, glassware, linens, quilts & advertising memorabilia. **Hrs:** Call ahead. **CC:** AX/V/MC/DIS **Dir:** Historic Waitsfield village. **Own:** Lois DeHeer.

The Store Antiques

Rte 100 • 05673
(802)496-4465 • (802)496-7719 (fax)
infor@vermontstore.com
www.vermontstore.com

A wide selection of 19th C American & British country furniture, prints & decorative accessories housed in a beautiful 1834 Methodist meeting house. **Pr:** $25.00-7,000 **Est:** 1965 **Hrs:** Daily 10-6. **Sz:** L **CC:** AX/V/MC **Assn:** VADA **Dir:** S on Rte 100, large red bldg on L. **Own:** Jacqueline Rose. **QC: 102 36 74**

Wallingford

Country House Antiques

Rte 7 • 05773
(802)446-2344

American country & formal furniture including large tables, beds, armoires, cupboards, stands & chests, accessories, primitives & stoneware. **Hrs:** Daily 10-5. **Assn:** VADA **Dir:** 1 mi S of Village. **Own:** Wayne & Eleanor Santwire. **QC: 102 106 31**

Old Tyme Shop

28 S Main St • 05773
(802)446-2828

17th & 18th C antique clocks including European, English & American, tall case, wall, mantle & carriage clocks. Also some smaller antiques. **Hrs:** Afternoons by chance/appt. **Assn:** NAWCC **Own:** Clayton & Arlene Doty. **QC: 35 S7**

Wallingford Antique Center [G]

Main St (Rte 7) • 05773
(802)446-2450

Country antiques, primitives, collectibles, paintings, quilts & accessories. **Hrs:** May-Oct daily 10-5. **CC:** V/MC **Dir:** Next door to shops at 16 S Main. **Own:** Richard & Helen Savery.

Waltham

C J Harris Antiques

Maple St Extension • 05491
(802)877-3961

Furniture in old paint, primitives, baskets, crockery, Shaker & folk art. **Hrs:** By appt only. **Dir:** 2-1/5 mi S of Vergennes. **QC: 48 106**

Warren

Warren Antiques

Main St • 05674
(802)496-4025 • 496-6834 (fax)
clobel@madriver.com

Victorian & turn-of-the-century furniture with related accessories. Huge selection of 20th C collectibles including wind-up toys, banks, Disneyana, advertising tins. **Est:** 1977 **Hrs:** Sum daily by chance. Call ahead if coming a long distance. **Sz:** L **CC:** V/MC **Dir:** Off Rte 100 in the Village; 30 min from Montpelier. Next to Town Hall. **Own:** Carl Lobel. **QC: 32 58 87 S1 S16 S8**

Waterbury

Early Vermont Antiques

Rte 100N • 05676
(802)244-5373

American country furniture & decorative accessories. **Pr:** $3.00-500 **Est:** 1975 **Hrs:** Daily 10-5. **Sz:** M **CC:** AX/V/MC/DIS **Dir:** 1 mi N of I-89 (Exit 10) on Rte 100, directly across from Ben & Jerry's. **Own:** Barbara Parker. **QC: 34 36 41**

Sir Richard's Antique Center [G]

Stowe Rd (Rte 100) • 05677
(802)244-8879

18th, 19th & 20th C American & Continental furnishings; fine porcelains plus almost every category pertaining to our past. **Est:** 1967 **Hrs:** Daily 10-5. **Sz:** L **Assn:** VADA **Dir:** I-89 Exit 10: 4 mi toward Stowe. **Own:** Richard & Barbara Woodward.

Wells River

S & S Village Barn

14 Main St • 05081
(802)757-2319

Books, toys & collectibles. **Hrs:** May-Nov Thu-Sun 11-5 or by chance. **QC: 32 87**

Westminster

Larson's Clock Shop

Main St (Rte 5) • 05158
(802)722-4203
muralsrp@sover.net

Hundreds of antique clocks in many styles & prices. **Hrs:** By chance/appt suggested. **Assn:** NAWCC VADA **Dir:** Across from Town Hall in village. **Own:** Lindy & Karen Larson. **QC: 35**

Weston

Drury House Antiques

On the Village Green • 05161
(802)824-4395 • (802)824-3635 (fax)
druryvt@together.net
www.druryhouse.com

Over 200 authentic original clocks professionally restored by a master clock maker. Period & country furniture, Georgian,

Victorian & Edwardian jewelry, Nippon & Noritake porcelain, nautical antiques, advertising, lighting & ephemera. **Est:** 1971 **Hrs:** May-Dec daily; Jan-Apr Sat-Sun & by appt. **Sz:** M **CC:** V/MC **Dir:** Yellow house on the village green in historic Weston across from the Museum & Playhouse. **Own:** Joe & Susanne Lyons. **QC: 35 52 79**

White River Junction

Reminiscence Antiques

74 Taft Ave • 05001
(802)295-6177

Country & formal American furniture & appropriate accessories with emphasis on 18th & early 19th C. **Hrs:** By appt only. **Assn:** GSAAA VADA **Own:** Anthony & Michelle Robinson.

Whiting

Bulwagga Books & Gallery

3 S Main St • 05778
(802)623-6800 • (802)623-6800 (fax)

Americana. **Hrs:** Tue-Sat 10-6, Sun-Mon by chance/appt. **Own:** John Travis. **QC: 19**

Williamsville

The Copper Penny

12 Dover Rd • 05362
(802)348-7400 • (802)348-9386 (fax)
miller@lmtiques
www.thecopperpenny.com

Two floors filled with country & formal furniture, primitives, lighting, china, glassware, pottery, accessories & collectibles. **Pr:** $5-5,000 **Est:** 1998 **Hrs:** Thu-Mon 10-5. **Sz:** L **CC:** AX/V/MC **Dir:** 10 mi N of Brattleboro off Rte 30 in the village of Williamsville. **Own:** Don & Linda Miller. **QC: 102 55 58**

> Use the Specialty QuickCode indexes at the back of the book to find dealers who specialize in your area of interest.

Wilmington

Austin's Antiquarian Books

123 W Main St • 05363
(802)464-3727
(800)556-3727
austbook@sover.net/'austbook/
www.sover.net/~austbook

Books, maps, prints & ephemera. **Hrs:** Daily 10-6; Nov-Apr closed Wed. **Assn:** VABA **Own:** Gary & Karen Austin. **QC: 19**

Left Bank Antiques [G]

Rtes 9 & 100 • 05363
(802)464-3224

Country furniture, jewelry, glassware, silver, china, trunks & early oil on canvas paintings. **Hrs:** Thu-Fri 12-5, Sat 11-5, Sun 11-4 or by chance. **CC:** V/MC **Own:** Arleen Songailo.

Pine Tree Hill Antiques

21 Warnock Rd • 05363
(802)464-2922

Quality country furniture, specializing in antique accessories, old paint, folk art & architecturals. **Hrs:** Daily 10-6 or by chance/appt. **Assn:** VADA **Dir:** 3 mi E of Rte 100. **Own:** Steve Gerben & Bob Buckley. **QC: 102 41 3**

Woodstock

American Classics

71 Central St • 03741
(802)457-4337 • (802)457-9270 (fax)

Quality Americana of the 18th, 19th & 20th C displayed elegantly in the upper-level gallery. Painted furniture, folk art, paintings & sculpture, textiles & smalls. **Hrs:** Thu-Tue 10:00-5:30 or by appt. **Assn:** NHADA VADA **Dir:** Just past Cardigan Mt School. **Own:** Meryl Weiss. **QC: 1 51 41**

Antiques & More

48 Rte 4 • 05091
(802)457-2615

A large selection of country furniture in as-found & refinished condition, folk art, brass lamps, mirrors & window mirrors, decoys, spongeware, yellowware, ironstone, advertising boxes & pieces. **Hrs:** May-Nov by chance/appt. **Sz:** M **CC:** V/MC **Dir:** 17 mi W of Woodstock on Rte 4. **Own:** Margot & Mal Beattie. **QC: 34 37 55**

Church Street Antiques Gallery

4 Church St (Rte 4) • 05091
(802)457-2628

Fine antiques, carefully chosen & arranged in a home setting. Period furniture, mirrors, lamps, porcelain, crystal, art work, accessories, majolica & Quimper, quilts & more. **Pr:** $10-10,000 **Est:** 1972 **Hrs:** Mon & Wed-Sat 10-5, Sun 1-5. **Sz:** M **CC:** AX/V/MC **Assn:** VADA **Dir:** Just W of the Woodstock Green, on Rte 4, near the churches. **Own:** Lillian Phelan. **QC: 52 68 23**

Old Dog Antiques

Rte 12 • 05091
(802)457-9800

18th & 19th C American country furniture in original paint & old finish. Folk art, primitives, Shaker, paintings & hooked rugs. **Est:** 1998 **Hrs:** By chance/appt. **Dir:** 1/2 mi N of Woodstock. **Own:** Robin & John Fernsell. **QC: 51 41 57**

Polo Antiques

65 Central St • 05091
(802)457-5837

18th & 19th C antiques from formal to good country furniture. Interesting selection of Canton, pewter & silver. Four rooms of paintings & prints. **Hrs:** Sum/Fall daily 10-5; Win Thu-Mon. **Own:** Steve Leninski. **QC: 74 48**

Praxis Antiques

51 Pleasant St (Rte 4) • 05091
(802)457-2396

Period, country & primitive furniture, furnishings & tools. **Hrs:** Daily; Win by chance/appt. **Own:** Peter Saman. **QC: 106 102 86**

Who Is Sylvia?

26 Central St • 05091
(802)457-1110

In the old village firehouse, two floors of Victorian to 1960s vintage clothing, accessories, fine antique linens, lace, curtains & bedspreads. **Hrs:** Daily 10-5. **Dir:** Near the int of Central & High Sts. **Own:** Virginia Ullery. **QC: 81 83**

Wigren & Barlow

29 Pleasant St • 05091
(802)457-2453

In a 19th C house & outbuildings, a large shop beautifully displayed with country & formal furnishings & accessories & garden appointments including urns, furniture, gates & architectural elements. **Est:** 1959 **Hrs:** Apr-Nov Mon-Sat 10-5, Sun 11-4; Win by chance. **Sz:** L **CC:** V/MC **Dir:** At the E end of town near the int of Ford St & Rte 4. **Own:** Jack Barlow. **QC: 3 48 60**

Windsor Galleries

20 Central St • 05091
(802)457-1702

Furniture, lamps, framed prints, porcelains & decorative items. **Hrs:** Mon-Sat 10-4. **Assn:** VADA **Dir:** In an old stone building by the brook near the int of High & Central St. **Own:** Betty & Tom McGuire. **QC: 65 74**

Part II

Services and Other Information

Services

Appraisers

Treasure Appraisal Services
1460 Fall River Ave (Rte 6), Ste 1
Seekonk, Massachusetts • 02771
(508)336-9294

Antiques & residential contents appraised. **Hrs:** By appt only. **Assn:** ISA **Own:** Sue Winokur. **QC: S1**

David J Le Beau Fine Antiques
Sheffield, Massachusetts • 01257
(413)229-3445 • (413)229-3247 (fax) **Hrs:** By appt only. **Assn:** ASA. **QC: S1**

The Appraisers' Registry
Westwood, Massachusetts • 02090
(781)329-4680 • (617)326-6762 (fax)
willson@gis.net

Appraisals of fine arts, jewelry, rare books, guns, Asian art, coins & stamps for insurance, estate & real estate purposes. **Est:** 1979 **Hrs:** By appt only. **Own:** Michael Wynne-Wilson. **QC: S1 S9**

Wizard of Odds & Ends
7 Main St
Wiscasset, Maine • 04535
(207)882-7870

Antiques appraised, estate sales conducted, buy & sell. Off season call (207)882-9628 or 633-7423. **Est:** 1962 **Hrs:** Apr-Nov 10-5. **Assn:** NEAA **Own:** Richard Plunkette. **QC: S1 S12**

Patricia Coughlin Antique & Estate Appraisals
22 Ash St #4
Hollis, New Hampshire • 03049
(603)465-3443 • (603)465-3732 (fax) **QC: S1**

Rupert W Fennell
Rte 203
Spencertown, New York • 12165
(518)392-0397 • (518)392-7232 (fax)
tte15605@taconic.net

Decorative arts appraiser including European, English & American furniture & decorations, silver, ceramics & textiles.

Barbara B Trask ASA Appraisals
Cheney Rd
Dorset, Vermont • 05251
(802)867-5370

Appraisals for insurance, estate settlement, donation, family distribution, sale. Senior member, ASA. **Hrs:** By appt only. **Assn:** ASA VADA **Own:** Barbara B Melhado. **QC: S1**

Art Restorers

Dorvan Manus Antiques & Restoration
179 Compo Rd S
Westport, Connecticut • 06880
(203)227-8602

Restoring precious objects: gilt frames, mirrors, lacquer trays, painted screens & furniture. Also select small antique furniture & accessories. **Est:** 1970 **Hrs:** Apr 10-Nov 13 by appt only. **Dir:** I-95 Exit 18: L on Post Rd, L on Campo Rd. **QC: 52 54 S16**

Art Restoration & Associates
244 Main St S
Woodbury, Connecticut • 06798
(203)263-7343

Museum-quality restorations. Trained in the conservation of paintings, frames & fine art. **Hrs:** By appt only. **Own:** Karen A Lumpkin. **QC: S16**

Vigues Art Studio
54 Flanders Rd
Woodbury, Connecticut • 06798
(203)263-4088 • (203)266-9118 (fax)
vigues@wtco.com

Conservation & restoration of oil paintings. Frames, paper, porcelain, china & glass. Free estimates & analysis. **Hrs:** Mon-Fri 10-5, Sat 10-2. **CC:** V/MC **Assn:** AIC **Dir:** I-84 Exit

15: L off ramp onto Rte 67N. L onto Flanders Rd. Shop on R, sign reads "Vigues Art Restorations." **Own:** Oscar & Debra Perez. **QC: S16**

Rosine Green Associates Inc
89 School St
Brookline, Massachusetts • 02146
(617)277-8368 • (617)731-3845 (fax)

Experts in restoration of art objects, Oriental lacquer, paintings, frames, porcelains, metals, furniture & designing display stands. **Est:** 1955 **Hrs:** Mon-Fri 9-5, Sat 10-12 appt suggested. **Assn:** AAA AIC **Dir:** Off Washington St betw Beacon St & Commonwealth Ave. **QC: S16 S17**

Peter Kostoulakos Painting Restoration
15 Sayles St
Lowell, Massachusetts • 01851
(978)453-8888

Oil paintings cleaned & restored, estimates for insurance, investment & conservation. **Est:** 1976 **Hrs:** By appt only. **Assn:** AIC **Dir:** Near U of Mass-Lowell (South Campus). **Own:** Peter Kostoulakos. **QC: 7 S16 S9**

Professional Art Conservation
3 Nobadeer Ave
Nantucket, Massachusetts • 02554
(508)228-3799

Preservation & restoration of fine art. Complete conservation services to dealers, private collectors & museums. **Est:** 1983 **Hrs:** By appt only. **Assn:** AIC **Own:** Craig Kay. **QC: 7 S16**

Fine Art Restoration
Brooks, Maine • 04921
(207)722-3464 • (207)722-3475 (fax)

Specializing in the conservation & restoration of oil paintings. Send size (unframed) of painting & photo. Free wood box for shipping of paintings will be supplied with free estimate. **Est:** 1960 **Hrs:** By appt only. **Dir:** 10 mi inland from Belfast ME. **Own:** John Squadra. **QC: S16**

Hays Sculpture Studio
17 Whitcomb Rd
East Swanzey, New Hampshire • 03446
(603)352-0572

A small studio offering personalized attention & museum quality restoration & reproduction of wood sculptures, specializing in carousel figures. **Hrs:** By appt only. **Own:** Rebecca Hays. **QC: S16**

Master Restorer
23 Krystal Dr
Somers, New York • 10589
(914)248-8289 • (914)248-5833 (fax)

Oil paintings, watercolor, pastels, drawings & frame restoration. **Est:** 1969 **Hrs:** By appt only. **Assn:** AAA **Own:** Leonard E Sasso. **QC: S16**

Rita Rogers
23 Third St
Newport, Rhode Island • 02840
(401)846-1709

Fine art restoration. **Hrs:** By appt only. **QC: S16**

Auctioneers

Park City Auction Service
Bridgeport, Connecticut • 06606
(203)333-5251

10% buyer's premium. **CC:** AX/V/MC/DIS **Own:** Art Zetomer. **QC: S2**

Canton Barn Auctions
75 Old Canton Rd
Canton, Connecticut • 06019
(860)693-0601

Auction every Sat night January-mid December at 7:30, preview 5-7:30, featuring Victorian & Colonial furniture, glass, china & lamps. Merchandise from homes & estates. No reserve, no buyer's premium, no children allowed. **Est:** 1945 **Sz:** L **Dir:** Off Rte 44, turn onto Old Canton Rd at Citgo station. **Own:** Richard Wacht. **QC: S2**

Sage Auction Galleries
221 Middlesex Ave (Rte 154)
Chester, Connecticut • 06412
(860)526-3036

Auctioning antiques & fine home furnishings from surrounding areas. No buyer's premium. **Hrs:** Call for appt or schedule. **Assn:** NEAA NAA **Own:** Paul Sage. **QC: S1 S2**

M J Tomasiewicz Auctioneer
2 South Rd
Harwinton, Connecticut • 06791-2300
(860)485-1779

Auctions every 4-6 weeks at the Litchfield Firehouse as well as on-premises auctions. 10% buyer's premium. **Est:** 1970 **Hrs:** Call for schedule. **CC:** AX/V/MC/DIS **Dir:** On the Green in historic Harwinton. **QC: S2**

Shannon's Fine Art Auctioneers
354 Woodmont Rd
Milford, Connecticut • 06460
(203)877-1711 • (203)877-1719 (fax)
info@shannonsauction.com
www.shannonsauction.com

Auctions paintings, sculpture & fine prints from 1600-1940. **Pr:** $1-100,000+ **Est:** 1997 **Hrs:** By appt only. **Sz:** L **CC:** V/MC **Dir:** I-95 Exit 40. **Own:** Gene & Mary Anne Shannon. **QC: 7 8 15 S2 S8 S12**

Mystic Fine Arts
47 Holmes St
Mystic, Connecticut • 06355
(860)572-8873 • (860)572-8895 (fax)

Auction house featuring 17th-20th C American & European paintings, watercolors, prints & sculpture. Buyer's premium 12%. **Est:** 1986 **Hrs:** Mon-Fri 10-5 or by appt. **Sz:** M **Dir:** I-95 Exit 90 (S or N): 1 mi to gallery. **QC: S1 S2 S8**

Watson Brothers Auctioneers & Appraisers
21 Wolcott Rd
Simsbury, Connecticut • 06070
(800)791-8606

Estate & commercial liquidation; antiques. 10% buyer's premium. **Hrs:** Thu-Sat 10-5. **CC:** AX/V/MC/DIS **Own:** Brett N Watson. **QC: S1**

Braswell Galleries
125 West Ave
South Norwalk, Connecticut • 06854
(203)899-7420 • (203)838-2159 (fax)
staff@braswellgalleries.com
www.braswellgalleries.com

Auctions about every 3 weeks with the contents of fine estates from New York City, Westchester, New Jersey & Connecticut: antiques, fine art, jewelry, sterling & fine porcelain. 15% buyer's premium. **Est:** 1985 **Hrs:** Mon-Fri 10-5 by appt only. **Sz:** L **CC:** V/MC **Dir:** From NYC: I-95 Exit 14: L on West Ave. From New Haven: I-95 Exit 15: follow signs for Maritime Center. **Own:** Gary Braswell. **QC: S2 S1**

Robert H Glass Associates Inc
Rte 14
Sterling, Connecticut • 06377
(860)564-7318 • (860)564-7660 (fax)

Own: Robert Glass, Gwendolyn Glass & Robert Glass Jr. **QC: S2**

Clearing House Auction Galleries
207 Church St
Wethersfield, Connecticut • 06109
(860)529-3344

Family-owned & operated full-time auction gallery, 1 sale per week. One major catalog auction per month, usually on Fri. Auctions every Wed at 7 PM, with a one-hour preview. 10% buyer's premium. **Est:** 1947 **Hrs:** Office Mon-Fri 8-4:30, gallery by appt only. **CC:** V/MC **Dir:** I-91 Exit 26 (Marsh St): S of Hartford. **QC: S1 S2**

Nadeau's Auction Gallery

25 Meadow Rd
Windsor, Connecticut • 06095
(860)246-2444 • (860)524-8735 (fax)
ed@nadeausauctions.com
www.nadeausauctions.com

10% buyer's premium. **Hrs:** Mon-Fri 8:30-5. **Dir:** From Hartford: I-91 N Exit 34. In the Metro Home Design Bldg. **Own:** Edwin Nadeau. **QC: S2**

Nutmeg Auction Gallery

125 Main St N
Woodbury, Connecticut • 06798
(203)263-5583 • (203)263-5599 (fax)

One of New England's foremost auction galleries. Appraisal & dispersal specialists. Auctions are held monthly. **Hrs:** Bi-monthly auctions. Please call for times. **CC:** V/MC **Assn:** WADA **Dir:** Rte 84 Exit 15: N on Rte 6 for 5 mi L on Rte 47 for 32 mi. On the L. **Own:** Paul B & Jason Leonard. **QC: S1 S2 S8**

Norman C Heckler & Co

79 Bradford Corner Rd
Woodstock Valley, Connecticut • 06282
(860)974-1634 • (860)974-2003 (fax)
www.hecklerauction.com

Full-service auction company specializing in auction sales of bottles, flasks, fruit jars & glass objects. Monthly sales at Woodstock Valley. 10% buyer's premium. Also estate auctions with other antiques. **Est:** 1988 **Hrs:** Mon-Fri 9-5 by appt. **QC: S2 S1**

John McInnis Auctioneers

76 Main St
Amesbury, Massachusetts • 01913
(978)388-0400 • (978)388-8863 (fax)
(800)822-1417

10% buyer's premium. **Hrs:** Call for schedule. **QC: S1 S2**

Coyle's Auction Gallery

21 Westminster Ave
Bellingham, Massachusetts • 02019
(508)883-1659

Permanent antique auction gallery featuring estate auctions every other Tue evening, specializing in antique, Victorian & custom mahogany, art, fine china, lamps, primitives & accessories. 10% buyer's premium. **Est:** 1985 **Hrs:** Daily 9-4; auctions every other Tue night. **Assn:** MFAA **Dir:** I-495 Exit 16: follow signs to Woonsocket, RI. Stay on King St to Rte 126, go S 300 yds. Behind Charter Gas. **Own:** James & Michael Coyle. **QC: S2**

Skinner Inc Auctioneers & Appraisers

Rte 117
Bolton, Massachusetts • 01740
(978)779-6241 • (508)779-5144 (fax)
www.skinnerinc.com

Bolton headquarters of New England's largest auctioneer & appraiser of antiques & fine art. Sixty scheduled auctions annually in 15 specialty depts: European, American, Arts & Crafts, Oriental furniture & decorative arts & fine jewelry. **Est:** 1962 **Hrs:** Mon-Sat 9-5. **Sz:** L **Dir:** I-495 Exit 27: E on Rte 117 toward Stow, Skinner is on the L. **QC: 7 1 48 S1 S2**

Beacon Hill Auctioneers & Appraisers

3 Louisburg Sq
Boston, Massachusetts
(978)682-9787

10% buyer's premium. **CC:** V/MC. **QC: S2**

Christie's

216 Newbury St
Boston, Massachusetts • 02116
(617)536-6000 • (617)536-0002 (fax)

New England office for this national auction house. **Hrs:** By appt only. **Dir:** At the W end of Newbury Street. **Own:** Elizabeth Chapin. **QC: S1 S2 S9**

Skinner Inc Auctioneers & Appraisers

63 Park Plaza
Boston, Massachusetts • 01740
(617)350-5400 • (617)350-5429 (fax)
www.skinnerinc.com

Boston headquarters of New England's largest auctioneer & appraiser of antiques & fine art. Sixty scheduled auctions annually in 15 specialty depts: European, American, Arts & Crafts, Oriental furniture & decorative arts & fine jewelry. **Est:** 1962 **Hrs:** Mon-Sat 9-5, auctions most frequently held on Fri or Sat. **Sz:** L **Dir:** Park Plaza, in the Heritage on the Garden, across from Public Garden. 1/2 blk E of Arlington St. **QC: 1 7 S1**

Sotheby's

67-1/2 Chestnut St
Boston, Massachusetts • 02108
(617)367-6323 • (617)367-4888 (fax)
www.sothebys.com

Boston office of the famous auction house specializing in the dispersal of antiques & fine art. **Est:** 1744 **Hrs:** Mon-Fri 9-5. **Dir:** In Back Bay at the New England Historical Genealogical Society on Newbury St betw Berkeley & Clarendon Sts. **QC: S2 S1**

Shute Auction Gallery

850 W Chestnut St
Brockton, Massachusetts • 02301
(508)588-0022 • (508)559-6687 (fax)

Liquidation of estates & fine antiques, china, glass, silver, paintings, statuary & sculpture, prints & collectibles. 12% buyer's premium. **Hrs:** Mon-Fri 9-5. **CC:** V/MC **Dir:** Rte 128 or I-495 to Rte 24 Exit 17A to Rte 123 (Brockton). Take 1st R at lights & L at end. Gallery 1/2 mi on R. **Own:** Philip Shute. **QC: S1 S2**

Sharon Boccelli & Co Auctioneers

358 Broadway
Cambridge, Massachusetts • 02139
(617)354-7919

A full service auction house specializing in estate auctions from 18th C antiques through 20th C custom furnishings, accessories & fine art. **Est:** 1978 **Hrs:** Mon-Fri 9-5 or by appt. **Sz:** M **CC:** V/MC **Own:** Sharon Boccelli. **QC: S2 S1**

F B Hubley & Co

364 Broadway
Cambridge, Massachusetts • 02139
(617)876-2030

Specializing in estate liquidation & consignments of antiques, fine arts & custom furniture or furnishings. Auctions held 1st & 3rd Wed at 10 AM; none in Jul-Aug. 10% buyer's premium. **Est:** 1935 **Hrs:** Mon-Fri 8:30-5. **Assn:** AAA **Dir:** Midway betw Harvard University & Kendall Sq. **Own:** Robert N Cann. **QC: S1 S2 S8**

Gabriel's Auction Co Inc

611 Neponset St
Canton, Massachusetts • 02021
(781)821-2992 • (781)821-6084 (fax)

Featuring bimonthly sales of antiques, art, collectibles, toy trains, fine furnishings, antique & modern firearms & militaria. Buyer's premium 12%. **Est:** 1974 **Hrs:** Mon-Sat 10-5, closed Sat in Sum except by appt. **Sz:** L **CC:** V/MC **Assn:** AAA CAI MSAA NAA NEAA **Dir:** I-95 Exit 11-A (Neponset St, Canton): 1/2 mi on L from hwy. **Own:** Evan Gavrilles. **QC: S1 S2**

Garrett Auctioneers

76 High St
Danvers, Massachusetts • 01923
(978)774-6008 • (508)774-4947 (fax)
garaycin@ix.net

Antiques & fine arts. **Assn:** CAI **Own:** Garrett D Healey. **QC: S2**

Grogan & Company

22 Harris St
Dedham, Massachusetts • 02026
(781)461-9530 • (781)461-9625 (fax)
www.groganco.com

A fine art auctioneer & appraisal company charging an auction commission of 15% of the successful bid price up to & including $50,000 & 10% on any amount in excess of $50,000. **Est:** 1987 **Hrs:** Mon-Fri 9-5, by appt. **Own:** Michael Grogan. **QC: 7 S1 S2**

Robert C Eldred Co Inc

1483 Main St (Rte 6A)
East Dennis, Massachusetts • 02641
(508)385-3116 • (508)385-7201 (fax)
www.eldreds.com

Cape Cod auction house with Sum auctions weekly; Sep-Jun auctions twice monthly. A variety of special auctions: Americana, European, Oriental antiques, marine, collectors, books & postcards. 10% buyer's premium. **Est:** 1950 **Hrs:** Office daily 8:30-5. **Dir:** Rte 6 Exit 9: L onto Rte 134, to int of Rte 6A, turn L again, 1/4 mi on L. **QC: S1 S2**

Blackwood/March Antiques, Auctioneers & Appraisers

3 Southern Ave
Essex, Massachusetts • 01929
(978)768-6943
www.blackwoodauction.com

Auctions of fine arts & antiques from local estates. 10% buyer's premium. Cape Ann art a specialty. **Hrs:** By appt only. **Dir:** At Burnham's Corner in S Essex. **Own:** Michael March. **QC: S2 S1**

Landry Appraisers & Auctioneers

Essex, Massachusetts
(978)768-6233
www.landryauctions.com

General auctioneers. **QC: S2 S1**

Stanton Auctions

106 E Longmeadow Rd
Hampden, Massachusetts • 01036
(413)566-3161 • (413)566-2023 (fax)

10% buyer's premium. **CC:** V/MC/DIS **Dir:** Accessible from Rte 91 N or S and/or Mass Pike (a suburb of Springfield, MA). **Own:** Peter Stanton Imler. **QC: S2**

Alcoholic Antiques III

Wine funnel: A small funnel made from silver or plate used for decanting wine. It had a filter at the top to catch any lees, and its spout was angled at the bottom to send the wine down the glass side of the decanter so that its color could be checked.

Taster: A small bowl, with one or two handles, made of silver or pewter, and used for tasting wine, beer, or other whiskey. They were sometimes hung on a cord round the neck of the cellar master as he moved round the cellar sampling his maturing stock. What a job!

Wine labels or spirit labels: Small shield-shaped labels hung on fine silver chains around the necks of decanters to identify their contents. Common from about 1775 until the end of the Victorian period and still reproduced, the labels most frequently found are Port, Madeira, Sherry, Whiskey, Gin, and Rum.

Corkscrew: The earliest ones, usually of steel, were made around 1600, and are now very rare. Much more common are silver handled ones, produced in Birmingham, England, from about 1775, and imported in large quantities for the rapidly growing American middle class. The 19th century saw a huge proliferation of corkscrews whose handles were made in almost every metal in forms that ranged from the beautiful through the curious to the obscene.

Caddigan Auctioneers

1130 Washington St
Hanover, Massachusetts • 02339
(781)826-8648 • (781)826-2438 (fax)
www.caddiganauctioneers.com

Antiques & collectibles auctions including antique tools, vintage clothing, toys & dolls; estate liquidations. Auctions held most Thus; 10% buyer's premium. **Hrs:** By chance/appt. **CC:** V/MC **Assn:** CAI MSAA NAA SSADA **Own:** Jeremy Caddigan. **QC: S2**

Lujohn's Auction Gallery

2130 Cape St (Rte 20)
Lee, Massachusetts • 01238
(413)443-3613
(800)243-4420

Monthly antique & consignment auctions. Featuring fine art & accessories, sterling silver, fine jewelry & furniture. Gemologist on premises. **Pr:** $25-200,000 **Est:** 1994 **Hrs:** May-Oct Sat-Sun or by appt. **CC:** V/MC **Assn:** NAA BCADA GIA **Dir:** I-90 Exit 2 (Lee): bear L after toll onto Rte 20 E for 4 mi. Gallery on R at Belden Restaurant & Tavern. **Own:** John Economou. **QC: S2 S1 S12**

Willis Henry Auctions

22 Main St
Marshfield, Massachusetts • 02050
(781)834-7774 • (617)826-3520 (fax)
wha@willishenry.com

Nation's only auction gallery featuring annual sales of Shaker furniture & accessories, also specializing in American Indian & African art, Americana & estate sales. 10% buyer's premium. **Hrs:** Mon-Fri 9-5 appt suggested. **CC:** V/MC **Dir:** Call for directions to specific auctions. **Own:** Willis & Karel Henry. **QC: S1 S2**

Mark J Enik Auctioneer & Appraiser

5 Miacomet Ave
Nantucket, Massachusetts • 02554
(508)325-5852

Nantucket's only year-round auction house. Also largest retail antique business open year-round. **Hrs:** Sum daily 10-5, Win daily 12-4. **Dir:** On Miacomet Ave, just off Surfside Rd. **QC: S1 S2**

Island Antiques & Auction House

5 Miacomet Ave
Nantucket, Massachusetts • 02554
(508)325-5852

Estates appraised, purchased & sold. **Hrs:** Year round. **Sz:** H **Dir:** Surfside Rd to Clam Shack next R, first large bldg on R. **QC: S1 S2 S8**

Rafael Osona Auctions

21 Washington St
Nantucket, Massachusetts • 02584
(508)228-3942 • (508)228-8778 (fax)

Nantucket's auctioneer for fine arts & antiques each year from Memorial Day to Christmas Stroll. 18th-20th C furniture, decorative accessories, paintings, marine artifacts, Nantucket baskets, folk art, rugs, porcelains & quilts. 10% buyer's premium. **Est:** 1980 **Hrs:** Auctions begin at 9:30; items may be viewed 2 days prior 10-5. **Own:** Rafael & Gail Osona. **QC: S2 S8 S12**

Stanley J Paine Auctioneer

373 Boylston St
Newton, Massachusetts • 02459
(617)731-4455 • (617)928-9806 (fax)
paineauct@aol.com
paineauctioneers.com

Auctioneers of local area estates, business liquidations, charity auctions. Buyer's premium 10%. **Hrs:** Mon-Sat 10-4. **CC:** AX/V/MC **Assn:** AAA NAA. **QC: S1 S2 S12**

Pioneer Auction of Amherst
Jct Rtes 116 N & 63
North Amherst, Massachusetts • 01059
(413)253-9914

Antique & estate auctions, including an annual Labor Day auction. 10% buyer's premium. **Hrs:** Call for appt or schedule. **CC:** AX/V/MC **Own:** Bruce Smebakken. **QC: S2**

Ken Miller & Son Inc
141 Warwick Rd
Northfield, Massachusetts • 01260
(413)498-2749

Antiques & estate auctions. 10% buyer's premium. **Own:** Velma Miller. **QC: S2**

Craftsman Auctions
1485 W Housatonic
Pittsfield, Massachusetts • 06260
(860)928-6662
www.artsncrafts.com

Specializing in Mission. Fully illustrated color catalog. **Hrs:** Call for schedule. **CC:** V/MC **Own:** Jerry Cohen & John Fontaine. **QC: 6 49 S2**

Fontaine's Auction Gallery
1485 Housatonic St
Pittsfield, Massachusetts • 01201
(413)448-8922 • (413)442-1550 (fax)
www.fontaineauction.com

Antiques & estate auctions. 10% buyer's premium. **Dir:** 1 mi E of Hancock Shaker Village. **Own:** John & Dina Fontaine. **QC: S2**

Atlantic Auction Gallery Ltd
Factory Outlet Rd
Sagamore, Massachusetts • 02561
(508)888-7220 • (508)833-8703 (fax)
atlauctn@capecod.net

Estate & antiques auctions. 13% buyer's premium, 3% discount for payment by cash/check. **Hrs:** Daily 9:30-5:30. **CC:** V/MC **Dir:** Over Sagamore Bridge, Rte 6 Exit 1: R onto Factory Outlet Rd. Over Bourne Bridge, E along canal to light, R on Factory Outlet Rd. **Own:** Frank Tammaro. **QC: S2**

Sandwich Auction House
15 Tupper Rd
Sandwich, Massachusetts • 02563
(508)888-1926 • (508)888-0716 (fax)
sandauct@capecod.net
www.capecod.net/sandauct

Special auctions include antiques auctions every six weeks, Oriental rug auctions monthly. 10% buyer's premium. **Hrs:** Auctions at 6:30, preview 2-6:30. **Own:** Donna Johnson. **QC: S2 S8 S1**

Bradford Galleries Ltd
725 Rte 7
Sheffield, Massachusetts • 01257
(413)229-6667 • (413)229-3278 (fax)

Monthly & specialty auctions featuring furniture & accessories, Oriental rugs, oil paintings, sterling silver, crystal, jewelry, vintage autos, firearms & more. Prepriced pavilion of used furniture & accessories on site. **Hrs:** Mon-Sat 9:30-4:30. **CC:** V/MC/DIS **Assn:** BCADA **Dir:** 6 mi S of Great Barrington. **Own:** William Bradford. **QC: S1 S2**

Douglas Auctioneers
Rte 5
South Deerfield, Massachusetts • 01373
(413)665-3530 • (413)665-2877 (fax)
www.douglasauctioneers.com

Western New England's largest auction gallery, two auctions a week year round. Regular estate auctions held weekly. Specialized auctions of antiques, furniture, paintings, jewelry, clocks, porcelain, glass, silver & books. 10% buyer's premium. **Est:** 1968 **Hrs:** Mon-Fri 8-4:30. **Assn:** CAI NAA **Dir:** I-91 Exit 24: 2 mi N. **Own:** Doris Bilodeau. **QC: S2**

Use the Service QuickCode indexes at the back of the book to find restorers, appraisers, refinishers, and other specialty service providers.

Kenneth W Van Blarcom Auctioneer

63 Eliot St
South Natick, Massachusetts • 01760
(508)653-7017 • (508)653-7725 (fax)

Individual antiques & estates appraised, purchased & sold on consignment. **Hrs:** By appt only. **QC: S1 S2 S8**

Slezik Auctions

Rte 12
Sterling, Massachusetts • 01564
(978)422-8464

10% buyer's premium. **CC:** AX/V/MC/DIS **Dir:** Midway betw Worcester & Leominster, mins from I-290, I190, Rte 2, I-495 & Mass Pike. **Own:** Joe & Adam Slezik. **QC: S2**

Bacon's Auctions & Appraisals

1740 Portland Rd
Arundel, Maine • 04046
(207)985-1401 • (207)985-4019 (fax)
bacon@cybertours.com

10% buyer's premium. **Own:** Tony Cacciapaglia. **QC: S2 S8**

James D Julia Inc

199 Skowhegan Rd (Rte 201)
Fairfield, Maine • 04937
(207)453-7125 • (207)453-2502 (fax)
(800)565-9298

Dealing in fine quality furniture, firearms, Americana, lamps & glass, dolls, antique advertising, jewelry, paintings. Special catalog auctions include fine arms, glass & lamps, toys, antique advertising, Americana & Victoriana. Buyer's premium 15%. **Pr:** $10-100,000 **Hrs:** Mon-Fri 8-5. **Sz:** M **Assn:** MAA NAA MADA **Dir:** I-95 Exit 36: on Rte 201, 1 mi N of Fairfield Village. **QC: S2 S1**

Gerald W Bell Jr Auctioneer

124 Gray Rd
Falmouth, Maine • 04105
(207)797-9386 • (207)878-8015 (fax)
gbell23@maine.rr.com

Auctioneer, appraiser & dealer in fine art, early American, Victorian & Oriental carpets.12-1/2% buyer's premium, 2% discount for cash or check. **Est:** 1976 **Hrs:** By chance, appt suggested. **Sz:** M **CC:** V/MC **Assn:** MADA **Dir:** I-95 ME Tpke Exit 10 (West Falmouth): L onto Rte 100 approx 3/4 mi on L. **QC: S1 S2 S12**

Cyr Auction Company

Rte 100 N
Gray, Maine • 04039
(207)657-5253 • (207)657-5256 (fax)
info@cyrauction.com
www.cyracution.com

10% buyer's premium. **CC:** V/MC **Dir:** Maine Tpke Exit 11: 1.5 mi N on Rte 100. **Own:** James Cyr.

Collins Galleries

35 Western Ave (Rte 9)
Kennebunk, Maine • 04043
(207)967-5004 • (207)967-5718 (fax)

Monthly estate auctions. 10% buyer's premium. **Est:** 1992 **Hrs:** Mon-Sat 9-5, Sun by appt.. **Own:** Bruce Collins. **QC: S2 S1**

J J Keating Inc

Rte 1 N
Kennebunk, Maine • 04043
(207)985-2097

Consignments & distinctive furnishings. Auctions year round at J J Keating auction field. **Est:** 1946 **Hrs:** May 1-Oct 30 Tue-Sat 11-5; Nov 1-Apr 30 Thu-Sat 11-5. **Sz:** H **CC:** V/MC **Assn:** CAI NAA **Dir:** I-95 Exit

3: Rte 35 N to US Rte 1, take L, 1 mi on L. **Own:** Richard & James Keating. **QC: S2 S8**

Robert L Foster Jr

Rte 1
Newcastle, Maine • 04553
(207)563-8150

Fine antiques, 15-20 estate sales per year, Aug 1-2 annual Sum auction: Americana, fine arts. 10% buyer's premium. **Est:** 1953 **Hrs:** Daily 9-4. **Assn:** MAA NAA **Dir:** From Wiscasset, 3 mi N, on L, on Rte 1. **QC: S2**

Young Fine Arts Auctions

North Berwick, Maine • 03906
(207)676-3104 • (207)676-3105 (fax)
gyoung@gwi.net
www.maine.com/yfa

Fine arts auctions of paintings, watercolors, drawings & prints held four or five times annually. 10% buyer's premium. **Hrs:** By appt only. **CC:** AX/V/MC **Dir:** Auctions at Frank Jones Center in Portsmouth, NH. **Own:** George Young. **QC: S2**

Andrews & Andrews Auctions & Appraisals

71 Cross St
Northport, Maine • 04849
(207)338-1386 • (207)338-2677 (fax)

Auctioneers offering antiques from area estates featuring estate merchandise, sterling silver & estate jewelry 10% buyer's premium. **Est:** 1985 **Hrs:** Call for appt or schedule. **Assn:** ISA MADA NAA **Own:** Daniel W & Elsie M Andrews. **QC: S1 S2**

F O Bailey Antiquarians

141 Middle St
Portland, Maine • 04101
(207)774-1479 • (207)774-7914 (fax)

One of Maine's oldest auction houses. Showroom of fine furniture, paintings, rugs, decorative lampshades & accessories. **Est:** 1819 **Hrs:** Mon-Fri 10-5, Sat 10-4. **Assn:** MADA **Dir:** I-295 exit Franklin St: at 5th set of lights turn R onto Middle St, gallery on R at next int. **Own:** Joy Piscopo. **QC: S1 S2**

Valyou/Abacus Auction Service

2 Millstream Ln
South Berwick, Maine • 03908
(207)384-5579
abacus-colonel@prodigy.net

10% buyer's premium. **Est:** 1973 **Hrs:** By appt only **Assn:** MAA MSAA NAA NHAA VAA **Own:** LeRoy Valyou. **QC: S2**

Kaja Veilleux Antiques / Thomaston Place Auction Gallery

US Rte 1
Thomaston, Maine • 04861
(207)354-8141 • (207)354-8565 (fax)
(888)VEILLEU

Coastal Maine's largest & most updated auction facility handling fresh estate merchandise on a daily basis. Biweekly Sat night auctions & an arts & antique feature auction every month. Private consignments welcomed. **Est:** 1996 **Hrs:** Mon-Fri 9-5, Sat for auctions (call ahead). **Sz:** L **CC:** AX/V/MC **Assn:** MADA NHADA **Dir:** N on Rte 1, just after Warren-Thomaston town line on L; S on Rte 1, 1 mi after Maine State Prison on R. **QC: S2 S1 S8**

Trueman Auction Co

Feyler's Corner
Waldoboro, Maine • 04572
(207)832-6062

Friendly auction company with low commission rates & prompt settlement of accounts. Entire estates or single items handled. 10% buyer's premium. **Hrs:** By chance/appt. **Assn:** MAA **Dir:** On Rte 220, approx 2-1/2 mi W of Moody's Diner in Waldoboro. **Own:** Lawrence Trueman. **QC: S2**

Gary Guyette & Frank Schmidt

West Farmington, Maine • 04992
(207)778-6256 • (207)778-6501 (fax)

World's leading decoy auction firm. **QC: 37 S2**

Maritime Antiques & Auctions
935 Rte 1
York, Maine • 03909
(207)363-4247

Nautical & marine items: ships wheels, navigational instruments, models, telescopes & quadrants. Nautical & firehouse memorabilia auctions. 10% buyer's premium. **Est:** 1975 **Hrs:** Mon-Fri 10-4, Sat-Sun by chance/appt. **QC: S2 S1**

Hap Moore Antiques Auctions
Rte 1
York, Maine • 03909
(207)363-6373
www.hapmoore.com

Estates & fine art. 10% buyer's premium. **CC:** V/MC. **QC: S2 S1**

Martin Willis Auctions & Appraisals
250A Cider Hill Rd
York, Maine • 03902-0760
(207)363-8592
mwauction@aol.com
members.aol.com/mwauction/collect/index.htm

10% buyer's premium. **QC: S2**

Sanders & Mock Associates Inc
Rte 16
Chocorua, New Hampshire • 03886
(603)323-8749 • (603)323-8784 (fax)

Full service auctioneers featuring on site & gallery auctions of antiques, decorative arts & fine furnishings. 10% buyer's premium. **Est:** 1972 **Sz:** L **Assn:** CAI NAA **Own:** Emory Sanders & Wayne Mock. **QC: S1 S2**

Garth Millett Auctions
126 Unit G, Hall St
Concord, New Hampshire • 03301
(603)224-3754
(800)370-2450
auctioneer4u@prodigy.net

On-site & weekly auctions every Mon & Thu at 6:00 PM. 10% buyer's premium. **CC:** V/MC. **QC: S1 S2 S8**

George S Foster III
386 Suncook Valley Hwy
Epsom, New Hampshire • 03234
(603)736-9240 • (603)736-3339 (fax)

Complete auction & appraisal service. 10% buyer's premium. **Hrs:** Call for schedule. **Assn:** CAI. **QC: S1 S2**

Regal Auction Services Inc
349 Central St
Franklin, New Hampshire • 03235
(603)934-5410 • (603)934-5424 (fax)
(800)22R-EGAL
www.theregal.com

Auctioneers, liquidators, appraisers, auction gallery. 10% buyer's premium. **CC:** V/MC **Own:** Paul D Morrissette Jr & Douglas R Rice. **QC: S1 S2**

Daniel Olmstead Antiques & Auctions
1119 Portsmouth Ave
Greenland, New Hampshire • 03840
(603)431-1644
www.olmsteadauctions.com

Featuring auctions of antiques fresh from New England private homes; Americana auctions, estate sales, specialty sales of tools, ephemera, advertising & toys. 10% buyer's premium. **Hrs:** By chance/appt. **Assn:** NHAA. **QC: S2 S12 S8**

Northeast Auctions
93 Pleasant St
Hampton, New Hampshire • 03842
(603)926-9800 • (603)926-3545 (fax)

Regular auctions of antique formal & country American & European furniture, clocks, paintings, decorative arts & Oriental carpets. 15% buyer's premium. **Est:** 1987 **Hrs:** Call for appt or schedule. **Assn:** NHADA **Dir:** Spr, Sum & Fall auctions at New Hampshire Holiday Inn (Manchester); maritime & China trade auction in Aug (Portsmouth). **Own:** Ronald Bourgeault. **QC: S2**

Paul McInnis Inc

356 Exeter Rd
Hampton Falls, New Hampshire • 03844
(603)778-8989 • (603)772-7452 (fax)

Auctions of antiques, Americana, automobiles & real estate. 10% buyer's premium. Free appraisal by appointment. **Est:** 1978 **Hrs:** Mon-Fri 8:30-5. **Assn:** CAI NAA **Dir:** I-95 Exit 2: Rte 51 W for 12 mi to Rte 111 exit, turn L to stop sign, then R onto Rte 27 W & go 12 mi, L onto Rte 88 for 1 mi. **QC: S2 S1**

Ronald J Rosenbleeth Inc

28 Western Ave
Henniker, New Hampshire • 03242
(603)428-7686

Auctioneer & appraiser specializing in fine estates, antiques & real estate. **Hrs:** Mon-Fri 8-5. **Assn:** NAA NEAA. **QC: S1 S2**

Richard W Withington Auctioneer

590 Center Rd
Hillsboro, New Hampshire • 03244
(603)464-3232

Antiques & fine furnishings, mostly estate auctions & doll auctions. 10% buyer's premium. **Est:** 1949 **Hrs:** Call for appts & schedule. **Assn:** MAA NAA NHAA VAA. **QC: S2 S1**

Your Country Auctioneer

63 Poor Farm Rd
Hillsboro, New Hampshire • 03244
(603)478-5723

Largest tool auctioneer in Northeast. Selling fine antique & more recent tools of the trade, including woodworking, blacksmithing & boatbuilding. **Est:** 1970 **Hrs:** Call for appt. **Assn:** AAA NEAA **Own:** Richard Crane. **QC: 86 S1 S2**

William Theo Auctioneer & Appraiser

Manchester, New Hampshire • 03104
(603)622-1524 • (603)622-1051 (fax)

Auctions of all types: antiques, classic automobiles & estates. 10% buyer's premium. **Est:** 1982 **Hrs:** By appt only. **Dir:** I-93 Exit 8: follow Bridge St. **Own:** William Theodosopoulos. **QC: S2 S1**

JC Devine Inc

20 S Street
Milford, New Hampshire • 03055
(603)673-4967 • (603)672-0328 (fax)
jcdevine@empire.net
www.jcdevine.com

World's leading specialty firearms auctioneer. **Own:** Joseph C Devine. **QC: 4 S2**

Gary R Wallace Auction Gallery

Rte 16
Ossipee, New Hampshire • 03864
(603)539-5276 • (603)539-3558 (fax)

Specializing in antique & estate liquidation; buy or take consignments/estates. 10% buyer's premium. **Hrs:** Daily 10-5, auctions most Sats. **QC: S1 S2**

William A Smith Inc

Rte 12A
Plainfield, New Hampshire • 03781
(603)675-2549 • (603)675-2227 (fax)

Auctioneer specializing in fine antiques. 12% buyer's premium (10% with cash or check). **Hrs:** Call for appt or schedule. **CC:** V/MC **Dir:** I-89 Exit 20: S on Rte 12A from West Lebanon Plaza 7 mi. **QC: S1 S2**

Gallery at Knotty Pine Auction Service

Rte 10
West Swanzey, New Hampshire • 03469
(603)352-2313 • (603)352-5019 (fax)
(800)352-5251

Estate liquidation. **Dir:** 4.5 mi S of Keene on Rte 10; 15 mi N of Bernardston from I-91. **Own:** John & Joan Pappas. **QC: S2**

MacPhail Auction Gallery

Rte 10
West Swanzey, New Hampshire • 03469
(603)352-4062

Two auctions weekly, Tue & Sat, featuring antiques, collectibles & general merchandise. Previews from 3-6; auctions begin at 6:00 p.m. 10% buyer's premium. No sales tax. **Est:** 1982 **Hrs:** By chance/appt only. **Assn:** ANA NHAA NHNA **Dir:** From Keene: 4 mi S of Ramada Inn From S: just past Swanzey Historical Museum. **QC: S2**

William J Jenack

37 Elkay Dr (Chester Industrial Park)
Chester, New York • 10918
(914)469-9095 • (914)469-8445 (fax)
wmjenack@frontiernet.net
www.jenack.com

Specializing in the delicate matters of estate liquidation. 10% buyer's premium. **Hrs:** Call for schedule. **QC: S1 S2**

Copake Country Auction

266 Rte 7A
Copake, New York • 12516
(518)329-1142 • (518)329-3369 (fax)
info@copakeauction.com
www.copakeauction.com

Country antique auction house with annual bicycles (1850-1950) auction in April. Related advertising, memorabilia, ephemera, medals, trophies, photos, toys, art, posters, prints & books. 10% buyer's premium. Shipping & storage available. **Hrs:** Mon-Fri 8-4:30. **CC:** V/MC **Assn:** ISA NEAA NSAA **Dir:** Off Taconic State Pkwy/NY Thruway/Mass Pike in Columbia County off Rte 22. **Own:** Michael E Fallon. **QC: S2**

Marquis Auctions

Rte 12 B
Earlville, New York • 13332
(315)691-4634

10% buyer's premium. **CC:** AX/V/MC/DIS. **QC: S2**

Mooney's Antique & Merchantile

Rte 145
East Durham, New York

10% buyer's premium. **CC:** V/MC/DIS **Dir:** NYS Thruway Exit 21 (Catskill): Rte 23 W to Rte 145 N into E Durham. Mooney's is betw 2nd & 3rd flashing yellow lights on R. **QC: S2**

Marc Stolfe Auction & Appraisal Services

42 Steve's Lane Industrial Park
Gardiner, New York • 12525
(914)255-7700
www.mstolfe.com

Antiques & estate auctions. 10% buyer's premium. **CC:** V/MC **Dir:** NY Thruway Exit 18 (New Paltz): L on Rte 299 to Rtes 32 or 208 (S) to Rtes 44-55, W to Gardiner. R onto Dusinberre Rd 1 mi to Steve's Lane Industrial Park. **QC: S2**

The Auction Gallery

11D River Rd
Glenmont, New York • 12077
(518)426-1353 • (518)686-9224 (fax)
leeauc@albany.net
www.auctiongallery2.com

Specializing in quality antique furniture, decorative arts, fine glass, china & collectibles. **Assn:** NEAA **Dir:** NYS Thruway Exit 23: R onto Rte 9W S. Go 2 traffic lights; L at 2nd light (Rte 32); proceed down hill. Gallery is on L. **Own:** Jon Lee, Joan Bohl. **QC: S2 S1 S8**

Meissner's Auction Service

Rtes 20 & 22
New Lebanon, New York • 12125
(518)766-5002

Antique & estate auctions. **Hrs:** Sat-Sun 10-5, Tue-Fri 9-5. **Own:** Keith & Dolores Meissner. **QC: S2**

Liberty Antique Warehouse

Rte 17 Quickway
Parksville, New York • 12768
(914)292-7450

10% buyer's premium. **CC:** V/MC/DIS **Dir:** 6 mi W of Liberty NY betw Exits 98 & 97. **QC: S2**

Cortlandt Auctions Inc

1000 N Division St
Peekskill, New York • 10566
(914)734-7414 • (914)734-7414 (fax)

Specializing in estate liquidation; consignments accepted. Auctions every other Wed night. 10% buyer's premium. **CC:** AX/V/MC **Dir:** NY Thruway Exit 9A to Bear Mountain Pkwy to Division St exit. L at bottom of ramp. **Own:** Joseph Mazrazino. **QC: S2**

Fifth Estate

106 Harmon Ave
Pelham, New York • 10803
(914)738-1806
tsc@fifthestate.com
www.fifthestate.com

Conduct on premises rare estate sales of provenanced art, antiques, clocks, tools, paintings, bronzes, collectibles, books, paper ephemera, jewelry, textiles, outdoor garden furnishings & decorative accessories. Privately buy/sell estate collections. **Pr:** $5-50,000 **Est:** 1989 **Hrs:** Daily by appt, estate sales Fri-Sat 9-4. **Sz:** L **Dir:** Hutchinson River Pwy or I-95 Exit E Lincoln Ave, turn onto Highbrook Ave, then Harmon Ave. **Own:** Terry Seldon Calhoun. **QC: S1 S2 S12**

Mark Vail Auction Co

Kelly Ave
Pine Bush, New York
(914)744-2120 • (914)744-2450 (fax)
www.markvail.com

10% buyer's premium. Absentee bids accepted. **CC:** V/MC **Dir:** NYS Thruway Exit 16 onto Rte 17W to Exit 119. R on Rte 302 to Pine Bush. I-84 Exit 8 onto Rte 52W to Pine Bush, L at Mobil station. **QC: S2**

Walsh Auction Service

32 River View Lane
Potsdam, New York • 13676
(315)265-9111 • (315)265-9222 (fax)
(800)371-9286
gwalsh@northnet.org

Antique auction service serving the north country since 1979. Conducting auctions on location & consignments at my auction building. Annual New Year's Day auctions. **Est:** 1979 **Sz:** L **CC:** V/MC **Dir:** 2.5 hrs N of Syracuse, 1.5 hrs S of Ottawa Canada. **Own:** Greg Walsh. **QC: S2**

Butterscotch Auction Gallery

Pound Ridge, New York • 10576
(914)764-4609 • (914)764-4609 (fax)
www.butterauction.com

Antiques & estate auctions. 15% buyer's premium. **Hrs:** . **CC:** V/MC **Assn:** ISA **Own:** Paul D Marinucci. **QC: S1 S2**

George W Cole Auctioneers & Appraisers

53 N Broadway
Red Hook, New York • 12571
(914)876-5215
bidbuy34@aol.com

A Hudson Valley tradition. **Est:** 1976 **Hrs:** Call for schedule. **Own:** George W Cole & Robin B Mizerak. **QC: S2 S1**

Patrick Thomas & Partners

858 Rte 212
Saugerties, New York • 12477
(914)247-8888 • (914)246-0589 (fax)
auctionptp@aol.com

Specializing in fine art & antiques. Consignments welcome. **Hrs:** Call for schedule. **Dir:** NYS Thruway Exit 20: W on Rte 212 approx 2 mi, auction on R. **QC: S1 S2**

Marty's Antique & Auction Service

Danielson Pike (Rte 6)
Foster, Rhode Island • 02814
(401)568-7196

Wide selection of quality furniture & accessories, primitives, collectibles, glass, china, Oriental rugs, Americana & much more. Auction every Tue at Auction Hall, Pole 52. **Hrs:** Tue 7 PM. **Assn:** SNEADA NAA **Dir:** I-395 to Rte 6 E: 5 mi over RI line. **Own:** Mary Austin. **QC: S2**

Gustave J S White Auctioneer

37 Bellevue Ave
Newport, Rhode Island • 02840
(401)841-5780 • (401)849-9310 (fax)

Auctions of antique & estate furniture, decorative accessories. 10% buyer's premium. Auctions on site or in Portsmouth, RI, auction gallery. **Hrs:** Daily 9-4. **QC: S2**

Corner Stone Auction Galleries

10 Brookfield Rd, Apt A3
Riverside, Rhode Island • 02915
(401)438-1338

Quality monthly auctions held on the second Mon except Jul at Brightridge Hall in East Providence. 10% buyer's premium. **Est:** 1979 **Hrs:** Call for more information. **CC:** V/MC **Own:** Bob Fricker. **QC: S2**

Martone's Gallery

699 New London Tpke
West Greenwich, Rhode Island • 02816
(401)885-3880

Auctioneer of antique furniture, rugs & glassware; auctions held every other Mon PM. 10% buyer's premium. **Hrs:** Call for appt or schedule. **CC:** V/MC **Dir:** I-95 Exit 7: 20 min from CT border. **Own:** Jack Martone. **QC: S2**

James Dickerson Auctioneers

710 Hinesburg Rd
Charlotte, Vermont • 05445
(802)425-3916

Own: James & Allison Dickerson. **QC: S2**

Wm E Barsalow Auctioneer & Appraiser

Jct Rtes 4 & 22
Fair Haven, Vermont • 05743
(802)265-2100

Early American, Victorian & golden oak furniture, jewelry, silver, glass, china, lamps & lighting, sporting collectibles, paintings, prints, clocks & watches. 5% buyer's premium. **Hrs:** Daily 10-5. **CC:** V/MC **Own:** Bill & Jane Barsalow. **QC: S1 S2**

Eric Nathan Auction Company Inc

West Road
Manchester, Vermont • 05254
(802)362-1016 (fax)
(800)700-8643
enathan@vermontel.com

Estate auctions, antiques & fine art. **Est:** 1985. **QC: S2 S1**

Use the Specialty QuickCode indexes at the back of the book to find dealers who specialize in your area of interest.

Wright's Enterprises/ Wright's Auction Services
Newport/Derby Rd (Rte 5)
Newport, Vermont • 05855
(802)334-6115 • (802)334-1591 (fax)

10% buyer's premium. **CC:** AX/V/MC/DIS **Own:** Ron Wright. **QC: S2**

Red Door Antiques & Auction Barn
Rupert, Vermont • 05768
(802)645-0328

5% buyer's premium. **Own:** Dick Perkins & Pam Petry. **QC: S2**

Townshend Auction Gallery
Rte 30
Townshend, Vermont • 05353
(802)365-4388

Specializing in estate, antique & farm auctions. 10% buyer's premium. **Hrs:** Call for auction dates & times. **Own:** Kit Martin & Art Monette. **QC: S2**

Merrill's Auction Gallery
27 James Brown Dr
Williston, Vermont • 05495
(802)878-2625 • (802)878-2625 (fax)

Specializing in estate & antique auctions, consignment day on Tue at gallery. 10% buyer's premium. **Dir:** I-89 Exit 12: N on Rte 2A 2.5 mi, turn L at Shell station. **Own:** Duane Merrill. **QC: S2 S1**

eHammer North
442 Woodstock Rd (Rte 4)
Woodstock, Vermont • 05062
(802)457-6119
tamica@ehammer.com
www.ehammer.com

A wide range of antiques & collectibles from weathervanes to postcards, from toys to fine art. **Hrs:** Daily 10-5. **Sz:** M **CC:** V/MC **Dir:** In the Gallery Place at the E end of Woodstock on Rte 4. **Own:** James Harley & Fred Giampietro. **QC: S2 S12 S1**

Building Materials

Gilyard's Antiques
1083 Rte 202
Bantam, Connecticut • 06750
(860)567-4204 • (860)567-9055 (fax)

18th C building supplies: hand-hewn beams, wide board flooring, granite steps, hardware. Also 18th & 19th C American country furniture. **Est:** 1971 **Hrs:** By appt only. **Sz:** L **Dir:** 4 mi W of Litchfield Green. **Own:** Kent & Yvonne Gilyard. **QC: 3 34 S18 S2 S4**

Olde New England Salvage Company
112 Sisson Rd
Lebanon, Connecticut • 06249
(860)887-2280

Antique buildings, building materials & components, stones & millstones, signposts, furniture & other architectural elements. Actively buying reclaimed & salvaged stock materials. **Hrs:** By appt only. **QC: 3 S18 S17 S4**

Chestnut Woodworking & Antique Flooring Co
West Cornwall, Connecticut • 06796
(860)672-4300 • (860)672-2441 (fax)

Antique wide board flooring & remilled tongue & groove flooring. 100% reclaimed, kiln dried. Rare chestnut, oak, white pine, heart pine, hemlock. Also furniture reproductions & harvest tables. **Own:** Bob Friedman. **QC: 56 S4 S17**

Ramase Genuine Old Building Material

661 Washington Rd
Woodbury, Connecticut • 06798
(203)263-4909
(800)WIDEOAK

General old building materials including hewn beams, wide flooring, paneled room ends, wall boards, doors, moldings, mantels, old window glass, old brick, early American hardware, cupboards & weathered barn siding. **Est:** 1960 **Hrs:** By appt only. **Dir:** 1-1/2 mi from int of Rtes 46 & 7. **Own:** Harold Cole. **QC: 3 S18 S4**

New England Demolition & Salvage

3065 Cranberry Hwy
East Wareham, Massachusetts • 02538
(508)291-7258 • (508)273-0274 (fax)
homeneds@aol.com
www.nedemolition.qpg.com

Architectural antiques, mantels, doors, windows, claw foot tubs, columns, radiators. **Est:** 1998 **Hrs:** Tue-Sun 9-6. **Sz:** H. **QC: 3 S4 S18**

Architectural Antiquities

Harborside, Maine • 04642
(207)326-4938

Architectural elegance in a seaside setting on Penobscot Bay. Components for home building restoration, primarily Victorian with 18th & 19th C period items including int/ext doors, windows, stained glass, brackets, columns, plumbing & accessories. **Est:** 1983 **Hrs:** By chance/appt suggested. **Sz:** H **Dir:** Call for directions. **Own:** John Jacobs. **QC: 3 89 S4 S18**

Old House Parts Co

Main St
Kennebunk, Maine • 04043
(207)985-1999

Architectural salvage, old house parts, whole structures & period rooms available. **Dir:** Behind the Mobil Station in Blue Wave Mall. **Own:** Tom & Diane Joyal. **QC: 3 S18 S4**

Architectural Salvage Inc

1A Mill St
Exeter, New Hampshire • 03833
(603)642-4348
arch@ttlc.net
www.oldhousesalvage.com

Dealing in all types of old house parts, from sash keepers to grand entrances, windows to clawfoot tubs. **Est:** 1996 **Hrs:** Sat-Sun 12-5 & by appt. **Sz:** L **Dir:** I-95 Exit 2 to Rte 101 to Rtes 108 & 33. L at bottom of ramp. 1.1 mi, go R, then L at bandstand. Mill St is last before tracks. **Own:** Chris McMahon. **QC: 3 S4 S18**

North Fields Restorations

Rte 1 N
Hampton Falls, New Hampshire • 03844
(603)926-5383

A complete line of antique building materials for 17th & 18th C house restoration, specializing in wide antique pine, oak & chestnut flooring. Also selling complete dismantled houses & barns delivered for reconstruction on a new site. **Hrs:** Mon-Fri 8-4, Sat by appt only. **Sz:** H **Dir:** I-95 N Exit 1: L on Rte 1, 1-1/2 mi on L. Look for windmill. **Own:** Mark Phillips. **QC: S18 S4**

Country Road Associates

Franklin Ave
Millbrook, New York • 12545
(914)677-6041 • (914)677-6532 (fax)
jrizzo4833@aol.com

19th C barnwood & 19th C style furniture made out of 19th C barnwood. Flooring in chestnut, wide-board pine, hemlock, oak & heart pine from 3 to 16 inches wide. Weathered barn siding in natural colors. **Hrs:** Tue-Sun 10-4. **CC:** AX/V/MC **Own:** Joe Rizzo. **QC: S18 S17 S4**

River House Wares Restoration

Rensselaer Falls, New York • 13680
(315)344-8882 • (315)344-7247 (fax)

2,000 period doors & windows, architectural restoration materials, authentic hardware, trim moldings, spindles, shutters, porch posts, railings, light fixtures, cast iron floor registers, claw foot bath tubs, pedestal & marble sinks & fireplace fronts. **QC: 3 54 S4 S18**

Historic Houseparts

540 South Ave
Rochester, New York • 14620
(716)325-2329 • (716)325-3613 (fax)
houseparts@msn.com
www.historichouseparts.com

Architectural salvage & restoration supplies. Offers a large selection of vintage hardware, plumbing, lighting, woodwork. Also carries a comprehensive selection of fine quality reproduction hardware, plumbing & lighting. **Est:** 1980 **Hrs:** Mon-Sat 9-6, **Sz:** H **CC:** AX/V/MC **Dir:** I-90 to I-490 E Exit 15 (South Ave): 1/2 mi on L. **Own:** Christina Jones. **QC: 3 65 20 S4 S18**

Boards & Beams

Rte 4
Whitehall, New York • 12887

Architectural salvage. Special request searches for architectural details, flooring, trim, doors & door jambs, windows, post & beam frames. **QC: 3 S18 S4**

Stephen Mack Associates

Chase Hill Farm
Ashaway, Rhode Island • 02804
(401)377-8041 • (401)377-2331 (fax)

Creating homes & estates using historic structures; providers of fine historic homes & barns. Specializing in design & construction of homes using transported historic structures that have been saved from destruction by meticulous disassembly. **Hrs:** By appt only. **Assn:** SPNEA **Dir:** S of I-95 at the CT-RI line, call for directions. **QC: S18 S4**

Domestic Arts

Fraktur: A Pennsylvanian Dutch certificate executed in traditional German gothic calligraphy, often surrounded by folk art motifs of birds, foliage, and figures. The certificates commemorated important domestic events, particularly births and deaths, and are now recognized as one of the most significant forms of folk art. After the mid-1830s, printed frakturs with spaces for handwritten names and dates gradually replaced the hand-made examples. The best are still beautiful, and many were hand-colored, but it is the earlier ones in traditional calligraphy that are obviously the most prized. "Fraktur" (literally "broken curve") is the German name for the traditional gothic script written with a broad nib that "broke" curves into thick and thin strokes.

Theorem: A stenciled painting, usually on velvet, but sometimes on Bristol board, of a still life of flowers and fruit, in a basket or urn, and occasionally with a bird or two. Theorem painting was an important accomplishment and art form for women and girls in the first half of the 19th century. It gradually replaced embroidery. The artist would first cut a number of stencils of different leaves, petals, and other motifs and design an arrangement from them. Though stenciled, no two theorems are the same. A thick, almost dry, watercolor was the preferred medium. Theorems are rarely signed, and today they are much appreciated examples of women's decorative art.

Mourning pictures: Mourning pictures were another accomplishment of girls in the early 19th century. The tomb, usually inscribed with the name of the deceased, occupied the center of the design, and was surrounded by conventional symbols of mourning — the weeping willow, the river (of life and death), a church and one or more mourners. They were either painted in water color or were worked in silk, in which case the faces and the inscription on the tomb were painted. George Washington's death provoked many mourning pictures.

The Barn People

Morgan Hill
South Woodstock, Vermont • 05071
(802)457-3356 • (802)457-3358 (fax)
(800)550-5578
barnman@sover.net

Vintage Vermont barn frames & outbuildings available for dismantling, restoration & reassembly on your choice lot anywhere in the United States. Custom-built small structures of hand-hewn timbers for home/office outbuildings. **Pr:** $12,000-100,000 **Est:** 1974 **Hrs:** Mon-Fri 8-4:30. **Sz:** H **Assn:** SPNEA **Dir:** I-91S Exit 9: L onto Rte 5 S, take L before 1st traffic light. Down hill to L of RR station go across RR tracks then R thru gate in chainlink fence. **Own:** Ken Epworth. **QC: 3 S4 S18 S16**

Cabinetmakers

Classics in Wood

271 Ashford Ctr Rd (Rte 44)
Ashford, Connecticut • 06278
(860)429-6020 • (860)429-8977 (fax)
www.classics@neca.com

Reproduction Windsor chairs, assorted tables & case pieces of the Colonial period. **Pr:** $250-4,000 **Est:** 1981 **Hrs:** Sat-Sun 10-5 or by appt. **Sz:** M **Dir:** 1 mi E of int Rtes 89 & 44, adjacent to Merrythought Antiques. **Own:** Gerald Dunphy. **QC: S17 S5**

Woody Mosch Cabinetmakers

23 Wood Creek Rd
Bethlehem, Connecticut • 06751
(203)266-7619 • (203)266-7619 (fax)

18th C & Shaker antique reproduction furniture, 18th C architectural woodworking & custom cabinetwork. **Est:** 1976 **Hrs:** By appt only. **Dir:** Call for directions. **QC: S5 S17 S18**

Stephen H Smith Handmade Furniture/Antiques

9 Old Post Rd
Clinton, Connecticut • 06413
(860)669-9172

Specializing in fine period reproduction furniture, period American antiques & accessories. Custom handmade furniture reproductions of exquisite detail & finish a specialty. **Pr:** $10-5,000 **Est:** 1985 **Hrs:** Mon-Sat 10-5, call ahead advised. **Sz:** S **Dir:** I-95 Exit 64: Rte 145 S to light at Rte 1; #9 is last house on R before Rte 1. **QC: 52 56 36 S17 S5**

New England Historical Connection

300 Danbury Rd
Wilton, Connecticut • 06897
(203)761-8646 • (203)761-1371 (fax)
(800)647-5719

A collection of handcrafted reproduction American country furniture & accessories including cupboards, highboys, lowboys, desks, Shaker chairs, beds, Windsor chairs & tables including dining, tea, breakfast & tavern; lamps, chandeliers & accessories. **Pr:** $25-15,000 **Est:** 1990 **Hrs:** Mon-Sat 10-5, Sun 12-5 or by appt. **Sz:** L **CC:** V/MC **Dir:** On Rte 7 at the int of Rte 33 & Rte 106. **Own:** John Schnefke. **QC: 36 56 S17**

R Loomis Furniture/Cabinetmaker

West Rd
Ashfield, Massachusetts • 01096
(413)628-3813

Fine furniture & cabinetmaking in all styles, but specializing in Queen Anne & Chippendale periods. Each piece museum quality, individually crafted, signed & dated. **Est:** 1974 **Hrs:** By appt only. **Dir:** I-91 Exit 19: L on Rte 9 to Williamsburg Ctr (9 mi), R onto North St, into Ashfield Rd, go 6 mi, L on Ludwig, into West Rd 1 mi on R. **Own:** Russ Loomis Jr. **QC: 56 S5 S17**

Marc Blanchette — Master Windsor Chairmaker

39 Coolidge Ave
Hampden, Maine • 04444
(207)942-4114
windsor@mint.net

Reproduction Windsor furniture. **QC: S17**

Windsor Chairmakers

Rte 1
Lincolnville, Maine • 04849
(800)789-5188

Visit this shop to watch chairs being made & "talk Windsors." Also make dining tables, any size or finish, with cabriole, spoonfoot, or tapered legs, in tiger maple, cherry or pine. Beds & case pieces too. **Pr:** $600-12,000 **Est:** 1987 **Hrs:** Jun-Oct daily 8-5; Nov-May Mon-Fri 8-5. **Sz:** L **Dir:** On the Maine Coast, 6 mi N of Camden on US Rte 1. **Own:** Jim Brown. **QC: 56 S17**

William Evans Fine Handmade Furniture

804 Main St
Waldoboro, Maine • 04572
(207)832-4175

A master cabinetmaker showing a changing selection of delicate boxes, inlaid desks, formal breakfronts & unique pieces. Period reproductions & restoration of quality period furniture. Trained by Dutch master cabinetmaker. **Est:** 1973 **Hrs:** By chance/appt advisable. **Dir:** In the village by the Medomak River. **QC: 56 S5 S17**

the Ball & Claw

55 America's Cup Ave
Newport, Rhode Island • 02840
(401)848-5600 • (401)848-5650 (fax)
www.theballandclaw.com

Historically accurate replicas of 18th C Townsend & Goddard designs. Showroom also includes accessories of period design including paintings, porcelain, textiles, weathervanes & lighting. **Pr:** $50-4,000 **Est:** 1988 **Hrs:** Jun-Sep Mon-Sat 10-10, Sun 11-6; Oct-May Mon-Fri 10-5, Sat 10-6, Sun 11-5. **Sz:** M **CC:** AX/V/MC **Dir:** From the N: I-95 S to Rte138 E to "Downtown Newport" exit. R off exit, then 2nd R onto America's Cup Ave at Bowen's Wharf. **Own:** Jeffrey & Christine Greene. **QC: 56 36 S5 S17**

Warren Chair Works

30 Cutler St
Warren, Rhode Island • 02885
(401)247-0426 • (401)247-2130 (fax)
chairs@loa.com
www.warrenchairworks.com

Authentically reproduced 18th C Windsor chairs, tavern & occasional tables. **Est:** 1981 **Hrs:** Please call for hrs. **Own:** David Wescott & Robert Barrow. **QC: 56 S17**

Chair Caning

Violet's Chair Caning

57 Pleasant St
Chester, Connecticut • 06412
(860)526-2874

Chair seats carefully restored. Woven cane, pressed cane, half-inch flat reed & fiber rush. **QC: S6**

Connecticut Cane & Reed Co

331 Broad St
Manchester, Connecticut • 06045
(860)646-6586 • (860)649-2221 (fax)
canereed@ntplx.net
www.caneandreed.com

Complete stock of all chair seating & wicker repair supplies. Largest selection on the East Coast. Reproduction Shaker furniture, smalls, books. **Hrs:** Sum Mon-Fri 9-5, Sat 10-4; Win Mon-Fri 9-6, Sat 10-5. **Sz:** M **CC:** AX/V/MC/DIS **Dir:** Off Cheney Silk Mill District. **QC: S6**

Heritage Caning Company

28 Foster St
Peabody, Massachusetts • 01960
(978)531-5094

Press & hand cane, fiber rush, porch weave, herringbone, Shaker tape, seat weaving of all kinds. **Est:** 1969 **Hrs:** Mon-Fri 8:30-4. **Dir:** In Peabody Sq 1-1/2 blks from Monument. **QC: S6**

Able to Cane

439 Main St
Warren, Maine • 04864
(207)273-3747
boz@mint.net

Caning, basketry, wicker material, Nantucket Lightship disks & basket molds. **Est:** 1975 **Hrs:** By chance/appt. **Sz:** S **Dir:** Off Rte 1 70 mi from Portland on the coast. **Own:** Bernard Zike. **QC: 91 S16 S6**

Steve's Chair Caning Service

241 Huxley Ave
Providence, Rhode Island • 02908
(401)751-5215
emma@steveemma.com
www.steveemma.com/caningservice.htm

Full chair caning service. Specializing in hand, press & binders cane, splint work, fiber rush, Shaker tape, Danish cord, seagrass, fancy patterns, vinyl strapping, historic restoration & other materials & patterns. **Est:** 1978 **Hrs:** Afternoons, eve. **CC:** V/MC **Own:** Steve Emma. **QC: S6 S16 S18**

The Chair Works

122 Elm St
Montpelier, Vermont • 05602
(802)229-4852
chairwks@together.net

Cane, splint, rush & wicker chair repair & refinishing as well as sales of a variety of cane seat chairs. **Est:** 1981 **Hrs:** Daily 9-5. **Sz:** S **Dir:** Three blks from the state capital. **Own:** Ronald Ball & Kitty Bammer. **QC: S6 S16**

Clock Repair

Strempel's Clocks

91 Main St (Rte 154)
Deep River, Connecticut • 06417
(860)526-5136
mokley@snet.net

Specializing in all phases of clock restoration. Heirloom quality antique & reproduction clocks including Chelsea Marine, Black Forest, cuckoo clocks, wall, mantle & grandfathers. **Pr:** $99-$3,000 **Est:** 1969 **Hrs:** Wed-Sun 10-5. **Sz:** M **CC:** V/MC **Assn:** NAWCC **Dir:** I-95 Exit 69: Rte 9N take Exit 5. R on Rte 80, straight thru 1 stop sign. L at 1st light, 4/10 mi on R. **Own:** Mark Strempel. **QC: 35 S7 S17 S16**

The Clockery

14 Van Zant St
East Norwalk, Connecticut • 06855
(203)838-1789

Antique clock specialists with over 50 clocks on display in the showroom. Repair everything from carriage clocks to tower clocks. **Pr:** $100-8,000 **Est:** 1972 **Hrs:** Tue-Sat 10-4:30. **CC:** V/MC **Assn:** AWI BHI NAWCC **Dir:** I-95 Exit 16: to Rte 136, 1/2 mi S. **Own:** JC Woodward & Bucky Taylor. **QC: 35 S7**

Clock Shoppe

8 Masaquet Ave
Nantucket, Massachusetts • 02554
(508)228-2727

Clock repair. **Own:** R Santos. **QC: S7**

Bill's Clock Repairs & Services

Sheffield, Massachusetts • 01257
(413)229-6635

Hrs: By appt only. **Own:** William Liebowitz. **QC: S7**

The Clock Shop at Pleasant Bay

403 S Orleans Rd (Rte 28)
South Orleans, Massachusetts • 02662
(508)240-0175 • (508)240-0223 (fax)
(800)325-6259
clockshop@capecod.net
www.3clock9.com

Antique & new clocks. Complete clock restoration & repair. **Pr:** $20-5,000 **Est:** 1990 **Hrs:** Mon-Sat 10-5. **Sz:** M **CC:** V/MC/DIS **Assn:** AWI CCADA NAWCC BHI **Dir:** Approx 2-1/2 mi outside of Orleans Center. **Own:** Gregory Scinto. **QC: 35 S7**

Scott's Clock Repair

76 Grove St
Peterborough, New Hampshire • 03458
(603)924-2072

Complete restoration service as well as American & European clocks for sale. **Hrs:** Wed-Sat 9:30-5. **Assn:** NHADA. **QC: 35 S7**

The Clock Man

541 Warren St
Hudson, New York • 12534
(518)828-8995

Expert clock repair & restoration. **Hrs:** Tue-Sat 10-6 or by appt. **Assn:** HADA **Own:** David & Barbara Fulton. **QC: 35 S7**

Antique Clock Restoration

79 Thames St
Newport, Rhode Island • 02840
(401)849-6690

Restoration, service & sales of fine antique clocks & timepieces. **Est:** 1965 **Hrs:** Tue-Sat 10-12 & 2-6, appts available. **Assn:** AWI NAWCC **Dir:** 1/2 blk N of Marlborough St on W side of Thames St. **Own:** W Edward Christiansen Jr. **QC: 35 S7**

Sign of the Dial Clock Shop

148 Eastern Ave
St Johnsbury, Vermont • 05819
(802)748-2193
r_and_n_dief@kingcon.net

Specializing in antique American & European clocks, pocket watches & older wristwatches. **Pr:** $100-6,000 **Est:** 1967 **Hrs:** Mon-Fri 9-5, Sat-Sun by appt. **Sz:** S **CC:** DIS **Assn:** AWI NAWCC VADA **Dir:** In the ctr of St Johnsbury across from Catamount Arts. **Own:** Richard Diefenbach. **QC: 35 S16 S1**

Green Mountain Clock Shop

73 Essex Rd (Rte 2A N)
Williston, Vermont • 05495
(802)879-4971 • (802)872-2619 (fax)
(800)844-4971
pboyden@together.net
www.VermontsClocks.com

Restoration & repair as well as sales of fine clocks, music boxes, tower & street clocks. **Pr:** $25-10,000 **Est:** 1974 **Hrs:** Mon-Fri 9-5, most Sats 9-3. **Sz:** M **CC:** AX/V/MC/DIS **Assn:** MBSI NAWCC NBSI **Dir:** I-89 Exit 12 (Williston-Essex Jct exit): 27 mi N. **Own:** Pat Boyden. **QC: 35 69 S7**

Consignment Shops

On Consignment

77 Wall St
Madison, Connecticut • 06443
(203)245-7012

Antiques, jewelry & Orientals. Furniture, china, crystal, artwork (oil paintings, lithographs, water colors), chandeliers, lamps, mirrors, collectibles. **Pr:** $10.00-10,000 **Est:** 1985 **Hrs:** Tue-Sat 10-5 **CC:** V/MC **Dir:** From Boston Post Rd: US Rte 1, L onto Wall St, betw library & PO **Own:** Jean Cowles. **QC: 48 65 7 S1 S8 S12**

Minot Hall Antiques Center [G100]

1721 Washington St
Boston, Massachusetts • 02118
(617)236-7800 • (617)247-7499 (fax)
minothall@aol.com

Furniture including formal, deco & early modern at very affordable prices. Jewelry, silver & smalls. Also pottery, glass & a large selection of decoratives. **Pr:** $50.00-$150.00 **Est:** 1998 **Hrs:** Tue-Sat 11-6, Sun 12-6. **Sz:** H **CC:** AX/V/MC **Dir:** Located at the int of Mass Ave & Washington St in Boston's South End. **QC: 48 36**

The White Elephant Shop

32 Main St
Essex, Massachusetts • 01929
(978)768-6901 • (978)768-7841 (fax)
elephant@shore.net
www.cape-ann.com/whiteelephant

One of New England's oldest consignment shops featuring collectibles, china, books & furniture **Pr:** $1-1,500 **Est:** 1953 **Hrs:** Mon-Sat 10-5, Sun 12-5 **Sz:** L **CC:** V/MC/DIS **Dir:** Rte 128 Exit 14. From NH: I- 95 to Rte 133 to Essex **Own:** Rick Grobe. **QC: 34 60 S8**

Flea Markets

Douglas Flea Market [G20]

634 N E Main St
Douglass, Massachusetts • 01516
(508)278-6027 • (508)278-6027 (fax)

Historic Dutch-hoop loft barn on Bosma Farm with 20 inside dealers: period furniture, collectibles, baseball cards, glass & vintage clothes. **Pr:** $1-5,000 **Est:** 1986 **Hrs:** Sat 10-4, Sun 8-4, tour groups anytime by appt. **Dir:** I-495 to Rte 16 to Mendon,

Uxbridge to Douglas. R at flashing light, sharp turn. Rte 146 from Worcester to Douglas, Lacky Mass Exit, bear R to 4 corner, 2 L's onto Charles L **Own:** Marlene & Henry Bosma. **QC: 64 67 52**

White Elephant Outlet

101 John Wise Ave (Rte 133)
Essex, Massachusetts
(978)768-3329 • (978)768-7841 (fax)
elephant@shore.net
www.cape-ann.com/whiteelephant

Greatest junk shop on the North Shore. **Est:** 1988 **Hrs:** Sat 10-5, Sun 12-5. **Own:** Rick & Jean Grobe.

Olde Hadley Flea Market

Lawrence Plain Rd (Rte 47 S)
Hadley, Massachusetts • 01035
(413)586-0352

Flea market with antiques, collectibles & other flea market merchandise. Free admission & parking. **Est:** 1980 **Hrs:** Sun 6-5. **Sz:** 200 spaces **Dir:** I-91N Exit 19: 2 mi from Hadley Ctr. **Own:** Marion & Raymond Szala.

Montsweag Flea Market

Rte 1
Woolwich, Maine • 04579
(207)443-2809
fleamkt@gwi.net

Flea market held four times weekly: Wed with antiques & collectibles only; Fri, Sat & Sun with general merchandise. **Hrs:** Mother's Day-Col Day Wed & Fri-Sun 6:30-3. **Dir:** 35 m N of Portland on Rte 1. 27 m S of Augusta on Rte 27 to Rte 1 S 4 mi. **Own:** Norma Scopino. **QC: 32**

Hollis Flea Market

436 Silver Lake Rd (Rte 122)
Hollis, New Hampshire • 03060
(603)882-6134 • (603)882-0927 (fax)
hollisflea@aol.com

Outdoor flea market featuring many dealers. China, estate jewelry, furniture, tools, books, dolls & collectibles. **Pr:** $1-600 **Est:** 1965 **Hrs:** Apr-mid-Nov Sun 7 til ? **Sz:** 125 spaces **Dir:** Rte 3 Exit 7 W: 8 mi to Rte 122, turn S 2 mi on R. **Own:** Gil & Alice Prieto. **QC: 33 52 64**

Nashua Antiques Shows

Saint Stans Hall
Nashua, New Hampshire • 02026
(781)329-1192

Weekly antiques show at St Stans Hall. Admission $4 9:30-10:30 a.m.; $1.50 10:30-12:30 p.m. **Est:** 1977 **Hrs:** Oct-Apr Sun 9:30-12:30. **Sz:** 45 dealers **Dir:** Rte 3 Exit 6: Rte 130 E 2nd L onto Blue Hill Ave. **Own:** Jack Donigan.

The Original Newfane Flea Market

Rte 30
Newfane, Vermont • 05345
(802)365-4000

The oldest & largest open-air flea market in Vermont. Always more than 100 dealers in antiques & collectibles. **Est:** 1963 **Hrs:** May-Oct Sun 7 AM.

Collectible Flea Mart

991 Rte 7
Salisbury, Vermont • 05769-9640
(802)352-4424
fleamart@together.net
homepages.together.net/~fleamart/

Indoor flea mart with antiques, baseball cards, collectibles, glass, china, jewelry & ephemera; barn with furniture. **Est:** 1983 **Hrs:** Daily 10-5. **CC:** V/MC **Dir:** 6 mi S of Middlebury. **Own:** Joyce McGettrick.

Framers

Arts & Framing

88 Main St
Putnam, Connecticut • 06260
(860)963-0105

Museum-quality period framing, art & frame restoration, gilding, fine antiques & gifts. **Hrs:** Tue-Sat 9-5:30, Sun 12-5. **CC:** V/MC **Own:** Barbara Lussier & Robert Craig. **QC: 7 68 74 S13 S16**

Picture This

606 Post Rd E
Westport, Connecticut • 06880
(203)227-6861 • (203)227-4362 (fax)

Custom framing & gallery. **QC: S13**

The Frame Gallery

2 Summit Ave
Brookline, Massachusetts • 02446
(617)232-2070

Hand-shaped, hand-carved & gilded picture frames custom designed. Creative French & English matting. Also restoration of gold leafing. Recreation of period frames. **Hrs:** Tue-Sat 10-6, appt suggested. **Sz:** M **CC:** V/MC **Dir:** Coolidge Corner, behind the Coolidge Theatre. **Own:** Michael Allen. **QC: S13 S16 S17**

Atelier Framing

170 Anderson St
Portland, Maine • 04112
(207)929-8822 • (207)929-8822 (fax)
carbon@mix.net.net

Gallery of handmade gilded, signed & numbered frames for your artwork. Conservation, restoration of gilded object including frames, clocks, furniture & weather vanes. Repair of ornament loss, scraffitto, pastiglia & punch work for gesso. **Est:** 1988 **Hrs:** By appt only. **Sz:** M **Assn:** SOG AIC **Dir:** E end of Congress St. **Own:** Michele A Caron. **QC: 36 68 11 S13 S16 S17**

Furniture Restorers

Leon Vanderbilt Antiques

370 Danbury Rd
New Milford, Connecticut • 06776
(860)354-5662

Fine furniture restoration & sales. **Hrs:** Mon-Sat 10-5, Sun by appt only. **QC: 48 S16**

Joseph Ransohoff

North Branford, Connecticut • 06471
(203)484-5273

Over 20 years experience in fine antique furniture restoration. Formal & painted finishes, turning, carving, inlay, veneer work & French polish. Museum experienced. **Dir:** 10 mi from New Haven, CT. **QC: S16**

Mario & Luigi's Fine Furniture Restoration

110 Pine Rock Rd
Southbury, Connecticut • 06488
(203)267-6300 • (203)267-6300 (fax)
ollenga1@aol.com

Own: Mario Agnello. **QC: 56 47 58 S16 S17 S5**

Raphael's Antique Restoration

655 Atlantic St
Stamford, Connecticut • 06902
(203)348-3079 • (860)358-0685 (fax)

Antique furniture restoration, veneer replacement, carving & French polishing. **Est:** 1947 **Hrs:** Tue-Fri 8-4:30, Sat 9-12. **Dir:** I-95S Exit 7 (Atlantic St): 2 blks turn L, under thruway & RR bridges, 1 blk on R. **QC: S16**

Antique Furniture Restoration

187 Washington Rd
Woodbury, Connecticut • 06798
(203)266-4295

French polishing, restoration of old finishes, veneers & inlays, complete & proper structural restoration. **Hrs:** Mon-Sat 9-5. **Dir:** From Canfield Corner 1 mi on L on Rte 47. **QC: S16 S1 S9**

J D Cushing Antique Restoration

113 Martin St
Essex, Massachusetts • 01929
(978)768-7356

Antique furniture restoration: repairs, hand

stripping, veneer work, lathe work, varnishes & shellac finishes. Consultation regarding restoration. **Hrs:** By appt only (essential). **Dir:** Rte 22 from ctr of Essex: 1/2 mi from jct of Rtes 22W & 133 on R side of road, sign in front. **Own:** John Cushing. **QC: S16 S9**

W Holtzman Antique Restoration

104 Bolton Rd
Harvard, Massachusetts • 01451
(978)456-6850
antique@tiac.net

Restoration & conservation of antique furniture: marquetry & inlay work; reproduction of missing parts; repair of splits, checks & warping; turning, carving; finishing, including authentic French polishing, gilt work; clock cleaning & case repair. **Hrs:** By appt only. **Assn:** NAWCC **Own:** Wade Holtzman. **QC: S16 S7**

The Woodcrafters Furniture Service

2135 GAR Hwy (Rte 6)
Swansea, Massachusetts • 02777
(508)379-0878

Stripping, repairing, regluing, refinishing & restoration. **Own:** Lawrence & Gail Gallagher. **QC: S16**

MacGruer Restorations

Rte 22
Austerlitz, New York • 12017
(518)325-7214
frankmac@taconic.net

Restoration & conservation services for furniture of all periods. French polish, veneers, inlays & replacement of missing parts. **Hrs:** Call for appt. **QC: S16**

Robert's Restoration Gallery

139 Parkway Rd
Bronxville, New York • 10708
(914)793-4870 • 793-4845 (fax)

Complete restoration, repairs & refinishing. Commercial & residential stripping. Antiques bought & sold. **Hrs:** Tue-Sat 10-5, Sun 10-2. **CC:** AX/V/MC **Own:** Robert Weis. **QC: S16**

John Hancock & Son

260 Warren St
Poughkeepsie, New York • 12601
(518)822-1858

Restoration of fine furniture & antiques, specializing in all types of seat weaving, repair/replication of decorative wood carving. Free estimates; pick up & delivery. **Hrs:** By appt only. **QC: S16 S6**

Furniture Restoration Center

27 Fulton St
White Plains, New York • 10606
(914)949-5056

Cold hand-stripping, antique refinishing & restorations, cane & rush seats, metal furniture sandblasted & refinished, kitchen cabinets, woodwork, dens, libraries refinished. **Own:** Aniello Imperati. **QC: S16 S6 S18**

Antiquity Restorations

22 Kersey Rd
Peacedale, Rhode Island • 02883
(401)789-2370

Furniture restoration, repair & refinishing as well as antique furniture sales & consignments. **Hrs:** Mon-Sat 9-5, Sun 12-4. **Dir:** On Rte 108. **Own:** Ben Rhodes. **QC: S16 S8**

Antique Furnishings/ Restoration

9 Newman Ave
Rumford, Rhode Island • 02916
(401)438-1672

Period furniture restoration services. **Hrs:** Mon-Fri 9-5. **Sz:** S **Own:** Raymond Dubois. **QC: S16**

Robert Sydorowich American Furniture

Andover, Vermont • 05149
(802)875-3154

Antique furniture restoration including lathe work, scroll work, band saw, joinery, molding duplication, veneer work, cabinetry, stripping, staining, finishing & grain painting in all woods used for period American furniture. **Est:** 1982 **Hrs:** By appt only. **Dir:** Call for directions. **QC: S16 S17**

E V Howard Agency

8 Raymond Ave
Poughkeepsie, New York • 12603
(914)471-5820 • (914)471-5864 (fax)

QC: S14

McBurnie Agency Inc

169 Old Post Rd
Rhinebeck, New York • 12572
(914)876-3005 • (914)876-0777 (fax)

Own: Charles Miele. **QC: S14**

Glass Restorers

Genovese Stained Glass Studio

15 Littell Rd
Brookline, Massachusetts • 02146
(617)738-4531

Repair & restoration of stained & leaded glass windows, lamps, mirrors & period pieces. Reframing & sizing of old panels. Brass, zinc, wood, glass etching & protective shields (lexan) installed. **Est:** 1982 **Hrs:** By chance/appt. **Dir:** In the heart of Brookline at Coolidge Corner, 3 blks S on Harvard St, L on Alton Pl, 1 blk, L on Littel Rd. **Own:** Emanuel Genovese. **QC: S16 S17**

Insurers

Lawrence V Toole Insurance Agency Inc

195 Main St
Lee, Massachusetts • 01238
(413)243-0089.

QC: S14

Metal Restorers

RC Metalcrafters

220 River Rd
Madison, Connecticut • 06443
(203)245-4708 • (203)245-4708 (fax)
rivercroft@aol.com

Repair, restoration & polishing of brass, copper, iron & perform fabrication, welding, brazing, soldering of metals & electrified lamps. **Hrs:** Mon-Fri 9-5 or by appt. **Dir:** I-95 Exit 62 S: L onto Rte 1, 1st L onto Mill Rd, 3/4 mi, sign hangs from tree at end of driveway on R. **Own:** Bob Cole. **QC: S16**

Orum Silver Co

51 S Vine St
Meriden, Connecticut • 06450
(203)237-3037 • (203)237-3037 (fax)
orum@ct1.nai.net
w3.nai.net/~maddog/orum.htm

Expert repair work of old silver & antiques, soldering, dents removed, fabrication of lost parts, buffing, cleaning & polishing of all types of metals. Dresser sets restored, knife blades replaced, sterling pieces repaired & refinished. **Est:** 1946 **Hrs:** Mon-Thu 8-4:30, Fri 8-1. **Sz:** S **Dir:** I-691 Exit 6 (W)/Exit 5 (E): Turn R (S) to W Main St. Turn R (W) to S Vine St. L on S Vine. Shop on R. **Own:** Joe Pistilli. **QC: 78 20 72 S16 S17**

Fleming's of Cohasset Village

24 Elm St
Cohasset, Massachusetts • 02025
(781)383-0684 • (781)659-1537 (fax)

Pewter, brass, copper, silver polishing, plating, repairing & lacquering. Free dent removal on all items silverplated. Repair twisted or broken sterling. Soldering. **Hrs:** Mon-Sat 9-5, Sun 12-5. **QC: S16**

HMS Antique Metal Restoration & Metal Finishing Supplies

40 Lake St
Somerville, Massachusetts • 02143
(617)666-9090 • (617)666-3452 (fax)
alchasen@aol.com. **QC: S16**

Patrick J Gill & Sons

9 Fowle St
Woburn, Massachusetts • 01801
(781)933-3275 • 78193-3751 (fax)
www.patrickgillcompany.com

Complete restoration of silver, pewter, brass & copper including repairing, refinishing & plating. Over 80 years experience specializing in plating (gold, silver & rhodium). All work performed on premises. Replace knife blades. **Est:** 1911 **Hrs:** Mon-Fri 9-6, Sat 9-5. **CC:** AX/V/MC/DIS **Dir:** I-93 Montvale Ave exit: to Woburn Ctr rotary. Take Rte 38 S, then L at 1st light onto Fowle. **QC: S16**

Jeffrey Herman

Chepachet, Rhode Island • 02814
(401)567-7800 • (401)461-7801 (fax)
(800)584-2352
jherman@silversmithing.com
www.silversmithing.com/jherman

Restoration & hand-finishing of sterling, coin, pewter & mixed metal hollowware, flatware & dresserware. Fully equipped silversmithing studio with a central alarm system. Your metalware deserves museum-quality care. Full line of silver care products. **Est:** 1984 **Hrs:** By appt only. **Assn:** SAS. **QC: S16 S9**

Metal Restoration Services

43 Wm S Canning Blvd (Rte 81S)
Tiverton, Rhode Island • 02878
(401)624-6486

Conservation, restoration, refinishing & spray coating of metal antiques made of gold, silver, bronze, copper, brass, pewter & tin. Lighting fixture work from lamps to chandeliers. No work done on jewelry. **Est:** 1980 **Hrs:** Mon-Fri 7:30-12 & 1-4, Sat 8-12; appt strongly recommended. **Sz:** L **Dir:** Rte 24 S of Fall River, MA, to Rte 81 S. 2nd driveway on R marked Canning Pl Bus Condos. **Own:** Peter Pflock. **QC: S16 S9**

Porcelain Restorers

Restoration Services

621 Main St #3
Waltham, Massachusetts • 02452
(781)647-9470
restserv@earthlink.net

Highest quality conservation & invisible restoration of antiques specializing in porcelain, glass & lacquer, as well as pottery, gold leaf, sculpture & ivory — the full range of objets d'art. **Hrs:** Mon-Fri 8-5, appt suggested. **Assn:** AIC NECA **Dir:** Directly across from Waltham City Hall on Main St (Rte 20), 2nd fl. **Own:** Nelson Dale. **QC: S16**

Terra Nuova Restorations

38 Cedar Heights Rd
Rhinebeck, New York • 12572
(914)876-3753

Ceramic restoration & conservation. **Hrs:** By appt only. **Own:** Roger Krokey. **QC: S16**

> Use the Specialty QuickCode indexes at the back of the book to find dealers who specialize in your area of interest.

Reproductions

Richard D Scofield Historic Lighting
One W Main St
Chester, Connecticut • 06412
(860)526-1800 • (860)526-2378 (fax)

Entirely handmade reproductions of 18th & early 19th C chandeliers, lanterns & sconces in copper, pewter, distressed tin & wood. **Pr:** $275-950 **Hrs:** Call for hrs. **CC:** V/MC/DIS. **QC: S17**

Horton Brasses Inc
Nooks Hill Rd
Cromwell, Connecticut • 06416
(860)635-4400 • (860)635-6473 (fax)
barb@horton-brasses.com
www.horton-brasses.com

Manufacturers of brass hardware for antique furniture. Superior reproductions of Queen Anne, Chippendale, Hepplewhite, Sheraton, Victorian & early 1900s drawer pulls, knobs, hinges, finials, escutcheons & iron. Catalogs available. **Est:** 1930 **Hrs:** Mon-Fri 8:30-4, closed in Aug. **CC:** V/MC **Dir:** I-91 Exit 21: call for directions. **Own:** Barbara Rockwell. **QC: S17**

Maurer & Shepherd Joyners
122 Naubuc Ave
Glastonbury, Connecticut • 06033
(860)633-2383 • (860)633-7231 (fax)

Reproduction of authentic 17th & 18th C Colonial joinery. **Est:** 1976 **Hrs:** Mon-Fri 8:30-5:30. **Dir:** 5 min outside of Hartford, off Rte 2. **QC: S17 S18**

Lamp Shades Plus
280 Boston Post Rd
Orange, Connecticut • 06477
(203)795-6628

Largest selection of lamp shades in CT including country & Victorian, custom lamps & shades, parchment. Over 9,000 shades in stock. Large selection of antique lamps, floorlamps & antique parts. Lamps repaired & restored. Silver & silverplate. **Pr:** $25-500 **Est:** 1977 **Hrs:** Mon-Sat 10-5:30, Oct-Dec open Sun, Jun-Jul closed Wed. **Sz:** L **CC:** V/MC **Dir:** I-95 Exit 41 (Marsh Hill Rd): from S, make L; from N, make R. Follow Marsh Hill Rd to Post Rd, make R, 1/4 mi on R. **Own:** Carol & Jim Tendler & Jill Pendergast. **QC: 65 78 S16**

The Tin Lantern
273 Back Rd
Windham, Connecticut • 06280
(860)423-5676

Over 100 reproductions of 18th & 19th C early American chandeliers, sconces, lanterns & reflector ovens. Selection of country antiques. **Hrs:** By chance/appt. **Dir:** 5 mi E of Willimantic at Windham Ctr. **Own:** Georgia Styger. **QC: S17**

The Lighting Barn
271 Washington Rd
Woodbury, Connecticut • 06798
(203)263-0010

Fine handcrafted reproduction & antique chandeliers, sconces & lamps in iron. **Pr:** $100-1,000 **Hrs:** Thu-Sat 1-5 by appt/chance. **Sz:** M **CC:** V/MC **Dir:** At the int of Rtes 47 & 132. **Own:** Paul Fierberg. **QC: 65 S17**

Country Bed Shop
328 Richardson Rd
Ashby, Massachusetts • 01431
(978)386-7550 • (978)386-7263 (fax)
alan@countrybed.com
www.countrybed.com

Country & high-style reproduction beds, chairs & tables. Each piece made to order. **Pr:** $1,000-8,000 **Est:** 1972 **Hrs:** Mon-Sat 8-5 (appt suggested). **Dir:** Call for directions. **Own:** Alan Pease. **QC: 52 56 S17 S5**

Smithers Metalsmithing

1057 Hawley Rd
Ashfield, Massachusetts • 01330
(413)625-2994

Hand-hammered silver hollowware & brass lighting, made using the tools & techniques of traditional silversmithing; designs inspired by the classic forms of early America. Restoration/conservation of fine early silver & brass. **Est:** 1979 **Hrs:** Appt suggested. **Sz:** M **Own:** Stephen Smithers. **QC: 78 20 65 S17 S16 S9**

Period Furniture Hardware Co Inc

123 Charles St
Boston, Massachusetts • 02114
(617)227-0758 • (617)227-2987 (fax)

A storehouse of brass hardware & accessories for the discriminating dealer or homeowner. Highest quality reproduction furniture & door hardware, light fixtures, bath accessories, fireplace equipment & weather vanes. **Pr:** $.50-5,000 **Hrs:** Sep-May Mon-Fri 8:30-5, Sat 10-2; Jun-Aug Mon-Fri 8:30-5. **Sz:** S **CC:** V/MC **Dir:** At the N end of Charles St on famed Beacon Hill. **Own:** Paul Drummey. **QC: 20 40 65 S17 S18**

Lamp Glass

2230 Massachusetts Ave
Cambridge, Massachusetts • 02140
(617)497-0770 • (617)497-2074 (fax)
lamps@lampglass.nu
www.lampglass.nu

Large selection of glass shades & antique reproductions including student shades, torchier, gas, GWTW globes, cased glass, etched sconce & chandelier glass & prisms. **Est:** 1984 **Hrs:** Wed & Fri-Sat 10-6, Thu 10-7. **Sz:** M **CC:** V/MC **Own:** Tania Maxwell. **QC: 65 S17**

Period Lighting Fixtures Inc

167 River Rd
Clarksburg, Massachusetts • 01247
(413)664-7141 • (413)664-0312 (fax)
(800)828-6990
www.periodlighting.com

Over 250 styles & designs created from period originals. **Pr:** $50-2950 **Est:** 1974 **Hrs:** Mon-Thu 9-5, Fri 9-4. **Sz:** S **CC:** V/MC **Dir:** From Boston: I-90 W to I-91 N to Rte 2 (Greenfield). Rte 2 W to jct Rte 8N (yellow blinking light). R on Rte 8N 1 mi on L. **Own:** Edward A Scofield. **QC: 65 S17**

Great Meadows Joinery

85 Main St
Concord, Massachusetts • 01742
(978)287-5955 • (978)287-5669 (fax)
gmj@ix.netcom.com

Large selection of reproduction early American crafts by more than 100 leading American crafters as well as Shaker & American country furniture reproductions. **Pr:** $800-5,000 **Est:** 1986 **Hrs:** Tue-Sat 10-5:30, Sun 12-5 exc hols. **CC:** AX/V/MC/DIS **Own:** Gene Cosloy. **QC: S17**

Old Fashioned Milk Paint Company

436 Main St
Groton, Massachusetts • 01450
(978)448-6336

Authentic early milk paint in powder form for restoration or reproduction on furniture, walls & woodwork. Sixteen environmentally safe, authentic colors. **Est:** 1974 **Hrs:** Mon-Fri 9-5. **Dir:** I-495 Exit 31W: 8 mi on Rte 119. 1 mi W of Groton on Rte 119 take driveway on R just before RR bridge. **Own:** Anne Thibean. **QC: S17 S16**

J R Burrows & Company

393 Union St
Rockland, Massachusetts • 02370
(781)982-1812

Historical design merchants specializing in imported carpets, wallpapers & textiles used for the restoration of historic buildings & interiors. **Est:** 1985 **Hrs:** By appt only. **CC:** V/MC **Dir:** Rte 3 Exit 14: corn of Exchange & Union Sts. **Own:** John Burrows. **QC: S17 S18**

Textile Reproductions

666 Worthington Rd
West Chesterfield, Massachusetts • 01084
(413)296-4437 • (413)296-0036 (fax)

Goods for 18th & 19th C reproduction textile furnishings. Fabrics, threads, tapes, hardware & other supplies for replicating textiles. Custom work also available (e.g. tall-post bed hangings). Vegetable-dyed linsey-woolsey. **Est:** 1983 **Hrs:** By appt only. **CC:** AX/V/MC/DIS **Assn:** NTHP SPNEA **Own:** Edmund & Kathleen Smith. **QC: S17**

Hammerworks

6 Freemont St
Worcester, Massachusetts • 01603
(508)755-3434

Handmade Colonial lighting including chandeliers, sconces, hardware, andirons & candlestands in copper, brass, iron & tin. **Hrs:** Mon-Fri 9-5, Sat 10-2. **Dir:** From E I-290 Hope Ave exit: less than 2 mi. **QC: 65 S17**

Copper House

1747 Dover Rd (Rte 4)
Epsom, New Hampshire • 03234
(603)736-9798
(800)281-9798
www.thecopperhouse.com

Copper & brass lighting in traditional styles, copper weather vanes & cupolas. **Est:** 1976 **Hrs:** Sat 12:30-5, Sun-Mon 10-5 or by appt. **Sz:** M **CC:** V/MC **Dir:** On Rte 4: 15 min E of Concord, 3/4 mi E of Epsom Traffic Circle. **QC: 65 S17**

Country Braid House

462 Main St
Tilton, New Hampshire • 03276
(603)286-4511 • (603)286-4155 (fax)
info@countrybraidhouse.com
www.countrybraidhouse.com

Custom-made wool braided rugs. Antique hooked & braided rugs. **Pr:** $25-3,000 **Est:** 1968 **Hrs:** Mon-Fri 9-5, Sat 9-4, Sun by chance/appt. **Sz:** M **CC:** V/MC/DIS **Dir:** I-93 Exit 20: R off ramp, 2 mi on L across from the high school. **Own:** Jan Jurta. **QC: 75 S16 S17**

Bournebrook Antiques & Table Company

44 Tivoli St
Albany, New York • 12207
(518)426-1066 • (518)426-1089 (fax)
(800)600-4763
www.bournebrook.com

Custom-made country harvest tables; 18th & 19th C craftsmanship with mortise-and-tenon joints & pegs; no nails, screws or bolts. **Hrs:** Mon-Fri 9-4, Sat 10-4. **CC:** V/MC **Own:** Mike & Claire Davis. **QC: 56 S17**

The Country Furniture Shop

Rte 20 E
Madison, New York • 13402
(315)893-7404

Windsor chairs, tall clocks & other reproductions made by hand. **Assn:** MBADA **Own:** Chris Harter. **QC: 56 S17**

Brassworks Ltd

379 Charles St
Providence, Rhode Island • 02904
(401)421-5815 • (401)421-4238 (fax)

Solid brass furniture hardware & accessories; brass, bronze & silver restoration. **Est:** 1979 **Hrs:** Mon-Fri 9-5; Sat 9-3. **Sz:** M **CC:** AX/V/MC **Dir:** I-95 Exit 24. **Own:** Anthony Palmer. **QC: S16 S17 S18**

Eighteenth Century Woodworks

272 James Tr
West Kingston, Rhode Island • 02892
(401)539-2558 • (401)539-6794 (fax)
clidence@aol.com

Reproduction Colonial beds & antique beds adapted to modern uses: cannonballs, pencil posts, canopy field beds, low posts & variations. Also tavern & tea tables. **Pr:** $2-8,000 **Est:** 1969 **Hrs:** Mon-Fri 9-5, Sat 9-12, Sun by appt. Call ahead advised. **Dir:** I-95 Exit 3A: Rte 138 approx 3 mi, L onto Hillsdale for 2-1/2 mi, R onto James Trail, go 1 mi. **Own:** Ray Clidence. **QC: S17 S16**

Authentic Designs

The Mill Rd
West Rupert, Vermont • 05776
(802)394-7713

Meticulously crafted reproduction lighting fixtures of Colonial & early American design in solid brass, maple, pewter & tin. Over 300 models displayed in room settings. Catalog $3. **Pr:** $100-5,000 **Est:** 1968 **Hrs:** Mon-Fri 8:30-4:30, Sat-Sun by appt. **Sz:** L **CC:** V/MC **Assn:** NEAA **Dir:** Off Rte 153. Follow state direction signs. **QC: 65 S17 S16**

Restoration (Other)

J Leeke Preservation Consultant

26 Higgins St
Portland, Maine • 04103
(207)773-2306 • (207)773-2306 (fax)
johnleeke@HistoricHomeWorks.com
www.HistoricHomeWorks.com

Onsite consulting and conditions surveys for historic buildings. Problem solving, project management, planning, maintenance programming & training. Practical restoration reports. Internships & assistantships available. Seminars. **Hrs:** By appt only - call or write for details. **CC:** V/MC. **QC: S9 S16 S17**

H H Perkins Co

10 S Bradley Rd
Woodbridge, Connecticut • 06525
(203)389-4011 (fax)
(800)462-6660
www.hhperkins.com

Seat weaving, basketry & restoration services. **Est:** 1917 **CC:** AX/V/MC/DIS **Own:** Steve & Mark DeFrancesco. **QC: S7 S17**

Rosenthal Paper Restoration

McClellan St
Amherst, Massachusetts • 01004
(413)256-0844

Conservation & restoration of flat printed paper. **Hrs:** By appt only. **Assn:** AIC NECA **Own:** Bernice Masse Rosenthal. **QC: S16**

Northeast Document Conservation Center

100 Brickstone Sq
Andover, Massachusetts • 01810
(978)470-1010 • (978)475-6021 (fax)
www.nedcc.org

The largest nonprofit regional conservation center in the United States specializing in the treatment of paper & related materials, including books, documents, photographs, maps, paper-based ephemera & works of art on paper. No appraisals. **Est:** 1973 **Hrs:** Mon-Fri 8:30-4:30. **Assn:** AIC **Dir:** I-93 to I-495 N to Exit 41A (Andover, Rte 28): go 1/4 mi, then turn L onto Rte 133 (Haverhill St). Brickstone Square on L. **QC: S16**

Craftsman Lumber Company

436 Main St
Groton, Massachusetts • 01450
(978)448-5621 • (978)448-2754 (fax)
mark@craftsmanlumber.com
www.craftsmanlumber.com

Specializing in wide pine boards & native hardwoods used widely in restoration or reproduction of furniture, flooring, wainscoting. Milled to customer specifications. **Hrs:** Mon-Fri 9-5; Sat 9-2. **Dir:** Rte 495 Exit 31W: 8 mi on Rte 119, 1 mi W of Groton on Rte 119 take driveway on R just before RR bridge. **Own:** Charles Thibeau. **QC: S18 S17**

SPNEA Conservation Center

Lyman Estate / 185 Lyman St
Waltham, Massachusetts • 02154
(781)891-1985

Technical expertise for conservation of early finishes: paint, wood, plaster & stone. State-of-the-art materials & expert craftsmanship for consolidation & repair. Historic buildings, furniture, upholstery & wood conservation. **Est:** 1972 **Hrs:** Mon-Fri 9-5 by appt only. **Assn:** AIC **Dir:** Rte 128 to Rte 20 E (Main St): go past City Hall, L onto Lyman St & immediate R at rotary. **QC: S16 S18 S9**

Ingrid Sanborn & Daughter

85 Church St
West Newbury, Massachusetts • 01985
(978)363-2253 • (508)363-2049 (fax)
sanborn@greennet.net
www.isd.pair.com

Restoration of reverse paintings & painting on glass, reproduction & custom work; graining, gold leaf etching on glass, decorative chair painting, marbleizing, paint matching, Japanning. **Hrs:** By appt only. **Dir:** I-95N Exit 57 (Rte 113 Newburyport): W 5 mi to ctr of W Newbury, R on Church St. **Own:** Ingrid Sanborn & Greta Shepard. **QC: S16 S17 S9**

The Beehive Reed Organ Service

11 Oak St
Alfred, Maine • 04002
(207)324-0990
beehive@cybertours.com

Emphasis on repair, rebuilding, restoring & refinishing of reed organs, melodeons, harmoniums, etc. Continues to offer for sale a few carefully restored reed instruments. **Pr:** $1600-6500 **Est:** 1973 **Hrs:** By appt only. **Sz:** S **CC:** DIS **Assn:** OHS ROS **Dir:** 15 min W of Maine Tpke Exit 4. In center of Alfred Village at 1 Oak St - tan house with green trim across from country store. **Own:** John Morningstar & Duane Smoot. **QC: 69 S16**

H Newman Restoration Conservation

55 Farewell St
Newport, Rhode Island • 02840
(401)846-4784 • (401)849-1522 (fax)
hhnewman@edgenet.net
www3.edgenet.net/hhnewman

Restoration & structural specialists. **Est:** 1989 **Hrs:** Daily 9-5. **Assn:** AIC **Dir:** Call for directions. **Own:** Howard Newman. **QC: S16**

Linda Eliason

Sykes Hollow Rd
Pawlet, Vermont • 05761
(802)325-3026

Hooked rug restoration. **Hrs:** By appt only. **Dir:** Call for directions. **QC: S16**

Shippers

Craters & Freighters of New England

1 Industrial Way, Ste 3
Portland, Maine • 04103
(207)797-8787 • (207)797-8783 (fax)
(800)335-9996
crandfrme@aol.com

Specialty packaging & shipping world wide. Pickup, door-to-door service, fully insured, quick turn around. Call for a free quote. **Est:** 1997 **Hrs:** Mon-Fri 8-5. **CC:** AX/V/MC/DIS **Dir:** Close to Exit 8 off the Maine Tpke. **Own:** Judy Sher. **QC: S19**

From Here to There Ltd

45 Winter St
Exeter, New Hampshire • 03833
(603)772-1964

Specializing in packing & shipping antiques. **QC: S19**

Richard Gauthier

Hudson, New York • 12534
(518)822-1618. **QC: S19**

Gero Bros Movers Inc

1 Gero Ct
Colchester, Vermont • 05446
(802)655-0803 • (802)655-7824 (fax)
(800)843-4200
gerobros@aol.com **Own:** Ken Marston.
QC: S19

Antiquing Periodicals

The New England antiques collector has plenty to read. Brief descriptions and subscription information for some of the more widely circulated antiques magazines and newspapers follow. A number of these publications are available free of charge at auctions, antiques shows, and group shops.

The Magazine ANTIQUES

The *Magazine ANTIQUES* covers the full range of the decorative and fine arts and is the most scholarly of the publications described here. Individual articles cover historic houses, ceramics, glass, silver, furniture, textiles, folk art, painting, sculpture, gardens, and architecture. Since 1922, *the* antiques publication in the United States and very much collected itself. Full color illustrations and advertisements add to its appeal and usefulness. Editor: Allison Eckardt Ledes.

Subscription rate: $34.95 (1 year).

The Magazine ANTIQUES, PO Box 37008, Boone, IA 500037; (800)925-9271.

Antique Collecting

"For collectors, by collectors, about collecting," *Antique Collecting* is the Journal of the Antique Collectors' Club of Great Britain. Although it emphasizes the European market, it includes informative general articles of interest to the intermediate and advanced collector. Auction and fair calendars.

Subscription rate: $40.00 (1 year).

Antique Collectors' Club Ltd, 5 Church St, Woodbridge, Suffolk IP12 1DS GREAT BRITAIN; 01394 385501, 01394 384434 (fax).

Antiques and the Arts Weekly

Known in the trade as the *Bee*, this is the only weekly New England antiques newspaper. Noted for its complete roster of auction and show advertisements, the *Bee* also contains numerous "wanted-to-buy" and "for sale" ads from individuals, along with dealer advertising. Editor: R. Scudder Smith.

Subscription rate: $58 (1 year).

Antiques and the Arts Weekly, PO Box 5503, Newtown, CT 06470-5503; (203)426-3141, (203)426-1394 (fax), www.thebee.com.

Art & Antiques

Art & Antiques, a monthly color magazine, emphasizes the fine & decorative arts but includes occasional articles on other aspects of antiquing. Editor: Paula Rackow.

Subscription rate: $23.93 (11 issues).

Art & Antiques, PO Box 660, Mt Morris, IL 61054-0660; (815)734-1162.

Art & Auction

Billed as the "magazine of the international art market," *Art & Auction* delves seriously into issues of finance and authenticity and includes thoughtful analyses of sales and trends. Editor: Bruce Wolmer.

Subscription rate: $37.50 (6 months, 11 issues); $67.00 (12 months, 22 issues).

Art & Auction, PO Box 11344, Des Moines, IA 50340-1134; (800)777-8718.

A-Plus

Supplement to five newspapers on Cape Cod (the *Cape Cod Chronicle*, the *Barnstable Patriot*, the *Falmouth Enterprise*, the *Mashpee Enterprise*, and the *Sandwich Enterprise*). Features on antiques, the arts and design as well as a calendar of arts and antiques events on Cape Cod. Editor: Laura Scheel.

A-PLUS, Publications of New England, PO Box 660, Yarmouth Port, MA 02675; (508)362-1440; (508)362-8845 (fax).

Early American Homes

Published bimonthly, including Christmas and Garden special issues, *Early American Homes* focuses on domestic life in the 17th, 18th, and early 19th centuries. Includes excellent informative articles about antiques, architecture & history, traditions, and period style. Source listings for period reproduction materials and accessories. Editor: Mimi Handler.

Subscription rate: $19.97 (1 year).

Early American Homes, PO Box 420235, Palm Coast, FL 32142; (800)829-3340.

Maine Antique Digest

A monthly paper in six to eight sections covering the whole of the American antiques market, *MAD* keeps its finger on the pulse of the antiques trade and attracts over 25,000 subscribers in 50 states and foreign countries. Detailed show and auction reviews, book reviews, specialty columns, and extensive advertising make this the primary information source for antiques dealers and serious collectors alike. A great read and an excellent web site! Publisher: Samuel Pennington.

Subscription rate: $43 (1 year).

Maine Antique Digest, PO Box 1429, Waldoboro, ME 04572-1429; (207)832-7534, www.maineantiquedigest.com

New England Antiques Journal

This monthly tabloid, first published in 1983, contains feature articles about antiques, auction previews and reviews, show reviews, a calendar of events, and information about shows at regional museums. The antiques dealer advertising is organized geographically. Editor: Jamie Mercier.

Subscription rate: $19.95 (1 year).

New England Antiques Journal, PO Box 120, Ware, MA 01082; (413)967-3505, (413)967-6009 (fax).

New Hampshire Antiques Monthly

New Hampshire's only monthly newspaper devoted to antiques. Show reports, auction advertising, and helpful columns designed for newer collectors. Editor: Charles W. Wibel.

Subscription rate: $17.95 (1 year).

New Hampshire Antiques Monthly, PO Box 546, Farmington, NH 03835; (603) 755-4568

Northeast

A monthly newspaper covering antiques, art, historic homes, country life, preservation and restoration, and interior design in upstate New York and western New England. Editor: Harold M. Hanson.

Northeast, PO Box 37, Hudson, NY 12534; (518)828-1616, (518)828-9437 (fax), www.northeastjournal.com.

The Vermont Antique Times

A new publication focusing exclusively on Vermont including general articles and a calendar of events.

Subscription rate: $20.00.

The Vermont Antique Times, PO Box 1880, Manchester Center, VT 05255; (802)362-3149, (800)542-4224.

Museums and Historic Homes

Touring early American homes and outstanding collections of decorative and fine arts can do much to enhance your knowledge of antiques, and New England is full of wonderful collections, from folk to formal, from which to learn. In addition to world-renowned museums in Salem, Boston, Providence, and New Haven, there are great collections at dozens of smaller institutions across the area from New York to Maine. From the outstanding collection of fine furniture and decorative arts at the Rhode Island School of Design Museum of Art, to the thousands of examples of folk art at the Shelburne Museum in Vermont, there are superb examples of American and European antiques at museums throughout New England.

In addition to public lectures and gallery talks, many institutions conduct courses and seminars around their collections. Many also have research libraries open to the scholarly antiquer. Members often qualify for reduced rates and special programs, and membership fees are generally quite reasonable.

We have provided basic information here concerning opening hours, rates, membership fees, and a general description of the collection, noting highlights where appropriate. Call or write for more detailed information.

Connecticut

Coventry

Nathan Hale Homestead

South St • 06238
(860) 742-6917

Hours: Mid-May to mid-Oct daily 1-5.

The rural family home and birthplace of Nathan Hale, who was hanged as an American spy by the British in 1776, the homestead was later used as a court and schoolhouse by Hale's brothers and appears much as it did in Revolutionary times. Run by The Antiquarian and Landmarks Society in Hartford.

Hartford

The Antiquarian and Landmarks Society

66 Forest St • 06105
(860) 247-8996 • (860) 249-4907 (fax)

Hours: Open mid-May to mid-Oct. Hours vary with individual houses.
Admission: Membership in society starts at $30.
Locations: Various.

Connecticut's oldest state-wide preservation group, founded in 1936. The society's nine house museums contain collections of decorative arts and furnishings that together document the history of domestic architecture and interior decoration in Connecticut during its first 300 years. The properties are authentically restored and outfitted to depict the evolution of life and culture in southern New England. The society offers special programs and sponsors tours. House museums of particular interest are listed under individual towns.

Butler McCook Homestead

396 Main St • 06103
(860) 522-1806

Hours: Mid-May to mid-Oct Tue, Thu & Sun 12-4.

This 1782 house has all original furnishings and houses Japanese armor, Victorian toys, fine American antiques, china, and paintings collected by the family over four generations. Run by The Antiquarian and Landmarks Society in Hartford.

Isham-Terry House

211 High St • 06105
(860) 247-8996

Hours: Open by appt only.

A significant ante-bellum Italianate house containing eclectic furnishings, original gas lighting fixtures, stained glass, decorative wall/ceiling treatments, and paintings. Run by The Antiquarian and Landmarks Society in Hartford.

Wadsworth Atheneum

600 Main St • 06103
(860) 278-2670
www.hartnet.org/~wadsworth

Hours: Tue-Sun 11-5. Evening hrs the first Thu of every month til 8. Closed New Year's Day, July 4, Thanksgiving and Christmas Day.
Admission: Adults $7, students and senior citizens $5, children ages 6-17 $3. Free all day Thu and before noon on Sat.
Location: On the Main Street side of Atheneum Square, next to the Travelers Tower.

The Wadsworth Atheneum, America's oldest continuously operating public art museum, houses more than 50,000 works of art and features excellent examples of furniture and decorative arts as well as period room installations dating from the 18th C. Its collections range from 15th C majolica to 18th C German silver, French and German porcelain, and decorative arts, to the famous Wallace Nutting Collection of early American furniture, which includes more Pilgrim C furniture than any other collection in America. The Atheneum is renowned for its collections of American art, including paintings of the Hudson River School; sculpture, drawings, and decorative arts; French impressionist paintings; 17th C European baroque paintings; and surrealist paintings from the 20th C. Also on display is an especially strong collection of American silver with approximately 800 pieces representing styles from the late 17th to the late 19th C.

Moodus

Amasa Day House

33 Plains Rd • 06469
(860)873-8144

Hours: Jun Sat-Sun 1-5, Jul-Aug Wed-Sun 1-5.

This stark white house, dating from 1816, has a cozy interior marked by stenciled floors and stairs. Run by The Antiquarian and Landmarks Society in Hartford.

Mystic

Mystic Seaport Museum

75 Greenmanville Ave
PO Box 6000 • 06355-0990
(860) 572-0711
www.mysticseaport.org

Hours: Daily: ships & exhibits 10-4, museum grounds 9-5. Closed Christmas Day.
Admission: Adults, $16, children ages 6-12, $8. Mystic Seaport members and children under 5 free. Second consecutive day free. Group rates on request.
Location: About 10 mi E of New London on Rte 27, approximately 1 mi S of I-95, Exit 90. Free parking.
Access: Some ships and buildings, gravel roads, and stone sidewalks may present barriers for physically challenged. Please call or visit web site for details.

Mystic Seaport Museum is an indoor-outdoor maritime museum including historic ships, boats, buildings, and formal exhibits relating to American maritime history. The primary emphasis is on the maritime commerce of the Atlantic coast during the 19th C and its impact on the economic, social, and cultural life of the United States. The exhibit area covers 17 acres along the Mystic River. The Museum comprises 60 historic buildings, four major vessels, over 430 boats, a research library, and substantial collections of maritime artifacts. Several large buildings are devoted to the display of maritime art and artifacts. The Stillman Building houses ship models, paintings, and scrimshaw. The Wendell Building houses an exhibit of British and American figureheads and wood carvings. The Schaefer Building has changing gallery exhibits of the museum's paintings, prints, and other artifacts.

New Haven

Yale University Art Gallery

1111 Chapel St
PO Box 2006 Yale Station • 06520
(203) 432-0600
www.yale.edu/artgallery

Hours: Tue-Sat 10-5, Sun 1-6. Closed Mon and major holidays.
Admission: Free, but a voluntary donation of $5 is appreciated to support the Gallery's programs.
Location: Campus of Yale University, at the corner of Chapel and York Streets, opposite the Center for British Art.
Access: Wheelchair access at 201 York St. Wheelchairs available within the museum. All exhibition areas can be reached by elevator. Strollers permitted unless otherwise noted. Back carriers are not allowed.

The American Decorative Arts Collection at the Yale University Art Gallery is comprehensive and contains many fine pieces. Displayed in a way that makes visual and chronological sense, the collection focuses on the Colonial and early Federal periods. Of special note are two furnished rooms from the mid-18th C Jonathan Rose house in North Branford, Connecticut, and a growing collection of late 19th and early 20th C objects. The Gallery also features good collections of furniture by Townsend and Goddard of Newport and by Stephen Badlam of Boston; and silver by American silversmiths Edward Winslow and Joseph Richardson.

New London

Hempsted Houses

11 Hempstead St • 06320
(860) 443-7949

Hours: Mid-May to mid-Oct Thu-Sun 12-4.

Two houses on one property. Joshua Hempsted House, built in 1678, survived the burning of New London during the American Revolution; it is furnished with many original family pieces and restored to suggest life in the colonial era as documented by the early 18th C diary of Joshua Hempsted. The other, the Nathaniel Hempsted or Huguenot House, is an unusual stone structure evocative of the Revolutionary period. Run by The Antiquarian and Landmarks Society in Hartford.

Old Lyme

Florence Griswold Museum

96 Lyme St • 06371
(860) 434-5542
www.flogris.org

Hours: Apr-Dec Tue-Sat 10-5, Sun 1-5; Jan-Mar Wed-Sun 1-5.

Admission: Adults $5, senior citizens $4, children under 12 and members free.
Location: Just N of I-95 Exit 70. From the N and E, turn R at end of ramp to second building on L. From the S and W, L at end of ramp, R on Halls Rd, L on Lyme St to the second building on L.

The Florence Griswold house occupies a unique place in the history of American art as some of the great early 20th C American impressionists gathered here each summer to enjoy Florence Griswold's encouragement, the pastoral landscapes, and the fellowship of their colleagues. The permanent collection of art includes over 900 paintings, drawings, watercolors, and prints by nearly 130 American artists. The archives contain information on the location of the thousands of Old Lyme art colony paintings collected elsewhere.

Suffield

Hatheway House

55 Main St • 06078
(860) 668-0055

Hours: May-Oct Wed, Sat, Sun 1-4; also open Thu & Fri in Jul &Aug.

Built in 1761 and expanded in 1794, and one of the most significant houses in New England, Hatheway House is known for its early neoclassical architecture, unique French wallpapers, and a collection of fine Early American furnishings. Run by The Antiquarian and Landmarks Society.

Wethersfield

Buttolph Williams House

249 Broad St • 06109
(860) 529-0460

Hours: May-Oct Wed-Mon 10-4.

This picturesque Pilgrim century house served as a model for the children's classic The Witch of Blackbird Pond and has been furnished to illustrate early colonial life. Run by The Antiquarian and Landmarks Society.

Woodstock

Bowen House, Roseland Cottage

Rte 169, on the Common • 06281
(860) 928-4074

Hours: Jun-Oct 15 Wed-Sun tours at 11, 12, 1, 2, 3, 4.
Admission: $4.

A rare and important surviving example of a Gothic Revival summer estate, notable for its different types of Gothic Revival furniture, Belter furniture, and Victorian accessories. A museum house run by the Society for the Preservation of New England Antiquities.

Maine

York Harbor

Sayward-Wheeler House

79 Barrell Ln • 03909
(603) 436-3205

Hours: Jun-Oct 15 Sat-Sun tours at 11, 12, 1, 2, 3, 4.
Admission: $4.

Mid- to late 18th C furniture, American portraits, 18th C glass, Chinese export porcelain, in a house that has remained virtually untouched since the 18th C. A museum house run by the Society for the Preservation of New England Antiquities.

Massachusetts

Beverly

The Trustees of Reservations

572 Essex St • 01915
(508) 921-1944

Admission: Varies at each property. Memberships include admission privileges to properties and the opportunity to attend special events held during the year.

Formed in 1891, the Trustees of Reservations is the world's first land trust. One of the largest privately supported land organizations in Massachusetts, TTOR owns and maintains 82 Massachusetts properties totaling more than 21,300 acres including beaches, wetlands, woodlands, and twelve historic houses and formal gardens open to the public. Two historic houses, Naumkeag in Stockbridge and the Stevens-Coolidge Place in North Andover, are notable for their decorative arts collections. Please see listings in those towns for more details.

Boston

Harrison Gray Otis House

141 Cambridge St • 02114
(617) 227-3956

Hours: Wed-Sun tours at 11, 12, 1, 2, 3, 4.
Admission: $4.

Free-standing brick mansion in the Federal style, furnished with American Federal furniture and decorative arts, with reproduction wallpapers and paint colors based on scientific analysis. A museum house run by the Society for the Preservation of New England Antiquities.

Museum of Fine Arts

465 Huntington Ave • 02115-5523
(617) 267-9300
www.mfa.org

Hours: Mon-Tue 10-4:45, Wed-Fri 10-9:45, Sat-Sun 10-5:45. Entrances to special exhibition galleries close 1/2 hour before Museum closing. Closed Thanksgiving and Christmas. Japanese Garden open 10-4:45, weather permitting.
Admission: Adults $10, senior citizens and college students with valid ID $8, children 17 and under and members free. Thu & Fri after 5 fees reduced by $2 (only West Wing galleries are open); Wed 4-9:45 by voluntary contribution. Membership starts at $60.
Location: Approx 1 mi SW of Copley Square in the Fenway. Take the Green Line "E" trolley to the Museum of Fine Arts stop. Adjacent indoor/outdoor parking.
Access: Wheelchair accessible.

One of the greatest strengths of the Museum of Fine Arts collection lies in its pre-Civil War New England objects. Holdings include silver objects such as Paul Revere's celebrated Liberty Bowl and a 17th C tankard by Robert Sanderson, the earliest recorded American silversmith. Among the numerous period rooms are three complete rooms from Oak Hill, an early 19th C home in Peabody, MA. Other rooms focus on Queen Anne and Chippendale-style furniture in the impressive Karolik Collection. The museum holds the finest collection of paintings by John Singleton Copley in the country, with over 50 works. Other American artists on view include Fitz Hugh Lane, Gilbert Stuart, and Winslow Homer.

Society for the Preservation of New England Antiquities

Harrison Gray Otis House
141 Cambridge St • 02114
(617) 227-3956

The Society for the Preservation of New England Antiquities (SPNEA) owns 35 historic properties in five states. Founded in 1910 by William Sumner Appleton, the country's first professional preservationist, SPNEA has the largest and best-documented collection of New England decorative arts. With a total of 50,000 objects — including furniture, wallpapers, ceramics, glass, metal, textiles, and toys — the house museums collectively document daily life in New England over three centuries. Membership starts at $35. Individual houses of particular interest to collectors are listed separately under individual states and towns.

Cambridge

The Fogg Art Museum

32 Quincy St • 02138
(617) 495-9400
www.artmuseums.harvard.edu

Hours: Mon-Sat 10-5, Sun 1-5, closed holidays.
Admission: General admission $5; non-Harvard University students $3, senior citizens $4; free to museum members, Harvard staff and students, children up to age 18; free on Sat mornings from 10-12 and all day Wed.
Location: Int of Broadway and Quincy Streets, 1 blk E of Harvard Square and adjacent to Harvard Yard.
Access: Wheelchair entrance on Prescott St at the entrance to the Fine Arts Library.

The Fogg Art Museum was founded in 1891 to house the growing Harvard art collection. The Fogg's Decorative Arts Gallery contains 17th, 18th & early 19th C decorative arts from

England and America, including an impressive collection of English and American silver. Among the 19th C French and British paintings are works from the time of the French Revolution and portraits by Reynolds and Gainsborough. Other paintings include works by Fra Angelico, Rubens, Ingres, Géricault, Van Gogh, Renoir, Monet, Degas, Homer, and Pollock, and drawings by renowned American and European artists. The Armand Hammer Galleries display Dutch art of the 17th C, including paintings by Rembrandt and van Ruisdael, along with examples of Dutch silver and furnishings. They also include American and French paintings of the 18th C and selections from the Hutchinson collection of English silver. On the second floor is the Wertheim Collection, one of America's finest collections of Impressionist and post-Impressionist works.

Concord

Concord Museum

200 Lexington Rd
PO Box 146 • 01742
(508) 369-9763
www.concordmuseum.org
email: cm1@concordmuseum.org

Hours: Mon-Sat 9-5, Sun 12-5, except Jan-Mar Mon-Sat 11-4, Sun 1-4.Closed Thanksgiving, Christmas, New Year's Day, and Easter.
Admission: Adults $6, senior citizens $5, students $4, children $3. Family rate $12. Memberships start at $30.
Location: Between Lexington Road and the Cambridge Turnpike, about 1-1/2 mi from Rte 2. The entrance is on the Cambridge Turnpike. Parking is free.

The Concord Museum is the home of the Concord Antiquarian Society. Fifteen period rooms and galleries vividly depict the growth and evolution of one of America's most historic communities. Decorative arts and domestic artifacts, either owned by Concord area residents or made by Concord area craftspeople, are attractively displayed. The collections are rich with examples of silver, furniture, clocks, and samplers produced in the area in the 17th and 18th C. Of special New England interest are the lantern hung from the steeple on the night of Paul Revere's ride, relics from the battle at the North Bridge, a large collection of artifacts relating to Thoreau, and the contents of Ralph Waldo Emerson's study.

Deerfield

Historic Deerfield

The Street
Box 321 • 01342
(413) 774-5581
www.historicdeerfield.org

Hours: Daily 9:30-4:30. Closed Thanksgiving, Christmas Eve, and Christmas.
Admission: Adults $12, children 6-17 $5. Special group rates for 20 or more with advance notice.

Location: 40 mi N of Springfield. I-91 to Exit 24 N: 6 mi N on Rtes 5/10, then turn L onto the village street. From Boston take Rte 2 W to Turners Falls. Go 5 mi to Deerfield.

Along a mile-long thoroughfare simply called The Street, 14 museum houses and the new Flynt Center of Early New England Life welcome visitors to Historic Deerfield year round. The old houses, filled with one of this country's finest Americana collections, date from the 18th and 19th C and are part of a remarkable survival of more than 50 buildings predating the American Revolution. The 300-year-old village of Deerfield, known as the best-documented community in America, lies within The Old Deerfield National Historic Landmark. Surrounded by more than 1,000 acres of prime farmland, the village is home to working farms and three boarding schools. Founded in 1952, Historic Deerfield offers daily tours, public lectures, workshops, a domestic and international travel program, forums, special events for families, an archaeological field school, and educational programs for students and visitors of all ages. On view at the Flynt Center of Early New England Life through 2001: Pursuing Refinement in Rural New England, 1750 to 1850, and The Museum's Attic: 3000 of Historic Deerfield's Choicest Antiques.

Memorial Hall/Pocumtuck Valley Memorial Association

8 Memorial St • 01342
(413) 774-7476
www.deerfield-ma.org

Hours: May 1-Oct 31 daily 9:30 to 4:30.
Admission: Adults $6, youths/students 6-21 $3. Free for members and children under 6. Joint ticket with Historic Deerfield: Adults $12, youths/students 6-21 $5. Ticket valid for one week.
Location: Corner of Memorial Street and Rtes 5/10 in Deerfield.

Opened in 1880 as the first historical society in western Massachusetts, Memorial Hall offers 19 exhibition rooms filled with treasures in a 19th C atmosphere. The museum contains five period rooms including an 1880 kitchen that is the oldest extant period room in America. Four Hadley chests, recognized as one of the most important regional furniture forms from the late 17th and early 18th C, are displayed in various rooms, while interesting exhibitions of glassware, ceramics, baskets, and more than 25 quilts, as well as samplers, beaded bags, clothing, and related accessories, are on view throughout the museum. Other items of note include the dolls and toys exhibited in the Children's Room, tools and agricultural equipment in the Tool Room, and arms in the Military Room.

Gloucester

Beauport

75 Eastern Point Blvd • 01930
(508) 283-0800

Hours: May 15-Sep 15 Mon-Fri 10-4; Sep 15-Oct 15 Mon-Sun 10-4.
Admission: $5.

Large collections of hooked rugs, glass, silhouettes, ceramics, and China trade material, arranged in period settings in a 40-room house overlooking the harbor. A museum house run by the Society for the Preservation of New England Antiquities.

Cape Ann Historical Museum

27 Pleasant St • 01930
(978) 283-0455

Hours: Tue-Sat 10-5. Closed holidays.
Admission: Adults $4.00, senior citizens $3.50, students $2.50, children under 6 and members free.
Location: In the heart of downtown Gloucester, 1 blk N of Main Street, 1 blk E of City Hall and the Sawyer Free Library. Parking available in adjacent lot.

The collections of the Cape Ann Historical Museum reflect the activities for which the area is best known: maritime trade including the China trade, fishing, and New England coastal art. Housed here is the nation's largest collection of paintings and drawings by New England's Fitz Hugh Lane, a 19th C Gloucester native now regarded as the best of the luminist maritime painters. Other American artists represented include Winslow Homer, Maurice Prendergast, Milton Avery, and John Sloan. Displays of American decorative arts include silver by Paul Revere, a large and beautiful collection of China trade porcelain, carved jades and fans, and more than 260 pieces of fine 19th C furniture. Collections of jewelry, glassware, basketry, and textiles, including early needlework, linens, and quilts, are also on view. The fisheries and maritime collections include attractively and meticulously arranged ship models, scale models, gear, rigging, tools, and sailmaking equipment. Also extensive library and archives.

Lincoln

Codman House

Codman Rd • 01773
(617) 259-8843

Hours: Jun-Oct 15 Wed-Sun tours at 12, 1, 2, 3, 4.
Admission: $4.

An 18th C country house with furnishings and interiors reflecting Georgian, Federal, Victorian, and classical periods; the boyhood home of the designer Ogden Codman, Jr. Furnished with French and American antiques, fine paneling, paintings, and sculpture, 1750-1930. Owned and run by the Society for the Preservation of New England Antiquities.

Milton

Captain Robert Bennet Forbes House

215 Adams St • 02186
(617) 696-181

Hours: Wed & Sun 1-4. Tours begin at 1, 2 & 3 pm. By appt on other weekdays.
Admission: Adults $3, senior citizens and students $1.50, children under 12 accompanied by an adult free. Memberships begin at $20 (individual) and $30 (family).
Location: Southeast Expressway (Rte 3) southbound exit 10; R at stop sign, which is Adams Street. The house is on the right.

The collection of this 19th C sea captain, merchant, and philanthropist and his family is housed in the Forbes family's former home, an 1833 treasure of a Greek Revival designed by Isaiah Rogers, one of New England's outstanding architects. The long-standing family connection with the China trade and shipping industry is apparent in the furniture, paintings, Asian export porcelain, silver, and textiles collected over a 150-year period. Fine examples of American furniture and Civil War mementos are also on display among the three floors of the house, as is a collection of items associated with Lincoln including autographs, letters, photographs, and a first edition of Harriet Beecher Stowe's *Uncle Tom's Cabin*. Also on the estate are a log cabin replica of Abraham Lincoln's birthplace, a carriage house dating from the 1830s, a plank house, a shed, and a prefabricated 1930s Hodgson building.

North Andover

Stevens-Coolidge Place

Andover St • 01845
(978)682-3580

Hours: May-Oct Sun 1-5, Wed 2-4; gardens open 8 til sunset.
Admission: Adults $3, children $0.50; garden only, adults $2, children $0.50.
Location: 1/2 mi from Rte 125 on Andover St.

This house contains pre-18th C ceramics for the Chinese domestic market, Anglo-Irish cut glass, Oriental rugs, and fine wall hangings. This house museum is run by The Trustees of Reservations.

Pittsfield

Hancock Shaker Village

Albany Rd (Rte 20)
PO Box 927 • 01202
(413) 443-0188 • (800) 817-1137
www.hancockshakervillage.org

Hours: Guided Tour Season: Mem Day weekend through the third week of Oct daily 9:30-5. Apr through late May and late Oct-Nov 10-3. Self-guided tours: May 14-Oct 24, 9:30-5 daily. Guided tours available by advance appointment Dec-Mar. Special events year round.
Admission: Guided tours: adults $10, youth (ages 6-17) $5, age 5 and under free, family (2 adults and all children under 18 in the immediate family) $25. Self-guided tours: adults $13.50, youth (ages 6 to 17) $5.50, age 5 and under free, family (2 adults and children under age 18 in the immediate family) $33.
Location: Jct of Rtes 20 and 41, 5 mi W of downtown Pittsfield.

Hancock Shaker Village is composed of 20 restored buildings on 1,200 scenic acres of meadow and woodland in the Berkshire Hills. It is a living history museum, exhibiting the country's largest and finest collection of Shaker furnishings and artifacts set in the context of an original village. Interpreters re-create the daily life and production of the Shaker village, including the faithful reproduction of 19th C Shaker goods such as furniture, oval boxes, textiles, iron items, and baskets. A festival of Shaker agriculture takes place during the fall foliage season.

Salem

Peabody Essex Museum

East India Square
Liberty and Essex Sts • 01970-3783
(508) 745-9500 (recorded message) • (800)745-4054

Hours: Mon-Sat 10-5, Sun 12-5. Open Mon Mem Day to Halloween. Closed on national holidays.
Admission: Adults $8.50, senior citizens & students $7.50, children 6 to 18 $5. Free to children under 6, residents of Salem, Massachusetts, and members.
Location: I-95 N to Rte 128 N to Rte 114 into Salem. Go 2.4 mi on Rte 114, then R onto Rte 107 N, Bridge Street. Take R opposite Parker Bros, onto St Peter Street, turn L, then R for municipal parking and Museum.

The Peabody Essex Museum, formed in 1799 by members of the East India Marine Society, comprises 300,000 objects relating to the maritime history of New England including the most beautiful collection of Chinese export porcelain in the country. Other exhibits include Chinese export gold and silver and decorative arts such as paintings, furniture, and textiles; Japanese export art; depictions of the China coast by Western artists; goods from Salem's trade with India and depictions of the Indian people; and architecture and landscapes of the 18th and 19th C. Featured in the American galleries are fine examples of New England furniture, paintings, silver, and textiles that date from the colonial period through the 20th C. The museum also has an important collection of ship models, paintings, and figureheads. Also has one of New England's premier research and rare book libraries, with extensive manuscripts, materials, and vintage photographs documenting more than three centuries of American life.

Sandwich

Heritage Plantation of Sandwich

Pine & Grove Sts
PO Box 566 • 02563
(508) 888-3300

Hours: May-Oct daily 10-5.
Admission: Adults $9, senior citizens $8, youths 6-18 $4.50, children under 5, free. Groups of 20 or more, $7 per person.
Location: From Rte 6A take Rte 130 to Pine St and the Museum. From the Mid-Cape Highway take Exit 2 and follow Rte 130 N to Grove St.

The Heritage Plantation of Sandwich consists of a Shaker round barn holding an antique automobile collection, a military museum, and an art museum that contains a restored and working carousel and an Americana Wing featuring folk art, landscape paintings, and Currier and Ives prints. Artifacts in the collection include Nantucket Lightship baskets, scrimshaw, weather vanes, toys, trade signs, and a vast collection of Anthony Elmer Crowell's bird carvings. There are cigar store figures by Samuel Anderson Robb; bronzes by Remington, Dallin, and Jackson; and early American paintings by Erastus Salisbury Field, William Matthew Prior, and Susan Waters. Heritage Plantation boasts one of the largest collections of Currier and Ives lithographs anywhere, vividly portraying events from America's past. Many of the top fifty large and small folio prints produced by the famous New York print firm are on display.

Sandwich Glass Museum

129 Main St
PO Box 103 • 02563
(508) 888-0251

Hours: Apr-Oct daily 9:30-5:00; Nov-Dec & Feb-Mar, Wed-Sun 9:30-4. Closed Jan and holidays during Nov-Dec.
Admission: Adults $3.50, children $1, under 6 free.
Location: From the Sagamore Bridge take Rte 6 to Exit 2. Turn L on Rte 130 toward Sandwich. Bear L at island. Museum is on R directly across from Town Hall.

Located in a charming white clapboard house on Town Hall Square, the Sandwich Glass Museum displays an extensive collection of the famous Sandwich Glass manufactured by the Boston and Sandwich Glass Company (1825-87) and the Cape Cod Glass Works (1859-69). The Museum is composed of 13 galleries, arranged chronologically. The exhibits take the viewer through the development and manufacture of several types of glass, starting with early free-blown glass and blown three-mold glass. Shapes and styles on display include candlesticks, tableware, vases, furniture knobs, and tiebacks; colorful mid-period pattern glass in canary, blue, green, and opalescent; and one-of-a-kind presentation pieces made to commemorate special occasions and events. A display of pressed glass includes the world-famous lacy glass developed at Sandwich. Impressively displayed are Sandwich paperweights and glass decorated by enameling and etching.

Stockbridge

Naumkeag

Prospect Hill Rd • 01262
(413) 298-3239

Hours: Mem Day to Col Day daily 10-5:15.
Admission: Adults $7, children $2.50; garden only, adults $5, children $3.
Location: From the intersection of Rtes 7 and 102 at the Red Lion Inn in Stockbridge center, take Pine St N. Bear L on Prospect Hill Rd 1/2 mi.

Naumkeag, a 26-room gabled mansion designed by Stanford White in 1885, contains notable collections of Chinese export porcelain, antique furniture, elegant rugs, and tapestries. Run by The Trustees of Reservations.

Sturbridge

Old Sturbridge Village

1 Old Sturbridge Village Rd • 01566
(508) 347-3362
www.osv.org

Hours: Apr-Oct daily 9-5, Nov-Mar daily 10-4. Open weekends only early Jan-mid Fed.

Closed Christmas, New Year's Day, and winter Mons.
Admission: Adults $16, senior citizens $15, children 6 to 15 $8, children under 6 free. Valid for two consecutive days. Group and school rates available with advance reservation. Membership and Kids Club available.
Location: I-90 Exit 9 or I-84 Exit 2. Follow the signs to Rte 20 W. Free parking.

Old Sturbridge Village is a living history museum, where historically costumed men and women interpret daily life in a rural New England town during the 1830s. The Sturbridge Village Common is surrounded by a Center Meetinghouse, Parsonage, Tavern, Bank and rural Store. The museum village also includes six restored houses furnished with antiques, such as the antique ceramics on display in the Salem Towne House. There are extensive collections of glass, clocks, and early lighting including a superb collection of New England clocks with examples by clockmakers Aaron, Benjamin, and Simon Willard; Eli Terry; and Seth Thomas.

Waltham

Gore Place

52 Gore St • 02154
(781) 894-2798

Hours: Mansion open for guided tours Apr 15-Nov 15, Tue-Sat 11-5, Sun 1-5. Last tour at 4 pm. Grounds open year round during daylight hours.
Admission: Adults $5, seniors over 65 and college students with a valid ID $4, children 5 to 12 $3. Memberships in Gore Place Society start at $15.
Location: From Rte 128/95 Exit 26: 3 mi E through Waltham center. From MA Turnpike I-90 Exit 17 through Watertown Square to Rte 20 W. Midway between Waltham Common and Watertown Square.

The Mansion at Gore is one of New England's finest examples of Federal period residential architecture. Noted for its oval rooms and its recently restored spiral staircase, it is filled with fine early American, European, and Oriental furnishings, many of which belonged to the Gore family. The 40-acre estate of gardens, cultivated fields, and woodlands also includes a 1793 coach house and an 1835 cottage. The Mansion houses an impressive collection of furniture, porcelain and silver, clothing, books, and letters. The furnishings have been assembled from many of the finest private collections in the Boston area and include masterpieces of American furniture from Baltimore, Philadelphia, Boston, and the New England area. Among family portraits are works by Copley, Trumbull, and Stuart. Decorative accessories from England, France, and China, spanning the period from ca 1740 to ca 1825, contribute to the elegance.

Williamstown

Clark Art Institute

225 South St • 01267
(413) 458-9545
www.clark.williams.edu

Hours: Tue-Sun 10-5. Closed Mon except Jul and Aug. Closed New Year's Day,

Thanksgiving and Christmas.
Admission: Free from Nov-Jun, Jul-Oct adults $5. Free on Tuesdays. Admission always free to members, students, and visitors under 18 years of age. Memberships start at $25.
Location: In the NW corner of Massachusetts in Williamstown, 1/2 m S of the jct of Rtes 2 and 7.
Access: Wheelchairs are available, and all galleries, auditorium, library and offices are wheelchair accessible, as is an entrance-level restroom.

The Institute's permanent collection of art ranges from the Renaissance to the 19th C. It is noted for an especially fine group of impressionist paintings, including a large number by Renoir that date between 1870 and 1880, as well as works by Monet, Degas, Pissarro, and Sisley. American painters represented include Homer, Sargent, Cassatt, and Remington. There is a large collection of silver, primarily English, that includes American, French, and Dutch as well. Decorative arts include porcelain from the Meissen, Chantilly, and Sèvres factories. Early American glass and French and American furniture are also displayed. One of the nation's premier art reference libraries for the study of European and American art.

Worcester

Worcester Art Museum

55 Salisbury St • 01609-3123
(508)799-4406
www.worcesterart.org

Hours: Wed-Fri 11-5, Sat 10-5, Sun 11-5. Closed Mon-Tue and major holidays.
Admission: Adults $8, senior citizens, full-time college students $6, members and youths 17 and under free. Free to all Sat 10-12. Memberships start at $40.
Location: From I-90 Exit 10 (Auburn): Take I-290 E to Worcester, Exit 17. Go L on Rte 9 to, and through, Lincoln Square to third set of lights at top of hill, turn R on Harvard Street. Museum on L at second traffic light.
Access: Most galleries and restrooms are accessible to handicapped. Park adjacent to Tuckerman St entrance. Wheelchairs and assistive listening devices are available upon request.

The Worcester Art Museum contains 30,000 objects and is the third largest fine arts museum in New England. Its collections cover the evolution of art, ranging from classical, Oriental, and medieval sculpture and tapestries to European and American painting, an American decorative arts gallery, and photographs, prints, and drawings. Of particular importance are works of New England portraiture including the double portraits of three members of the Freake family, which are considered two of the finest existing examples of 17th C American portraiture. Portrait artists from the 18th C represented in the collection include John Singleton Copley, Charles Willson Peale, Joseph Blackburn, Christian Gullager, and Ralph and James Earle. The collection of American impressionist paintings includes oils by Childe Hassam, Frank Benson, Edmund Tarbell, Mary Cassatt, Maurice Prendergast, John Singer Sargent and James A. McN. Whisler. The watercolor art of Winslow Homer, John Singer Sargent, John La Farge, and Maurice Prendergast is also on display.

Yarmouth Port

Winslow Crocker House

250 Rte 6A • 02675
(508) 362-4385

Hours: Jun-Oct 15 Sat-Sun tours at 11, 12, 1, 2, 3, 4.
Admission: $4.

Mid to late 18th C furniture, American portraits, Chinese export porcelain, and 18th C glass, in a Georgian shingle house. A museum house run by the Society for the Preservation of New England Antiquities.

New Hampshire

Manchester

Currier Gallery of Art

201 Myrtle Way • 03104
(603) 669-6144
www.currier.org

Hours: Mon, Wed, Thu, Sun 11-5, Fri 11-8, Sat 10-5. Closed Tue and most national holidays.
Admission: Adults $5, students and senior citizens $4. Free to children under age 18 and to members. Special exhibitions $1 extra. Memberships begin at $20.
Location: From I-293: Exit 6 (Amoskeag Bridge) to Elm Street. Turn R, then L at the first traffic light onto Bridge Street. Continue through fourth traffic light and turn L onto Ash Street, where museum drive will be the third L. From I-93, take Exit 8 (Bridge St) , R 2 m onto Ash Street, where museum drive will be the third L.
Access: Wheelchair accessible.

The Currier's collections of New England decorative arts are strong in works from the 18th through the late 19th C. New Hampshire furniture makers are well represented with chests, chairs, tables, and lowboys, including a number of pieces by the Dunlap family. Handsome pieces by Boston and Charlestown, Massachusetts, cabinetmakers are also displayed. Folk art paintings include works by Joseph Davis and Zedekiah Belknap, and portraits by Ammi Phillips and Samuel Miller. Among important American artists represented are Albert Bierstadt, Thomas Eakins, William Merritt Chase, Willard Metcalf, Childe Hassam, John Singer Sargent, Winslow Homer, Edward Hopper, and Thomas Hart Benton. Works by Hudson River School artists are prominent throughout the museum. The silver collections feature pieces by John Coney and Paul Revere I and II, and a growing collection of Arts and Crafts silver by Arthur Stone, George Gebelein, and Karl Leinonen. The Currier is well known for an enormous glass collection that ranges from very early American pieces to pressed glass, cameo glass, and other English, Continental, and American pieces.

New Ipswich

Barrett House

Main St • 03071
(603) 878-2517

Hours: Jun-Oct 15 Sat-Sun tours 11, 12, 1, 2, 3, 4.
Admission: $4.

Elegant Federal mansion with late 18th and early 19th C furnishings, musical instruments, and scenic wallpaper. A museum house run by the Society for the Preservation of New England Antiquities.

Portsmouth

Rundlet-May House

364 Middle St • 03802
(603) 436-3205.

Hours: Jun-Oct 15 Sat-Sun tours 11, 12, 1, 2, 3, 4.
Admission: $4.

A collection of early 19th C Portsmouth Federal furniture; English and American prints, glass, and ceramics; and English and Canton china in a Federal mansion with gardens and outbuildings. A museum house run by the Society for the Preservation of New England Antiquities.

Strawbery Banke

Marcy St
PO Box 300 • 03802
(603) 433-1100
www.strawberybanke.org

Hours: Apr-Oct daily 10-5. Evenings during the first two weekends in December for the Candlelight Stroll.
Admission: Adults $12, children 6 to 17 $8, families $28. Group rates available. Individual memberships start at $30. Senior and student memberships start at $20.
Location: I-95 Exit 7: Take Market Street and follow the signs. Located on Marcy Street opposite Prescott Park and the Portsmouth waterfront.

Strawbery Banke Museum is a 10-acre waterfront settlement of over 40 historic homes ranging from the 17th to the 20th C, still on their original foundations. Period gardens, craft shops, and exhibitions depict more than 350 years of architectural and social change in one of America's oldest neighborhoods, established in 1630. Visitors can stroll through the 1796 Walsh House with its display of interior woodwork and neoclassical furniture, view early craftsmen's tools in the Lowd House, and puzzle over the "Split" Drisco House. The Governor Ichabod Goodwin House includes decorative arts from the 1860s. The ca 1762 Chase House contains a collection of important Portsmouth furniture and objects originally owned by the Wendell family. One of the newest additions to the museum is the Shapiro House, containing items from a Russian Jewish immigrant family from the early 20th C.

New York

Annandale-on-Hudson

Montgomery Place

PO Box 32 • 12504
(914) 758-5461

Hours: Apr-Oct daily 10-5, closed Tue. Weekends only in Nov and first two weeks of Dec, Sat-Sun 10-5. Closed Jan, Feb, Thanksgiving, and Christmas.
Admission: Adults $6, senior citizens $5, youths 6 to 17 $3, under 6 free. Grounds-only pass $3.
Location: From I-87 Exit 19 to Rte 209/199 E across Kingston/Rhinecliff Bridge, L on Rte 9G 3 mi and L on Annandale Road, bear L onto River Road to entrance. From Taconic State Parkway: Pine Plains/Red Hook Exit to Rte 199, proceed 10 mi through Red Hook, R onto Rte 9G, L on Annandale Road as above.

A magnificent Hudson River and Catskill Mountains landscape surrounds Montgomery Place, the Federal-style mansion built in 1804-05 for Janet Livingston Montgomery, widow of Revolutionary War hero General Richard Montgomery. Today Montgomery Place's 435 acres offer a pristine view, and the grounds are open for picnicking and hiking, as once enjoyed by the Montgomery and Livingston families. Two hundred years of family possessions, including antique furniture, crystal chandeliers, and Livingston family portraits by Gilbert Stuart and Rembrandt Peale, grace the interior of the house. A fine collection of miniatures is also on display.

Essex

Greystone House & Gardens

By the Ferry Dock • 12936
(518)963-8058 • (518)963-4650

Hours: Jul-Aug Wed-Mon 1-5. Mem Day-Col Day Sat-Sun 1-5.
Admission: Open by appointment only. Small admission fee.
Location: Essex, New York, is located approximately 2 hrs N of Albany, 1-1/2 hours S of Montreal, 30 min S of Plattsburgh and 40 min E of Lake Placid. From Burlington, Vermont, take the 20-minute ferry ride.

Good collection of Empire-style furnishings from the 1840s-1850s located on the shore of Lake Champlain.

Glens Falls

Hyde Collection

161 Warren St • 12801
(518) 792-1761
Hours: Jan-Apr Tue-Sun 12-5, May-Dec Tue-Sun 10-5. Tours from 1-3. Closed Mons and holidays.
Admission: Adults $3.50, senior citizens and students $2.50, children under 5 free. Family

rate of $10. Free admission Sun 10-2.
Location: Glens Falls, 15 mi N of Saratoga Springs. I-87 Exit 18: approximately 2-1/2 mi E.
Access: Facility accessible to wheelchairs.

The Hyde Collection consists of more than 100 works of art collected by and featured in the former home of Charlotte Pruyen Hyde and her husband, Louis Fiske Hyde. Paintings and sculpture by major artists from the late Gothic period to the early 20th C, including Rubens, Botticelli, and Degas, reflect the diverse styles represented in the collection. A fine collection of American paintings by Thomas Eakins, Winslow Homer, and Childe Hassam, as well as 19th and 20th C American sculpture and prints, are on display. Distinguished decorative arts pieces include Italian Renaissance and 18th C French furniture, as well as European tapestries, textiles, pewter, and ceramics.

Hyde Park

Vanderbilt Mansion

Rte 9 • 12538
(914) 229-9115

Hours: Apr-Oct daily 9-5. Closed Thanksgiving, Christmas, and New Year's Day and two days a week in the winter. Grounds open dawn to dusk daily.
Admission: Adults $8, senior citizens and children under 16 free.
Location: North of Hyde Park on Rte 9.

This 54-room beaux arts-style mansion was built between 1896 and 1899 for Frederick Vanderbilt. Designed by the prominent architectural firm McKim, Mead & White, the building was meant to evoke the ancestral homes of the European nobility. The interior is a prime example of ornate Gilded Age style. First-floor rooms are filled with rugs, tapestries, Italian wood-carved ceilings, and Renaissance chairs. Displayed in Frederick's bedroom on the second floor are lavish fabrics and elaborately carved furniture from Europe. Situated on the grounds are a coach house and stables, gardener's cottage, and a pavilion that has been converted into a visitor center.

Hudson

Olana

Rte 9G • 12534
(518) 828-0135

Hours: Guided tours only. Reservations are recommended. Apr 15-May 31 and mid-Oct-Oct 31 10-5. Last tour starts at 4. June 1-mid-Oct 10-6, last tour starts at 5. Visitor Center and Museum shop open Apr-Oct daily at 9:30.
Admission: Adults $3, senior citizens $2, children $1.
Location: On Rte 9G, 1 mi S of Rip Van Winkle Bridge.
Access: House tour is on one floor. An elevator provides access to the tour floor. Visitor Center and restrooms are also accessible. An orientation film, "Frederic Church's Olana" is closed-captioned. New York State Access Passes are accepted.

Olana is a Persian-style villa created by Frederick Edwin Church, foremost artist of the Hudson River School, and built between 1870 and 1876 as a rural home for his family.

Church's sublime landscapes, many of which depict the view of the Hudson River from Olana, are displayed throughout the house along with paintings by his mentor, Thomas Cole. Exotic artifacts and furnishings are included in an eclectic mix of Shaker chairs; Lockwood de Forest workshop furniture; Asian, pre-Columbian, and European art; and decorative art objects and textiles brought back from the Middle East.

Rhode Island

Providence

Rhode Island School of Design Museum of Art

224 Benefit St • 02903-2723
(401) 454-6500

Hours: Wed-Sun 10-5, Fri til 8. Closed Thanksgiving, Christmas, New Year's Day, Easter Sunday and July 4.
Admission: Adults $5, senior citizens $4, children 5 to 18 $1, college students $2.
Location: I-95 Exit 22 to downtown Providence. Continue straight on Memorial Blvd; at third set of lights, L onto Waterman St Halfway up hill, turn R onto Benefit St. Museum is on R. From I-195W, take Exit 2 to S Main St and continue for 1/2 mi until the first set of traffic lights. R onto College St, then L onto Benefit St. Museum on L.
Access: Main entrance in Daphne Farago Wing is handicapped accessible.

The Museum of Art was founded in 1877 as an integral part of the Rhode Island School of Design. Three floors of galleries arranged around a courtyard house the museum's collection of over 65,000 works of art. The Pendleton collection contains outstanding examples from all the major urban cabinetmaking centers between Portsmouth, New Hampshire, and Baltimore. Other noteworthy items include two superlative Goddard and Townsend six-shell desks and an important Philadelphia slab table. Also displayed are 17th and early 18th C furniture by both urban and rural turners and joiners and collections of American decorative arts, painting, and sculpture.

Vermont

Bennington

The Bennington Museum

W Main St • 05201
(802) 447-1571
www.benningtonmuseum.com
bennmuse@sover.net

Hours: Open daily, Nov-May 9-5, Jun-Oct 9-6. Closed Thanksgiving Day, Christmas, and New Year's Day.
Admission: Adults $6.00, senior citizens and students $5.00, group (10 or more with reservation) $4.50 per person, children under 12 free.

Location: West Main Street (Rte 9), 1 mi W of the int of Rtes 7 and 9 in downtown Bennington.

The Bennington Museum boasts the largest collection of Bennington pottery in existence (over 3,000 pieces) as well as a huge American-made glass collection including 1,000 different patterns in pressed glass goblets and examples of free-blown, cut, engraved, and art glass. Also, American furniture from the 18th and 19th C, including the largest public collection of Vermont furniture. A geneology and local history library contains more than 4,000 volumes. The Museum also houses a collection of 30 paintings by the famous primitive painter Grandma Moses, a native of nearby Eagle Bridge, New York, who began her painting career at the age of 58, lived in Bennington for eight years, and painted several views of the town. Works by other American painters including Joseph Blackburn, Rembrandt Peale, William Jennys, Erastus Salisbury Field, William Morris Hunt, Henry Inman, and William Merritt Chase are also on display, along with one of the oldest known American landscape paintings, "A View of Bennington," painted in 1798.

Shelburne

Shelburne Museum

Rte 7
PO Box 10 • 05482
(802) 985-3346 • (800)253-0191
www.shelburnemuseum.org

Hours: Mid-May to mid-Oct daily 10-5. From mid-Oct to mid-May there are daily tours of selected buildings, with advance reservations.
Admission: Adults $17.50, children ages 6 to 14 $7, $40 maximum for parents and children under 16. Valid for the recommended two consecutive days.
Location: On Rte 7, 7 mi S of Burlington and 300 mi N of New York City.

The Shelburne Museum, founded in 1947 by Electra Havemeyer Webb, is one of the special treasures of New England. Located on 45 well-tended acres, this assemblage of 37 buildings, predominantly historic, and 200,000-plus artifacts includes an outstanding collection of American folk art. There are superb collections of furnishings and decorative accessories, rugs, quilts, pewter, glass, pottery, and porcelain. The Colchester Reef Lighthouse contains galleries of marine art, including paintings, figureheads, an scrimshaw. The Stagecoach Inn houses American folk sculpture with weather vanes, cigar-store Indians, circus and carousel figures, symbolic eagles, and ship's figures. Dorset House contains a collection of over 1,000 decoys: ducks, geese, swans and shorebirds. The quilt collection, numbering over 700, is noted for quality and superb designs. The 140 horse-drawn carriages, wagons, sleighs, and coaches in the Horseshoe Barn are regarded by many as the outstanding exhibit at the Shelburne. The Webb Gallery contains works representing 300 years of American painting, including primitive portraits of the Colonial period, luminist painters such as Fitz Hugh Lane and landscapes from the Hudson River School.

Weston

Farrar-Mansur House

Rte 100 • 05161
(802) 824-8190

Hours: Memorial Day-Jun, Sat-Sun 1-4; July 1-Labor Day daily 1-4.
Location: Located on the village green in Weston, just off Rte 100.
Admission: Adults $2.
Access: Not wheelchair accessible.

Built as a tavern in 1797, the house is now a museum operated by the Weston Historical Society. Collection includes many items from original families in the area with a focus on 18th-19th C decorative arts and furnishings.

Antiques Show Promoters

Allman Promotions
Stephen Allman
PO Box 470
Clayton, NY 13624
(315)686-5789
allman@gisco.net

Holliston Show, Holiday Inn Turf, Winter Greater Rochester Expo, Greater Syracuse Expo, Round Lake NY Festival, Honolulu Holiday Show.

Antique Photo Shows
Russell Norton
PO Box 1070
New Haven, CT 06504
(203)281-0066
oldphoto@connix.com
stereoview.com

DC Antique Photo Image Show, Boston Antique Photo Image Show.

Antiquefest
Bobi Dallas
PO Box 2284
Liverpool, NY 13089
(315)695-1723

Great American Antiquefest.

Antiques Council
PO Box 574
Southport, CT 06490
(203)396-0192
(203)396-0193 (fax)

Nantucket Historical Assn Annual August Show, Cleveland Show, Southport-Westport Show, Gladstone Show, Maryland Historical Society Show.

Marjorie Barry Antique Shows
Marjorie Green
1222 US Rte 5N
Fairlee, VT 05045
(802)333-9083

Lebanon NH Show.

Bernice & David Bornstein Shows
Bernice & David Bornstein
PO Box 2204
Peabody, MA 01960
(978)774-2731
(978)741-3771 (fax)
bbshows@aol.com
www.bornsteinshows.com

Jewelry, Silver, Smalls Etc Show; Ephemera City Show; Great Indoor/Outdoor Show (Topsfield MA); Antiques in Stockbridge Show; Searles Castle Show; Paper & Collectible Show; Doll, Teddy & Toy Show.

Brimfield Acres North Inc
Robert Hopfe & Colleen James
120 Richards Ave
Paxton, MA 01612
(508)754-4185
brim1@splusnet.com

Brimfield's Heart-O-The-Mart

Pam Moriarty
PO Box 26
Brimfield, MA 01010
(413)245-9556
(413)245-3542
info@brimfield-hotm.com
www.brimfield-hotm.com

Heart-O-The-Mart.

Coastal Promotions

Paul & Cordie Davis
PO Box 799
Newcastle, ME 04553
(207)563-1013
cpishows@lincoln.midcoast.com

Portsmouth Antiques Market, NE Winter Antiques Show, Concord Armory Show, Bar Harbor Antiques Market, Maine Antiques Festival, NE Fall Antiques Show, Millis Antiques Show.

Don & Joyce Coffman

Box 592
Great Barrington, MA 02130
(413)229-2433
(413)528-0493 (fax)
ccamjc@vgernet.net
www.antiquejunction.com/coffmans

Antiques at Christmas Show.

Connelly Productions

Sallie Connelly
205 State Street
Binghamton, NY 13901-2711
(607)722-3544
(607)722-1266 (fax)
connelly@clarityconnect.com

Cord Shows Ltd

Vivien Cord
4 Whippoorwill Lane
Armonk, NY 10504
(914)273-4667
(914)273-4656 (fax)
cordshows@aol.com
www.cordshows.com

Danbury Fair, Antiquesmart III, Winter in Rye Show, Mt Kisco Show, Lasdon Show, New Milford Village Fair, Ulster Fairgrounds Show, Back To The Good Olde Days, Antique Stocking Stuffers Show.

Country Cape Antiques Shows

Jan & Chuck Thompson
PO Box 556
Old Mystic, CT 06372
(860)536-7729

Country Cape Mystic, Country Cape Norwich, Country Cape at the Y Westerly, Pine Point School Show, Old Lyme Show.

Jack Donigian

97 Richards St
Dedham, MA 02026
(617)329-1192

Nashua NH Antiques Show.

Faxon's

Lori Faxon
PO Box 28
Fiskdale, MA 01518
(508)347-3929
(508)347-3929 (fax)

The Dealer's Choice, Faxon's Midway, Faxon's Treasure Chest.

Forbes & Turner Antiques Shows

Linda Turner
45 Larchwood Rd
South Portland, ME 04106
(207)767-3967

Hildene & Dorset Shows, Connecticut Spring Antiques Show, Riverside Antiques Show, Bath Area Show, Bunker Hill Market, Fall Hartford Antiques Show.

The Gallagher Show

Bob Gallagher
417 Hoyt Street
Darien, CT 06820
(203)329-1516
bobspaper@aol.com

Movie & Paper Collectible Show, Salute the Stars Movie Convention.

Goosefare Antiques & Promos

John & Elizabeth DeSimone
PO Box 45
Saco, ME 04072
(207)284-8657
(800)641-6908
goosefare@int-usa.com

Quincy Antiques Show, Hingham Antiques Show, Tufts Antiques Show, Westwood Antiques Show, Maine's Spring Antiques Expo, Camden-Rockport Historical Society Antiques Show, Boothbay Harbor Antiques, Kennebunk Antiques Show, Barnstable Show, Falmouth Show.

Guernsey's

Arlan Ettinger
108 East 73rd Street
New York, NY 10021
(212)794-2280
(212)744-3638 (fax)
aettin7472@aol.com
www.guernseys.com

Hillcrest Promotions

Paul Gipstein
PO Box 290152
Wethersfield, CT 06109
(860)529-7582
(860)563-9975 (fax)

Merle L Hornstein

176800 Village Walk
Guilford, CT 06437
(203)457-0368
antiques@connix.com

Rotary Club Fairfield Show.

J & J Promotions: Antiques & Collectible Shows

PO Box 385 (Rte 20)
Brimfield, MA 01010-0385
(413)245-3436
jnjbrimfld@meganet.net
www.jandj-brimfield.com

Brimfield.

JLD Promotions

John & Lynn Doldoorian
231 Carpenter Rd
Whitinsville, MA 01588
(508)234-2477
(508)234-0360 (fax)
mjmed@tiac.net

Grafton on the Common Show, Capertown Antique Show.

N Pendergast Jones

158 Water St
Stonington, CT 06378
(860)535-1995

Antiques in Alexandria, Carnegie Museum of Art Show, NY Botanical Garden Show, Repertory Theatre of St Louis, Gunn Memorial Museum, Antiquarias, Boys & Girls Clubs of Boston.

Ellen Katona and Bob Lutz Antique Show Promotions

Ellen Katona & Bob Lutz
231 Atlantic Hwy
Northport, ME 04849
(207)338-1444
(207)338-5213 (fax)
ellenbob@mint.net

Heart of Bucks Show, Wenham Museum Show, Prallsville Mills Spring Show, Tinicum Outdoor Show, Bucks Co Antique Dealers Show.

Malden Bridge Productions Inc

Jackie Sideli
303 Ridge St
Fall River, MA 02721
(508)324-1837
(508)636-3454 (fax)

Boston Antiques Show, Boston International Fine Arts Show, Tivertown 4 Corners Antique Shows.

The Maven Company/Young Management Company

Richard Robbins
PO Box 937
Plandome, NY 11030
(914)248-4646
(800)344-7469
(914)248-0800 (fax)
maven@mavencompany.com
www.mavencompany.com

NE Holiday Antiques & Collectibles Show, Antique-A-Rama, Eastern States Antique Show, Stratford Shows.

May's Antique Market Inc

Richard May
PO Box 416
Brimfield, MA 01010
(413)245-9271
(413)245-9509

May's Antique Market (Brimfield).

Trisha McElroy

PO Box 40
Exeter, NH 03833
(603)778-8842

MCG Antiques Promotions Inc

Marilyn Gould
10 Chicken St
Wilton, CT 06897
(203)762-3525

Wilton Antiques Marketplace.

New England Events Mgt

Cathy & Frank Sykes
320 Pork Hill Rd
Wolfeboro, NH 03894
(603)569-0000
(603)569-0000 (fax)
neevents@worldpath.net
antiquefest.com

Lake Memorabilia & Classic Boat Auction, Winnipesaukee Antiques Festival, 46th Wolfeboro Antiques Fair, Hopkinton New Hampshire Antiques & Collectibles Festival, Vermont Antique Festival.

Oliver & Gannon Associates

PO Box 651
Altamont, NY 12009
(518)861-5062
(518)861-5062 (fax)
shows@albany.net
www.showsfairsfestivals.com

Westchester Antiquarian Book & Ephemera Fairs, MARIAB Spring Book Fairs, Columbia County Historical Society Festival, Altamont Fair, Southampton Show, Adirondack Museum Show, Albany Institute Fair.

Michael Payeur's Festival Promotions

Michael Payeur
18 Lasher Ave
Germantown, NY 12526
(518)537-4861

Montgomery Place Show, Kingston Armory Show.

Elias Pekale

PO Box 263
Merrick, NY 11566-0263
(516)868-2751

Bridgehampton Antiques & Collectibles Show, Roslyn LI Antiques & Collectibles Street Fair.

PT Promotions Inc

Polly Thibodeau
PO Box 333
Bath, ME 04530-9998
(207)443-8983
ptantiques@clinic.net

Bath Antiques Shows, Waldoboro Antiques Show.

Revival Promotions

Bob & Abbey McInnis
PO Box 388
Grafton, MA 01519
(508)839-9735

(800)494-0051
(508)839-4635 (fax)
bretrk@aol.com
www.farmington-antiques.com

Farmington Antiques Weekend.

Jean Sinenberg

PO Box 877
Wainscott, NY 11975
(516)537-0333
(516)537-0333 (fax)
antiqueshows@hamptons.com

Hampton's Garden Shows, Historic Mulford Farm Show, Sagaponack Outdoor Antiques Show, Hampton's Summer Antiques Festival.

Sanford Smith & Associates

Sanford Smith
68 East 7 Street
New York, NY 10003
(212)777-5218
(212)477-6490 (fax)
smith@freeverse.com

Philadelphia Show, Chelsea Int'l Antiquarian Book Fair, NY Photography Fair, Print Fair, Modernism & Photography, Fall Show, Outsider Art Fair, National Black Fine Art, The Art Show, Works on Paper, NY Antiquarian Book Fair, Chicago Int'l Fine Art.

Stella Show Mgmt Co

147 West 24th St
New York, NY 10011
(212)255-0020
(212)255-0020 (fax)
jstella327@aol.com
www.antiqnet.com/Stella

Americana at the Piers, Antiques at the "Other" Armory, Gramercy ,Triple Pier Expo, Great American Country Fair, Morristown, Waterloo Fair, Liberty Collectibles Expo, Vintage Home Restoration Show, Cape May, Modern Show, Manhattan Show.

Christine Vining

131 Charles St
Boston, MA 02114
(617)720-7808

Peabody Essex Museum Show.

Bill Walter Shows Inc

Jimi Barton
PO Box 310
Rhinebeck, NY 12572-0838
(914)758-6186
(914)876-6387 (fax)
rhbantfair@aol.com
www.northerndutchess.com/rhinebeckantiquesfair.htm

Rhinebeck Antiques Festival.

Wendy Management

Meg Wendy
PO Box 707
Rye, NY 10580
(914)698-3442
(914)698-6273 (fax

Morristown Shows, NY Armory Shows, White Plains Shows, Park Avenue Show, Sacred Heart Schools Shows, Pound Ridge Show, Twig of United Hospital Show.

Part III

Indexes

Index I: Alphabetical Index to Dealers

Index II: QuickCode Index to Specialties

1 Americana

2 Antiquities

3 Architectural Antiques

4 Arms/Military Antiques

4 – Arms/Military Antiques

5 Art Deco/Art Nouveau

6 Arts & Crafts

7 Art (General)

8 Art (Landscapes/Townscapes)

18 Books/Manuscripts

Connecticut

Maine

Massachusetts

New Hampshire

22 Ceramics (American, General)

23 Ceramics (English/Continental)

24 Ceramics (Oriental, General)

25 Ceramics (Chinese Export)

26 Ceramics (Creamware/Pearlware)

27 Ceramics (Delft/Faience)

28 Ceramics (Imari)

29 Ceramics (Redware/Yellowware)

30 Ceramics (Staffordshire)

31 Ceramics (Stoneware)

32 Collectibles

New York

Rhode Island

Vermont

35 Clocks/Watches

36 Decorative Accessories

New Hampshire

New York

37 Decoys

38 Dolls

107 English Antiques

39 Ephemera

40 Fireplace Accessories

41 Folk Art (General)

New Hampshire

New York

Vermont

42 Folk Art (Native American)

Connecticut

Maine

New York

Rhode Island

44 Folk Art (Trade Signs)

Connecticut

New York

45 Folk Art (Weathervanes)

Connecticut

Maine

Massachusetts

New Hampshire

New York

47 French Antiques

Connecticut

Maine

Massachusetts

New York

Rhode Island

Vermont

48 Furniture (General)

Connecticut

Maine

Massachusetts

New Hampshire

102 Furniture (Country)

51 Furniture (Paint)

52 Furniture (Period American)

Maine

Massachusetts

New Hampshire

New York

53 Furniture (Period Continental)

54 Furniture (Period English)

55 Furniture (Pine)

56 Furniture (Reproduction)

57 Furniture (Shaker)

58 Furniture (Victorian)

61 Glass/Bottles (General)

103 Glass (Pattern)

64 Jewelry (Estate)

65 Lighting

66 Maps/Globes

71 Oriental Antiques/Export Trade

72 Pewter

73 Photography

106 Primitives

74 Prints

75 Rugs (Hooked/Braided)

Connecticut

Maine

Massachusetts

New Hampshire

New York

Vermont

76 Rugs (Oriental)

Connecticut

Maine

Massachusetts

New Hampshire

Rhode Island

Vermont

77 Scientific/Medical Instruments

Connecticut

Maine

Massachusetts

New Hampshire

New York

78 Silver

Connecticut

Maine

Massachusetts

New Hampshire

New York

Rhode Island

Vermont

79 Sporting Antiques

Connecticut

Maine

Massachusetts

New Hampshire

New York

Vermont

80 Textiles (General)

Connecticut

Maine

Massachusetts

New Hampshire

New York

Rhode Island

Vermont

81 Textiles (Lace/Linen)

82 Textiles (Needlework/Samplers)

83 Textiles (Vintage Clothing)

84 Textiles (Quilts)

90 Vintage Cars/Carriages

91 Wicker

Index III: QuickCode Index to Services

S1 Appraisal

New Hampshire

S2 Auction

S3 Bookbinding/Restoration

Massachusetts

New Hampshire

S4 Building Materials

Connecticut

Maine

Massachusetts

New Hampshire

New York

Rhode Island

Vermont

S5 Cabinetmakers

Connecticut

Maine

Massachusetts

New Hampshire

Rhode Island

Vermont

S6 Chair Caning

Connecticut

Maine

Massachusetts

New Hampshire

S7 Clock Repair

S8 Consignment

S9 Consultation/Research

S10 Display Stands/Glass

S11 Doll Hospital

S12 Estate Purchases

S13 Framing

S14 Insurance

S15 Interior Design

S16 Repair/Restoration/Conservation

New Hampshire

New York

Rhode Island

Vermont

S17 Reproduction/Replication

Connecticut

Maine

Massachusetts

New Hampshire

New York

Rhode Island

S18 Services to Period Homes

Connecticut

S19 Shipping/Packing/Storage

About the Editors

Lisa Freeman and John Fiske are co-owners of Fiske & Freeman: Fine and Early Antiques, specializing in period formal and high-country furniture and appropriate accessories. They exhibit at shows throughout New England and the Midwest. Their articles on married furniture, drawers, Rockingham pottery, make-dos, restoration, and other subjects have appeared in *Early American Homes*, the *New England Antiques Journal*, and *Art & Antiques*. They have previously edited the sixth edition *of Sloan's Green Guide to Antiquing in New England* and the *Green Guide to Antiquing in the Midwest* (October 1998). They live in southern Vermont.